Microeconomic Theory:
A Mathematical Approach

Economics Handbook Series

Seymour E. Harris, Editor

The Board of Advisors

Microeconomic Theory
A MATHEMATICAL APPROACH

Second Edition

JAMES M. HENDERSON
Professor of Economics
University of Minnesota

RICHARD E. QUANDT
Professor of Economics
Princeton University

McGraw-Hill Book Company
New York   St. Louis   San Francisco
Düsseldorf   Johannesburg   Kuala Lumpur
London   Mexico   Montreal
New Delhi   Panama   Rio de Janeiro
Singapore   Sydney   Toronto

Microeconomic Theory: A Mathematical Approach

Library of Congress Catalog Card Number 72-140956

07-028089-4

10 11 12 13   D O D O   7 9 8 7

Preface to the Second Edition

The experience of using *Microeconomic Theory* in graduate and advanced undergraduate courses over a number of years, the many helpful suggestions of colleagues and students, and recent developments in economics have all provided incentives for a major revision. The second (enlarged) edition differs from the first in three major respects. There have also been some minor changes in the mathematical tools used in the text.

First, an attempt has been made to include a fair amount of new material that either appeared in the economic literature since the publication of the first edition or was considered too new or difficult for inclusion at the earlier time. Examples are the constant-elasticity-of-substitution production function (Chap. 3), a proof for the existence of equilibrium in a competitive economy (Chap. 5), the case of the revenue-maximizing monopolist (Chap. 6), and the theory of second best (Chap. 7). Many other extensions are included in the appropriate chapters.

A second change of major significance is the addition of a new chapter on linear models. It replaces the fragmentary treatments of linear programming, input-output analysis, and game theory which are in three different chapters of the first edition. These topics are now covered in an extended and unified manner in Chap. 9. Unlike the first eight chapters, this new chapter is method oriented rather than subject oriented.

The inclusion of exercises at the end of each chapter is the third major change. Their inclusion was the most frequent recommendation for change received from users of the first edition. The exercises contain both concrete illustrations and extensions of the materials in the text. The ability to work the exercises is an important aspect of gaining a working knowledge of microeconomic theory. The more difficult exercises are marked with an asterisk (*).

The level of mathematics has remained substantially unchanged. The emphasis remains upon methods and applications rather than detailed proofs. The calculus is the basic mathematical tool. A treatment of simple differential equations has been added. The concepts of convex and concave functions, which have gained increased importance in the economic literature, are introduced. Elementary convex-set theory is employed in Chaps. 5 and 9. In only one instance is significantly more advanced mathematics, namely Brouwer's fixed-point theorem, employed. It is used to prove the existence of competitive equilibrium in Chap. 5. As before, readers are urged to refresh their memories about the mathematics and fill whatever gaps may exist by reading the Appendix (and working its exercises) before beginning Chap. 2.

Suggestions for improvements in the first edition have been made by many colleagues and students to whom profound thanks are hereby expressed. It is hoped that few new errors have been introduced. As before, the authors' work is thoroughly intermingled and they take equal responsibility for the final result.

James M. Henderson
Richard E. Quandt

Preface to the First Edition

The last two decades have witnessed an increasing application of mathematical methods to nearly every branch of economics. The theories of individual optimizing units and market equilibrium which are included within the microeconomics branch are no exception. Traditional theory has been formulated in mathematical terms, and the classical results proved or disproved. The use of mathematics has also allowed the derivation of many new results. Mathematical methods are particularly useful in this field since the underlying premises of utility and profit maximization are basically mathematical in character.

In the early stages of this development economists were rather sharply divided into two groups: the mathematical economists and the literary, or nonmathematical, economists. Fortunately, this sharp division is breaking down with the passage of time. More and more economists and students of economics are becoming acquainted with at least elementary mathematics and are learning to appreciate the advantages of its use in economics. On the other side, many mathematically inclined economists are becoming more aware of the limitations of mathematics. It seems a safe prediction that before too many more years have passed the question of the use of mathematics in microeconomic theory will be only a matter of degree.

As the number of economists and students of economics with mathematical training increases, the basic problem shifts from that of teaching mathematics to economists to that of teaching them economics in mathematical terms. The present volume is intended for economists and students of economics who have some mathematical training but do not possess a high degree of mathematical sophistication. It is not intended as a textbook on mathematics for economists. The basic concepts of microeconomic theory are developed with the aid of intermediate mathematics. The selection of topics and the order of presentation are indicated by economic, rather than mathematical, content.

This volume is intended for readers who possess some knowledge, though not necessarily a great deal, of both economics and mathematics. The audience at which it is aimed includes advanced undergraduate and graduate students in economics and professional economists who desire to see how intermediate mathematics contributes to the understanding of some familiar concepts. Advanced knowledge in one of these fields can partially compensate for a lack of training in the other. The reader with a weak background in microeconomics will not fully appreciate its problems or the limitations of the mathematical methods unless he consults some of the purely literary works in this area. A limited number of these are contained in the lists of selected references at the end of each chapter.

A one-year college course in calculus, or its equivalent, is sufficient mathematical preparation for the present volume.[1] A review of the mathematical concepts employed in the text is contained in the Appendix. The Appendix is not adequate for a reader who has never been exposed to calculus, but it should serve the dual purpose of refreshing the reader's memory on topics with which he has some familiarity and of introducing him to the few concepts that are employed in the text but are not usually covered in a first course in calculus—specifically, Cramer's rule, Lagrange multipliers, and simple difference equations. The reader interested in extending his knowledge of specific mathematical concepts will find a list of references at the end of the Appendix.

In order to simplify the reader's introduction to the use of mathematical methods in microeconomic theory, two- and three-variable cases are emphasized in Chapters 2 and 3. The more general cases are empha-

---

[1] The reader without this background is referred to the first fifteen chapters of R. G. D. Allen, *Mathematical Analysis for Economists* (London: Macmillan, 1938).

sized in the later chapters. The analysis is frequently accompanied by diagrams, in order to provide a geometric interpretation of the formal results. The formal analysis is also illustrated with specific numerical examples. The reader may test his comprehension by working through the examples and working out the proofs and extensions of the analysis that are occasionally left as exercises.

The authors have both served as senior partners in the preparation of this volume, with each contributing approximately one-half of the material. Henderson is primarily responsible for Chapters 3, 5, 6, and 8, and Quandt is primarily responsible for Chapters 2, 4, 7, and the Appendix. However, the manuscript was prepared in very close collaboration, and each author helped plan, review, and revise the work of the other. Therefore, all errors and defects are the responsibility of both.

The authors are indebted to many of their teachers, colleagues, and students for direct and indirect aid in the production of this volume. Their greatest debt is to their former teacher, Wassily W. Leontief. His general outlook is in evidence throughout the volume, and he is responsible for much of the authors' affection for microeconomic theory. The authors gratefully acknowledge the advice and criticism of William J. Baumol, who read the entire manuscript in an intermediate stage and offered numerous suggestions for its improvement. Others who deserve specific mention are Robert Dorfman, W. Eric Gustafson, Franklin M. Fisher, Carl Kaysen, and Seymour E. Harris. The marginal productivities of the inputs of the authors' above-mentioned friends are strictly positive in all cases.

The authors also owe a very significant debt to the economists who pioneered the application of mathematical methods to microeconomic theory. Their written works provide the framework for this book. The outstanding pioneers are J. R. Hicks and Paul A. Samuelson, but there are many others. The names and works of many of the pioneers can be found in the lists of selected references at the end of each chapter.

James M. Henderson
Richard E. Quandt

Contents

1
Introduction

Economics is not a clearly defined discipline. Its frontiers are constantly changing, and their definition is frequently a subject of controversy. A commonly used definition characterizes economics as the study of the use of limited resources for the achievement of alternative ends. This definition is adequate if interpreted broadly enough to include the study of unemployed resources and to cover situations in which the ends are selected by economists themselves. More specifically, economics may be defined as a social science which covers the actions of individuals and groups of individuals in the processes of producing, exchanging, and consuming goods and services.

1-1 THE ROLE OF THEORY

Explanation and prediction are the goals of economics as well as most other sciences. Both theoretical analyses and empirical investigations are necessary for the achievement of these goals. The two are usually inextricably intertwined in concrete examples of research; yet there is a

1

real distinction between them.   Theories employ abstract deductive reasoning whereby conclusions are drawn from sets of initial assumptions.
Purely empirical studies are inductive in nature.   The two approaches
are complementary, since theories provide guides for empirical studies
and empirical studies provide tests of the assumptions and conclusions
of theories.

Basically, a theory contains three sets of elements: (1) data which
play the role of parameters and are assumed to be given from outside the
analytical framework; (2) variables, the magnitudes of which are determined within the theory; and (3) behavior assumptions or postulates
which define the set of operations by which the values of the variables
are determined.   The conclusions of a theoretical argument are always
of a *what would happen if* nature.   They state what the results of
economic processes would be if the initial assumptions were satisfied, i.e., if the data were in fact given and the behavior assumptions
justified.

Empirical investigations allow comparisons of the assumptions and
conclusions of theories with observed facts.   However, the requirement
of a strict conformity between theory and fact would defeat the very purpose of theory.   Theories represent simplifications and generalizations
of reality and therefore do not completely describe particular situations.
The data-variable distinctions and behavior assumptions of the theories
presented in subsequent chapters are satisfied by few, if any, actual
market situations.   A stricter conformity to facts would require a separate, highly detailed theory for each individual market situation, since
each possesses its own distinctive characteristics.   Applied theories of
this nature, however valuable for specific research projects, are of little
general value.   The more general theories are fruitful because they contain statements which abstract from particulars and find elements which
many situations have in common.   Increased understanding is realized
at the cost of the sacrificed detail.   It is then possible to go from the
general to the specific.   The cases described by pure theories provide
insight into economic processes and serve as a background and starting
point for applied theories and specific empirical studies.

1-2 MICROECONOMICS

Like most other disciplines, economics is divided into branches and sub-
branches.   The major branches are *microeconomics*, which is the study
of the economic actions of individuals and well-defined groups of individuals, and *macroeconomics*, which is the study of broad aggregates such
as total employment and national income.   This dichotomy is in a sense
artificial, since aggregates are merely sums of individual figures.   How-

ever, it is justified by the basic differences in the objectives and methods of the two branches.

The microscopic versus the macroscopic view of the economy is the fundamental, but not the only, difference between these two branches of economics. Before the micro-macro distinction came into vogue, the fundamental distinction was between price and income analyses. This distinction can be carried over into the micro and macro branches. Prices play a major role in microeconomic theories, and their goal is generally the analysis of price determination and the allocation of specific resources to particular uses. On the other hand, the goals of macroeconomic theories generally are the determination of the levels of national income and aggregate resource employment.

One cannot say that income concepts are ignored in micro theories or that prices are nonexistent in macro theories. However, in micro theories the determination of the incomes of individuals is encompassed within the general pricing process: individuals earn their incomes by selling factors of production, the prices of which are determined in the same manner as all other prices. On the other hand, prices are relevant in macro theories, but macro theorists usually abstract from the problems of determining individual prices and their relations to one another and deal with aggregate price indices as determined by the level of aggregate spending.

Since the problems of individual price determination are assumed away in macro theory, the relationship between individual units and the aggregates is not clear. If it were, the analysis would be classified as micro theory. The simplifications introduced by aggregation are not without reward, since they make it possible to describe the position and progress of the economy as a whole in terms of a few simple aggregates. This would be impossible if the micro emphasis on individual behavior and relative prices were maintained.

Following this established separation of subject matter, the present volume is limited to a systematic exposition of traditional microeconomic theory. The theories of individual behavior and price determination for a perfectly competitive economy are developed in three stages of increasing generality in Chaps. 2 through 5. The behavior of individual consumers (Chap. 2) and producers (Chap. 3) is the focal point of the first stage. Each individual is assumed to consider the prices of the goods that he buys and sells as given parameters, the magnitudes of which he is unable to influence. The quantities of his purchases and sales are the variables determined in these theories. The market for a single commodity is the focal point of the second stage (Chap. 4). The prices of all other commodities are assumed to be given parameters, and the price of the commodity in question, as well as the volume of its purchases and sales, is shown to be determined by the independent actions of all its buyers and sellers. Finally, in the third stage (Chap. 5) the interrelations between the various markets in the system are explicitly taken into account, and all prices are determined simultaneously.

Microeconomic theories are sufficiently flexible to permit many variations in their underlying assumptions. For example, the assumption that no single individual is able to influence prices or the actions of other individuals is modified in Chap. 6. Despite the variation of this basic premise, the family resemblance between the analyses of Chap. 6 and those of earlier chapters is quite evident. The assumption of a static world in which consumers and producers do not plan for the future is relaxed in Chap. 8. Again the logical connection with the earlier chapters is easily discernible. The possibility of relaxing these and other assumptions increases the flexibility and generality of the basic theories.

Another important use of theory is to serve as a guide to *what ought to be*. The subbranch of microeconomics which covers these problems is known as welfare economics and is the subject of Chap. 7. The degree of conformity between theory and fact is of great importance in welfare economics. If one were interested in pure description, a divergence between theory and fact would suggest that the theory is faulty for that particular purpose. When the theory becomes a welfare ideal, such a divergence leads to the conclusion that the actual situation is faulty and should be remedied.

The manner in which some of the problems in Chaps. 2 through 8 are treated represents a particular and mathematically easily tractable form of abstraction from reality. An alternative linear approach to microeconomics, and particularly to the theory of production, is covered in Chap. 9.

1-3 THE ROLE OF MATHEMATICS

The theories of the present volume are cast in mathematical terms. The mathematics is not an end in itself, but rather a set of tools which facilitates the derivation and exposition of the economic theories. Mathematics is useful for translating verbal arguments into concise and consistent forms. However, it does more than this. Mathematics provides the economist with a set of tools often more powerful than ordinary speech in that mathematics possesses concepts and allows operations for which no manageable verbal equivalents exist. The use of mathematics enlarges the economist's tool kit and widens the range of possible inferences from initial assumptions.

Purely verbal analysis was the first stage in the historical development of economic theory. However, as quantitative relationships were formulated in increasing numbers and as theories became increasingly complex, purely verbal analyses became more tedious and more difficult to formulate consistently. Mathematical relations underlay most of these early theories, though they were seldom made explicit. The recognition that more rigorous formulations were often necessary led to the acceptance of plane geometry as an important tool of analysis. Plane geometry was and is highly useful, but possesses many limitations. One of the most serious of these is the limitation of theoretical arguments to two, or at most three, variables. The increasing use of other mathematical tools reflects the belief that plane geometry is not adequate for rigorous economic reasoning in many cases.

The calculus and some simple concepts of simultaneous-equation systems are the major mathematical tools used in the present volume. Some notions of convex sets and a fixed-point theorem are used in particular discussions. Some general results are illustrated by two-dimensional geometry. The explicit use of mathematics does not mean that the authors believe that all verbal analyses should be discarded. Verbal analyses are preferable to mathematical analyses for some purposes. They serve to fill in many details, state important qualifications, and suggest new topics for rigorous investigation.

The mathematical concepts used in the text are reviewed in the Appendix. All except the mathematically most sophisticated readers should read, or at least skim, the Appendix *before* beginning Chap. 2.

2
The Theory of Consumer Behavior

The postulate of rationality is the customary point of departure in the theory of the consumer's behavior. The consumer is assumed to choose among the alternatives available to him in such a manner that the satisfaction derived from consuming commodities (in the broadest sense) is as large as possible. This implies that he is aware of the alternatives facing him and is capable of evaluating them. All information pertaining to the satisfaction that the consumer derives from various quantities of commodities is contained in his *utility function*.

The concepts of utility and its maximization are void of any sensuous connotation. The assertion that a consumer derives more satisfaction or utility from an automobile than from a suit of clothes means that if he were presented with the alternatives of receiving as a gift either an automobile or a suit of clothes, he would choose the former. Things that are necessary for survival—such as vaccine when a smallpox epidemic threatens—may give the consumer the most utility, although the act of consuming such a commodity has no pleasurable sensations connected with it.

The nineteenth-century economists W. Stanley Jevons, Léon Walras, and Alfred Marshall considered utility measurable, just as the weight of objects is measurable. The consumer was assumed to possess a *cardinal* measure of utility; i.e., he was assumed to be capable of assigning to every commodity or combination of commodities a number representing the amount or degree of utility associated with it. The numbers representing amounts of utility could be manipulated in the same fashion as weights. Assume, for example, that the utility of A is 15 units and the utility of B 45 units. The consumer would "like" B three times as strongly as A. The differences between utility numbers could be compared, and the comparison could lead to a statement such as "A is preferred to B twice as much as C is preferred to D." It was also assumed by the nineteenth-century economists that the additions to a consumer's total utility resulting from consuming additional units of a commodity decrease as he consumes more of it. The consumer's behavior can be deduced from the above assumptions. Imagine that a certain price, say 2 dollars, is charged for coconuts. The consumer, confronted with coconuts, will not buy any if the amount of utility he surrenders by paying the price of a coconut (i.e., by parting with purchasing power) is greater than the utility he gains by consuming it. Assume that the utility of a dollar is 5 utils and remains approximately constant for small variations in income and that the consumer derives the following increments of utility by consuming an additional coconut:

Unit	Additional utility
Coconut 1	20
Coconut 2	9
Coconut 3	7

He will buy at least one coconut, because he surrenders 10 utils in exchange for 20 utils and thus increases his total utility.[1] He will not buy a second coconut, because the utility loss exceeds the gain. In general, the consumer will not add to his consumption of a commodity if an additional unit involves a net utility loss. He will increase his consumption only if he realizes a net gain of utility from it. For example, assume that the price of coconuts falls to 1.6 dollars. Two coconuts will now be bought. A fall in the price has increased the quantity bought. This is the sense in which the theory predicts the consumer's behavior.

---

[1] The price is 2 dollars; the consumer loses 5 utils per dollar surrendered. Therefore the gross loss is 10 utils, and the gross gain is 20 utils.

The assumptions on which the theory of cardinal utility is built are very restrictive. Equivalent conclusions can be deduced from much weaker assumptions. Therefore it will *not* be assumed in the remainder of this chapter that the consumer possesses a cardinal measure of utility or that the additional utility derived from increasing his consumption of a commodity diminishes.

If the consumer derives more utility from alternative A than from alternative B, he is said to prefer A to B.† The postulate of rationality is equivalent to the following statements: (1) for all possible pairs of alternatives A and B the consumer knows whether he prefers A to B or B to A, or whether he is indifferent between them; (2) only one of the three possibilities is true for any pair of alternatives; (3) if the consumer prefers A to B and B to C, he will prefer A to C. The last statement ensures that the consumer's preferences are consistent or *transitive:* if he prefers an automobile to a suit of clothes and a suit of clothes to a bowl of soup, he must prefer an automobile to a bowl of soup.

The postulate of rationality, as stated above, merely requires that the consumer be able to rank commodities in order of preference. The consumer possesses an *ordinal* utility measure; i.e., he need not be able to assign numbers that represent (in arbitrary units) the degree or amount of utility that he derives from commodities. His ranking of commodities is expressed mathematically by his utility function. It associates certain numbers with various quantities of commodities consumed, but these numbers provide only a ranking or ordering of preferences. If the utility of alternative A is 15 and the utility of B is 45 (i.e., if the utility function associates the number 15 with alternative or commodity A and the number 45 with alternative B), one can only say that B is preferred to A, but it is meaningless to say that B is liked three times as strongly as A. This reformulation of the postulates of the theory of consumer behavior was effected only around the turn of the last century. It is remarkable that the consumer's behavior can be explained just as well in terms of an ordinal utility function as in terms of a cardinal one. Intuitively one can see that the consumer's choices are completely determinate if he possesses a ranking (and only a ranking) of commodity bundles according to his preferences. One could visualize the consumer as possessing a list of all commodity bundles that can be purchased for one dollar in decreasing order of desirability; when the consumer receives his income, he starts purchasing bundles from the top of the list and descends as

---

† A chain of definitions must eventually come to an end. The word "prefer" could be defined to mean "would rather have than," but then this expression must be left undefined. The term "prefer" is also void of any connotation of sensuous pleasure.

far as his income allows.[1] Therefore it is not necessary to assume that he possesses a cardinal measure of utility. The much weaker assumption that he possesses a consistent ranking of preferences is sufficient.

The basic tools of analysis and the nature of the utility function are discussed in Sec. 2-1. Two alternative but equivalent methods are employed for the determination of the individual consumer's optimum consumption levels in Sec. 2-2. It is shown in Sec. 2-3 that the solution of the consumer's maximum problem is invariant with respect to monotonic transformations of his utility function. Demand functions are derived in Sec. 2-4, and the analysis is extended to the problem of choice between income and leisure in Sec. 2-5. The effect of price and income variations on consumption levels is examined in Sec. 2-6. The theory is generalized to an arbitrary number of commodities in Sec. 2-7 and is reformulated in terms of an alternative approach, the theory of revealed preference, in Sec. 2-8. Finally, the problem of choice is analyzed with respect to situations with uncertain outcomes in Sec. 2-9.

2-1 BASIC CONCEPTS

THE NATURE OF THE UTILITY FUNCTION

Consider the simple case in which the consumer's purchases are limited to two commodities. His ordinal utility function is

$$U = f(q_1, q_2) \tag{2-1}$$

where q_1 and q_2 are the quantities of the two commodities Q_1 and Q_2 which he consumes. It is assumed that $f(q_1, q_2)$ is continuous and has continuous first- and second-order partial derivatives. The consumer's utility function is not unique (see Sec. 2-3). In general, any single-valued increasing function of q_1 and q_2 can serve as a utility function. The utility number U^0 assigned to any particular commodity combination indicates that it is preferable or superior to all combinations with lower numbers and inferior to those with higher numbers.

The utility function is defined with reference to consumption during a specified period of time. The level of satisfaction that the consumer derives from a particular commodity combination depends upon the length of the period during which he consumes it. Different levels of satisfaction are derived from consuming ten portions of ice cream within one hour and within one month. There is no unique time period for which the utility function *should* be defined. However, there are restrictions upon the possible length of the period. The consumer usually

---

[1] How much a particular item on the list is liked is irrelevant; an item which is higher on the list will always be chosen before one which comes later.

derives utility from variety in his diet and diversification among the commodities he consumes.   Therefore, the utility function must not be defined for a period so short that the desire for variety cannot be satisfied. On the other hand, tastes (the shape of the function) may change if it is defined for too long a period.   Any intermediate period is satisfactory for the static theory of consumer behavior.[1]   The present theory is static in the sense that the utility function is defined with reference to a single time period, and the consumer's optimal expenditure pattern is analyzed only with respect to this period.   No account is taken of the possibility of transferring consumption expenditures from one period to another.[2]

INDIFFERENCE CURVES

A particular level of utility or satisfaction can be derived from many different combinations of Q_1 and Q_2.†   For a given level of utility U^0, Eq. (2-1) becomes

$$U^0 = f(q_1, q_2) \tag{2-2}$$

where U^0 is a constant.   Since the utility function is continuous, (2-2) is satisfied by an infinite number of combinations of Q_1 and Q_2.   Imagine that the consumer derives a given level of satisfaction U^0 from 5 units of Q_1 and 3 units of Q_2.   If his consumption of Q_1 were decreased from 5 to 4 without an increase in his consumption of Q_2, his satisfaction would certainly decrease.   In general, it is possible to compensate him for the loss of 1 unit of Q_1 by allowing an increase in his consumption of Q_2. Imagine that an increase of 3 units in his consumption of Q_2 makes him indifferent between the two alternative combinations.   Other commodity combinations which yield the consumer the same level of satisfaction can be discovered in a similar manner.   The locus of all commodity combinations from which the consumer derives the same level of satisfaction forms an *indifference curve*.   An *indifference map* is a collection

[1] The theory would break down if it were impossible to define a period that is neither too short from the first point of view nor too long from the second.
[2] The present analysis is static in that it does not consider what happens after the current income period.   The consumer makes his calculations for only one such period at a time.   At the end of the period he repeats his calculations for the next one. If he were capable of borrowing, one would consider his total liquid resources available in any time period instead of his income proper.   Conversely, he may save, i.e., not spend all his income on consumption goods.   Provision can be made for both possibilities without changing the essential points of the analysis (see Sec. 8-2).
† By definition, a commodity is an item of which the consumer would rather have more than less.   Otherwise he is dealing with a discommodity.   In reality a commodity may become a discommodity if its quantity is sufficiently large.   For example, if the consumer partakes of too many portions of ice cream, it may become a discommodity for him.   It is assumed in the remainder of the chapter that such a point of saturation has not been reached.

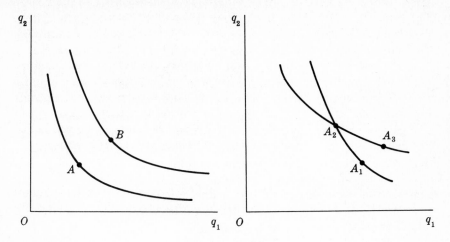

Fig. 2-1   **Fig. 2-2**

of indifference curves corresponding to different levels of satisfaction. The quantities q_1 and q_2 are measured along the axes of Fig. 2-1. One indifference curve passes through every point in the positive quadrant of the q_1q_2 plane. Indifference curves correspond to higher and higher levels of satisfaction as one moves in a northeasterly direction in Fig. 2-1. A movement from point A to point B would increase the consumption of both Q_1 and Q_2. Therefore B must correspond to a higher level of satisfaction than A.†

Indifference curves cannot intersect as shown in Fig. 2-2. Consider the points A_1, A_2, and A_3. Let the consumer derive the satisfaction U_1 from the batch of commodities represented by A_1 and similarly U_2 and U_3 from A_2 and A_3. The consumer has more of both commodities at A_3 than at A_1, and therefore $U_3 > U_1$. Since A_1 and A_2 are on the same indifference curve, $U_1 = U_2$. The points A_2 and A_3 are also on the same indifference curve, and therefore $U_2 = U_3$. This implies $U_1 = U_3$. Therefore, A_1 and A_3 are on the same indifference curve contrary to assumption.

THE RATE OF COMMODITY SUBSTITUTION

The total differential of the utility function is

$$dU = f_1\,dq_1 + f_2\,dq_2 \tag{2-3}$$

† The term "level of satisfaction" should not mislead the reader to think in terms of a cardinal measure of utility. The term is relevant only in that a particular level of satisfaction is *higher* or *lower* than some other level. Only the ordinal properties of levels of satisfaction are relevant.

where f_1 and f_2 are the partial derivatives of U with respect to q_1 and q_2. The total change in utility (compared to an initial situation) caused by variations in q_1 and q_2 is approximately the change in q_1 multiplied by the change in utility resulting from a unit change of q_1 plus the change in q_2 multiplied by the change in utility resulting from a unit change in q_2. Let the consumer move along one of his indifference curves by giving up some Q_1 in exchange for Q_2. If his consumption of Q_1 decreases by dq_1 (therefore, $dq_1 < 0$), the resulting loss of utility is approximately $f_1 \, dq_1$. The gain of utility caused by acquiring some Q_2 is approximately $f_2 \, dq_2$ for similar reasons. Taking arbitrarily small increments, the sum of these two terms must equal zero in the limit, since the total change in utility along an indifference curve is zero by definition.[1] Since the analysis runs in terms of ordinal utility functions, the magnitudes of $f_1 \, dq_1$ and $f_2 \, dq_2$ are not known. However, it must still be true that the sum of these two terms is zero. Setting $dU = 0$,

$$f_1 \, dq_1 + f_2 \, dq_2 = 0$$

yields

$$-\frac{dq_2}{dq_1} = \frac{f_1}{f_2} \tag{2-4}$$

The slope of an indifference curve, dq_2/dq_1, is the rate at which a consumer would be willing to substitute Q_1 for Q_2 or Q_2 for Q_1 in order to maintain a given level of utility. The negative of the slope, $-dq_2/dq_1$, is the *rate of commodity substitution* (RCS) of Q_1 for Q_2 or Q_2 for Q_1, and it equals the ratio of the partial derivatives of the utility function.[2] The RCS at a point on an indifference curve is the same for movements in either direction. It is immaterial whether the verbal definition is in terms of substituting Q_1 for Q_2 or vice versa.

In a cardinal analysis the partial derivatives f_1 and f_2 are defined as the *marginal utilities* of the commodities Q_1 and Q_2.† This definition is retained in the present ordinal analysis. However, the partial derivative of an ordinal utility function cannot be given a cardinal interpretation. Therefore, the numerical magnitudes of individual marginal utilities are

---

[1] Imagine the utility function as a surface in three-dimensional space. Then the total differential (2-3) is the equation of the tangent plane to this surface at some point. This justifies the use of the word approximate in the above argument (see Sec. A-3).

[2] The rate of commodity substitution is frequently referred to in the literature of economics as the *marginal* rate of substitution. Cf. J. R. Hicks, *Value and Capital* (2d ed.; Oxford: Clarendon Press, 1946), pt. I.

† The marginal utility of a commodity is often loosely defined as the increase in utility resulting from a unit increase in its consumption.

without meaning. The consumer is not assumed to be aware of the existence of marginal utilities, and only the economist need know that the consumer's RCS equals the ratio of marginal utilities. The signs as well as the ratios of marginal utilities are meaningful in an ordinal analysis. A positive value for f_1 signifies that an increase in q_1 will increase the consumer's satisfaction level and move him to a higher indifference curve.

EXISTENCE OF THE UTILITY FUNCTION

It is not obvious that real-valued functions that can serve as utility functions exist for all consumers. A consumer's preferences must satisfy certain conditions in order to be representable by a utility function. A set of sufficient conditions for the existence of a utility function is as follows:

1. The various commodity combinations available to the consumer stand in a relation to each other, denoted by R. The meaning of R is "is at least as well liked as." The relation R is complete: For any pair of commodity combinations $\mathbf{A}_1$ and $\mathbf{A}_2$ either $\mathbf{A}_1 R \mathbf{A}_2$, $\mathbf{A}_2 R \mathbf{A}_1$, or both. Further, R is reflexive: $\mathbf{A}_1 R \mathbf{A}_1$, whatever $\mathbf{A}_1$ may be. Finally, R is transitive: If $\mathbf{A}_1 R \mathbf{A}_2$ and $\mathbf{A}_2 R \mathbf{A}_3$, then $\mathbf{A}_1 R \mathbf{A}_3$.
2. The set of all commodity combinations available to the consumer is connected. If $\mathbf{A}_1$ and $\mathbf{A}_2$ are available to the consumer, one can find a continuous path of available combinations connecting $\mathbf{A}_1$ and $\mathbf{A}_2$.
3. Given some commodity combination $\mathbf{A}_1$, one may consider the set of all combinations at least as well liked as $\mathbf{A}_1$ and the set of all combinations not more liked than $\mathbf{A}_1$. These two sets are closed. This means that if one selected for consideration an infinite sequence of commodity combinations which converged to some limiting combination $\mathbf{A}_0$ and if each member of the sequence were at least as well liked as $\mathbf{A}_1$, then the limiting combination would also be at least as well liked as $\mathbf{A}_1$. This condition ensures the continuity of the consumer's preferences and rules out "jumps." It ensures, for example, that if two commodity combinations differ from each other only slightly and if one of these is preferred to some given combination $\mathbf{A}_1$ then the other will be at least as well liked as $\mathbf{A}_1$.

It might seem that these conditions are so unrestrictive as to be almost always satisfied. It is easy, however, to cite preference structures that do not satisfy them. Consider the following case. Let there be two commodities Q_1 and Q_2, and consider two commodity combinations $\mathbf{A}_1 = (q_1^{(1)}, q_2^{(1)})$ and $\mathbf{A}_2 = (q_1^{(2)}, q_2^{(2)})$. Imagine that the preference structure of the consumer is given by the following rule: $\mathbf{A}_1$ is preferred to $\mathbf{A}_2$ if either $q_1^{(1)} > q_1^{(2)}$ or $q_1^{(1)} = q_1^{(2)}$ and $q_2^{(1)} > q_2^{(2)}$. In this situation the preference ordering is said to be *lexicographic* and no utility function exists.

2-2 THE MAXIMIZATION OF UTILITY

The rational consumer desires to purchase a combination of Q_1 and Q_2 from which he derives the highest level of satisfaction. His problem is one of maximization. However, his income is limited, and he is not able to purchase unlimited amounts of the commodities. The consumer's budget constraint can be written as

$$y^0 = p_1q_1 + p_2q_2 \tag{2-5}$$

where y^0 is his (fixed) income and p_1 and p_2 are the prices of Q_1 and Q_2 respectively. The amount he spends on the first commodity (p_1q_1) plus the amount he spends on the second (p_2q_2) equals his income (y^0).

METHOD 1

In order to maximize the utility function subject to the budget constraint the consumer must find a combination of commodities that satisfies (2-5) and also maximizes the utility function (2-1). Transposing p_1q_1 to the left in (2-5) and dividing through by p_2, the budget constraint becomes

$$\frac{y^0 - p_1q_1}{p_2} = q_2$$

Substituting this value of q_2 into (2-1), the utility function becomes a function of q_1 alone:

$$U = f\left(q_1, \frac{y^0 - p_1q_1}{p_2}\right) \tag{2-6}$$

Because of the fixed relationship between q_1 and q_2 via the budget constraint, it is sufficient to maximize (2-6) with respect to q_1. Sufficient conditions are satisfied if $dU/dq_1 = 0$ (first-order condition) and $d^2U/dq_1^2 < 0$ (second-order condition).

Setting the first derivative of (2-6) equal to zero,[1]

$$\frac{dU}{dq_1} = f_1 + f_2\left(-\frac{p_1}{p_2}\right) = 0 \tag{2-7}$$

[1] The composite-function rule and the function of a function rule have been used (see Secs. A-2 and A-3).

Transposing the second term of (2-7) to the right and dividing by f_2 yields

$$\frac{f_1}{f_2} = \frac{p_1}{p_2} \tag{2-8}$$

The ratio of the marginal utilities must equal the ratio of prices for a maximum. Since f_1/f_2 is the RCS, the first-order condition for a maximum is expressed by the equality of the RCS and the price ratio. Equation (2-8) can be rewritten as

$$\frac{f_1}{p_1} = \frac{f_2}{p_2} \tag{2-9}$$

Marginal utility divided by price must be the same for all commodities. This ratio gives the rate at which satisfaction would increase if an additional dollar were spent on a particular commodity. If more satisfaction could be gained by spending an additional dollar on Q_1 rather than Q_2, the consumer would not be maximizing utility. He could increase his satisfaction by shifting some of his expenditure from Q_2 to Q_1. Equation (2-8) is derived from the first-order conditions for a maximum, but it does not ensure that a maximum is actually reached.

Denoting the second direct partial derivatives of (2-1) by f_{11} and f_{22} and the second cross partial derivatives by f_{12} and f_{21}, the second-order condition for a maximum requires that

$$\frac{d^2 U}{dq_1^2} = f_{11} + 2f_{12}\left(-\frac{p_1}{p_2}\right) + f_{22}\left(-\frac{p_1}{p_2}\right)^2 < 0$$

Substituting $p_1/p_2 = f_1/f_2$ from (2-8) and multiplying through by $f_2^2 > 0$, the second-order condition becomes

$$f_{11}f_2^2 - 2f_{12}f_1f_2 + f_{22}f_1^2 < 0 \tag{2-10}$$

A maximum is obtained if (2-10) holds in addition to (2-8).

By further differentiation of (2-4) the rate of change of the slope of the indifference curve is[1]

$$\frac{d^2 q_2}{dq_1^2} = -\frac{1}{f_2^3}(f_{11}f_2^2 - 2f_{12}f_1f_2 + f_{22}f_1^2) \tag{2-11}$$

Inequality (2-10) ensures that the parenthesized term on the right-hand side of (2-11) is negative. Since $f_2 > 0$, the second-order condition requires that $d^2 q_2/dq_1^2$ be positive at an equilibrium point.

---

[1] Note that (2-11) is obtained by taking the total derivative of the slope of the indifference curve instead of the partial derivative.

It is frequently assumed that (2-11) is positive for a wide range of nonnegative values for q_1 and q_2. This assumption places a restriction upon the shape of indifference curves that allows the second-order condition to be satisfied for a wide range of values for p_1/p_2, and ensures that all maxima will be global maxima. A function of one variable is strictly convex (see Sec. A-2) if its second derivative is positive. Thus in the two-commodity case, the positivity assumption means that each indifference curve gives q_2 as a strictly convex function of q_1 (and q_1 as a strictly convex function of q_2). Such indifference curves are bowed toward the origin as illustrated in Fig. 2-1. Throughout this volume, indifference curves are assumed to possess this convexity unless otherwise specified.

The assumption of convex indifference curves means that the consumer's RCS as given by (2-4) decreases as he moves from left to right along an indifference curve. The negative slope of the indifference curve becomes larger algebraically and smaller in absolute value as Q_1 is substituted for Q_2. The indifference curve becomes flatter, and the RCS, which is the absolute value of its slope, decreases. As the consumer moves along an indifference curve he acquires more Q_1 and less Q_2, and the rate at which he is willing to sacrifice Q_2 to acquire yet more Q_1 declines. The increasing relative scarcity of Q_2 increases its relative value to the consumer, and the increasing relative abundance of Q_1 decreases its relative value.

Assume that the utility function is $U = q_1 q_2$, that $p_1 = 2$ dollars, $p_2 = 5$ dollars, and that the consumer's income for the period is 100 dollars. The budget constraint is

$$100 - 2q_1 - 5q_2 = 0$$

Expressing q_2 as a function of q_1 from the budget constraint,

$$q_2 = 20 - \frac{2q_1}{5}$$

Substituting into the utility function,

$$U = 20q_1 - \frac{2q_1^2}{5}$$

Therefore

$$\frac{dU}{dq_1} = 20 - \frac{4q_1}{5}$$

Setting dU/dq_1 equal to zero and solving for q_1 gives $q_1 = 25$. Substituting this into the budget constraint gives $q_2 = 10$. The second derivative of the utility function is negative for these values of q_1 and q_2, as

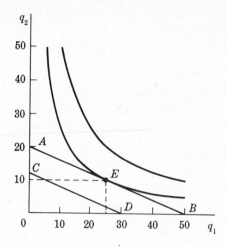

Fig. 2-3

the reader may verify by performing the necessary differentiation. The consumer maximizes utility by consuming this combination.

Figure 2-3 contains a graphic presentation of this example. The price line AB is the geometric counterpart of the budget constraint and shows all possible combinations of Q_1 and Q_2 that the consumer *can* purchase. Its equation is $100 - 2q_1 - 5q_2 = 0$. The consumer can purchase 50 units of Q_1 if he buys no Q_2, 20 units of Q_2 if he buys no Q_1, etc. A different price line corresponds to each possible level of income; if the consumer's income were 60 dollars, the relevant price line would be CD. The indifference curves in this example are a family of rectangular hyperbolas.[1] The consumer desires to reach the highest indifference curve that has at least one point in common with AB. His equilibrium is at point E, at which AB is tangent to an indifference curve. Movements in either direction from point E result in a diminished level of utility. The constant slope of the price line, $-p_1/p_2$ or $-\frac{2}{5}$ in the present example, must equal the slope of the indifference curve. Forming the ratio of the partial derivatives of the utility function, the slope of the indifference curves in the present example is $-q_2/q_1$, and hence the RCS equals $q_2/q_1 = \frac{10}{25}$, which equals the ratio of prices $\frac{2}{5}$ as required. The second-order condition is satisfied. The indifference curves are convex, and the RCS is decreasing at the equilibrium point: $-d^2q_2/dq_1^2 = -2q_2/q_1^2 < 0$.

The first-order condition (2-8) or (2-9) is not always necessary for a maximum. Two exceptions are pictured in Fig. 2-4. In the first case (see Fig. 2-4a) the indifference curves are concave rather than convex. They are bowed away from the origin, and the RCS is increasing

[1] Hyperbolas the asymptotes of which coincide with the coordinate axes.

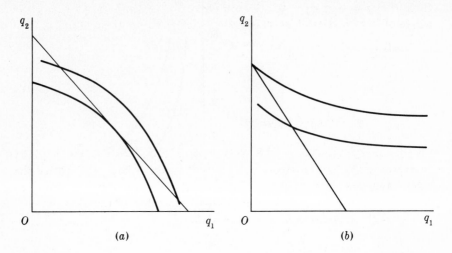

Fig. 2-4

throughout. The first-order condition for a maximum is satisfied at the point of tangency between the price line and an indifference curve, but the second-order condition is not. Therefore this point represents a situation of minimum utility, and the consumer can increase his utility by moving from the point of tangency toward either axis. He consumes only one commodity at the optimum. If he spends all his income on one commodity, he can buy y^0/p_1 units of Q_1 or y^0/p_2 units of Q_2. Therefore he will buy only Q_1 or only Q_2, depending upon whether $f(y^0/p_1,0) \gtrless f(0,y^0/p_2)$. In the example shown in Fig. 2-4a he will buy only Q_2. In the second case (see Fig. 2-4b) the indifference curves have the appropriate shape, but they are everywhere less steep than the price line. Tangency is not possible; the first-order condition cannot be fulfilled because of the restrictions $q_1 \geqq 0$, $q_2 \geqq 0$. The consumer's optimum position is again given by a corner solution, and he purchases only Q_2 at the optimum.

METHOD 2

The same conclusions can be obtained by using the technique of Lagrange multipliers. From the utility function (2-1) and the budget constraint (2-5) form the function

$$V = f(q_1,q_2) + \lambda(y^0 - p_1q_1 - p_2q_2) \tag{2-12}$$

where λ is the as yet undetermined Lagrange multiplier (see Sec. A-3). V is a function of q_1, q_2, and λ. Moreover, V is identically equal to U for those values of q_1 and q_2 which satisfy the budget constraint, since

$$\frac{\partial^2 Z}{\partial q_1\, \partial q_2} = F'' f_1 f_2 + F' f_{12}$$

$$\frac{\partial^2 Z}{\partial q_2\, \partial q_1} = F'' f_1 f_2 + F' f_{21}$$

$$\frac{\partial^2 Z}{\partial q_1\, \partial \lambda} = -p_1$$

$$\frac{\partial^2 Z}{\partial q_2\, \partial \lambda} = -p_2$$

The second-order condition for a maximum states that

$$\mathbf{A} = \begin{vmatrix} F'' f_1^2 + F' f_{11} & F'' f_1 f_2 + F' f_{12} & -p_1 \\ F'' f_1 f_2 + F' f_{21} & F'' f_2^2 + F' f_{22} & -p_2 \\ -p_1 & -p_2 & 0 \end{vmatrix} > 0 \qquad (2\text{-}18)$$

This determinant can be shown to be the same as (2-14). The value of a determinant does not change if a multiple of one row is added to some other row or if a multiple of a column is added to some other column. Multiplying a row or a column of the array by a given number is equivalent to multiplying the value of the determinant by that number (see Sec. A-1). From the first two equations of (2-16)

$$p_1 = \frac{F' f_1}{\lambda}$$

$$p_2 = \frac{F' f_2}{\lambda}$$

Substituting these values of p_1 and p_2 into (2-18),

$$\mathbf{A} = \begin{vmatrix} F'' f_1^2 + F' f_{11} & F'' f_1 f_2 + F' f_{12} & -F' f_1/\lambda \\ F'' f_1 f_2 + F' f_{21} & F'' f_2^2 + F' f_{22} & -F' f_2/\lambda \\ -F' f_1/\lambda & -F' f_2/\lambda & 0 \end{vmatrix} > 0 \qquad (2\text{-}19)$$

Multiplying the last row and the last column of (2-19) by λ/F',

$$\mathbf{A} = \left(\frac{F'}{\lambda}\right)^2 \begin{vmatrix} F'' f_1^2 + F' f_{11} & F'' f_1 f_2 + F' f_{12} & -f_1 \\ F'' f_1 f_2 + F' f_{21} & F'' f_2^2 + F' f_{22} & -f_2 \\ -f_1 & -f_2 & 0 \end{vmatrix} > 0$$

Now add $F'' f_1$ times the last row to the first row and $F'' f_2$ times the last row to the second row. This leaves $\mathbf{A}$ unchanged:

$$\mathbf{A} = \left(\frac{F'}{\lambda}\right)^2 \begin{vmatrix} F' f_{11} & F' f_{12} & -f_1 \\ F' f_{21} & F' f_{22} & -f_2 \\ -f_1 & -f_2 & 0 \end{vmatrix} > 0$$

Substitute $-\lambda p_1/F'$ for $-f_1$ and $-\lambda p_2/F'$ for $-f_2$ from the first two equations of (2-16) and then multiply the last row and the last column by F'/λ:

$$\mathbf{A} = \begin{vmatrix} F'f_{11} & F'f_{12} & -p_1 \\ F'f_{21} & F'f_{22} & -p_2 \\ -p_1 & -p_2 & 0 \end{vmatrix} > 0$$

Now multiply the last column by F' and divide the first two rows by F':

$$\mathbf{A} = \begin{vmatrix} f_{11} & f_{12} & -p_1 \\ f_{21} & f_{22} & -p_2 \\ -p_1 & -p_2 & 0 \end{vmatrix} (F') > 0 \tag{2-20}$$

F is a monotonic transformation by hypothesis; hence F' is positive, and the sign of $\mathbf{A}$ is the same as the sign of the determinant on the right-hand side of (2-20). However, the determinant on the right-hand side of (2-20) is identical with that given by (2-14). This proves that the second-order condition is invariant with respect to the choice of the utility index. It follows from the invariance of the first- and second-order conditions that if the utility index U is maximized, so will be the utility index W. It can be concluded that if the consumer maximizes his utility subject to the budget constraint for one given utility index, he will behave in identical fashion irrespective of the utility index chosen, as long as the index selected is a monotonic transformation of the original one. If a utility function is maximized by a particular batch of commodities, the same batch will maximize all other utility functions that are monotonic transformations of it. The consumer's utility function is unique except for a monotonic transformation.[1]

Choose the utility index $U^* = q_1^2 q_2^2$, which is a monotonic transformation of $U = q_1 q_2$.† Form the function

$$V^* = q_1^2 q_2^2 + \lambda(y^0 - 2q_1 - 5q_2)$$

and set its partial derivatives equal to zero:

$$\frac{\partial V^*}{\partial q_1} = 2q_1 q_2^2 - 2\lambda = 0$$

$$\frac{\partial V^*}{\partial q_2} = 2q_1^2 q_2 - 5\lambda = 0$$

$$\frac{\partial V^*}{\partial \lambda} = y^0 - 2q_1 - 5q_2 = 0$$

---

[1] This proposition can be proved intuitively as follows. Any single-valued function U can serve as a utility function if it is *order-preserving;* that is, $U(A) > U(B)$ if and only if A is preferred to B. If $F(U)$ is a monotonic transformation, $F[U(A)] > F[U(B)]$, and the function $F(U)$ is itself order-preserving.

† The new utility function is obtained by squaring the original one. Squaring is not a monotonic transformation if negative numbers are admissible. However, squaring is proper for the present purposes, since the possibility of negative purchases by the consumer is not admitted.

Substituting $y^0 = 100$ and solving for q_1 and q_2, the same values are obtained as before: $q_1 = 25$ and $q_2 = 10$.

2-4 DEMAND FUNCTIONS

ORDINARY DEMAND FUNCTIONS

A consumer's ordinary demand function (sometimes called a Marshallian demand function) gives the quantity of a commodity that he will buy as a function of commodity prices and his income. Ordinary demand functions are called simply demand functions unless it is necessary to distinguish them from another type of demand function. They can be derived from the analysis of utility maximization. The first-order conditions for maximization (2-13) consist of three equations in the three unknowns: q_1, q_2, and λ.[†] The demand functions are obtained by solving this system for the unknowns. The solutions for q_1 and q_2 are in terms of the parameters p_1, p_2, and y^0. The quantity of Q_1 (or Q_2) that the consumer purchases in the general case depends upon the prices of all commodities and his income.

As above, assume that the utility function is $U = q_1 q_2$ and the budget constraint $y^0 - p_1 q_1 - p_2 q_2 = 0$. Form the expression

$$V = q_1 q_2 + \lambda(y^0 - p_1 q_1 - p_2 q_2)$$

and set its partial derivatives equal to zero:

$$\frac{\partial V}{\partial q_1} = q_2 - p_1 \lambda = 0$$

$$\frac{\partial V}{\partial q_2} = q_1 - p_2 \lambda = 0$$

$$\frac{\partial V}{\partial \lambda} = y^0 - p_1 q_1 - p_2 q_2 = 0$$

Solving for q_1 and q_2 gives the demand functions:[1]

$$q_1 = \frac{y^0}{2p_1} \qquad q_2 = \frac{y^0}{2p_2}$$

The demand functions derived in this fashion are contingent on continued optimizing behavior by the consumer. Given the consumer's income and prices of commodities, the quantities demanded by him can be determined from his demand functions. Of course, these quantities are the

---

[†] Assume that the second-order conditions are fulfilled.
[1] Notice that these demand functions are a special case in which the demand for each commodity depends only upon its own price and income.

same as those obtained directly from the utility function. Substituting $y^0 = 100$, $p_1 = 2$, $p_2 = 5$ in the demand functions gives $q_1 = 25$ and $q_2 = 10$, as in Sec. 2-2.

Two important properties of demand functions can be deduced: (1) the demand for any commodity is a single-valued function of prices and income, and (2) demand functions are homogeneous of degree zero in prices and income; i.e., if all prices and income change in the same proportion, the quantities demanded remain unchanged.

The first property follows from the convexity of the indifference curves: a single maximum, and therefore a single commodity combination, corresponds to a given set of prices and income. To prove the second property assume that all prices and income change in the same proportion. The budget constraint becomes

$$ky^0 - kp_1q_1 - kp_2q_2 = 0$$

where k is the factor of proportionality. Expression (2-12) becomes

$$V = f(q_1,q_2) + \lambda(ky^0 - kp_1q_1 - kp_2q_2)$$

and the first-order conditions are

$$\begin{aligned} f_1 - \lambda kp_1 &= 0 \\ f_2 - \lambda kp_2 &= 0 \\ ky^0 - kp_1q_1 - kp_2q_2 &= 0 \end{aligned} \qquad (2\text{-}21)$$

The last equation of (2-21) is the partial derivative of V with respect to the Lagrange multiplier and can be written as

$$k(y^0 - p_1q_1 - p_2q_2) = 0$$

Since $k \neq 0$,

$$y^0 - p_1q_1 - p_2q_2 = 0$$

Eliminating k from the first two equations of (2-21) by moving the second terms to the right-hand side and dividing the first equation by the second,

$$\frac{f_1}{f_2} = \frac{p_1}{p_2}$$

The last two equations are the same as (2-5) and (2-8). Therefore the demand function for the price-income set (kp_1,kp_2,ky^0) is derived from the same equations as for the price-income set (p_1,p_2,y^0). It is also easy to demonstrate that the second-order conditions are unaffected. This proves that the demand functions are homogeneous of degree zero in prices and income.   If all prices and the consumer's income are increased in the same proportion, the quantities demanded by the consumer do not change.   This implies a relevant and empirically testable restriction upon the consumer's behavior; it means that he will not behave as if he were richer (or poorer) in terms of real income if his income and prices rise in the same proportion.   A rise in money income is desirable for the consumer, *ceteris paribus*, but its benefits are illusory if prices change proportionately.   If such proportionate changes leave his behavior unaltered, there is an absence of "money illusion."[1]

COMPENSATED DEMAND FUNCTIONS

Imagine a situation in which some public authority taxes or subsidizes a consumer in such a way as to leave his utility unchanged after a price change.   Assume that this is done by providing a lump-sum payment that will give the consumer the minimum income necessary to achieve his initial utility level.   The consumer's compensated demand functions give the quantities of the commodities that he will buy as functions of commodity prices under these conditions.   They are obtained by minimizing the consumer's expenditures subject to the constraint that his utility is at the fixed level U^0.

Assume again that the utility function is $U = q_1q_2$.   Form the expression

$$Z = p_1q_1 + p_2q_2 + \mu(U^0 - q_1q_2)$$

and set its partial derivatives equal to zero:

$$\frac{\partial Z}{\partial q_1} = p_1 - \mu q_2 = 0$$

$$\frac{\partial Z}{\partial q_2} = p_2 - \mu q_1 = 0$$

$$\frac{\partial Z}{\partial \mu} = U^0 - q_1q_2 = 0$$

Solving for q_1 and q_2 gives the compensated demand functions:

$$q_1 = \sqrt{\frac{U^0 p_2}{p_1}} \qquad q_2 = \sqrt{\frac{U^0 p_1}{p_2}}$$

The reader can easily verify that these functions are homogeneous of degree zero in prices.

---

[1] If the consumer possesses a hoard of cash, he may feel richer in spite of a proportional fall in commodity prices and income, since the purchasing power of his hoard increases.   He may consequently increase his demand for commodities.   This is the real balance effect.

DEMAND CURVES

In general, the consumer's ordinary demand function for Q_1 is written as

$$q_1 = \phi(p_1, p_2, y^0)$$

or, assuming that p_2 and y^0 are given parameters,[1]

$$q_1 = D(p_1)$$

The shape of the demand function depends upon the properties of the consumer's utility function. It is generally assumed that demand curves are negatively sloped: the lower the price, the greater the quantity demanded. In exceptional cases the opposite relationship may hold. An example is provided by ostentatious consumption: if the consumer derives utility from a high price, the demand function may have a positive slope. The nature of price-induced changes in the quantity demanded is analyzed in detail in Sec. 2-6. Elsewhere in this volume it is assumed that demand functions are negatively sloped.

The consumer's compensated demand curve for Q_1 is constructed in a similar fashion with p_2 and U^0 as given parameters. In Sec. 2-6 it is shown that the convexity of the indifference curves ensures that compensated demand curves are always downward sloping.

Possible shapes for ordinary and compensated demand curves are shown in Fig. 2-5. The ordinary demand curve is labeled DD and the compensated demand curve is labeled $D'D'$. The values at their point of intersection, p_1^0 and q_1^0, satisfy both functions. At this point the utility level achieved for the ordinary demand curve equals the level prescribed for the compensated demand curve, and the minimum income for the compensated demand curve equals the fixed income for the ordinary demand curve. At prices greater than p_1^0 income compensation will be positive, and the compensated demand curve will yield higher quantities for each price. At prices less than p_1^0 income compensation will be negative, and the compensated demand curve will yield lower quantities for each price.

---

[1] In general, the demand curve can also be written as $p_1 = \psi(q_1)$. If the price is p_1^0, and the consumer purchases q_1^0 units, his total expenditure on the commodity is $p_1^0 q_1^0$ dollars. It has been argued that the area under the demand curve up to the point $q_1 = q_1^0$ represents the sum of money that the consumer would be willing to pay for q_1^0 units rather than not have the commodity at all. The difference between what he would be willing to pay and what he actually pays, $\int_0^{q_1^0} \psi(q_1)\, dq_1 - p_1^0 q_1^0$, is the "consumer surplus," i.e., a measure of the net benefit he derives from buying Q_1. There are several alternative definitions of consumer surplus, and the concept has been refined considerably.

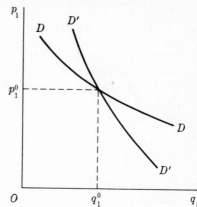

Fig. 2-5

PRICE AND INCOME ELASTICITIES OF DEMAND

The own elasticity of demand for $Q_1(\varepsilon_{11})$ is defined as the proportionate rate of change of q_1 divided by the proportionate rate of change of its own price with p_2 and y^0 constant:

$$\varepsilon_{11} = \frac{\partial(\log q_1)}{\partial(\log p_1)} = \frac{p_1}{q_1}\frac{\partial q_1}{\partial p_1} \qquad (2\text{-}22)$$

Price elasticities of demand are pure numbers independent of the units in which prices and outputs are measured. The elasticity ε_{11} is negative if the corresponding demand curve is downward sloping.

The consumer's expenditure on Q_1 is p_1q_1, and

$$\frac{\partial(p_1q_1)}{\partial p_1} = q_1 + p_1\frac{\partial q_1}{\partial p_1} = q_1\left(1 + \frac{p_1}{q_1}\frac{\partial q_1}{\partial p_1}\right) = q_1(1 + \varepsilon_{11})$$

The consumer's expenditures on Q_1 will increase with p_1 if $\varepsilon_{11} > -1$, remain unchanged if $\varepsilon_{11} = -1$, and decrease if $\varepsilon_{11} < -1$.

A cross-price elasticity of demand for the ordinary demand function relates the proportionate change in one quantity to the proportionate change in the other price. For example,

$$\varepsilon_{21} = \frac{\partial(\log q_2)}{\partial(\log p_1)} = \frac{p_1}{q_2}\frac{\partial q_2}{\partial p_1} \qquad (2\text{-}23)$$

Cross-price elasticities may be either positive or negative.

Taking the total differential of the budget constraint (2-5) and letting $dy^0 = dp_2 = 0$,

$$p_1\, dq_1 + q_1\, dp_1 + p_2\, dq_2 = 0$$

Multiplying through by $p_1q_1q_2/y^0q_1q_2\,dp_1$, and rearranging terms,

$$\alpha_1\varepsilon_{11} + \alpha_2\varepsilon_{21} = -\alpha_1 \qquad\qquad (2\text{-}24)$$

where $\alpha_1 = p_1q_1/y^0$ and $\alpha_2 = p_2q_2/y^0$ are the proportions of total expenditures for the two goods. If the own-price elasticity of demand for Q_1 is known, (2-24) can be used to evaluate the cross-price elasticity of demand for Q_2. If $\varepsilon_{11} = -1$, $\varepsilon_{21} = 0$. If $\varepsilon_{11} < -1$, $\varepsilon_{21} > 0$, and if $\varepsilon_{11} > -1$, $\varepsilon_{21} < 0$.

Own- and cross-price elasticities of demand for compensated demand functions can be defined in an analogous manner by inserting compensated rather than ordinary demand functions in (2-22) and (2-23). Equation (2-24) does not hold for compensated demand functions. Taking the total differential of the utility function (2-1) and letting $dU = 0$,

$$f_1\,dq_1 + f_2\,dq_2 = 0$$

Using the first-order condition $p_1/p_2 = f_1/f_2$, multiplying through by $p_1q_1q_2/y^0q_1q_2\,dp_1$, and rearranging terms,

$$\alpha_1\xi_{11} + \alpha_2\xi_{21} = 0 \qquad\qquad (2\text{-}25)$$

where the compensated price elasticities are denoted by ξ_{11} and ξ_{21}. Since $\xi_{11} < 0$, it follows from (2-25) that $\xi_{21} > 0$.

Returning to the example $U = q_1q_2$, the own- and cross-price elasticities for the ordinary demand function are

$$\varepsilon_{11} = -\frac{p_1}{q_1}\frac{y^0}{2p_1^2} = -\frac{p_1}{y^0/2p_1}\frac{y^0}{2p_1^2} = -1$$

$$\varepsilon_{21} = \frac{p_1}{q_2}0 = 0$$

This is a special case. Not all demand functions have unit own and zero cross elasticities or even constant elasticities. In general, elasticities are a function of p_1, p_2, and y^0. The reader can verify that the compensated elasticities for this example are $\xi_{11} = -\frac{1}{2}$ and $\xi_{21} = \frac{1}{2}$.

An income elasticity of demand for an ordinary demand function is defined as the proportionate change in the purchases of a commodity relative to the proportionate change in income with prices constant:

$$\eta_1 = \frac{\partial(\log q_1)}{\partial(\log y)} = \frac{y}{q_1}\frac{\partial\phi(p_1,p_2,y)}{\partial y} \qquad\qquad (2\text{-}26)$$

where η_1 denotes the income elasticity of demand for q_1. Income elasticities can be positive, negative, or zero, but are normally assumed to be positive.

Taking the total differential of the budget constraint (2-5),

$$p_1\,dq_1 + p_2\,dq_2 = dy$$

Multiplying through by y/y, multiplying the first term on the left by q_1/q_1 and the second by q_2/q_2,

$$\alpha_1\eta_1 + \alpha_2\eta_2 = 1 \tag{2-27}$$

The sum of the income elasticities weighted by total expenditure proportions equals unity. Income elasticities cannot be derived for compensated demand functions since income is not an argument of these functions.

2-5 INCOME AND LEISURE

If the consumer's income is payment for work performed by him, the optimum amount of work that he performs can be derived from the analysis of utility maximization. One can also derive the consumer's demand curve for income from this analysis. Assume that the consumer's satisfaction depends on income and leisure. His utility function is

$$U = g(L,y) \tag{2-28}$$

where L denotes leisure. Both income and leisure are desirable. In the preceding sections it is assumed that the consumer derives utility from the commodities he purchases with his income. In the construction of (2-28) it is assumed that he buys the various commodities in fixed proportions at constant prices, and income is thereby treated as generalized purchasing power.

The rate of substitution of income for leisure is

$$-\frac{dy}{dL} = \frac{g_1}{g_2}$$

Denote the amount of work performed by the consumer by W and the wage rate by r. By definition,

$$L = T - W \tag{2-29}$$

where T is the total amount of available time.[1] The budget constraint is

$$y = rW \tag{2-30}$$

Substituting (2-29) and (2-30) into (2-28),

$$U = g(T - W, rW) \tag{2-31}$$

[1] For example, if the period for which the utility function is defined is one day, $T = 24$ hours.

To maximize utility set the derivative of (2-31) with respect to W equal to zero:[1]

$$\frac{dU}{dW} = -g_1 + g_2 r = 0$$

and therefore

$$-\frac{dy}{dL} = \frac{g_1}{g_2} = r \qquad\qquad (2\text{-}32)$$

which states that the rate of substitution of income for leisure equals the wage rate.   The second-order condition states

$$\frac{d^2U}{dW^2} = g_{11} - 2g_{12}r + g_{22}r^2 < 0$$

Equation (2-32) is a relation in terms of W and r and is based on the individual consumer's optimizing behavior.   It is therefore the consumer's supply curve for work and states how much he will work at various wage rates.   Since the supply of work is equivalent to the demand for income, (2-32) indirectly provides the consumer's demand curve for income.

Assume that the utility function is of the same form as in previous sections: $U = Ly$.   Then

$$U = (T - W)Wr$$

and setting the derivative equal to zero,

$$\frac{dU}{dW} = Tr - 2Wr = 0$$

Therefore

$$W = \frac{T}{2}$$

and substituting this in (2-30),

$$y = \frac{rT}{2}$$

One can infer that the consumer will work 12 hours per day irrespective of the wage level.   The second-order condition is fulfilled:

$$\frac{d^2U}{dW^2} = -2r < 0$$

An alternative example is provided by the utility function

$$U = Ly - 0.1L^2 - 0.1y^2 = (T - W)Wr - 0.1(T - W)^2 - 0.1W^2r^2$$

---

[1] The composite-function rule is employed.

Then

$$\frac{dU}{dW} = -Wr + (T - W)r + 0.2(T - W) - 0.2Wr^2 = 0$$

and

$$W = \frac{T(r + 0.2)}{2(0.1 + r + 0.1r^2)}$$

The amount of work performed now depends upon the wage rate. If $r = 1$ dollar, the individual will work 12 hours per day. The second-order condition is fulfilled:

$$\frac{d^2U}{dW^2} = -2(0.1 + r + 0.1r^2) < 0$$

2-6 SUBSTITUTION AND INCOME EFFECTS

THE SLUTSKY EQUATION

The quantities purchased by a rational consumer will always satisfy Eqs. (2-13). Changes in prices and income will normally alter his expenditure pattern, but the new quantities (and prices and income) will still satisfy (2-13). In order to find the magnitude of the effect of price and income changes on the consumer's purchases, allow all variables to vary simultaneously. This is accomplished by total differentiation of Eqs. (2-13):

$$
\begin{aligned}
f_{11}\, dq_1 + f_{12}\, dq_2 - p_1\, d\lambda &= \lambda\, dp_1 \\
f_{21}\, dq_1 + f_{22}\, dq_2 - p_2\, d\lambda &= \lambda\, dp_2 \\
-p_1\, dq_1 - p_2\, dq_2 &= -dy + q_1\, dp_1 + q_2\, dp_2
\end{aligned}
\tag{2-33}
$$

In order to solve this system of three equations for the three unknowns, dq_1, dq_2, and $d\lambda$, the terms on the right must be regarded as constants. The array of coefficients formed by (2-33) is the same as the bordered Hessian determinant (2-14). Denoting this determinant by $\mathbf{D}$ and the cofactor of the element in the first row and the first column by $\mathbf{D}_{11}$, the cofactor of the element in the first row and second column by $\mathbf{D}_{12}$, etc., the solution of (2-33) by Cramer's rule (see Sec. A-1) is

$$dq_1 = \frac{\lambda \mathbf{D}_{11}\, dp_1 + \lambda \mathbf{D}_{21}\, dp_2 + \mathbf{D}_{31}(-dy + q_1\, dp_1 + q_2\, dp_2)}{\mathbf{D}} \tag{2-34}$$

$$dq_2 = \frac{\lambda \mathbf{D}_{12}\, dp_1 + \lambda \mathbf{D}_{22}\, dp_2 + \mathbf{D}_{32}(-dy + q_1\, dp_1 + q_2\, dp_2)}{\mathbf{D}} \tag{2-35}$$

Dividing both sides of (2-34) by dp_1 and assuming that p_2 and y do not change ($dp_2 = dy = 0$),

$$\frac{\partial q_1}{\partial p_1} = \frac{\mathbf{D}_{11}\lambda}{\mathbf{D}} + q_1 \frac{\mathbf{D}_{31}}{\mathbf{D}} \tag{2-36}$$

The partial derivative on the left-hand side of (2-36) is the rate of change of the consumer's purchases of Q_1 with respect to changes in p_1, all other things being equal. *Ceteris paribus*, the rate of change with respect to income is

$$\frac{\partial q_1}{\partial y} = -\frac{\mathbf{D}_{31}}{\mathbf{D}} \tag{2-37}$$

Changes in commodity prices change the consumer's level of satisfaction, since a new equilibrium is established which lies on a different indifference curve.

Consider a price change that is compensated by an income change that leaves the consumer on his initial indifference curve. An increase in the price of a commodity is accompanied by a corresponding increase in his income such that $dU = 0$ and $f_1\,dq_1 + f_2\,dq_2 = 0$ by (2-3). Since $f_1/f_2 = p_1/p_2$, it is also true that $p_1\,dq_1 + p_2\,dq_2 = 0$. Hence, from the last equation of (2-33), $-dy + q_1\,dp_1 + q_2\,dp_2 = 0$, and

$$\left(\frac{\partial q_1}{\partial p_1}\right)_{U=\text{const}} = \frac{\mathbf{D}_{11}\lambda}{\mathbf{D}} \tag{2-38}$$

Equation (2-36) can now be rewritten as

$$\frac{\partial q_1}{\partial p_1} = \left(\frac{\partial q_1}{\partial p_1}\right)_{U=\text{const}} - q_1\left(\frac{\partial q_1}{\partial y}\right)_{\text{prices=const}} \tag{2-39}$$

Equation (2-39) is known as the *Slutsky equation*. The quantity $\partial q_1/\partial p_1$ is the slope of the ordinary demand curve for Q_1, and the first term on the right is the slope of the compensated demand curve for Q_1.

The Slutsky equation may be expressed in terms of the price and income elasticities described in Sec. 2-4. Multiplying (2-39) through by p_1/q_1 and multiplying the last term on the right by y/y,

$$\varepsilon_{11} = \xi_{11} - \alpha_1\eta_1 \tag{2-40}$$

The price elasticity of the ordinary demand curve equals the price elasticity of the compensated demand curve less the corresponding income elasticity multiplied by the proportion of total expenditures spent on Q_1. Hence, the ordinary demand curve will have a greater demand elasticity than the compensated demand curve, that is, ε_{11} will be more negative than ξ_{11}, if the income elasticity of demand is positive.

DIRECT EFFECTS

The first term on the right-hand side of (2-39) is the *substitution effect*, or the rate at which the consumer substitutes Q_1 for other commodities when the price of Q_1 changes and he moves along a given indifference

curve.[1]   The second term on the right is the *income effect*, which states
the consumer's reaction with respect to purchases of Q_1 to changes in his
income, prices remaining constant.   The sum of the two terms gives the
total effect on the consumer's purchases of Q_1 as p_1 changes.   Imagine
that the price of Q_1 falls.   The consumer may wish to substitute Q_1
for Q_2 because (1) Q_1 has become cheaper and (2) the fall in the price
of Q_1 is equivalent to an increase in the consumer's income.   The substitution effect describes the reallocation that will take place among the
consumer's purchases if a price change is compensated by a simultaneous income change which forces him to remain on the same indifference
curve.   The discrepancy between this point and the final point of equilibrium is accounted for by the income effect.   These concepts are illustrated in Fig. 2-6.   The original price line is AB, and the corresponding point of equilibrium is at R.   After the change in p_1 the price line
is represented by AC, and the final equilibrium is at T.   The movement
from R to T can be decomposed into the steps from R to S and from
S to T.   The point S is the tangency point between the original indifference curve and a price line DE which has the same slope (and therefore
represents the same price ratio) as AC.   The movement from R to S is
accounted for by the substitution and the movement from S to T by the
income effect.[2]

[1] Slutsky called this the *residual variability* of the commodity in question.
[2] Figure 2-6 is not an exact representation of the foregoing mathematical discussion.
The Slutsky equation involves rates of change which cannot be represented directly
in an indifference-curve diagram.   In Fig. 2-6 the sum of two discrete changes (rather
than of two rates) is the total discrete change (rather than the total rate of change).
These two discrete changes *correspond to* (rather than *are*) the substitution effect and
the income effect.

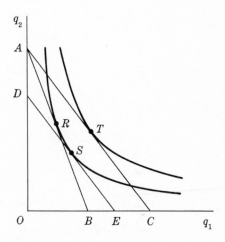

Fig. 2-6

In the present case the multiplier λ is the derivative of utility with respect to income with prices constant and quantities variable. From the utility function (2-1) it follows that $\partial U/\partial y = f_1(\partial q_1/\partial y) + f_2(\partial q_2/\partial y)$. Substituting $f_1 = \lambda p_1$ and $f_2 = \lambda p_2$,

$$\frac{\partial U}{\partial y} = \lambda \left(p_1 \frac{\partial q_1}{\partial y} + p_2 \frac{\partial q_2}{\partial y} \right) = \lambda$$

which follows from the partial derivative of the budget constraint (2-8) with respect to y: $1 = p_1(\partial q_1/\partial y) + p_2(\partial q_2/\partial y)$. The marginal utility of income λ is positive if the marginal utilities of the two commodities are positive as assumed.

By (2-38) the substitution effect is $\mathbf{D}_{11}\lambda/\mathbf{D}$. The determinant $\mathbf{D}$, which is the same as (2-14), is positive. Expanding $\mathbf{D}_{11}$,

$$\mathbf{D}_{11} = -p_2^2$$

which is clearly negative. This proves that the sign of the substitution effect is always negative and that the compensated demand curve is always downward sloping.

A change in real income may cause a reallocation of the consumer's resources even if prices do not change or if they change in the same proportion. The income effect is $-q_1(\partial q_1/\partial y)_{\text{prices=const}}$ and may be of either sign. The final effect of a price change on the purchases of the commodity is thus unknown. However, an important conclusion can still be derived: the smaller the quantity of Q_1, the less significant is the income effect. A commodity Q_1 is called an *inferior good* if the consumer's purchases decrease as income rises and increase as income falls; i.e., if $\partial q_1/\partial y$ is negative, which makes the income effect positive. A *Giffen good* is an inferior good with an income effect large enough to offset the negative substitution effect and make $\partial q_1/\partial p_1$ positive. This means that as the price of Q_1 falls, the consumer's purchases of Q_1 will also fall. This may occur if a consumer is sufficiently poor so that a considerable portion of his income is spent on a commodity such as potatoes which he needs for his subsistence. Assume now that the price of potatoes falls. The consumer who is not very fond of potatoes may suddenly discover that his real income has increased as a result of the price fall. He will then buy fewer potatoes and purchase a more palatable diet with the remainder of his income.

The Slutsky equation can be derived for the specific utility function assumed in the previous examples. State the budget constraint in the general implicit form $y - p_1 q_1 - p_2 q_2 = 0$, and form the function

$$V = q_1 q_2 + \lambda(y - p_1 q_1 - p_2 q_2)$$

Setting the partial derivatives equal to zero,

$$q_2 - \lambda p_1 = 0$$
$$q_1 - \lambda p_2 = 0$$
$$y - p_1 q_1 - p_2 q_2 = 0$$

The total differentials of these equations are

$$dq_2 - p_1 \, d\lambda = \lambda \, dp_1$$
$$dq_1 - p_2 \, d\lambda = \lambda \, dp_2$$
$$-p_1 \, dq_1 - p_2 \, dq_2 = -dy + q_1 \, dp_1 + q_2 \, dp_2$$

Denote the determinant of the coefficients of these equations by $\mathbf{D}$ and the cofactor of the element in the ith row and jth column by $\mathbf{D}_{ij}$. Simple calculations show that

$$\mathbf{D} = 2p_1 p_2$$
$$\mathbf{D}_{11} = -p_2^2$$
$$\mathbf{D}_{21} = p_1 p_2$$
$$\mathbf{D}_{31} = -p_2$$

Solving for dq_1 by Cramer's rule gives

$$dq_1 = \frac{-p_2^2 \lambda \, dp_1 + p_1 p_2 \lambda \, dp_2 - p_2(-dy + q_1 \, dp_1 + q_2 \, dp_2)}{2p_1 p_2}$$

Assuming that only the price of the first commodity varies,

$$\frac{\partial q_1}{\partial p_1} = -\frac{p_2 \lambda}{2p_1} - \frac{q_1}{2p_1}$$

The value of λ is obtained by substituting the values of q_1 and q_2 from the first two equations of the first-order conditions into the third and solving for λ in terms of the parameters p_1, p_2, and y. Thus $\lambda = y/2p_1 p_2$. Substituting this value into the above equation and then introducing into it the values of the parameters ($y = 100$, $p_1 = 2$, $p_2 = 5$) and also the equilibrium value of q_1 (25), a numerical answer is obtained:

$$\frac{\partial q_1}{\partial p_1} = -12.5$$

The meaning of this answer is the following: if, starting from the initial equilibrium situation, p_1 were to change, *ceteris paribus*, the consumer's purchases would change at the rate of 12.5 units of Q_1 per dollar of change in the price of Q_1; furthermore the direction of the change in the consumer's purchases is opposite to the direction of the price change. The expression $-p_2 \lambda/2p_1$ is the substitution effect, and its value in the present example is -6.25. The expression $-q_1/2p_1$ is the income effect, also with a value of -6.25.

CROSS EFFECTS

The Slutsky equation (2-39) and its elasticity representation (2-40) can be extended to account for changes in the demand for one commodity resulting from changes in the price of the other. The generalized forms are

$$\frac{\partial q_i}{\partial p_j} = \frac{\mathbf{D}_{ji}\lambda}{\mathbf{D}} + q_j \frac{\mathbf{D}_{3i}}{\mathbf{D}} = \left(\frac{\partial q_i}{\partial p_j}\right)_{U=\text{const}} - q_j \left(\frac{\partial q_i}{\partial y}\right)_{\text{prices}=\text{const}} \qquad (2\text{-}41)$$

and

$$\varepsilon_{ij} = \xi_{ij} - \alpha_j \eta_i \qquad (2\text{-}42)$$

for $i, j = 1, 2$. The signs of the cross-substitution effects ($i \neq j$) are not known in general. Let $S_{ij} = \mathbf{D}_{ji}\lambda/\mathbf{D}$ denote the substitution effect when the quantity of the ith commodity is adjusted as a result of a variation in the jth price. Since $\mathbf{D}$ is a symmetric determinant,[1] $\mathbf{D}_{12} = \mathbf{D}_{21}$, and it follows that $S_{ij} = S_{ji}$. The substitution effect on the ith commodity resulting from a change in the jth price is the same as the substitution effect on the jth commodity resulting from a change in the ith price.

This is a remarkable conclusion. Imagine that the consumer's demand for tea increases at the rate of 2 cups of tea per 1-cent increase in the price of coffee. One can infer from this that his purchases of coffee would increase at the rate of 2 cups of coffee per 1-cent increase in the price of tea.

Sum the compensated demand elasticities for Q_1 as a result of changes in p_1 and p_2:

$$\xi_{11} + \xi_{12} = \frac{p_1 \mathbf{D}_{11}\lambda}{q_1 \mathbf{D}} + \frac{p_2 \mathbf{D}_{21}\lambda}{q_1 \mathbf{D}} = \frac{\lambda(p_1 \mathbf{D}_{11} + p_2 \mathbf{D}_{21})}{q_1 \mathbf{D}} = 0 \qquad (2\text{-}43)$$

The term in parentheses equals zero since it is an expansion of the determinant of (2-33) in terms of alien cofactors; i.e., the cofactors of the elements of the first column are multiplied by the negative of the elements in the last column. Thus, the negative compensated elasticity for Q_1 with respect to p_1 equals in absolute value the positive compensated elasticity for Q_1 with respect to p_2.

Sum the negative of the ordinary demand elasticities for Q_1 as a result of changes in p_1 and p_2 as given by (2-42):

$$-(\varepsilon_{11} + \varepsilon_{12}) = -(\xi_{11} + \xi_{12}) + (\alpha_1 + \alpha_2)\eta_1 = \eta_1 \qquad (2\text{-}44)$$

from (2-43) and $\alpha_1 + \alpha_2 = 1$. The income elasticity of demand for a commodity equals the negative of the sum of ordinary price elasticities of demand for that commodity with respect to its own and the other price.

---

[1] A determinant is symmetric if its array is symmetric around the principal diagonal.

SUBSTITUTES AND COMPLEMENTS

Two commodities are substitutes if both can satisfy the same need of the consumer; they are complements if they are consumed jointly in order to satisfy some particular need. These are loose definitions, but everyday experience may suggest some plausible examples. Coffee and tea are most likely substitutes, whereas coffee and sugar are most likely complements. A more rigorous definition of substitutability and complementarity is provided by the cross-substitution term of the Slutsky equation (2-41). Accordingly, Q_1 and Q_2 are substitutes if the substitution effect $\mathbf{D}_{21}\lambda/\mathbf{D}$ is positive; they are complements if it is negative. If Q_1 and Q_2 are substitutes (in the everyday sense) and if compensating variations in income keep the consumer on the same indifference curve, an increase in the price of Q_1 will induce the consumer to substitute Q_2 for Q_1. Then $\left(\dfrac{\partial q_2}{\partial p_1}\right)_{U=\text{const}} > 0$. For analogous reasons, $\left(\dfrac{\partial q_2}{\partial p_1}\right)_{U=\text{const}} < 0$ in the case of complements.[1]

All commodities cannot be complements for each other. Hence only substitutability can occur in the present two-variable case. This theorem is easily proved. Multiply (2-36) by p_1, (2-37) by y, and (2-41) for $i = 1$ and $j = 2$ by p_2, and add:

$$\frac{\mathbf{D}_{11}\lambda}{\mathbf{D}}\, p_1 + q_1 \frac{\mathbf{D}_{31}}{\mathbf{D}}\, p_1 + \frac{\mathbf{D}_{21}\lambda}{\mathbf{D}}\, p_2 + q_2 \frac{\mathbf{D}_{31}}{\mathbf{D}}\, p_2 - \frac{\mathbf{D}_{31}}{\mathbf{D}}\, y$$

$$= \frac{1}{\mathbf{D}}\left[\mathbf{D}_{11}\lambda p_1 + \mathbf{D}_{21}\lambda p_2 - \mathbf{D}_{31}(y - p_1 q_1 - p_2 q_2)\right]$$

$$= \frac{1}{\mathbf{D}}\left[\mathbf{D}_{11}\lambda p_1 + \mathbf{D}_{21}\lambda p_2 - \mathbf{D}_{31}(0)\right] = 0$$

The final bracketed term equals zero since it is an expansion in terms of alien cofactors as in (2-43). Substituting $S_{ij} = \mathbf{D}_{ji}\lambda/\mathbf{D}$,

$$S_{11}p_1 + S_{12}p_2 = 0 \tag{2-45}$$

The substitution effect for Q_1 resulting from changes in p_1, S_{11}, is known to be negative. Hence (2-45) implies that S_{12} must be positive, and in terms of the definitions of substitutability and complementarity this means that Q_1 and Q_2 are necessarily substitutes.

2-7 GENERALIZATION TO n VARIABLES

The foregoing analysis of the consumer is now generalized to the case of n commodities. The generalization is not carried out in detail, but the

---

[1] This provides a rationale for the definitions. When $\left(\dfrac{\partial q_2}{\partial p_1}\right)_{U=\text{const}} = 0$, Q_1 and Q_2 are independent.

first few steps are indicated. If there are n commodities, the utility function is

$$U = f(q_1, q_2, \ldots, q_n)$$

and the budget constraint is given by

$$y - \sum_{i=1}^{n} p_i q_i = 0$$

Forming the Lagrangian function as above,

$$V = f(q_1, q_2, \ldots, q_n) + \lambda\left(y - \sum_{i=1}^{n} p_i q_i\right)$$

Setting the partial derivatives equal to zero,

$$\frac{\partial V}{\partial q_i} = f_i - \lambda p_i = 0 \qquad i = 1, \ldots, n \tag{2-46}$$

Conditions (2-46) can be modified to state the equality for all commodities of marginal utility divided by price. The partial derivative of V with respect to λ is again the budget constraint. There are a total of $(n + 1)$ equations in $(n + 1)$ variables (n q's and λ). The demand curves for the n commodities can be obtained by solving for the q's. Conditions (2-46) can be stated alternatively as

$$-\frac{\partial q_i}{\partial q_j} = \frac{p_j}{p_i}$$

for all i and j; i.e., the rate of commodity substitution of commodity i for commodity j must equal the price ratio p_j/p_i. Second-order conditions must be fulfilled in order to ensure that a batch of commodities that satisfies (2-46) is optimal. The bordered Hessian determinants must alternate in sign:

$$\begin{vmatrix} f_{11} & f_{12} & -p_1 \\ f_{21} & f_{22} & -p_2 \\ -p_1 & -p_2 & 0 \end{vmatrix} > 0, \qquad \begin{vmatrix} f_{11} & f_{12} & f_{13} & -p_1 \\ f_{21} & f_{22} & f_{23} & -p_2 \\ f_{31} & f_{32} & f_{33} & -p_3 \\ -p_1 & -p_2 & -p_3 & 0 \end{vmatrix} < 0,$$

$$\ldots, (-1)^n \begin{vmatrix} f_{11} & f_{12} & \cdots & f_{1n} & -p_1 \\ f_{21} & f_{22} & \cdots & f_{2n} & -p_2 \\ \cdots & \cdots & \cdots & \cdots & \cdots \\ f_{n1} & f_{n2} & \cdots & f_{nn} & -p_n \\ -p_1 & -p_2 & \cdots & -p_n & 0 \end{vmatrix} > 0$$

which is a generalization of condition (2-14).

The assumption of convexity for indifference curves in two dimensions may also be extended to indifference hypersurfaces in n dimensions.

The first of the second-order conditions for the n-dimensional case is the same as the second-order condition for the two-dimensional case which was demonstrated to imply a decreasing RCS between the commodities. In n dimensions it implies decreasing RCSs between every pair of commodities. If the second-order conditions are satisfied for a range of nonnegative values for the q's, the utility function will be *quasi-concave*. This means that the set of all commodity combinations which yield a utility level equal to or greater than the level prescribed for an indifference hypersurface, U^0, will form a closed strictly convex set.[1]

Other theorems can also be generalized in straightforward fashion. The Slutsky equations (2-41) and (2-42) hold for $i, j = 1, \ldots, n$. The generalization of (2-45) is

$$\sum_{j=1}^{n} S_{ij}p_j = 0 \qquad i = 1, \ldots, n \tag{2-47}$$

It still follows that all commodities cannot be complements for each other. However, some pairs of commodities can be complements; i.e., some $S_{ij} < 0$ for $i \neq j$.

All the elasticity relations generalize. The n-commodity forms for (2-24), (2-25), and (2-27) respectively are

$$\sum_{i=1}^{n} \alpha_i \varepsilon_{ij} = -\alpha_j \qquad j = 1, \ldots, n$$

$$\sum_{i=1}^{n} \alpha_i \xi_{ij} = 0 \qquad j = 1, \ldots, n$$

$$\sum_{j=1}^{n} \alpha_j \eta_j = 1$$

and the general forms for (2-43) and (2-44) respectively are

$$\sum_{j=1}^{n} \xi_{ij} = 0 \qquad i = 1, \ldots, n$$

$$-\sum_{j=1}^{n} \varepsilon_{ij} = \eta_i \qquad i = 1, \ldots, n$$

2-8 THE THEORY OF REVEALED PREFERENCE

It was assumed in the previous sections that the consumer possesses a utility function. If his behavior conforms to certain simple axioms, the existence and nature of his indifference map can be inferred from his actions.

[1] Convex sets are discussed in Secs. 5-4 and 9-2.

Assume that there are n commodities. A particular set of prices p_1^0, $p_2^0, \ldots, p_n^0$ is denoted by $\mathbf{p}^0$, and the corresponding quantities bought by the consumer by $\mathbf{q}^0$. The consumer's total expenditures are given by $\mathbf{p}^0\mathbf{q}^0$ which is defined as the sum $\Sigma_{i=1}^{n} p_i^0 q_i^0$.

Consider an alternative batch of commodities $\mathbf{q}^1$ that could have been purchased by the consumer but was not. The total cost of $\mathbf{q}^1$ at prices $\mathbf{p}^0$ must be no greater than the total cost of $\mathbf{q}^0$:

$$\mathbf{p}^0\mathbf{q}^1 \leqq \mathbf{p}^0\mathbf{q}^0 \tag{2-48}$$

Since $\mathbf{q}^0$ is at least as expensive a combination of commodities as $\mathbf{q}^1$, and since the consumer refused to choose combination $\mathbf{q}^1$, $\mathbf{q}^0$ is "revealed" to be preferred to $\mathbf{q}^1$.

WEAK AXIOM OF REVEALED PREFERENCE

If $\mathbf{q}^0$ is revealed to be preferred to $\mathbf{q}^1$, the latter must never be revealed to be preferred to $\mathbf{q}^0$.

The only way in which $\mathbf{q}^1$ can be revealed to be preferred to $\mathbf{q}^0$ is to have the consumer purchase the combination $\mathbf{q}^1$ in some price situation in which he could also afford to buy $\mathbf{q}^0$. In other words, $\mathbf{q}^1$ is revealed to be preferred if

$$\mathbf{p}^1\mathbf{q}^0 \leqq \mathbf{p}^1\mathbf{q}^1 \tag{2-49}$$

The axiom states that (2-49) can never hold if (2-48) does. Consequently (2-48) implies the opposite of (2-49) or

$$\mathbf{p}^0\mathbf{q}^1 \leqq \mathbf{p}^0\mathbf{q}^0 \quad \text{implies that} \quad \mathbf{p}^1\mathbf{q}^0 > \mathbf{p}^1\mathbf{q}^1 \tag{2-50}$$

STRONG AXIOM OF REVEALED PREFERENCE

If $\mathbf{q}^0$ is revealed to be preferred to $\mathbf{q}^1$, which is revealed to be preferred to $\mathbf{q}^2, \ldots,$ which is revealed to be preferred to $\mathbf{q}^k$, $\mathbf{q}^k$ must never be revealed to be preferred to $\mathbf{q}^0$. This axiom ensures the transitivity of revealed preferences, but is stronger than the usual transitivity condition.

At the beginning of this chapter the cardinal approach to utility theory was rejected on the grounds that there is no reason to assume that the consumer possesses a cardinal measure of utility. By the same token one could question whether he even possesses an indifference map. It can fortunately be proved that a consumer who always conforms to the above axioms must possess an indifference map. His indifference map could be constructed with a high degree of accuracy (the "true" indifference map could be approximated as closely as is desired) by confronting him with various appropriately chosen price sets and observing his purchases.[1]   If the consumer does not conform to the axioms, he is irrational by the definition of the earlier sections.   If he is irrational and acts inconsistently, he does not possess an indifference map, and the shape of his utility function cannot be determined by observing his behavior.

The meaning of the Weak axiom is illustrated in Fig. 2-7 for the two-commodity case.   Assume that when prices were given by the lines designated by $\mathbf{p}^0$ the consumer purchased commodity combination $\mathbf{q}^0$, and when prices were given by $\mathbf{p}^1$ he purchased $\mathbf{q}^1$.   In both of the cases shown in Fig. 2-7 he could have purchased $\mathbf{q}^1$ at the $\mathbf{p}^0$ prices since $\mathbf{q}^1$ lies below the line $\mathbf{p}^0$.   Given this choice, the Weak axiom states that $\mathbf{q}^0$ must be unobtainable when he purchases $\mathbf{q}^1$; that is, $\mathbf{q}^0$ must lie above the line $\mathbf{p}^1$.   The Weak axiom is satisfied by the behavior shown in Fig. 2-7a.   It is violated by the behavior shown in Fig. 2-7b.   In this case it is not possible to find convex indifference curves with the property that one curve is tangent to $\mathbf{p}^0$ at $\mathbf{q}^0$ and another is tangent to $\mathbf{p}^1$ at $\mathbf{q}^1$.

THE SUBSTITUTION EFFECT

It can be proved from revealed-preference theory that the substitution effect is negative.[2]   Assume that the consumer is forced to move along a

[1] The proof of this theorem is somewhat difficult and is not reproduced here.   See H. S. Houthakker, "Revealed Preference and the Utility Function," *Economica*, n.s., vol. 17 (May, 1950), pp. 159–174.

[2] This is only one of several theorems that can be deduced from the theory.   Others are (1) the homogeneity of the demand functions of zero degree in prices and incomes (Sec. 2-4), and (2) the equality of the cross-substitution effects (Sec. 2-6).   See P. A. Samuelson, *Foundations of Economic Analysis* (Cambridge, Mass.: Harvard, 1948), pp. 111–112; and J. R. Hicks, *A Revision of Demand Theory* (Oxford: Clarendon Press, 1956), p. 127.

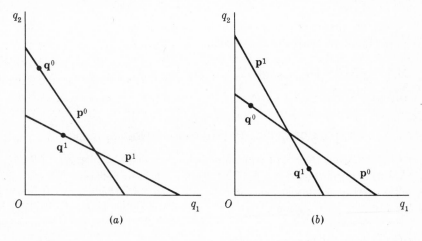

(a)   (b)

Fig. 2-7

given indifference hypersurface in n dimensions. When prices are given by $\mathbf{p}^0$, he purchases the batch $\mathbf{q}^0$ rather than the batch $\mathbf{q}^1$ which lies on the same indifference hypersurface. Since he is indifferent between $\mathbf{q}^0$ and $\mathbf{q}^1$ and yet purchases $\mathbf{q}^0$, the latter combination must not be more expensive than the former:

$$\mathbf{p}^0 \mathbf{q}^0 \leqq \mathbf{p}^0 \mathbf{q}^1 \tag{2-51}$$

The combination $\mathbf{q}^1$ is purchased at prices $\mathbf{p}^1$. This implies that $\mathbf{q}^0$ must not be cheaper at the $\mathbf{p}^1$ prices than $\mathbf{q}^1$:

$$\mathbf{p}^1 \mathbf{q}^1 \leqq \mathbf{p}^1 \mathbf{q}^0 \tag{2-52}$$

Moving the right-hand terms in (2-51) and (2-52) to the left,[1]

$$\mathbf{p}^0 \mathbf{q}^0 - \mathbf{p}^0 \mathbf{q}^1 = \mathbf{p}^0(\mathbf{q}^0 - \mathbf{q}^1) = -\mathbf{p}^0(\mathbf{q}^1 - \mathbf{q}^0) \leqq 0 \tag{2-53}$$
$$\mathbf{p}^1 \mathbf{q}^1 - \mathbf{p}^1 \mathbf{q}^0 = \mathbf{p}^1(\mathbf{q}^1 - \mathbf{q}^0) \leqq 0 \tag{2-54}$$

Adding together (2-53) and (2-54),

$$-\mathbf{p}^0(\mathbf{q}^1 - \mathbf{q}^0) + \mathbf{p}^1(\mathbf{q}^1 - \mathbf{q}^0) = (\mathbf{p}^1 - \mathbf{p}^0)(\mathbf{q}^1 - \mathbf{q}^0) \leqq 0 \tag{2-55}$$

This inequality asserts that the sum of all quantity changes multiplied by the corresponding price changes is nonpositive if the consumer moves along a given indifference curve. Assume now that only the price of the first commodity changes, all other prices remaining constant. Then (2-55) reduces to

$$(p_1^1 - p_1^0)(q_1^1 - q_1^0) < 0 \tag{2-56}$$

The strict inequality must hold in (2-56) by the assumption that the price change is nonzero and that q_1^1 and q_1^0 are distinct, i.e., that price is a single-valued function of demand. If the price increases, the quantity bought must decrease and vice versa. This proves that the substitution effect is negative.

2-9 THE PROBLEM OF CHOICE IN SITUATIONS INVOLVING RISK

The traditional theory of consumer behavior does not include an analysis of uncertain situations. Von Neumann and Morgenstern showed that under certain circumstances it is possible to construct a set of numbers for a particular consumer that can be used to predict his choices in uncer-

---

[1] The term $\mathbf{q}^0 - \mathbf{q}^1$ denotes the n differences $q_1^0 - q_1^1,\ q_2^0 - q_2^1,\ \ldots,\ q_n^0 - q_n^1$.

tain situations. Great controversy has centered around the question of whether the resulting utility index is ordinal or cardinal. It will be shown that von Neumann–Morgenstern utilities possess at least some cardinal properties.

The previous analysis is unrealistic in the sense that it assumes that particular actions on the part of the consumer are followed by particular, determinate consequences which are knowable in advance. All automobiles of the same model and produced in the same factory do not always have the same performance characteristics. As a result of random accidents in the production process some substandard automobiles are occasionally produced and sold. The consumer has no way of knowing ahead of time whether the particular automobile which he purchases is of standard quality or not. Let A represent the situation in which the consumer possesses a satisfactory automobile, B a situation in which he possesses no automobile, and C one in which he possesses a substandard automobile. Assume that the consumer prefers A to B and B to C.† Present him with a choice between two alternatives: (1) He can maintain the status quo and have no car at all. This is a choice with certain outcome, i.e., the probability of the outcome equals unity. (2) He can obtain a lottery ticket with a chance of winning either a satisfactory automobile (alternative A) or an unsatisfactory one (alternative C). The consumer may prefer to retain his income (or money) with certainty, or he may prefer the lottery ticket with dubious outcome, or he may be indifferent between them. His decision will depend upon the chances of winning or losing in this particular lottery. If the probability of C is very high, he might prefer to retain his money with certainty; if the probability of A is very high, he might prefer the lottery ticket.

THE AXIOMS

It is possible to construct a utility index which can be used to predict choice in uncertain situations if the consumer conforms to the following five axioms:

Complete-ordering axiom For the two alternatives A and B one of the following must be true: the consumer prefers A to B, he prefers B to A, or he is indifferent between them. The consumer's evaluation of alternatives is transitive: if he prefers A to B and B to C, he prefers A to C.

Continuity axiom Assume that A is preferred to B and B to C. The axiom asserts that there exists some probability P, $0 < P < 1$, such that the consumer is indifferent between outcome B with certainty and a

† Not having a car is assumed preferable to owning a substandard one because of the nuisance and expense involved in its upkeep.

lottery ticket offering the outcomes A and C with probabilities P and $1 - P$ respectively.

Independence axiom   Assume that the consumer is indifferent between A and B and that C is any outcome whatever.   If one lottery ticket offers outcomes A and C with probabilities P and $1 - P$ respectively and another the outcomes B and C with the same probabilities P and $1 - P$, the consumer is indifferent between the two lottery tickets.

Unequal-probability axiom   Assume that the consumer prefers A to B. If two lottery tickets, L_1 and L_2, both offer the same outcomes, A and B, the consumer prefers the lottery ticket L_2 if and only if the probability of winning A is greater for L_2 than for L_1.

Axiom of complexity   Assume that a person engages in the following game of chance: he throws a die, and if a one or two comes up, his opponent pays him 9 dollars.   He pays his opponent 3 dollars in every other case. The probability of a win is $\frac{1}{3}$, and the probability of a loss $\frac{2}{3}$.   The player can expect to win, on the average,

$$(\tfrac{1}{3})(9) + (\tfrac{2}{3})(-3) = 1 \text{ dollar per game}$$

If A and B are the money values of two outcomes with probabilities P and $1 - P$, the mathematical expectation of the game, or the expected win, is $PA + (1 - P)B$.   Assume now that the consumer is offered a choice between two lottery tickets.   The first one, L_1, offers the outcomes A and B with given probabilities.   The other, L_2, is a complex one in the sense that the prizes themselves are lottery tickets: if the consumer chooses L_2 and wins, he gets a lottery ticket L_3 (offering A and B with some given probabilities); if he loses he is given another lottery ticket L_4 (also offering A and B with some given probabilities).   Assume finally that the probabilities of winning on each ticket happen to be such that the consumer's expectation of winning (as defined above) is the same whether he chooses L_1 or L_2.   The axiom asserts that the consumer is then indifferent between L_1 and L_2.

These axioms are very general, and it may be difficult to object to them on the grounds that they place unreasonable restrictions upon the consumer's behavior.   However, they rule out some types of plausible behavior.   Consider a person who derives satisfaction from the sheer act of gambling.   It is conceivable that there exists no P other than $P = 1$ or $P = 0$ for such a person, so that he is indifferent between outcome B with certainty and the uncertain prospect consisting of A and C: he will always prefer the gamble.   If he has a fear of gambling, he may always prefer the "sure thing" to the dubious prospect.   This type of behavior is ruled out by the continuity axiom and the axiom of complexity.

CONSTRUCTION OF THE UTILITY NUMBERS

Imagine that the consumer derives the satisfaction U_A from outcome A and U_C from outcome C.   Given that these outcomes have the probabilities P and $1 - P$, the consumer's expected utility is $PU_A + (1 - P)U_C$. It can be proved that a consumer who conforms to the axioms will maximize expected utility.   If he faces a set of uncertain prospects (i.e., he has to decide which lottery ticket to select), he will choose the one with the highest expected utility.   The consumer's prospects can be arranged in order of decreasing expected utility or desirability.   In the special case in which a prospect has a certain (rather than uncertain or dubious) outcome, the expected utility of the prospect equals the utility number associated with the (single) outcome.   Thus the utility numbers associated with various outcomes are an ordinal utility index and provide a correct ranking.

Consider the earlier example in which the outcomes A, B, and C represented the possession of a satisfactory automobile, no automobile, or a substandard one.   The consumer prefers A to B and B to C.   In order to derive a utility index, an origin and a unit have to be chosen. This can be accomplished by assigning numbers to represent the utilities of any two outcomes.   These numbers are completely arbitrary, except for the fact that a higher number must be assigned to the preferred outcome.   The utility index $U_A = 100$ and $U_C = 10$ can be used, since A is preferred to C.   The continuity axiom ensures that there exists some probability P for which the consumer is indifferent between B and a chance between A and C.   Since the consumer is an expected-utility maximizer, the utility of B with certainty must equal, for some value of P, the expected utility of the prospect (or lottery ticket) involving A and C, or

$$U_B = PU_A + (1 - P)U_C$$

He could be asked to reveal the value of P for which he is indifferent between B with certainty and a chance between A and C.   Assume that this value is $P = 0.1$.   Then

$$U_B = (0.1)(100) + (0.9)(10) = 19$$

Proceeding in this fashion one can find utility numbers U_A, U_B, U_C, U_D, . . . , etc., for all possible quantities and combinations of all commodities; hence a complete utility index can be derived by taking two arbitrary starting points and successively confronting the consumer with various choice situations involving probabilities or risk. For example, if the consumer is indifferent between a satisfactory automobile with certainty and a 0.8 chance of winning a yacht (outcome D) or a 0.2 chance of winning a substandard car, the application of the previous technique gives 122.5 as the utility of a yacht. The consumer's choice between more complicated alternatives can be predicted on the basis of these utility numbers. The rational consumer would prefer a 40:60 chance of D and B to a 50:50 chance of A and C, since

$$(0.5)(100) + (0.5)(10) < (0.4)(122.5) + (0.6)(19)$$

UNIQUENESS OF THE UTILITY INDEX

Imagine that a set of utility numbers satisfying the above axioms has been found for a particular consumer. Ordinal utility functions have been demonstrated to be unique except for a monotonic transformation. The results obtained from the present utility index might change under some monotonic transformations. This can be illustrated with reference to the example used above. As before,

$$U_A = 100 \qquad U_B = 19$$
$$U_C = 10 \qquad U_D = 122.5$$

The consumer prefers a 40:60 chance of D and B to a 50:50 chance of A and C. Perform a monotonic transformation on these numbers such that they become[1]

$$U_A = 120 \qquad U_B = 20$$
$$U_C = 18 \qquad U_D = 125$$

The consumer will now prefer the 50:50 chance of A and C. It is no longer true that any monotonic transformation of a utility index in the present sense can also serve as a utility index. However, monotonic linear transformations of utility functions are also utility functions.[2] $U_B = PU_A + (1 - P)U_C$ for some P. Transform the utility function so that $U^* = aU + b$, $a > 0$. Then $U = (U^* - b)/a$ or $U = cU^* + d$ (where $c = 1/a$ and $d = -b/a$), and

$$cU_B^* + d = P(cU_A^* + d) + (1 - P)(cU_C^* + d)$$
$$= PcU_A^* + (1 - P)cU_C^* + d$$

Hence

$$cU_B^* = PcU_A^* + c(1 - P)U_C^*$$

---

[1] The exact form of the transformation is not indicated. The reader may check that the transformation is monotonic.
[2] Y is a monotonic linear transformation of X if $Y = aX + b$ and $a > 0$.

and therefore

$$U_B^* = PU_A^* + (1 - P)U_C^*$$

This proves that a monotonic linear transformation of the original utility function is itself a utility function giving the same results.

The utilities in the von Neumann–Morgenstern analysis are cardinal in a restricted sense. They are derived from the consumer's risk behavior and are valid for predicting his choices as long as he maximizes expected utility. They are derived by presenting him with mutually exclusive choices; therefore, it is meaningless to attempt to infer from the utility of event A and the utility of event B the utility of the joint event A and B. Von Neumann–Morgenstern utilities possess some, but not all, the properties of cardinal measures. Let the utilities of three alternatives be $U_A = 10$, $U_B = 30$, and $U_C = 70$. It is not meaningful to assert that the consumer prefers C "seven times as much" as A, since the choice of the origin is arbitrary: the same preferences are described by $U_A = 1$, $U_B = 21$, and $U_C = 61$. Utility numbers differ from measures of weight, distance, or volume. It can be meaningfully asserted that one object weighs seven times as much as another. However, the utility numbers provide an *interval* scale and differences between them are meaningful. This follows from the fact that the relative magnitudes of differences between utility numbers are invariant with respect to linear transformations. In the above example

$$U_C - U_B > U_B - U_A$$

Choose a linear transformation $U = cU^* + d$, $c > 0$, and substitute in the above inequality:

$$cU_C^* + d - cU_B^* - d > cU_B^* + d - cU_A^* - d$$

and

$$U_C^* - U_B^* > U_B^* - U_A^*$$

In contrast to the traditional theory of the consumer, the sign of the rate of change of marginal utility (the second derivative of the utility function) is relevant, since it is invariant with respect to linear transformations. Such comparisons do not imply, however, that the consumer would prefer to have C over B to B over A, since the chosen alternative must have the highest utility number

Interpersonal comparisons of utility are still impossible. However, the construction of von Neumann–Morgenstern utilities does permit (1) the complete ranking of alternatives in situations characterized by certainty, (2) the comparison of utility differences by virtue of the above cardinal property, and (3) the calculation of expected utilities, thus making it possible to deal with the consumer's behavior under conditions of uncertainty.

2-10 SUMMARY

Nineteenth-century economic theorists explained the consumer's behavior on the assumption that utility is measurable. This restrictive assumption was abandoned around the turn of the last century, and the consumer was assumed to be capable only of ranking commodity combinations consistently in order of preference. This ranking is described mathematically by the consumer's ordinal utility function, which always assigns a higher number to a more desirable combination of commodities. The consumer is normally assumed to have convex indifference curves which reflect a decreasing rate of commodity substitution (RCS).

The basic postulate of the theory of consumer behavior is that the consumer maximizes utility. Since his income is limited, he maximizes utility subject to a budget constraint, which expresses his income limitation in mathematical form. The consumer's RCS must equal the price ratio for a maximum. In diagrammatic terms, the optimum commodity combination is given by the point at which his income line is tangent to an indifference curve. The second-order condition for a maximum is guaranteed by the convexity assumption.

The consumer's utility function is not unique. If a particular function describes appropriately the consumer's preferences, so does any other function which is a monotonic transformation of the first. Other kinds of transformations do not preserve the correct ranking, and the utility function is unique up to a monotonic transformation.

The consumer's ordinary demand functions for commodities can be derived from his first-order conditions for utility maximization. These state quantities demanded as functions of all prices and the consumer's income. Ordinary demand functions are single-valued and homogeneous of degree zero in prices and income: a proportionate change in all prices and the consumer's income leaves the quantity demanded unchanged. The consumer's compensated demand functions for commodities are constructed on the assumption that his income is increased or decreased following a price change in order to leave him at his initial utility level. The compensated demand functions state quantities demanded as functions of all prices. They are single-valued and homogeneous of degree zero in prices. A demand curve is obtained by stating quantity demanded as a function of own price on the assumption that the other arguments of the demand function are given parameters. Price elasticities are defined for both types of demand functions, and income elasticities are defined for ordinary demand functions.

In general, the amount of labor performed by a consumer affects his level of utility. The amount of labor performed by the consumer can be determined on the basis of the rational-decision criterion of utility maximization. The equilibrium conditions are similar to those which hold for the selection of an optimal commodity combination.

The consumer's reaction to price and income changes can be analyzed in terms of substitution and income effects. The effect of a given price change can be analytically decomposed into a substitution effect, which measures the rate at which he would substitute commodities for each other by moving along the same indifference curve, and an income effect as a residual category. If the price of a commodity changes, the quantity demanded changes in the opposite direction if the consumer is forced to move along the same indifference curve: the substitution effect is negative. If the income effect is positive, the commodity is an inferior good. If the total effect is positive, it is also a Giffen good. Substitutes and complements are defined in terms of the sign of the substitution effect for one commodity when the price of another changes: a positive cross-substitution effect means substitutability, and a negative one, complementarity.

The theory can be generalized to an arbitrary number of commodities. It can also be restated in terms of the theory of revealed preference, which makes no use of differential calculus and arrives at essentially the same conclusions as the preceding analysis. The results are obtained by presenting the consumer with hypothetical price-income situations and observing his choices. His indifference curves can be derived, and future choices can be predicted on the basis of past choices if his behavior satisfies the fundamental axioms of revealed preference.

The approach of von Neumann and Morgenstern is concerned with the consumer's behavior in situations characterized by uncertainty. If the consumer's behavior satisfies certain crucial axioms, his utility function can be derived by presenting him with a series of choices between a certain outcome on the one hand and a probabilistic combination of two uncertain outcomes on the other. The utility function thus derived is unique up to a linear transformation and provides a ranking of alternatives in situations that do not involve risk. Consumers maximize expected utility, and von Neumann–Morgenstern utilities are cardinal in the sense that they can be combined to calculate expected utilities and can be used to compare differences in utilities. The expected utility calculation can be used to determine the consumer's choices in situations involving risk.

EXERCISES

2-1. Determine whether or not the following utility functions have convex indifference curves: $U = q_1^\gamma q_2$; $U = aq_1 + q_2$; $U = q_1 q_2$; $U = q_1^2 + q_2^2$; $U = q_1 + q_2 + 2q_1 q_2$; $U = q_1 + q_2 + 2q_1 q_2 - 0.01(q_1^2 + q_2^2)$; and $U = q_1 q_2 + q_1 q_3 + q_2 q_3$.

2-2. Find the optimum commodity purchases for a consumer whose utility function and budget constraint are $U = q_1^{1.5}q_2$ and $3q_1 + 4q_2 = 100$ respectively.

2-3. The locus of points of tangency between income lines and indifference curves for given prices p_1^0, p_2^0 and a changing value of income is called an income expansion line or Engel curve. Show that the Engel curve is a straight line if the utility function is given by $U = q_1^\gamma q_2$, $\gamma > 0$.

2-4. Show that the utility functions $U = Aq_1^\alpha q_2^\beta$ and $W = q_1^{\alpha/\beta}q_2$ are monotonic transformations of each other where A, α, and β are positive.

2-5. Construct ordinary and compensated demand functions for Q_1 for the utility function $U = 2q_1q_2 + q_2$. Construct expressions for ϵ_{11}, ξ_{12}, and η_1.

2-6. Derive the elasticity of supply of work with respect to the wage rate for each of the two supply curves for work given by the examples in Sec. 2-5.

2-7. Prove that Q_1 and Q_2 cannot both be inferior goods.

2-8. Verify that $S_{11}p_1 + S_{12}p_2 = 0$ for the utility function $U = q_1^\gamma q_2$.

2-9. A consumer is observed to purchase $q_1 = 20$, $q_2 = 10$ at the prices $p_1 = 2$, $p_2 = 6$. He is also observed to purchase $q_1 = 18$, $q_2 = 4$ at the prices $p_1 = 3$, $p_2 = 5$. Is his behavior consistent with the axioms of the theory of revealed preference?

2-10. A consumer who conforms to the von Neumann–Morgenstern axioms is faced with four situations A, B, C, and D. He prefers A to B, B to C, and C to D. Experimentation reveals that the consumer is indifferent between B and a lottery ticket with probabilities of 0.4 and 0.6 for A and D respectively, and that he is indifferent between C and a lottery ticket with probabilities of 0.2 and 0.8 for B and D respectively. Construct a set of von Neumann–Morgenstern utility numbers for the four situations.

*2-11. Imagine that point rationing is in effect so that each commodity has two prices: a dollar price and a ration-coupon price. Assume that there are three commodities and that the consumer has a dollar income y and a ration-coupon allotment z. Also assume that this allotment is not so liberal that any commodity combination that he can afford to purchase with his dollar income can also be purchased with his coupons. Formulate his constrained-utility-maximization problem. Derive first- and second-order conditions for a maximum. Interpret the first-order conditions from an economic point of view. Find a sufficient condition which guarantees that the imposition of rationing does not alter the consumer's purchases.

* Hereinafter, the more difficult exercises will be marked with an asterisk.

SELECTED REFERENCES

Debreu, Gerard, *Theory of Value* (New York: Wiley, 1959). The theory of the consumer is discussed in chap. 4 from an advanced and modern mathematical point of view.

Ellsberg, D., "Classic and Current Notions of 'Measurable Utility,'" *Economic Journal*, vol. 64 (September, 1954), pp. 528–556. A comparison of the nineteenth-century concept of measurable utility with the von Neumann-Morgenstern index. Nonmathematical.

Friedman, M., *Essays in Positive Economics* (Chicago: University of Chicago Press, 1953), "The Marshallian Demand Curve," pp. 47–99. An analysis of the various types of demand functions and demand curves.

———, and L. J. Savage, "The Utility Analysis of Choices Involving Risk," *Journal of Political Economy*, vol. 56 (August, 1948), pp. 279–304. Also reprinted in

American Economic Association, *Readings in Price Theory* (Homewood, Ill.: Irwin, 1952), pp. 57–96. An analysis of situations with uncertain outcomes leading to a hypothesis concerning utility as a function of income. Simple mathematics.

Georgescu-Roegen, N., "The Pure Theory of Consumer Behavior," *Quarterly Journal of Economics*, vol. 50 (August, 1936), pp. 545–593. A mathematical analysis of ordinal utility theory.

Hicks, J. R., *A Revision of Demand Theory* (Oxford: Clarendon Press, 1956). A discussion of consumer theory relying on the theory of revealed preference and employing little mathematics.

———, *Value and Capital* (2d ed.; Oxford: Clarendon Press, 1946). Chapters I–III contain an exposition of ordinal utility theory. The mathematical analysis is in an appendix.

Houthakker, H. S., "Revealed Preference and the Utility Function," *Economica*, n.s., vol. 17 (May, 1950), pp. 159–174. Contains a proof of the existence of indifference curves for consumers who satisfy the axioms of revealed-preference theory.

Lancaster, K. J., "A New Approach to Consumer Theory," *Journal of Political Economy*, vol. 74 (April, 1966), pp. 132–157. An analysis of consumer's choice on the assumption that the consumer derives utility from the attributes of commodities.

Marschak, J., "Rational Behavior, Uncertain Prospects and Measurable Utility," *Econometrica*, vol. 18 (April, 1950), pp. 111–141. A further development of the von Neumann–Morgenstern approach. Moderately difficult mathematics.

Marshall, Alfred, *Principles of Economics* (8th ed.; London: Macmillan, 1920). Chapters I–IV, Book III, contain a nonmathematical discussion of wants, utility, marginal utility, and demand from the cardinalist viewpoint.

Neumann, J. von, and O. Morgenstern, *Theory of Games and Economic Behavior* (2d ed.; Princeton, N.J.: Princeton, 1947). Chapter 1 and an appendix contain the original statement of the von Neumann–Morgenstern approach.

Richter, M. K., "Revealed Preference Theory," *Econometrica*, vol. 34 (July, 1966), pp. 635–645. A modern approach using advanced mathematics.

Samuelson, Paul A., "Consumption Theory in Terms of Revealed Preference," *Economica*, n.s., vol. 15 (November, 1948), pp. 243–253. Presents a proof that the revealed-preference approach can lead to the determination of indifference curves.

———, *Foundations of Economic Analysis* (Cambridge, Mass.: Harvard, 1948). Chapters V and VII contain a comprehensive analysis of utility theory using fairly advanced mathematics.

Slutsky, E. E., "On the Theory of the Budget of the Consumer," *Giornale degli Economisti*, vol. 51 (July, 1915), pp. 1–26. Also reprinted in American Economic Association, *Readings in Price Theory* (Homewood, Ill,: Irwin, 1952), pp. 27–56. The article upon which the modern mathematical theory of consumer behavior is based. Fairly difficult mathematics.

3
The Theory of the Firm

A firm is a technical unit in which commodities are produced. Its entrepreneur (owner and manager) decides how much of and how one or more commodities will be produced, and gains the profit or bears the loss which results from his decision. An entrepreneur transforms inputs into outputs, subject to the technical rules specified by his production function. The difference between his revenue from the sale of outputs and the cost of his inputs is his profit, if positive, or his loss, if negative.

The entrepreneur's production function gives mathematical expression to the relationship between the quantities of inputs he employs and the quantities of outputs he produces. The concept is perfectly general. A specific production function may be given by a single point, a single continuous or discontinuous function, or a system of equations. This chapter is limited to production functions given by a single continuous function with continuous first- and second-order partial derivatives. The analysis is first developed for the relatively simple case in which two inputs are combined for the production of a single output, and then extended to more general cases.

An input is any good or service which contributes to the production of an output. An entrepreneur normally will use many different inputs for the production of an output. Some of his inputs may be the outputs of other firms. For example, steel is an input for an automobile producer and an output for a steel producer. Other inputs—such as labor, land, and mineral resources—are not produced. For a specified period of time, inputs are classified as either fixed or variable. A fixed input is necessary for production, but its quantity is invariant with respect to the quantity of output produced. Its costs are incurred by the entrepreneur regardless of his *short-run* maximizing decisions. The necessary quantity of a variable input depends upon the quantity of output produced. The distinction between fixed and variable inputs is temporal. Inputs which are fixed for one period of time are variable for a longer period. The entrepreneur of a machine shop may require a period of three months in order to buy new machinery or dispose of existing machinery. He will consider machinery as a fixed input in planning production for a one-month period, and as a variable input in planning production for a one-year period. All inputs are variable, given a sufficiently long period of time.

The formal analysis of the firm is similar to the formal analysis of the consumer in a number of respects. The consumer purchases commodities with which he "produces" satisfaction; the entrepreneur purchases inputs with which he produces commodities. The consumer possesses a utility function; the firm, a production function. The consumer's budget equation is a linear function of the amounts of commodities he purchases; the competitive firm's cost equation is a linear function of the amounts of inputs it purchases. The postulate of rational maximizing behavior has a counterpart in the theory of the firm. The rational consumer desires to maximize the utility he obtains from the consumption of commodities; the rational entrepreneur desires to maximize the profit he obtains from the production and sale of commodities.

The differences between the analyses of the consumer and firm are not quite as obvious as the similarities. A utility function is subjective, and utility does not possess an unambiguous cardinal measure; a production function is objective, and the output of a firm is easily measured. A single firm may produce more than one output. The maximization process of the entrepreneur usually goes one step beyond that of the consumer. The rational consumer maximizes utility for a given income. The analogous action for the entrepreneur is to maximize the quantity of his output for a given cost level, but generally his cost is variable, and he desires to maximize his profit.

The problems of an entrepreneur who uses two inputs for the production of a single output are discussed in the first three sections of this chapter.   The first covers the nature of his production function and the derivation of productivity curves and isoquants, the second covers alternative modes of optimizing behavior, and the third covers factor demands derived from optimizing behavior.   In Sec. 3-4 cost functions are derived from production relations.   Homogeneous production functions are considered in Sec. 3-5, and CES (constant elasticity of substitution) production functions are considered in Sec. 3-6.   The problems of an entrepreneur who uses one input for the production of two outputs are covered in Sec. 3-7, and the analysis is generalized for arbitrary numbers of inputs and outputs in Sec. 3-8.

3-1 BASIC CONCEPTS

THE PRODUCTION FUNCTION

Consider a simple production process in which an entrepreneur utilizes two variable inputs (X_1 and X_2) and one or more fixed inputs in order to produce a single output (Q).   His production function states the quantity of his output (q) as a function of the quantities of his variable inputs (x_1 and x_2):

$$q = f(x_1, x_2) \tag{3-1}$$

where (3-1) is assumed to be a single-valued continuous function with continuous first- and second-order partial derivatives.   The production function is defined only for nonnegative values of the input and output levels.   Negative values are meaningless within the present context. The production function is constructed on the assumption that the quantities of the fixed inputs are at predetermined levels which the entrepreneur is unable to alter during the time period under consideration.

The entrepreneur is able to use many different combinations of X_1 and X_2 for the production of a given level of output.   In fact, since (3-1) is continuous, the number of possible combinations is infinite.   The entrepreneur's technology is all the technical information about the combination of inputs necessary for the production of his output.   It includes all physical possibilities.   The technology may state that a single combination of X_1 and X_2 can be utilized in a number of different ways and therefore can yield a number of different output levels.   The production function differs from the technology in that it presupposes technical efficiency and states the *maximum* output obtainable from every possible input combination.   The best utilization of any particular input combination is a technical, not an economic, problem.   The selection of the best input combination for the production of a particular output level depends upon input and output prices and is the subject of economic analysis.

Input and output levels are rates of flow per unit of time. The period of time for which these flows, and hence the short-run production function, are defined is subject to three general restrictions: it must be (1) sufficiently short so that the entrepreneur is unable to alter the levels of his fixed inputs, (2) sufficiently short so that the shape of the production function is not altered through technological improvements, and (3) sufficiently long to allow the completion of the necessary technical processes. The selection of a particular time period within the specified limits is arbitrary. The analysis can be shifted to a long-run basis by relaxing condition (1) and defining the production function for a period long enough to allow variation of the heretofore fixed inputs. The major difference between a short-run and long-run analysis is the number of variable inputs. Nearly all the results for a short-run period will follow in a slightly altered form for a long-run period.

PRODUCTIVITY CURVES

The total productivity of X_1 in the production of Q is defined as the quantity of Q that can be secured from the input of X_1 if X_2 is assigned the fixed value x_2^0:

$$q = f(x_1, x_2^0) \tag{3-2}$$

The input level x_2^0 is treated as a parameter, and q becomes a function of x_1 alone. The relation between q and x_1 may be altered by changing x_2^0. A representative family of total productivity curves is presented in Fig. 3-1. Each curve gives the relationship between q and x_1 for a different value of x_2^0. Normally, an increase of x_2^0 will result in a reduction of the quantity of X_1 necessary to produce each output level within the feasible range. If one total productivity curve lies to the left of another, it corresponds to a higher value for x_2^0: $x_2^{(1)} > x_2^{(2)} > x_2^{(3)}$.

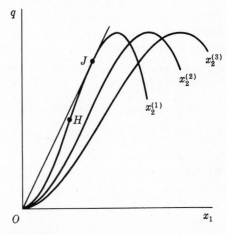

Fig. 3-1

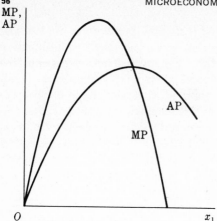

Fig. 3-2

Average and marginal productivities for X_1 are defined in an analogous manner for particular values of x_2^0. The *average productivity* (AP) of X_1 is its total productivity divided by its quantity:

$$AP = \frac{q}{x_1} = \frac{f(x_1, x_2^0)}{x_1}$$

The *marginal productivity* (MP) of X_1 is the rate of change of its total productivity with respect to variations of its quantity, i.e., the partial derivative of (3-1) with respect to x_1:

$$MP = \frac{\partial q}{\partial x_1} = f_1(x_1, x_2^0) \tag{3-3}$$

Families of AP and MP curves can be constructed by assigning different values to x_2^0.

The AP and MP curves corresponding to one of the total productivity curves in Fig. 3-1 are presented in Fig. 3-2. Both AP and MP increase and then decline as the application of X_1 is expanded. The MP curve reaches a maximum at a lower input level than the AP curve and intersects the AP curve at its maximum point.[1] The input level at

---

[1] To determine the maximum value of AP, set its partial derivative with respect to x_1 equal to zero:

$$\frac{\partial AP}{\partial x_1} = \frac{x_1 f_1(x_1, x_2^0) - f(x_1 x_2^0)}{x_1^2} = 0$$

If a fraction equals zero, its numerator must equal zero:

$$x_1 f_1(x_1, x_2^0) - f(x_1, x_2^0) = 0$$

Moving the second term to the right, and dividing through by x_1,

$$f_1(x_1, x_2^0) = \frac{f(x_1, x_2^0)}{x_1}$$

MP and AP are equal at the point of maximum AP if such a point exists.

which MP equals zero is the same as the input level at which the corresponding total productivity curve is at a maximum, i.e., the point at which the slope of its tangent equals zero. The input level at which MP reaches a maximum is the same as the input level at the point of inflection on the corresponding total productivity curve, i.e., the point at which the slope of its tangent is at a maximum (see point H on curve $x_2^{(1)}$ in Fig. 3-1). The input level at which the AP curve reaches a maximum is the same as the input level at which the slope of a vector drawn from the origin to the total productivity curve reaches a maximum (see point J on curve $x_2^{(1)}$ in Fig. 3-1).

(margin notes:) ① $MP = 0$ ② $MP\ max.$ ③ $AP\ max.$

The productivity curves given in Figs. 3-1 and 3-2 satisfy the almost universal *law of diminishing marginal productivity:* The MP of X_1 will eventually decline as x_1 is increased with x_2^0 remaining unchanged.[1] This law does not rule out the initial phase of increasing MP exhibited in the present example. Consider a production process in which labor and land are combined for the production of wheat and compute the quantity of wheat produced as more and more labor is applied to a fixed amount of land. Initially an increase in the number of laborers employed may allow specialization and result in an increasing MP of labor. However, after these initial economies have been realized, increasing applications of labor will result in smaller and smaller increases in the output of wheat. The quantity of labor becomes greater and greater relative to the fixed quantity of land. The law of diminishing marginal productivity concerns the relative quantities of the inputs and is not applicable if both inputs are increased.

The output elasticity of X_1, denoted by ω_1, is defined as the proportionate rate of change of Q with respect to X_1:

$$\omega_1 = \frac{\partial(\log q)}{\partial(\log x_1)} = \frac{x_1}{q}\frac{\partial q}{\partial x_1} = \frac{\text{MP}}{\text{AP}} \tag{3-4}$$

Output elasticities may be expressed as ratios of marginal and average productivities and are positive if MP and AP are positive. The output elasticity of an input will be greater than, equal to, or less than unity as its MP is respectively greater than, equal to, or less than its AP. The entire productivity analysis may be applied to variations of x_2 with x_1 as a parameter.

For a specific example, consider the production function given by the sixth-degree equation

$$q = A x_1^2 x_2^2 - B x_1^3 x_2^3 \tag{3-5}$$

[1] This law has been stated in a number of alternative forms. See K. Menger, "The Laws of Return," in O. Morgenstern (ed.), *Economic Activity Analysis* (New York: Wiley, 1954), pp. 419–482.

where $A, B > 0$.   The corresponding productivity curves are depicted in
Figs. 3-1 and 3-2.†   Letting $Ax_2^2 = k_1$ and $Bx_2^3 = k_2$, the family of total
productivity curves for X_1 is given by the cubic equation

$$q = k_1x_1^2 - k_2x_1^3$$

where k_1 and k_2 depend upon the fixed value assigned to x_2.   The AP and
MP curves are given by the quadratic equations

$$\text{AP} = k_1x_1 - k_2x_1^2 \qquad \text{MP} = 2k_1x_1 - 3k_2x_1^2$$

AP reaches a maximum at $x_1 = k_1/2k_2$, and MP reaches a maximum
at $x_1 = k_1/3k_2$.   Since x_1, k_1, $k_2 > 0$, MP reaches its maximum at
a smaller input of X_1 than AP.   The reader may verify that AP = MP at
$x_1 = k_1/2k_2$.   The output elasticity for X_1 is

$$\omega_1 = \frac{2k_1 - 3k_2x_1}{k_1 - k_2x_1}$$

The reader may verify that ω_1 declines as x_1 increases.

Another and somewhat different example is provided by the pro-
duction function $q = x_1^\alpha x_2^{1-\alpha}$ with $0 < \alpha < 1$.   The MP and AP for
X_1 decline continuously and are not equal for any value of x_1:

$$\text{AP} = \frac{q}{x_1} \qquad \text{MP} = \alpha \frac{q}{x_1}$$

The output elasticity for X_1 equals the constant α.

ISOQUANTS

An isoquant is the firm's counterpart of the consumer's indifference curve.
It is the locus of all combinations of x_1 and x_2 which yield a specified
output level.   For a given output level, (3-1) becomes

$$q^0 = f(x_1,x_2) \tag{3-6}$$

where q^0 is a parameter.   The locus of all the combinations of x_1 and x_2
which satisfy (3-6) forms an isoquant.   Since the production function is
continuous, an infinite number of input combinations lie on each isoquant.
Three curves from a family of isoquants are shown in Fig. 3-3.   All the
input combinations which lie on an isoquant will result in the output
indicated for that curve.   Within the relevant range of operation an
increase of both inputs will result in an increased output.   The further an
isoquant lies from the origin, the greater the output level which it represents: $q^{(3)} > q^{(2)} > q^{(1)}$.

† The values $A = 0.09$ and $B = 0.0001$ were used for the construction of the curves
in Figs. 3-1 and 3-2.

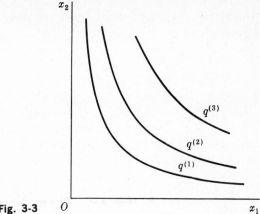

Fig. 3-3

The slope of the tangent to a point on an isoquant is the rate at which X_1 must be substituted for X_2 (or X_2 for X_1) in order to maintain the corresponding output level. The negative of the slope is defined as the *rate of technical substitution* (RTS):

$$\text{RTS} = -\frac{dx_2}{dx_1}$$

The RTS for the firm is analogous to the RCS for the consumer. The RTS at any point is the same for movements in either direction.

The total differential of the production function is

$$dq = f_1\, dx_1 + f_2\, dx_2 \tag{3-7}$$

where f_1 and f_2 are the partial derivatives of q with respect to x_1 and x_2 (the MPs of X_1 and X_2). Since $dq = 0$ for movements along an isoquant,

$$0 = f_1\, dx_1 + f_2\, dx_2$$

and

$$\text{RTS} = -\frac{dx_2}{dx_1} = \frac{f_1}{f_2} \tag{3-8}$$

The RTS at a point equals the ratio of the MP of X_1 to the MP of X_2 at that point.

Isoquants of the shape presented in Fig. 3-3 (rectangular hyperbolas which are negatively sloped throughout) can be derived for the production function given by (3-5). Let $z = x_1 x_2$, and rewrite (3-5) as

$$q^0 = Az^2 - Bz^3$$

Form the cubic equation

$$Bz^3 - Az^2 + q^0 = 0$$

which can be solved for z. Treat the smallest positive real root as the solution for z. The value of z depends upon the parameter q^0:

$$z = \psi(q^0) \qquad \text{or} \qquad x_1 x_2 = \psi(q^0)$$

which defines the isoquants as a family of rectangular hyperbolas, since $\psi(q^0)$ is constant for any fixed value of q^0.

The MP of X_1 may become negative if the application of X_1 is sufficiently large. One can imagine a situation in which the quantity of labor employed relative to the quantities of the other inputs is so large that an increase of labor would result in congestion and inefficiency. The definition of the production function as giving the maximum output for every possible input combination does not rule out this possibility. If the MP of X_1 is negative and the MP of X_2 positive,[1] the RTS is negative, as at point A in Fig. 3-4. A movement along the isoquant from A to B would result in a reduction of both x_1 and x_2. Clearly, point B is preferable to A if the entrepreneur must pay positive prices for the inputs. A rational entrepreneur will never operate on a positively sloped section of an isoquant; i.e., he will never use a factor combination which results in a negative MP for one of the inputs. The *ridge lines* OC and OD enclose the area of rational operation.

SHAPE OF THE PRODUCTION FUNCTION

Production functions are normally assumed to possess convex isoquants, bowed toward the origin with a decreasing RTS as X_1 is substituted for X_2 along an isoquant. The isoquants in Fig. 3-3 are of this shape, and those in Fig. 3-4 are of this shape within the area defined by the ridge

[1] This situation will never arise for the production function given by (3-5). If the MP of one of its inputs is negative, the MP of the other must also be negative.

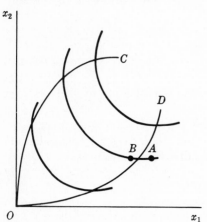

O x_1 **Fig. 3-4**

lines.   Production functions and utility functions are alike in this regard.
The similarity ends here.   The production function itself is normally
assumed to be concave (and often it is assumed to be strictly concave) for
at least a region of positive values for the inputs.[1]   In the two-dimensional
case a production function is concave over a region (see Sec. A-2) if

$$f_{11} \leqq 0 \qquad f_{22} \leqq 0$$

and

$$\begin{vmatrix} f_{11} & f_{12} \\ f_{21} & f_{22} \end{vmatrix} = f_{11}f_{22} - f_{12}^2 \geqq 0 \tag{3-9}$$

over that region.   It is strictly concave if the strict inequalities hold.
Consider the class of production functions given by $q = Ax_1^\alpha x_2^\beta$
with $\alpha, \beta > 0$.   The convexity of the isoquants for these functions for
$x_1, x_2 > 0$ is easily verified:

$$x_2 = \left(\frac{q^0}{A} \right)^{1/\beta} x_1^{-\alpha/\beta}$$

$$\frac{\partial^2 x_2}{\partial x_1^2} = \frac{\alpha(\alpha + \beta)}{\beta^2} \left(\frac{q^0}{A} \right)^{1/\beta} x_1^{-(\alpha+2\beta)/\beta} > 0$$

The isoquants will be of the desired shape for any positive values of α and
β.   The second direct partials of the production function will be negative
as required for its concavity if α and β are each less than one:

$$f_{11} = \alpha(\alpha - 1) \frac{q}{x_1^2} \qquad f_{22} = \beta(\beta - 1) \frac{q}{x_2^2}$$

An evaluation of (3-9) yields

$$\alpha(\alpha - 1) \frac{q}{x_1^2} \beta(\beta - 1) \frac{q}{x_2^2} - \left(\frac{\alpha\beta q}{x_1 x_2} \right)^2 = (1 - \alpha - \beta) \frac{\alpha\beta q^2}{x_1^2 x_2^2}$$

which can be positive, negative, or zero depending upon the values of
α and β.   If $\alpha + \beta < 1$, it is positive and the production function is
strictly concave for all positive values of x_1 and x_2.   If $\alpha + \beta = 1$, it is
zero and the production function is concave but not strictly concave.
If $\alpha + \beta > 1$, it is negative and the production function is neither concave
nor convex.
The production function given by (3-5), $q = Ax_1^2 x_2^2 - Bx_1^3 x_2^3$, is not
as well behaved.   Its isoquants are rectangular hyperbolas with the
appropriate convexity for all positive output levels yielded by the function.   The second direct partials are negative for $x_1 x_2 > A/3B$.   The

---

[1] Isoquants will be strictly convex if the production function is strictly concave and
will be either convex or strictly convex if the production function is concave, but not
strictly concave.

Hessian (3-9) is positive only for the region

$$\frac{2A}{5B} < x_1 x_2 < \frac{2A}{3B}$$

The production function is strictly concave within this region. The MPs of both factors are positive and decreasing within this region.

ELASTICITY OF SUBSTITUTION

If a production function has convex isoquants, the RTS of X_1 for X_2 and the input ratio x_2/x_1 will both decline as X_1 is substituted for X_2 along an isoquant. The elasticity of substitution (σ) is a pure number that measures the rate at which substitution takes place. It is defined as the proportionate rate of change of the input ratio divided by the proportionate rate of change of the RTS:

$$\sigma = \frac{d \log (x_2/x_1)}{d \log (f_1/f_2)} = \frac{f_1/f_2}{x_2/x_1} \frac{d(x_2/x_1)}{d(f_1/f_2)}$$

Substituting $d(x_2/x_1) = (x_1 \, dx_2 - x_2 \, dx_1)/x_1^2$,

$$d(f_1/f_2) = \frac{\partial(f_1/f_2)}{\partial x_1} \, dx_1 + \frac{\partial(f_1/f_2)}{\partial x_2} \, dx_2 \quad \text{and} \quad dx_2 = -(f_1/f_2) \, dx_1$$

from (3-8),

$$\sigma = \frac{f_1(f_1 x_1 + f_2 x_2)}{f_2 x_1 x_2 \left[f_1 \dfrac{\partial(f_1/f_2)}{\partial x_2} - f_2 \dfrac{\partial(f_1/f_2)}{\partial x_1} \right]}$$

and evaluating the bracketed term in the denominator from (3-8)

$$\sigma = \frac{f_1 f_2 (f_1 x_1 + f_2 x_2)}{x_1 x_2 \mathbf{D}} \tag{3-10}$$

where $\mathbf{D} = 2f_{12}f_1 f_2 - f_1^2 f_{22} - f_2^2 f_{11}$ is positive by the assumption of convex isoquants.[1] Since all of the terms in (3-10) are positive, the elasticity of substitution will be positive. Some production functions have constant elasticities of substitution, but in general σ will vary from point-to-point on the production function. The value of $\mathbf{D}$ reflects the rate of change of the slope of an isoquant. As $\mathbf{D}$ becomes larger the isoquant becomes more highly curved.

Consider the class of production functions given by $q = A x_1^{\alpha} x_2^{\beta}$ with $\alpha, \beta > 0$. Evaluating (3-10),

$$\sigma = \frac{\alpha q}{x_1} \frac{\beta q}{x_2} \frac{(\alpha q + \beta q)}{x_1 x_2} \frac{x_1^2 x_2^2}{q^3 \alpha \beta (\alpha + \beta)} = 1$$

Production functions of this class have unit elasticity of substitution throughout.

[1] Compare with Eq.(2-11).

3-2 OPTIMIZING BEHAVIOR

The present analysis is limited to the case in which the entrepreneur purchases X_1 and X_2 in perfectly competitive markets at constant unit prices. His total cost of production (C) is given by the linear equation

$$C = r_1 x_1 + r_2 x_2 + b \qquad (3\text{-}11)$$

cost equation

where r_1 and r_2 are the respective prices of X_1 and X_2, and b is the cost of the fixed inputs. An isocost line is defined as the locus of input combinations that may be purchased for a specified total cost:

$$C^0 = r_1 x_1 + r_2 x_2 + b \qquad (3\text{-}12)$$

where C^0 is a parameter.

Solving (3-12) for x_1,

$$x_1 = \frac{C^0 - b}{r_1} - \frac{r_2}{r_1} x_2$$

The slopes of the isocost lines equal the negative of the input price ratio. The intercept of an isocost line on the x_1 axis $[(C^0 - b)/r_1]$ is the amount of X_1 that could be purchased if the entire outlay, exclusive of the cost of the fixed inputs, were expended upon X_1 and the intercept on the x_2 axis $[(C^0 - b)/r_2]$ is the amount of X_2 that could be purchased if this amount were expended upon X_2. Three of a family of isocost lines are given in Fig. 3-5. The greater the total outlay to which an isocost line corresponds, the greater the intercepts on the x_1 and x_2 axes, and therefore the further it lies from the origin: $C^{(3)} > C^{(2)} > C^{(1)}$. The family of isocost lines completely fills the positive quadrant of the $x_1 x_2$ plane.

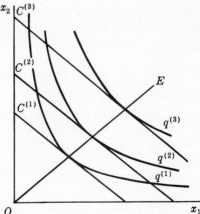

Fig. 3-5

CONSTRAINED OUTPUT MAXIMIZATION

The consumer maximizes utility subject to his budget constraint. The analogous problem for the firm is the maximization of output (3-1) subject to a cost constraint (3-12). The entrepreneur would desire to obtain the greatest possible output for a given cost outlay. Form the function

$$V = f(x_1, x_2) + \mu(C^0 - r_1 x_1 - r_2 x_2 - b)$$

where $\mu \neq 0$ is an undetermined Lagrange multiplier, and set the partial derivatives of V with respect to x_1, x_2, and μ equal to zero:

$$\frac{\partial V}{\partial x_1} = f_1 - \mu r_1 = 0$$

$$\frac{\partial V}{\partial x_2} = f_2 - \mu r_2 = 0$$

$$\frac{\partial V}{\partial \mu} = C^0 - r_1 x_1 - r_2 x_2 - b = 0$$

Moving the price terms to the right of the first two equations and dividing the first by the second,

$$\frac{f_1}{f_2} = \frac{r_1}{r_2} \tag{3-13}$$

First-order conditions state that the ratio of the MPs of X_1 and X_2 must be equated with the ratio of their prices.

The first-order conditions may be stated in a number of equivalent forms. Solving the first two equations for μ,

$$\mu = \frac{f_1}{r_1} = \frac{f_2}{r_2} \tag{3-14}$$

The contribution to output of the last dollar expended upon each input must equal μ. The multiplier μ is the derivative of output with respect to cost with prices constant and quantities variable.[1]

---

[1] Assuming that cost is variable, the differential of the cost equation (3-11) is

$$dC = r_1 \, dx_1 + r_2 \, dx_2$$

Substituting $r_1 = f_1/\mu$ and $r_2 = f_2/\mu$ from the first-order conditions,

$$dC = \frac{1}{\mu} (f_1 \, dx_1 + f_2 \, dx_2)$$

Dividing this expression into the differential of the production function (3-7), the derivative of output with respect to cost with prices constant is

$$\frac{dq}{dC} = \mu \frac{f_1 \, dx_1 + f_2 \, dx_2}{f_1 \, dx_1 + f_2 \, dx_2} = \mu$$

THE THEORY OF THE FIRM

Finally, substituting RTS $= f_1/f_2$ from (3-8) into (3-13),

$$\text{RTS} = \frac{r_1}{r_2} \tag{3-15}$$

The first-order conditions may also be expressed as the equality of the RTS and the input price ratio. The three formulations of the first-order conditions given by (3-13), (3-14), and (3-15) are equivalent alternatives. If one is satisfied, all three are satisfied.

The formulation given by (3-15) has a clear geometric interpretation. The optimum input combination is given by the point of tangency between an isoquant and the relevant isocost line. If $C^{(3)}$ (see Fig. 3-5) is the predetermined level of cost, the maximum output is $q^{(3)}$. The outputs corresponding to all other isoquants which have points in common with the given isocost line, such as $q^{(1)}$ and $q^{(2)}$, are less than $q^{(3)}$.

Second-order conditions require that the relevant bordered Hessian determinant be positive:

$$\begin{vmatrix} f_{11} & f_{12} & -r_1 \\ f_{21} & f_{22} & -r_2 \\ -r_1 & -r_2 & 0 \end{vmatrix} > 0$$

The second-order conditions may be utilized to demonstrate that the rate of change of the slope of the tangent to an isoquant must be positive $(d^2x_2/dx_1^2 > 0)$ at the point of tangency with an isocost line.[1] This means that the isoquants must be convex as shown in Fig. 3-5.

CONSTRAINED COST MINIMIZATION

The entrepreneur may desire to minimize the cost of producing a prescribed level of output. In this case (3-11) is minimized subject to (3-6). Form the function

$$Z = r_1 x_1 + r_2 x_2 + b + \lambda[q^0 - f(x_1, x_2)]$$

and set the partial derivatives of Z with respect to x_1, x_2, and λ equal to zero:

$$\frac{\partial Z}{\partial x_1} = r_1 - \lambda f_1 = 0$$

$$\frac{\partial Z}{\partial x_2} = r_2 - \lambda f_2 = 0$$

$$\frac{\partial Z}{\partial \lambda} = q^0 - f(x_1, x_2) = 0$$

---

[1] The formal derivation is identical with that used to demonstrate that the rate of change of the slope of the indifference curve must be positive at the point of maximum utility (see Sec. 2-2).

Since r_1 and f_1 are both positive, λ is also positive. Moving the price terms of the first two equations to the right, and dividing the first by the second,

$$\frac{f_1}{f_2} = \frac{r_1}{r_2} \quad \text{or} \quad \frac{1}{\lambda} = \frac{f_1}{r_1} = \frac{f_2}{r_2} \quad \text{or} \quad \text{RTS} = \frac{r_1}{r_2}$$

The first-order conditions for the minimization of cost subject to an output constraint are similar to those for the maximization of output subject to a cost constraint. The multiplier λ is the reciprocal of the multiplier μ, or the derivative of cost with respect to output level (defined as marginal cost in Sec. 3-4). In the present case, the entrepreneur finds the lowest isocost line which has at least one point in common with a selected isoquant. He could produce $q^{(1)}$ (see Fig. 3-5) at a cost of $C^{(3)}$ or $C^{(2)}$, but $C^{(1)}$ is lower than either of these. His minimum cost is given by the isocost line which is tangent to the selected isoquant.

The second-order condition requires that the relevant bordered Hessian determinant be negative:

$$\begin{vmatrix} -\lambda f_{11} & -\lambda f_{12} & -f_1 \\ -\lambda f_{21} & -\lambda f_{22} & -f_2 \\ -f_1 & -f_2 & 0 \end{vmatrix} < 0$$

Substituting $-f_1 = -r_1/\lambda$ and $-f_2 = -r_2/\lambda$, multiplying the first two columns of the array by $-1/\lambda$, and then multiplying the third row by $-\lambda^2$ and the third column by λ,†

$$\begin{vmatrix} -\lambda f_{11} & -\lambda f_{12} & -\dfrac{r_1}{\lambda} \\ -\lambda f_{21} & -\lambda f_{22} & -\dfrac{r_2}{\lambda} \\ -\dfrac{r_1}{\lambda} & -\dfrac{r_2}{\lambda} & 0 \end{vmatrix} = \lambda^2 \begin{vmatrix} f_{11} & f_{12} & -\dfrac{r_1}{\lambda} \\ f_{21} & f_{22} & -\dfrac{r_2}{\lambda} \\ \dfrac{r_1}{\lambda^2} & \dfrac{r_2}{\lambda^2} & 0 \end{vmatrix}$$

$$= -\frac{1}{\lambda} \begin{vmatrix} f_{11} & f_{12} & -r_1 \\ f_{21} & f_{22} & -r_2 \\ -r_1 & -r_2 & 0 \end{vmatrix} < 0$$

Since $\lambda > 0$,

$$\begin{vmatrix} f_{11} & f_{12} & -r_1 \\ f_{21} & f_{22} & -r_2 \\ -r_1 & -r_2 & 0 \end{vmatrix} > 0$$

† The multiplication of the first column by $-1/\lambda$ increases the value of the determinant by the same multiple. The multiplication of both the first and second columns by $-1/\lambda$ increases the value of the determinant by $1/\lambda^2$. Its value is left unchanged if the entire array is now multiplied by λ^2 (see Sec. A-1).

The second-order condition is the same as that for the constrained-cost minimization case.

If the second-order condition is satisfied, every point of tangency between an isoquant and an isocost line is the solution of both a constrained-maximum and a constrained-minimum problem. If $q^{(1)}$ (see Fig. 3-5) is the maximum output which can be obtained from an outlay of $C^{(1)}$ dollars, $C^{(1)}$ dollars is the minimum cost for which the output $q^{(1)}$ can be produced. The locus of tangency points (OE in Fig. 3-5) gives the _expansion path_ of the firm. The rational entrepreneur will select only input combinations which lie on his expansion path. Formally, the expansion path is an implicit function of x_1 and x_2:

$$g(x_1,x_2) = 0 \tag{3-16}$$

for which the first- and second-order conditions for constrained maxima and minima are fulfilled.

If the isoquants are convex, the second-order conditions will always be satisfied, and the expansion path can be derived from the first-order conditions. Consider the production function given by (3-5) as an example. Compute the ratio of the MPs of X_1 and X_2:

$$\frac{f_1}{f_2} = \frac{2Ax_1x_2^2 - 3Bx_1^2x_2^3}{2Ax_1^2x_2 - 3Bx_1^3x_2^2} = \frac{x_2(2Ax_1x_2 - 3Bx_1^2x_2^2)}{x_1(2Ax_1x_2 - 3Bx_1^2x_2^2)} = \frac{x_2}{x_1}$$

and set it equal to the ratio of the input prices

$$\frac{x_2}{x_1} = \frac{r_1}{r_2}$$

Putting this first-order condition in the form of an implicit function, the expansion path is given by the linear equation

$$r_1x_1 - r_2x_2 = 0 \qquad \textit{expansion path}$$

This corresponds to the expansion path OE in Fig. 3-5.

PROFIT MAXIMIZATION

The entrepreneur is usually free to vary the levels of both cost and output, and his ultimate aim is the maximization of profit rather than the solution of constrained-maximum and -minimum problems. The total revenue of an entrepreneur who sells his output in a perfectly competitive market is given by the number of units he sells multiplied by the fixed unit price (p) he receives. His profit (π) is the difference between his total revenue and his total cost:

$$\pi = pq - C$$

or substituting $q = f(x_1,x_2)$ from (3-1) and $C = r_1x_1 + r_2x_2 + b$ from (3-11),

profit

$$\pi = pf(x_1,x_2) - r_1x_1 - r_2x_2 - b$$

Profit is a function of x_1 and x_2 and is maximized with respect to these variables.

Setting the partial derivatives of π with respect to x_1 and x_2 equal to zero,

$$\frac{\partial \pi}{\partial x_1} = pf_1 - r_1 = 0 \qquad \frac{\partial \pi}{\partial x_2} = pf_2 - r_2 = 0$$

Moving the input-price terms to the right,

$$pf_1 = r_1 \qquad pf_2 = r_2 \tag{3-17}$$

The partial derivatives of the production function with respect to the inputs are the MPs of the inputs. The value of the MP of X_1 (pf_1) is the rate at which the entrepreneur's revenue would increase with further application of X_1. The first-order conditions for profit maximization (3-17) require that each input be utilized up to a point at which the value of its MP equals its price. The entrepreneur can increase his profit as long as the addition to his revenue from the employment of an additional unit of X_1 exceeds its cost. The maximum profit-input combination lies on the expansion path, since (3-17) is a special case of (3-13).

Second-order conditions require that the principal minors of the relevant Hessian determinant alternate in sign:

$$\frac{\partial^2 \pi}{\partial x_1^2} = pf_{11} < 0 \qquad \frac{\partial^2 \pi}{\partial x_2^2} = pf_{22} < 0 \tag{3-18}$$

and

$$\begin{vmatrix} \dfrac{\partial^2 \pi}{\partial x_1^2} & \dfrac{\partial^2 \pi}{\partial x_1 \, \partial x_2} \\[2mm] \dfrac{\partial^2 \pi}{\partial x_2 \, \partial x_1} & \dfrac{\partial^2 \pi}{\partial x_2^2} \end{vmatrix} = p^2 \begin{vmatrix} f_{11} & f_{12} \\ f_{21} & f_{22} \end{vmatrix} > 0 \tag{3-19}$$

Conditions (3-18) imply that profit must be decreasing with respect to further applications of *either* X_1 or X_2. Condition (3-19) ensures profit is decreasing with respect to further applications of *both* X_1 and X_2. Since $p > 0$, conditions (3-18) require that the MPs of both inputs be decreasing. If the MP of one of the inputs were increasing, a small movement from the point at which the first-order conditions are satisfied would result in an increase in the value of its MP. Since its price is constant, the entrepreneur could increase his profit by increasing its quantity.

Conditions (3-18) and (3-19) require that the production function be strictly concave in the neighborhood of a point at which the first-order conditions are satisfied with x_1, $x_2 \geq 0$ if such a point exists. Solutions are limited to strictly concave regions of the production function with nonnegative input and output levels. If the production function possesses no such region, competitive profit-maximization solutions of the type described here cannot be achieved.

3-3 INPUT DEMAND FUNCTIONS

The producer's input demands are derived from the underlying demand for the commodity which he produces. His input demand functions are obtained by solving his first-order conditions (3-17) for x_1 and x_2 as functions of r_1, r_2, and p. These are defined for strictly concave regions of his production function where his second-order conditions are satisfied. The producer's input demand functions are analogous to the consumer's ordinary demand functions in many regards. It is obvious from (3-17) that input demand functions are homogeneous of degree zero in the three prices (cf. Sec. 2-4). Elasticities may be defined for each of the inputs with respect to each of the prices. The input demand curve for X_1 is obtained by graphing the input demand function as a function of r_1 alone on the assumption that r_2 and p are given parameters.

Consider the class of production functions given by $q = Ax_1^{\alpha}x_2^{\beta}$ with $\alpha, \beta > 0$ and $\alpha + \beta < 1$ which were shown in Sec. 3-1 to be strictly concave for x_1, $x_2 \geq 0$. Form the profit function

$$\pi = pAx_1^{\alpha}x_2^{\beta} - r_1x_1 - r_2x_2$$

and set its partial derivatives equal to zero:

$$\frac{\partial \pi}{\partial x_1} = p\alpha Ax_1^{\alpha-1}x_2^{\beta} - r_1 = 0$$

$$\frac{\partial \pi}{\partial x_2} = p\beta Ax_1^{\alpha}x_2^{\beta-1} - r_2 = 0$$

Solving these equations for x_1 and x_2, the corresponding input demand functions are

$$x_1 = \left(\frac{\alpha}{r_1}\right)^{(1-\beta)/\gamma} \left(\frac{\beta}{r_2}\right)^{\beta/\gamma} (Ap)^{1/\gamma}$$

$$x_2 = \left(\frac{\alpha}{r_1}\right)^{\alpha/\gamma} \left(\frac{\beta}{r_2}\right)^{(1-\alpha)/\gamma} (Ap)^{1/\gamma}$$

where $\gamma = 1 - \alpha - \beta$. The demand for each input will decrease as r_1 or r_2 increases, and increase as p increases.

As prices change the producer will alter his input levels to satisfy his first-order conditions (3-17). Differentiating (3-17) totally and rearranging terms,

$$pf_{11}\,dx_1 + pf_{12}\,dx_2 = -f_1\,dp + dr_1$$
$$pf_{21}\,dx_1 + pf_{22}\,dx_2 = -f_2\,dp + dr_2 \tag{3-20}$$

Solving (3-20) for dx_1 and dx_2 by Cramer's rule,

$$dx_1 = \frac{p}{\mathbf{H}}\,[f_{22}\,dr_1 - f_{12}\,dr_2 + (f_{12}f_2 - f_{22}f_1)\,dp]$$
$$dx_2 = \frac{p}{\mathbf{H}}\,[-f_{21}\,dr_1 + f_{11}\,dr_2 + (f_{21}f_1 - f_{11}f_2)\,dp] \tag{3-21}$$

where $\mathbf{H} = p^2(f_{11}f_{22} - f_{12}^2) > 0$ by (3-19).

Dividing both sides of the first equation of (3-21) by dr_1 and letting $dr_2 = dp = 0$,

$$\frac{\partial x_1}{\partial r_1} = \frac{pf_{22}}{\mathbf{H}} < 0$$

Since $p > 0$ and $f_{22} < 0$ by (3-18), the rate of change of the producer's purchases of X_1 with respect to changes in its price with all other prices constant is always negative, and producer's input demand curves are always downward sloping. This is one of the few cases in economics in which the sign of a derivative is unambiguous. There is only a substitution effect. There is no counterpart for the income effect of the consumer in the theory of the profit-maximizing producer.

Dividing both sides of the first equation of (3-21) by dr_2 and letting $dr_1 = dp = 0$,

$$\frac{\partial x_1}{\partial r_2} = -\frac{pf_{12}}{\mathbf{H}}$$

This derivative will have a sign the opposite of the second cross partial f_{12}. In most cases considered by economists an increase in the quantity of one input will increase the marginal product of the other; that is, $f_{12} > 0$. Therefore, an increase in one input price normally will reduce the usage of the other input.

3-4 COST FUNCTIONS

The economist frequently assumes that the problem of optimum input combinations has been solved and conducts his analysis of the firm in terms of its revenues and costs expressed as functions of output. The problem of the entrepreneur is then to select an output at which his profits are maximized.

SHORT-RUN COST FUNCTIONS

Cost functions can be derived from the information contained in Secs. 3-1 and 3-2.† Consider the system of equations consisting of the production function (3-1), the cost equation (3-11), and the expansion path function (3-16):

$$q = f(x_1, x_2)$$
$$C = r_1 x_1 + r_2 x_2 + b$$
$$0 = g(x_1, x_2)$$

reduce these 3 equations to one below

Assume that this system of three equations in four variables can be reduced to a single equation in which <u>cost is stated as an explicit function of the level of output plus the cost of the fixed inputs</u>:

$$C = \phi(q) + b \qquad (3\text{-}22)$$

The cost of the fixed inputs, *the fixed cost*, must be paid regardless of how much the firm produces, or whether it produces at all. The cost function gives the minimum cost of producing each output and is derived on the assumption that the entrepreneur acts rationally. A cost-output combination for (3-22) can be obtained as follows: (1) select a point on the expansion path, (2) substitute the corresponding values of the input levels into the production function to obtain the corresponding output level, (3) multiply the input levels by the fixed input prices to obtain the total variable cost for this output level, and (4) add the fixed cost.

A number of special cost relations which are also functions of the level of output can be derived from (3-22). Average total (ATC), average variable (AVC), and average fixed (AFC) costs are defined as the respective total, variable, and fixed costs divided by the level of output:

$$\text{ATC} = \frac{\phi(q) + b}{q} \qquad \text{AVC} = \frac{\phi(q)}{q} \qquad \text{AFC} = \frac{b}{q}$$

ATC is the sum of AVC and AFC. Marginal cost (MC) is the derivative of total cost with respect to output:

$$\text{MC} = \frac{dC}{dq} = \phi'(q)$$

The derivatives of total and total variable cost are identical since the fixed-cost term vanishes upon differentiation.

Specific cost functions may assume many different shapes. One possibility which exhibits properties often assumed by economists is

† The term *cost function* is used to denote cost expressed as a function of output. The term *cost equation* is used to denote cost expressed in terms of input levels and input prices.

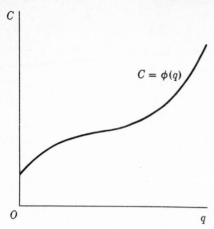

Fig. 3-6

depicted in Figs. 3-6 and 3-7.   Total cost is a cubic function of output.
ATC, AVC, and MC are all second-degree curves which first decline and
then increase as output is expanded.   MC reaches its minimum before
ATC and AVC, and AVC reaches its minimum before ATC.   The reader
may verify that the MC curve passes through the minimum points of
both the AVC and ATC curves.[1]   The AFC curve is a rectangular hyper-
bola regardless of the shapes of the other cost curves; the fixed cost is
spread over a larger number of units as output is expanded, and therefore
AFC declines monotonically.   The vertical distance between the ATC
and AVC curves equals AFC and hence decreases as output is increased.

[1] Set the derivative of ATC (or AVC) equal to zero, and put the equation in a form
which states the equality between ATC (or AVC) and MC (see Sec. A-2).

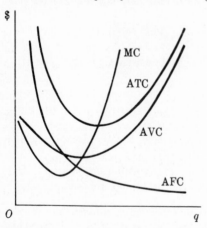

Fig. 3-7

The revenue of an entrepreneur who sells his output at a fixed price is also a function of the level of his output. Therefore, his profit is a function of the level of his output:

$$\pi = pq - \phi(q) - b \qquad \text{profit equation re-written}$$

To maximize profit, set its derivative with respect to q equal to zero:

$$\frac{d\pi}{dq} = p - \phi'(q) = 0 \qquad \text{note this simple derivation}$$

Moving the MC to the right,

$$p = \phi'(q) \qquad\qquad\qquad (3\text{-}23)$$

The entrepreneur must equate his MC with the constant selling price of his output. He can increase his profit by expanding his output if the addition to his revenue (p) of selling another unit exceeds the addition to his cost (MC).

The second-order condition for profit maximization requires that

$$\frac{d^2\pi}{dq^2} = -\frac{d^2C}{dq^2} < 0$$

or multiplying by -1 and reversing the inequality,

$$\frac{d^2C}{dq^2} > 0$$

MC must be increasing at the profit-maximizing output. If MC were decreasing, the equality of price and MC would give a point of minimum profit. *note mathematical explanation*

The level of the entrepreneur's fixed cost (b) generally has no effect upon his optimizing decisions during a short-run period. It must be paid regardless of the level of his output and merely adds a constant term to his profit equation. The fixed-cost term vanishes upon differentiation, and MC is independent of its level. Since the first- and second-order conditions for profit maximization are expressed in terms of MC, the equilibrium output level is unaffected by the level of fixed cost. The mathematical analyses of optimization in the present section and in Sec. 3-2 can generally be carried out on the basis of variable cost alone.

The level of fixed cost has significance for the analysis of short-run profit maximization in one special case. The entrepreneur has an option not recognized by the calculus. He can discontinue production and accept a loss equal to his fixed cost. This option is optimal if his maximum profit from the production of a positive output level is a negative

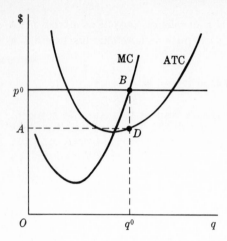

Fig. 3-8

amount (a loss) with a greater absolute value than the level of his fixed cost. The entrepreneur need never lose more than the amount of his fixed cost. He will produce at a loss in the short run if his loss is less than the amount of his fixed cost, i.e., if revenue exceeds total variable cost, and he is able to recover a portion of his outlay on the fixed inputs.

A geometric description of profit maximization is contained in Fig. 3-8. The optimum output (q^0) is given by the intersection of a horizontal line drawn at the level of the going price (p^0) and the rising portion of the MC curve. The entrepreneur's revenue is given by the area of the rectangle Op^0Bq^0, total cost by $OADq^0$, and profit by Ap^0BD.

As an example consider the cubic total cost function

$$C = 0.04q^3 - 0.9q^2 + 10q + 5 \qquad (3\text{-}24)$$

Assume that the price of q is 4 dollars per unit. Equating MC and price,

$$0.12q^2 - 1.8q + 10 = 4$$

which yields the quadratic equation

$$q^2 - 15q + 50 = 0$$

the roots of which are $q = 5$ and $q = 10$. Two different outputs satisfy the first-order condition for profit maximization, and the rate of change of MC must be calculated for both. The rate of change of MC:

$$\frac{d^2C}{dq^2} = 0.24q - 1.8$$

is negative for $q = 5$ and positive for $q = 10$. An output of 10 units yields a maximum profit, and an output of 5 a minimum. Profit at 10 units, however, is negative:

$$\pi = 4q - (0.04q^3 - 0.9q^2 + 10q + 5)$$
$$= 40 - 55 = -15$$

The entrepreneur's ATC curve lies above the price line for every output, and his maximum profit is a loss of 15 dollars. He should discontinue production, since his fixed cost (5 dollars) is less than the smallest loss which he can incur from a positive output level.

LONG-RUN COST FUNCTIONS

Let the levels of the entrepreneur's fixed inputs be represented by a parameter k, which gives the "size of his plant"—the greater the value of k, the greater the size of his plant. The entrepreneur's short-run problems concern the optimal utilization of a plant of given size. In the long run he is free to vary k and select a plant of optimum size. The shapes of the entrepreneur's production and cost functions depend upon his plant size. These are uniquely determined in the short run. In the long run he can choose between cost and production functions with different shapes. The number of his alternatives equals the number of different values which k may assume. Once he has selected the shapes of these functions, i.e., selected a value for k, he is faced with the conventional short-run optimization problems.

As an illustration, consider the case of an entrepreneur operating a grocery store. The "size of his plant" is given by the number of square feet of selling space which he possesses. Assume that the only possible alternatives are 5,000, 10,000, and 20,000 square feet and that he currently possesses 10,000. His present plant size is the result of a long-run decision made in the past. When the time comes for the replacement of his store, he will be able to select his plant size anew. If conditions have not changed since his last decision, he will again select 10,000 square feet. If the store has been crowded and he anticipates a long-run increase in sales, he will build 20,000 square feet. Under other conditions he may build a store with 5,000 square feet. Once he has built a new store, his problems concern the optimal utilization of a selling area of given size.

Assume that k is continuously variable and introduce it explicitly into the production function, cost equation, and expansion path function:

$$q = f(x_1, x_2, k)$$
$$C = r_1 x_1 + r_2 x_2 + \psi(k)$$
$$0 = g(x_1, x_2, k)$$

$k = $ "size of production plant"

Fixed cost is an increasing function of plant size: $\psi'(k) > 0$. The shapes of the families of isoquants and isocost lines and the shape of the expansion path depend upon the value assigned to the parameter k. Generally, two of the above relations may be utilized to eliminate x_1 and x_2, and total cost may be expressed as a function of output level and plant size:

$$C = \phi(q,k) + \psi(k) \tag{3-25}$$

which describes a family of total cost curves generated by assigning different values to the parameter k. As soon as plant size is assigned a particular value $k = k^{(0)}$, (3-25) is equivalent to the particular total cost function given by (3-22), and the short-run analysis is applicable.

The entrepreneur's long-run total cost function gives the minimum cost of producing each output level if he is free to vary the size of his plant. For a given output level he computes the total cost for each possible plant size and selects the plant size for which total cost is a minimum. Figure 3-9 contains the total cost curves corresponding to three different plant sizes. The entrepreneur can produce the output OR in any of the plants. His total cost would be RS for plant size $k^{(1)}$, RT for $k^{(2)}$, and RU for $k^{(3)}$. The plant size $k^{(1)}$ gives the minimum production cost for the output OR. Therefore, the point S lies on the long-run total cost curve. This process is repeated for every output level, and the long-run total cost curve is defined as the locus of the minimum-cost points.

The long-run cost curve is the envelope of the short-run curves; it touches each and intersects none. Write the equation for the family of short-run cost functions (3-25) in implicit form:

$$C - \phi(q,k) - \psi(k) = G(C,q,k) = 0 \tag{3-26}$$

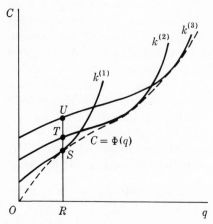

Fig. 3-9

and set the partial derivative of (3-26) with respect to k equal to zero:

$$G_k(C,q,k) = 0 \qquad\qquad (3\text{-}27)$$

The equation of the envelope curve (the long-run cost curve) is obtained by eliminating k from (3-26) and (3-27) and solving for C as a function of q (see Sec. A-3):

$$C = \Phi(q) \qquad \text{envelope curve w/o } k$$

Long-run total cost is a function of output level, given the condition that each output level is produced in a plant of optimum size. The long-run cost curve is not something apart from the short-run cost curves. It is constructed from points on the short-run curves. Since k is assumed continuously variable, the long-run cost curve (see Fig. 3-9) has one and only one point in common with each of the infinite number of short-run cost curves.

Since AC equals total cost divided by output level, the minimum AC of producing a particular output level is attained at the same plant size as the minimum total cost of producing that output level. The long-run AC curve can be derived by dividing long-run total cost by output level, or by constructing the envelope of the short-run AC curves. The two constructions are equivalent.

2 alternative ways of constructing LR AC curve

The long-run MC curve can be constructed by plotting the derivative of long-run total cost with respect to output level, or can be derived from the short-run MC curves. However, the long-run MC curve is not the envelope of the short-run MC curves. Short-run MC equals the rate of change of short-run variable cost with respect to output level; long-run MC is the rate of change of total cost assuming that all costs are variable. Therefore, portions of short-run MC curves may lie below the long-run MC curve. The long-run MC curve may be defined as the locus of those points on the short-run MC curves which correspond to the optimum plant size for each output.[1] The equivalence of the two methods of deriving the long-run MC curve is obvious in Fig. 3-9. The long-run total cost curve is tangent to each short-run curve at the output for which the short-run curve in question represents optimum plant size. Since the MCs are defined as the slopes of the tangents of these curves, the long-run and short-run MCs are equal at such points.

Assume that the entrepreneur desires to construct a plant for use during a number of short-run periods and that he expects to receive the same price for his product during each of the short-run periods. Since

---

[1] It *is not correct* to construct the long-run MC curve by selecting the points on the short-run MC curves which correspond to the optimum output (i.e., point of minimum AC) for each plant size.

conditions remain unchanged from one period to the next, he will produce the same level of output in each period. His profit during one of
the periods is the difference between his revenue and cost with plant size
variable:

$$\pi = pq - \Phi(q)$$

Set the derivative of π equal to zero:

$$\frac{d\pi}{dq} = p - \Phi'(q) = 0$$

$(3\text{-}26)\ \ C - \phi(q,k) - \psi(k) = G(C,q,\ =0$

$(3\text{-}27)\ \ G_K(C,q,k) = 0$

or

$$p = \Phi'(q)$$

Profits are maximized by equating long-run MC to price, if long-run MC
is increasing (second-order condition). Once the optimum output is
determined, the optimum value for k can be determined from (3-26) and
(3-27).

Consider the family of short-run cost curves generated by

$$C = 0.04q^3 - 0.9q^2 + (11 - k)q + 5k^2 \qquad (3\text{-}28)$$

For the plant size $k = 1$, the short-run cost curve is the one given by
(3-24). Setting the partial derivative of the implicit form of (3-28) with
respect to k equal to zero,

$$G_k(C,q,k) = -q + 10k = 0$$

which has the solution $k = 0.1q$. Substituting into (3-28) gives the long-
run cost function:

$$\begin{aligned}
C &= 0.04q^3 - 0.9q^2 + (11 - 0.1q)q + 5(0.1q)^2 \\
&= 0.04q^3 - 0.95q^2 + 11q
\end{aligned}$$

Long-run fixed cost equals zero.

Let the price of the entrepreneur's product be 4 dollars, as in the
example for a short-run cost function. Setting price equal to long-run
MC,

$$4 = 0.12q^2 - 1.9q + 11$$

which yields the quadratic equation

$$0.12q^2 - 1.9q + 7 = 0$$

with the roots $q = 5.83$ and $q = 10$. Profit is maximized at an output
of 10 units. Utilizing the relation $k = 0.1q$, the optimum-size plant is
given by $k = 1$. The entrepreneur's profit per short-run period is

$$\pi = pq - (0.04q^3 - 0.95q^2 + 11q) = 40 - 55 = -15$$

As in the last example, the maximum operating profit is a loss of 15 dollars.   In the long run the entrepreneur is unable to earn a positive profit *note !* and will not construct a plant of any size.

The situation is quite different if price is increased to 6 dollars. Setting long-run MC equal to price yields the quadratic equation

$$0.12q^2 - 1.9q + 5 = 0$$

with the roots $q = 3.3$ and $q = 12.5$.   Profit is maximized at an output of 12.5 units.   Profit is positive for this plant size:

$$\pi = 75 - 67.1875 = 7.8125$$

and the entrepreneur will construct a plant of the optimum size ($k = 1.25$).

3-5 HOMOGENEOUS PRODUCTION FUNCTIONS

"Returns to scale" describes the output response to a proportionate increase of all inputs.   If output increases by the same proportion, returns to scale are constant for the range of input combinations under consideration.   They are increasing if output increases by a greater proportion and decreasing if it increases by a smaller proportion.   A single production function may exhibit all three types of returns.   Some economists assume that production functions exhibit increasing returns for small amounts of the inputs, then pass through a stage of constant returns, and finally exhibit decreasing returns to scale as the quantities of the inputs become greater and greater.

PROPERTIES

Returns to scale are easily defined for homogeneous production functions. A production function is homogeneous of degree k if

$$f(tx_1, tx_2) = t^k f(x_1, x_2) \tag{3-29}$$

where k is a constant and t is any positive real number.   If both inputs are increased by the factor t, output is increased by the factor t^k.   Returns to scale are increasing if $k > 1$, constant if $k = 1$, and decreasing if $k < 1$.   Homogeneity of degree one is most commonly assumed for production functions.[1]

The partial derivatives of a function homogeneous of degree k are homogeneous of degree $k - 1$.   Differentiate (3-29) partially with

---

[1] A function which is homogeneous of degree one is said to be linearly homogeneous. This, of course, does not imply that the production function is linear.

respect to x_1 using the function of a function rule (see Sec. A-2) on the left:

$$tf_1(tx_1,tx_2) = t^k f_1(x_1,x_2)$$

Dividing through by t,

$$f_1(tx_1,tx_2) = t^{k-1} f_1(x_1,x_2)$$

which is the definition of homogeneity of degree $k-1$. If a production function is homogeneous of degree one, the marginal productivities of X_1 and X_2 are homogeneous of degree zero; i.e., they remain unchanged for proportionate changes of both inputs:

$$f_1(x_1,x_2) = f_1(tx_1,tx_2)$$
$$f_2(x_1,x_2) = f_2(tx_1,tx_2)$$

The MPs depend only upon the proportion in which X_1 and X_2 are used.

A straight line from the origin in the isoquant plane is defined by $(0,0)$ and any arbitrary point (x_1^0,x_2^0). Such a line is the locus of all points (tx_1^0,tx_2^0) for $t \geqq 0$. The RTS at any arbitrarily selected point on the line equals the ratio of the marginal productivities for the input combination corresponding to that point:

$$\frac{f_1(tx_1^0,tx_2^0)}{f_2(tx_1^0,tx_2^0)} = \frac{t^{k-1}f_1(x_1^0,x_2^0)}{t^{k-1}f_2(x_1^0,x_2^0)} = \frac{f_1(x_1^0,x_2^0)}{f_2(x_1^0,x_2^0)}$$

The RTS at (tx_1^0,tx_2^0) equals the RTS at (x_1^0,x_2^0). The expansion path which is the locus of points with RTS equal to the fixed-input-price ratio is a straight line if the production function is homogeneous of any degree. A straight-line expansion path, however, does not necessarily imply a homogeneous production function. The production function given by (3-5) possesses a straight-line expansion path, but it is not homogeneous.

One of the most widely used homogeneous production functions is the Cobb-Douglas function:

$$q = A x_1^\alpha x_2^{1-\alpha} \tag{3-30}$$

where $0 < \alpha < 1$. Increasing the levels of both inputs by the factor t,

$$f(tx_1,tx_2) = A(tx_1)^\alpha (tx_2)^{1-\alpha} = tA x_1^\alpha x_2^{1-\alpha}$$

The Cobb-Douglas function is homogeneous of degree one. The MPs of both inputs are homogeneous of degree zero:

$$f_1(x_1,x_2) = \alpha A x_1^{\alpha-1} x_2^{1-\alpha}$$
$$f_2(x_1,x_2) = (1-\alpha) A x_1^\alpha x_2^{-\alpha}$$
$$f_1(tx_1,tx_2) = \alpha A t^{\alpha-1} x_1^{\alpha-1} t^{1-\alpha} x_2^{1-\alpha} = \alpha A x_1^{\alpha-1} x_2^{1-\alpha}$$
$$f_2(tx_1,tx_2) = (1-\alpha) A t^\alpha x_1^\alpha t^{-\alpha} x_2^{-\alpha} = (1-\alpha) A x_1^\alpha x_2^{-\alpha}$$

The expansion path generated by the Cobb-Douglas function is linear. The first-order conditions for a constrained optimum require that

$$\frac{r_1}{r_2} = \frac{f_1}{f_2} = \frac{\alpha A x_1^{\alpha-1} x_2^{1-\alpha}}{(1-\alpha) A x_1^{\alpha} x_2^{-\alpha}} = \frac{\alpha x_2}{(1-\alpha) x_1}$$

Therefore, the expansion path is given by the implicit function

$$(1-\alpha) r_1 x_1 - \alpha r_2 x_2 = 0$$

which describes a straight line emanating from the origin in the isoquant plane.

EULER'S THEOREM AND DISTRIBUTION

Euler's theorem states that the following condition is satisfied by a homogeneous function:[1]

$$x_1 f_1 + x_2 f_2 = k f(x_1, x_2) \tag{3-31}$$

This theorem yields a number of results of interest in economics. For example, dividing (3-31) by q,

$$\omega_1 + \omega_2 = k$$

The sum of the output elasticities [see Eq. (3-4)] for X_1 and X_2 equals the degree of homogeneity.

Assuming that the production function is homogeneous of degree one, and substituting $q = f(x_1, x_2)$,

$$x_1 f_1 + x_2 f_2 = q \tag{3-32}$$

Total output equals the MP of X_1 multiplied by its quantity plus the MP of X_2 multiplied by its quantity. If the firm were to pay the suppliers of each input its marginal physical product, total output would be just exhausted. Total payments would exceed output if the degree of homogeneity were greater than one and would be less than output if it were less than one.

Euler's theorem played a major role in the development of the marginal-productivity theory of distribution. The basic postulates of this theory are: (1) each input is paid the value of its marginal product, and

---

[1] Differentiating (3-29) partially with respect to t using the composite-function rule on the left,

$$x_1 f_1(t x_1, t x_2) + x_2 f_2(t x_1, t x_2) = k t^{k-1} f(x_1, x_2)$$

Equation (3-31) is obtained by substituting $t = 1$.

(2) total output is just exhausted. Since these conditions are satisfied by production functions homogeneous of degree one, it was mistakenly assumed that all production functions must be of this type.

The Cobb-Douglas function was utilized to attempt an empirical verification of the marginal-productivity theory of distribution. The variable q represented aggregate output, and x_1 and x_2 were aggregate inputs of labor and capital respectively. Euler's theorem is satisfied:

$$q = x_1(\alpha A x_1^{\alpha-1} x_2^{1-\alpha}) + x_2[(1-\alpha) A x_1^{\alpha} x_2^{-\alpha}]$$
$$= \alpha A x_1^{\alpha} x_2^{1-\alpha} + (1-\alpha) A x_1^{\alpha} x_2^{1-\alpha}$$

Substituting from (3-30),

$$q = \alpha q + (1-\alpha)q$$

If each factor is paid its marginal product, total output is distributed between labor and capital in the respective proportions α and $(1-\alpha)$. Paul Douglas estimated α from aggregate time-series data and compared his estimates with labor's share of total output.[1]

The condition of product exhaustion is equivalent to the condition that maximum long-run profit equal zero. Multiplying (3-32) through by the price of the product

$$x_1(pf_1) + x_2(pf_2) = pq$$

Substituting $r_1 = pf_1$ and $r_2 = pf_2$ from the first-order conditions for profit maximization,

$$r_1 x_1 + r_2 x_2 = pq \qquad\qquad (3\text{-}33)$$

Long-run total outlay equals long-run total revenue. Following the assumptions of the marginal-productivity theory, Eq. (3-33) leads to the startling conclusion that long-run profit equals zero regardless of the level of the product price.

The analysis of the marginal-productivity theory of distribution is misleading, if not erroneous. The conventional analysis of profit maximization breaks down if the entrepreneur sells his output at a constant price and possesses a production function which is homogeneous of degree one. The reader can verify that in this case his profit function is also homogeneous of degree one:

$$t\pi = pf(tx_1, tx_2) - r_1 tx_1 - r_2 tx_2$$

[1] See the references listed at the end of this chapter.

Three outcomes are possible. If the prices are such that some factor combination yields a positive profit, profit can be increased to any level by selecting a sufficiently large value for t. In this case the profit function has no finite maximum. If the prices are such that every factor combination yields a negative profit, the entrepreneur will go out of business.

The third possibility, to which the marginal-productivity theorists generally limited their analysis, is the most interesting. In this case there is no factor combination which will yield a positive profit, but the combination (x_1^0, x_2^0) yields a zero profit. From the homogeneity of the profit function it follows that the factor combination (tx_1^0, tx_2^0) will also yield a zero profit. Maximum long-run profit equals zero, but the size of the firm is indeterminate. If the entrepreneur can earn a zero profit for a particular factor combination, his profit remains unchanged if he doubles or halves his scale of operations. If an arbitrary scale of operations is imposed upon the entrepreneur, Euler's theorem holds, and his product is just exhausted.

The assumption of a homogeneous production function is not necessary for the fulfillment of the postulates of the marginal-productivity theory. The postulates are fulfilled if (1) the production function is not homogeneous, (2) the first- and second-order conditions for profit maximization are fulfilled, and (3) the entrepreneur's maximum profit equals zero. Conditions (1) and (2) have been assumed throughout the development of the theory of the firm in Secs. 3-1 and 3-2. In Chap. 4 it will be demonstrated that the free entry and exit of competing firms will result in the satisfaction of condition (3). Condition (3) requires that

$$\pi = pq - r_1 x_1 - r_2 x_2 = 0$$

Substituting $r_1 = pf_1$ and $r_2 = pf_2$ (the first-order conditions), and solving for q,

$$q = x_1 f_1 + x_2 f_2$$

Here the result of (3-32) is attained without the use of Euler's theorem. Furthermore, since the production function is not homogeneous, the entrepreneur's optimum factor combination is generally determinate.

The indeterminacy problem can be viewed in terms of the inability of the entrepreneur to satisfy his second-order conditions for profit maximization. Differentiate (3-32) totally,

$$(f_1 + x_1 f_{11} + x_2 f_{21})\, dx_1 + (f_2 + x_1 f_{12} + x_2 f_{22})\, dx_2 = dq$$

Alternately, let $dx_2 = 0$ and divide by dx_1, and let $dx_1 = 0$ and divide by dx_2:

$$f_1 + x_1 f_{11} + x_2 f_{21} = \frac{\partial q}{\partial x_1} = f_1$$

$$f_2 + x_1 f_{12} + x_2 f_{22} = \frac{\partial q}{\partial x_2} = f_2$$

Subtract f_1 from both sides of the first equation and solve for f_{11}, and subtract f_2 from both sides of the second and solve for f_{22}:

$$f_{11} = -\frac{x_2}{x_1} f_{21} \qquad f_{22} = -\frac{x_1}{x_2} f_{12} \tag{3-34}$$

Thus, $f_{12} = f_{21}$ is positive if f_{11} and f_{22} are negative as assumed. Evaluating the Hessian of the production function using (3-34),

$$f_{11} f_{22} - f_{12}^2 = \left(-\frac{x_2}{x_1} f_{12} \right) \left(-\frac{x_1}{x_2} f_{12} \right) - f_{12}^2 = 0$$

A production function homogeneous of degree one is concave, but it has linear subregions in which it is not strictly concave.

Production functions homogeneous of degree one are used often and meaningfully in economics despite the indeterminacy problems for the individual firm. A number of assumptions are invoked to cope with this problem. Two possible assumptions are: (1) Firm size and firm numbers are determined by some arbitrary mechanism subject to the condition that industry output satisfies industry demand. (2) An industry possesses a production function homogeneous of degree one even though the individual firms within the industry do not possess such production functions. In Chap. 6 it is shown that firm size may be determinate if firms operate under conditions of imperfect competition.

LONG-RUN COST FUNCTIONS

It is possible to construct long-run cost functions with all inputs variable for homogeneous production functions with convex indifference curves. Let (x_1^0, x_2^0) be the optimum input combination for the production of one unit of Q. The corresponding production cost is $a = r_1 x_1^0 + r_2 x_2^0$. Since the expansion path for a homogeneous production function is linear, all optimum input combinations may be written as $(t x_1^0, t x_2^0)$. Therefore, the production function and cost equation may be written as

$$q = f(t x_1^0, t x_2^0) = t^k$$
$$C = (r_1 x_1^0 + r_2 x_2^0) t = at$$

Solving the first equation for t and substituting into the second, the total cost function is

$$C = a q^{1/k}$$

with

$$\frac{dC}{dq} = \frac{a}{k} q^{(1-k)/k} \qquad \frac{d^2C}{dq^2} = \frac{a(1-k)}{k^2} q^{(1-2k)/k}$$

Functions homogeneous of degree one have constant MC and ATC and a linear long-run total cost function. MC is increasing throughout for $k < 1$ and decreasing throughout for $k > 1$. The second-order condition that MC be increasing can be satisfied only if the degree of homogeneity is less than one.

The total cost function for the Cobb-Douglas production function can be derived more easily in the conventional manner. Writing out the production function, cost equation, and expansion path function,

$$q = A x_1^\alpha x_2^{1-\alpha}$$
$$C = r_1 x_1 + r_2 x_2$$
$$(1 - \alpha) r_1 x_1 - \alpha r_2 x_2 = 0$$

Solving the second and third equations for x_1 and x_2,

$$x_1 = \frac{\alpha C}{r_1} \qquad x_2 = \frac{(1 - \alpha)C}{r_2}$$

and substituting these values into the production function,

$$q = A \left(\frac{\alpha C}{r_1}\right)^\alpha \left[\frac{(1 - \alpha)C}{r_2}\right]^{1-\alpha}$$

Solving for C in terms of q and the parameters, the total cost function is

$$C = aq$$

where

$$a = \frac{r_1^\alpha r_2^{1-\alpha}}{A\alpha^\alpha (1 - \alpha)^{1-\alpha}}$$

3-6 CES PRODUCTION FUNCTIONS

A production function which belongs to the CES class has two major characteristics: (1) it is homogeneous of degree one, and (2) it has a constant elasticity of substitution (see Sec. 3-1). Production functions which lack one or both of these characteristics do not belong to the CES class. In Sec. 3-1 it was shown that the production functions $q = A x_1^\alpha x_2^\beta$ have constant unit elasticities of substitution. Thus, all production functions in this class satisfy criterion (2). However, criterion (1) is satisfied only for $\alpha + \beta = 1$, that is, for the Cobb-Douglas function. The production function $q = A x_1^\alpha x_2^{1-\alpha} + x_1$ is homogeneous of degree one, but does not have a constant elasticity of substitution and is not a member of the CES class.

PROPERTIES

By advanced methods it has been shown that the class of CES production functions may be expressed in the form[1]

$$q = A[\alpha x_1^{-\rho} + (1 - \alpha)x_2^{-\rho}]^{-1/\rho} \tag{3-35}$$

where the parameters $A > 0$ and $0 < \alpha < 1$. It is easily verified that (3-35) is homogeneous of degree one:

$$A[\alpha(tx_1)^{-\rho} + (1 - \alpha)(tx_2)^{-\rho}]^{-1/\rho} = tA[\alpha x_1^{-\rho} + (1 - \alpha)x_2^{-\rho}]^{-1/\rho}$$

The marginal productivities of the inputs are

$$\frac{\partial q}{\partial x_1} = \frac{\alpha}{A^\rho}\left(\frac{q}{x_1}\right)^{\rho+1} \qquad \frac{\partial q}{\partial x_2} = \frac{1 - \alpha}{A^\rho}\left(\frac{q}{x_2}\right)^{\rho+1}$$

and the rate of technical substitution is

$$\text{RTS} = \frac{\alpha}{1 - \alpha}\left(\frac{x_2}{x_1}\right)^{\rho+1} \tag{3-36}$$

An expression for the elasticity of substitution for production functions homogeneous of degree one is obtained by substituting (3-34) into (3-10)

$$\sigma = \frac{f_1 f_2(x_1 f_1 + x_2 f_2)}{f_{12}(x_1 f_1 + x_2 f_2)^2}$$

and invoking Euler's theorem (3-31),

$$\sigma = \frac{f_1 f_2}{f_{12}q} \tag{3-37}$$

For (3-35),

$$f_{12} = \frac{(1 + \rho)\alpha(1 - \alpha)q^{1+2\rho}}{A^{2\rho}(x_1 x_2)^{1+\rho}}$$

Evaluating (3-37) for (3-35),

$$\sigma = \frac{1}{1 + \rho} \qquad \rho = \frac{1 - \sigma}{\sigma} \tag{3-38}$$

Thus, the parameter ρ is closely related to the constant elasticity of substitution.

---

[1] See K. Arrow, H. B. Chenery, B. Minhas, and R. M. Solow, "Capital-Labor Substitution and Economic Efficiency," *Review of Economics and Statistics*, vol. 43 (August, 1961), pp. 228–232.

ISOQUANTS

Differentiating (3-36),

$$- \frac{d^2x_2}{dx_1^2} = -(\rho + 1) \frac{\alpha}{(1 - \alpha)^2} \frac{x_2^{\rho+1}}{x_1^{2(\rho+1)}} [(1 - \alpha)x_1^\rho + \alpha x_2^\rho]$$

The RTS is decreasing and isoquants are convex if $\rho > -1$. The particular shape of the convex isoquants generated by a CES function depends upon the value of σ. Two limits and three intermediate cases describe the possible isoquant configurations.

Case 1 $\sigma \to 0$, $\rho \to +\infty$. The RTS (3-36) approaches zero if $x_1 > x_2$ or $+\infty$ if $x_1 < x_2$, and in the limit substitution is impossible. The curvature of the isoquants approaches a right angle.

Case 2 $0 < \sigma < 1$, $\rho > 0$. The isoquants for (3-35) can be written as

$$\alpha x_1^{-\rho} + (1 - \alpha)x_2^{-\rho} = \left(\frac{q}{A}\right)^{-\rho} = K \tag{3-39}$$

where K is a positive constant for any selected positive value of q. Neither term on the left-hand side of (3-39) can be negative. Therefore, neither term can exceed K in value. As $x_1 \to 0$, $ax_1^{-\rho} \to +\infty$. Since there is an upper limit K on the value of $ax_1^{-\rho}$, x_1 cannot equal zero. By similar reasoning, x_2 cannot equal zero. Thus, an isoquant neither cuts nor approaches the axes. It is asymptotic to $x_1 = (K/\alpha)^{-1/\rho}$ and $x_2 = [K/(1 - \alpha)]^{-1/\rho}$.

Case 3 $\sigma = 1$, $\rho = 0$. It has been observed that the CES production function becomes the Cobb-Douglas function for $\sigma = 1$. The interpretation of this case is not obvious from (3-35). When the parameter $\rho = 0$, (3-39) becomes an identity and is not helpful in establishing the properties of this case. These properties may be examined by making use of L'Hôpital's rule which states that[1] if

$$\lim_{z \to b} h(z) = 0 \qquad \text{and} \qquad \lim_{z \to b} g(z) = 0$$

and if

$$\lim_{z \to b} \frac{h'(z)}{g'(z)} = \alpha$$

then

$$\lim_{z \to b} \frac{h(z)}{g(z)} = \alpha$$

---

[1] See W. Rudin, *Principles of Mathematical Analysis* (New York: McGraw-Hill, 1953), pp. 82–83.

Write the natural logarithm of (3-35) as the quotient of two functions of ρ:

$$\log q - \log A = \frac{-\log [\alpha x_1^{-\rho} + (1 - \alpha)x_2^{-\rho}]}{\rho} = \frac{h(\rho)}{g(\rho)}$$

where $h(\rho) \to 0$ and $g(\rho) \to 0$ as $\rho \to 0$. Taking the derivative of the numerator,

$$h'(\rho) = \frac{\alpha x_1^{-\rho} \log x_1 + (1 - \alpha)x_2^{-\rho} \log x_2}{\varkappa x_1^{-\rho} + (1 - \alpha)x_2^{-\rho}}$$

which converges to $\alpha \log x_1 + (1 - \alpha) \log x_2$ as $\rho \to 0$. Finally, $g'(\rho) = 1$. By L'Hôpital's rule the limiting case is

$$\log q - \log A = \alpha \log x_1 + (1 - \alpha) \log x_2$$

and $q = A x_1^{\alpha} x_2^{1-\alpha}$ which is the Cobb-Douglas function.

Case 4 $\sigma > 1$, $-1 < \rho < 0$. The exponents of the terms on the left of (3-39) are positive. Isoquants will meet both axes. If $x_1 = 0$, $x_2 = [K/(1 - \alpha)]^{-\rho}$, and if $x_2 = 0$, $x_1 = (K/\alpha)^{-\rho}$.

Case 5 $\sigma \to +\infty$, $\rho \to -1$. In the limit the exponents of both terms on the left of (3-39) are one, and the isoquants are straight lines. The inputs are perfect substitutes in this limiting case.

THE EQUILIBRIUM CONDITION

The CES production function (3-35) is cumbersome and difficult to manipulate. Its RTS, however, is quite simple and this is one of the reasons for its popularity and wide use. Substituting for σ from (3-38), and letting the RTS (3-36) equal the input-price ratio,

$$\frac{\alpha}{1 - \alpha}\left(\frac{x_2}{x_1}\right)^{1/\sigma} = \frac{r_1}{r_2}$$

and

$$\frac{x_2}{x_1} = a\left(\frac{r_1}{r_2}\right)^{\sigma} \tag{3-40}$$

where $a = [(1 - \alpha)/\alpha]^{\sigma}$. The reader can verify from (3-40) that the constant elasticity of substitution is also the constant elasticity of the input-use ratio (x_2/x_1) with respect to the input-price ratio.

Equation (3-40) states that the input-use ratio is a simple power function of the input-price ratio. Since this function is linear in the logarithms of the variables, the parameters a and σ are amenable to estimation by linear regression analysis from time-series data. If x_1 and x_2 are labor and capital respectively, (3-40) shows how the capital-labor ratio for a particular good changes with changes in the wage-capital rental ratio.   This type of analysis has proved particularly useful for the study of problems in the theory of international trade.[1]

3-7   JOINT PRODUCTS

Some production processes will yield more than one output.   Sheep raising is the classic example of such a process.   Two outputs, wool and mutton, can be produced in varying proportions by a single production process.[2]   The case of joint products is distinguished on technical rather than organizational grounds and exists whenever the quantities of two or more outputs are technically interdependent.   Cases in which a single firm produces two or more technically independent products are excluded by this definition.

BASIC CONCEPTS

Consider the simplest case in which an entrepreneur uses a single input (X) for the production of two outputs $(Q_1$ and $Q_2)$.   In implicit form his production function is

$$H(q_1,q_2,x) = 0 \tag{3-41}$$

where q_1, q_2, and x are the respective quantities of Q_1, Q_2, and X.   Assume that (3-41) can be solved explicitly for x:

$$x = h(q_1,q_2) \tag{3-42}$$

The cost of production *in terms of* X is a function of the quantities of the two outputs.

A *product transformation curve* is defined as the locus of output combinations that can be secured from a given input of X:

$$x^0 = h(q_1,q_2)$$

Three of a family of product transformation curves are presented in Fig. 3-10.   The further a curve lies from the origin, the greater the input of X to which it corresponds:

$$x^{(3)} > x^{(2)} > x^{(1)}$$

---

[1] See B. S. Minhas, "The Homohypallagic Production Function, Factor-intensity Reversals, and the Heckscher-Ohlin Theorem," *Journal of Political Economy*, vol. 70 (April, 1962), pp. 138–156.

[2] The production of joint products does not require an extended analysis unless they can be produced in varying proportions.   If two products are always produced in a fixed proportion: $q_1/q_2 = k$ where k is a constant, the analysis for a single output can be applied.   Define a compound unit of output as k units of Q_1 and 1 unit of Q_2 with a price of $kp_1 + p_2$ and treat it as a single output.

The slope of the tangent to a point on a product transformation curve is the rate at which Q_2 must be sacrificed to obtain more Q_1 (or Q_1 sacrificed to obtain more Q_2) without varying the input of X. The negative of the slope is defined as the *rate of product transformation* (RPT):

$$\text{RPT} = -\frac{dq_2}{dq_1}$$

Taking the total differential of (3-42),

$$dx = h_1\,dq_1 + h_2\,dq_2$$

Since $dx = 0$ for movements along a product transformation curve,

$$\text{RPT} = -\frac{dq_2}{dq_1} = \frac{h_1}{h_2} \tag{3-43}$$

The RPT at a point on a product transformation curve equals the ratio of the marginal cost of Q_1 *in terms of* X to the marginal cost of Q_2 *in terms of* X at that point.

Alternatively, the RPT can be expressed in terms of the MPs. The inverse-function rule applies:

$$\frac{\partial q_1}{\partial x} = \frac{1}{h_1} \qquad \frac{\partial q_2}{\partial x} = \frac{1}{h_2} \tag{3-44}$$

Substituting into (3-43),

$$\text{RPT} = -\frac{dq_2}{dq_1} = \frac{\partial q_2/\partial x}{\partial q_1/\partial x} \tag{3-45}$$

The RPT equals the ratio of the MP of X in the production of Q_2 to the MP of X in the production of Q_1. If both MPs are positive, as rational operation requires, the slopes of the product transformation curves are negative, and the RPT positive.

Taking the total derivative of (3-43), the rate of change of the RPT is

$$-\frac{d^2q_2}{dq_1^2} = \frac{1}{h_2^3}\left(h_{11}h_2^2 - 2h_{12}h_1h_2 + h_{22}h_1^2\right) \tag{3-46}$$

It is normally assumed that (3-46) is positive, i.e., that the RPT increases as a movement is made from left to right along a product transformation curve. As more Q_1 and less Q_2 is produced with a fixed input quantity, an increasing amount of Q_2 must be sacrificed per unit of Q_1. If (3-46) is positive, a product transformation curve gives q_2 as a function of q_1 with negative second derivative, i.e., q_2 as a strictly concave function of q_1 (see Sec. A-2). Such product transformation curves are bowed away from the origin as pictured in Fig. 3-10.

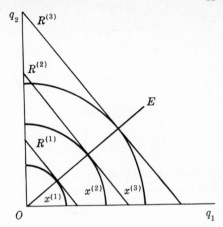

Fig. 3-10

The system of product transformation curves in Fig. 3-10 is generated by the implicit production function

$$q_1^2 + q_2^2 - x = 0$$

The product transformation curves are concentric circles:

$$x^0 = q_1^2 + q_2^2$$

with RPT $= q_1/q_2$. For q_1, $q_2 > 0$, the slopes of the product transformation curves are negative, and the RPT positive. The rate of change of the RPT as given by (3-46) equals $(q_1^2 + q_2^2)/q_2^3$ in this case.

CONSTRAINED REVENUE MAXIMIZATION

If the entrepreneur sells his outputs at fixed prices, his revenue is given by the linear equation

$$R = p_1q_1 + p_2q_2 \tag{3-47}$$

where p_1 and p_2 are the prices of Q_1 and Q_2 respectively. An isorevenue line is the revenue counterpart of an isocost line and is defined as the locus of output combinations that will earn a specified revenue. Three of a system of isorevenue lines are presented in Fig. 3-10. They are parallel straight lines with slopes equal to the negative of the ratio of the output prices $(-p_1/p_2)$.

To solve the constrained-maximization problem of an entrepreneur who desires to maximize revenue for a specified input of X, form the function

$$W = p_1q_1 + p_2q_2 + \mu[x^0 - h(q_1,q_2)]$$

where μ is an undetermined Lagrange multiplier, and set its partial derivatives equal to zero:

$$\frac{\partial W}{\partial q_1} = p_1 - \mu h_1 = 0$$

$$\frac{\partial W}{\partial q_2} = p_2 - \mu h_2 = 0$$

$$\frac{\partial W}{\partial \mu} = x^0 - h(q_1,q_2) = 0$$

Moving the second terms of the first two equations to the right and dividing the first by the second,

$$\frac{p_1}{p_2} = \frac{h_1}{h_2} = \text{RPT}$$

or substituting from (3-44),

$$\frac{p_1}{p_2} = \frac{\partial q_2/\partial x}{\partial q_1/\partial x} = \text{RPT} \tag{3-48}$$

The RPT must be equated with the fixed price ratio. In geometric terms, the specified product transformation curve must be tangent to an isorevenue line.

The first-order conditions may also be stated as

$$\mu = \frac{p_1}{h_1} = \frac{p_2}{h_2}$$

or substituting from (3-44),

$$\mu = p_1 \frac{\partial q_1}{\partial x} = p_2 \frac{\partial q_2}{\partial x}$$

The value of the MP of X in the production of each output must equal μ, the derivative of R with respect to x with prices constant.[1]

---

[1] The total differential of (3-47) is

$$dR = p_1 \, dq_1 + p_2 \, dq_2$$

or substituting $p_1 = \mu h_1$ and $p_2 = \mu h_2$,

$$dR = \mu(h_1 \, dq_1 + h_2 \, dq_2)$$

Dividing this by the differential of (3-42), the total derivative of R with respect to x with prices constant is

$$\frac{dR}{dx} = \frac{\mu(h_1 \, dq_1 + h_2 \, dq_2)}{h_1 \, dq_1 + h_2 \, dq_2} = \mu$$

and is called the marginal-revenue productivity of X.

The second-order condition requires that the relevant bordered Hessian determinant be positive:

$$\begin{vmatrix} -\mu h_{11} & -\mu h_{12} & -h_1 \\ -\mu h_{21} & -\mu h_{22} & -h_2 \\ -h_1 & -h_2 & 0 \end{vmatrix} > 0$$

Expanding,

$$\mu(h_{11}h_2^2 - 2h_{12}h_1h_2 + h_{22}h_1^2) > 0$$

Since $\mu > 0$,

$$(h_{11}h_2^2 - 2h_{12}h_1h_2 + h_{22}h_1^2) > 0$$

With $h_2 > 0$ as required by the first-order condition, it follows from (3-46) that the second-order condition requires that the product transformation curve have an increasing RPT.

An entrepreneur might desire to minimize the amount of X necessary to obtain a specified revenue. In this case he would minimize (3-42) subject to a revenue constraint. Geometrically, he desires to reach the lowest product transformation curve that has a common point with a specified isorevenue line. For constrained revenue maximization he desires to reach the highest isorevenue line possessing a common point with a specified product transformation curve. If the product transformation curves are strictly concave, every point of tangency between an isorevenue line and a product transformation curve represents the solution of both a constrained-revenue-maximization and a constrained-input-minimization problem. The locus of all points of tangency (see OE in Fig. 3-10) is an *output expansion path* similar in interpretation to the input expansion path of the single-product firm.

PROFIT MAXIMIZATION

Express profit as a function of q_1 and q_2:

$$\pi = p_1q_1 + p_2q_2 - rh(q_1,q_2)$$

and set its partial derivatives equal to zero:

$$\frac{\partial \pi}{\partial q_1} = p_1 - rh_1 = 0$$

$$\frac{\partial \pi}{\partial q_2} = p_2 - rh_2 = 0$$

Moving the price terms to the right and dividing by the marginal costs in terms of X,

$$r = \frac{p_1}{h_1} = \frac{p_2}{h_2}$$

or substituting from (3-44),

$$r = p_1 \frac{\partial q_1}{\partial x} = p_2 \frac{\partial q_2}{\partial x} \tag{3-49}$$

The value of the MP of X for the production of each output must be equated to the price of X.† The entrepreneur could increase his profit by increasing his employment of X if its return in the production of either product exceeded its cost.

Second-order conditions require that

$$-rh_{11} < 0 \qquad \begin{vmatrix} -rh_{11} & -rh_{12} \\ -rh_{21} & -rh_{22} \end{vmatrix} > 0$$

Expanding the second determinant,

$$r^2[h_{11}h_{22} - (h_{12})^2] > 0$$

Since $r > 0$, the second-order conditions can be stated as

$$h_{11} > 0 \qquad h_{11}h_{22} - (h_{12})^2 > 0 \tag{3-50}$$

Both together imply that $h_{22} > 0$. The marginal cost of each output in terms of X must be increasing. Conditions (3-50) require that the production relation (3-42) be strictly convex in a neighborhood about a point at which the first-order conditions (3-49) are satisfied.[1] If (3-42) is strictly convex throughout, any maximum that is achieved will be a global maximum.

Consider profit maximization by an entrepreneur whose product transformation curves are given by a system of concentric circles. His profit is

$$\pi = p_1q_1 + p_2q_2 - r(q_1^2 + q_2^2)$$

Setting the partial derivatives equal to zero

$$\frac{\partial \pi}{\partial q_1} = p_1 - 2rq_1 = 0 \qquad \frac{\partial \pi}{\partial q_2} = p_2 - 2rq_2 = 0$$

The first-order conditions can be stated as

$$r = \frac{p_1}{2q_1} = \frac{p_2}{2q_2}$$

---

† Following the derivations of (3-48) and the note on p. 92, it is not surprising to learn that profit maximization requires that $r = dR/dx$. The rate at which the application of an additional unit of X would increase the entrepreneur's revenue must equal its price.

[1] Strict convexity for (3-42) implies a strictly concave product transformation curve.

Second-order conditions (3-50) are satisfied:

$$2 > 0 \qquad 4 - 0 = 4 > 0$$

3-8 GENERALIZATION TO m VARIABLES

The analysis of the firm is easily generalized to cover a production process with s outputs and n inputs. The production function is stated in implicit form as

$$F(q_1, \ldots ,q_s,x_1, \ldots ,x_n) = 0 \tag{3-51}$$

where (3-51) is assumed to possess continuous first- and second-order partial derivatives which are different from zero for all its nontrivial solutions. It is assumed that (3-51) is written in such a way that its partial derivatives for outputs are normally positive and its partial derivatives for inputs are normally negative. For example, the concentric-circle production relation may be written in implicit form as either $q_1^2 + q_2^2 - x_1 = 0$ or $x_1 - q_1^2 - q_2^2 = 0$. It is assumed that the first variant is used. The Cobb-Douglas function is written as

$$q_1 - Ax_1^\alpha x_2^{1-\alpha} = 0$$

PROFIT MAXIMIZATION

Profit is the difference between the total revenue from the sale of all outputs and the expenditure upon all inputs.

$$\pi = \sum_{i=1}^{s} p_i q_i - \sum_{j=1}^{n} r_j x_j \tag{3-52}$$

The entrepreneur desires to maximize profit subject to the technical rules given by his production function. Form the function

$$J = \sum_{i=1}^{s} p_i q_i - \sum_{j=1}^{n} r_j x_j + \lambda F(q_1, \ldots ,x_n)$$

and set each of its $(s + n + 1)$ partial derivatives equal to zero:

$$\frac{\partial J}{\partial q_i} = p_i + \lambda F_i = 0 \qquad i = 1, \ldots , s$$

$$\frac{\partial J}{\partial x_j} = -r_j + \lambda F_{s+j} = 0 \qquad j = 1, \ldots , n \tag{3-53}$$

$$\frac{\partial J}{\partial \lambda} = F(q_1, \ldots ,x_n) = 0$$

where $F_i(i = 1, \ldots , s + n = m)$ is the partial derivative of (3-51) with respect to its ith argument.

Select any two of the first s equations of (3-53), move the second terms to the right, and divide one by the other:[1]

$$\frac{p_j}{p_k} = \frac{F_j}{F_k} = -\frac{\partial q_k}{\partial q_j} \qquad j, k = 1, \ldots, s \tag{3-54}$$

The RPT for every pair of outputs—holding the levels of all other outputs and all inputs constant—must equal the ratio of their prices. For the kth output and the jth input, (3-53) implies that

$$\frac{r_j}{p_k} = -\frac{F_{s+j}}{F_k} = \frac{\partial q_k}{\partial x_j} \qquad \text{or} \qquad r_j = p_k \frac{\partial q_k}{\partial x_j} \qquad \begin{matrix} k = 1, \ldots, s \\ j = 1, \ldots, n \end{matrix}$$

The value of the marginal product of each input with respect to each output is equated to the input price. Finally, consider two inputs. The first-order conditions become

$$\frac{r_j}{r_k} = -\frac{\partial x_k}{\partial x_j} \qquad j, k = 1, \ldots, n$$

The RTS for every pair of inputs—holding the levels of all outputs and all other inputs constant—must equal the ratio of their prices.

The second-order conditions for the maximization of profit require that the relevant bordered Hessian determinants alternate in sign:

$$\begin{vmatrix} \lambda F_{11} & \lambda F_{12} & F_1 \\ \lambda F_{21} & \lambda F_{22} & F_2 \\ F_1 & F_2 & 0 \end{vmatrix} > 0, \ldots, (-1)^m \begin{vmatrix} \lambda F_{11} & \cdots & \lambda F_{1m} & F_1 \\ \cdots & \cdots & \cdots & \cdots \\ \lambda F_{m1} & \cdots & \lambda F_{mm} & F_m \\ F_1 & \cdots & F_m & 0 \end{vmatrix} > 0 \tag{3-55}$$

Multiplying the first two columns of the first array and the first m of the last by $1/\lambda$, and multiplying the last row of both arrays by λ,

$$\lambda \begin{vmatrix} F_{11} & F_{12} & F_1 \\ F_{21} & F_{22} & F_2 \\ F_1 & F_2 & 0 \end{vmatrix} > 0, \ldots, (-1)^m \lambda^{m-1} \begin{vmatrix} F_{11} & \cdots & F_{1m} & F_1 \\ \cdots & \cdots & \cdots & \cdots \\ F_{m1} & \cdots & F_{mm} & F_m \\ F_1 & \cdots & F_m & 0 \end{vmatrix} > 0$$

Since $\lambda < 0$ from (3-53), the second-order conditions require that

$$\begin{vmatrix} F_{11} & F_{12} & F_1 \\ F_{21} & F_{22} & F_2 \\ F_1 & F_2 & 0 \end{vmatrix} < 0, \ldots, \begin{vmatrix} F_{11} & \cdots & F_{1m} & F_1 \\ \cdots & \cdots & \cdots & \cdots \\ F_{m1} & \cdots & F_{mm} & F_m \\ F_1 & \cdots & F_m & 0 \end{vmatrix} < 0 \tag{3-56}$$

[1] The implicit-function rule, $F_i/F_j = -\partial q_j/\partial q_i$, is utilized in (3-54) (see Sec. A-3).

Conditions (3-56) imply that the input-output combinations defined by

$$F(q_1, \ldots ,q_s, x_1, \ldots ,x_n) \leqq 0$$

form a closed strictly convex point set (see Sec. 5-4 or Sec. 9-2) in the neighborhood of a point at which the first-order conditions (3-53) are satisfied. These general conditions encompass the second-order conditions derived in the earlier sections of this chapter as special cases.

If (3-56) is satisfied over a range of input and output values, all one-output production functions obtained by fixing the values of the other $(s - 1)$ outputs will be strictly concave over this range, and all one-input production functions obtained by fixing the values of the other $(n - 1)$ inputs will be strictly convex. Consider a one-output–two-input case. The implicit production function is $q - f(x_1,x_2) = 0$ with the partial derivatives $F_1 = 1$, $F_2 = -f_1$, and $F_3 = -f_2$. In this case, conditions (3-56) are

$$\begin{vmatrix} 0 & 0 & 1 \\ 0 & -f_{11} & -f_1 \\ 1 & -f_1 & 0 \end{vmatrix} < 0 \qquad \begin{vmatrix} 0 & 0 & 0 & 1 \\ 0 & -f_{11} & -f_{12} & -f_1 \\ 0 & -f_{21} & -f_{22} & -f_2 \\ 1 & -f_1 & -f_2 & 0 \end{vmatrix} < 0$$

Expand each determinant by the last element in its first row, then by the last element in its first column; multiply both columns of the second determinant by -1, and finally multiply the second determinant by -1:

$$f_{11} < 0 \qquad \begin{vmatrix} f_{11} & f_{12} \\ f_{21} & f_{22} \end{vmatrix} > 0$$

which imply the strict concavity of (3-1). This result is easily generalized to the one-output–n-input case. It also can be shown that conditions (3-56) for the implicit form of the s-output–one-input production relation is equivalent to strict convexity for the explicit form of this relation.

SUBSTITUTION EFFECTS

The profit-maximizing entrepreneur will respond to changes in his input and output prices by varying his input and output levels in order to continue to satisfy the first-order conditions (3-53). By total differentiation of (3-53),

$$\lambda F_{11} \, dq_1 + \cdots + \lambda F_{1m} \, dx_n + F_1 \, d\lambda = -dp_1$$
$$\cdots \cdots \cdots \cdots \cdots \cdots \cdots \cdots \cdots \cdots \cdots \cdots$$
$$\lambda F_{m1} \, dq_1 + \cdots + \lambda F_{mm} \, dx_n + F_m \, d\lambda = dr_n \qquad (3\text{-}57)$$
$$F_1 \, dq_1 + \cdots + F_m \, dx_n \qquad\qquad = 0$$

Assume that the price changes are given and treat (3-57) as a system of $(m + 1)$ equations in $(m + 1)$ variables: $dq_i(i = 1, \ldots , s)$,

$dx_j (j = 1, \ldots, n)$, and $d\lambda$. Using Cramer's rule (see Sec. A-1) to solve (3-57) for dq_j and dx_j,

$$dq_j = \frac{-\mathbf{D}_{1j} \, dp_1 - \cdots + \mathbf{D}_{mj} \, dr_n}{\mathbf{D}} \qquad j = 1, \ldots, s$$

$$dx_j = \frac{-\mathbf{D}_{1,s+j} \, dp_1 - \cdots + \mathbf{D}_{m,s+j} \, dr_n}{\mathbf{D}} \qquad j = 1, \ldots, n \tag{3-58}$$

where $\mathbf{D}$ is the determinant of the coefficients of (3-57) and $\mathbf{D}_{ij}$ is the cofactor of the element in the ith row and jth column of the array. The determinant $\mathbf{D}$ is the same as the highest-order determinant of (3-55).

The rate of change of quantity with respect to a price is determined by dividing both sides of (3-58) by the price differential and letting the remaining price differentials equal zero:

$$\frac{\partial q_j}{\partial p_k} = \frac{\partial q_k}{\partial p_j} = -\frac{\mathbf{D}_{kj}}{\mathbf{D}} \qquad j, k = 1, \ldots, s$$

$$\frac{\partial x_j}{\partial r_k} = \frac{\partial x_k}{\partial r_j} = \frac{\mathbf{D}_{s+k,s+j}}{\mathbf{D}} \qquad j, k = 1, \ldots, n \tag{3-59}$$

$$\frac{\partial q_j}{\partial r_k} = \frac{\partial x_k}{\partial p_j} = \frac{\mathbf{D}_{s+k,j}}{\mathbf{D}} \qquad \begin{array}{l} j = 1, \ldots, s \\ k = 1, \ldots, n \end{array}$$

Since $\mathbf{D}$ is a symmetric determinant, the partial derivatives (3-59) are also symmetric. There is no counterpart of the consumer's nonsymmetric income effect in the theory of the firm. The total effect for the firm is a symmetric substitution effect.

Most of the derivatives of (3-59) may be of either sign depending upon the particular form of the implicit production function. The signs of own-price effects, however, can be determined. It follows from (3-55) that $\mathbf{D}_{jj}$ and $\mathbf{D}$ must be of opposite sign for $j = 1, \ldots, m$. Therefore,

$$\frac{\partial q_j}{\partial p_j} > 0 \qquad j = 1, \ldots, s \qquad \frac{\partial x_k}{\partial r_k} < 0 \qquad k = 1, \ldots, n$$

An increase of the jth output price, with other prices constant, will always increase the production of the jth output. An increase of the kth input price, with other prices constant, will always decrease the use of the kth input.

3-9 SUMMARY

The production function for the one-output–two-variable-inputs case gives the maximum output level that can be secured from each possible input combination. Productivity curves are obtained by treating the quantity of one of the variable inputs as a parameter and expressing output as a function of the quantity of the other. An output elasticity for an input is the proportionate rate of change of output per one percent change of the input. An isoquant is the locus of all input combinations that yield a specified output level. The production function normally is assumed to have convex isoquants. The elasticity of substitution relates proportionate changes in the input ratio to proportionate changes in the rate of technical substitution along an isoquant.

The entrepreneur may desire to maximize his output level for a given cost, or he may desire to minimize the cost of producing a given output level. The first-order conditions for both problems require that the rate of technical substitution between the inputs be equated to their price ratio. In diagrammatic terms, both require tangency between an isoquant and an isocost line. The locus of such tangency points is the expansion path of the firm. The entrepreneur may allow both output level and cost to vary and maximize his profit. First-order conditions require that the value of the marginal physical productivity of each input be equated to its price. Second-order conditions require that the production function be strictly concave in the neighborhood of a point at which the first-order conditions are satisfied. The marginal productivities of both inputs must be decreasing.

The producer's demand for an input is derived from the underlying demand for the commodity which he produces. His input demand functions are obtained by solving his first-order conditions for his input levels as functions of input and output prices. An input demand curve relates the demand for an input to its own price; these curves are always downward sloping.

Given the entrepreneur's production function, cost equation, and expansion path function, his total cost can be expressed as a function of his output level. In the short run, the cost of his fixed inputs must be paid, regardless of his output level. The first-order condition for profit maximization requires the entrepreneur to equate his marginal cost to the selling price of his output. The second-order condition requires that marginal cost be increasing. The entrepreneur is able to vary the levels of his fixed inputs in the long run and therefore is able to select a particular short-run cost function. His long-run total cost function is the envelope of his alternative short-run total cost functions. Long-run profit maximization requires that long-run marginal cost be equated to selling price and that long-run marginal cost be increasing.

A number of interesting results arise if the entrepreneur's production function is homogeneous of degree one. A proportionate variation of all input levels results in a proportionate change of output level and leaves the marginal productivities of the inputs unchanged. The sum of the output elasticities for the inputs equals one. Euler's theorem has been utilized to demonstrate that total output is just exhausted if each input is paid its marginal physical productivity. However, the assumptions of competitive profit maximization break down if the entrepreneur's long-run production function is homogeneous of degree one.

A CES production function is homogeneous of degree one and has a constant elasticity of substitution throughout. The isoquants for CES functions range from right angles to straight lines as the elasticity of substitution ranges from its limits of zero to $+\infty$. The Cobb-Douglas production function has a constant elasticity of substitution of unity and is a member of the CES class. The first-order conditions for a CES function state the input use ratio as a function, linear in logarithms, of the input price ratio.

Two or more outputs are often produced jointly in a single production process. In the simplest case the quantities of two outputs can be expressed as a function of the quantity of a single input. A product transformation curve is the locus of all output combinations that can be secured from a given input level. The production relation normally is assumed to have concave product transformation curves. The entrepreneur may desire to maximize the revenue he obtains from a given input level. First-order conditions require that he equate the rate of product transformation to the ratio of his output prices. In diagrammatic terms he will operate at a point at which an isorevenue line is tangent to a particular product transformation curve. If he desires to maximize profit, he must equate the value of the marginal productivity of the input with respect to each output to its price. Second-order conditions require that the production relation be strictly convex in the neighborhood of a point at which the first-order conditions are satisfied.

In the general case n inputs are used for the production of s outputs, and the production function is stated in implicit form. The first-order conditions for profit maximization require that: (1) the rate of product transformation between every pair of outputs equal their price ratio, (2) the value of the marginal productivity of each input with respect to each output equal the input price, and (3) the rate of technical substitution between every pair of inputs equal their price ratio. Substitution effects with respect to price variations can be computed, but there is no counterpart of the consumer's nonsymmetric income effect.

EXERCISES

3-1. Construct the average and marginal productivity functions for X_1 which correspond to the production function $q = x_1x_2 - 0.2x_1^2 - 0.8x_2^2$. Let $x_2 = 10$. At what respective values of x_1 will the AP and MP of X_1 equal zero?

3-2. Determine the output elasticities for X_1 and X_2 which correspond to the CES production function (3-35). Prove that their sum equals one.

3-3. Derive an input expansion path for the production function $q = A x_1^\alpha x_2^\beta$ where $\alpha, \beta > 0$.

3-4. Assume that an entrepreneur's short-run total cost function is $C = q^3 - 10q^2 + 17q + 66$. Determine the output level at which he maximizes profit if $p = 5$. Compute the output elasticity of cost at this output.

3-5. Each of the following production functions is homogeneous of degree one. In each case, derive the marginal productivities for X_1 and X_2 and demonstrate that they are homogeneous of degree zero:

    (a) $q = (ax_1x_2 - bx_1^2 - cx_2^2)/(\alpha x_1 + \beta x_2)$.

    (b) $q = A x_1^\alpha x_2^{1-\alpha} + bx_1 + cx_2$.

3-6. An entrepreneur uses two distinct production processes to produce two distinct goods, Q_1 and Q_2. The production function for each good is CES, and the entrepreneur obeys the equilibrium condition (3-40) for each. Assume that Q_1 has a higher elasticity of substitution and a lower value for the parameter a than Q_2. Determine the input price ratio at which the input use ratio would be the same for both goods. Which good would have the higher input use ratio if the input price ratio were lower? Which would have the higher use ratio if the price ratio were higher?

3-7. An entrepreneur uses one input to produce two outputs subject to the production relation $x = A(q_1^\alpha + q_2^\beta)$ where $\alpha, \beta > 1$. He buys the input and sells the outputs at fixed prices. Express his profit-maximizing outputs as functions of the prices. Prove that his production relation is strictly convex for $q_1, q_2 > 0$.

*3-8. An entrepreneur produces one output with two inputs using the Cobb-Douglas production function (3-30). He buys the inputs and sells the outputs at fixed prices. He is subject to a quota which allows him to purchase no more than x_1^0 units of X_1. He would have purchased more in the absence of the quota. Determine the entrepreneur's conditions for profit maximization. What is the optimal relation between the value of the marginal product of each input and its price? What is the optimal relation between the RTS and the input price ratio?

SELECTED REFERENCES

Allen, R. G. D., *Mathematical Economics* (London: Macmillan, 1956). Chapter 18 contains a mathematical statement of the theory of the firm. The necessary algebra is developed in the text.

Arrow, K., H. B. Chenery, B. Minhas, and R. M. Solow, "Capital-Labor Substitution and Economic Efficiency," *Review of Economics and Statistics*, vol. 43 (August, 1961), pp. 228–232. The original statement of the properties of the CES production function.

Bronfenbrenner, M., and Paul H. Douglas, "Cross-section Studies in the Cobb-Douglas Function," *Journal of Political Economy*, vol. 47 (December, 1939), pp. 761–785. A general discussion of the Cobb-Douglas production function.

Carlson, Sune, *A Study on the Theory of Production* (New York: Kelley & Millman, 1956). An exposition of the theory of the firm in terms of simple mathematics.

Frisch, Ragnar, *Theory of Production* (Chicago: Rand McNally, 1965). Differential and integral calculus are used extensively in this treatise.

Hicks, J. R., *Value and Capital* (2d ed.; Oxford: Clarendon Press, 1946). The theory of the firm is developed in chaps. VI–VII. The mathematical analysis is contained in an appendix.

McFadden, Daniel, "Constant Elasticity of Substitution Production Functions," *Review of Economic Studies*, vol. 30 (June, 1963), pp. 73–83. Fairly advanced mathematics are employed.

Menger, K., "The Laws of Return," in O. Morgenstern (ed.), *Economic Activity Analysis* (New York: Wiley, 1954), pp. 419–482. A mathematical study of alternative formulations of the law of diminishing returns.

Samuelson, Paul A., *Foundations of Economic Analysis* (Cambridge, Mass.: Harvard, 1948). Chapter 4 contains a mathematical statement of the theory of the firm.

Shephard, Ronald W., *Cost and Production Functions* (Princeton, N.J.: Princeton, 1953). Calculus and convex-set theory are used.

4
Market Equilibrium

The behavior of consumers and entrepreneurs has been analyzed on the assumption that they are unable to affect the prices at which they buy and sell. The isolated consumer is confronted with given prices, and he purchases the commodity combination that maximizes his utility. The entrepreneur faces given output and input prices and decides to produce an output level for which his profit is maximized. Each must solve a maximum problem. The individual actions of all consumers and entrepreneurs together determine the prices which are considered parameters by each one alone. Prices are determined in the market where consumers and entrepreneurs meet and exchange commodities. The consumer is the buyer and the entrepreneur the seller in the market for a final good. Their roles are reversed in a market for a primary input such as labor. Some inputs are outputs of other firms. Wheat is an input for the milling industry, but an output of agriculture. Both buyers and sellers are entrepreneurs in the markets for such intermediate goods. The analysis of market equilibrium seeks to describe the determination of the market price and the quantity bought and sold.   The present chapter is focused upon behavior in individual markets.

The basic assumptions and characteristics of a perfectly competitive market are outlined in Sec. 4-1.   Market demand functions are derived in Sec. 4-2.   Market supply functions are derived for short-run and long-run periods in Sec. 4-3, which also contains a discussion of external economies and diseconomies.   Demand and supply functions are used for the determination of commodity-market equilibria in Sec. 4-4.   The analysis is applied to the case of spatially separated firms and a problem in taxation in Sec. 4-5.   The market equilibrium analysis is extended to factor markets in Sec. 4-6.   The existence and uniqueness of market equilibrium are discussed in Sec. 4-7; stability is discussed in Sec. 4-8.   The properties of equilibrium in markets with lagged supply reactions is the subject of Sec. 4-9.   Throughout this chapter it is assumed that the market or markets under consideration are perfectly competitive and that prices remain unchanged in all other markets.

4-1 THE ASSUMPTIONS OF PERFECT COMPETITION

A perfectly competitive commodity market satisfies the following conditions: (1) firms produce a homogeneous commodity, and consumers are identical from the sellers' point of view in that there are no advantages or disadvantages associated with selling to a particular consumer; (2) both firms and consumers are numerous, and the sales or purchases of each individual unit are small in relation to the aggregate volume of transactions; (3) both firms and consumers possess perfect information about the prevailing price and current bids, and they take advantage of every opportunity to increase profits and utility respectively; (4) entry into and exit from the market is free for firms and consumers in the long run.

Condition (1) ensures the anonymity of firms and consumers.   With regard to the firm, it is equivalent to the statement that the product of the firm is indistinguishable from products of others: trademarks, patents, special brand labels, etc., do not exist.   Consumers have no reason to prefer the product of one firm to that of another.   The uniformity of consumers ensures that an entrepreneur will sell to the highest bidder. Custom and other institutional rules of thumb (such as the "first-come-first-served" rule) for distributing output among consumers are nonexistent.

Condition (2) ensures that many sellers face many buyers.   If firms are numerous, an individual entrepreneur can increase or reduce his output level without noticeably altering the market price.   An individual consumer's demand for the commodity may rise or fall without any perceptible influence on the price. The individual buyer or seller acts as if he had no influence on price and merely adjusts to what he considers a given market situation.

Condition (3) guarantees perfect information on both sides of the market. Buyers and sellers possess complete information with respect to the quality and nature of the product and the prevailing price. Since there are no uninformed buyers, entrepreneurs cannot attempt to charge more than the prevailing price. Consumers cannot buy from some entrepreneurs at less than the prevailing price for analogous reasons. Since the product is homogeneous and everybody possesses perfect information, a single price must prevail in a perfectly competitive market. This can be proved by assuming on the contrary that the commodity is sold at two different prices. By hypothesis, consumers are aware of the facts that (1) the commodity can be bought at two different prices, (2) one unit of the commodity is exactly the same as any other. Since consumers are utility maximizers, they will not buy the commodity at the higher price. Therefore a single price must prevail.

The last condition ensures the unimpeded flow of resources between alternative occupations in the long run. It assumes that resources are mobile and always move into occupations from which they derive the greatest advantage. Firms move into markets in which they can make profits and leave those in which they incur losses. Resources such as labor tend to be attracted to industries the products of which are in great demand. Inefficient firms are eliminated from the market and are replaced by efficient ones.

Perfect competition among sellers prevails if an individual seller has only an imperceptible influence on the market price and on the actions of others. Each seller acts as if he had no influence. Analogous conditions must hold for perfect competition among buyers. A market is perfectly competitive if perfect competition prevails on both the sellers' and the buyers' sides of the market. The market price which was considered a parameter in previous chapters is now a variable, and its magnitude is determined jointly by the actions of buyers and sellers.

4-2 DEMAND FUNCTIONS

The market demand function for a commodity is obtained by summing the demand functions of individual consumers. An individual producer, however, because of his small size relative to the market does not face the market demand function. His demand function reflects his assumption that he can sell all that he desires at a going market price.

MICROECONOMIC THEORY: A MATHEMATICAL APPROACH

MARKET DEMAND

Following the derivation of Sec. 2-4 as generalized in Sec. 2-7, the ith consumer's demand for Q_j depends upon the price of Q_j, the prices of all other commodities, and his income:

$$D_{ij} = D_{ij}(p_1, p_2, \ldots, p_m, y_i)$$

The consumer's demand functions are obtained from his first-order conditions for utility maximization, assuming that his second-order conditions are fulfilled. He will react to price and income changes by changing his commodity demands so as to maintain the equality of his RCS and the price ratio for every pair of commodities and, at the same time, to satisfy his budget constraint.

The consumer's demand for Q_j may vary as a result of a change in p_k ($k \neq j$), even though p_j remains unchanged, or in response to changes in his income, all prices remaining constant. All other prices and the consumer's income are assumed constant in order to isolate behavior in the jth market. His demand for Q_j is then a function of p_j alone:

$$D_{ij} = D_{ij}(p_j) \tag{4-1}$$

The quantity demanded still depends upon the prices of other commodities and the consumer's income, but these variables are now treated as parameters. To satisfy his first-order conditions the consumer will vary his demands for commodities other than Q_j as p_j changes. These variations generally are ignored in an analysis centered upon the market for Q_j.

Omitting the commodity subscript j in (4-1),

$$D_i = D_i(p) \qquad i = 1, 2, \ldots, n$$

The aggregate demand for Q at any price is the sum of the quantities demanded by the n individual consumers at that price:

$$D = \sum_{i=1}^{n} D_i(p) = D(p) \tag{4-2}$$

where D is the aggregate demand. The form of (4-2) is the result of the assumptions that all other prices and the incomes of all n consumers are constant. The demands of individual consumers normally are assumed to be monotonically decreasing functions of price, but the possibility of an increasing function of price exists for a Giffen good (see Sec. 2-6). Clearly, if the individual demand functions are monotonically decreasing, the aggregate demand function is also monotonically decreasing.

The aggregate demand curve for a commodity is obtained by plotting (4-2). The shape and position of the aggregate demand curve may

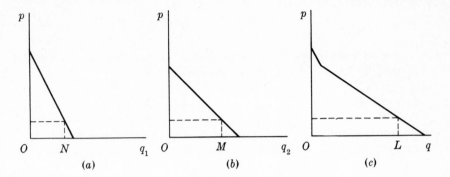

Fig. 4-1

change as the parameters of (4-2) change, i.e., as the prices of other commodities and consumers' incomes change. In fact, the aggregate demand curve may shift with changes in the distribution of income without any variation in aggregate income. If one consumer's income is reduced and another's increased by exactly the same amount, the corresponding individual demand curves are likely to shift, and the aggregate demand curve will be affected unless the shifts exactly compensate each other.

In terms of the conventional diagrams the aggregate demand curve is the horizontal sum of the individual demand curves. Parts (a) and (b) of Fig. 4-1 represent the demand curves of the only two consumers in a hypothetical competitive market.[1] Part (c) is their aggregate demand curve which is constructed by letting the distance OL equal the sum of the distances ON and OM.

PRODUCER DEMAND

The aggregate or market demand function confronts the aggregate of all sellers. The individual entrepreneur considers himself incapable of influencing market price. A change in his output results in an imperceptible movement along the market demand curve, and he believes that he can sell any quantity that he is able to produce at the prevailing price. The demand curve for the output of an individual entrepreneur appears to him as a horizontal line given by

$$p = \text{constant}$$

The market demand curve is not the horizontal sum of the demand curves faced by individual firms.

---

[1] Two consumers do not constitute the large number necessary for perfect competition. They are simply used to illustrate the behavior of a larger number.

The firm's total revenue is

$$R = pq$$

Marginal revenue is the rate at which total revenue increases as a result of a small increase in sales. In mathematical terms,

$$\frac{dR}{dq} = p$$

since p is a constant. The marginal revenue curve faced by the individual firm is identical with its demand curve.

4-3 SUPPLY FUNCTIONS

The cost functions of individual firms can be defined for (1) a very short period during which output level cannot vary, (2) a short run during which output level can be varied but plant size cannot, and (3) a long run in which all inputs are variable.

THE VERY SHORT PERIOD

Assume that the entrepreneur decides every morning how much to produce that day. His output decision is instantly implemented, and he spends the rest of the day trying to sell his output at the highest possible price. He cannot increase his output during the day and sells a given stock of the commodity.[1] Since an output q^0 has already been produced, the marginal cost of any output less than q^0 is zero. Output cannot be increased beyond this point in the very short period, and the marginal cost of higher outputs may be considered infinite. The marginal cost curve is represented by a vertical line at this point.

  The firm maximizes profit by selling a quantity for which MC = p. Since the MC of any output less than q^0 is zero and the MC of any output greater than q^0 is infinite, the equality MC = p cannot be satisfied, and the firm will expand sales to the point at which price ceases to exceed MC. Therefore, it will sell its entire output (i.e., its entire stock of the commodity) at the prevailing price.[2] This maximizes profit, because the prevailing price is the highest price at which the output can be sold. Quantity sold does not respond to price changes. In general, the

---

[1] The present analysis is simplified by assuming that production and all other adjustments occur instantaneously. It may be more realistic to assume that output is produced as a continuous and steady stream. If production is a time-consuming process, a change in the level of output cannot be realized immediately. The very short period is then any length of time shorter than the period which elapses between the change in the level of inputs and the corresponding change in the output level.
[2] Since the present analysis is static, the costs of holding inventories are neglected.

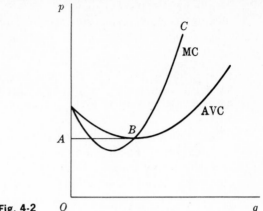

Fig. 4-2

aggregate supply function states the quantity that will be supplied by all producers as a function of the price. Since the output of each firm is fixed, the aggregate supply of the commodity is also given and does not depend upon the price. The supply curve is a vertical line, and its distance from the price axis is equal to the sum of the outputs of the individual firms.

THE SHORT RUN

The supply function of a perfectly competitive firm states the quantity that it will produce as a function of market price and can be derived from the first-order condition for profit maximization. The horizontal coordinate of a point on the rising portion of the MC curve corresponding to a given price measures the quantity that the firm would supply at that price. The firm's short-run supply curve is identical with that portion of its short-run MC curve which lies above its AVC curve. Its supply function is not defined for outputs less than the abscissa of the intersection of its MC and AVC curves. Quantity supplied would be zero at all prices less than the ordinate of this point. The firm's supply curve consists of the segments OA and BC in Fig. 4-2.

The ith firm's short-run MC is a function of its output:

$$\text{MC}_i = \Phi_i'(q_i) \qquad\qquad\qquad (4\text{-}3)$$

The supply function of the ith firm is obtained from its first-order condition for profit maximization by letting $p = \text{MC}$ and solving (4-3) for $q_i = S_i$:

$$S_i = S_i(p) \qquad \text{for } p \geqq \min \text{AVC}$$
$$S_i = 0 \qquad\quad\ \text{for } p < \min \text{AVC}$$

The aggregate supply function for Q is obtained by summing the n individual supply functions. The aggregate supply is

$$S = \sum_{i=1}^{n} S_i(p) = S(p)$$

The aggregate supply curve is the horizontal sum of the individual supply curves.

The second-order condition for maximum profit requires the MC curve to be rising. The firm's supply function is therefore monotonically increasing for prices at or above minimum AVC. The horizontal sum of monotonically increasing functions is itself monotonically increasing, and thus the short-run aggregate supply function has positive slope.[1]

Let the total cost curve be

$$C_i = 0.1q_i^3 - 2q_i^2 + 15q_i + 10$$

Then

$$\text{MC}_i = 0.3q_i^2 - 4q_i + 15$$

Setting $\text{MC}_i = p$ and solving for q_i,[†]

$$q_i = S_i = \frac{4 + \sqrt{1.2p - 2}}{0.6} \tag{4-4}$$

The individual supply function is relevant for all prices greater than, or equal to, minimum AVC. The AVC function is

$$\text{AVC}_i = 0.1q_i^2 - 2q_i + 15$$

The minimum point on the AVC function is located by setting the derivative with respect to q_i equal to zero and solving for q_i:[‡]

$$\frac{d(\text{AVC}_i)}{dq_i} = 0.2q_i - 2 = 0 \qquad q_i = 10$$

Substituting $q_i = 10$ in the AVC function gives the value 5. When the price is less than 5 dollars, the firm will find it most profitable to produce

[1] The aggregate supply curve will coincide with the price axis for prices below the minimum AVC of all firms. For this segment supply is a nondecreasing function of price; i.e., no output is produced as price increases. It is possible that the MC curves of individual firms may have negatively sloped portions in the relevant range where MC > AVC. The individual firm's supply curve will then be discontinuous. In an exceptional case the aggregate supply curve could be discontinuous.

[†] The mathematical solution (4-4) describes a curve with two branches corresponding to the + and − signs before the square root. The branch corresponding to the − sign has a negative slope and can be disregarded, since the second-order condition requires MC to be rising.

[‡] The reader may verify that the second-order condition for a minimum is satisfied.

no output.   The firm's supply function is

$$S_i = \frac{4 + \sqrt{1.2p - 2}}{0.6} \qquad \text{if } p \geqq 5$$
$$S_i = 0 \qquad\qquad\qquad \text{if } p < 5$$

Assuming that the industry consists of one hundred identical firms, the aggregate supply function is

$$S = 100\,\frac{4 + \sqrt{1.2p - 2}}{0.6} \qquad \text{if } p \geqq 5$$

$$S = 0 \qquad\qquad\qquad\qquad \text{if } p < 5$$

At a price of 22.50 dollars the aggregate supply will be 1,500 units.

THE LONG RUN

The firm's long-run optimal output is determined by the equality of price and long-run MC.   Zero output is produced at prices less than AC, and the firm's long-run supply function consists of that portion of its long-run MC function for which MC exceeds AC.   The mathematical derivation of the long-run aggregate supply function is similar to the derivation of the short-run supply function.   The MC function of the ith firm is

$$\text{MC}_i = \Phi_i'(q_i) \qquad i = 1, \ldots, n$$

Setting $p = \text{MC}_i$ and solving for $q_i = S_i$

$$S_i = S_i(p) \qquad i = 1, \ldots, n \tag{4-5}$$

The aggregate supply function is then obtained by adding the n individual supply functions in (4-5).   In the absence of external effects the long-run supply function is positively sloped for the same reason as the short-run supply function.

EXTERNAL ECONOMIES AND DISECONOMIES

The individual firm's total costs have been assumed to be a function of only its output level.   However, the firm's total costs may frequently depend upon the output level of the industry as a whole.   External economies are realized if an expansion of industry output lowers the total cost curve of each firm in the industry.   External diseconomies are realized if an expansion of industry output raises the total cost curve of each firm.[1]   External economies or diseconomies may be caused by many

[1] External effects need not be unambiguously economies or diseconomies.   It is possible that an increase in industry output will raise the total cost curves of some firms and lower the total cost curves of others.

factors. An expansion of the industry's output may lead to a better trained and more efficient labor force, with a consequent reduction in the costs of the ith firm without any diminution of its own output; a reduction of the industry's output may lead to less training and a consequent increase in the costs of the ith firm. External diseconomies could occur if an increase in the industry's output drove up the prices of raw materials and thus increased the total costs of the ith firm.

Assume in general that the long-run costs of the ith firm depend upon the industry output level as well as its own output level:

$$C_i = \Phi_i(q_i, q) \qquad i = 1, 2, \ldots, n$$

where q_i is the output of the ith firm and $q = \Sigma_{i=1}^{n} q_i$. Each entrepreneur provides a small part of industry output and maximizes profit with respect to his own output on the assumption that his output level does not affect the industry output level. The profit functions are

$$\pi_i = R_i - C_i \qquad i = 1, 2, \ldots, n$$

where $R_i = pq_i$. Differentiate π_1 with respect to q_1 (considering q constant), π_2 with respect to q_2, etc., and set the resulting partial derivatives equal to zero:

$$\frac{\partial \pi_i}{\partial q_i} = p - \frac{\partial \Phi_i(q_i, q)}{\partial q_i} = 0 \qquad i = 1, 2, \ldots, n \tag{4-6}$$

The second-order conditions require that $\partial^2 \Phi_i(q_i, q)/\partial q_i^2 > 0$ for all $i = 1, 2, \ldots, n$. Substituting $q = \Sigma_{i=1}^{n} q_i$, solving the system of n equations given by (4-6) for the q_i, and writing $S_i = q_i$,

$$\begin{aligned} S_1 &= S_1(p) \\ S_2 &= S_2(p) \\ &\cdots \cdots \cdots \\ S_n &= S_n(p) \end{aligned} \tag{4-7}$$

Each entrepreneur bases his behavior on his own MC function. Each observes or anticipates industry output and selects his output to equate price and marginal cost. If all entrepreneurs anticipate the same industry output and if this industry output is consistent with their individual output levels, no further adjustment is necessary. Otherwise some or all individual MC curves will shift from their anticipated positions, and entrepreneurs will adjust their output levels correspondingly. This sequence will continue until no further adjustments are necessary. The supply functions (4-7) state each firm's optimal supply as a function of the price after all these adjustments have taken place. The aggregate supply function is obtained as before by adding the individual supply functions (4-7):

$$S = \sum_{i=1}^{n} S_i(p) = S(p)$$

The aggregate supply function may have negative slope in the presence of external economies. The second-order conditions require that the individual MC curves be rising when the output of the industry is assumed to be a given parameter.

Consider a simplified example in which the industry is represented by two competitive firms with the total cost functions

$$C_1 = \alpha q_1^2 - \beta q_1 + b q_1 q \qquad C_2 = \alpha q_2^2 - \beta q_2 + b q_2 q$$

where $q = q_1 + q_2$ and the coefficients α and β are positive. If $b < 0$, there are external economies, and if $b > 0$, there are external diseconomies. The first-order conditions corresponding to (4-6) are

$$p - 2\alpha q_1 + \beta - bq = 0 \qquad p - 2\alpha q_2 + \beta - bq = 0$$

Solving these equations for $q_1 = S_1$ and $q_2 = S_2$,

$$S_1 = S_2 = \frac{p + \beta}{2(\alpha + b)}$$

Therefore, the aggregate supply function is linear in this case:

$$S = S_1 + S_2 = \frac{p + \beta}{\alpha + b}$$

If there are external diseconomies ($b > 0$), the supply curve will have a positive slope, and supply will increase less rapidly with price than in the absence of such diseconomies. If there are external economies ($b < 0$), the supply curve will have positive or negative slope as the denominator of the aggregate supply function is positive or negative.[1] The long-run supply curve will be negatively sloped only if the cost reductions due to expanding industry output are sufficiently large to swamp the cost increases due to expanding firm outputs.

4-4 COMMODITY–MARKET EQUILIBRIUM

SHORT–RUN EQUILIBRIUM

The market forces which determine the price and the quantity sold can be regarded as manifesting themselves through the aggregate demand

[1] If the denominator equals zero, the supply curve is a horizontal straight line.

and supply functions. The slope of the demand function $[D'(p)]$ is normally negative. The slope of the supply function $[S'(p)]$ is positive in the absence of external economies. $S'(p)$ will be assumed to be positive, unless otherwise specified.

Imagine that buyers and sellers arrive in the market without any foreknowledge as to what will become the going price. Since the commodity is homogeneous, a single price must prevail. The quantity demanded must equal the quantity supplied at the equilibrium price:

equilibrium condition

$$D(p) - S(p) = 0 \qquad\qquad (4\text{-}8)$$

If the equality does not hold for some $p = p^0$, buyers' and sellers' desires are inconsistent: either buyers want to purchase more than sellers are supplying, or sellers are supplying more than buyers wish to purchase. The equality in (4-8) is necessary and sufficient for the buyers' and sellers' desires to be consistent.

Assume that production is instantaneous and producers arrive in the market without any actual output. When the market is open for trading, buyers and sellers begin to bid and attempt to enter into contracts that are favorable to them. Whenever a buyer and seller enter into a contract, they both reserve themselves the right to *recontract* with any person who makes a more favorable offer. It is thus permitted to break existing contracts. Assume that some consumer makes an initial bid and offers a price of p^0 dollars for the commodity. This price is recorded and made public by an auctioneer who is an impartial observer of the trading process. Imagine that the initial price is lower than the equilibrium price. Buyers and sellers will attempt to enter into contracts with each other at the price p^0. Consumers who are willing to buy at this price find that the quantity offered is not sufficient to satisfy their desires; i.e., sellers are not willing to contract for as large a quantity as buyers desire. Some of the consumers who have not been able to satisfy their demand will be induced to raise their bids in the hope of tempting sellers away from other consumers. As soon as this higher price $p^{(1)}$ is recorded and made public by the auctioneer, sellers break their old contracts and recontract at the higher price. As higher prices are offered, the quantity demanded declines, since marginal consumers are driven out of the market and each consumer demands less. Simultaneously the quantity offered by sellers increases. The process of recontracting continues as long as the price announced by the auctioneer is below the equilibrium price, i.e., as long as the quantity demanded exceeds the quantity supplied. When the equilibrium price is reached, neither consumers nor producers have an incentive to recontract any further. Recontracting is discontinued, entrepreneurs instantaneously produce and deliver the output for which they have contracted, and the exchange is completed.   If the arbitrary initial price p^0 happens to exceed p_e (equilibrium price), some producers will be unable to sell the quantity which is the optimal quantity for them at that price.   They cannot find consumers who want to enter into contracts with them.   In order to avoid such an outcome, the sellers who have been unable to find buyers at the initial price will reduce the price.   Consumers who have contracted at the higher price will find it advantageous to recontract.   The process of recontracting continues until the equilibrium price is reached.   When p_e is established, both buyers' and sellers' desires are satisfied, and no one can benefit from further recontracting.

The equilibrium price-quantity combination must satisfy both the demand and supply functions.   This is the only price-quantity combination for which the desires of buyers and sellers are consistent with each other.   The equilibrium price is determined by solving the *equilibrium condition* (4-8) for p.   The equilibrium quantity is determined by substituting the equilibrium price in either the demand or the supply function.   Since the equilibrium price-quantity combination satisfies both the demand curve and the supply curve, the above operation is equivalent to finding the coordinates of the intersection point of the demand and supply curves.

Assume that the demand and supply curves are

$$D = -50p + 250 \qquad S = 25p + 25$$

Setting $D - S = 0$,

$$-50p + 250 - 25p - 25 = 0$$

and therefore

$$p = 3 \qquad D = S = 100$$

These functions are illustrated in Fig. 4-3.

LONG-RUN EQUILIBRIUM

If the plant size is variable, the equilibrium of the *existing* firms in the market is given by the intersection of the long-run supply curve with the corresponding demand curve.   The long-run cost and supply curves include "normal profit," i.e., the minimum remuneration necessary for the firm to remain in existence.   It is the profit that accrues to the entrepreneur as payment for managerial services, for providing organization, for risk-bearing, etc.   If the intersection of the demand curve and the long-run supply curve occurs at a price at which firms in the industry earn more than normal profit, new entrepreneurs may be induced to enter.

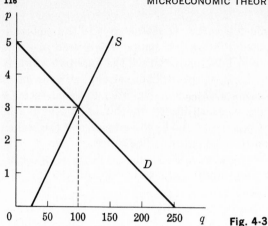

Fig. 4-3

The assumption of free entry guarantees that they are able to enter the industry, produce the same homogeneous product, and possess the same complete information as the old firms. The new producers will add their supplies to the already existing supply, and as a result the long-run supply curve will shift to the right. New producers will continue to enter as long as they can make positive profits, and the supply curve will continue to shift to the right until its intersection with the demand curve determines a price at which new entrants would earn zero profits.

The converse argument can be made for the case in which existing firms make losses. Some firms will withdraw from the industry, and the aggregate supply will diminish; the supply curve will shift to the left. Firms will continue to leave the industry until the intersection of the demand curve with the supply curve determines a price for which losses (and therefore profits) are zero for the highest cost firm in the industry.

Demand must equal supply, and the potential profits of new entrants must equal zero for long-run equilibrium. The supply function of the ith firm is $S_i = S_i(p)$. Let n be the number of firms in the industry. Assuming that all firms are identical with respect to their cost functions, the aggregate supply function is

$$S(p) = nS_i(p) \tag{4-9}$$

As before, the aggregate demand function is

$$D = D(p) \tag{4-10}$$

In addition to the equality of demand and supply, long-run equilibrium requires that profit equal zero for each firm:

$$\pi_i = pS_i - \Phi(S_i) = 0 \tag{4-11}$$

where $\Phi(S_i)$ is the long-run total cost of the ith firm for an output $q_i = S_i = S/n$. Equation (4-11) requires the equality of price and AC: $p = \Phi(S_i)/S_i$. Equations (4-8) to (4-11) can generally be solved for the variables (D, S_i, p, n). In the long run the forces of perfect competition determine not only the price and the quantity, but the number of firms within the industry as well.

The argument is illustrated in Fig. 4-4. The left-hand side of the diagram shows the cost curves of a typical or "representative" firm. The right-hand side shows the market demand and supply curves with the horizontal scale compressed. The final equilibrium from the industry's point of view is at the intersection of the demand and supply curves, provided that profits are zero. From the entrepreneur's point of view, equilibrium is attained when price equals MC and AC. Optimality is ensured by $p = \text{MC}$, and zero profits by $p = \text{AC}$. Every firm operates at the minimum point of its AC curve in long-run equilibrium, since MC = AC at the minimum point of the AC curve.

The long-run supply curve S is defined to include the supplies offered by firms already in the market, but not the supplies of potential producers. Firms are making positive profits in the situation characterized by the supply curve S (Fig. 4-4). New firms enter, and the supply curve shifts to S'. If the supply curve had been defined to include all supplies (by actual and potential producers, as in S^*), the intersection of the demand and supply curves would have determined the final equilibrium without any shifting. The supply curve S is given for fixed n in (4-9). S^* is obtained from (4-11) by letting p equal minimum AC. The hori-

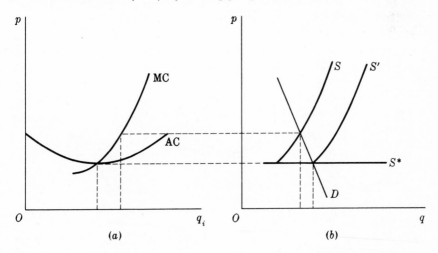

(a) (b)

Fig. 4-4

zontal long-run industry supply curve S^* is also the industry's long-run
AC curve and its long-run MC curve in the present case. In Sec. 3-5
it was shown that production functions homogeneous of degree one
generate constant AC = MC for fixed factor prices and generate zero
profit levels by Euler's theorem if inputs are paid the values of their
marginal products. These conditions are the same as those for the industry as a whole in the situation pictured in Fig. 4-4. Therefore, it is
often assumed that the industry has a long-run production function homogeneous of degree one even though the firms within the industry do not.

Long-run supply curves are not always horizontal. The supply
curve will be upward sloping if firms do not have identical cost functions
and there are no offsetting external economies. External economies (diseconomies) can generate downward (upward) sloping long-run supply
curves in the identical-cost-function case.

DIFFERENTIAL COST CONDITIONS AND RENT

The symmetry assumption is convenient for purposes of exposition, but
is not necessary for the attainment of equilibrium. Firms may choose
their own technology, entrepreneurs may differ with respect to organizing
ability, and they may have built plants of different size as a result of
divergent price expectations. Some entrepreneurs may possess scarce
factors such as fertile land that are not available to others. Under any
of these conditions the cost functions of all firms will not be identical.

Assume that there are two distinct types of firms. Their long-run
AC and MC curves are shown in parts (a) and (b) of Fig. 4-5. Part (c)
shows the industry supply curve and five hypothetical demand curves.
The supply curve is based on the assumption that there are fifty firms in
each category. Assume that the number of firms in each category cannot be increased. For example, the number of low-cost producers (cate-

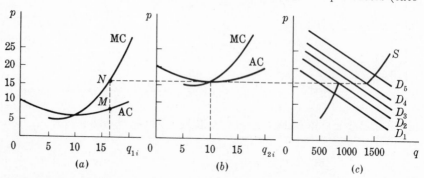

Fig. 4-5

gory I) may be unalterably given by the quantity of some scarce resource such as fertile land. New firms are unable to enter category I even though the firms in this category are making profits.

Consider the demand curve D_4. Each low-cost firm produces an output of 16 units, and each of the other firms produces an output of 10 units. The latter operate at the minimum point of their AC curves and earn normal profits. Each low-cost firm earns a unit of profit NM above normal. If the demand curve shifted to D_2, all high-cost firms (category II) would leave the industry, but each low-cost firm would still earn the same positive profit. They would earn positive profits even if the demand curve were D_1. With D_3 some, but not all, of the high-cost firms would leave the industry. Those remaining would earn a normal profit. If the demand curve were D_5, all firms in the industry would earn profits in excess of normal, and a third group of firms (not shown in Fig. 4-5) might find it profitable to enter the industry. The low-cost firms would still be in the more favorable position.

Assume that the total cost functions of representative firms in the two categories are

$$C_{1i} = 0.04q_{1i}^3 - 0.8q_{1i}^2 + 10q_{1i} \qquad C_{2i} = 0.04q_{2i}^3 - 0.8q_{2i}^2 + 20q_{2i}$$

The corresponding average and marginal cost functions are

$$MC_{1i} = 0.12q_{1i}^2 - 1.6q_{1i} + 10 \qquad MC_{2i} = 0.12q_{2i}^2 - 1.6q_{2i} + 20$$
$$AC_{1i} = 0.04q_{1i}^2 - 0.8q_{1i} + 10 \qquad AC_{2i} = 0.04q_{2i}^2 - 0.8q_{2i} + 20$$

The minimum points of the respective average cost curves are at the points $q_{1i} = 10$, $p = 6$, and $q_{2i} = 10$, $p = 16$. The supply curve of an individual low-cost firm is derived by setting $MC_{1i} = p$:

$$p = 0.12q_{1i}^2 - 1.6q_{1i} + 10$$

Solving this quadratic equation for q_{1i},

$$q_{1i} = \frac{1.6 \pm \sqrt{2.56 - 0.48(10 - p)}}{0.24}$$

The minus sign preceding the square root must be disregarded because it corresponds to the situation in which the individual firm's second-order condition for maximization is not fulfilled. Substituting S_{1i} for q_{1i}, the supply curve is

$$S_{1i} = 0 \qquad\qquad\qquad\qquad\qquad \text{if } p < 6$$
$$S_{1i} = \frac{1.6 + \sqrt{2.56 - 0.48(10 - p)}}{0.24} \qquad \text{if } p \geq 6$$

By analogous reasoning the supply curve of the representative high-cost firm is

$$S_{2i} = 0 \qquad\qquad\qquad\qquad\qquad \text{if } p < 16$$
$$S_{2i} = \frac{1.6 + \sqrt{2.56 - 0.48(20 - p)}}{0.24} \qquad \text{if } p \geqq 16$$

Maintaining the assumption that there are fifty firms in each category, the aggregate supply function is described by the following set of three equations:

$$S = 0 \qquad\qquad\qquad\qquad\qquad\qquad \text{if } 0 \leqq p < 6$$
$$S = 50\,\frac{1.6 + \sqrt{2.56 - 0.48(10 - p)}}{0.24} \qquad \text{if } 6 \leqq p < 16$$
$$S = \frac{160}{0.24} + \frac{50}{0.24}\,[\sqrt{2.56 - 0.48(10 - p)}$$
$$+ \sqrt{2.56 - 0.48(20 - p)}] \qquad \text{if } p \geqq 16$$

Assume that the relevant demand curve is D_i which has the equation

$$D = -100p + 2050$$

The relevant segment of the supply curve is given by

$$S = 50\,\frac{1.6 + \sqrt{2.56 - 0.48(10 - p)}}{0.24}$$

Setting $D = S$ and solving for p and S gives $p = 13$, $S = 750$.† If $p = 13$, each low-cost firm will produce 15 units at an average cost of 7 dollars. The high-cost firms produce nothing. The total quantity is, as determined by solving the demand and supply relations, $(50)(15) = 750$ units. Each low-cost firm earns a 90-dollar profit.

Low-cost firms can produce at a lower AC than the others because they possess some scarce factor, such as fertile land, which is not available to the latter. If the demand curve intersects the supply curve at a point at which some firms earn more than normal profit, a considerable profit advantage is enjoyed by those who possess the scarce resource. Some (potential) producers, seeing the large profits made by the low-cost firms, would want to persuade the owners of the fertile land (landlords) to hire it out to them rather than to the firms currently employing it. They would try to accomplish this by offering to pay more for the use of the

---

† If it is not obvious by inspection which supply-curve segment is the relevant one, let $D = S$ for each of the three supply-curve segments separately and solve for the price. Only one of the three prices calculated will be in the range that is appropriate for the particular supply-curve segment used. This segment is the relevant one.

land than existing firms are paying. The present users would match these offers until competition drove up the amount paid for the use of fertile land to the point where no differential profit advantage could be derived from employing it. The owners will thus be able to exact from the firms using the scarce resource their entire profit in excess of normal. The sums thus exacted are the *rent* paid by the entrepreneur for the use of the scarce resource. One may conclude that no advantage can be derived from being a more efficient (low-cost) producer: the differential profit advantage is wiped out by the extra rent that the low-cost producer must pay. In the present example, the scarce resources employed by each low-cost firm earn a rent of 90 dollars. If an entrepreneur happened to own the scarce resource himself, no actual payment would take place, and the rent would accrue to him. Otherwise the entrepreneur would have to pay 90 dollars for renting the land. Rent is thus defined to be that part of a person's or firm's income which is above the minimum amount necessary to keep that person or firm in its given occupation. Whether it is actually paid to the owner of the scarce resource is immaterial. Distributive shares are distinguished by function, and not by the individual to whom they accrue.

4-5 APPLICATIONS OF THE ANALYSIS

The theory of perfect competition can be applied to numerous special cases. Two examples are considered in the present section. The first is an extension of the analysis to the case of spatially distributed firms. The second contains an analysis of the effects of taxation on perfectly competitive output.

SPATIALLY DISTRIBUTED FIRMS

Production and consumption are generally assumed to take place at a single point in space. In reality there are many markets in which producers and consumers are spatially separated. Geographic locations and transport costs are frequently factors of considerable importance. It is illustrated below how the theory of perfectly competitive markets can be extended to a case in which producers are spatially separated.

Many central markets are supplied by a number of firms located at some distance from them. Examples are provided by city milk markets. Farmers from the surrounding area supply a central market at varying unit transport costs. If an entrepreneur produces at any distance from his market, his total cost consists of production and transportation costs:

$$C_i = \phi_i(q_i) + b_i + \beta_i q_i$$

where β_i is the cost of transporting 1 unit of his product to the central market. His profit is the difference between his total revenue and his total cost of production and transportation:

$$\pi_i = pq_i - \phi_i(q_i) - b_i - \beta_i q_i \tag{4-12}$$

Setting the derivative of (4-12) equal to zero,

$$\frac{d\pi_i}{dq_i} = p - \phi_i'(q_i) - \beta_i = 0$$

or

$$p = \phi_i'(q_i) + \beta_i$$

The first-order condition for profit maximization requires that the entrepreneur equate his marginal cost of production plus his unit transport cost to the market price of his product. The second-order condition, as before, requires that his marginal cost of production be increasing.

The entrepreneur's MC and AVC curves are raised vertically by a distance equal to the amount of his unit transport cost (see Fig. 4-6). His output is determined by the intersection of the rising portion of his $MC + \beta_i$ curve and the horizontal demand curve. Since the entrepreneur will not supply at prices less than $AVC + \beta_i$, his supply curve coincides with the rising portion of his $MC + \beta_i$ curve which lies above his $AVC + \beta_i$ curve. An entrepreneur who is not located at the market will supply less at every price (at which he supplies a nonzero amount) than one who is if their production cost functions are identical.

The aggregate supply function for the central market is the horizontal sum of the supply curves of the n individual producers:

$$S = \sum_{i=1}^{n} S_i(p) = S(p)$$

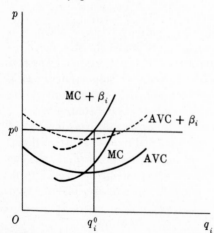

Fig. 4-6

where $S_i(p)$ is the supply function of the ith producer. Market equilibrium is attained when supply equals demand.

Assume that fifty of the one hundred firms supplying commodity Q are at location I and the other fifty at location II. It costs 6 dollars to transport to the market a unit of Q from I and 10 dollars from II. All firms possess the same production cost functions, and the total costs of representative firms are

$$C_1 = 0.5q_1^2 + 6q_1 \qquad C_2 = 0.5q_2^2 + 10q_2$$

where the subscripts 1 and 2 denote firms at locations I and II respectively. The first-order conditions for profit maximization are $p = q_1 + 6$ and $p = q_2 + 10$. Supply functions are obtained by substituting $q_1 = S_1$ and $q_2 = S_2$ into the first-order conditions and invoking the condition that $S_i = 0$ unless $p > \text{AVC} + \beta_i$:

$$
\begin{aligned}
S_1 &= 0 & &\text{if } 0 \leq p < 6 \\
S_1 &= p - 6 & &\text{if } 6 \leq p \\
S_2 &= 0 & &\text{if } 0 \leq p < 10 \\
S_2 &= p - 10 & &\text{if } 10 \leq p
\end{aligned}
\qquad (4\text{-}13)
$$

An entrepreneur at I will supply no output if the market price is less than 6 dollars, and an entrepreneur at II will not supply if the market price is less than 10 dollars. The $\text{MC} + \beta_1$ curve for an entrepreneur at I is given by $q_1 + 6$, and his $\text{AVC} + \beta_1$ by $0.5q_1 + 6$. His supply curve coincides with his $\text{MC} + \beta_1$ curve for prices of 6 dollars or more.

The aggregate supply for the central market is given by the following three equations:

$$
\begin{aligned}
S &= 0 & &\text{if } 0 \leq p < 6 \\
S &= 50(p - 6) = 50p - 300 & &\text{if } 6 \leq p < 10 \\
S &= 50(p - 6) + 50(p - 10) \\
&\quad\quad\quad = 100p - 800 & &\text{if } 10 \leq p
\end{aligned}
\qquad (4\text{-}14)
$$

Aggregate supply is zero if price is less than 6 dollars. The fifty entrepreneurs at I will supply a positive amount if the price exceeds 6 dollars, and the fifty entrepreneurs at II will supply if it exceeds 10.

Assume that the aggregate demand function is

$$D = -20p + 1,600$$

The appropriate segment of the supply function is given by the third equation of (4-14). Setting $D = S$,

$$
\begin{aligned}
-20p + 1,600 &= 100p - 800 \\
p = 20 \qquad S &= D = 1,200
\end{aligned}
$$

From (4-13), each entrepreneur at I supplies 14 units and earns a 98-dollar profit, and each entrepreneur at II supplies 10 units and earns a 50-dollar profit.   In general, if all entrepreneurs produce under the same cost conditions, output and profit are inversely related to the level of unit transport cost.

The existence of more favorable locations may give rise in the long run to rent payments if sites are scarce in the more favorable locations. Competition for the more favorable sites will enable the owners of these sites to charge entrepreneurs a rent which exceeds the rent in the less advantageous location by an amount equal to the profit difference between the two locations, i.e., by 48 dollars.[1]

TAXATION AND PERFECTLY COMPETITIVE OUTPUT

A sales tax generally changes the individual entrepreneur's optimum output level.   It shifts the individual supply curves and therefore also the aggregate supply curve.   This alters the equilibrium price-quantity combination.   Sales taxes are either *specific* or *ad valorem*.   A specific tax is stated in terms of the number of dollars which the entrepreneur has to pay per unit sold.   An ad valorem tax is stated in terms of à percentage of the sales price.

Assume that the sales tax is a specific tax of t dollars per unit.   The total costs of the representative entrepreneur are

$$C_i = \phi(q_i) + b_i + tq_i$$

The first-order condition for profit maximization requires him to produce the output level for which $\mathrm{MC} = p$:

$$\phi'(q_i) + t = p$$

or

$$\phi'(q_i) = p - t \tag{4-15}$$

The entrepreneur equates the marginal cost of production plus the unit tax to the price.   The second-order condition requires that the MC curve be rising.   The entrepreneur's supply function is obtained by solving (4-15) for q_i and setting $q_i = S_i$ for all prices greater than, or equal to, minimum AVC:

$$S_i = S_i(p - t)$$

The aggregate supply function is obtained by summing the individual supply functions:

$$S = \sum_{i=1}^{n} S_i(p - t) = S(p - t)$$

---

[1] The analysis can be easily extended to the case in which consumers are spatially distributed.

The aggregate supply is a function of the net price $(p - t)$ received by sellers. If, in the absence of a sales tax, aggregate supply is $S^{(0)}$ units at the price of $p^{(0)}$ dollars, entrepreneurs will supply the same quantity $S^{(0)}$ with a sales tax of 1 dollar if the price paid by consumers is $p^{(0)} + 1$ dollars. This is equivalent to a vertical upward shift of the supply curve by 1 dollar. Entrepreneurs are willing to supply less than before at every price. In order to determine the equilibrium price-quantity combination, set demand equal to supply,

$$D(p) - S(p - t) = 0$$

and solve for p.

Let an ad valorem tax rate be $100v$ percent of the sales price. Total costs are

$$C_i = \phi(q_i) + b + vpq_i$$

Setting MC plus unit tax equal to price,

$$\phi'(q_i) + vp = p$$

or

$$\phi'(q_i) = p(1 - v)$$

Therefore the individual supply function is

$$S_i = S_i[p(1 - v)]$$

and the aggregate supply function is

$$S = \sum_{i=1}^{n} S_i[p(1 - v)] = S[p(1 - v)]$$

Aggregate supply is a function of the net price, and the sales tax involves an upward shift of the supply curve which is proportional to the height of the original supply curve above the quantity axis. The equilibrium price-quantity combination is again determined by setting demand equal to supply.

Let the industry consist of 100 firms with identical cost functions

$$C_i = 0.1q_i^2 + q_i + 10$$

Setting MC equal to price, solving for q_i, and setting $q_i = S_i$,

$$S_i = 0 \qquad \text{if } p < 1$$
$$S_i = 5p - 5 \qquad \text{if } p \geq 1$$

The aggregate supply function is

$$S = 0 \qquad \text{if } p < 1$$
$$S = 500p - 500 \qquad \text{if } p \geq 1$$

Assume that the demand function is

$$D = -400p + 4,000$$

Setting demand equal to supply, the equilibrium price-quantity combination is

$$p = 5 \qquad D = S = 2,000$$

Assume now that a specific tax of t dollars is imposed. The representative total cost function becomes

$$C_i = 0.1q_i^2 + (1 + t)q_i + 10$$

Setting MC equal to price and solving for $q_i = S_i$,

$$S_i = 0 \qquad\qquad \text{if } p < 1 + t$$
$$S_i = 5(p - t) - 5 \qquad \text{if } p \geq 1 + t$$

Hence the aggregate supply function is

$$S = 0 \qquad\qquad\qquad \text{if } p < 1 + t$$
$$S = 500(p - t) - 500 \qquad \text{if } p \geq 1 + t$$

Setting demand equal to supply and solving for p,

$$p = 5 + \tfrac{5}{9}t$$

If the tax rate is 90 cents per unit of sales, the equilibrium price-quantity combination is

$$p = 5.50 \qquad D = S = 1,800$$

The price rises and the quantity sold diminishes as a result of the tax. The price rise is less than the amount of the unit tax. The 50-cent increase in the price represents that portion of the unit tax that is passed on to the consumer; the remainder of 40 cents is the burden on the entrepreneur. The example is pictured in Fig. 4-7. The supply curve is S before and S' after the tax is imposed. The tax is 90 cents, the vertical distance between S and S'. The price paid rises from 5 dollars to 5.50, and the price received by entrepreneurs falls to 4.60. The reader may verify that the proportion of the unit tax passed on to the consumer is the greater, the smaller are the slopes (algebraically) of the demand and supply curves. *Ceteris paribus*, the price varies directly, and the quantity inversely with the tax rate.[1]

---

[1] The analysis can be used to show the effects of subsidies by treating a subsidy as a negative tax.

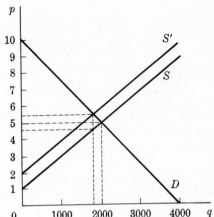

Fig. 4-7

4-6 FACTOR-MARKET EQUILIBRIUM

The foregoing sections are limited to perfectly competitive commodity markets. Analogous conclusions can be reached with respect to markets for inputs which are nonproduced factors of production. A factor market is perfectly competitive if (1) the factor is homogeneous and different buyers are indistinguishable from the sellers' point of view, (2) buyers and sellers are numerous, (3) both buyers and sellers possess perfect information, (4) buyers and sellers are free to enter or leave in the long run. Consumers purchase commodities because they derive satisfaction from them. Inputs are purchased for the sake of the contribution they make to production. The demand curves for final products are derived from the consumers' utility functions on the assumption of utility maximization. The demand curves for inputs are derived from production functions on the assumption of profit maximization.

DEMAND FUNCTIONS

A rational entrepreneur's optimum input combination satisfies the condition that the price of each input equals the value of its MP. The first-order conditions for profit maximization were solved in Sec. 3-3 to obtain the firm's input demands as functions of input prices and the product price. For the one-output–two-input case:

$$D_{i1} = D_{i1}(r_1, r_2, p)$$
$$D_{i2} = D_{i2}(r_1, r_2, p)$$

where D_{ij} is the ith firm's demand for the jth input. Assuming that all other prices are constant, and neglecting the input subscripts, the ith firm's demand function for a particular input is

$$D_i = D_i(r)$$

where r is the price of the input. The aggregate demand function is obtained by summing the individual demand functions. If there are m firms demanding the input,

$$D = \sum_{i=1}^{m} D_i(r) = D(r)$$

In Sec. 3-3 it was shown that individual input demand curves are always negatively sloped. Therefore, aggregate input demand curves also are always negatively sloped; that is, $\partial D / \partial r < 0$.

SUPPLY FUNCTIONS

Inputs are either primary or produced. Produced inputs are the outputs of some other firms. The supply function of a produced input is the aggregate supply function of the firms that produce it. Such functions are derived in Sec. 4-3. Different procedures are employed for non-produced factors such as labor, which normally are assumed to be in the possession of consumers who sell them to producers in order to obtain income to purchase commodities. Sometimes it is assumed that the consumers will sell their entire stock at whatever market price may prevail. In this circumstance the factor supply function is a vertical straight line with abscissa equal to the aggregate factor stock. A more interesting case is one in which consumers gain utility from retaining some of or all their factor stocks.

For the case of labor it was assumed in Sec. 2-5 that utility is a function of leisure and income:

$$U = g(T - W, y)$$

where T is the total amount of available time (the length of the period for which the utility function is defined) and W the amount of work performed in terms of hours. It was shown that the utility-maximizing individual allocates his time between work and leisure in such fashion that

$$\frac{g_1}{g_2} = r \tag{4-16}$$

where r is the wage rate and g_i is the partial derivative of the utility function with respect to its ith argument. The g_i's depend upon income and the amount of work performed. Since $y = rW$, (4-16) contains only the variables r and W. Solving (4-16) for W and setting $W = S_i$, the labor supply function of the ith individual is

$$S_i = S_i(r)$$

The supply function states the amounts of work that the individual is willing to perform as a function of the wage rate. The aggregate supply function is obtained by summing the individual supply functions. If there are n individuals who are willing to supply labor at some wage rate, the aggregate supply function is

$$S = \sum_{i=1}^{n} S_i(r) = S(r)$$

The supply curve may have negative slope, positive slope, or both. If individuals value leisure highly and are more concerned with increasing their time for leisure than raising their incomes, the supply curve of labor may be negatively sloped: the higher the wage, the less work is performed.

MARKET EQUILIBRIUM

Given the demand and supply functions for an input the equilibrium price-quantity combination is determined by invoking the equilibrium condition $D = S$. Market forces similar to those discussed in Sec. 4-4 will change the existing situation whenever the actual price differs from the equilibrium price. Equilibrium is reached only when the quantity demanded equals the quantity supplied. As in product markets, no participant can improve his position by recontracting after equilibrium has been reached.

Since the equilibrium price-quantity combination must lie on both the demand and supply curves, it must also satisfy the producer's equilibrium conditions from which the demand curve is derived. The equilibrium price of an input is always equal to the value of its marginal product; i.e., the value of the marginal dollar spent on inputs is the same in every use.[1] This equality is a necessary condition for profit maximization, and every entrepreneur can reach his optimum point in a perfectly competitive market if his second-order conditions for maximization are fulfilled.

4-7 THE EXISTENCE AND UNIQUENESS OF EQUILIBRIUM

Thus far, the analysis of market equilibrium has been based upon the assumption that a unique price-quantity equilibrium exists for each isolated market under investigation. It is not difficult to construct examples for which this existence assumption is violated: supply and

---

[1] This has an analog in the theory of consumer behavior. Recall that $f_1 = \lambda p_1$ is one of the equilibrium conditions for the consumer, where f_1 is the marginal utility of the first good and λ is the marginal utility of money. Then $f_1(1/\lambda) = p_1$, or the price of the commodity must equal its marginal utility multiplied by the additional amount of money that has to be paid per unit of additional utility $(1/\lambda)$.

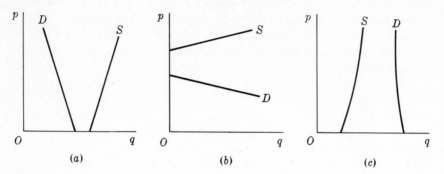

Fig. 4-8

demand are not equal at any nonnegative price-quantity combination. Likewise, examples exist for which the assumption of uniqueness is violated: supply and demand are equal at more than one nonnegative price-quantity combination. This section is limited to general observations and the discussion of some specific cases. The problems of existence and uniqueness are considered more deeply within a multimarket framework in Chap. 5.

EXISTENCE

A competitive market equilibrium will exist if there is one or more nonnegative prices at which demand and supply are equal and nonnegative. In terms of the conventional diagram, equilibrium will exist if the demand and supply curves have at least one point in common in the nonnegative quadrant.

Three situations in which the supply and demand curves have no point in common are pictured in Fig. 4-8. Supply exceeds demand at every nonnegative price for the case pictured in Fig. 4-8a. No equilibrium exists according to the definition given above. The definition of equilibrium is easily broadened to cover this case. Let $p = 0$ if $S(0) > D(0)$. A *free good* has a price of zero and is characterized by an excess of supply over demand. Consumers can get all they want for nothing. Air and water may be considered free goods. Up to some critical point water may be there for the taking. Beyond this point purification and transportation may become necessary and lead to a positive supply price.

Figure 4-8b covers a case in which the demand price is less than the supply price at each nonnegative output. The amounts that consumers are willing to pay is inadequate to compensate producers. Market equilibrium does not exist by the definitions thus far given. Again it is possible to broaden the definitions to cover such cases. An equilibrium exists with zero output if supply price exceeds demand price for all non-

negative outputs. It is technologically possible to produce solid-gold
school-lunch boxes, but none are produced because parents are not willing
to pay enough to allow producers to cover their costs.

The free-good and zero-production cases are meaningful. They are
covered by the general methods described in Chap. 5. Many other cases
in which equilibrium cannot be achieved are the result of poor model
specification. If such cases are encountered, the assumptions of their
underlying producer and consumer models must be altered in order to
provide a meaningful framework for analysis. Figure 4-8c provides an
example. Demand exceeds supply for every price, and there is no meaningful interpretation that can be placed upon this situation.

UNIQUENESS

It is possible that more than one equilibrium exists, i.e., that demand and
supply are equal at more than one nonnegative price-quantity combination. Points A and B in Fig. 4-9a are both equilibria. The demand
curve is downward sloping in the normal fashion, but the supply curve
bends back as price increases. Quantity is a single-valued function of
price, but price is not a single-valued function of quantity. Some economists have found evidence that a "backward-bending" supply curve
exists for labor markets in some underdeveloped countries. The supply
curve is positively sloped at relatively low wage rates, and an increase in
the wage rate brings forth an increased supply of labor. However, as
the wage rate continues to increase and the income of each worker
increases, a point is reached at which the workers prefer leisure to yet
more income.

Let δ be the difference in the slopes of the demand and supply
curves: $\delta = D'(p) - S'(p)$. If the demand curve is negatively sloped
throughout and the supply curve is positively sloped throughout, $\delta < 0$
for all prices and there cannot be more than one equilibrium point. If

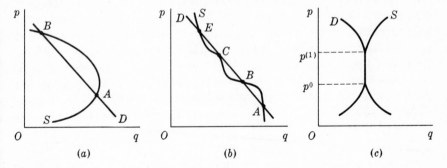

(a)   (b)   (c)

Fig. 4-9

$\delta < 0$ at an equilibrium price p^0, demand will be less than supply at a price slightly higher than p^0 and will be greater than supply at a price slightly lower than p^0. As long as $\delta < 0$ the demand curve will remain to the left of the supply curve at prices above p^0 and to the right at prices below p^0. Hence, there cannot be a second equilibrium point. A similar argument can be utilized to prove that there cannot be more than one equilibrium point if $\delta > 0$ throughout.

In Fig. 4-9a $\delta < 0$ for equilibrium point A. At B the demand and supply curves are both negatively sloped. The demand curve is more steeply sloped than the supply curve and $\delta > 0$ at B.† Four equilibrium points are shown in Fig. 4-9b. The supply curve has negative slope throughout, reflecting external economies. The values of δ are negative at equilibrium point A, positive at B, zero at C, and negative at E. In general, ignoring equilibrium points at which $\delta = 0$, δ must alternate in sign at adjacent equilibrium points. Equilibrium points with $\delta = 0$ may lie between or on either side of the points with alternating sign.

There will be a range of equilibrium points with $\delta = 0$ if the demand and supply curves are coincident for all or a portion of their lengths. Such a case is shown in Fig. 4-9c. Here, the equilibrium quantity is unique, but any price from p^0 through $p^{(1)}$ is an equilibrium price.

4-8 THE STABILITY OF EQUILIBRIUM

Equilibrium price and quantity are determined by the equality of demand and supply. Equilibrium is characterized by the acquiescence of buyers and sellers in the *status quo:* no participant in the market has an incentive to modify his behavior. However, the existence of an equilibrium point does not guarantee that it will be attained. There is no guarantee that the equilibrium price will be established if the market is not in equilibrium when the contracting begins. There is also no reason to assume that the initial price will happen to be the equilibrium price. Moreover, changes in consumer preferences will generally shift the demand curve, and innovations will shift the supply curve. Both factors tend to disturb an established equilibrium situation. The change defines a new equilibrium, but there is again no guarantee that it will be attained.

In general, a disturbance denotes a situation in which the actual price is different from the equilibrium price. An equilibrium is *stable* if a disturbance results in a return to equilibrium and *unstable* if it does not.[1]

---

† The derivatives $D'(p)$ and $S'(p)$ are functions of price. Hence, a steeper downward slope for the demand curve means that $D'(p) > S'(p)$.

[1] This is not a rigorous definition of stability and is only one of several alternative definitions. See P. A. Samuelson, *Foundations of Economic Analysis* (Cambridge, Mass.: Harvard, 1948), pp. 260–262.

It was implicitly assumed in the discussion of equilibrium in Sec. 4-4 that the market equilibrium was stable.

STATIC STABILITY

A disturbance usually creates an adjustment process in the market.   For example, if the actual price is less than the equilibrium price, the adjustment may consist of some buyers raising their bids for the commodity. Static analysis abstracts from the time path of the adjustment process and considers only the nature of the change, i.e., whether it is toward, or away from, equilibrium.

Define

$$E(p) = D(p) - S(p)$$

as the excess demand at price p.   In Fig. 4-10 excess demand is positive at the price p^0, negative at the price $p^{(1)}$.   Stability conditions are derived from assumptions about the market behavior of buyers and sellers.   The *Walrasian stability condition* is based on the assumption that buyers tend to raise their bids if excess demand is positive and sellers tend to lower their prices if it is negative.   If this behavior assumption is correct, a market is stable if a price rise diminishes excess demand, i.e., if

$$\frac{dE(p)}{dp} = E'(p) = D'(p) - S'(p) < 0 \qquad (4\text{-}17)$$

Writing p_d for the price at which a given quantity is demanded, p_s for the price at which that same quantity is supplied, and setting $D = S = q$, the demand and supply functions can be solved for the demand price p_d and the supply price p_s:

$$p_d = D^{-1}(q)$$
$$p_s = S^{-1}(q)$$

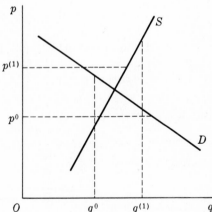

Fig. 4-10

where D^{-1} and S^{-1} are the inverses of the functions D and S.† The excess demand price is defined as

$$F(q) = D^{-1}(q) - S^{-1}(q)$$

It is the difference between the price that buyers are willing to pay and the price that sellers are charging for a given quantity. In Fig. 4-10 there is a positive excess demand price at q^0 and a negative excess demand price at $q^{(1)}$. The behavior assumption underlying the *Marshallian stability condition* for a market states that producers will tend to raise their output when the excess demand price is positive and lower it when it is negative. If excess demand price is positive, the producer realizes that consumers are offering a higher price than he is charging and concludes that he can profitably increase the quantity supplied. Analogous reasoning holds for the converse case. Equilibrium is stable in the Marshallian sense if an increase in quantity reduces the excess demand price, i.e., if

$$\frac{dF(q)}{dq} = F'(q) = D^{-1\prime}(q) - S^{-1\prime}(q) < 0 \tag{4-18}$$

If the demand curve has negative slope and the supply curve has positive slope, (4-17) and (4-18) are both satisfied.[1] The ordinary supply-demand situation is therefore stable according to both the Walrasian and Marshallian definitions.

If the demand and supply curves are both negatively sloped, an equilibrium cannot be stable according to both definitions. Dividing both sides of (4-18) by $D^{-1\prime}(q)S^{-1\prime}(q)$,

$$\frac{1}{S^{-1\prime}(q)} - \frac{1}{D^{-1\prime}(q)} < 0 \tag{4-19}$$

In the usual diagram in which quantity is plotted along the horizontal axis, $D^{-1\prime}(q)$ and $S^{-1\prime}(q)$ are the slopes of the demand and supply curves. By the inverse-function rule,

$$\frac{1}{D^{-1\prime}(q)} = D'(p) \qquad \frac{1}{S^{-1\prime}(q)} = S'(p)$$

Substituting these values into (4-19),

$$S'(p) - D'(p) < 0 \tag{4-20}$$

---

† If $y = f(x)$ can be solved for x, the solution is written as $x = f^{-1}(y)$. The function denoted by f^{-1} is the *inverse* of the function $f(x)$.

[1] The sign of $D'(p)$ is the same as the sign of $D^{-1\prime}(q)$; the sign of $S'(p)$ is the same as that of $S^{-1\prime}(q)$. See the inverse-function rule, Sec. A-2.

Conditions (4-17) and (4-20) cannot be fulfilled simultaneously. If an equilibrium is stable in the Walrasian sense, (4-17) holds, and the equilibrium is unstable in the Marshallian sense. The converse statement holds if (4-20) is fulfilled.[1]

If the demand and supply curves are both positively sloped, Marshallian stability again implies (4-20) which is inconsistent with the Walrasian condition (4-17). Finally, if the demand curve is positively sloped and the supply curve is negatively sloped, the two conditions give the same result.

It follows from (4-17) and (4-20) that equilibrium is stable in the Walrasian sense if the supply curve is steeper than the demand curve $[S^{-1\prime}(q) < D^{-1\prime}(q)$ or $D'(p) < S'(p)]$ and unstable in the opposite case. Equilibrium is stable in the Marshallian sense if the supply curve is less steep than the demand curve and unstable in the opposite case. These concepts are illustrated in Fig. 4-11. At the price p^0 the excess demand is MN; therefore competition among consumers will tend to raise the price, and excess demand diminishes. However, the quantity supplied at the price of p^0 is q^0; the corresponding excess demand price RM is positive. The quantity produced will tend to increase, but the excess demand price increases too. The actual price and quantity move farther away from equilibrium.

The negatively sloped supply curve depicted in Fig. 4-9b yields four equilibrium points. The successive equilibrium points A, B, and E are alternately stable and unstable by the Walrasian behavior assumption

---

[1] No contradiction exists between the two conditions if the demand and supply curves have slopes of opposite sign. When (4-18) is divided by $D^{-1\prime}(q)S^{-1\prime}(q)$, the direction of the inequality in (4-19) and (4-20) is reversed because of the division by a negative number. Inequality (4-20) becomes $S'(p) - D'(p) > 0$, which is the same as (4-17).

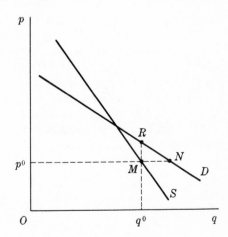

Fig. 4-11

(4-17).† The supply curve is steeper than the demand curve at A, and the equilibrium is stable at this point. Another intersection B can exist only if the supply curve becomes less steep than the demand curve; B is therefore unstable. By similar reasoning, E is again stable. The stability condition (4-17) is not sufficient to cover equilibrium point C. Excess demand is positive at prices less than p^0 and also at prices higher than p^0. The price will tend to rise for downward *or* upward deviations from equilibrium. Point C is classed as semistable.

Assertions about the stability of equilibrium depend upon the assumptions made concerning the mechanism of the market and the behavior of the participants. One cannot say a priori whether the Walrasian or Marshallian condition is more plausible in reality. In any concrete situation stability of equilibrium can be assessed only after empirical information has been gathered concerning the behavior patterns of the participants in the market.

DYNAMIC STABILITY: LAGGED ADJUSTMENT

The static stability conditions are stated in terms of the rate of change of excess demand with respect to price or the rate of change of excess demand price with respect to quantity. The static analysis of stability makes no attempt to investigate the time path of the adjustment process. One would not expect instantaneous adjustments in the present model. If the initial price is not equal to the equilibrium price, it changes, and recontracting takes place. If the new price is still different from the equilibrium price, it is again forced to change. The dynamic nature of the recontracting model may be formally stated as follows. When the market opens some consumer makes an initial bid. This bid is recorded and made public by the auctioneer. After this price is announced, the participants have a specified amount of time (say, one hour) to enter into favorable contracts with each other at this price. After one hour new bids are permitted. The first new bids are recorded and made public by the auctioneer, and a one-hour period of recontracting begins. This process continues until equilibrium is reached. A price is observed in each one-hour period, and the analysis of dynamic stability investigates the course of price over time, i.e., from period to period.[1] Equilibrium is stable in the dynamic sense if the price converges to (or approaches) the equilibrium price over time; it is unstable if the price change is away from equilibrium. Dynamic stability can also be defined in terms of the convergence of the quantity supplied to the equilibrium quantity.

† An analogous argument can be made in terms of the Marshallian assumption.
[1] The prices which are recorded from period to period are potential, rather than realized, prices until equilibrium is reached. As long as $D \neq S$, none of the contracts is executed, and recontracting continues.

The former definition corresponds to the Walrasian and the latter to the Marshallian definition of stability.

Assuming the Walrasian mechanism to operate in the market, a positive excess demand tends to raise the price. This is expressed mathematically as

$$p_t - p_{t-1} = kE(p_{t-1}) \qquad (4\text{-}21)$$

where p_t is the price in period t and k is a positive constant. Equation (4-21) expresses one possible type of behavior for buyers and sellers. Assuming that there is a positive excess demand $E(p_{t-1})$ in period $(t-1)$, it expresses the assumption that an excess demand of $E(p_{t-1})$ induces buyers to bid a price $p_t = p_{t-1} + kE(p_{t-1}) > p_{t-1}$ in the following period. Assume that the demand and supply functions are

$$D_t = ap_t + b \qquad (4\text{-}22)$$
$$S_t = Ap_t + B \qquad (4\text{-}23)$$

Excess demand in period $(t-1)$ is

$$E(p_{t-1}) = (a - A)p_{t-1} + b - B$$

Substituting this into (4-21),

$$p_t - p_{t-1} = k[(a - A)p_{t-1} + b - B]$$

and

$$p_t = [1 + k(a - A)]p_{t-1} + k(b - B) \qquad (4\text{-}24)$$

The first-order difference equation (4-24) describes the time path of price on the basis of the behavior assumption contained in (4-21). Given the initial condition $p = p_0$ when $t = 0$, its solution is

$$p_t = \left(p_0 - \frac{b - B}{A - a}\right)[1 + k(a - A)]^t + \frac{b - B}{A - a} \qquad (4\text{-}25)$$

Excess demand is zero in equilibrium. The equilibrium price p_e can be found from (4-22) and (4-23) by setting $D_t - S_t = 0$. Solving for $p_t = p_e$,

$$p_e = \frac{b - B}{A - a}$$

Therefore the constant term in (4-25) is the equilibrium price. The equilibrium is stable if the actual price level approaches the equilibrium level as t increases. The price level converges to p_e without oscillations if $0 < 1 + k(a - A) < 1$. The right-hand side of this inequality holds if

$$a < A \qquad (4\text{-}26)$$

The left-hand side holds if

$$k < \frac{1}{A - a}$$

Condition (4-26) is automatically fulfilled if the supply curve has positive slope $(A > 0)$. The price level moves upward over time if the initial price is less than the equilibrium price: $p_0 - (b - B)/(A - a) < 0$, and downward if it is greater. If the slope of the supply curve is negative, stability requires that the slope of the demand curve $(1/a)$ be algebraically greater than the slope of the supply curve $(1/A)$; i.e., the supply curve must cut the demand curve from above.[1] Equilibrium is unstable if the supply curve cuts the demand curve from below, and any deviation from equilibrium is followed by increasing deviations from it. If k is sufficiently large and $a - A$ is negative, $1 + k(a - A)$ is also negative, and the price level must oscillate over time.[2]

Both static and dynamic stability depend upon the slopes of the demand and supply curves. Dynamic stability depends in addition on the magnitude of the parameter k which indicates the extent to which the market adjusts to a discrepancy between the quantities demanded and supplied per unit of time. A large k indicates that buyers and sellers tend to "overadjust": if excess demand is positive, bidding by buyers is sufficiently active to raise the price above the equilibrium level. For example, assume that the equilibrium price is 5 dollars and the actual price bid by buyers is 3 dollars in a given period. Buyers realize that there is an excess demand, but overestimate the adjustment necessary to equilibrate the market and bid 6 dollars in the following period. Sellers become aware of the excess supply and lower their price, but also overestimate the extent of the required adjustment: the price falls to 4 dollars. Each adjustment is in the right direction, but is exaggerated in magnitude. Dynamic analysis thus takes into account the strength of reactions to disturbances.

The dynamic stability of equilibrium can be analyzed diagrammatically in the following fashion. Plotting price along the horizontal axis, the dotted line in Fig. 4-12a represents the excess demand function. Assuming that $k < 1$, the solid line represents $kE(p_{t-1})$. The 45-degree

---

[1] Equations (4-22) and (4-23) state the demand and supply functions with price as the independent variable. Quantity is measured along the horizontal axis and price along the vertical in the customary diagram. Thus the slope of the demand curve is $1/a$, and the slope of the supply curve, $1/A$.

[2] If $1 + k(a - A)$ is greater than -1 (but less than zero), the amplitude of the oscillations decreases over time, and the time path approaches the equilibrium level. If it is less than -1, the market is subject to increasing price fluctuations.

line in Fig. 4-12*b* represents the locus of points defined by $p_t = p_{t-1}$. The function

$$p_t = p_{t-1} + kE(p_{t-1}) = f(p_{t-1})$$

is obtained by adding the ordinates (corresponding to the same abscissa) of the solid lines in Figs. 4-12*a* and 4-12*b*. The result is shown in Fig. 4-12*c*. Assume that the initial price is p_0. The price in the following period, p_1, is given by the ordinate of the point on $f(p_{t-1})$ directly above p_0. In order to calculate the price in the following period, p_1 is transferred to the horizontal axis by drawing a horizontal line from K to L. L lies on a 45-degree line, and the abscissa of each point on it equals its ordinate. The price p_2 is found by moving vertically to M on $f(p_{t-1})$. All subsequent prices are found in this manner. The price level converges in the present example to the equilibrium price given by the intersection of $f(p_{t-1})$ and the 45-degree line.[1] The stability of equilibrium depends upon the slope of the excess demand function and the magnitude of k. If the excess demand function in Fig. 4-12*a* were positively sloped, the function $f(p_{t-1})$ would cut the 45-degree line from below, and the equilibrium would be unstable. If the excess demand function had negative slope, as in Fig. 4-12*a*, but k were very large, $f(p_{t-1})$ would have negative slope, and the price level would oscillate.

A dynamic statement of the Marshallian stability condition can be formulated in similar fashion. The conclusions of the static analysis of stability are maintained: equilibrium is dynamically stable in both the

---

[1] It can be easily verified that point N is the equilibrium point. At N, $p_t = p_{t-1}$ (for the 45-degree line) and $p_t = p_{t-1} + kE(p_{t-1})$. Substituting p_{t-1} for p_t,

$$p_{t-1} = p_{t-1} + kE(p_{t-1})$$

or $kE(p_{t-1}) = 0$. Excess demand equals zero at point N.

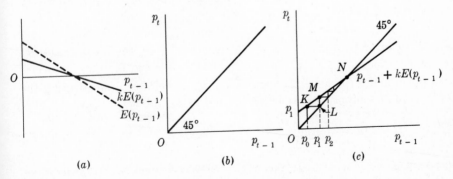

Fig. 4-12

Walrasian and Marshallian senses if the demand curve has negative and the supply curve positive slope, and is dynamically unstable in both senses if the demand curve has positive and the supply curve negative slope. An equilibrium is stable according to one definition and unstable according to the other if both curves are sloped in the same direction.

The static and dynamic approaches to stability are fundamentally different. Static stability need not imply dynamic stability, but dynamic stability implies static stability. The reason for this discrepancy is that dynamic analysis is a more inclusive tool for investigating the properties of equilibrium. Static analysis concerns itself only with the direction of the adjustment and neglects the magnitude of the adjustment from period to period.

Let

$$D_t = -0.5p_t + 100$$
$$S_t = -0.1p_t + 50$$

and let $k = 6$.† The equilibrium is stable in the static Walrasian sense if $D'(p) - S'(p) < 0$. Substituting from the demand and supply functions, $-0.5 - (-0.1) = -0.4 < 0$. Dynamic stability requires $-1 < 1 + k(a - A) < 1$. Substituting the appropriate values gives

$$1 + k(a - A) = -1.4$$

and the required left-hand inequality does not hold. The market will exhibit explosive oscillations.

DYNAMIC STABILITY: CONTINUOUS ADJUSTMENT

Equation (4-21) describes a price adjustment process that occurs over discrete intervals of time. An alternative approach is based on the assumption that adjustment takes place continuously. Equation (4-21) is then replaced by

$$\frac{dp}{dt} = kE(p) \tag{4-27}$$

where k and $E(p)$ have the same meaning as before.[1] Substituting the demand and supply functions (4-22) and (4-23), (4-27) becomes

$$\frac{dp}{dt} = k(a - A)p + k(b - B) \tag{4-28}$$

---

† The high value for k indicates that buyers and sellers react violently to disturbances.
[1] The value of p is defined for all values of t. It is customary in this case to omit the subscript t. The dependence of p on t may be indicated explicitly by writing p_t.

which is a first-order differential equation. Its solution (see Sec. A-6) is

$$p = \left(p_0 - \frac{b - B}{A - a}\right)e^{k(a-A)t} + \frac{b - B}{A - a}$$

where p_0 is the initial price at $t = 0$ and $e = 2.71828 \ldots$ is the base of the system of natural logarithms.

The equilibrium price $p_e = (b - B)/(A - a)$ is dynamically stable, that is, $p \to p_e$ as $t \to \infty$, if $a - A < 0$, which will be the case if the demand function is negatively and the supply function positively sloped. The magnitude of the adjustment coefficient influences the speed with which convergence or divergence takes place, but in contrast to the lagged adjustment model it plays no role in determining whether an equilibrium is stable or not. The static and dynamic stability conditions are identical in this case.

An equilibrium point is *locally* stable if the system returns to it, given a small initial deviation from equilibrium. It is *globally* stable if the system returns to it for any initial deviation from equilibrium. Linear models such as (4-28) have unique equilibrium points in general, and if they are locally stable, they are also globally stable. Nonlinear models may have several equilibrium points, and, in any event, the local stability of an equilibrium point does not guarantee its global stability.

A linear approximation is useful in determining the local stability of nonlinear models. Assume that the excess demand function $E(p)$ is some complicated function of p so that the differential equation (4-27) is difficult or impossible to solve directly. The approximate equality

$$\frac{E(p) - E(p_e)}{p - p_e} \approx E'(p_e) \tag{4-29}$$

where p_e is an equilibrium price, follows from the definition of a derivative [see Eq. (A-5)]. In the limit, as $p \to p_e$, (4-29) holds exactly, and for small deviations of p from p_e the approximation may be expected to be good. Substituting $E(p_e) = 0$, solving (4-29) for $E(p)$, and substituting the result on the right-hand side of (4-27),

$$\frac{dp}{dt} = kE'(p_e)(p - p_e)$$

which is a linear equation since $E'(p_e)$, the derivative of excess demand evaluated at p_e, is a constant. The root of the characteristic equation (valid in the neighborhood of p_e) is $kE'(p_e)$. Thus, if the excess demand function is negatively sloped in the neighborhood of p_e, the equilibrium is locally stable. The static and dynamic conditions again are identical.

The existence of global stability can often be ascertained by a technique known as *Liapunov's direct method*. First find a Liapunov function, $V(p)$, such that $V(p) > 0$ if $p \neq p_e$ and $V(p_e) = 0$. If dV/dt is negative whenever $p \neq p_e$, the equilibrium solution is globally stable.[1] An appropriate Liapunov function is often provided by

$$V(p) = (p - p_e)^2 \qquad (4\text{-}30)$$

the squared distance of the actual point p at time t from the equilibrium point.

For illustration, consider the excess demand function $E = b/p - a$ where $p_e = b/a$ with $a, b > 0$, and

$$\frac{dp}{dt} \doteq k\left(\frac{b}{p} - a\right)$$

Utilizing (4-30),

$$\frac{dV}{dt} = 2(p - p_e)\frac{dp}{dt}$$

Substituting for p_e and dp/dt,

$$\frac{dV}{dt} = -\frac{2k(ap - b)^2}{ap}$$

which is negative for all $p \neq p_e$ since k, a, and p are positive. Thus, an equilibrium for this model is globally stable.

4-9 DYNAMIC EQUILIBRIUM WITH LAGGED ADJUSTMENT

Producers' supply functions show how they adjust their outputs to the prevailing price. Since production takes time, the adjustment may not be instantaneous, but may become perceptible in the market only after a period of time. Agricultural commodities often provide good examples of lagged supply. An individual farmer may base his production plans on the market price in the fall; the output materializes only during the following summer.

LAGGED ADJUSTMENT IN A SINGLE MARKET

Consider the market for winter wheat as an example of a market with lagged supply reaction. Production plans are made after the harvest. The output corresponding to these production plans appears on the market a year later. Assume that the demand and supply functions are

$$D_t = ap_t + b \qquad (4\text{-}31)$$
$$S_t = Ap_{t-1} + B \qquad (4\text{-}32)$$

[1] More advanced treatises distinguish between *stability* and *asymptotic stability*. See J. La Salle and S. Lefschetz, *Stability by Liapunov's Direct Method* (New York: Academic, 1961), pp. 31–32.

The quantity demanded in any period depends upon the price in that period, but the quantity supplied depends upon the price in the previous period. It is assumed that the quantity supplied in period t is always equal to the quantity demanded in that period; that is, p_t adjusts to bring about the equality of D_t and S_t as soon as S_t appears on the market. This implies that no producer is left with unsold stocks and no consumer with an unsatisfied demand. Therefore

$$D_t - S_t = 0$$

Substituting from (4-31) and (4-32),

$$ap_t + b - Ap_{t-1} - B = 0$$

Solving for p_t,

$$p_t = \frac{A}{a} p_{t-1} + \frac{B-b}{a} \qquad (4\text{-}33)$$

Assuming that the initial condition is given by $p = p_0$ when $t = 0$, the solution of the first-order difference equation (4-33) is

$$p_t = \left(p_0 - \frac{B-b}{a-A}\right)\left(\frac{A}{a}\right)^t + \frac{B-b}{a-A} \qquad (4\text{-}34)$$

The solution (4-34) describes the path of the price as a function of time. Some of the possible time paths are illustrated in Figs. 4-13a and 4-13b.

Assume that the initial supply does not equal the equilibrium amount as a result of a disturbance such as a drought. Let the initial supply equal q_0 in Fig. 4-13a. The corresponding initial price is p_0.

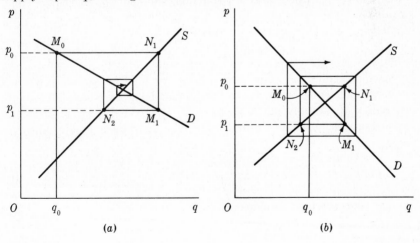

(a)   (b)

Fig. 4-13

Consumers demand $p_0 M_0$, and this quantity equals the initial supply. The price p_0 induces entrepreneurs to supply the quantity $p_0 N_1$ in the next period. The price falls instantaneously to p_1. The quantity demanded is then $p_1 M_1$ (which equals $p_0 N_1$, the quantity supplied in that period). In the following period the price p_1 induces a supply of $p_1 N_2$. This process continues indefinitely, producing a cobweb pattern. The price level fluctuates, but converges to the equilibrium level indicated by the intersection of the demand and supply curves. The same mechanism operates in Fig. 4-13b, but the price fluctuations tend to become larger and larger: the market is subject to explosive oscillations.

The conditions for convergence to an equilibrium price can be ascertained from (4-34). The market is in dynamic equilibrium if the price remains unchanged from period to period, i.e., if $p_t = p_{t-1}$. The constant term $(B - b)/(a - A)$ in (4-34) is the only such equilibrium price.[1] The market is dynamically stable if $p_t \to p_e$ as $t \to \infty$. If the absolute value of the quotient (A/a) is less than one, the first term on the right of (4-34) will vanish as $t \to \infty$, and the market will be dynamically stable. If the slopes of the demand $(1/a)$ and supply curves $(1/A)$ have opposite sign, price will oscillate about the equilibrium price level. If the slope of the demand curve has smaller absolute value than the slope of the supply curve, $1/|a| < 1/|A|$, the oscillations will decrease in amplitude, and the market is dynamically stable as shown in Fig. 4-13a. If the slope of the demand curve has greater absolute value than the slope of the supply curve, $1/|a| > 1/|A|$, the oscillations will increase in amplitude, and the market is dynamically unstable as shown in Fig. 4-13b. Finally, if the slopes of the demand and supply curves are equal in absolute value, $1/|a| = 1/|A|$, the oscillations will have constant amplitude, and the market is dynamically unstable.

If the demand and supply curves slope in the same direction, A/a is positive, and the price level will not oscillate, but will either increase or decrease continually.[2] The same conditions hold as above: price will converge to its equilibrium value if the demand curve has smaller absolute slope than the supply curve (Fig. 4-14), and will diverge in either an upward or downward direction if the demand curve has greater absolute slope.

The conditions for dynamic stability are not the same as in the simple dynamic case. Buyers and sellers react to excess demand in the simple dynamic case. Excess demand is zero in cobweb situations. Buyers react to given supplies in terms of the prices they offer. Sellers

---

[1] Set $D_t = S_t$ and $p_{t-1} = p_t$ in (4-31) and (4-32) and solve for p_t.
[2] The price may remain constant if the demand and supply curves coincide. No unique equilibrium is defined in this case. See Sec. 4-7.

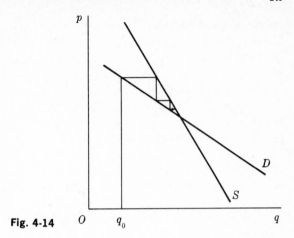

Fig. 4-14 O q_0 q

respond to given prices in terms of the quantities they supply in the following period.

LAGGED ADJUSTMENT IN TWO INTERRELATED MARKETS

Interesting oscillatory behavior can be obtained in the case of two interrelated markets.   A case in point is the noted "corn–hog" cycle.   A
simplified version of this type of market is discussed below.   The complete solution is not derived, and the discussion is confined to developing
the conditions under which the two markets are stable or unstable.

Let the subscripts c and h refer to corn and hogs respectively.   The
demand and supply functions for corn are

$$D_{ct} = a_{11}p_{ct} + b_1 \tag{4-35}$$
$$S_{ct} = a_{21}p_{c,t-1} + b_2 \tag{4-36}$$

The corn market possesses the same characteristics which were assumed
for the winter wheat market.   The demand for corn in any period
depends upon the price of corn in the same period, and the corn supply is
lagged and depends upon the corn price in the previous period.   The
demand and supply functions for hogs are

$$D_{ht} = a_{31}p_{ht} + b_3 \tag{4-37}$$
$$S_{ht} = a_{41}p_{h,t-1} + a_{42}p_{c,t-1} + b_4 \tag{4-38}$$

The demand for hogs is a function of the price of hogs in the same period.
The supply of hogs depends both upon the price of hogs and the price of
corn in the previous period.   Equation (4-38) contains two assumptions
concerning the behavior of hog producers: their production plans for any
period t depend upon (1) the price of their output at time $(t - 1)$, and

(2) the price of corn at time $(t - 1)$. The second assumption reflects the fact that corn is an important input in producing hogs. The price of corn thus tends to affect the hog producer's production plans. A change of $p_{c,t-1}$ results in a shift of the conventional hog supply function.

Equations (4-35) to (4-38) are a system of four simultaneous difference equations which must be solved in order to derive the conditions under which p_{ct} and p_{ht} approach their equilibrium values. Equating aggregate supply and demand in each market,

$$D_{ct} - S_{ct} = 0$$
$$D_{ht} - S_{ht} = 0$$

Substituting from (4-35) — (4-38),

$$a_{11}p_{ct} - a_{21}p_{c,t-1} \qquad\qquad = b_2 - b_1 \qquad\qquad (4\text{-}39)$$
$$a_{31}p_{ht} - a_{41}p_{h,t-1} - a_{42}p_{c,t-1} = b_4 - b_3 \qquad\qquad (4\text{-}40)$$

Equations (4-39) and (4-40) describe the behavior of prices in the corn and hog markets respectively. The behavior of the corn price is independent of the hog price, since the latter does not enter (4-39). The corn cycle is self-contained and independent of whatever fluctuations may exist in the movement of the hog price. However, the hog price in period t depends upon the corn price in period $(t - 1)$. The hog cycle is not independent of the corn cycle. In order to find a solution for p_{ht}, one must derive an equation which does not contain the price of corn. Solving (4-40) for $p_{c,t-1}$,

$$p_{c,t-1} = \frac{a_{31}p_{ht} - a_{41}p_{h,t-1} - b_4 + b_3}{a_{42}} \qquad\qquad (4\text{-}41)$$

Equation (4-41) holds for any value of t; thus,

$$p_{ct} = \frac{a_{31}p_{h,t+1} - a_{41}p_{ht} - b_4 + b_3}{a_{42}} \qquad\qquad (4\text{-}42)$$

Substituting (4-41) and (4-42) into (4-39),

$$p_{ht} - \left(\frac{a_{41}}{a_{31}} + \frac{a_{21}}{a_{11}}\right) p_{h,t-1} + \frac{a_{21}a_{41}}{a_{11}a_{31}} p_{h,t-2} = K \qquad\qquad (4\text{-}43)$$

where $K = [(b_2 - b_1)a_{42} + (b_4 - b_3)(a_{11} - a_{21})]/a_{11}a_{31}$. The behavior of price in the hog market is described by a second-order difference equation, and two initial conditions are necessary to obtain a general solution. The general solution of (4-43) is of the form

$$p_{ht} = c_1 x_1^t + c_2 x_2^t + Q$$

where c_1 and c_2 are constants determined in accordance with the initial conditions and where Q is the particular solution (see Sec. A-5). Whether the time path is explosive or convergent depends upon the magnitudes of x_1 and x_2 which are the roots of the quadratic equation derived from (4-43) by neglecting the constant term on the right-hand side. The homogeneous equation corresponding to (4-43) is

$$p_{ht} - \left(\frac{a_{41}}{a_{31}} + \frac{a_{21}}{a_{11}}\right) p_{h,t-1} + \frac{a_{21}a_{41}}{a_{11}a_{31}} p_{h,t-2} = 0$$

Assume that the solution is of the form x^t. Setting $p_{ht} = x^t$ and dividing through by x^{t-2},

$$x^2 - \left(\frac{a_{41}}{a_{31}} + \frac{a_{21}}{a_{11}}\right) x + \frac{a_{21}a_{41}}{a_{11}a_{31}} = 0$$

The solution of this quadratic characteristic equation is

$$x = \frac{\frac{a_{41}}{a_{31}} + \frac{a_{21}}{a_{11}} \pm \sqrt{\left(\frac{a_{41}}{a_{31}} + \frac{a_{21}}{a_{11}}\right)^2 - 4\frac{a_{21}a_{41}}{a_{11}a_{31}}}}{2}$$

$$= \frac{\frac{a_{41}}{a_{31}} + \frac{a_{21}}{a_{11}} \pm \left(\frac{a_{41}}{a_{31}} - \frac{a_{21}}{a_{11}}\right)}{2}$$

Therefore

$$x_1 = \frac{a_{41}}{a_{31}} \qquad x_2 = \frac{a_{21}}{a_{11}}$$

The time path of the hog price will converge if both roots are less than unity in absolute value. This requirement is fulfilled if the demand curve is less steep than the supply curve in both markets. Consequently the time paths of prices in the two markets *taken separately* must converge. The assertion that $|x_2| < 1$ is a necessary condition for dynamic stability in the corn market. The assertion that $|x_1| < 1$ is a necessary condition for dynamic stability in the hog market, considering corn prices to be constant. The two assertions together are necessary for stability in the hog market if the effect of changes in corn prices is considered. Stability in the two interrelated markets taken together implies stability in each of them separately, but stability in the corn market alone does not imply stability in both.

A diagrammatic representation may clarify the analysis. Let Fig. 4-15a represent the corn market and Fig. 4-15b the hog market. A change in the price of corn shifts the supply curve for hogs according to

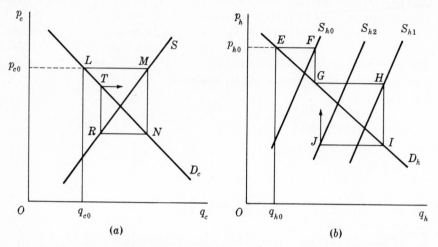

Fig. 4-15

(4-38).   Denote the initial quantities in the corn and hog markets by q_{c0} and q_{h0} and the initial prices by p_{c0} and p_{h0} respectively.   Assume that the relevant supply curve for hogs is S_{h0} if the price of corn is p_{c0}.   The movement in the corn market is traced out by the lines LM and MN in Fig. 4-15a.   The corresponding movement in the hog market is EF, FG. But the price of corn has fallen by the amount MN.   The supply curve for hogs is therefore shifted to the position S_{h1}, and the subsequent move-ment in the hog market is from G to H and from H to I.   During the same time, the supply of corn is reduced by RN, and the corn price is raised by RT.   This increase in the price of corn shifts the hog supply curve in the reverse direction to position S_{h2}, and the hog supply is reduced by the amount IJ.   These results are based on the assumption that a_{42} in (4-38) is negative; i.e., the higher the price of corn in period $(t-1)$, the lower the supply of hogs in period t.   The conclusion that overall stability requires both markets to be stable separately is now clear: if the corn market were unstable, fluctuations in the price of corn would tend to become larger and larger, and the hog supply curve would also shift by larger and larger amounts in subsequent periods.   The hog market could not be stable.   Even if the corn market were stable, and consequently the successive shifts in the supply curve for hogs were of decreasing magnitude, the price of hogs would still exhibit increasing oscillations if the demand curve for hogs were steeper than the supply curve.

If hog producers purchased a sizable portion of the total corn supply, it might be reasonable to assume that the demand for corn depended upon the prices of both corn and hogs. This assumption would increase the complexity of the model, but would not alter the basic tools of analysis.[1]

4-10 SUMMARY

The theory of perfect competition analyzes the factors that determine price and quantity in markets in which (1) the product is homogeneous and buyers are uniform, (2) buyers and sellers are numerous, (3) buyers and sellers possess perfect information, (4) there are free entry and exit for both buyers and sellers in the long run. The participants in the market act as if they had no influence on the price, and each individual regards it as a given parameter.

The price and the quantity bought and sold are determined by supply and demand. The aggregate demand function is derived from the demand functions of individual consumers, which, in turn, are derived from the individual consumers' first-order conditions for utility maximization. The aggregate supply function is derived from individual supply functions which are based on the individual firms' first-order conditions for profit maximization. Equilibrium is attained when demand equals supply. The equality of demand and supply guarantees that buyers' and sellers' desires are consistent. The analysis of a perfectly competitive market is extended to spatially distributed firms and some problems of taxation.

The analysis of perfectly competitive factor markets is similar to the analysis of commodity markets. The equilibrium price-quantity combination is determined by demand and supply, and the equality of demand and supply ensures the consistency of buyers' and sellers' desires. The demand function for a factor is derived from the individual firms' first-order conditions for profit maximization. The supply function for a primary input such as labor is derived from the individual laborers' first-order conditions for utility maximization. Equilibrium in a factor market ensures that the price of a factor equals the value of its marginal product.

The existence of demand and supply functions does not necessarily imply that demand and supply are equal at one or more nonnegative price-quantity combinations. The concept of market equilibrium is extended to cover two situations in which demand and supply are not equal. A *free-good* equilibrium is characterized by an excess of supply over demand at a zero price. A *zero-production* equilibrium is characterized by supply price exceeding demand price for all nonnegative out-

---

[1] The results of Sec. 4-9 are based on the assumption that the demand and supply functions are linear. If this assumption is relaxed, the variety of possible results increases considerably.

puts.   It is possible that more than one price-quantity equilibrium may exist for a market.   Multiple equilibria cannot occur if the difference in the slopes of the demand and supply curves is negative for all prices, or if the difference is positive for all prices.

The existence of an equilibrium point does not guarantee its attainment.   The analysis of the stability of equilibrium is concerned with the effects of disturbances.   Equilibrium is stable if a disturbance is followed by a return to equilibrium and unstable if it is not.   The static analysis of stability considers merely the direction of the adjustment which follows the disturbance; dynamic analysis considers the time sequence of the adjustment process as well.   A dynamic model with lagged adjustment demonstrates that a market which is stable according to the static analysis may be dynamically unstable.   A dynamic model with continuous adjustment enriches the static model by describing the path of price over time following a disturbance.   Both static and dynamic analyses contain assumptions about the behavior of buyers and sellers.   According to the assumption of the Walrasian stability condition, buyers and sellers react to excess demand.   According to the Marshallian assumption, sellers react to excess demand price.   These assumptions are not generally equivalent, and their plausibility must be verified empirically.

Special dynamic problems arise in markets in which supply reactions are lagged.   In markets of this type both buyers and sellers are assumed to react to price.   The time path of the market price oscillates and produces a cobweb-like path pattern if the demand and supply curves have slopes of opposite sign; an equilibrium is stable if the absolute value of the slope of the demand curve is less than the absolute value of the slope of the supply curve.   The analysis is extended to cases in which two markets are interrelated, and stability conditions are derived in analogous fashion.

EXERCISES

4-1. Two hundred consumers derive utility from the consumption of two goods.   Each has the utility function $U = 10q_1 + 5q_2 + q_1q_2$.   Each has a fixed income of 100 dollars.   Assume that the price of Q_2 is 4 dollars per unit.   Express the aggregate demand for Q_1 as a function of p_1.   Is the aggregate demand curve downward sloping?

4-2. Construct a short-run supply function for an entrepreneur whose short-run cost function is $C = 0.04q^3 - 0.8q^2 + 10q + 5$.

4-3. A good Q is produced using only one input X.   The market for Q is supplied by 100 identical competitive firms each of which has the production function $q = x^\beta$ where $0 < \beta < 1$.   Each firm behaves as if the price of X were constant.   However, the industry as a whole faces an upward sloping supply curve for X: $r = b(100x)$ where $b > 0$.   Derive the industry's long-run supply curve.

4-4. The long-run cost function for each firm that supplies Q is $C = q^3 - 4q^2 + 8q$. Firms will enter the industry if profits are positive and leave the industry if profits are negative. Describe the industry's long-run supply function. Assume that the corresponding demand function is $D = 2{,}000 - 100p$. Determine equilibrium price, aggregate quantity, and number of firms.

4-5. Determine equilibrium price and quantity for a market with the following demand and supply functions: $D = 20 - 2p$ and $S = 40 - 6p$. Assume that a specific tax of 1 dollar per unit is imposed. Compute the changes in equilibrium price and quantity.

4-6. A consumer allocates a fixed amount of time to labor and leisure. He derives satisfaction from the time he retains as leisure, L, and the income, y, that he secures by selling his labor at a fixed wage rate. His utility function is $U = Ly + aL$ where a is a positive parameter. Derive the consumer's supply function for labor. Is his labor supply curve upward sloping?

4-7. Determine whether equilibrium solutions exist for markets with the following demand and supply functions:

   (a) $D = 12 - 3p; S = -10 + 2p$.
   (b) $D = 16 - 2p; S = 20 - 2p$.
   (c) $D = 50 - 4p; S = 10 + 10p - p^2$.
   (d) $D = 50 - 4p; S = 2 + 10p - p^2$.

4-8. Assume that the aggregate demand and supply functions are given by $D = 25/p$ and $S = \sqrt{5p}$. Is the dynamic process defined by (4-27) locally stable?

4-9. Consider the following markets which are characterized by lagged supply response:

   (a) $D_t = 40 - 10p_t; S_t = 2 + 9p_{t-1}$.
   (b) $D_t = 30 - 5p_t; S_t = 20 - p_{t-1}$.

Determine equilibrium price and quantity for each market. Assume an initial price 20 percent below the equilibrium price for each market, and determine the number of periods necessary for each price to adjust to within 1 percent of equilibrium.

***4-10.** Consider an industry with n identical firms in which the ith firm's total cost function is $C_i = aq_i^2 + bq_iq$ ($i = 1, \ldots, n$), where $q = q_1 + q_2 + \cdots + q_n$. Derive the industry's supply function.

SELECTED REFERENCES

Baumol, W. J., *Economic Dynamics* (2d ed.; New York: Macmillan, 1959). Chapter 7 contains a nonmathematical discussion of comparative statics, dynamics, and the cobweb theorem.

Boulding, K. E., *Economic Analysis: Microeconomics* (4th ed.; New York: Harper & Row, 1966), vol. I. The model of a perfectly competitive economy is developed in nonmathematical terms in pt. I.

Buchanan, N. S., "A Reconsideration of the Cobweb Theorem," *Journal of Political Economy*, vol. 47 (February, 1939), pp. 67–81. An extension of the cobweb theorem with the use of geometry.

Ellis, H. S., and William Fellner, "External Economies and Diseconomies," *American Economic Review*, vol. 33 (September, 1943), pp. 493–511. Also reprinted in American Economic Association, *Readings in Price Theory* (Chicago: Irwin, 1952), pp. 242–263. A geometric elucidation of these concepts.

Knight, F. H., *Risk, Uncertainty and Profit* (Boston: Houghton Mifflin, 1921). Also reprinted by the London School of Economics in 1937. A nonmathematical analysis of a perfectly competitive economy with emphasis on the effect of uncertainty on profits.

Marshall, Alfred, *Principles of Economics* (8th ed.; London: Macmillan, 1920). Book
  V contains a nonmathematical analysis of supply and demand and the determination of market equilibrium.
Samuelson, Paul A., *Foundations of Economic Analysis* (Cambridge, Mass.: Harvard,
  1948). Chapter IX contains a discussion of market stability. A knowledge
  of advanced calculus is necessary.
Schneider, Erich, *Pricing and Equilibrium* (London: William Hodge, 1952). Chapter 4 contains a discussion of equilibrium in a single perfectly competitive market
  in geometric terms.
Stigler, George J., *The Theory of Price* (3d ed.; New York: Macmillan, 1966). Theories of perfect competition are developed in chap. 10 without the use of
  mathematics.

5
Multimarket Equilibrium

The analysis of price determination and allocation can be performed on three levels of increasing generality: (1) the equilibrium of an individual consumer or producer, (2) the equilibrium of a single market, and (3) the simultaneous equilibrium of all markets. The first type of analysis is the subject of Chaps. 2 and 3, and the second is the subject of Chap. 4. The present chapter is devoted to the third.

A theoretical analysis contains data, variables, and behavior assumptions that allow the determination of specific values for the variables once the data are known. Consider the analysis of an individual consumer. The data are his utility function, his income, and commodity prices. The variables are the quantities of the commodities he purchases and consumes, and the basic behavior assumption is his desire to maximize utility. The analysis of an individual producer is similar. The data are his production function and the prices of all outputs and inputs. The variables are the quantities of the inputs he purchases and the quantity of the output he produces and sells. The behavior assumption is his desire to maximize profit. The analysis of an individual unit sheds no light upon the determination of perfectly competitive prices, however, since all prices are considered parameters.

The analysis of equilibrium in a single market is somewhat more general.   A single price is determined as the result of optimizing behavior on the part of a large number of consumers and a large number of producers.   The data for the analysis of equilibrium in a commodity market are the utility and production functions of all consumers and producers, the incomes of all consumers, the prices of all factors, and the prices of all commodities other than the one under consideration.   The explicit variables are the price of the commodity and the purchases and sales of each consumer and producer.   The condition that the market must be cleared, i.e., aggregate demand must equal aggregate supply, is added to the assumptions of utility and profit maximization.   The analysis of a single factor market is similar except that the consumers' incomes are determined by their factor sales.

A consumer's demand functions are derived from his equilibrium conditions for utility maximization.   If he purchases and consumes two commodities, his demand for each is a function of both prices and his income:

$$D_1 = D_1(p_1, p_2, y) \qquad D_2 = D_2(p_1, p_2, y)$$

In a single-market equilibrium analysis for Q_1, p_2 and y become parameters, and D_1 becomes a function of p_1 alone:

$$D_1 = D_1(p_1, p_2^0, y^0) \qquad D_2 = D_2(p_1, p_2^0, y^0)$$

As a result of these assumptions D_2 is also a function of p_1 alone, although this relation is seldom explicit.   If the consumer alters his purchases of Q_1 with a change of p_1, he normally also alters his purchases of Q_2.   The quantities that the consumer purchases of all commodities other than the one under consideration are implicit variables for the equilibrium analysis of a single market.   Similar considerations apply to producers.   The quantities of the inputs a producer employs become functions of his output price alone.

Every factor and commodity price is a variable for the analysis of its own market and a parameter for the analysis of all other markets.   There is no assurance that a consistent set of prices will result from a piecemeal solution, taking one market at a time.   It is only by chance that the price assumed for Q_j in the analysis of the market for Q_k will be the same as the price determined in the analysis of the market for Q_j in isolation.

All markets are interrelated.   Consumers spend their incomes for all commodities, and the demand for each commodity depends upon all prices.   If the goods Q_1 and Q_2 are gross substitutes, an increase in the price of Q_1 will induce consumers as a whole to substitute Q_2 for Q_1.   If two goods are complements, an increase in the price of one may induce consumers to restrict their consumption of both (see Sec. 2-6).   Pairs of inputs may also be defined as substitutes or complements.   Furthermore, production and consumption are not independent.   Consumers earn their incomes from the sale of labor services and other productive factors to producers.   As a result of these interrelationships, equilibria for all product and factor markets must be determined simultaneously in order to secure a consistent set of prices.

The data for the determination of a general multimarket equilibrium are the utility and production functions of all producers and consumers and their initial endowments of factors and/or commodities.   The variables are the prices of all factors and commodities and the quantities purchased and sold by each consumer and producer.   The behavior assumptions require utility and profit maximization together with the condition that every market be cleared.

A multimarket equilibrium analysis is developed for a pure-exchange system in Sec. 5-1 and then extended to include production in Sec. 5-2. The problems of absolute price determination and the choice of a standard of value are considered in Sec. 5-3.   Section 5-4 contains a discussion of the existence of multimarket equilibria.   Static and dynamic stability conditions are extended to multimarket systems, and the uniqueness of equilibrium is considered in Sec. 5-5.

5-1 PURE EXCHANGE

Pure exchange deals with the pricing and allocation problems of a society in which n individuals exchange and consume fixed quantities of m commodities.   Each individual possesses an initial endowment of one or more of the commodities and is free to buy and sell at the prevailing market prices.   Purchases and sales may be interpreted as barter transactions.   Imagine a consumer whose initial endowment consists of twenty pears and three apples and assume that there are no other commodities. The prevailing market prices determine the terms on which he can barter pears for apples or apples for pears.   If the prices are 5 cents for pears and 10 cents for apples, he can obtain one apple by selling two pears or two pears by selling one apple.   Given market prices and initial endowments, each consumer's trading will be determined by his ordinal utility function. It would be a rare case if none of the consumers was able to increase his satisfaction level through exchange.   A consumer will sell a portion of his initial endowment of some commodities and add to his stocks of others as long as he is able to increase his utility index.

EQUILIBRIUM OF THE iTH CONSUMER

The excess demand of the ith consumer for the jth commodity (E_{ij}) is defined as the difference between the quantity he consumes (q_{ij}) and his initial endowment (q_{ij}^0):

$$E_{ij} = q_{ij} - q_{ij}^0 \qquad j = 1, \ldots, m \tag{5-1}$$

If his consumption of Q_j exceeds his initial endowment, his excess demand is positive; he purchases Q_j in the market. If his consumption is less than his initial endowment, his excess demand is negative; he sells Q_j in the market. It is not possible to determine the signs of his excess demands a priori. He may either sell or buy Q_j. The sharp distinction between buyers and sellers used throughout Chap. 4 is no longer possible.

The consumer's income equals the value of his initial endowment:

$$y_i = \sum_{j=1}^{m} p_j q_{ij}^0 \tag{5-2}$$

This is the amount of purchasing power that he would obtain if he sold his entire endowment. In order to relate the present analysis to that of Chap. 2, assume for the moment that he sells his entire endowment and uses the proceeds to purchase commodities at the prevailing market prices. The value of the commodities that he purchases and consumes must equal his income as given by (5-2):

$$y_i = \sum_{j=1}^{m} p_j q_{ij} \tag{5-3}$$

His purchases will most likely include some of the commodities that he sold, but this does not matter since the acts of buying and selling are assumed costless. The self-canceling transactions can be omitted without affecting the analysis. Therefore, it is henceforth assumed that the consumer does not both buy and sell the same commodity. His budget constraint can be expressed in terms of his excess demands. Subtracting (5-2) from (5-3) and substituting from (5-1),

$$\sum_{j=1}^{m} p_j(q_{ij} - q_{ij}^0) = \sum_{j=1}^{m} p_j E_{ij} = 0 \tag{5-4}$$

The net value of the consumer's excess demands must equal zero. His budget constraint in this form states that the value of the commodities he buys must equal the value of the commodities he sells.

The equilibrium analysis of the consumer as developed in Chap. 2 needs slight modification to be applicable to a consumer in a pure-exchange economy. The consumer's utility index is a function of the quantities of the commodities he consumes, but can be stated as a function of his excess demands and initial endowments by substituting $q_{ij} = E_{ij} + q_{ij}^0$ from (5-1):

$$U_i = U_i(q_{i1}, \ldots, q_{im}) = U_i(E_{i1} + q_{i1}^0, \ldots, E_{im} + q_{im}^0) \qquad (5\text{-}5)$$

The consumer desires to maximize the value of his utility index subject to a budget constraint. Using the form of the utility function given by (5-5) and the budget constraint (5-4), form the function

$$V_i = U_i(E_{i1} + q_{i1}^0, \ldots, E_{im} + q_{im}^0) - \lambda \left(\sum_{j=1}^{m} p_j E_{ij} \right) \qquad (5\text{-}6)$$

and set the partial derivatives of V_i with respect to the excess demands and λ equal to zero:

$$\frac{\partial V_i}{\partial E_{ij}} = \frac{\partial U_i}{\partial E_{ij}} - \lambda p_j = 0 \qquad j = 1, \ldots, m$$

$$\frac{\partial V_i}{\partial \lambda} = - \sum_{j=1}^{m} p_j E_{ij} = 0 \qquad\qquad (5\text{-}7)$$

Since $dE_{ij}/dq_{ij} = 1$, the first set of equations of (5-7) can be expressed in terms of the utility-index increments:

$$\frac{\partial U_i}{\partial E_{ij}} \frac{dE_{ij}}{dq_{ij}} - \lambda p_j = \frac{\partial U_i}{\partial q_{ij}} - \lambda p_j = 0 \qquad j = 1, \ldots, m$$

The first-order conditions for the individual consumer are the familiar ones developed in Chap. 2. He buys and sells commodities until the rate of commodity substitution for every pair of commodities (the ratio of their utility-index increments) equals their price ratio. Second-order conditions require that the relevant bordered Hessian determinants alternate in sign (see Sec. 2-7).

If the second-order conditions are satisfied, the ith consumer's excess demand functions can be derived from the first-order conditions. Eliminate λ from (5-7) and solve for the m excess demands as functions of commodity prices:

$$E_{ij} = E_{ij}(p_1, \ldots, p_m) \qquad j = 1, \ldots, m \qquad\qquad (5\text{-}8)$$

The consumer's excess demands depend upon the prices of all commodities. If his endowment of Q_j is not zero, his excess demand for Q_j may be positive for some sets of prices and negative for others.

It was proved in Sec. 2-4 that consumer demand functions are homogeneous of degree zero in income and prices. A similar theorem can be proved for the pure-exchange barter economy: the consumer's excess

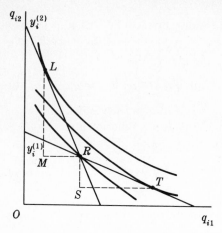

Fig. 5-1

demand functions are homogeneous of degree zero in prices; i.e., the excess demands will remain unchanged if all prices are increased or decreased by the same proportion.[1]   A doubling of all prices would double both the value of the consumer's initial endowment and the cost of the commodities he purchases.   If the consumer's endowment consisted of pears and apples and their prices increased from 5 and 10 cents to 10 and 20 respectively, he could still obtain one apple for two pears or two pears for one apple.   In a barter economy of this type the consumer is interested in market exchange ratios rather than absolute price levels.

A graphic description of an individual consumer's equilibrium is contained in Fig. 5-1.   His initial endowment is given by the coordinates of R.   His income line is the locus of all quantity combinations with the same market value as his initial endowment.   If $y_i^{(1)}$ is his income line, he will maximize utility by moving to T.   He will sell RS units of Q_2 and purchase ST units of Q_1 in moving from R to T.   His excess demand for Q_1 is positive, and his excess demand for Q_2 negative.

Assume that the price of Q_1 increases relative to the price of Q_2 and that the consumer's new income line is $y_i^{(2)}$.   Point L is the position of maximum utility on this income line.   The consumer will sell MR units of Q_1 and purchase ML units of Q_2 in moving from R to L.   A price change has resulted in a change of the signs of his excess demands.   His excess demand for Q_1 is now negative, and his excess demand for Q_2 positive.

---

[1] The proof is similar to that used in Sec. 2-4.   Substitute kp_j into the budget constraint in (5-6), set its partial derivatives equal to zero to obtain a system similar to (5-7), divide the first $(m - 1)$ equations by the mth to eliminate λ and k, and factor k out of the $(m + 1)$th.

The irrelevance of absolute price levels is obvious in the graphic analysis. The consumer's initial endowment is given by a point representing physical quantities. His income line is drawn through this point with a slope equal to the negative of the ratio of commodity prices. A proportionate change of both prices will leave their ratio unaffected, and neither the slope nor the position of the income line will change.

MARKET EQUILIBRIUM

An aggregate excess demand function for Q_j is constructed by summing the individual excess demand functions of the n consumers:

$$E_j = \sum_{i=1}^{n} E_{ij}(p_1, \ldots, p_j, \ldots, p_m) = E_j(p_1, \ldots, p_j, \ldots, p_m)$$

Aggregate excess demand is also a function of the m commodity prices. Partial equilibrium is attained in the jth market if the excess demand for Q_j equals zero when the remaining $(m - 1)$ prices are assigned fixed values:

$$E_j(p_1^0, \ldots, p_j, \ldots, p_m^0) = 0 \qquad (5\text{-}9)$$

Condition (5-9) is equivalent to the condition that supply equal demand. The equilibrium price for Q_j is obtained by solving (5-9) for p_j and depends upon the prices assigned to the other $(m - 1)$ commodities. The purchases and sales of the individual consumers are determined by substituting the equilibrium price into the individual excess demand functions.

MULTIMARKET EQUILIBRIUM

Now treat all prices as variables and consider the simultaneous equilibrium of all m markets. Aggregate excess demand must equal zero in every market:

$$E_j(p_1, \ldots, p_m) = 0 \qquad j = 1, \ldots, m \qquad (5\text{-}10)$$

The equilibrium conditions form a system of m equations in m variables. However, (5-10) contains no more than $(m - 1)$ independent equations.

The budget constraints of each of the n consumers are not equilibrium conditions, but are identities satisfied for any set of prices. Summing the budget constraints given by (5-4) for all consumers:

$$\sum_{i=1}^{n} \sum_{j=1}^{m} p_j E_{ij} = \sum_{j=1}^{m} p_j E_j = 0 \qquad (5\text{-}11)$$

since $E_j = \Sigma_{i=1}^{n} E_{ij}$. The aggregate form of the budget constraint is also an identity satisfied for any set of prices. This identity is called *Walras' law*. The equilibrium conditions require that every aggregate excess demand equal zero. Clearly if $E_j = 0$, the value of the excess demand for Q_j $(p_j E_j)$ must also equal zero. If the first $(m - 1)$ markets are in equilibrium, the aggregate value of their excess demands equals zero:

$$\sum_{j=1}^{m-1} p_j E_j = 0 \tag{5-12}$$

Subtracting (5-12) from (5-11),

$$\sum_{j=1}^{m} p_j E_j - \sum_{j=1}^{m-1} p_j E_j = p_m E_m = 0$$

It follows that $E_m = 0$, since $p_m \neq 0$. If equilibrium is attained in $(m - 1)$ markets, it is automatically attained in the mth.

Multimarket equilibrium is completely described by any $(m - 1)$ equations of (5-10). The addition of an mth equation which is dependent upon the other $(m - 1)$ adds no new information. Since equations of (5-10) are functionally dependent, their Jacobian is identically zero, and a locally unique solution does not exist for the p_j (see Sec. A-3). The inability to determine absolute price levels should not be a surprising result if it is remembered that consumers are interested only in exchange ratios in a barter-type economy.

Since the excess demand functions are homogeneous of degree zero in prices, the number of variables can be reduced to $(m - 1)$ by dividing the m absolute prices by the price of an arbitrarily selected commodity. If Q_1 is selected, (5-10) may be rewritten as

$$E_j = E_j \left(1, \frac{p_2}{p_1}, \cdots, \frac{p_m}{p_1} \right) \qquad j = 1, \ldots, m \tag{5-13}$$

The variables of (5-13) are the prices of the Q_j $(j \neq 1)$ relative to the price of Q_1, i.e., the exchange ratios relative to Q_1. Omit any one of the equations in (5-13) to obtain a system of $(m - 1)$ equations. This system of differentiable equations has a unique mathematical solution for the $(m - 1)$ price ratios if its Jacobian does not vanish in a small neighborhood. The mathematical solution is a multimarket equilibrium if it contains real, nonnegative price ratios and quantities. It is possible to construct specific multimarket systems that have equilibrium solutions, and it is possible to construct specific systems that do not. Through Sec. 5-3 attention is limited to systems for which equilibria exist. The conditions under which equilibrium solutions do and do not exist are considered in Sec. 5-4.

Once the equilibrium exchange ratios are determined from (5-13), the purchases and sales of each individual can be determined by substituting into the individual excess demand functions. However, a multimarket equilibrium can be determined directly without recourse to aggregate excess demand functions. The individual excess demand functions are homogeneous of degree zero in prices and can be written in the same form as (5-13):

$$E_{ij} = E_{ij}\left(1, \frac{p_2}{p_1}, \cdots, \frac{p_m}{p_1}\right) \quad \begin{array}{l} i = 1, \ldots, n \\ j = 1, \ldots, m \end{array} \qquad (5\text{-}14)$$

Now add the condition that every market must be cleared:

$$\sum_{i=1}^{n} E_{ij} = 0 \quad j = 1, \ldots, m \qquad (5\text{-}15)$$

The system formed by (5-14) and (5-15) contains $(mn + m)$ equations with the mn individual excess demands and the $(m - 1)$ exchange ratios as variables. As before, the system is functionally dependent and cannot be solved for absolute price levels.

TWO-COMMODITY EXCHANGE

The analysis of pure exchange can be illustrated through an example in which two commodities are exchanged by two individuals. Assume that individual I is endowed with 78 units of Q_1 and no Q_2, and that his utility function is

$$U_1 = q_{11}q_{12} + 2q_{11} + 5q_{12}$$

Substitute $q_{11} = E_{11} + 78$ and $q_{12} = E_{12}$ into his utility function and form the function

$$V_1 = (E_{11} + 78)E_{12} + 2(E_{11} + 78) + 5E_{12} - \lambda(p_1 E_{11} + p_2 E_{12})$$

Set the partial derivatives of V_1 equal to zero:

$$\frac{\partial V_1}{\partial E_{11}} = E_{12} + 2 - \lambda p_1 = 0$$

$$\frac{\partial V_1}{\partial E_{12}} = E_{11} + 83 - \lambda p_2 = 0$$

$$\frac{\partial V_1}{\partial \lambda} = -(p_1 E_{11} + p_2 E_{12}) = 0$$

The reader can verify that the second-order condition presented in Sec. 2-2 is satisfied.

Eliminating λ and solving the first-order conditions for E_{11} and E_{12}, I's excess demand functions are

$$E_{11} = \frac{p_2}{p_1} - 41.5 \qquad E_{12} = 41.5\frac{p_1}{p_2} - 1$$

His excess demands are functions of the commodity price ratio and are homogeneous of degree zero in prices. I's budget constraint is satisfied for any set of prices:

$$p_1 \left(\frac{p_2}{p_1} - 41.5 \right) + p_2 \left(41.5 \frac{p_1}{p_2} - 1 \right) = 0$$

The excess demand functions possess the usual properties. An increase of p_1 relative to p_2 will decrease E_{11} and increase E_{12}. An increase of p_2 relative to p_1 will increase E_{11} and decrease E_{12}.

Assume that II's utility function is

$$U_2 = q_{21}q_{22} + 4q_{21} + 2q_{22}$$

and that his endowment consists of 164 units of Q_2 and no Q_1. A derivation similar to that employed for I yields the excess demand functions

$$E_{21} = 84 \frac{p_2}{p_1} - 1 \qquad E_{22} = \frac{p_1}{p_2} - 84$$

II's budget constraint is always fulfilled, and his excess demands are homogeneous of degree zero in prices.

Invoking the condition that each market must be cleared

$$E_1 = E_{11} + E_{21} = 85 \frac{p_2}{p_1} - 42.5 = 0$$

$$E_2 = E_{12} + E_{22} = 42.5 \frac{p_1}{p_2} - 85 = 0$$

Either equation is sufficient for the determination of the equilibrium exchange ratio. Solving the first equation, $p_2/p_1 = 0.5$. Solving the second, $p_1/p_2 = 2$. The solutions are identical. In equilibrium 1 unit of Q_1 can be exchanged for 2 units of Q_2.

Substituting the equilibrium price ratio into the individual excess demand functions,

$$E_{11} = -41 \qquad E_{12} = 82 \qquad E_{21} = 41 \qquad E_{22} = -82$$

I gives 41 units of Q_1 to II in exchange for 82 units of Q_2.

THE EDGEWORTH BOX

A geometric picture of a two-person, two-commodity, pure-exchange economy is provided by the *Edgeworth box diagram*. Individual I's indifference map is pictured in the usual way with the origin, O_1, in the southwest corner. Three of his indifference curves are shown in Fig. 5-2a with $U_1^{(1)} < U_1^{(2)} < U_1^{(3)}$. Individual II's indifference-curve diagram is

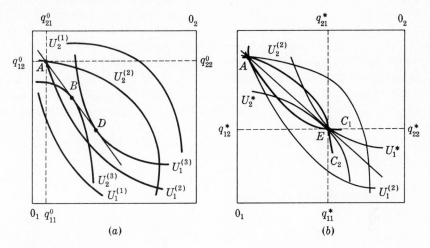

Fig. 5-2

rotated 180 degrees so that its origin, O_2, is in the northeast corner. The quantities q_{21} and q_{22} are measured from right to left and from top to bottom respectively as II moves away from his origin. Utility increases as he moves downward: $U_2^{(1)} < U_2^{(2)} < U_2^{(3)}$. The two indifference-curve diagrams are joined to form a "box" with a width equal to the sum of the two consumers' endowments of Q_1 and a height equal to the sum of their endowments of Q_2. Every point within the box and on its boundary describes a particular distribution of the fixed quantities of the two commodities. For example, O_2 describes the case in which I has all of both commodities.

Consider the initial endowments of q_{11}^0 and q_{12}^0 for I and q_{21}^0 and q_{22}^0 for II described by point A in Fig. 5-2a. The budget constraint for each consumer is represented by a line through A with a slope equal to the negative of the price ratio. Consider the budget line that passes through points B and D. Individual I would maximize his utility by exchanging Q_2 for Q_1 to move from A to D where his RCS equals the price ratio. Similarly, II would maximize his utility by exchanging Q_1 for Q_2 to move from A to B. This price ratio does not provide a multimarket equilibrium. The RCSs of the two consumers are equal, but I desires to buy more Q_1 than II desires to sell and desires to sell more Q_2 than II desires to buy.

An *offer curve* for I is the locus of the utility maximization points, such as D, that are obtained as the budget line is rotated about A to represent different price ratios. His offer curve is labeled C_1 in Fig. 5-2b. It passes through A since A would be his utility maximization point if the price ratio equalled the slope of his indifference curve at A. If the budget line were more steeply sloped, he would sell Q_1 and buy Q_2. If the budget line were less steeply sloped, he would buy Q_1 and sell Q_2. His offer curve lies above his initial indifference curve, $U_1^{(2)}$, except at A where the two coincide. Individual II's offer curve, labeled C_2, is constructed in an analogous manner. Point E in Fig. 5-2b where C_1 and C_2 intersect is a multimarket equilibrium. The equilibrium price ratio is given by the negative of the slope of the budget line passing through A and E. The equilibrium utility levels for I and II are U_1^* and U_2^* respectively. Consumer I trades $(q_{12}^0 - q_{12}^*)$ units of Q_2 to II in exchange for $(q_{21}^0 - q_{21}^*)$ units of Q_1.

5-2 PRODUCTION AND EXCHANGE

The multimarket equilibrium analysis is now extended to an economy in which goods are both produced and exchanged. The consumers' initial endowments consist of primary factors such as land and labor power. In addition all profits earned by firms are distributed to consumers. A consumer generally sells factors and uses the proceeds together with his profit income to purchase commodities. He may withhold a portion of his factor endowment for direct consumption. Labor power provides an example. The consumer will seldom supply the full amount of his labor power, but will generally reserve a portion for final consumption in the form of leisure. If a consumer possesses a factor from which he derives no utility, he will supply his entire endowment of that factor regardless of commodity and factor prices. Some consumers may sell one factor and purchase another. An example is provided by a landlord who employs domestic servants. Entrepreneurs use both factors and produced goods for the production of commodities. The produced commodities are useful both as inputs and final consumption goods.[1]

EQUILIBRIUM OF THE iTH CONSUMER

Each of the n consumers is endowed with initial stocks of one or more of s primary goods. The initial endowment of the ith consumer is denoted by $q_{i1}^0, q_{i2}^0, \ldots, q_{is}^0$. He may sell (and buy) at the prevailing market prices $(p_1, p_2, \ldots, p_s)$. The consumer derives utility from the quantities of the primary factors he retains and the quantities of the $(m - s)$ produced commodities he purchases:

$$U_i = U_i(q_{i1}, q_{i2}, \ldots, q_{im}) \qquad (5\text{-}16)$$

where the produced commodities are numbered from $(s + 1)$ through m.

---

[1] It is sometimes necessary to distinguish pure intermediate goods which are not desired by consumers. They are produced by entrepreneurs and used as inputs.

The consumer's excess demand for a factor equals the quantity he consumes less his initial stock, and his excess demand for a commodity equals the quantity he consumes:

$$E_{ij} = q_{ij} - q_{ij}^0 \qquad j = 1, \ldots, s$$
$$E_{ij} = q_{ij} \qquad\qquad j = s+1, \ldots, m \tag{5-17}$$

The excess demand for a factor may be positive, negative, or zero, but will most often be negative, since the consumer generally sells factors in order to buy commodities. His excess demands for commodities must be positive or zero. The consumer's income equals the value of his factor endowment plus his profit earnings:

$$y_i = \sum_{j=1}^{s} p_j q_{ij}^0 + \sum_{k=s+1}^{m} \sum_{h=1}^{N_k} \theta_{ihk}\pi_{hk} \tag{5-18}$$

where N_k is the number of firms producing the kth commodity, π_{hk} are the profits of the hth firm which produces the kth commodity, and $\theta_{ihk} \geqq 0$ is the ith consumer's proportionate share of these profits.[1]

The value of the factors and commodities that an individual consumes must also equal his income:

$$y_i = \sum_{j=1}^{m} p_j q_{ij} \tag{5-19}$$

The consumer's budget constraint is obtained by subtracting (5-18) from (5-19) and substituting from (5-17):

$$\sum_{j=1}^{m} p_j E_{ij} - \sum_{h=s+1}^{m} \sum_{k=1}^{N_k} \theta_{ihk}\pi_{hk} = 0 \tag{5-20}$$

The net value of his excess demands equals his profit earnings, or losses if negative.

The consumer again desires to maximize his utility level subject to his budget constraint. Form the function

$$Z_i = U_i(E_{i1} + q_{i1}^0, \ldots, E_{is} + q_{is}^0, E_{i,s+1}, \ldots, E_{im})$$
$$- \mu \Big(\sum_{j=1}^{m} p_j E_{ij} - \sum_{h=s+1}^{m} \sum_{k=1}^{N_k} \theta_{ihk}\pi_{hk} \Big)$$

and set the partial derivatives of Z_i equal to zero:

$$\frac{\partial Z_i}{\partial E_{ij}} = \frac{\partial U_i}{\partial E_{ij}} - \mu p_j = 0 \qquad j = 1, \ldots, m$$
$$\frac{\partial Z_i}{\partial \mu} = - \Big(\sum_{j=1}^{m} p_j E_{ij} - \sum_{h=s+1}^{m} \sum_{k=1}^{N_k} \theta_{ihk}\pi_{hk} \Big) = 0 \tag{5-21}$$

---

[1] It is assumed that each firm produces a single product. The indices of summation in (5-18) would have to be revised if firms produced joint products.

First-order conditions require that the consumer equate the RCS for every pair of goods to their price ratio.

Second-order conditions require that the appropriate determinants alternate in sign for a point at which (5-21) is satisfied:

$$
\begin{vmatrix} U_{11} & U_{12} & -p_1 \\ U_{21} & U_{22} & -p_2 \\ -p_1 & -p_2 & 0 \end{vmatrix} > 0, \quad
\begin{vmatrix} U_{11} & U_{12} & U_{13} & -p_1 \\ U_{21} & U_{22} & U_{23} & -p_2 \\ U_{31} & U_{32} & U_{33} & -p_3 \\ -p_1 & -p_2 & -p_3 & 0 \end{vmatrix} < 0,
$$

$$
\ldots, \; (-1)^m
\begin{vmatrix} U_{11} & U_{12} & \cdots & U_{1m} & -p_1 \\ U_{21} & U_{22} & \cdots & U_{2m} & -p_2 \\ \cdots & \cdots & \cdots & \cdots & \cdots \\ U_{m1} & U_{m2} & \cdots & U_{mm} & -p_m \\ -p_1 & -p_2 & \cdots & -p_m & 0 \end{vmatrix} > 0 \quad (5\text{-}22a)
$$

where $U_{jk} = \partial^2 U_i / \partial E_{ij} \, \partial E_{ik}$. Substituting $p_j = U_j / \mu$ $(j = 1, \ldots, m)$ from (5-21), where $U_j = \partial U_i / \partial E_{ij}$, multiplying the last row and column of each determinant of (5-22a) by $-\mu$, and omitting $1/\mu^2 > 0$, the conditions (5-22a) will be satisfied if

$$
\begin{vmatrix} U_{11} & U_{12} & U_1 \\ U_{21} & U_{22} & U_2 \\ U_1 & U_2 & 0 \end{vmatrix} > 0, \quad
\begin{vmatrix} U_{11} & U_{12} & U_{13} & U_1 \\ U_{21} & U_{22} & U_{23} & U_2 \\ U_{31} & U_{32} & U_{33} & U_3 \\ U_1 & U_2 & U_3 & 0 \end{vmatrix} < 0,
$$

$$
\ldots, \; (-1)^m
\begin{vmatrix} U_{11} & U_{12} & \cdots & U_{1m} & U_1 \\ U_{21} & U_{22} & \cdots & U_{2m} & U_2 \\ \cdots & \cdots & \cdots & \cdots & \cdots \\ U_{m1} & U_{m2} & \cdots & U_{mm} & U_m \\ U_1 & U_2 & \cdots & U_m & 0 \end{vmatrix} > 0 \quad (5\text{-}22b)
$$

If the second-order conditions are satisfied over a region, the consumer's excess demand functions for that region are obtained by solving (5-21) for the m excess demands, as functions of the profit levels in which he has an interest, and the m prices. It is shown below that profits may be expressed as functions of commodity and factor prices. Therefore, the ith consumer's excess demands may be expressed as functions of the prices alone:

$$
E_{ij} = E_{ij}(p_1, \ldots, p_m) \quad j = 1, \ldots, m \quad (5\text{-}23)
$$

Profits are homogeneous of degree one with respect to prices. It is easily verified that the consumer's excess demands are homogeneous of degree zero with respect to the prices of all commodities and factors.

EQUILIBRIUM OF THE hTH FIRM IN THE jTH INDUSTRY

Each firm combines inputs for the production of a single commodity according to the technical rules specified in its production function:[1]

$$\bar{q}_{hj} = f_{hj}(q^*_{hj1}, \ \ldots \ ,q^*_{hjm})$$

where $\bar{q}_{hj}$ is the output level of the hth firm in the jth industry and q^*_{hjk} is the quantity of the kth good which the entrepreneur uses as an input. Both the s factors and $(m - s)$ commodities serve as inputs.

The entrepreneur's profit is his competitive revenue less the cost of his inputs:

$$\pi_{hj} = p_j f_{hj}(q^*_{hj1}, \ \ldots \ ,q^*_{hjm}) - \sum_{k=1}^{m} p_k q^*_{hjk}$$

Setting the partial derivatives of profit with respect to each of the inputs equal to zero,

$$\frac{\partial \pi_{hj}}{\partial q^*_{hjk}} = p_j \frac{\partial \bar{q}_{hj}}{\partial q^*_{hjk}} - p_k = 0 \qquad k = 1, \ \ldots \ , m \tag{5-24}$$

The entrepreneur will utilize each input up to a point at which the value of its marginal physical productivity equals its price. The second-order conditions require that the principal minors of the relevant Hessian determinant alternate in sign:

$$f_{11} < 0, \begin{vmatrix} f_{11} & f_{12} \\ f_{21} & f_{22} \end{vmatrix} > 0, \ \ldots \ , (-1)^m \begin{vmatrix} f_{11} & \cdots & f_{1m} \\ \cdots & \cdots & \cdots \\ f_{m1} & \cdots & f_{mm} \end{vmatrix} > 0 \tag{5-25}$$

where $f_{ku} = \partial^2 \bar{q}_{hj}/\partial q^*_{hjk} \, \partial q^*_{hju}$. If the production function is strictly concave over a region, the second-order conditions (5-25) will be satisfied over that region (see Sec. A-3).

Conditions (5-24) imply that $\partial \bar{q}_{hj}/\partial q^*_{hjj} = 1$. If the entrepreneur utilizes his own output as an input—as a wheat farmer utilizes wheat for seed—he will utilize it up to a point at which its marginal physical productivity equals unity.

The entrepreneur's excess demand functions for his inputs for a strictly concave region of his production function are obtained by solving the m equations of (5-24) for $q^*_{hjk} = E^*_{hjk}$:

$$E^*_{hjk} = E^*_{hjk}(p_1, \ \ldots \ ,p_m) \qquad k = 1, \ \ldots \ , m \tag{5-26}$$

---

[1] Production is sometimes introduced with the alternative assumption that each firm jointly produces all commodities.

The quantity of each input he purchases is a function of all prices. Since the entrepreneur never supplies (sells) inputs, his excess demands are always nonnegative.

If the jth industry contains N_j identical firms, its aggregate excess demand for the kth input equals the excess demand of a representative firm multiplied by the number of firms within the industry:

$$E_{jk}^* = N_j E_{hjk}^*(p_1, \ldots, p_m) = E_{jk}^*(p_1, \ldots, p_m, N_j) \qquad (5\text{-}27)$$

An industry's excess demand for an input is a function of all prices and the number of firms within the industry.

The entrepreneur's excess demand for (supply of) his own output is determined by substituting the excess demand functions for his inputs (5-26) into his production function and letting $\bar{E}_{hj} = -\bar{q}_{hj}$:†

$$\bar{E}_{hj} = -f_{hj}[E_{hj1}^*(p_1, \ldots, p_m), \ldots, E_{hjm}^*(p_1, \ldots, p_m)]$$

or more simply

$$\bar{E}_{hj} = \bar{E}_{hj}(p_1, \ldots, p_m)$$

The excess demand for the industry as a whole equals the excess demand of a representative firm multiplied by the number of firms:

$$\bar{E}_j = N_j \bar{E}_{hj}(p_1, \ldots, p_m) = \bar{E}_j(p_1, \ldots, p_m, N_j) \qquad (5\text{-}28)$$

The industry's excess demand depends upon the prices of all goods and the number of firms within the industry.

The entrepreneur's excess demand functions for his output and inputs are homogeneous of degree zero in all prices. If all prices are changed by the factor $t > 0$, profit becomes

$$\pi_{hj} = t p_j f_{hj}(q_{hj1}^*, \ldots, q_{hjm}^*) - \sum_{k=1}^{m} t p_k q_{hjk}^*$$

Setting the partial derivatives equal to zero,

$$\frac{\partial \pi_{hj}}{\partial q_{hjk}^*} = t p_j \frac{\partial \bar{q}_{hj}}{\partial q_{hjk}^*} - t p_k = 0 \qquad k = 1, \ldots, m$$

or

$$t \left(p_j \frac{\partial \bar{q}_{hj}}{\partial q_{hjk}^*} - p_k \right) = 0 \qquad k = 1, \ldots, m$$

Since $t \neq 0$,

$$p_j \frac{\partial \bar{q}_{hj}}{\partial q_{hjk}^*} - p_k = 0 \qquad k = 1, \ldots, m$$

† Separate excess demand functions are defined for Q_j as an output and as an input. The two could be combined into a single net excess demand without affecting the analysis.

The first-order conditions from which the excess demands are obtained can be stated in a form identical with (5-24). Since the second-order conditions also remain unchanged, the excess demands are unaffected by a proportionate change of all prices.

MARKET EQUILIBRIUM

The excess demand functions of the consumers and entrepreneurs can be aggregated for both types of goods. The aggregate excess demand for a factor is the sum of the excess demands of the n consumers (5-23) and the $(m - s)$ industries on input account (5-27):

$$E_j = \sum_{i=1}^{n} E_{ij}(p_1, \ldots, p_m)$$

$$+ \sum_{k=s+1}^{m} E^*_{kj}(p_1, \ldots, p_m, N_k) \qquad j = 1, \ldots, s \quad (5\text{-}29)$$

The aggregate excess demand for a commodity is the sum of the excess demands by the n consumers (5-23), the $(m - s)$ industries on input account (5-27), and its producers (5-28):

$$E_j = \sum_{i=1}^{n} E_{ij}(p_1, \ldots, p_m) + \sum_{k=s+1}^{m} E^*_{kj}(p_1, \ldots, p_m, N_k)$$

$$+ \bar{E}_j(p_1, \ldots, p_m, N_j) \qquad j = s + 1, \ldots, m \quad (5\text{-}30)$$

The aggregate excess demands given by (5-29) and (5-30) can be stated simply as

$$E_j = E_j(p_1, \ldots, p_m, N_{s+1}, \ldots, N_m) \qquad j = 1, \ldots, m$$

The excess demand for each good is a function of the m prices and the numbers of firms within the $(m - s)$ producing industries.

It is assumed that a short-run equilibrium price can be determined for any of the m markets considered in isolation from the other $(m - 1)$ markets by setting the aggregate excess demand for the good under consideration equal to zero. In the short run the number of firms in the industry as well as the prices of the other $(m - 1)$ goods and the numbers of firms within the other $(m - s - 1)$ industries are treated as parameters. Utility, production, and excess demand functions are defined for a longer period of time in a long-run analysis. In addition, the number of firms within the industry is a variable in the determination of a long-run equilibrium for a commodity market. Excess demand and profit are both set equal to zero, and the resultant two equations are solved for profit and the number of firms. Short- and long-run equilibrium prices are nonnegative and generate consumption and production quantities within the region for which the excess demand functions are defined.

WALRAS' LAW

Expressing the profit of the hth firm in the jth industry in terms of excess demands and rearranging terms,

$$p_j \bar{E}_{hj} + \sum_{k=1}^{m} p_k E_{hjk}^* + \pi_{hj} = 0 \tag{5-31}$$

The net value of a firm's excess demands equals the negative of its profit. Summing (5-20) over all consumers and (5-31) over all producers yields the result

$$\sum_{j=1}^{m} p_j E_j = 0$$

Thus, Walras' law holds as an identity for any set of prices in the production and exchange system. The existence of positive profits does not affect this result. Total profits appear as a negative term in the aggregation of (5-20) and as a positive term in the aggregation of (5-31).

MULTIMARKET EQUILIBRIUM

A long-run multimarket equilibrium requires that every market be cleared and that profit equal zero in every industry:[1]

$$\begin{aligned}
E_j(p_1, \ldots, p_m, N_{s+1}, \ldots, N_m) &= 0 \qquad j = 1, \ldots, m \\
\pi_j(p_1, \ldots, p_m) &= 0 \qquad j = s+1, \ldots, m
\end{aligned}$$

$$\tag{5-32}$$

where π_j is the profit of a representative firm in the jth industry. Again Walras' law results in a functional dependence among the excess demands, and it is not possible to solve (5-32) for absolute price levels.

Equilibrium again is defined in terms of relative, rather than absolute, prices. Since the excess demands of every consumer and producer are homogeneous of degree zero in prices, the aggregate excess demands are homogeneous of degree zero in prices. The profits of each entrepreneur are homogeneous of degree one in prices. If all prices are doubled, the entrepreneur's input and output levels will remain unchanged, but his total revenue and total cost, and hence his profit, will be doubled. However, if a long-run equilibrium is established for one set of prices, the system will remain in equilibrium if all prices are changed by the same proportion. A doubling of all prices will leave the excess demands

[1] The profit equations are omitted and the numbers of firms are assumed predetermined for a short-run multimarket equilibrium analysis.

equal to zero. The representative firms' revenues and costs will be doubled, but profit levels will remain equal to zero, and no new firms will be induced to enter any industry.

The number of variables in (5-32) can be reduced by one by dividing the m absolute prices by the price of an arbitrarily selected commodity. If Q_1 is selected, (5-32) can be rewritten as

$$E_j\left(1, \frac{p_2}{p_1}, \ldots, \frac{p_m}{p_1}, N_{s+1}, \ldots, N_m\right) = 0 \qquad j = 1, \ldots, m$$

$$ \tag{5-33}$$

$$\pi_j\left(1, \frac{p_2}{p_1}, \ldots, \frac{p_m}{p_1}\right) = 0 \qquad j = s+1, \ldots, m$$

It is assumed that this system contains $(2m - s - 1)$ independent equations that can be solved for the equilibrium values of the $(m - 1)$ exchange ratios relative to Q_1 and the $(m - s)$ firm numbers. The equilibrium values of the variables are all nonnegative.

Once the equilibrium exchange ratios and firm numbers are determined, the excess demands of every consumer and entrepreneur can be computed by substituting their values into the individual excess demand functions. A long-run equilibrium solution satisfies the following conditions: (1) every consumer maximizes utility, (2) every entrepreneur maximizes profit, (3) every market is cleared, and (4) every entrepreneur earns a zero profit. The equilibrium values of the individual consumption and production levels are within the regions for which the individual excess demand functions are defined.

5-3 THE NUMERAIRE, MONEY, AND SAY'S LAW

General equilibrium has been established in Secs. 5-1 and 5-2 for barter-type economies in which circulating money is nonexistent. Commodities and factors are exchanged for other commodities and factors, and the conditions of exchange are completely described by exchange ratios. These systems have been solved for the $(m - 1)$ exchange ratios relative to an arbitrarily selected good, generally called the numéraire. Any set of absolute prices that yields the equilibrium exchange ratios is an equilibrium solution. If there is one such solution, there is an infinite number.

A number of different kinds of money can be introduced into a general equilibrium system. One good may be selected as a standard of value and serve as money in the sense that all prices are expressed in terms of its units. Money can be established as an abstract unit of account which serves as a standard of value but does not circulate. Under some circumstances circulating paper money can be introduced.

Under different circumstances an attempt to introduce paper money leads to a contradiction.

THE NUMÉRAIRE

For m goods there are m^2 exchange ratios taking two commodities at a time: p_j/p_k (j, $k = 1, \ldots ,m$). Of these m are identities which state that the exchange ratio of a good for itself equals unity: $p_j/p_k = 1$ for $j = k$. The m^2 exchange ratios are not independent. Consider the identity and the $(m - 1)$ exchange ratios with Q_1 as numéraire. The other $m(m - 1)$ exchange ratios and identities can be derived from these:

$$\frac{p_j}{p_k} = \frac{p_j}{p_1} : \frac{p_k}{p_1} \qquad j, k = 1, \ldots , m \tag{5-34}$$

Imagine that Q_1 is pears, Q_2 oranges, and Q_3 apples, and that two oranges exchange for one pear ($p_2/p_1 = 0.5$) and one apple for two pears ($p_3/p_1 = 2$). Utilizing (5-34), four oranges will exchange for one apple: $p_3/p_2 = 4$. The complete set of exchange ratios is given either directly or indirectly by the $(m - 1)$ exchange ratios and the identity for the numéraire.

The numéraire can be changed from Q_1 to Q_k by dividing the exchange ratios and identity for Q_1 by p_k/p_1:

$$\frac{1}{p_k/p_1} \left(1, \frac{p_2}{p_1}, \ldots , \frac{p_k}{p_1}, \ldots , \frac{p_m}{p_1} \right) = \left(\frac{p_1}{p_k}, \frac{p_2}{p_k}, \ldots , 1, \ldots , \frac{p_m}{p_k} \right)$$

The exchange ratios are unaffected by this transformation, and the selection of the numéraire is truly arbitrary.

The numéraire can also serve as a standard of value. Setting its price identically equal to unity, the exchange ratios become $p_j/p_1 = p_j$. The equilibrium exchange ratios are unaffected by this transformation. The equilibrium price of each good is expressed as the number of units of the numéraire which must be exchanged to obtain 1 unit of that good. The price of oranges becomes 0.5 pears per orange, and the price of apples 2 pears per apple. The price of apples is four times as great as the price of oranges, and one apple still exchanges for four oranges in equilibrium. The numéraire has become money in the sense that its units serve as a standard of value. However, it does not serve as a store of value, since it is desired only as a productive factor or consumable commodity on the same basis as all other goods. Any good may serve as a standard of value in this sense.

The expression of prices in terms of a good such as pears is not common practice. Prices are generally expressed in terms of a monetary unit such as dollars. An accounting money is easily introduced into the framework of a general equilibrium system. There is no reason why the price of the numéraire should equal unity. It could be set equal to 2, $\sqrt{2}$, 25, or 200 million. The equilibrium exchange ratios would be unaffected. Accounting money can be introduced by setting the price of the numéraire (or any other good) equal to a specified number of monetary units. Money prices can then be derived for all other goods. If Q_1 is numéraire and p_1 is set equal to β dollars, the dollar price of Q_k (ρ_k) is

$$\rho_k = \beta \frac{p_k}{p_1} \qquad k = 2, \ldots, m$$

If the price of a pear is set equal to 2 dollars, the price of an orange is 1 dollar and the price of an apple 4 dollars. In this case money only serves as an abstract unit of account. It does not exist in a physical sense. Goods still exchange for goods. No one holds money, and no one desires to hold money. Accounting money serves as a standard, but not a store, of value.[1]

It is sometimes convenient to normalize prices by defining a unit of account such that $\Sigma_{i=1}^{m} p_i = 1$. In this case a composite of all factors and commodities, rather than a single good, serves as a valuation base. The composite definition avoids the difficulties that would arise if a pre-selected numéraire factor or commodity were a free good in equilibrium (see Sec. 5-4).

MONETARY EQUILIBRIUM

Commodity money and accounting money are quite different from circulating money which serves as a store of value. The classical economists of the nineteenth century frequently divided the economy into two sectors with regard to equilibrium price determination: the real sector in which exchange ratios are determined, and the monetary sector in which absolute money prices are determined by the quantity of money in existence. The real sector is described in Secs. 5-1 and 5-2. The present task is to add the monetary sector to this analysis. For simplicity the analysis is developed for the case of pure exchange though it is easily extended to cover production and exchange.

Assume that the n consumers also possess initial stocks of paper money denoted by the subscript $(m + 1)$: $(q_{1,m+1}^0, \ldots, q_{n,m+1}^0)$. Paper money serves as a store of value, but does not enter the consumers'

---

[1] The assumption that money is only a unit of account is implicit throughout the analyses of the consumer and entrepreneur. The consumer's income may be expressed in monetary units, but he spends his entire income and does not desire to hold money. The entrepreneur maximizes his money profit, but he also has no desire to hold money. If he earns a positive profit, he will spend it in his role as a consumer.

utility functions. The ith consumer's excess demand for paper money is defined as the stock he desires to hold less his initial stock:

$$E_{i,m+1} = q_{i,m+1} - q_{i,m+1}^0 \tag{5-35}$$

His excess demand is positive if he adds to his initial stock of money and negative if he reduces it. The consumer's budget constraint (5-4) must be redefined to include money:

$$\sum_{j=1}^{m+1} p_j E_{ij} = 0 \tag{5-36}$$

where p_j is the price of the jth commodity. The price of money p_{m+1} equals unity by definition. The consumer may exchange money for commodities or commodities for money. If his excess demand for money is positive, the value of the commodities he sells is greater than the value of those he buys, and he is exchanging commodities for money.

Since money does not enter the consumer's utility function, his excess demand for money cannot be determined by the principles of utility maximization. It is usually assumed that the consumer finds it convenient to hold money in order to facilitate commodity transactions. Assume that the ith consumer desires to hold a quantity of money which is a fixed proportion of the monetary value of his initial endowment of commodities:

$$q_{i,m+1} = \alpha_i \sum_{j=1}^{m} p_j q_{ij}^0 \tag{5-37}$$

where α_i is a constant. Substituting (5-37) into (5-35),

$$E_{i,m+1} = \alpha_i \sum_{j=1}^{m} p_j q_{ij}^0 - q_{i,m+1}^0 \tag{5-38}$$

The aggregate excess demand for money is obtained by summing (5-38) for all n consumers:

$$E_{m+1} = \alpha \sum_{i=1}^{n} \sum_{j=1}^{m} p_j q_{ij}^0 - \sum_{i=1}^{n} q_{i,m+1}^0 = E_{m+1}(p_1, \ldots, p_m) \tag{5-39}$$

No essentials are lost by assuming that $\alpha_i = \alpha$ for $i = 1, \ldots, n$. If the initial endowments of commodities and money are fixed, the excess demand for money is a function of the m commodity prices.

The excess demand functions for the m commodities are determined by maximizing utility for each consumer subject to his budget constraint, including money, solving the first-order conditions in order to obtain individual excess demand functions, and then summing for all consumers.

A general equilibrium is established if the excess demand for each commodity and money equals zero:

$$E_j(p_1, \ldots ,p_m) = 0 \qquad j = 1, \ldots , m + 1 \tag{5-40}$$

This gives a system of $(m + 1)$ equations in the m variable commodity prices. By Walras' law functional dependence exists among the $(m + 1)$ excess demand functions. If the m commodity markets were in equilibrium, the money market would also be in equilibrium; i.e., consumers as a whole would not desire to exchange commodities for money or money for commodities. The quantity of money that consumers desired to hold would equal the quantity in existence. It is assumed that (5-40) contains m independent equations that can be solved for the equilibrium money prices of the m commodities.

The excess demands for commodities and money are not homogeneous of degree zero in commodity prices. If all commodity prices are increased by the factor $t > 0$, the excess demand for money (5-39) becomes

$$E_{m+1} = \alpha \sum_{i=1}^{n} \sum_{j=1}^{m} tp_j q_{ij}^0 - \sum_{i=1}^{n} q_{i,m+1}^0 \tag{5-41}$$

The partial derivative of (5-41) with respect to t is

$$\frac{\partial E_{m+1}}{\partial t} = \alpha \sum_{i=1}^{n} \sum_{j=1}^{m} p_j q_{ij}^0 > 0$$

A proportionate increase of all commodity prices will increase the excess demand for money. If the system is in equilibrium before the price increase, consumers will desire to exchange commodities for money in order to bring their monetary stocks into the desired relation with the monetary values of their initial endowments of commodities. However, there will not be a corresponding negative excess demand for commodities. Any proportionate change of the equilibrium commodity prices will throw the system out of equilibrium.

The excess demands for commodities and money are homogeneous of degree zero in commodity prices and initial money stocks. The excess demand for money becomes

$$E_{m+1} = \alpha \sum_{i=1}^{n} \sum_{j=1}^{m} tp_j q_{ij}^0 - \sum_{i=1}^{n} tq_{i,m+1}^0$$

and

$$\frac{\partial E_{m+1}}{\partial t} = \alpha \sum_{i=1}^{n} \sum_{j=1}^{m} p_j q_{ij}^0 - \sum_{i=1}^{n} q_{i,m+1}^0$$

which equals zero if the money market was in equilibrium before the price change.   Each consumer's money stock retains the desired relation to the value of his commodity endowment, and he will not desire to exchange commodities for money or money for commodities.

It can also be demonstrated that a change of the money stock of each consumer by the factor t will result in a change of the money price of each commodity by the same factor, but will leave the real sector unaffected. If equilibrium has been established and then each money stock is increased by the factor t, each consumer will desire to exchange money for commodities, but no one will desire to exchange commodities for money.   As a result commodity prices will increase until the existing stocks of money no longer exceed the stocks that consumers desire to hold.

Monetary equilibrium will be reestablished when the values of all commodity stocks are increased by the factor t

$$\sum_{i=1}^{n} \sum_{j=1}^{m} \rho_j q_{ij}^0 = t \sum_{i=1}^{n} \sum_{j=1}^{m} p_j q_{ij}^0 \tag{5-42}$$

where ρ_j is the price of the jth commodity after equilibrium has been reestablished.   Proportionate increases of all commodity prices: $\rho_j = t p_j$ $(j = 1, \ldots, m)$, will satisfy (5-42), but so will many other price constellations.   Consider a nonproportionate set of price changes which satisfies (5-42).   It follows that $\rho_h = u p_h$ and $\rho_k = v p_k$ where $u > t > v$ for some h and k.   The exchange ratio between Q_h and Q_k is now $u p_h / v p_k > p_h / p_k$. The price of Q_h has increased relative to the price of Q_k, and consumers will desire to exchange Q_h for Q_k.   If the system was in equilibrium at the initial exchange ratio, the new exchange ratio will result in a positive aggregate excess demand for Q_k and a negative aggregate excess demand for Q_h.   The aggregate excess demands for all commodities will equal zero if and only if $\rho_h / \rho_k = p_h / p_k$ for $h, k = 1, \ldots, m$.   This is consistent with monetary equilibrium if and only if $\rho_j = t p_j$ $(j = 1, \ldots, m)$. The dichotomization of equilibrium price determination is complete. Equilibrium exchange ratios are determined by the consumers' utility functions and the real values of their initial endowments.   Money prices are determined by the quantity of money.

The introduction of circulating paper money into a static general equilibrium system is possible, but rather artificial.   Equation (5-37) postulates a mode of behavior that is logically, though not mathematically, inconsistent with utility maximization: the consumer desires to hold a stock of money from which he derives no utility rather than spend it on commodities from which he does.   It is difficult to find motives for holding money in a static system that is in no way connected with preceding or succeeding points in time.   The interesting problems of money only arise in a dynamic analysis in which behavior is considered over time.

SAY'S LAW

The classical economists frequently denied the possibility of a positive excess demand for all commodities. In terms of the present analysis this can be interpreted as the statement that

$$\sum_{j=1}^{m} p_j E_j = 0 \tag{5-43}$$

where the excess demand for all commodities is measured in monetary terms. This proposition has become known as Say's law in honor of its promulgator, the nineteenth-century French economist Jean Baptiste Say. Unfortunately, Say did not use mathematics and was vague regarding the conditions under which his law applies. Some twentieth-century economists have interpreted it as an equilibrium condition, and others as an identity that holds regardless of whether or not the system is in equilibrium. The quantity of money will determine the absolute price level if (5-43) is an equilibrium condition, but will not if it is an identity.

Monetary equilibrium has been established for the case in which Walras' law (5-36) is the relevant identity. It holds for all commodities and money, and (5-43) is an equilibrium condition. In equilibrium, consumers do not desire to exchange money for commodities or commodities for money.

If (5-43) is an identity, consumers will never desire to exchange money for commodities or commodities for money. This implies that the excess demand for money is identically equal to zero:

$$E_{m+1} \equiv 0 \tag{5-44}$$

Regardless of commodity prices consumers will never desire to increase or decrease their money stocks. This implied behavior is inconsistent with the introduction of quantity equations, such as (5-37), which state that the consumers' excess demands for money depend upon commodity prices. Therefore, the quantity of money cannot serve to determine absolute price levels. If (5-43) is an identity, equilibrium in $(m-1)$ of the commodity markets ensures equilibrium in the mth. The general equilibrium system contains at most $(m-1)$ independent equations to be solved for $(m-1)$ exchange ratios. The statement that the money market is always in equilibrium adds no useful information, and absolute prices are indeterminate. The crucial point in considering Say's law and money is whether or not money is included in the consumers' budget constraints. If it is, (5-43) is an equilibrium condition. If it is not, (5-43) is an identity.

5-4 THE EXISTENCE OF EQUILIBRIUM

The mere formulation of a multimarket system gives no assurance of the existence of an equilibrium solution. Some systems have no mathematical solution; others have many. The existence of a mathematical solution may not be adequate. Economics places bounds upon the admissible values for the variables. Prices must be given by nonnegative,[1] real numbers. Furthermore, the consumption levels of each consumer and the input and output levels of each firm must be nonnegative. A mathematical solution which contains, for example, negative consumption levels is meaningless.

The question of the existence of an admissible solution may be considered on two different levels. One may desire to determine whether or not a particular numerically implemented multimarket system possesses an equilibrium solution. On a more general level one may desire to prove an existence theorem which states that equilibrium solutions exist for all multimarket systems that satisfy a number of general assumptions.

This section begins with a discussion of existence for particular sets of excess demand functions. Attention is then turned to the general problem of existence for a short-run version of the production and exchange system presented in Sec. 5-2. First, restrictions are placed upon individual utility and production functions that ensure the existence of appropriate individual and aggregate excess demand functions. Next, the mathematical techniques underlying Brouwer's fixed-point theorem are introduced. This theorem is then used to prove that multimarket equilibria exist for all systems with utility and production functions that conform to the stated restrictions. Finally, Debreu's more advanced existence theorem based upon more general restrictions is outlined.

---

[1] If the price of a commodity were negative, purchasing power would be transferred from sellers to buyers rather than from buyers to sellers. Negative prices are not always nonsensical. The possession of discommodities such as garbage will reduce a consumer's utility level, and he will generally be willing to pay for their removal. The possibility of meaningful negative prices is eliminated by centering attention upon the commodity counterparts of discommodities. The consumer may be considered to buy garbage-removal service rather than sell garbage, and the garbage collector may be considered to sell garbage-removal service rather than buy garbage. The price of garbage-removal service is positive and equal in absolute value to the negative price of garbage.

SOLUTIONS FOR PARTICULAR SYSTEMS

A locally univalent solution of N differentiable equations in N variables exists if its Jacobian does not vanish in a small neighborhood (see Sec. A-3). The system of m equations obtained by setting the excess demands equal to zero cannot be solved for the absolute values of the m prices. Since the aggregate budget constraint is always satisfied, the excess demands are functionally dependent, and their Jacobian vanishes identically. The nonexistence of a locally unique solution for absolute prices is meaningful from the economic viewpoint, since the excess demands are homogeneous of degree zero in all prices.

By letting $p_1 = 1$ and omitting the excess demand equation for Q_1 the system is reduced to $(m - 1)$ equations in $(m - 1)$ variable prices. Thus far, it has been assumed that these equations are independent and a univalent solution exists for the reduced system. This assumption is not necessarily true. Consider the three-commodity reduced system given by

$$E_2 = -2p_2 - 4p_3 + 10 = 0$$
$$E_3 = -3p_2 - 6p_3 + 15 = 0$$

The Jacobian of this system vanishes identically, and it cannot be solved for unique values of p_2 and p_3. The excess demand functions for Q_2 and Q_3 are not independent. The functional dependence in this case is $E_3 = 1.5E_2$. Society as a whole always demands and supplies Q_2 and Q_3 in a fixed proportion. Any set of values for p_2 and p_3 which satisfies $p_2 = 5 - 2p_3$ will result in multimarket equilibrium. Examples are $p_2 = 1$, $p_3 = 2$, and $p_2 = 3$, $p_3 = 1$. In this case the Jacobian test states that a locally univalent solution does not exist, but it provides no aid in determining that other solutions do exist.

A system that passes the Jacobian test has a unique mathematical solution, but its solution might contain negative prices or imply negative consumption and production levels for some market participants, and not be admissible as a multimarket equilibrium. Each numerical multimarket system may be treated individually. First apply the nonvanishing Jacobian condition to determine whether a locally unique mathematical solution exists. If one does, attempt to solve the system and examine its solution(s) from the viewpoint of admissibility. If the Jacobian of the system vanishes, one must apply whatever methods appear appropriate in the particular circumstances to determine whether or not equilibrium solutions exist.

BROUWER'S FIXED-POINT THEOREM

The solution method proposed for particular systems is not helpful for a consideration of existence for abstract multimarket systems that are not numerically implemented. In this case it is necessary to prove an existence theorem which states that all multimarket systems satisfying stated assumptions possess equilibrium solutions. Most existence proofs rest on one or another of a class of mathematical theorems called fixed-point theorems. Brouwer's fixed-point theorem is one of the least difficult of those used in economics. The mathematical techniques upon which it is based are discussed now.

A *point-to-point mapping* in n-dimensional space is a rule or set of rules which associates a point in n-dimensional space with some other point in this space. Let (x_1, x_2) denote a point in two-dimensional space, and let (x'_1, x'_2) denote its associated point. The rules $x'_1 = x_1 + x_2$ and $x'_2 = x_1^2 x_2$ provide an example of a mapping in two-dimensional space. Both x'_1 and x'_2 may be expressed as functions of x_1 and x_2. In general, a mapping in n-dimensional space may be written as

$$x'_i = f_i(x_1, \ldots, x_n) \qquad i = 1, \ldots, n$$

or in more compact notation it may be written as $\mathbf{x}' = F(\mathbf{x})$ where $\mathbf{x} = (x_1, \ldots, x_n)$ and $\mathbf{x}' = (x'_1, \ldots, x'_n)$. This is analogous to the way in which functions are denoted, except that $\mathbf{x}$ and $\mathbf{x}'$ represent points with n coordinates rather than single numbers. The point $\mathbf{x}'$ is called the *image* of point $\mathbf{x}$. A mapping is *continuous* if each of the functions $f_i(\mathbf{x})$ $(i = 1, \ldots, n)$ composing it is continuous.

A mapping may be defined for some subset of points in its coordinate space. For example, the mapping $F(\mathbf{x})$ may be defined only for points lying on a circle with center at the origin and radius equal to unity, i.e., for points the coordinates of which satisfy $x_1^2 + x_2^2 = 1$. A mapping is *into itself* if the associated points also lie in the point set for which the mapping is defined. The following functions provide an example of a mapping of the set of points lying on the unit circle into itself:[1]

$$x'_1 = \frac{x_1}{\sqrt{(x_1^2 + x_2^2)}} \qquad x'_2 = \frac{x_2}{\sqrt{(x_1^2 + x_2^2)}}$$

A point set is *convex* if every point on a straight-line segment connecting any two points in the set is also in the set. The point set formed by the circumference of a circle is not convex since a line segment joining two distinct points in the set contains points inside the circle which are not in the set. The point set formed by the circumference and interior of a circle is convex.

---

[1] If $F(\mathbf{x})$ were defined for all points in two-dimensional space, the mapping would carry two-dimensional space into the unit circle and would not be into itself.

A point set in n-dimensional space is *bounded from above* if there exists a set of n finite numbers $\mathbf{x}^* = (x_1^*, \ldots, x_n^*)$ such that $x_i^* \geqq x_i$ for all $\mathbf{x} = (x_1, \ldots, x_n)$ in the set. It is *bounded from below* if there exists a set of n finite numbers $\mathbf{x}^0 = (x_1^0, \ldots, x_n^0)$ such that $x_i^0 \leqq x_i$ for all $\mathbf{x} = (x_1, \ldots, x_n)$ in the set. A *bounded* set is bounded from both above and below. The point set formed by the circumference of a circle is bounded, but the point set formed by the positive quadrant of the coordinate space is not.

A point set is *closed* if, whenever every point of a convergent infinite sequence is in the set, the limit point of that sequence is also in the set.[1] The point set defined by $0 < x < 1$ is not closed because every point in the infinite sequence $\frac{1}{2}$, $\frac{1}{3}$, $\frac{1}{4}$, $\ldots$, $1/n$, $\ldots$ is in the set, but the limit of the sequence, zero, is not. The point set defined by $0 \leqq x \leqq 1$ is closed.

Brouwer's fixed-point theorem states that *a continuous mapping of a closed, bounded, convex set into itself has a fixed point;* i.e., if $F(\mathbf{x})$ is the mapping, there exists a point $\mathbf{x}^*$ in the set on which the mapping is defined such that $\mathbf{x}^* = F(\mathbf{x}^*)$. At least one point gets mapped into itself. Consider as an example the mapping $F(x)$ shown in Fig. 5-3. The mapping is defined in the interval $0 \leqq x \leqq 1$ which is a closed, bounded, and convex set of points on the real line. The mapping is also continuous. Hence, there must be at least one point where the graph of $F(x)$ intersects a 45-degree line through the origin. Point A in Fig. 5-3 is such an intersection with the property that $x^* = F(x^*)$.

An illustrative existence proof using Brouwer's fixed-point theorem is now formulated for a short-run version of the multimarket system

[1] A different, but equivalent, definition of a closed point set is given in Sec. 9-2.

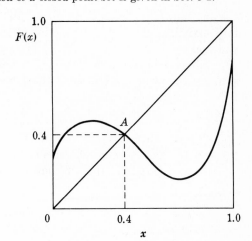

Fig. 5-3

developed in Sec. 5-2.   In this context short run means that the number of firms in each industry is predetermined, and the profits of individual firms need not equal zero.   The proof proceeds in two stages.   First, the existence of aggregate excess demand functions with suitable properties is proved.   Second, the existence of equilibrium prices satisfying these functions is proved.

THE EXISTENCE OF EXCESS DEMAND FUNCTIONS

The typical ith consumer is assumed to be endowed with stocks of each of s primary goods.   He may sell portions of these stocks and buy the s primary and $(m - s)$ produced goods in competitive markets at nonnegative prices.   He selects a consumption bundle that maximizes his utility subject to his budget constraint, which requires that the value of his consumption bundle equal the value of his initial primary-goods stocks plus his share of profits from production.   For simplicity it is assumed that he receives profits from at least one firm in each industry.   His utility function is defined for nonnegative consumption levels.   It is continuous and has continuous first- and second-order partial derivatives.   It is assumed that the utility function also has the following properties for $q_{ij} > 0$ $(j = 1, \ldots ,m)$: (1) it is strictly concave or has a monotonic transformation that is (2) $\partial U_i/\partial q_{ij} > 0$ $(j = 1, \ldots ,m)$, and (3) $U_i = U_i^0$, where U_i^0 is a constant, if $q_{ij} = 0$ for any j, and $U_i > U_i^0$ if $q_{ij} > 0$ for all j. Restriction (1) ensures a decreasing RCS between every pair of goods. Restriction (2) implies that the consumer can always increase utility by increasing his consumption of any good.   Restriction (3) extends the definition of the utility function to cover zero consumption levels for one or more goods.   It rules out the possibility of corner solutions similar to the one shown in Fig. 2-4b which violate the familiar marginal conditions for maximization.   This restriction is not necessary in more advanced analyses.

Single-valued excess demand functions will exist for the ith consumer if the principal minors of the Jacobian $(\mathbf{J})$ of (5-21):

$$\mathbf{J} = \begin{vmatrix} U_{11} & \cdots & U_{1m} & -p_1 \\ \cdots\cdots\cdots\cdots\cdots\cdots \\ U_{m1} & \cdots & U_{mm} & -p_m \\ -p_1 & \cdots & -p_m & 0 \end{vmatrix}$$

alternate in sign (see Nikaido, *Convex Structures*, chap. VII).   Restriction (1) guarantees that the minors will have the correct signs within the domain of the utility function.   Restrictions (2) and (3) ensure that the first-order conditions will be fulfilled with all consumption levels positive if all prices are positive.[1] Thus, single-valued excess demand functions of the form

$$E_{ij} = E_{ij}(p_1, \ldots, p_m) \qquad j = 1, \ldots, m \qquad (5\text{-}45)$$

exist for the ith consumer. These functions are continuous and homogeneous of degree zero in prices.

It is convenient to limit attention to price combinations that lie within the normalized price set, i.e., numbers $(p_1, \ldots, p_m)$ which satisfy

$$\sum_{j=1}^{m} p_j = 1 \qquad p_j \geqq 0 \qquad (5\text{-}46)$$

Since the excess demand functions considered here are homogeneous of degree zero in prices, no generality is lost by limiting attention to the normalized price set (see Sec. 5-3).[2]

The excess demand functions (5-45) have the domain $p_k > 0$ $(k = 1, \ldots, m)$. They do not directly accommodate zero prices. The restrictions placed upon the utility functions imply that $E_{ij} \to \infty$ as $p_j \to 0$. The application of Brouwer's fixed-point theorem that will be used to prove the existence of equilibrium prices requires that finite excess demands be generated by zero prices. This requirement can be met by the use of an artifice. Define the numbers k_j $(j = 1, \ldots, m)$ such that for a primary good $(j = 1, \ldots, s)$, k_j exceeds the total endowment of all consumers, and for a produced good $(j = s + 1, \ldots, m)$, k_j exceeds the maximum output of Q_j that could be secured if the economy's entire endowment of primary goods were devoted to the production of Q_j.

Now, construct a set of *pseudo excess demand functions* on the assumption that the ith consumer maximizes utility subject to his budget constraint and the additional requirements that $E_{ij} \leqq k_j$ $(j = 1, \ldots, m)$. These functions have the normalized price set (5-46) as their domain. The pseudo functions are the same as the conventional functions (5-45) for all price points for which

$$E_{ij}(p_1, \ldots, p_m) \leqq k_j \qquad j = 1, \ldots, m$$

However, these inequalities are not satisfied for all points in the normalized price set. One or more of the inequalities are violated if one or more

---

[1] This result would not hold in general if it were possible for the consumer to receive a negative profit income sufficiently large to make his total income zero or negative. For the system considered here the possibility of a negative profit income is excluded by assumptions covering production.

[2] The normalized price set does not cover the situation in which all prices are zero. This is no loss, however, since such a situation cannot be a multimarket equilibrium.

prices are either zero or sufficiently small to generate excess demands larger than the corresponding upper bounds.

Assume that u of the upper bounds are effective as strict equalities, and renumber the goods so that $E_{ij} = k_j$ $(j = 1, \ldots ,u)$. Substitute these equalities and form the Lagrange function

$$Z_i = U_i(k_1, \ldots ,k_u, E_{i,u+1}, \ldots ,E_{im})$$
$$- \mu \left(\sum_{j=m}^{u} p_j k_j + \sum_{j=u+1}^{m} p_j E_{ij} - \sum_{k=s+1}^{m} \sum_{h=1}^{N_k} \theta_{ihk}\pi_{hk} \right)$$

Set the $(m - u + 1)$ partial derivatives of this function equal to zero:

$$\frac{\partial Z_i}{\partial E_{ij}} = U_j - \mu p_j = 0 \qquad j = u + 1, \ldots , m$$
$$\frac{\partial Z_i}{\partial \mu} = - \left(\sum_{j=1}^{u} p_j k_j + \sum_{j=u+1}^{m} p_j E_{ij} - \sum_{k=s+1}^{m} \sum_{h=1}^{N_k} \theta_{ihk}\pi_{hk} \right) = 0$$

where $U_j = \partial U_i / \partial E_{ij}$. The Jacobian of this system is

$$\mathbf{H} = \begin{vmatrix} U_{u+1,u+1} & \cdots & U_{u+1,m} & -p_{u+1} \\ \cdots\cdots\cdots\cdots\cdots\cdots\cdots\cdots \\ U_{m,u+1} & \cdots & U_{mm} & -p_m \\ -p_{u+1} & \cdots & -p_m & 0 \end{vmatrix}$$

where $U_{jh} = \partial^2 U_i / \partial E_{ij} \partial E_{ih}$. By construction

$$p_j > 0 \; (j = u + 1, \ldots ,m)$$

The restrictions placed upon the ith consumer's utility function ensure that the principal minors of $\mathbf{H}$, a subset of those of $\mathbf{J}$, will alternate in sign. Thus, limited excess demand functions exist on the assumption that u of the excess demands equal their upper bounds. These limited functions are the pseudo excess demand functions for all price points for which the values they generate for the $(m - u)$ unconstrained excess demands do not exceed their upper bounds.

The conventional excess demand functions (5-45) cover the case $u = 0$. The index u may assume values from 0 through $(m - 1)$. The assumptions underlying the utility function and the construction of the k_js exclude the case in which all upper bounds are effective; that is, $u = m$. There are $m!/(m - u)!u!$ combinations[1] of the m possible upper bounds in which a particular number u are effective. The total

---

[1] The number $n!$ (read n factorial) is the product of the integers 1 through n: $n! = 1 \cdot 2 \cdot 3 \cdots (n - 1)n$. By definition $0! = 1$.

number of sets of limited excess demand functions (L) for all possible combinations is

$$L = \sum_{u=1}^{m-1} \frac{m!}{(m-u)!u!} = 2^m - 1$$

The number L may be very large, but is finite. Pseudo excess demand functions for the ith consumer, denoted by

$$E_{ij} = \hat{E}_{ij}(p_1, \ldots, p_m) \qquad j = 1, \ldots, m \tag{5-47}$$

are formed from the L sets of limited excess demand functions. The pseudo functions are not given by a single set of m individual equations as has been the practice in most cases heretofore. They are given by L sets of m individual equations each and rules that specify which set is appropriate for each price point. By advanced methods it can be proved that the pseudo excess demand functions (1) have the normalized price set (5-46) as their domain, (2) are single-valued; i.e., if more than one set of limited excess demand functions is valid for a price point, each valid set will give identical values for the E_{ij} at that point, and (3) are continuous but in general do not have continuous first- and second-order partial derivatives. Since the underlying L sets of limited excess demand functions satisfy the consumer's budget constraint, the pseudo functions also satisfy it. The construction of pseudo functions would be a formidable task for even relatively small numbers of commodities. Fortunately, their construction is not necessary. It is only necessary to know that they exist and to know their properties.

The procedures for constructing excess demand functions for the firm are similar to those employed for the consumer. The entrepreneur of the hth firm in the jth industry uses the m goods as inputs for the production of the jth. He sells his output and buys his inputs in competitive markets at nonnegative prices. His production function is defined for nonnegative input and output levels. It is continuous and has continuous first- and second-order partial derivatives. He maximizes his profit which he distributes among consumers in predetermined shares. The following restrictions are also placed on the firm's production function: (1) it is strictly concave, (2) $\partial \bar{q}_{hj}/\partial q_{hjk}^* > 0$ if $q_{hjk}^* > 0$, (3) $\bar{q}_{hj} = 0$ if $q_{hjk}^* = 0$ for any k, and $\bar{q}_{hj} > 0$ if $q_{hjk}^* > 0$ for every k, and (4) $\lim \bar{q}_{hj} = 0$ and $\lim \partial \bar{q}_{hj}/\partial q_{hjk}^* = +\infty$ as $q_{hjk}^* \to 0$. The first and second restrictions imply that the RTS between every pair of inputs is increasing and that the marginal product of every input is always positive and decreasing. The third and fourth restrictions extend the definition of the production function to cover zero input levels and exclude corner solutions.

Single-valued excess demand functions will exist for the hth firm in the jth industry if the principal minors of the Jacobian ($\mathbf{K}$) of the first-order conditions (5-24):

$$\mathbf{K} = p_j^m \begin{vmatrix} f_{11} & \cdots & f_{1m} \\ \cdots & \cdots & \cdots \\ f_{m1} & \cdots & f_{mm} \end{vmatrix}$$

where $f_{ku} = \partial^2 \bar{q}_{hj}/\partial q^*_{hjk} \, \partial q^*_{hju}$, alternate in sign. Strict concavity ensures that the second-order conditions (5-25) are satisfied if $p_j > 0$, and that the minors of $\mathbf{K}$ will have the appropriate signs. The firm's conventional excess demand functions for inputs and output respectively are of the form

$$\begin{aligned} E^*_{hjk} &= E^*_{hjk}(p_1, \, \ldots \, ,p_m) \qquad k = 1, \, \ldots \, , \, m \\ \bar{E}_{hj} &= \bar{E}_{hj}(p_1, \, \ldots \, ,p_m) \end{aligned} \qquad (5\text{-}48)$$

These functions have the domain $p_i > 0$ $(i = 1, \, \ldots \, ,m)$. The restrictions placed upon the production function imply ranges of $E^*_{hjk} > 0$ $(k = 1, \, \ldots \, ,m)$ and $\bar{E}_{hj} < 0$.

The conventional functions (5-48) do not directly accommodate zero prices. Pseudo excess demand functions are defined for the producer on the assumption that he maximizes profit subject to the additional requirements that $E^*_{hju} = q^*_{hju} \leqq k_u$ $(u = 1, \, \ldots \, ,m)$. No direct limit is placed upon his output level. Output and input levels are assumed to equal zero if output price equals zero: $\bar{q}_{hj} = q^*_{hj1} = \cdots = q^*_{hjm} = 0$ if $p_j = 0$. Limited excess demand functions are defined for each possible combination of effective upper bounds by substituting the appropriate $q^*_{hju} = k_u$ into the firm's profit equation and determining optimal values as functions of prices for the remaining input levels and the output level. Pseudo excess demand functions for the jth firm in the hth industry, denoted by

$$\begin{aligned} E^*_{hjk} &= \hat{E}^*_{hjk}(p_1, \, \ldots \, ,p_m) \qquad k = 1, \, \ldots \, , \, m \\ \bar{E}_{hj} &= \hat{E}_{hj}(p_1, \, \ldots \, ,p_m) \end{aligned} \qquad (5\text{-}49)$$

are formed from the limited functions. As in the case of the consumer, it can be proved that (1) the pseudo functions have the normalized price set as their domain, (2) they are single-valued, and (3) they are continuous.

By advanced methods it can be proved that each firm's maximum profit is positive if its output price is positive and zero if its output price is zero. The significance of this is twofold. First, it means that no firm will produce at a negative profit. Second, it means that each consumer will have a positive income if any price is positive. Each consumer has a positive stock of each primary good, and will have a positive income if the price of any primary good is positive. If the prices of all primary goods are zero, he will still have a positive profit income if any output price is positive. This is a consequence of the assumption that each consumer has a share of profits from at least one firm in every industry.

Conventional aggregate excess demand functions for the domain $p_k > 0$ $(k = 1, \ldots, m)$,

$$E_j = E_j(p_1, \ldots, p_m) \qquad j = 1, \ldots, m \tag{5-50}$$

are obtained by summing the conventional functions for the individual consumers and producers given by (5-45) and (5-48) respectively. Aggregate pseudo excess demand functions with the normalized price set as their domain, denoted by

$$E_j = \hat{E}_j(p_1, \ldots, p_m) \qquad j = 1, \ldots, m \tag{5-51}$$

are formed from the pseudo functions for the individual consumers and producers given by (5-47) and (5-49) respectively. For each price point the aggregate pseudo functions give the sums of the excess demands dictated by the appropriate limited functions for each individual consumer and producer. The continuity of both sets of aggregate functions follows from the continuity of the corresponding individual functions. Each set of aggregate functions satisfies Walras' law. An important property of the aggregate pseudo functions from the viewpoint of an existence proof is that E_j is positive and finite if $p_j = 0$.

THE EXISTENCE OF EQUILIBRIUM PRICES[1]

In general, a multimarket equilibrium exists if there is at least one normalized price point such that

$$E_j = 0 \quad \text{if } p_j > 0 \quad \text{and} \quad E_j \leqq 0 \quad \text{if } p_j = 0 \quad j = 1, \ldots, m$$

For notational convenience let a point in the normalized price set be denoted by $\mathbf{p} = (p_1, \ldots, p_m)$. The normalized price set is closed, bounded, and convex. For $m = 2$ it is a line from $(1,0)$ to $(0,1)$. For $m = 3$ it is a triangle. The existence proof proceeds by devising a suitable mapping of the normalized price set into itself, showing that it has a fixed point, and demonstrating that the fixed point defines a multimarket equilibrium.

---

[1] The general form of the existence proof used here was suggested by J. G. Kemeny and J. L. Snell, *Mathematical Methods in the Social Sciences* (Boston: Ginn, 1962), pp. 38–39.

Define m functions by

$$g_j(\mathbf{p}) = \max\,[p_j + \hat{E}_j(\mathbf{p}),\, 0.5p_j] > 0 \qquad j = 1,\, \ldots,\, m \qquad (5\text{-}52)$$

Since by (5-46) prices cannot be negative and since a zero price implies a positive excess demand, it follows that all the functions of (5-52) always have positive values. Let

$$h(\mathbf{p}) = \sum_{j=1}^{m} g_j(\mathbf{p}) > 0 \qquad\qquad\qquad (5\text{-}53)$$

Since $h(\mathbf{p})$ is always positive, division by it is a legitimate operation. Define m new functions by

$$f_j(\mathbf{p}) = \frac{g_j(\mathbf{p})}{h(\mathbf{p})} > 0 \qquad j = 1,\, \ldots,\, m \qquad\qquad (5\text{-}54)$$

These functions define a continuous mapping of prices. The continuity of the mapping follows from the continuity of (5-52) and (5-53). Since

$$\sum_{j=1}^{m} f_j(\mathbf{p}) = \frac{\displaystyle\sum_{j=1}^{m} g_j(\mathbf{p})}{h(\mathbf{p})} = 1$$

by (5-53), the image points satisfy the definitions of the normalized price set, and (5-54) maps this set into itself. It follows from Brouwer's fixed-point theorem that the normalized price set contains at least one point $\mathbf{p}^*$ such that

$$p_j^* = f_j(\mathbf{p}^*) = \frac{g_j(\mathbf{p}^*)}{h(\mathbf{p}^*)} > 0 \qquad j = 1,\, \ldots,\, m \qquad (5\text{-}55)$$

All components of $\mathbf{p}^*$ are positive since (5-55) is a special case of (5-54). It remains to be shown that all excess demands equal zero at a point defined by (5-55) before it can be concluded that such a point constitutes a multimarket equilibrium.

If each $g_j(\mathbf{p}^*)$ were equal to its lower limit, $0.5p_j^*$, the sum $h(\mathbf{p}^*)$ would equal its lower limit of 0.5 as established by (5-52) and (5-46). If any $g_j(\mathbf{p}^*)$ exceeds $0.5p_j^*$, $h(\mathbf{p}^*)$ will exceed 0.5. If all $g_j(\mathbf{p}^*) = 0.5p_j^*$, it follows from (5-52) that all $\hat{E}_j(\mathbf{p}^*) < 0$. This implies that $\Sigma_{j=1}^{m} p_j^* \hat{E}_j(\mathbf{p}^*)$ < 0 which contradicts Walras' law. Thus, it cannot be true that $g_j(\mathbf{p}^*) = 0.5p_j^*$ for all j. Assume that it is true for some j. Then from (5-55)

$$p_j^* = \frac{g_j(\mathbf{p}^*)}{h(\mathbf{p}^*)} = \frac{0.5p_j^*}{h(\mathbf{p}^*)} < p_j^*$$

since $h(\mathbf{p}^*) > 0.5$, but this is also a contradiction. It then follows from (5-52) and (5-55) that

$$p_j^* = \frac{p_j^* + \hat{E}_j(\mathbf{p}^*)}{h(\mathbf{p}^*)} \qquad j = 1, \ldots, m \qquad (5\text{-}56)$$

Multiplying both sides of the jth equation of (5-56) by $\hat{E}_j(\mathbf{p}^*)$ and adding the resultant m equations,

$$\sum_{j=1}^{m} p_j^* \hat{E}_j(\mathbf{p}^*) = \frac{\displaystyle\sum_{j=1}^{m} p_j^* \hat{E}_j(\mathbf{p}^*) + \sum_{j=1}^{m} [\hat{E}_j(\mathbf{p}^*)]^2}{h(\mathbf{p}^*)}$$

It follows from Walras' law that the left-hand side and the first term in the numerator on the right-hand side are zero. Thus,

$$\sum_{j=1}^{m} [\hat{E}_j(\mathbf{p}^*)]^2 = 0$$

A sum of squares can equal zero only if each term equals zero; hence $\hat{E}_j(\mathbf{p}^*) = 0$ for all j, and the fixed point $\mathbf{p}^*$ is a multimarket equilibrium set of prices. Since all equilibrium prices are positive, (5-50) gives the aggregate excess demands, and (5-45) and (5-48) give the individual excess demands. The consumption level for each good by each consumer is positive and finite. The output and input levels for each producer are positive and finite.

A great deal of effort was expended in defining pseudo excess demands for zero prices only to discover that the restrictions placed upon the individual utility and production functions always generate positive equilibrium prices. However, if the zero-price case had not been accommodated, it would not have been possible to define a mapping of the *closed* normalized price set (5-46), and Brouwer's fixed-point theorem would not have been applicable.

ADVANCED EXISTENCE PROOFS

Existence was proved for a competitive economy for which individual utility and production functions are continuous with continuous first- and second-order partial derivatives and obey stated restrictions. This, as all other existence proofs, is based upon a sufficiency rather than a necessity argument. All systems that satisfy the restrictions possess equilibrium points, but there are systems with equilibrium points that do not satisfy them. A number of authors have employed advanced mathematics to formulate existence proofs that are based upon generally weaker restrictions.[1]

One of the most complete and least restrictive existence proofs was formulated by Gerard Debreu.[2] It is summarized in approximate form here. Analysis is in terms of point sets rather than functions. To prove existence, Debreu utilizes the Kakutani fixed-point theorem, which generalizes the Brouwer theorem from point-to-point to point-to-set mappings. A consumption set for the ith consumer is defined as the collection of all possible points representing commodity consumption levels (nonnegative numbers) and endowments (nonpositive numbers). It is assumed that each consumer's consumption set (1) is closed, convex, and bounded from below, (2) contains no saturation point, and (3) contains a bundle strictly smaller than the consumer's initial endowment. Assumptions about consumer preferences are based upon rankings. A consumer's optimum consumption bundle for a given set of prices need not be unique.

A firm is allowed to produce more than one good. Outputs are described by positive and inputs by negative numbers. It is assumed that each firm may remain idle using no inputs. Debreu's remaining assumptions about production cover the economy as a whole rather than individual firms. An aggregate production set is defined as all possible input and output combinations for the economy as a whole. The aggregate production set is assumed to be closed and convex. Thus, increasing returns are not possible for the economy, but they are possible for individual firms. Free disposal of inputs is allowed. Production is assumed to be irreversible; i.e., inputs cannot be produced with outputs. All competitive economies that fulfill Debreu's assumptions have one or more equilibrium points. However, there are systems that violate one or more of his assumptions that possess equilibrium points.

EMPIRICAL APPLICATIONS

The knowledge that abstract multimarket systems possess equilibrium solutions is of limited usefulness for empirical studies. A simple system with 2 primary goods, 50 produced goods, 10,000 consumers, and 2,000 firms has more than 600,000 individual excess demand functions. Numerical solutions are impractical for systems of this size even if the necessary data could be obtained. If the economist desires to make empirical applications, he is normally limited to a somewhat simplified

---

[1] An excellent summary of the assumptions employed by different authors is given by James Quirk and Rubin Saposnik, *Introduction to General Equilibrium Theory and Welfare Economics* (New York: McGraw-Hill, 1968), chap. 3.

[2] *Theory of Value* (New York: Wiley, 1959).

version of the partial equilibrium analysis or a greatly simplified version of the general equilibrium analysis.

5-5 THE STABILITY AND UNIQUENESS OF EQUILIBRIUM

Once existence has been proved, one may ask under what conditions a system will return to an equilibrium point following a disturbance, and under what conditions a system will have only one equilibrium point. Meaningful statements can be made about stability and uniqueness for systems that conform to the general assumptions considered in the preceding section. As yet, little can be said about systems that adhere to the relatively weak assumptions of the Debreu existence proof. Since the analysis of stability provides guidelines for the analysis of uniqueness, stability is considered first.

The effects of a disturbance in one market upon the equilibria in other markets are ignored in Sec. 4-8 in accordance with the assumptions of partial equilibrium analysis. A general equilibrium analysis involves an explicit recognition of the interrelated nature of all markets. The excess demand for each good is a function of the prices of all goods. A disturbance in one market normally will upset equilibrium in other markets. The stability of a single market depends upon the adjustments following the induced disturbances in other markets. Both the static and dynamic conditions for stability in a single market are extended to a multimarket system in the present section. The static conditions are often called the *Hicksian* conditions in honor of their formulator, J. R. Hicks. The Walrasian behavior assumptions (see Sec. 4-8) are employed throughout the present section.

STATIC STABILITY

Return to the assumption that the multimarket system does not contain money. Let Q_1 serve as numéraire and set its price identically equal to unity.

The stability condition for a two-market system is the same as the condition for a single market. There is only one independent equation and only one variable price: $E_1 = E_1(p_2)$ and $E_2 = E_2(p_2)$. The aggregate budget constraint, Walras' law, $E_1 + p_2 E_2 = 0$, is always satisfied. A relaxation of the equilibrium condition for Q_2 so that $E_2 \neq 0$ necessarily implies a relaxation of the equilibrium condition for Q_1 such that $dE_1 + p_2\, dE_2 = 0$. The differentials dE_1 and dE_2 and therefore the derivatives dE_1/dp_2 and dE_2/dp_2 must be of opposite sign except for the trivial case in which both equal zero. Equilibrium is stable according to the static Walrasian assumption if $dE_2/dp_2 < 0$ (or equivalently if $dE_1/dp_2 > 0$). If equilibrium is restored in the market for Q_2, equilibrium is automatically restored in the market for the numéraire; i.e., if

E_2 equals zero, E_1 must also equal zero. The unique problems of multi-market stability arise only for systems with three or more interrelated markets.

If $\partial E_k / \partial p_j \neq 0$, a displacement of equilibrium in the market for Q_j will cause a displacement of equilibrium in the market for Q_k. Walrasian stability for an isolated market requires that $\partial E_j / \partial p_j < 0$ where $\partial E_j / \partial p_j$ is a partial derivative and all other prices are assumed to remain unchanged. The total derivative dE_j / dp_j must be utilized for a multimarket analysis. Its value may be computed under a number of alternative assumptions regarding the adjustment of other markets. One possibility is to assume that equilibrium is restored in all markets other than those for Q_j and the numéraire.[1] There are many possible price-adjustment patterns other than the case of complete inflexibility, in which none of the other $(m - 2)$ markets adjusts, and the case of complete flexibility, in which they all adjust. In general, one can imagine a system with M "rigid prices" which will not change from their initial equilibrium values during the period under consideration where M may be any number from one through $(m - 1)$. The price of the numéraire is always rigid as a result of its definition.

The most stringent stability conditions for the market for Q_j $(j \neq 1)$ require that the total derivative dE_j / dp_j be negative for all possible combinations of rigid and flexible prices. The market for Q_j is perfectly stable by the Hicksian definition if $dE_j / dp_j < 0$ under the following conditions: (1) if all the $(m - 1)$ prices other than p_j are rigid, (2) if $(m - 2)$ of the prices are rigid but p_h is flexible and adjusts so that $E_h = 0$, (3) if $(m - 3)$ of the prices are rigid but p_h and p_k are flexible and adjust so that $E_h = 0$ and $E_k = 0$, and so on up to the final case in which the prices of all goods other than the numéraire are flexible. The system as a whole is perfectly stable if the $(m - 1)$ markets for the goods other than the numéraire are perfectly stable.

The excess demand functions for a system with m goods are

$$E_j = E_j(p_2, \ldots, p_m) \qquad j = 2, \ldots, m \tag{5-57}$$

The excess demand function for the numéraire may be omitted, since it can be derived from the other $(m - 1)$. The effects of price changes upon the excess demands are computed by total differentiation of (5-57),

$$
\begin{aligned}
dE_2 &= b_{22}\, dp_2 + b_{23}\, dp_3 + \cdots + b_{2m}\, dp_m \\
dE_3 &= b_{32}\, dp_2 + b_{33}\, dp_3 + \cdots + b_{3m}\, dp_m \\
&\cdots\cdots\cdots\cdots\cdots\cdots\cdots\cdots\cdots\cdots \\
dE_m &= b_{m2}\, dp_2 + b_{m3}\, dp_3 + \cdots + b_{mm}\, dp_m
\end{aligned}
\tag{5-58}
$$

---

[1] Since the aggregate budget constraint is always satisfied, $p_j E_j + E_1 = 0$ if Q_1 is numéraire. The violation of the equilibrium condition for the numéraire provides the slack necessary to allow the excess demand for Q_j to take on a nonzero value.

where $b_{jk} = \partial E_j/\partial p_k$. Since b_{jk} may be assumed constant in a small neighborhood about an equilibrium point, (5-58) forms a system of $(m - 1)$ simultaneous linear equations in the $(m - 1)$ variables $(dp_2,$ . . . ,$dp_m)$. The coefficients of (5-58) form the Jacobian of $E_2,$ . . . , E_m with respect to $p_2,$ . . . , p_m.

Consider the case in which equilibrium is displaced in the market for Q_j and all other prices are rigid. Substituting $dp_k = 0$ for $k = 2,$ . . . , m and $j \neq k$ into (5-58) the $(j - 1)$st equation becomes[1]

$$dE_j = b_{jj}\, dp_j$$

Dividing through by dp_j, the first condition for the perfect stability of the market for Q_j is

$$\frac{dE_j}{dp_j} = b_{jj} < 0 \qquad\qquad (5\text{-}59)$$

Condition (5-59) is identical with the stability requirement for an isolated market. Perfect stability for the system as a whole requires that (5-59) hold for $j = 2,$ . . . , m, and thus the first condition for perfect stability requires the isolated stability of every market in the system.

Now consider the case in which equilibrium is displaced in the market for Q_j, p_h adjusts, and all other prices are rigid. Substituting $dE_h = 0$ and $dp_k = 0$ for $k \neq j, h$ into (5-58), the equations for Q_j and Q_h become

$$dE_j = b_{jj}\, dp_j + b_{jh}\, dp_h$$
$$0 = b_{hj}\, dp_j + b_{hh}\, dp_h$$

Using Cramer's rule to solve for dp_j,

$$dp_j = \frac{\begin{vmatrix} dE_j & b_{jh} \\ 0 & b_{hh} \end{vmatrix}}{\begin{vmatrix} b_{jj} & b_{jh} \\ b_{hj} & b_{hh} \end{vmatrix}} = dE_j \frac{b_{hh}}{\begin{vmatrix} b_{jj} & b_{jh} \\ b_{hj} & b_{hh} \end{vmatrix}}$$

Dividing through by the constant term on the right and by dp_j, the second condition for the perfect stability of the market for Q_j is

$$\frac{dE_j}{dp_j} = \frac{\begin{vmatrix} b_{jj} & b_{jh} \\ b_{hj} & b_{hh} \end{vmatrix}}{b_{hh}} < 0 \qquad\qquad (5\text{-}60)$$

[1] A displacement of equilibrium in the market for Q_j will cause displacements of the equilibria in the other markets. The other equations of (5-58) become

$$dE_k = b_{kj}\, dp_j$$

Since the other prices are assumed rigid, these displacements will not react back upon the excess demand for Q_j, and nonzero excess demands will continue to exist in the other markets.

Perfect stability of the market for Q_h requires that the denominator of (5-60) be negative.   Therefore, perfect stability for the system as a whole requires that the numerator of (5-60) be positive.

Finally, consider the case in which equilibrium is displaced in the market for Q_j, p_h and p_i adjust, and the other $(m-4)$ prices are rigid. Substituting $dE_h = dE_i = 0$ and $dp_k = 0$ for the other $(m-4)$ prices into (5-58), the relevant equations become

$$dE_j = b_{jj}\, dp_j + b_{jh}\, dp_h + b_{ji}\, dp_i$$
$$0 = b_{hj}\, dp_j + b_{hh}\, dp_h + b_{hi}\, dp_i$$
$$0 = b_{ij}\, dp_j + b_{ih}\, dp_h + b_{ii}\, dp_i$$

Using Cramer's rule to solve for dp_j,

$$dp_j = \begin{vmatrix} dE_j & b_{jh} & b_{ji} \\ 0 & b_{hh} & b_{hi} \\ 0 & b_{ih} & b_{ii} \end{vmatrix} : \begin{vmatrix} b_{jj} & b_{jh} & b_{ji} \\ b_{hj} & b_{hh} & b_{hi} \\ b_{ij} & b_{ih} & b_{ii} \end{vmatrix}$$

Expanding the numerator by its first column and solving for dE_j/dp_j, the third condition for the perfect stability of the market for Q_j is

$$\frac{dE_j}{dp_j} = \begin{vmatrix} b_{jj} & b_{jh} & b_{ji} \\ b_{hj} & b_{hh} & b_{hi} \\ b_{ij} & b_{ih} & b_{ii} \end{vmatrix} : \begin{vmatrix} b_{hh} & b_{hi} \\ b_{ih} & b_{ii} \end{vmatrix} < 0 \qquad (5\text{-}61)$$

Letting $j = h$ and $h = i$ in requirement (5-60), perfect stability of the market for Q_h requires that the denominator of (5-61) be positive. Therefore, perfect stability for the system as a whole requires that the numerator of (5-61) be negative.

Perfect stability for the system as a whole requires that the Jacobian determinants of order $[1,2,3, \ldots ,(m-1)]$:

$$b_{jj}, \begin{vmatrix} b_{jj} & b_{jh} \\ b_{hj} & b_{hh} \end{vmatrix}, \begin{vmatrix} b_{jj} & b_{jh} & b_{ji} \\ b_{hj} & b_{hh} & b_{hi} \\ b_{ij} & b_{ih} & b_{ii} \end{vmatrix}, \ldots$$

be alternatively negative and positive for all values of j, h, i, $\ldots$.

The conditions for perfect stability are stronger than necessary for the consideration of many multimarket systems.   If the system contains no rigid prices, the only relevant value for dE_j/dp_j is the one computed on the assumption that the other $(m-2)$ markets adjust.   Following the computational procedure outlined above, the market for Q_2 is stable if

$$\frac{dE_2}{dp_2} = \frac{\mathbf{B}}{\mathbf{B}_{22}} < 0 \qquad (5\text{-}62)$$

where $\mathbf{B}$ is the Jacobian determinant of the complete system given by (5-58) and $\mathbf{B}_{22}$ is the cofactor of b_{22}.   In the Hicksian terminology the system as a whole is *imperfectly stable* if a condition similar to (5-62) holds for all goods other than the numéraire. It is interesting to note that imperfect stability does not necessarily imply the isolated stability of each market.

Consider the following excess demand functions for three-commodity systems:

(1) $E_2 = -2p_2 + 3p_3 - 5$ $\qquad E_3 = 4p_2 - 8p_3 + 16$
(2) $E_2 = 2p_2 - 3p_3 + 5$ $\qquad E_3 = -4p_2 + 4p_3 - 4$
(3) $E_2 = 2p_2 + 3p_3 - 13$ $\qquad E_3 = 4p_2 - 8p_3 + 16$

The equilibrium prices are $p_2 = 2$ and $p_3 = 3$ for all three examples. System (1) satisfies all the conditions for perfect stability:

$$\frac{dE_2}{dp_2} = \frac{\partial E_2}{\partial p_2} = -2 < 0 \qquad \frac{dE_2}{dp_2} = \frac{\begin{vmatrix} -2 & 3 \\ 4 & -8 \end{vmatrix}}{-8} = -0.5 < 0$$

$$\frac{dE_3}{dp_3} = \frac{\partial E_3}{\partial p_3} = -8 < 0 \qquad \frac{dE_3}{dp_3} = \frac{\begin{vmatrix} -2 & 3 \\ 4 & -8 \end{vmatrix}}{-2} = -2 < 0$$

System (2) fails to satisfy the conditions for perfect stability, but satisfies the conditions for imperfect stability:

$$\frac{dE_2}{dp_2} = \frac{\begin{vmatrix} 2 & -3 \\ -4 & 4 \end{vmatrix}}{4} = -1 < 0 \qquad \frac{dE_3}{dp_3} = \frac{\begin{vmatrix} 2 & -3 \\ -4 & 4 \end{vmatrix}}{2} = -2 < 0$$

The markets for both Q_2 and Q_3 are unstable when considered in isolation, but the system as a whole is stable if both prices adjust. System (3) fails to satisfy the conditions for either perfect or imperfect stability.

DYNAMIC STABILITY: LAGGED ADJUSTMENT

The conditions for the dynamic stability of a multimarket system with lagged adjustment represent a generalization of the condition for the dynamic stability of a single market with lagged adjustment as presented in Sec. 4-8. An explicit statement of the laws of price change is introduced, and the time paths of the prices following a disturbance are investigated. Many different types of dynamic adjustment processes may be introduced to describe the behavior of the participants in particular systems. In general, a multimarket equilibrium is dynamically stable if every price approaches its equilibrium level over time following a slight displacement from equilibrium, i.e., if

$$\lim_{t \to \infty} p_{jt} = p_{je} \qquad j = 2, \ldots, m$$

where p_{jt} is the price of Q_j at time t and p_{je} is the equilibrium price of Q_j.

Much of the mathematics necessary for a full development of dynamic stability is beyond the scope of the present volume, but the general nature of the analysis can be indicated with the aid of a linear example for a three-commodity system:

$$E_{2t} = a_{22}p_{2t} + a_{23}p_{3t} + a_{20}$$
$$E_{3t} = a_{32}p_{2t} + a_{33}p_{3t} + a_{30}$$
$$(5\text{-}63)$$

Equilibrium prices can be computed by setting E_{2t} and E_{3t} equal to zero and solving for p_{2t} and p_{3t}:

$$p_{2e} = \frac{a_{23}a_{30} - a_{33}a_{20}}{a_{22}a_{33} - a_{23}a_{32}} \qquad p_{3e} = \frac{a_{32}a_{20} - a_{22}a_{30}}{a_{22}a_{33} - a_{23}a_{32}} \qquad (5\text{-}64)$$

Assume that the dynamic laws of price adjustment are given by the linear equations

$$p_{2,t+1} - p_{2t} = kE_{2t}$$
$$p_{3,t+1} - p_{3t} = kE_{3t}$$
$$(5\text{-}65)$$

where $k > 0$ is the "speed of adjustment," i.e., the amount that price will increase (or decrease) per unit of excess demand. The price-adjustment process which is described by (5-65) follows the Walrasian behavior assumptions. A positive excess demand means that buyers desire to purchase more than is being offered at the current price. Competition among buyers will then lead to an increase of price. A negative excess demand means that sellers offer more than buyers desire to purchase at the current price. Competition among sellers will then lead to a decrease of price. Neither price will change if both markets are in equilibrium, i.e., if the excess demand for each good equals zero. The "speed of adjustment" need not be the same for both markets, but no generality is lost by assuming that it is, since the units in which the goods are measured are arbitrary.

Substitute the values of the excess demands from (5-63) into (5-65) and write the equations in implicit form:

$$p_{2,t+1} - (1 + ka_{22})p_{2t} - ka_{23}p_{3t} - ka_{20} = 0$$
$$p_{3,t+1} - (1 + ka_{33})p_{3t} - ka_{32}p_{2t} - ka_{30} = 0$$
$$(5\text{-}66)$$

Solve the second equation of (5-66) for p_{2t}:

$$p_{2t} = \frac{1}{ka_{32}} p_{3,t+1} - \frac{1 + ka_{33}}{ka_{32}} p_{3t} - \frac{a_{30}}{a_{32}} \qquad (5\text{-}67)$$

Now substitute the values of p_{2t} and $p_{2,t+1}$ given by (5-67) into the first equation of (5-66):

$$p_{3,t+2} + \alpha_3 p_{3,t+1} + \beta_3 p_{3t} + \gamma_3 = 0 \qquad (5\text{-}68)$$

where $\alpha_3 = -(2 + ka_{33} + ka_{22})$

$\beta_3 = 1 + ka_{33} + ka_{22} + k^2a_{22}a_{33} - k^2a_{23}a_{32}$

$\gamma_3 = k^2a_{22}a_{30} - k^2a_{32}a_{20}$

The time path of the price of Q_3 is described by a second-order, non-homogeneous difference equation with constant coefficients. The solution of (5-68) (see Sec. A-5) is

$$p_{3t} = A_3\sigma_{31}^t + B_3\sigma_{32}^t + \frac{a_{32}a_{20} - a_{22}a_{30}}{a_{22}a_{33} - a_{23}a_{32}} \tag{5-69}$$

where σ_{31} and σ_{32} are the roots of the homogeneous part of (5-68), and A_3 and B_3 are constants determined by the initial conditions. The constant term of (5-69) is the equilibrium price of Q_3 as given by (5-64).†

The time path of p_{2t} can be described by an equation similar to (5-69). Substituting p_{3e} for the constant term in (5-69) and writing a similar equation for the price of Q_2,

$$p_{2t} = A_2\sigma_{21}^t + B_2\sigma_{22}' + p_{2e}$$
$$p_{3t} = A_3\sigma_{31}^t + B_3\sigma_{32}' + p_{3e}$$

The system is dynamically stable and p_{2t} and p_{3t} will approach their equilibrium values over time if $-1 < \sigma_{ij} < 1$ ($i = 2, 3; j = 1, 2$). The absolute values of the roots of the homogeneous parts of (5-68) and the corresponding equation for Q_2 must be less than unity.

The roots σ_{ij}, and therefore dynamic stability, depend upon the "speed of adjustment" as well as the coefficients of the excess demand equations. Hicksian stability depends only upon the values of the coefficients. A system which satisfies the Hicksian conditions for perfect stability will prove dynamically unstable for some values of k. Consider the system given by

$$E_2 = -2p_2 + 3p_3 - 5$$
$$E_3 = 4p_2 - 8p_3 + 16$$

which was demonstrated to satisfy the Hicksian conditions for perfect stability. Assume the dynamic adjustment process is described by (5-65). For this example (5-68) becomes

$$p_{3,t+2} + (10k - 2)p_{3,t+1} + (4k^2 - 10k + 1)p_{3t} - 12k^2 = 0$$

The roots of the homogeneous part are

$$\sigma_{31} = -0.41k + 1 \qquad \sigma_{32} = -9.58k + 1$$

† The reader can verify this by substituting $p_{3t} = K$ into (5-68) and solving

$$K + \alpha_3 K + \beta_3 K + \gamma_3 = 0$$

for K.

Since $k > 0$, σ_{31} and $\sigma_{32} < 1$ for all admissible speeds of adjustment, and the market for Q_3 is dynamically stable if the value of k is such that both roots are greater than -1. Since $\sigma_{32} < \sigma_{31}$, dynamic stability requires that $\sigma_{32} > -1$, or equivalently that $k < 0.21$. If k were greater than 0.21, the market for Q_3 would be characterized by overadjustment on the part of buyers and sellers, and p_{3t} would exhibit ever-increasing fluctuations about p_{3e}.

DYNAMIC STABILITY: CONTINUOUS ADJUSTMENT

The single market analysis of dynamic stability with continuous adjustment presented in Sec. 4-8 also may be generalized to a multimarket system. Assume that the first of the m goods is again numéraire. The dynamic adjustment equations are

$$\frac{dp_j}{dt} = k_j E_j(p_2, \ldots, p_m) \qquad j = 2, \ldots, m \tag{5-70}$$

where the $k_j > 0$ are speed of adjustment coefficients. Assume that units are defined so that all k_j equal one.

The total differential of the jth excess demand function is

$$dE_j = \sum_{k=2}^{m} \frac{\partial E_j}{\partial p_k} dp_k \qquad j = 2, \ldots, m$$

An analog to the approximation (4-29) for a single market is obtained by replacing the differentials dE_j and dp_k with deviations from equilibrium values, $E_j - E_{je}$ and $p_k - p_{ke}$:

$$E_j \approx \sum_{k=2}^{m} \frac{\partial E_j}{\partial p_k} (p_k - p_{ke}) \qquad j = 2, \ldots, m \tag{5-71}$$

since $E_{je} = 0$. Substituting from (5-71) into (5-70),

$$\frac{dp_j}{dt} = b_{j2}p_2 + \cdots + b_{jm}p_m + c_j \qquad j = 2, \ldots, m \tag{5-72}$$

where the c_j are constants that depend upon the equilibrium values of the prices. The local stability properties of (5-70) are ascertained from an examination of the solution of this system of simultaneous linear differential equations. A solution of (5-72) (see Sec. A-6) is of the form[1]

$$p_j = a_{j2}e^{\lambda_2 t} + \cdots + a_{jm}e^{\lambda_m t} + p_{je} \qquad j = 2, \ldots, m \tag{5-73}$$

---

[1] The form of (5-73) requires slight modification if two or more of the roots are identical. The local stability condition, however, remains unchanged.

where the a_{jk} are coefficients depending on the initial conditions and the λ_k are the $(m-1)$ roots of the polynomial given by

$$\begin{vmatrix} b_{22} - \lambda & \cdots & b_{2m} \\ \cdots\cdots\cdots\cdots\cdots \\ b_{m2} & \cdots & b_{mm} - \lambda \end{vmatrix} = \beta_{m-1}\lambda^{m-1} + \cdots + \beta_1\lambda + \beta_0 = 0$$

(5-74)

The time paths of the p_j will converge to their equilibrium values p_{je} if each of the $(m-1)$ roots of (5-74) is negative or has a negative real part.

In general, Hicksian stability is neither necessary nor sufficient for dynamic stability in the case of continuous adjustment. Advanced mathematics have been used to prove theorems about the conditions under which (5-70) is stable and the conditions under which Hicksian and dynamic stability are synonymous.[1] An important theorem states that *the dynamic system is locally stable and also has Hicksian stability if all commodities are strict gross substitutes;* that is, $b_{ii} < 0$ for all i, and $b_{ij} > 0$ for all $j \neq i$.

This theorem is now proved for the three-good case. Hicksian stability requires that

$$b_{22} < 0 \qquad b_{33} < 0 \qquad b_{22}b_{33} - b_{23}b_{32} > 0 \tag{5-75}$$

The first two inequalities of (5-75) follow immediately from gross substitutability. Differentiating the aggregate budget constraint totally,

$$dE_1 + p_2\,dE_2 + E_2\,dp_2 + p_3\,dE_3 + E_3\,dp_3 = 0$$

Let $dp_3 = 0$, and alternately let $dp_2 = 0$:

$$b_{12} + p_2b_{22} + E_2 + p_3b_{32} = 0$$
$$b_{13} + p_2b_{23} + p_3b_{33} + E_3 = 0$$

At equilibrium $E_2 = E_3 = 0$:

$$p_2b_{22} + p_3b_{32} = -b_{12} < 0$$
$$p_2b_{23} + p_3b_{33} = -b_{13} < 0$$

and

$$-p_2b_{22} > p_3b_{32} \qquad -p_3b_{33} > p_2b_{23}$$

---

[1] The major source of stability theorems is K. J. Arrow and L. Hurwicz, "On the Stability of Competitive Equilibrium, I," *Econometrica*, vol. 26 (October, 1958), pp. 522–552; and K. J. Arrow, H. D. Block, and L. Hurwicz, "On the Stability of Competitive Equilibrium, II," *ibid.*, vol. 27 (January, 1959), pp. 82–109. Advanced mathematics are employed in these articles. Simplified discussions of these and other stability theorems are given by J. Quirk and R. Saposnik, *op. cit.*, chap. 5.

Since the right-hand sides in these inequalities are positive by assumption, all four terms are positive, and their product is

$$p_2 p_3 b_{22} b_{33} > p_2 p_3 b_{23} b_{32}$$

which establishes the third inequality of (5-75). Therefore, gross substitutability implies Hicksian stability.

For the three-good case the polynomial of (5-74) is

$$\lambda^2 + \beta_1 \lambda + \beta_0 = \lambda^2 - (b_{22} + b_{33})\lambda + (b_{22} b_{33} - b_{23} b_{32}) = 0$$

Since β_1 and β_0 are both positive, both roots are negative if real, or have negative real parts if complex. Therefore, gross substitutability implies that the dynamic system is locally stable.

A system is *globally stable* if it will return to equilibrium following a disturbance of any magnitude. The analysis of global stability for a unique equilibrium using a Liapunov function (see Sec. 4-8) is easily extended to multimarket systems. Define a Liapunov function, $V(t)$, as the sum of the squared distances of the prices from their equilibrium values:

$$V(t) = \sum_{j=1}^{m} [p_j - p_{je}]^2 \tag{5-76}$$

This function has the necessary properties: it equals zero if all prices are at their equilibrium values and is positive if one or more prices are not. A system is globally stable if $dV(t)/dt < 0$ whenever $p_j \neq p_{je}$ for some j.

The analysis is illustrated by proving the following theorem: *a system that possesses a unique equilibrium and satisfies the Weak axiom of revealed preference (see Sec. 2-8) in the aggregate is globally stable.* Differentiating (5-76), substituting $dp_j/dt = E_j$ from (5-70), and invoking Walras' law,

$$\frac{dV(t)}{dt} = 2 \sum_{j=1}^{m} (p_j - p_{je}) \frac{dp_j}{dt} = 2 \sum_{j=1}^{m} (p_j - p_{je})E_j = -2 \sum_{j=1}^{m} p_{je} E_j \tag{5-77}$$

In terms of excess demands the Weak axiom states that

$$\sum_{j=1}^{m} p_j E_{je} \leqq \sum_{j=1}^{m} p_j E_j \quad \text{implies} \quad \sum_{j=1}^{m} p_{je} E_{je} < \sum_{j=1}^{m} p_{je} E_j \tag{5-78}$$

where the p_j are prices such that $p_j \neq p_{je}$ for one or more j, and the E_j are the excess demands that correspond to these prices. The left side of the first expression in (5-78) equals zero because $E_{je} = 0$ for all j, and the right side equals zero by Walras' law. Thus, the strict equality holds for the first expression, and the second expression is valid. The left side of the second expression in (5-78) also equals zero.   Therefore, $\Sigma_{j=1}^{m}p_{je}E_j > 0$, the derivative (5-77) is negative, and the system is globally stable.

UNIQUENESS

Most existence proofs state that classes of multimarket systems have one or more equilibrium points.   Uniqueness proofs state that subclasses of systems satisfying existence proofs have unique equilibrium points. Most of the observations about uniqueness for a single market in Sec. 4-7 can be extended to multimarket systems.   In general, if the total derivatives dE_j/dp_j $(j = 2, \ldots ,m)$ do not change sign and do not equal zero for any values of the p_j, there cannot be more than one equilibrium point.   This is a sufficient, but not necessary, condition for uniqueness.

A variety of cases is illustrated for two-commodity systems in Fig. 5-4.   In Fig. 5-4a, $dE_2/dp_2 < 0$ throughout, but there is no equilibrium point, and a consideration of uniqueness is meaningless.   This

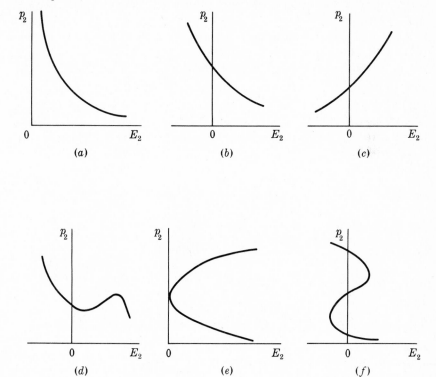

Fig. 5-4

case emphasizes that an existence proof must precede a uniqueness proof. In Fig. 5-4b, $dE_2/dp_2 < 0$ throughout, there is a unique equilibrium point, and it is globally stable. In Fig. 5-4c, $dE_2/dp_2 > 0$ throughout, there is a unique equilibrium point, but it is unstable. Cases of this type are of limited interest because of their instability. The systems illustrated in Fig. 5-4d and Fig. 5-4e have unique equilibrium points, but do not satisfy the condition for dE_2/dp_2. In Fig. 5-4f the condition is violated, and there are multiple equilibrium points.

Hicksian stability [see Eqs. (5-59) to (5-62)] requires that $dE_j/dp_j < 0$ for all j in a neighborhood of equilibrium. A system that satisfies the Hicksian stability conditions throughout has a unique equilibrium. Thus, a uniqueness proof can proceed by proving Hicksian stability throughout. In the last subsection it was proved that gross substitutability for a three-good system implies Hicksian stability throughout. Thereby, gross substitutability for a three-good system implies a unique equilibrium point. This theorem may be generalized to m goods.

If the Weak axiom (5-78) holds for the aggregate excess demands, uniqueness follows trivially. Proof is by contradiction. Assume that there are two equilibrium points, and evaluate (5-78) for these points. The first relation of (5-78) is satisfied because $E_{je} = E_j = 0$. For the same reason both terms in the second relation of (5-78) are zero, and it becomes $0 < 0$ which is a contradiction.

5-6 SUMMARY

A multimarket equilibrium analysis allows the determination of a consistent set of prices for all goods. In a pure-exchange system individuals are endowed with commodity stocks. Each is free to buy and sell commodities at prevailing prices subject to his budget constraint, which states that the value of his sales must equal the value of his purchases. Individual excess demand functions are derived from the first-order conditions for utility maximization. Aggregate functions are obtained by summing the individual functions for each commodity. The sum of the aggregate excess demands multiplied by prices is identically equal to zero. This follows from the individual budget constraints and is known as *Walras' law*. All the individual, and therefore the aggregate, functions are homogeneous of degree zero in prices. Consumer behavior is determined by exchange ratios rather than absolute prices. Multimarket equilibrium requires that the excess demand for every commodity equal zero. The m excess demands are functionally dependent as a result of Walras' law, and an equilibrium solution for the system is expressed in terms of the $(m - 1)$ exchange ratios for the commodities relative to an arbitrarily selected numéraire.

Production is introduced in the second stage of the analysis. The consumers' endowments are assumed to consist of primary factors which they generally sell to entrepreneurs in order to be able to purchase produced commodities. The consumer receives predetermined proportions of the profits and losses earned by firms. The consumer's excess demand functions for factors and commodities are derived from his first-order conditions for utility maximization. Each entrepreneur uses both factors and commodities as inputs for the production of a single commodity. An entrepreneur's excess demand functions for his inputs are derived from his first-order conditions for profit maximization. The excess demand for his output is obtained by substituting the input values into his production function. The entrepreneur's excess demands are also homogeneous of degree zero in prices. Aggregate excess demand functions for each factor and commodity are obtained by summing the functions of the individual consumers and entrepreneurs. Walras' law again holds for the aggregate functions. A symmetry assumption is introduced, and the aggregate excess demands become functions of prices and the number of firms in each industry. Long-run equilibrium requires that every market be cleared and that the profit of the representative firm in each industry equal zero. Again, the excess demands are functionally dependent. A long-run equilibrium solution is expressed in terms of $(m - 1)$ exchange ratios and the number of firms in each industry.

The exchange ratios between every pair of commodities can be determined from the exchange ratios relative to the numéraire. The numéraire can serve as money in the standard-of-value sense. Its price can be set equal to unity and all other prices expressed in terms of its units. Alternatively, prices can be normalized by setting their sum equal to unity. Abstract accounting money can serve as a standard of value. Circulating paper money can be introduced, and its quantity will determine the level of absolute prices if Say's law is interpreted as an equilibrium condition and money is included in the budget constraints. The quantity of money cannot determine the level of absolute prices if Say's law is interpreted as an identity and money is excluded from the budget constraints.

The mere formulation of a multimarket system gives no assurance that an equilibrium solution exists. Particular numerical systems may be examined individually to determine existence. An existence proof states that systems which satisfy a number of general restrictions possess equilibrium solutions. The existence of excess demand functions is proved for an illustrative system. Then Brouwer's fixed-point theorem is used to prove that one or more equilibrium price sets exist for the system. The Debreu existence proof which is based upon much weaker assumptions is outlined.

The static and dynamic conditions for multimarket stability represent a generalization of the Walrasian condition for a single market. Perfect stability in the static Hicksian sense requires that the total derivatives dE_j/dp_j ($j = 2, \ldots ,m$) be negative for all possible combinations of rigid and flexible prices. Imperfect stability requires that the total derivatives be negative, given the assumption that all prices are flexible. An analysis of dynamic stability requires an explicit statement of the laws of price adjustment over time. A multimarket system is dynamically stable if all prices approach their equilibrium values over time following a disturbance. The dynamic stability of a system with lagged adjustment depends upon the speed with which adjustment takes place as well as the form of the excess demand functions. Dynamic stability and Hicksian stability are synonymous for a system with continuous adjustment if all commodities are strict gross substitutes. A system with a unique equilibrium is globally stable if its excess demand functions satisfy the Weak axiom of revealed preference. If a solution exists for a system that satisfies the Hicksian conditions for perfect stability throughout, the solution is unique. The Weak axiom also implies uniqueness.

EXERCISES

5-1. Consider a two-person, two-commodity, pure-exchange, competitive economy. The consumers' utility functions are $U_1 = q_{11}q_{12} + 12q_{11} + 3q_{12}$ and $U_2 = q_{21}q_{22} + 8q_{21} + 9q_{22}$. Consumer I has initial endowments of 8 and 30 units of Q_1 and Q_2 respectively; II has endowments of 10 units of each commodity. Determine excess demand functions for the two consumers. Determine an equilibrium price ratio for this economy.

5-2. Construct offer curves as mathematical functions from the first-order conditions for the two consumers described in Exercise 5-1. Show that the equilibrium derived in Exercise 5-1 satisfies both offer curves.

5-3. Derive excess demand functions for the inputs and output of a representative firm with the production function $\bar{q}_{hj} = (q_{hj1}^{*})^{\alpha}(q_{hj2}^{*})^{\beta}$ where $\alpha, \beta > 0$ and $\alpha + \beta < 1$.

5-4. Consider a two-person, two-commodity, pure-exchange economy with paper money. The utility functions are $U_1 = q_{11}q_{12}^{0.5}$ and $U_2 = q_{21}q_{22}^{0.5}$. Consumer I has initial endowments of 30 units of Q_1, 5 units of Q_2, and 43 units of money; II has respective endowments of 20, 10, and 2. Each of the consumers desires to hold a money stock equal to one-fifth of the value of his initial commodity endowment. Determine equilibrium money prices for Q_1 and Q_2. Show that the equilibrium prices would triple if the initial money stocks of I and II were increased to 129 and 6 respectively.

5-5. Use a Jacobian test to determine whether solutions exist for the following three-commodity systems:

(a) $E_2 = -8p_2 + 24p_3 + 6 = 0$; $E_3 = 10p_2 - 30p_3 + 8 = 0$.
(b) $E_2 = -3p_2 - p_2p_3 + p_3 = 0$; $E_3 = p_2 - p_2p_3 - 3p_3 = 0$.
(c) $E_2 = -4p_2 + 8p_3 + 4 = 0$; $E_3 = p_2^2 - 2p_2 - 4p_2p_3 + 4p_3 + 4p_3^2 + 1 = 0$.

5-6. Consider the system (5-58) with $b_{ii} < 0$ $(i = 2, \ldots ,m)$ and $b_{ij} = 0$ for $i > j$. Show that the system possesses perfect Hicksian stability in this case.

5-7. Find equilibrium prices for the three-commodity system given by

$$E_2 = 2p_2^2 + 22p_2 - 13p_2p_3 - 64p_3 + 20p_3^2 + 48 = 0$$
$$E_3 = p_2 - 2p_3 + 2 = 0$$

5-8. Assuming continuous adjustment, do the solutions for Exercise 5-7 satisfy the conditions for dynamic local stability?

*5-9. Consider a system with one primary good, Q_1, and one produced good, Q_2. Assume that each consumer has a positive initial endowment of the primary good, and a positive share of the profits of at least one firm. Assume that all individual utility functions are of the form $U_i = q_{i1}q_{i2}$ $(i = 1, \ldots ,n)$, and that the production function for a representative firm is of the form $\bar{q}_{h2} = (q_{h21}^*)^\alpha (q_{h22}^*)^\beta$ with $\alpha, \beta > 0$ and $\alpha + \beta < 1$. Show that this system meets the assumptions underlying the existence proof of Sec. 5-4.

SELECTED REFERENCES

Allen, R. G. D., *Mathematical Economics* (London: Macmillan, 1956). Multimarket equilibrium is covered in chap. 10, and multimarket stability in chap. 13. The necessary mathematical concepts beyond the calculus are developed in the text.

Debreu, Gerard, *Theory of Value* (New York: Wiley, 1959). Advanced mathematics is used to prove the existence of competitive equilibrium.

Hicks, J. R., *Value and Capital* (2d ed.; Oxford: Clarendon Press, 1946). Multimarket equilibrium is covered in chaps. IV–VIII. The mathematical development is contained in an appendix.

Kuenne, Robert E., *The Theory of General Economic Equilibrium* (Princeton, N.J.: Princeton, 1963). A detailed treatise using fairly simple mathematics.

Lancaster, Kelvin, *Mathematical Economics* (New York: Macmillan, 1968). Existence and stability are covered in chaps. 9 and 12 respectively. Advanced mathematical concepts are developed in appendices.

Lange, Oscar, "Say's Law: A Restatement and Criticism," in Lange, McIntyre, and Yntema (eds.), *Studies in Mathematical Economics and Econometrics* (Chicago: University of Chicago Press, 1942), pp. 49–68. A mathematical statement of alternative versions of Say's law and the possibility of introducing money into a multimarket equilibrium system.

Metzler, Lloyd A., "Stability of Multiple Markets: The Hicks Conditions," *Econometrica*, vol. 13 (October, 1945), pp. 277–292. An advanced mathematical discussion of the Hicksian and dynamic multimarket stability conditions.

Nikaido, Hukukane, *Convex Structures and Economic Theory* (New York: Academic, 1968). Existence, stability, and uniqueness are covered in this volume for the mathematically sophisticated reader.

Quirk, James, and Rubin Saposnik, *Introduction to General Equilibrium Theory and Welfare Economics* (New York: McGraw-Hill, 1968). Existence and stability are treated in chaps. 3 and 5 respectively. Mathematical concepts are simplified and developed in the text.

Samuelson, Paul A., *Foundations of Economic Analysis* (Cambridge, Mass.: Harvard, 1948). Dynamic multimarket stability is discussed in chap. IX.

Walras, Léon, *Elements of Pure Economics*, trans. by William Jaffé (Homewood, Ill.: Irwin, 1954). The original statement of multimarket equilibrium theory.

6
Imperfect Competition

Thus far, conditions of perfect competition have been assumed to prevail in all markets. A perfectly competitive industry contains a large number of firms selling a homogeneous product. Input and output prices are unaffected by the actions of any individual firm. Each firm faces a horizontal demand curve and maximizes profit by selecting an output level at which marginal cost equals market price.

A market is imperfectly competitive if the actions of one or more buyers or sellers have a perceptible influence on price. This broad definition of imperfect competition encompasses markets of many different types, which can be distinguished by further classification. Product and input markets are frequently classified according to the numbers of sellers and buyers which they contain. A market with a single seller is a *monopoly*, one with two a *duopoly*, and one with a small number greater than two an *oligopoly*. A market with a single buyer is a *monopsony*, one with two a *duopsony*, and one with a small number greater than two an *oligopsony*. Any combination of buyer and seller relationships is possible. A firm might be a perfect competitor in the markets for its inputs and a monopolist in the market for its output. Another firm might be a duopsonist in the markets for its inputs and an oligopolist in the market for its output. In fact, a single firm might purchase its various inputs in markets of quite different organization.

Product markets can be further classified with regard to differentiation. The theory of perfect competition is based upon the assumption that all firms within an industry produce a single homogeneous product and that buyers do not distinguish between the outputs of the various firms. However, the reader need not look far to discover industries in which the products of the various firms are close substitutes but differentiated in the eyes of the buyers. The cigarette industry provides a good example. Camels and Chesterfields are not the same product, though they satisfy the same need, and the demand for one depends upon the price of the other. The cigarette industry is an oligopoly *with product differentiation*.

Imperfect competition is not limited to markets with small numbers of buyers and sellers. Product differentiation alone is sufficient for its existence. An industry with a large number of firms selling closely related, but differentiated, products is a special case of imperfect competition called *monopolistic competition*. Each firm, though small in relation to the market as a whole, possesses some control over the price at which it sells.

The market demand curve for a commodity gives consumers' purchases as a function of price on the assumption that the prices of all other commodities remain unchanged. The relation between price and sales for an individual seller depends upon the organization of the market in which he sells. A monopolist's demand curve is the same as the corresponding market demand curve. A perfect competitor's demand curve is not directly related to the market demand curve for his output, since he is unable to influence price. His price-sales relationship is represented by a horizontal line at the going market price. His sales would fall off to zero if he attempted to charge more than the going price. He is able to sell his entire output at this price and would not be acting rationally if he lowered it. As a result, the individual seller's demand curve is constructed on the assumption that all sellers charge the same price.

The construction of individual demand curves for duopolists and oligopolists presents a number of new problems. First, consider the market for a homogeneous product. Competition among buyers will result in a single price for all sellers, but each seller is sufficiently large in relation to the market so that his actions will have noticeable effects upon his rivals. An output change on the part of one seller will affect the price received by all. The consequences of attempted price variations on the part of an individual seller are uncertain. His rivals may follow his change, or they may not, but he can no longer assume that they will not notice it. The results of any move on the part of a duopolist or oligopolist depend upon the reactions of his rivals. Since, in general, reaction patterns are uncertain, general price-sales relationships cannot be defined for an individual firm.

The scope for individual action is greater if the product is differentiated. An individual seller will not lose all his sales if he charges a higher price than his competitors. Some former buyers will switch to his competitors, but some of his more loyal customers will continue to purchase his differentiated product at a higher price because of their relatively strong preference for it. A market demand curve covering the entire industry cannot be defined, since each member of the market produces a commodity which is distinct in the eyes of consumers. Each producer faces a separate demand curve. The quantity sold by an individual producer is a function of his price and the prices of all his competitors. His actions are generally governed by the actions and reactions of his competitors.

A profit-maximizing monopolist operates unfettered by the competition of close rivals. An individual producer in a large group selling a differentiated product knows that his actions will have a negligible effect upon each of his competitors, and he is able to maximize his profit in a manner similar to that of an individual producer under conditions of perfect competition. The actions of individual sellers (or buyers) are highly interdependent in all other forms of imperfect competition. The actions of one firm have significant effects upon the quantities, prices, and profits of the others. Unqualified profit maximization is not possible, since an individual firm does not have control over all the variables that affect its profit. If an entrepreneur desires to maximize profit, he must take account of the reactions of his rivals to his decisions. There is a very large number of possible reaction patterns for duopolistic and oligopolistic markets, and as a result there is a very large number of theories of duopoly and oligopoly. Only a few of the many possible reaction patterns can be presented within the confines of the present chapter.

The traditional theory of monopoly, the one-firm industy, is developed in Sec. 6-1 and applied to special situations in Sec. 6-2. In Sec. 6-3 which concerns the problems of industries containing a small number of firms, product differentiation and five different theories of duopoly and oligopoly are discussed. Monopolistic competition is described in Sec. 6-4. Monopsony, duopsony, and oligopsony are outlined in Sec. 6-5, and bilateral monopoly is covered in Sec. 6-6.

6-1 MONOPOLY: BASIC THEORY

There is no distinction between the industry and the firm in a monopolistic market. The monopolistic firm is the industry; it has no com-

petitors.[1] A monopolist's individual demand curve possesses the same
general properties as the industry demand curve for a perfectly competitive market. It is an aggregate of the demand curves of individual
consumers and is assumed to be negatively sloped. The quantity of
his sales is a single-valued function of the price which he charges:

$$q = f(p) \qquad\qquad (6\text{-}1)$$

where $dq/dp < 0$. The demand curve has a unique inverse, and price
may be expressed as a single-valued function of quantity:

$$p = F(q) \qquad\qquad (6\text{-}2)$$

where $dp/dq < 0$. A major difference between a monopolist and a perfect competitor is that the monopolist's price decreases as he increases his
sales. A perfect competitor accepts price as a parameter and maximizes
profit with respect to variations of his output level; a monopolist may
maximize profit with respect to variations of either output or price. Of
course, he cannot set both independently since his price (output level) is
uniquely determined by his demand curve once he has selected his output
level (price). The price-quantity combination which maximizes profit is
invariant with respect to his choice of the independent variable.

AVERAGE AND MARGINAL REVENUE

The monopolist's total revenue (R) is price multiplied by quantity sold:

$$R = pq \qquad\qquad (6\text{-}3)$$

His marginal revenue (MR) is the derivative of his total revenue with
respect to his output level. Differentiating (6-3) with respect to q,

$$\text{MR} = \frac{dR}{dq} = p + q\,\frac{dp}{dq} \qquad\qquad (6\text{-}4)$$

Since $dp/dq < 0$, MR is less than price. The MR of a perfect competitor
is also defined by (6-4). His MR equals price since $dp/dq = 0$. The
monopolist's MR equals price less the rate of change of price with respect
to quantity multiplied by quantity. If the perfect competitor expands
his sales by 1 unit, his revenue will increase by the market value of the
additional unit. The monopolist must decrease the price he receives for
every unit in order to sell an additional unit.

---

[1] In a broad sense all products compete for the limited incomes of consumers. The
term monopoly defines a situation in which a single firm produces a commodity for
which there are no *close* substitutes. The prices of all other commodities are assumed
constant, as is always the case for the analysis of a single market, and the competition
of other commodities for the consumer's income is reflected in the position and shape
of the monopolist's demand curve.

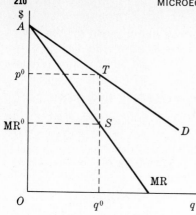

Fig. 6-1

Linear demand and MR curves are pictured in Fig. 6-1. Demand is monotonically decreasing, and MR is less than price for every output greater than zero. The rate of decline of MR is twice the rate of decline of price:

$$p = a - bq \qquad R = aq - bq^2 \qquad \text{MR} = \frac{dR}{dq} = a - 2bq$$

Since $dp/dq = -b$ is a constant, the distance between the two curves $\left(q\frac{dp}{dq} = bq \right)$ is a linear function of output. Total revenue for the price-quantity combination (p^0, q^0) equals the area of the rectangle Op^0Tq^0. The area $OASq^0$ which lies under the MR curve also equals total revenue:

$$\int_0^q (a - 2bq)\, dq = aq - bq^2 = R$$

This result is applicable to demand curves which are not linear. In general

$$\int_0^q \left(p + q\frac{dp}{dq} \right) dq = pq = R$$

since the integration constant always equals zero. Total revenue is given by the area lying under the MR curve.

The elasticity of demand (e) at a point on a demand curve is defined as the absolute value of the rate of percentage change of output divided by the rate of percentage change of price:[1]

$$e = -\frac{d(\log q)}{d(\log p)} = -\frac{p}{q}\frac{dq}{dp} \tag{6-5}$$

[1] Since attention is limited to negatively sloped demand curves, it is convenient to define the elasticity of demand as a positive number. This is in contrast to Sec. 2-4 where elasticities of demand take the signs of the slopes of the demand curves to which they refer.

MR as given by (6-4) can be expressed in terms of price and demand elasticity:

$$\text{MR} = p\left(1 + \frac{q}{p}\frac{dp}{dq}\right) = p\left(1 - \frac{1}{e}\right) \tag{6-6}$$

MR is positive if $e > 1$, zero if $e = 1$, and negative if $e < 1$. The difference between MR and price decreases as demand elasticity increases, and MR approaches price as demand elasticity approaches infinity.

A parabolic total revenue curve which corresponds to the linear demand curve of Fig. 6-1 is presented in Fig. 6-2. The first derivative of total revenue (MR) is monotonically decreasing and reaches zero at the output level q^0. Total revenue is increasing and $e > 1$ for $q < q^0$, is at a maximum and $e = 1$ for $q = q^0$, and is declining and $e < 1$ for $q > q^0$.

PROFIT MAXIMIZATION: COST FUNCTION

The monopolist's total revenue and total cost can both be expressed as functions of output:

$$R = R(q) \qquad C = C(q)$$

His profit is the difference between his total revenue and total cost:

$$\pi = R(q) - C(q) \tag{6-7}$$

To maximize profit set the derivative of (6-7) with respect to q equal to zero:

$$\frac{d\pi}{dq} = R'(q) - C'(q) = 0$$

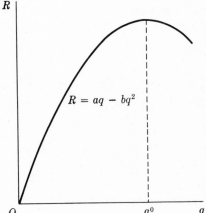

Fig. 6-2

or

$$R'(q) = C'(q) \tag{6-8}$$

MR must equal MC for profit maximization. The monopolist can increase his profit by expanding (or contracting) his output, as long as the addition to his revenue (MR) exceeds (or is less than) the addition to his cost (MC). Since MR is positive for a profit-maximizing output, it follows from (6-6) that the monopolist will always select an elastic point on his demand curve, i.e., a point at which $e > 1$. There is no similar restriction upon the equilibrium value of e for a competitive market.

The second-order condition for profit maximization requires that

$$\frac{d^2\pi}{dq^2} = R''(q) - C''(q) < 0$$

or adding $C''(q)$ to both sides of the inequality,

$$R''(q) < C''(q) \tag{6-9}$$

The rate of increase of MR must be less than the rate of increase of MC. The second-order condition is *a fortiori* satisfied if MR is decreasing and MC increasing, as is generally assumed. If MC is decreasing, (6-9) requires that MR be decreasing at a more rapid rate. If both conditions for profit maximization are satisfied for more than one output level, the one which yields the greatest profit can be selected by inspection.

The first-order condition can be satisfied in each of the three cases presented in Fig. 6-3. The equalization of MR and MC for (a) determines a quantity of q^0 and a price of p^0. The monopolist can set the price p^0 and allow the consumers to purchase q^0, or he can offer q^0 for sale and allow the consumers to determine a price of p^0. The second-order condition requires that the algebraic value of the slope of the MC curve

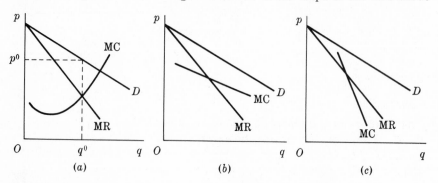

Fig. 6-3

exceed that of the MR curve, i.e., the MC curve must cut the MR curve from below. This condition is satisfied at the intersection points in (a) and (b). MR = MC does not yield a point of maximum profit in (c) since the MC curve cuts the MR curve from above at their only point of intersection. The first-order condition can be satisfied, but the second-order condition cannot.

If a monopolist followed the rule of a perfect competitor and equated MC to price, he would produce a greater output and charge a lower price. This is obvious by Fig. 6-3a. The coordinates of the intersection point of the MC and demand curves give a price less than p^0 and a quantity greater than q^0.

Consider a monopolist who faces a linear demand curve:

$$p = 100 - 4q \qquad R = pq = 100q - 4q^2 \tag{6-10}$$

and produces at a constant MC of 20 dollars. His total cost is a linear function of his output level:

$$C = 50 + 20q \tag{6-11}$$

His profit is

$$\pi = (100q - 4q^2) - (50 + 20q)$$

Setting MR equal to MC,

$$100 - 8q = 20$$
$$q = 10 \qquad p = 60 \qquad \pi = 350$$

The second-order condition is satisfied: the rate of change of MC (zero) exceeds the rate of change of MR (-8). If the monopolist were to follow the rule of the perfect competitor and set price equal to MC:

$$100 - 4q = 20$$
$$q = 20 \qquad p = 20 \qquad \pi = -50$$

he would sell a larger quantity at a lower price and earn a smaller profit. In this example the monopolist's 350 dollar profit would be reduced to a 50 dollar loss.

PROFIT MAXIMIZATION: PRODUCTION FUNCTION

The analysis of monopoly is usually conducted in terms of cost functions. There are situations, however, in which it is desirable to consider a monopolist's production function and input purchases explicitly. Assume that a monopolist uses two inputs which he purchases in competitive markets to produce his output. His profit is

$$\pi = R(q) - r_1 x_1 - r_2 x_2$$

Setting the partial derivatives of profit with respect to inputs equal to zero,

$$\frac{\partial \pi}{\partial x_i} = R'(q)h_i - r_i = 0 \qquad i = 1, 2 \tag{6-12}$$

where $q = h(x_1,x_2)$ and $h_i = \partial q/\partial x_i$. Rearranging terms,

$$R'(q)h_i = r_i \qquad i = 1, 2$$

Profit maximization requires that the monopolist set the value of the *marginal-revenue product* of each input equal to its price. In monopoly marginal revenue times marginal product equals input price; in perfect competition output price times marginal product equals input price.

The second-order conditions for profit maximization require that

$$\pi_{11} < 0 \qquad \pi_{22} < 0 \qquad \pi_{11}\pi_{22} - \pi_{12}^2 > 0 \tag{6-13}$$

where $\pi_{ij} = \partial^2 \pi/\partial x_i\, \partial x_j$. By further differentiation of (6-12),

$$\pi_{ii} = R'(q)h_{ii} + R''(q)h_i^2 < 0 \qquad i = 1, 2$$

or by rearranging terms and substituting from (6-12),[1]

$$R''(q) < -\frac{R'(q)h_{ii}}{h_i^2} = -\frac{r_i h_{ii}}{h_i^3} = C''(q) \qquad i = 1, 2 \tag{6-14}$$

The MC obtained by varying either of the inputs cannot exceed MR. The third inequality of (6-13) requires that the MC obtained by varying both of the inputs cannot exceed MR.

Since $R''(q) = 0$ for a perfect competitor, his $C''(q)$ must be positive, or equivalently, his production function must be strictly concave in the neighborhood of an equilibrium point. Since $R''(q)$ is normally negative for a monopolist, his $C''(q)$ may also be negative and still satisfy (6-14). Thus, it is possible to have a monopoly equilibrium at a point at which the production function is not strictly concave, i.e., a point

---

[1] Let $F(q,x_1,x_2) = q - h(x_1,x_2)$, and

$$\frac{\partial x_i}{\partial q} = -\frac{F_q}{F_{x_i}} = -\frac{1}{h_i}$$

and by further differentiation,

$$\frac{\partial^2 x_i}{\partial q^2} = \frac{h_{ii}(\partial x_i/\partial q)}{h_i^2} = -\frac{h_{ii}}{h_i^3}$$

The last equality of (6-14) is derived using the composite-function rule:

$$C''(q) = \frac{\partial^2 C}{\partial x_i^2}\left(\frac{\partial x_i}{\partial q}\right)^2 + \frac{\partial C}{\partial x_i}\frac{\partial^2 x_i}{\partial q^2} = -\frac{r_i h_{ii}}{h_i^3}$$

at which $h_{ii} > 0$. Strict concavity of the production function at a point at which (6-12) is satisfied is sufficient for monopoly equilibrium, but not necessary.

6-2 MONOPOLY: APPLICATIONS

The basic theory of monopoly may be modified to cover a wide variety of situations. Four applications are considered in this section.

THE DISCRIMINATING MONOPOLIST

The monopolist need not always sell his entire output in a single market for a uniform price. In some situations he is able to sell in two or more distinct markets at different prices and thereby increase his profit. Price discrimination is feasible only if buyers are unable to purchase the product in one market and resell it in another. Otherwise, speculators would buy in a low-price market and resell in a high-price market at a profit, and thereby equalize price in all markets. Personal services are seldom transferable, and their sale frequently provides an opportunity for price discrimination. The resale of such commodities as electricity, gas, and water, which require physical connections between the facilities of the producer and consumer, is extremely difficult, and price discrimination is widely followed in setting utility rates. Price discrimination is often possible in spatially separated markets such as the "home" and "foreign" markets of a monopolist who sells abroad; resale can be prevented by a sufficiently high tariff.

If a monopolist practices price discrimination in two distinct markets, his profit is the difference between his total revenue from both markets and his total cost of production:

$$\pi = R_1(q_1) + R_2(q_2) - C(q_1 + q_2) \tag{6-15}$$

where q_1 and q_2 are the quantities which he sells in the two markets, $R_1(q_1)$ and $R_2(q_2)$ are his revenue functions, and $C(q_1 + q_2)$ is his cost function. Setting the partial derivatives of (6-15) equal to zero,

$$\frac{\partial \pi}{\partial q_1} = R_1'(q_1) - C'(q_1 + q_2) = 0$$

$$\frac{\partial \pi}{\partial q_2} = R_2'(q_2) - C'(q_1 + q_2) = 0$$

or

$$R_1'(q_1) = R_2'(q_2) = C'(q_1 + q_2)$$

The MR in each market must equal the MC of the output as a whole. If the MRs were not equal, the monopolist could increase total revenue without affecting total cost by shifting sales from the low MR market to the high one. The equality of the MRs does not necessarily imply the equality of prices in the two markets. Denoting the prices and the demand elasticities in the two markets by p_1, p_2, e_1, and e_2 and utilizing (6-6), the equality of the MRs implies

$$p_1\left(1 - \frac{1}{e_1}\right) = p_2\left(1 - \frac{1}{e_2}\right)$$

and

$$\frac{p_1}{p_2} = \frac{1 - 1/e_2}{1 - 1/e_1}$$

Price will be lower in the market with the greater demand elasticity. The prices will be equal if and only if the demand elasticities are equal.

Second-order conditions require that the principal minors of the relevant Hessian determinant

$$\begin{vmatrix} R_1'' - C'' & -C'' \\ -C'' & R_2'' - C'' \end{vmatrix}$$

alternate in sign beginning with the negative sign. Expanding the principal minors,

$$R_1'' - C'' < 0 \qquad (R_1'' - C'')(R_2'' - C'') - (C'')^2 > 0$$

These imply that $R_2'' - C'' < 0$. The MR in each market must be increasing less rapidly than the MC for the output as a whole.

Assume that the monopolist whose demand and cost functions are given by (6-10) and (6-11) is able to separate his consumers into two distinct markets:[1]

$$\begin{aligned} p_1 &= 80 - 5q_1 & R_1 &= 80q_1 - 5q_1^2 \\ p_2 &= 180 - 20q_2 & R_2 &= 180q_2 - 20q_2^2 \\ C &= 50 + 20(q_1 + q_2) \end{aligned}$$

----

[1] His aggregate demand curve remains unchanged. Solving the demand equations for q_1 and q_2,

$$q_1 = 16 - 0.2p_1 \qquad q_2 = 9 - 0.05p_2$$

The total demand at any price (p) is the sum of the demands in the two markets:

$$q = q_1 + q_2 = 16 - 0.2p + 9 - 0.05p = 25 - 0.25p$$

Solving for p,

$$p = 100 - 4q$$

which is the demand function (6-10).

Setting the MR in each market equal to the MC of the output as a whole,

$$80 - 10q_1 = 20 \qquad 180 - 40q_2 = 20$$

Solving for q_1 and q_2 and substituting into the demand, profit, and elasticity equations,

$$q_1 = 6 \qquad p_1 = 50 \qquad e_1 = 1.67$$
$$q_2 = 4 \qquad p_2 = 100 \qquad e_2 = 1.25$$
$$\pi = 450$$

Second-order conditions are satisfied:

$$-10 < 0 \qquad \begin{vmatrix} -10 & 0 \\ 0 & -40 \end{vmatrix} = 400 > 0$$

The monopolist has increased his profit from 350 to 450 dollars through discrimination. Price is lower in the market with the greater demand elasticity. Further discrimination would be profitable if the monopolist were able to subdivide his consumers into a larger number of groups with different demand elasticities.

Each point on the demand curve gives the highest single price that consumers are willing to pay for the corresponding quantity of output. Some consumers would be willing to pay more rather than forego consumption of the commodity. They gain a *consumers' surplus* from a single price system. For simplicity assume that income effects are zero so that the ordinary and compensated demand curves coincide (see Sec. 2-4). Consumers' surplus then equals the area under the demand curve less the amount that consumers pay for the commodity.

The *perfectly discriminating monopolist* is able to subdivide his market to such a degree that he sells each successive unit of his commodity for the maximum amount that consumers are willing to pay. The monopolist, thereby, extracts all the consumers' surplus. His total revenue is the area under his demand curve and his profit is

$$\pi = \int_0^q F(q)\, dq - C(q)$$

Setting the derivative of profit with respect to output equal to zero,

$$\frac{d\pi}{dq} = F(q) - C'(q) = 0$$

and $F(q) = C'(q)$. Profit is maximized by equating marginal price and marginal cost. In diagrammatic terms the perfectly discriminating monopolist operates at a point at which his MC curve intersects his demand curve. The second-order condition for profit maximization:

$$\frac{d^2\pi}{dq^2} = F'(q) - C''(q) < 0$$

requires that the slope of his MC curve be greater than the slope of his demand curve.

Assuming perfect discrimination for the example given by (6-10) and (6-11), profit is

$$\pi = \int_0^q (100 - 4q)\, dq - (50 + 20q)$$

and setting marginal price equal to MC,

$$100 - 4q = 20 \qquad q = 20 \qquad \pi = 750$$

The perfectly discriminating monopolist produces more than the 10 units produced by the simple monopolist and earns a higher profit than the 350 earned by the simple monopolist. His marginal price is 20, but his average revenue per unit sold is 100, contrasted with a uniform price of 60 for the simple monopolist.

THE MULTIPLE-PLANT MONOPOLIST

Consider a monopolist selling in a single market, who can produce his output in two separate plants. His profit is the difference between his total revenue and his total production costs for both plants:

$$\pi = R(q_1 + q_2) - C_1(q_1) - C_2(q_2) \tag{6-16}$$

where q_1 and q_2 are the quantities which he produces in the two plants, $R(q_1 + q_2)$ is his revenue function, and $C_1(q_1)$ and $C_2(q_2)$ are his cost functions. Setting the partial derivatives of (6-16) equal to zero,

$$\frac{\partial \pi}{\partial q_1} = R'(q_1 + q_2) - C_1'(q_1) = 0$$

$$\frac{\partial \pi}{\partial q_2} = R'(q_1 + q_2) - C_2'(q_2) = 0$$

or

$$R'(q_1 + q_2) = C_1'(q_1) = C_2'(q_2)$$

The MC in each plant must equal the MR of the output as a whole. Second-order conditions require that the principal minors of the relevant Hessian determinant

$$\begin{vmatrix} R'' - C_1'' & R'' \\ R'' & R'' - C_2'' \end{vmatrix} \tag{6-17}$$

alternate in sign beginning with the negative sign.   The reader can verify that (6-17) requires that the MC in each plant must be increasing more rapidly than the MR of the output as a whole.

TAXATION AND MONOPOLY OUTPUT

A lump-sum or a profit tax (with a marginal rate less than 100 percent) will reduce the profit after taxes of a profit-maximizing monopolist, but will not affect his optimum price-quantity combination.   A sales tax, whether based upon quantity sold or value of sales, will reduce his profit and output level and increase his price.

The monopolist cannot avoid a lump-sum tax.   It must be paid regardless of the physical quantity or value of his sales or the amount of his profit.   His profit becomes

$$\pi = R(q) - C(q) - T \tag{6-18}$$

where T is the amount of the lump-sum tax and π is his profit after the tax payment.   Setting the derivative of (6-18) equal to zero,

$$\frac{d\pi}{dq} = R'(q) - C'(q) = 0 \qquad R'(q) = C'(q)$$

Since T is a constant, it vanishes upon differentiation, and the monopolist's output level and price are determined by the equality of MR and MC as would be the case if no tax were imposed.[1]

A profit tax requires that the monopolist pay the government a specified proportion of the difference between his total revenue and total cost.   If the tax is a flat rate (constant proportion), his profit after tax payment is

$$\pi = R(q) - C(q) - t[R(q) - C(q)] = (1 - t)[R(q) - C(q)] \tag{6-19}$$

where $0 < t < 1$.   Setting the derivative of (6-19) equal to zero,

$$\frac{d\pi}{dq} = (1 - t)[R'(q) - C'(q)] = 0$$

Since $1 - t \neq 0$,

$$R'(q) - C'(q) = 0 \qquad R'(q) = C'(q)$$

Since the first-order condition is the same as (6-8), output level and price are unaffected.   The only way a monopolist can avoid a profit tax is to reduce his profit before taxes.   If he is able to keep a fraction of an increase of profit before taxes, he will maximize his profit after taxes by equating MR and MC.

[1] Second-order conditions are henceforth assumed to be satisfied unless otherwise stated.

If a specific sales tax of α dollars per unit of output is imposed,

$$\pi = R(q) - C(q) - \alpha q$$

and

$$\frac{d\pi}{dq} = R'(q) - C'(q) - \alpha = 0 \qquad R'(q) = C'(q) + \alpha \qquad (6\text{-}20)$$

The monopolist maximizes profit after tax payment by equating MR with MC plus the unit tax. Taking the total differential of (6-20),

$$R''(q)\, dq = C''(q)\, dq + d\alpha$$

and

$$\frac{dq}{d\alpha} = \frac{1}{R''(q) - C''(q)}$$

Since $R''(q) - C''(q) < 0$ by the assumption that the second-order condition is fulfilled, $dq/d\alpha < 0$, and the optimum output level declines as the tax rate increases. The imposition of a specific sales tax results in a smaller quantity sold and a higher price.

Return to the example given by (6-10) and (6-11) and assume that the government imposes a tax of 8 dollars per unit upon the monopolist's output:

$$\pi = (100q - 4q^2) - (50 + 20q) - 8q$$
$$\frac{d\pi}{dq} = 72 - 8q = 0 \qquad q = 9 \qquad p = 64 \qquad \pi = 274$$

Sales diminish by 1 unit, price increases by 4 dollars, and the monopolist's profit diminishes by 76 dollars as a result of the imposition of the tax. Price increases by less than the unit tax, but the monopolist's profit decreases by more than the 72 dollar tax revenue. If the government imposed a 72 dollar lump-sum tax upon the monopolist, it would receive the same revenue, the monopolist's profit would be decreased by 4 dollars less, and the consumers would not have to pay a higher price for the product. As a result it is frequently argued that a lump-sum tax is preferable to a sales tax.

The results are similar if the sales tax is a proportion of the value of sales (total revenue),

$$\pi = R(q) - C(q) - sR(q) = (1 - s)R(q) - C(q)$$
$$\frac{d\pi}{dq} = (1 - s)R'(q) - C'(q) = 0 \qquad (1 - s)R'(q) = C'(q) \qquad (6\text{-}21)$$

where $0 < s < 1$. Profits are maximized by equating MC to the portion of the MR that the monopolist is allowed to retain. Taking the total differential of (6-21),

$$(1 - s)R''(q)\, dq - R'(q)\, ds = C''(q)\, dq$$

and

$$\frac{dq}{ds} = \frac{R'(q)}{(1 - s)R''(q) - C''(q)} \tag{6-22}$$

Since the first-order condition requires that MR be positive and the second-order condition requires that the denominator of (6-22) be negative, $dq/ds < 0$. The imposition of an ad valorem sales tax also results in a reduced output level and an increased price.

THE REVENUE–MAXIMIZING MONOPOLIST

It has been suggested that many large firms do not maximize profit, but rather maximize sales revenue subject to the constraint that profit equal or exceed some minimum acceptable level.[1] The monopolist desires to maximize $R(q)$ subject to

$$\pi = R(q) - C(q) \geqq \pi^0 \tag{6-23}$$

where π^0 is the minimum acceptable profit.

Assume that a unique unrestricted maximum profit, π^*, exists at the output q^* with $R'(q^*) > 0$, $C''(q) > 0$ for $q \geqq q^*$, and $R''(q) < 0$ for $q > 0$. If $\pi^0 > \pi^*$, (6-23) cannot be satisfied and the maximum-revenue problem has no solution. A solution will exist if $\pi^0 \leqq \pi^*$. If $\pi^0 = \pi^*$, q^* is the maximum-revenue solution since it is the only output that satisfies (6-23). If $\pi^0 < \pi^*$, revenue will increase and profit decrease as q is increased beyond q^*. Thus, the monopolist will continue to increase q until either he reaches the unrestricted maximum of $R(q)$ or (6-23) is satisfied as an equality, whichever occurs at the lower output. Under these conditions the maximum-revenue output can be determined as follows: First, find the q that gives an unrestricted maximum for $R(q)$. This is the solution if the corresponding profit satisfies (6-23). If it does not, the solution is obtained by solving the equality of (6-23) for q.

Consider again the example given by (6-10) and (6-11). Assume that $334 = \pi^0 < \pi^* = 350$. The unrestricted maximum for $R(q)$ is 625 which occurs at $q = 12.5$ with $\pi = 325$. This option may be excluded because it yields too low a profit. The equality of (6-23) is

$$(100q - 4q^2) - (50 + 20q) = 334$$

which may also be written as

$$q^2 - 20q + 96 = 0$$

This quadratic equation has the roots 8 and 12 with respective total revenues of 544 and 624. Thus, the revenue-maximizing monopolist

---

[1] See William J. Baumol, *Business Behavior, Value and Growth* (rev. ed.; New York: Harcourt, Brace & World, 1967), chap. 6.

produces 12 units which he sells at a price of 52 to gain a total revenue of 624 and a profit of 334. By contrast, the simple monopolist produces 10 units which he sells at a price of 60 to gain a total revenue of 600 and a profit of 350.

The revenue-maximizing monopolist, unlike the simple monopolist, may alter his output if a profit tax is introduced. Consider a case in which his output is determined by the equality of (6-23) both before and after a tax is imposed. Assume that the tax, $0 < t < 1$, is a constant fraction of profit. The equality of (6-23) becomes

$$(1 - t)[R(q) - C(q)] = \pi^0 \tag{6-24}$$

Taking the total differential of (6-24),

$$\frac{dq}{dt} = \frac{R(q) - C(q)}{(1 - t)[R'(q) - C'(q)]}$$

Since the value of q that satisfies (6-24) is greater than q^*, $R'(q) - C'(q)$ is negative. Since $R(q) - C(q)$ and $1 - t$ are positive, $dq/dt < 0$; that is, an increase in the profit-tax rate reduces the maximum-revenue output. If the output for an unrestricted maximum revenue yielded a profit at least as great as the minimum acceptable level both before and after the imposition of a tax, the monopolist would not alter this output.

6-3 DUOPOLY AND OLIGOPOLY

A duopolistic industry contains two sellers. An oligopolistic industry contains a number sufficiently small so that the actions of any individual seller have a perceptible influence upon his rivals. It is not sufficient to distinguish oligopoly from perfect competition for a homogeneous product or from the many-sellers case of monopolistic competition for a differentiated product on the basis of the number of sellers alone. The essential distinguishing feature is the interdependence of the various sellers' actions. If the influence of one seller's quantity decision upon the profit of another, $\partial \pi_i / \partial q_j$, is imperceptible, the industry satisfies the basic requirement for either perfect competition or the many-sellers case of monopolistic competition. If $\partial \pi_i / \partial q_j$ is of a noticeable order of magnitude, it is duopolistic or oligopolistic.[1]

---

[1] Market symmetry is assumed throughout the present chapter, in the sense that the partial derivatives $\partial \pi_i / \partial q_j$ are assumed to be of the same order of magnitude for all i and j except $i = j$. Many asymmetric market situations can be analyzed by modifying and combining the analyses for symmetric markets. Consider the case of partial monopoly, i.e., a market containing one large seller and a large number of small ones. The partial derivatives $\partial \pi_i / \partial q_j$ are of an imperceptible order of magni-

The price-quantity combination and profit of a duopolist or oligopolist depend upon the actions of all members of his market. He can control his own output level (or price, if his product is differentiated), but he has no direct control over the other variables which affect his profit. The profit of each seller is the result of the interaction of the decisions of all market members. There are no generally accepted behavior assumptions for oligopolists and duopolists as there are for perfect competitors and monopolists. There are many different solutions for duopolistic and oligopolistic markets. Each solution is based upon a different set of behavior assumptions. Five of the more interesting solutions are described in the present section. Each is developed for a duopolistic market, but all except the Stackelberg solution are easily generalized for oligopolistic markets. The Cournot, collusion, and Stackelberg solutions are developed for markets with homogeneous products, but are easily extended to cover markets with differentiated products. The market-shares and kinked-demand-curve solutions are developed for differentiated products. The former can be modified to cover homogeneous products, but the latter cannot.

THE COURNOT SOLUTION

The classical solution of the duopoly (and oligopoly) problem is associated with the name of Augustin Cournot, an early-nineteenth-century French economist. Two firms are assumed to produce a homogeneous product. The inverse demand function states price as a function of the aggregate quantity sold:

$$p = F(q_1 + q_2) \tag{6-25}$$

where q_1 and q_2 are the levels of the duopolists' outputs. The total revenue of each duopolist depends upon his own output level and that of his rival:

$$R_1 = q_1 F(q_1 + q_2) = R_1(q_1, q_2)$$
$$R_2 = q_2 F(q_1 + q_2) = R_2(q_1, q_2)$$

---

tude for $i = 1, \ldots, n$; $j = 2, \ldots, n$; and $i \neq j$; and $\partial \pi_i / \partial q_1$ is of a noticeable order of magnitude for all i where the subscript 1 denotes the large seller.

A theory of partial monopoly can be formulated by combining the theories of pure monopoly and perfect competition. The small firms will accept the going price and adjust their output levels to maximize profit in the same manner as a perfect competitor. The partial monopolist's effective demand function is obtained by subtracting the supply of the small firms, a function of price, from the market demand curve, also a function of price. Using this net demand function, the partial monopolist maximizes profit by selecting either a price or output level in the same manner as a pure monopolist.

The profit of each equals his total revenue less his cost, which depends upon his output level alone:

$$\pi_1 = R_1(q_1,q_2) - C_1(q_1)$$
$$\pi_2 = R_2(q_1,q_2) - C_2(q_2) \tag{6-26}$$

The basic behavior assumption of the Cournot solution is that each duopolist maximizes his profit on the assumption that the quantity produced by his rival is invariant with respect to his own quantity decision. The first duopolist (I for short) maximizes π_1 with respect to q_1, treating q_2 as a parameter, and the second (II for short) maximizes π_2 with respect to q_2, treating q_1 as a parameter.

Setting the appropriate partial derivatives of (6-26) equal to zero,

$$\frac{\partial \pi_1}{\partial q_1} = \frac{\partial R_1}{\partial q_1} - \frac{dC_1}{dq_1} = 0 \qquad \frac{\partial R_1}{\partial q_1} = \frac{dC_1}{dq_1}$$
$$\frac{\partial \pi_2}{\partial q_2} = \frac{\partial R_2}{\partial q_2} - \frac{dC_2}{dq_2} = 0 \qquad \frac{\partial R_2}{\partial q_2} = \frac{dC_2}{dq_2} \tag{6-27}$$

First-order conditions require that each duopolist equate his MC to his MR. The MRs of the duopolists are not necessarily equal. Let $q = q_1 + q_2$ and $\partial q/\partial q_1 = \partial q/\partial q_2 = 1$. The MRs of the duopolists are

$$\frac{\partial R_i}{\partial q} = p + q_i \frac{dp}{dq} \qquad i = 1, 2$$

The duopolist with the greater output will have the smaller MR. An increase of output by either duopolist acting alone will result in a reduction of price, i.e., a movement down the market demand curve, and the total revenues of both will be affected. The rates of change of the total revenues depend upon the output levels. Imagine that price decreases at the rate of 1 dollar per unit increase of aggregate sales, and that $q_1 = 100$ and $q_2 = 200$. If I increases his output to 101 units, he will receive 100 dollars less for the 100 units he had previously sold at a higher price. If II's output remains unchanged, he will lose 200 dollars of revenue as a result of I's action, but this is of no concern to I within the framework of the Cournot assumptions. If II increases his output by 1 unit, with I's output level unchanged, he will receive 200 dollars less for the units he had previously sold.

The second-order condition for each duopolist requires that

$$\frac{\partial^2 \pi_i}{\partial q_i^2} = \frac{\partial^2 R_i}{\partial q_i^2} - \frac{d^2 C_i}{dq_i^2} < 0 \qquad i = 1, 2$$

or

$$\frac{\partial^2 R_i}{\partial q_i^2} < \frac{d^2 C_i}{dq_i^2} \qquad i = 1, 2 \tag{6-28}$$

Each duopolist's MR must be increasing less rapidly than his MC.   The maximization process for the Cournot solution is not the same as in the case of the two-plant monopolist, where a single individual controls the values of both output levels.   Here each duopolist maximizes his profit with respect to the single variable under his control.

The duopolistic market is in equilibrium if the values of q_1 and q_2 are such that each duopolist maximizes his profit, given the output of the other, and neither desires to alter his output.   The equilibrium solution can be obtained by solving (6-27) for q_1 and q_2 if (6-28) is satisfied. The market process can be described more fully by introducing an additional step before solving for the equilibrium output levels.   Reaction functions which express the output of each duopolist as a function of his rival's output are determined by solving the first equation of (6-27) for q_1 and the second for q_2:

$$q_1 = \Psi_1(q_2)$$
$$q_2 = \Psi_2(q_1)$$
\hfill (6-29)

I's reaction function gives a relationship between q_1 and q_2 with the property that for any specified value of q_2 the corresponding value of q_1 maximizes π_1.   II's reaction function gives the value of q_2 which maximizes π_2 for any specified value of q_1.   An equilibrium solution is a pair of values for q_1 and q_2 which satisfy both reaction functions.

If the demand and cost functions are

$$p = A - B(q_1 + q_2) \qquad C_1 = a_1 q_1 + b_1 q_1^2 \qquad C_2 = a_2 q_2 + b_2 q_2^2$$

with all parameters positive, the profits of the duopolists are

$$\pi_1 = A q_1 - B(q_1 + q_2)q_1 - a_1 q_1 - b_1 q_1^2$$
$$\pi_2 = A q_2 - B(q_1 + q_2)q_2 - a_2 q_2 - b_2 q_2^2$$

Setting the appropriate partial derivatives equal to zero,

$$\frac{\partial \pi_1}{\partial q_1} = A - B(2q_1 + q_2) - a_1 - 2b_1 q_1 = 0$$

$$\frac{\partial \pi_2}{\partial q_2} = A - B(q_1 + 2q_2) - a_2 - 2b_2 q_2 = 0$$

The corresponding reaction functions are

$$q_1 = \frac{A - a_1}{2(B + b_1)} - \frac{B}{2(B + b_1)} q_2 \qquad q_2 = \frac{A - a_2}{2(B + b_2)} - \frac{B}{2(B + b_2)} q_1$$
\hfill (6-30)

Since B, b_1, and b_2 are all positive, a rise of either duopolist's output will cause a reduction of the other's optimum output.   The reaction func-

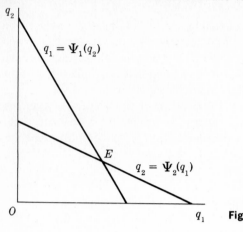

Fig. 6-4

tions are linear as pictured in Fig. 6-4. An equilibrium is provided by a solution of (6-30), or equivalently, by an intersection point for the reaction curves, such as E in Fig. 6-4. The solution of (6-30) is

$$q_1 = \frac{2(B + b_2)(A - a_1) - B(A - a_2)}{4(B + b_1)(B + b_2) - B^2}$$

$$q_2 = \frac{2(B + b_1)(A - a_2) - B(A - a_1)}{4(B + b_1)(B + b_2) - B^2}$$

The second-order conditions are satisfied by the linear demand and quadratic cost functions:

$$\frac{\partial^2 \pi_1}{\partial q_1^2} = -2(B + b_1) < 0 \qquad \frac{\partial^2 \pi_2}{\partial q_2^2} = -2(B + b_2) < 0$$

For illustration, let the demand and cost functions be given by

$$p = 100 - 0.5(q_1 + q_2) \qquad C_1 = 5q_1 \qquad C_2 = 0.5q_2^2 \tag{6-31}$$

The reader may verify that the reaction functions are

$$q_1 = 95 - 0.5q_2 \qquad q_2 = 50 - 0.25q_1 \tag{6-32}$$

and that the equilibrium solution is

$$q_1 = 80 \qquad q_2 = 30 \qquad p = 45 \qquad \pi_1 = 3{,}200 \qquad \pi_2 = 900$$

Thus far, it has been assumed that a Cournot equilibrium is reached through a sequence of instantaneous adjustments. It is of interest to ask whether a Cournot equilibrium will be reached if each of the sequential quantity adjustments takes a finite length of time. An explicit dynamic adjustment process must be introduced before this question can be answered.   Assume that each duopolist begins with an arbitrarily selected output level which he changes from period to period in proportion to the discrepancy between his desired and actual output levels in the preceding period:

$$q_{1t} - q_{1,t-1} = k[\Psi_1(q_{2,t-1}) - q_{1,t-1}]$$
$$q_{2t} - q_{2,t-1} = k[\Psi_2(q_{1,t-1}) - q_{2,t-1}]$$
$$(6\text{-}33)$$

where k is a positive constant.   For simplicity, it is assumed that a single value of the adjustment coefficient, k, is applicable for both duopolists.   The duopolists' desired output levels are given by their reaction functions.

For illustration, consider the demand function $p = 100 - q_1 - q_2$ and the cost functions $C_1 = 3q_1$, $C_2 = 2q_2$.   Forming the profit functions and setting the appropriate derivatives equal to zero yields the reaction functions

$$2q_1 + q_2 = 97 \qquad q_1 + 2q_2 = 98$$

for I and II respectively.   The equilibrium output levels are $q_1 = 32$, $q_2 = 33$.   Substituting these reaction functions into (6-33) and rearranging terms,

$$q_{1t} - (1 - k)q_{1,t-1} + 0.5kq_{2,t-1} - 48.5k = 0$$
$$q_{2t} - (1 - k)q_{2,t-1} + 0.5kq_{1,t-1} - 49k \quad = 0$$

Following the procedures of Sec. 4-8, solve the first equation for $q_{2,t-1}$ and substitute this result with appropriate change of the lags for q_{2t} and $q_{2,t-1}$ in the second equation:

$$q_{1t} - 2(1 - k)q_{1,t-1} + [(1 - k)^2 - 0.25k^2]q_{1,t-2} - 24k^2 = 0$$

which is a second-order nonhomogeneous difference equation (see Sec. A-5).   The solution of this equation is

$$q_{1t} = c_1(1 - 0.5k)^t + c_2(1 - 1.5k)^t + 32$$

where c_1 and c_2 depend on initial conditions.   The constant term, 32, is the equilibrium value of q_1.   The first two terms will approach zero as t approaches ∞ if the parenthesized roots are each less than one in absolute value.   Since $k > 0$, both roots are less than $+1$.   The second root is smaller than the first.   Therefore, the system will be stable and approach the Cournot equilibrium if the second root is greater than -1, which will be the case if $k < \frac{4}{3}$.   A sufficiently strong speed of adjustment, k, can render the equilibrium unattainable.   The reader may verify that the speed of adjustment will not have this effect if a differential-equation version of the adjustment process is used.

The basic behavior assumption of the Cournot solution is rather weak. Each duopolist acts as if his rival's output were fixed. However, this is not the case. Equilibrium is reached through a sequence of instantaneous adjustments. One sets an output; this induces the other to adjust his output, which in turn induces the first to adjust his, and so on. It is rather unlikely that each will assume that his quantity decisions do not affect his rival's quantity decision if each of his adjustments is immediately followed by a reaction on the part of his rival. Others have assumed that each maximizes his profit on the assumption that his rival's price remains unchanged, but this is an even more unrealistic assumption if the product is homogeneous. Duopolists and oligopolists generally recognize the mutual interdependence of their decisions and those of their rivals.

The Cournot solution is easily extended to markets containing more than two sellers. As the number of sellers is increased, the output of each represents a progressively smaller proportion of the industry total, and the effects of an individual seller's actions upon his rivals become less and less noticeable. Under various simplifying assumptions the Cournot solution approaches in the limit the perfectly competitive result. An individual seller will be unable to influence price, his MR will equal the market price, and his individual actions will not induce reactions on the part of his rivals.

THE COLLUSION SOLUTION

Duopolists (or oligopolists) may recognize their mutual interdependence and agree to act in unison in order to maximize the total profit of the industry. Both variables are then under a single control, and the industry is, in effect, a monopoly. Maximization proceeds in the same manner as for the two-plant monopolist.

Consider the example given by (6-31). Industry profit is

$$\pi = \pi_1 + \pi_2 = 100(q_1 + q_2) - 0.5(q_1 + q_2)^2 - 5q_1 - 0.5q_2^2$$

Setting the partial derivatives of π equal to zero,

$$\frac{\partial \pi}{\partial q_1} = 95 - q_1 - q_2 = 0 \qquad \frac{\partial \pi}{\partial q_2} = 100 - q_1 - 2q_2 = 0$$

Solving for q_1 and q_2 and substituting in the profit and demand equations,

$$q_1 = 90 \qquad q_2 = 5 \qquad \pi = 4,525 \qquad p = 52.5$$

Comparison with the Cournot solution shows that the colluding duopolists produce a smaller total output at a higher price for a larger total profit. From the viewpoint of the industry as a whole, it is advantageous for the firm with the lower MC (I in this example) to increase its relative share of total output.   The equilibrium MCs of the two firms are equal for the collusion solution.

THE STACKELBERG SOLUTION

Generally, the profit of each duopolist is a function of the output levels of both:

$$\pi_1 = h_1(q_1,q_2) \qquad \pi_2 = h_2(q_1,q_2) \tag{6-34}$$

The Cournot solution is obtained by maximizing π_1 with respect to q_1 and π_2 with respect to q_2.   The collusion solution is obtained by maximizing $\pi_1 + \pi_2$ with respect to both q_1 and q_2.   Many other modes of maximizing behavior are possible for the duopolists whose profit functions are given by (6-34).   One of the more interesting is the analysis of leadership and followership formulated by the German economist Heinrich von Stackelberg.

A *follower* obeys his reaction function (6-29) and adjusts his output level to maximize his profit, given the quantity decision of his rival, whom he assumes to be a leader.   A *leader* does not obey his reaction function.   He assumes that his rival acts as a follower, and maximizes his profit, given his rival's reaction function.   If I desires to play the role of a leader, he assumes that II's reaction function is valid and substitutes this relation into his profit function:

$$\pi_1 = h_1[q_1,\Psi(q_1)]$$

I's profit is now a function of q_1 alone and can be maximized with respect to this single variable.   II can also determine his maximum profit from leadership on the assumption that I obeys his reaction function and acts as a follower.   I's maximum profit from followership is determined by substituting II's optimum leadership output level in I's reaction function, and II's maximum profit from followership is determined by substituting I's optimum leadership output level in II's reaction function.

Each duopolist determines his maximum profit levels from both leadership and followership and desires to play the role which yields the larger maximum.   Four outcomes are possible: (1) I desires to be a leader, and II a follower; (2) II desires to be a leader, and I a follower; (3) both desire to be leaders; or (4) both desire to be followers.   Outcome (1) results in consistent behavior patterns and therefore a determinate equilibrium.[1]   I assumes that II will act as a follower, and he does; II assumes that I will act as a leader, and he does.   Likewise (2) results in a determinate equilibrium.   If both desire to be followers, their expecta-

---

[1] The first- and second-order conditions for maxima are assumed to be fulfilled in all cases.

tions are not realized, since each assumes that the other will act as a leader. The duopolists must revise their expectations. Under the Stackelberg assumptions, the Cournot solution is achieved if each desires to act as a follower, knowing that the other will also act as a follower. Otherwise, one must change his behavior pattern and act as a leader before equilibrium can be achieved.

If both desire to be leaders, each assumes that the other's behavior is governed by his reaction function, but, in fact, neither of the reaction functions is obeyed, and a *Stackelberg disequilibrium* is encountered. Stackelberg believed that this disequilibrium is the most frequent outcome. The final result of a Stackelberg disequilibrium cannot be predicted a priori. If Stackelberg was correct, this situation will result in economic warfare, and equilibrium will not be achieved until one has succumbed to the leadership of the other or a collusive agreement has been reached.

Return again to the example given by (6-31). The maximum leadership profit of I is obtained by substituting II's reaction function (6-32) into I's profit equation:

$$\pi_1 = 100q_1 - 0.5q_1^2 - 0.5q_1(50 - 0.25q_1) - 5q_1$$
$$= 70q_1 - 0.375q_1^2$$

Maximizing with respect to q_1,

$$\frac{d\pi_1}{dq_1} = 70 - 0.75q_1 = 0 \qquad q_1 = 93\tfrac{1}{3} \qquad \pi_1 = 3{,}266\tfrac{2}{3}$$

Likewise for II,

$$\pi_2 = 100q_2 - 0.5q_2^2 - 0.5q_2(95 - 0.5q_2) - 0.5q_2^2$$
$$= 52.5q_2 - 0.75q_2^2$$
$$\frac{d\pi_2}{dq_2} = 52.5 - 1.5q_2 = 0 \qquad q_2 = 35 \qquad \pi_2 = 918.75$$

To determine I's maximum followership profit, first determine his output by substituting the leadership output of II (35 units) into his reaction function (6-32), and then compute his profit:

$$q_1 = 95 - 0.5q_2 = 77.5 \qquad \pi_1 = 3{,}003.125$$

Likewise substitute $93\tfrac{1}{3}$ into II's reaction function and then compute his profit:

$$q_2 = 50 - 0.25q_1 = 26\tfrac{2}{3} \qquad \pi_2 = 155\tfrac{5}{9}$$

Each duopolist receives a greater profit from leadership, and both desire to act as leaders. An example in which the Cournot solution is easily determined has become a Stackelberg disequilibrium as the result of an alteration of the basic behavior assumptions.

PRODUCT DIFFERENTIATION

The individual producer of a differentiated product in an oligopolistic market faces his own distinct demand curve. The quantity which he can sell depends upon the price decisions of all members of the industry:

$$q_i = f_i(p_1, p_2, \ldots, p_n) \qquad i = 1, \ldots, n \qquad (6\text{-}35)$$

where $\partial q_i/\partial p_i < 0$ and $\partial q_i/\partial p_j > 0$ for all $i \neq j$. An increase of price on the part of the ith seller with all other prices remaining unchanged results in a reduction of his output level. Some of his customers will turn to his competitors. If some other seller should increase his price, the ith seller can sell a larger quantity at a fixed price. Some of his competitor's customers will turn to him.

Individual producers can set either price or quantity. Demand functions may be expressed in inverse form with output levels as independent variables:[1]

$$p_i = F_i(q_1, q_2, \ldots, q_n) \qquad i = 1, \ldots, n \qquad (6\text{-}36)$$

All partial derivatives of (6-36) are negative. If the ith seller increases his output level, with all other output levels constant, p_i will decline, since a larger quantity brings a lower price. If some other seller increases his output level, his price will decline, and the price of the ith firm must also decline in order to maintain q_i at a constant level. Otherwise some of his customers would turn to the firm with the lowered price.

The Cournot, collusion, and Stackelberg solutions are easily modified for product differentiation by replacing $p = F(q_1 + q_2)$ with individual demand functions:

$$p_1 = F_1(q_1, q_2) \qquad p_2 = F_2(q_1, q_2)$$

The analysis can also be extended to cases in which prices are the independent variables:

$$q_1 = f_1(p_1, p_2) \qquad q_2 = f_2(p_1, p_2)$$

Profits were expressed as functions of quantities:

$$\pi_1 = h_1(q_1, q_2) \qquad \pi_2 = h_2(q_1, q_2)$$

[1] The demand functions may be constructed to describe a situation in which price is the independent variable for some sellers and quantity for others. The dependent variable of each seller is then expressed as a function of the independent variables of all sellers.

By substitution,

$$\pi_1 = h_1[f_1(p_1,p_2), \, f_2(p_1,p_2)] = H_1(p_1,p_2)$$
$$\pi_2 = h_2[f_1(p_1,p_2), \, f_2(p_1,p_2)] = H_2(p_1,p_2)$$

The profit of each duopolist is a function of both prices, and maximization may proceed with respect to prices.

In the case of differentiated products the duopolists' profits may also depend upon the amounts of their advertising expenditures. If advertising is effective, it allows a firm to sell a larger quantity at a given price or a given quantity at a higher price. The demand curves are

$$p_1 = F_1(q_1,q_2,A_1,A_2) \qquad p_2 = F_2(q_1,q_2,A_1,A_2)$$

where A_1 and A_2 are the amounts of advertising expenditure by I and II respectively. The profit functions become

$$\pi_1 = q_1 F_1(q_1,q_2,A_1,A_2) - C_1(q_1) - A_1$$
$$\pi_2 = q_2 F_2(q_1,q_2,A_1,A_2) - C_2(q_2) - A_2$$

Each duopolist must now maximize his profit with respect to his advertising expenditure as well as his output level.

THE MARKET-SHARES SOLUTION

Assume that II desires to maintain a fixed share of the total sales of a differentiated product, regardless of the effects of his actions on his short-run profits. His major concern is with the long-run advantages that are derived from maintaining a given market share. A quantity change on the part of I will be immediately followed by a proportionate change on the part of II. The relation

$$\frac{q_2}{q_1 + q_2} = k \qquad q_2 = \frac{kq_1}{1 - k} \tag{6-37}$$

where k is II's desired market share, will always hold. I is a market leader in the sense that his actions will always be followed by II in a predetermined manner.

I's demand function is $p_1 = F_1(q_1,q_2)$, and his profit function is

$$\pi_1 = q_1 F_1(q_1,q_2) - C_1(q_1)$$

Substituting from (6-37) for q_2,

$$\pi_1 = q_1 F_1\left(q_1, \frac{kq_1}{1 - k}\right) - C_1(q_1)$$

I's profit is a function of q_1 alone and may be maximized with respect to this single variable as long as II reacts to maintain his market share.

Let I's demand and cost functions be

$$p_1 = 100 - 2q_1 - q_2 \qquad C_1 = 2.5q_1^2 \tag{6-38}$$

Let $k = \frac{1}{3}$, and therefore $q_2 = 0.5q_1$. I's profit is

$$\pi_1 = q_1(100 - 2q_1 - 0.5q_1) - 2.5q_1^2 = 100q_1 - 5q_1^2 \tag{6-39}$$

Setting the first derivative of (6-39) equal to zero, solving for q_1, and substituting in the above relations,

$$\frac{d\pi_1}{dq_1} = 100 - 10q_1 = 0$$

$$q_1 = 10 \qquad q_2 = 5 \qquad p_1 = 75 \qquad \pi_1 = 500 \tag{6-40}$$

I maximizes his profit at an output of 10 units, and II reacts by producing 5 units.

THE KINKED-DEMAND-CURVE SOLUTION

Some duopolistic and oligopolistic markets are characterized by infrequent price changes. Firms in such markets usually do not change their price-quantity combinations in response to small shifts of their cost curves as the foregoing market analyses would suggest. The kinked-demand-curve solution presents a theoretical analysis which is consistent with this observed behavior. Starting from predetermined price-quantity combinations, if one of the duopolists lowers his price (increases his quantity), the other is assumed to react by lowering his price (increasing his quantity) in order to maintain his market share. If one of the duopolists raises his price, his rival is assumed to leave his own price unchanged and thereby increase his market share. Price decreases will be followed, but price increases will not.

Assume that the demand and cost functions of the duopolists are

$$\begin{aligned} p_1 &= 100 - 2q_1 - q_2 \qquad C_1 = 2.5q_1^2 \\ p_2 &= 95 - q_1 - 3q_2 \qquad C_2 = 25q_2 \end{aligned} \tag{6-41}$$

and that the currently established prices and quantities are $p_1 = 70$, $q_1 = 10$, $p_2 = 55$, and $q_2 = 10$.† If I increased his price, II would leave

---

† The reader can verify that these price-quantity combinations represent a Cournot solution. MC equals MR for each duopolist, on the assumption that his rival's output level remains unchanged. The method by which initial price-quantity combinations are achieved is of little concern for the kinked-demand-curve analysis.

his own price unchanged at 55 dollars. Substituting $p_2 = 55$ into II's demand function (6-41) and solving for q_2,

$$q_2 = \frac{40 - q_1}{3} \tag{6-42}$$

II's output level and market share will increase as I increases his price and thereby decreases his output level. Substituting the value for q_2 given by (6-42) into I's demand function (6-41),

$$p_1 = \frac{260 - 5q_1}{3} \tag{6-43}$$

I's price is a function of q_1 alone given the assumption that II maintains his price at 55 dollars. Starting from the initial position, (6-43) is only valid for $p_1 > 70$ and $q_1 < 10$. I's MR function for price increases can be derived by forming his total revenue function from (6-43):

$$R_1 = q_1 \left(\frac{260 - 5q_1}{3} \right)$$

and

$$\frac{dR_1}{dq_1} = \frac{260 - 10q_1}{3} \tag{6-44}$$

At $q_1 = 10$, I's MR for a price increase is $53\frac{1}{3}$ dollars.

The demand and MR functions given by (6-43) and (6-44) are not valid if I reduces his price. In this case, II will follow by lowering his price by an amount sufficient to allow him to retain half the total volume of sales. II must increase his output level by the same amount as I in order to maintain his market share: $q_2 = q_1$. Substituting $q_2 = q_1$ into I's demand function (6-41),

$$p_1 = 100 - 3q_1 \tag{6-45}$$

I's price is a function of q_1 alone given the fact that II maintains his market share. The demand function given by (6-45) is valid for $p_1 < 70$ and $q_1 > 10$. I's MR function for price decreases can be derived by forming a total revenue function from (6-45):

$$R_1 = q_1(100 - 3q_1)$$

and

$$\frac{dR_1}{dq_1} = 100 - 6q_1 \tag{6-46}$$

At $q_1 = 10$, I's MR for a price decrease is 40 dollars.

The initial position represents a maximum-profit point for I. His MC for an output of 10 units is 50 dollars. He cannot increase his profit by increasing his price (reducing his output level), since MR exceeds MC

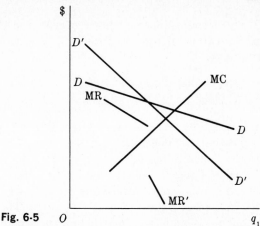

Fig. 6-5

$(53\frac{1}{3} > 50)$ and this difference would be increased by a price increase. He cannot increase his profit by reducing his price (increasing his output level), since MR is less than MC $(40 < 50)$ and this difference would be increased by a price reduction.   His initial price-quantity combination is optimal for any value of MC from $53\frac{1}{3}$ to 40 dollars.   A reduction of his MC by an amount not greater than 10 dollars would not induce him to lower his price and expand his sales.   Likewise, an increase of MC by an amount not greater than $3\frac{1}{3}$ dollars would not induce him to increase his price and contract his sales.

Graphically, I's effective demand curve is "kinked" and his effective MR curve discontinuous at his initial output level.   His demand curve is $D'D'$ (see Fig. 6-5) if II reacts by maintaining his market share and DD if II reacts by maintaining his price. DD is valid for price increases, and $D'D'$ for price decreases.   His effective MR curve follows the MR curve corresponding to DD to the left of his initial output level and the MR curve corresponding to $D'D'$ to the right of his initial output level.   I is unable to equate MR and MC.

6-4 MONOPOLISTIC COMPETITION

Monopolistic competition contains elements of both monopoly and perfect competition.[1]   It is akin to perfect competition in that the number of sellers is sufficiently large so that the actions of an individual seller have no perceptible influence upon his competitors.   It is akin to monopoly and differentiated oligopoly in that each seller possesses a negatively sloped demand curve for his distinct product.

[1] See Edward H. Chamberlin, *The Theory of Monopolistic Competition* (7th ed.; Cambridge, Mass.: Harvard, 1956).

Assuming linear demand curves, the price received by each seller is a function of the quantities sold by each of the n firms within the industry:

$$p_k = A_k - a_{kk}q_k - \sum_{\substack{i=1 \\ i \neq k}}^{n} b_{ki}q_i \qquad k = 1, \ldots, n \qquad (6\text{-}47)$$

where $\partial p_k/\partial q_i = -b_{ki}$ is negative, but numerically small. To facilitate exposition, assume that all firms have identical demand and cost functions; that is, $b_{ki} = b$ for all k and i except $k = i$, $a_{kk} = a$, $A_k = A$, and $C_k(q_k) = C(q_k)$ for all k. Assuming initial price-quantity combinations which are the same for all firms, the industry can be described in terms of the actions of a "representative" firm. The revenue and cost functions of all firms and their maximizing behavior are identical, though their products are differentiated in the eyes of consumers. The demand curve facing the representative firm is

$$p_k = A - aq_k - b \sum_{\substack{i=1 \\ i \neq k}}^{n} q_i \qquad (6\text{-}48)$$

The profit of the representative firm is

$$\pi_k = q_k \left(A - aq_k - b \sum_{\substack{i=1 \\ i \neq k}}^{n} q_i \right) - C(q_k) \qquad (6\text{-}49)$$

Since b is numerically small and a quantity change on the part of the representative firm affects each of its $(n-1)$ competitors to the same degree, the effects of his movements upon the price of any particular competitor are negligible. Therefore, the entrepreneur of the representative firm acts as if his actions had no effects upon his competitors. Equating his MR and MC on the assumption that the output levels of his competitors remain unchanged:

$$A - 2aq_k - b \sum_{\substack{i=1 \\ i \neq k}}^{n} q_i = C'(q_k) \qquad (6\text{-}50)$$

The second-order condition requires that his MC be increasing more rapidly than his MR. The optimum output level for the kth firm depends upon the aggregate output level of its competitors.

The symmetry assumption ensures that if it is profitable for the representative firm to make a particular move, it is profitable for all other firms to make the same move. All firms will attempt to maximize profit simultaneously, and quantity variations by the kth firm will be accompanied by identical variations on the part of all the other firms within the industry. The representative firm will not move along the demand curve (6-48) which is constructed upon the assumption that the output levels of the other firms remain unchanged. Its effective demand curve is constructed by substituting $q_k = q_i$ into (6-48):

$$p_k = A - [a + (n - 1)b]q_k \qquad\qquad\qquad (6\text{-}51)$$

The number $(n - 1)$ is not of a negligible order of magnitude. A 1 percent increase in the output level of one competitor may cause p_k to decrease by 0.02 percent, but a simultaneous 1 percent increase on the part of 1,000 firms may decrease p_k by 20 percent or more. The effective demand curve (6-51) which accounts for simultaneous and identical movements on the part of all sellers has a steeper slope than (6-48). The entrepreneur of the representative firm may realize that he is unable to move along his individual demand curve, but this information is of no use to him, since he has no control over the output levels of his competitors. The other firms change their output levels because they can increase their profits. Their actions are not governed by the actions of the representative firm. The representative firm must take advantage of its opportunity to increase profit and act in the same manner as the other firms.

The representative firm starting from some arbitrary initial price-quantity combination faces two separate demand curves. In Fig. 6-6a, DD is its demand curve for variations of its output level alone, and $D'D'$ is its effective demand curve for identical variations of the output levels of all firms within the industry. The two intersect at the initial price-

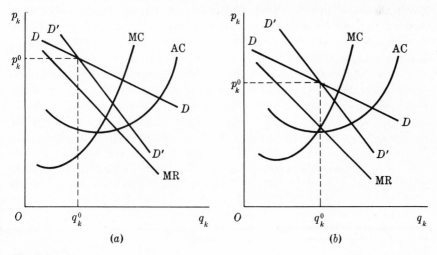

(a)   (b)

Fig. 6-6

quantity combination. As all firms increase their output levels, the shape and position of $D'D'$, which is a function of q_k alone [see (6-51)], remain unchanged, and DD, the position of which is dependent upon the outputs of all firms [see (6-48)], "slides" along $D'D'$, always intersecting it at the current output level of the representative firm.

The industry reaches an equilibrium when MR equals MC for all firms. The n simultaneous equations of (6-50) must be solved for the n unknown quantities. It can be proved by advanced methods that the symmetry assumption guarantees that (6-50) will result in equal output levels for all n firms. Therefore, the solution can be obtained by substituting $q_k = q_i$ in (6-50) and solving

$$A - [2a + (n - 1)b]q_k = C'(q_k) \qquad (6\text{-}52)$$

for q_k.† The latter formulation involves only one equation and one variable. The maximum profit and optimum price-quantity combination are the same for all firms. A graphic description of short-run equilibrium is presented in Fig. 6-6b. MR equals MC, and DD intersects $D'D'$ at the equilibrium price-quantity combination.

Free entry and exit drive pure profit to zero in a perfectly competitive industry and can have the same effect in monopolistic competition. The profit of the representative firm can be expressed as a function of its output and the number of firms within the industry if $q_k = q_i$ is substituted in (6-49):

$$\pi_k = Aq_k - [a + (n - 1)b]q_k^2 - C(q_k) \qquad (6\text{-}53)$$

Setting π_k equal to zero, (6-52) and (6-53) are a system of two equations in the two variables q_k and n. The solution of these equations gives the long-run equilibrium values for the output level of the representative firm and the number of firms.

The long-run equilibrium position of the representative firm is pictured in Fig. 6-7. New firms will be induced to enter the industry if the pure profit of the representative firm is greater than zero. As the number of firms increases, the representative firm can sell a smaller output at any given price; i.e., both DD and $D'D'$ are shifted to the left. Long-run equilibrium is attained when MR equals MC, DD is tangent to the average cost curve (indicating that total revenue equals total cost and therefore profit equals zero), and the tangency point is intersected by $D'D'$.

---

† This solution is not the same as that for an oligopolistic market in which one of the entrepreneurs knows that (6-51) is his effective demand curve. MR is $A - [2a + 2(n - 1)b]q_k$ in this case, or $(n - 1)bq_k$ dollars less for every output level. The output level at which MR and MC are equated is smaller than that obtained from a solution of (6-52).

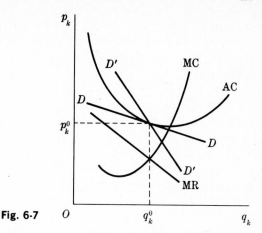

Fig. 6-7

The long-run equilibrium point for the representative firm is to the left of the minimum point on its average total cost curve. Price equals average cost, as is true for the representative firm in perfect competition, but price does not equal MC. Contrasted with the results of perfect competition, the representative firm produces a smaller output at a greater average total cost.

6-5 MONOPSONY, DUOPSONY, AND OLIGOPSONY

The preceding sections deal with entrepreneurs who purchase their inputs in perfectly competitive markets. Input prices are invariant with respect to the quantities which they buy. In some input markets the number of buyers is so small that the assumption of competitive purchases at invariant prices is not viable. Such markets are considered in this section. A market with one buyer and many competitive sellers is a *monopsony*. A market with two buyers is a *duopsony*, and one with a small number greater than two is an *oligopsony*.

MONOPSONY

A monopsonist cannot purchase an unlimited amount of an input at a uniform price; the price which he must pay for each quantity purchased is given by the market supply curve for the input. Since the supply curves for most inputs are positively sloped, the price which the monopsonist must pay is generally an increasing function of the quantity he purchases.

First consider the case of a monopsonist who uses a single input, which we shall call labor, for the production of a commodity which he sells in a perfectly competitive market. An example might be provided by a producer who is the sole purchaser in a local labor market and sells his output in a competitive national or international market. His production function states output as a function of the quantity of labor (x) employed:

$$q = h(x) \tag{6-54}$$

The cost equation and revenue function are, as before:

$$R = pq \qquad C = rx$$

where r is the price of labor. However, the price of labor is now an increasing function of the amount employed:

$$r = g(x) \tag{6-55}$$

where $dr/dx > 0$. The *marginal cost of labor* is the rate of change of its cost with respect to the quantity employed:[1]

$$\frac{dC}{dx} = r + xg'(x) \tag{6-56}$$

Since $g'(x) > 0$, the marginal cost of labor exceeds its price for $x > 0$.

The monopsonist's profit can be expressed as a function of the amount of labor which he employs:

$$\pi = R - C = ph(x) - rx \tag{6-57}$$

Setting the derivative of (6-57) with respect to x equal to zero,

$$\frac{d\pi}{dx} = ph'(x) - r - xg'(x) = 0$$

$$ph'(x) = r + xg'(x) \tag{6-58}$$

The first-order condition for profit maximization requires that labor be employed up to a point at which the value of its marginal product equals its marginal cost. The second-order condition requires that the rate of change of the value of the marginal product of labor be less than the rate of change of its marginal cost:

$$\frac{d^2\pi}{dx^2} = ph''(x) - 2g'(x) - xg''(x) < 0$$

$$ph''(x) < 2g'(x) + xg''(x) \tag{6-59}$$

The monopsonist's optimum output and the price of labor are determined by solving (6-58) for x and substituting a value for which the second-order condition is satisfied into (6-54) and (6-55).

---

[1] The reader should note that marginal cost is here defined with respect to the quantity of labor employed rather than the quantity of output produced. The abbreviated form (MC) is reserved for marginal cost with respect to output level.

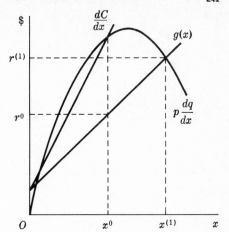

Fig. 6-8

The profit-maximizing monopsonist (see Fig. 6-8) will employ x^0 units of labor at a wage rate of r^0 dollars. The equality of the price of labor with the value of its marginal product, the equilibrium point for an entrepreneur who purchases labor in a perfectly competitive market, would result in the employment of $x^{(1)}$ units of labor at a wage rate of $r^{(1)}$. The monopsonist employs a smaller quantity of labor at a lower wage rate.

If the monopsonist's production and labor supply functions are

$$q = 15x^2 - 0.2x^2 \qquad r = 144 + 23.4x$$

and he sells his output in a perfectly competitive market at a price of 3 dollars, his total revenue function and cost equation are

$$R = 45x^2 - 0.6x^3 \qquad C = 144x + 23.4x^2$$

Setting the value of the marginal product of labor equal to its marginal cost,

$$90x - 1.8x^2 = 144 + 46.8x$$

which yields the quadratic equation:

$$1.8x^2 - 43.2x + 144 = 0$$

with the roots $x = 4$ and $x = 20$. The second-order condition

$$90 - 3.6x < 46.8$$

is satisfied for $x = 20$. The solution $x = 4$ is a minimum-profit position. Substituting $x = 20$ into the appropriate functions,

$$q = 4{,}400 \qquad r = 612 \qquad \pi = 960$$

If a monopsonist is also a· monopolist in the market for his output, the price he receives is a function of the quantity which he sells:

$$p = F(q)$$

His profit may again be expressed as a function of the quantity of labor which he employs:

$$\pi = pq - rx = F[h(x)]h(x) - rx$$

or more simply,

$$\pi = R(x) - C(x) \qquad (6\text{-}60)$$

where total revenue and total cost are expressed as functions of the quantity of labor employed. Setting the derivative of (6-60) equal to zero yields the first-order condition that the rate of increase of total revenue from the employment of another unit of labor (the *marginal-revenue product* of labor) must equal its marginal cost. The second-order condition requires that the marginal-revenue product of labor increase less rapidly than its marginal cost.

DUOPSONY AND OLIGOPSONY

A market situation with a small number of buyers is similar to one with a small number of sellers. There are no generally accepted behavior assumptions. Each buyer can control the level of his purchases, but each is noticeably affected by the actions of the other buyers. Most theories of duopoly and oligopoly covering undifferentiated products can be modified to cover duopsony and oligopsony. For illustration, a modified version of the Cournot solution is considered here.

Consider a local labor market in which two firms buy from many competitive sellers. As before, the price of labor is an increasing function of quantity:

$$r = g(x_1 + x_2)$$

where x_1 and x_2 are the amounts purchased by the two firms. Each buyer is assumed to use labor alone to produce a commodity which he sells in a competitive national market at a fixed price. Their production functions are

$$q_1 = h_1(x_1) \qquad q_2 = h_2(x_2)$$

and their profits are

$$\begin{aligned}
\pi_1 &= p_1 h_1(x_1) - g(x_1 + x_2)x_1 \\
\pi_2 &= p_2 h_2(x_2) - g(x_1 + x_2)x_2
\end{aligned} \qquad (6\text{-}61)$$

The basic Cournot behavior assumption is invoked. Each duopsonist maximizes his profit on the assumption that the other is unaffected by his actions.

Setting the appropriate partial derivatives of (6-61) equal to zero,

$$\frac{\partial \pi_1}{\partial x_1} = p_1 h_1'(x_1) - r - x_1 g'(x_1 + x_2) = 0$$

$$\frac{\partial \pi_2}{\partial x_2} = p_2 h_2'(x_2) - r - x_2 g'(x_1 + x_2) = 0$$

and

$$\begin{aligned} p_1 h_1'(x_1) &= r + x_1 g'(x_1 + x_2) \\ p_2 h_2'(x_2) &= r + x_2 g'(x_1 + x_2) \end{aligned} \tag{6-62}$$

Each duopsonist equates the value of his marginal product to his marginal cost for the input. The duopsonists will not have the same marginal cost in equilibrium unless $x_1 = x_2$. The duopsonist with the higher purchase level will have the higher marginal cost. The second-order conditions are a straightforward generalization of (6-59): the value of the marginal product of each duopsonist must increase less rapidly than his marginal cost.

Input reaction functions which express the purchases of each duopsonist as a function of the other's purchases are determined by solving the first equation of (6-62) for x_1 and the second for x_2:

$$\begin{aligned} x_1 &= \Phi_1(x_2) \\ x_2 &= \Phi_2(x_1) \end{aligned}$$

Consider the specific case in which the input supply function and production functions are

$$r = 2 + 0.1(x_1 + x_2)$$
$$q_1 = 13x_1 - 0.2x_1^2 \qquad q_2 = 12x_2 - 0.1x_2^2$$

Assume that $p_1 = 2$ and $p_2 = 3$. The profit functions are

$$\begin{aligned} \pi_1 &= 2(13x_1 - 0.2x_1^2) - [2 + 0.1(x_1 + x_2)]x_1 \\ \pi_2 &= 3(12x_2 - 0.1x_2^2) - [2 + 0.1(x_1 + x_2)]x_2 \end{aligned}$$

Setting the appropriate partial derivatives equal to zero yields the input reaction functions

$$x_1 = 24 - 0.1x_2 \qquad x_2 = 42.5 - 0.125x_1$$

The reader may verify that in equilibrium $r = 8$ and

$$\begin{array}{lll} x_1 = 20 & q_1 = 180 & \pi_1 = 200 \\ x_2 = 40 & q_2 = 320 & \pi_2 = 640 \end{array}$$

6-6 BILATERAL MONOPOLY

A monopolist does not have an output supply function relating price and quantity. He selects a point on his buyers' demand function that maximizes his profit. Similarly, a monopsonist does not have an input demand function. He selects a point on his sellers' supply function that maximizes his profit. Bilateral monopoly is a market situation with a single buyer and a single seller. It is not possible for the seller to behave as a monopolist and the buyer to behave as a monopsonist at the same time. The seller cannot exploit a demand function that does not exist, and the buyer cannot exploit a supply function that does not exist. Something must give. Three general outcomes are possible: (1) one of the participants may dominate and force the other to accept his price and/or quantity decisions, (2) the buyer and seller may collude or bargain to set price and quantity, or (3) the market mechanism may break down. The theories of monopoly and monopsony provide guidelines for a consideration of the first two outcomes.

REFERENCE SOLUTIONS

Consider a case of bilateral monopoly in the market for a produced good, Q_2. The buyer uses Q_2 as an input to produce Q_1 according to his production function: $q_1 = h(q_2)$. He sells Q_1 in a competitive market at the fixed price p_1. The seller uses a single input X for the production of Q_2. He buys X in a competitive market at the fixed price r. Assume that his production function can be expressed in inverse form as $x = H(q_2)$. The solutions that would be achieved by monopoly, monopsony, and competition provide useful reference points for an analysis of this market.

A monopoly solution would be achieved if the seller dominated and forced the buyer to accept whatever price he set. The buyer's profit is

$$\pi_B = p_1 h(q_2) - p_2 q_2$$

He sets $d\pi_B/dq_2$ equal to zero to maximize profit:

$$\frac{d\pi_B}{dq_2} = p_1 h'(q_2) - p_2 = 0$$

and

$$p_2 = p_1 h'(q_2) \tag{6-63}$$

which is the buyer's demand function for Q_2.† The buyer purchases Q_2 up to a point at which the value of his marginal product equals the price

---

† The term demand function is used in this section to describe price as a function of quantity; in more common usage quantity is described as a function of price. The term supply function is similarly defined.

set by the seller. The monopolistic seller substitutes from (6-63) for p_2 and maximizes his profit:

$$\pi_S = p_1 h'(q_2)q_2 - rH(q_2)$$

$$\frac{d\pi_S}{dq_2} = p_1[h'(q_2) + h''(q_2)q_2] - rH'(q_2) = 0$$

$$p_1[h'(q_2) + h''(q_2)q_2] = rH'(q_2) \tag{6-64}$$

The equilibrium condition (6-64) states that the seller equates his MR and MC. Solve (6-64) for the monopoly output, q_{2S}^*, and substitute this value into (6-63) to obtain the monopoly price, p_{2S}^*. An example of a monopoly solution is given by point S in Fig. 6-9.

A monopsony solution would be achieved if the buyer dominated and forced the seller to accept whatever price he set. The seller's profit is

$$\pi_S = p_2 q_2 - rH(q_2)$$

He sets $d\pi_S/dq_2$ equal to zero to maximize profit:

$$\frac{d\pi_S}{dq_2} = p_2 - rH'(q_2) = 0$$

and

$$p_2 = rH'(q_2) \tag{6-65}$$

which is the seller's supply function for Q_2. The seller produces and sells Q_2 up to a point at which his marginal cost equals the price set by the buyer. The monopsonistic buyer substitutes from (6-65) for p_2 and maximizes his profit:

$$\pi_B = p_1 h(q_2) - rH'(q_2)q_2$$

$$\frac{d\pi_B}{dq_2} = p_1 h'(q_2) - r[H'(q_2) + H''(q_2)q_2] = 0$$

$$p_1 h'(q_2) = r[H'(q_2) + H''(q_2)q_2] \tag{6-66}$$

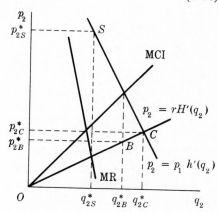

Fig. 6-9

The equilibrium condition (6-66) states that the buyer equates the value of his marginal product to the marginal cost of the input (MCI). Solve (6-66) for the monopsony output, q_{2B}^*, and substitute this value into (6-65) to obtain the monopsony price, p_{2B}^*. An example of a monopsony solution is given by point B in Fig. 6-9.

Finally, consider the price and quantity that would be achieved if both seller and buyer were price takers. The demand (6-63) and supply (6-65) functions would both be effective in this case. The competitive quantity, q_{2C}^*, is determined by equating demand price and supply price:

$$p_{2C}^* = p_1 h'(q_{2C}^*) = rH'(q_{2C}^*) \tag{6-67}$$

The competitive price, p_{2C}^*, equals both the value of the marginal product of the buyer and the marginal cost of the seller. This competitive result may not be a likely outcome for a market characterized by bilateral monopoly, but it provides another useful reference point. An example of a competitive solution is given by point C in Fig. 6-9.

Some of the results of a comparison of the monopoly (B), monopsony (S), and competitive (C) solutions in Fig. 6-9 may be generalized to cover all cases in which the demand curve $[p_1 h'(q_2)]$ has negative slope and the supply curve $[rH'(q_2)]$ has positive slope, i.e., cases in which $h''(q_2) < 0$ and $H''(q_2) > 0$. The monopoly and monopsony equilibrium points will always lie to the left of the demand and supply curve intersection. Thus, q_{2C}^* is always greater than q_{2B}^* and q_{2S}^*. In Fig. 6-9, $q_{2B}^* > q_{2S}^*$. This result does not always hold. The monopoly and monopsony outputs depend upon the slopes of the demand and supply curves. The reader may construct a case in which $q_{2B}^* < q_{2S}^*$. The competitive price will always lie between the monopoly and monopsony prices. Since the monopoly equilibrium lies on the demand curve to the left of the competitive equilibrium, $p_{2S}^* > p_{2C}^*$, and since the monopsony equilibrium lies on the supply curve to the left of the competitive equilibrium, $p_{2C}^* > p_{2B}^*$. Let π_{SS}^*, π_{SC}^*, and π_{SB}^* denote the seller's profit levels in the three cases. In general,

$$\pi_{SS}^* > \pi_{SC}^* > \pi_{SB}^*$$

Let π_{BS}^*, π_{BC}^*, and π_{BB}^* denote the buyer's profit levels. In general,

$$\pi_{BS}^* < \pi_{BC}^* < \pi_{BB}^*$$

The proof of these propositions is left as an exercise for the reader.

COLLUSION AND BARGAINING

It is often assumed that the market participants will recognize their mutual interdependence and reach a mutually satisfactory agreement as to price and quantity. The bargaining process can be separated into two steps. First, the participants determine a quantity that maximizes their joint profit, and then determine a price that distributes the joint profit among them. Their joint profit is

$$\pi = \pi_B + \pi_S = [p_1 h(q_2) - p_2 q_2] + [p_2 q_2 - rH(q_2)]$$
$$= p_1 h(q_2) - rH(q_2)$$

Setting $d\pi/dq_2$ equal to zero,

$$\frac{d\pi}{dq_2} = p_1 h'(q_2) - rH'(q_2) = 0$$

and

$$p_1 h'(q_2) = rH'(q_2)$$

Joint profit is maximized at an output at which the value of the buyer's marginal product equals the seller's marginal cost. This is the same as the competitive solution given by (6-67). The optimal collusive output level is the same as the competitive output level, q_{2C}^*. A collusive bilateral monopoly will behave in the same way as a competitive industry insofar as the outside world is concerned.

The competitive price does not necessarily follow from a collusive solution. For the prescribed quantity the seller desires as high a price as possible, and the buyer desires as low a price as possible. Let the upper limit be the price that would force the buyer's profit to zero, and the lower limit be the price that would force the seller's profit to zero:

$$\frac{p_1 h(q_{2C}^*)}{q_{2C}^*} \geqq p_2 \geqq \frac{rH(q_{2C}^*)}{q_{2C}^*} \tag{6-68}$$

Since a negative profit would force one of the firms to discontinue operations, price cannot be set beyond these limits.

An alternative is to assume that the buyer can do no worse than the monopoly solution, and that the seller can do no worse than the monopsony solution:

$$p_1 h(q_{2C}^*) - p_2 q_{2C}^* \geqq \pi_{BS}^*$$
$$p_2 q_{2C}^* - rH(q_{2C}^*) \geqq \pi_{SB}^*$$

Solving each inequality for p_2,

$$\frac{p_1 h(q_{2C}^*) - \pi_{BS}^*}{q_{2C}^*} \geqq p_2 \geqq \frac{rH(q_{2C}^*) + \pi_{SB}^*}{q_{2C}^*} \tag{6-69}$$

These limits can be determined from the reference solutions. If π_{BS}^* and π_{SB}^* are positive, (6-69) provides a narrower range for bargaining than (6-68). In either case the determination of a specific price within the bargaining limits will depend upon the relative bargaining power of the buyer and seller.

AN EXAMPLE

The supply and demand curves in Fig. 6-9 correspond to a market for which the production functions are

$$q_1 = 270q_2 - 2q_2^2 \qquad q_2 = 2\sqrt{x} \qquad x = 0.25q_2^2$$

with the external prices $p_1 = 3$ and $r = 6$. For the monopoly case the buyer's profit maximum is derived from

$$\pi_B = 3(270q_2 - 2q_2^2) - p_2q_2$$
$$\frac{d\pi_B}{dq_2} = 810 - 12q_2 - p_2 = 0$$

and the demand function is

$$p_2 = 810 - 12q_2 \tag{6-70}$$

The monopolistic seller's profit maximum is derived from

$$\pi_S = (810 - 12q_2)q_2 - 1.5q_2^2$$
$$\frac{d\pi_S}{dq_2} = 810 - 27q_2 = 0$$

The monopoly solution is

$$q_{2S}^* = 30 \qquad p_{2S}^* = 450 \qquad \pi_{BS}^* = 5{,}400 \qquad \pi_{SS}^* = 12{,}150$$

For the monopsony case the seller's profit maximum is derived from

$$\pi_S = p_2q_2 - 1.5q_2^2$$
$$\frac{d\pi_S}{dq_2} = p_2 - 3q_2 = 0$$

and the supply function is

$$p_2 = 3q_2 \tag{6-71}$$

The monopsonistic buyer's profit maximum is derived from

$$\pi_B = 3(270q_2 - 2q_2^2) - (3q_2)q_2$$
$$\frac{d\pi_B}{dq_2} = 810 - 18q_2 = 0$$

The monopsony solution is

$$q_{2B}^* = 45 \qquad p_{2B}^* = 135 \qquad \pi_{SB}^* = 3{,}037.50 \qquad \pi_{BB}^* = 18{,}225$$

The competitive solution is obtained by equating (6-70) and (6-71)

$$q_{2C}^* = 54 \qquad p_{2C}^* = 162 \qquad \pi_{2C}^* = 4{,}374 \qquad \pi_{BC}^* = 17{,}496$$

The competitive output is also the collusive output. The maximum joint profit, $\pi^* = 21{,}870$, is the sum of the competitive profits.

Evaluation of (6-68) gives the bargaining limits for the zero profit assumption:

$$486 \geqq p_2 \geqq 81$$

and evaluation of (6-69) gives the bargaining limits that correspond to the profit limits of π^*_{BS} and π^*_{SB}:

$$386 \geqq p_2 \geqq 137.25$$

It is interesting to note that in this example the upper limit for price, 386, to assure the buyer a minimum profit of π^*_{BS} is considerably less than $p^*_{2S} = 450$.

6-7 SUMMARY

A monopolistic firm constitutes an industry and is unfettered by the competition of close rivals. A monopolist is free to select any price-quantity combination which lies on his negatively sloped demand curve. Since an expansion of his output results in a reduction of his price, his MR is less than his price. His first-order condition for profit maximization requires the equality of MR and MC. His second-order condition requires that MC be increasing more rapidly than MR. When his production function is introduced explicitly, the monopolist maximizes profit by equating the marginal-revenue product of each input to its price.

If second-order conditions are satisfied, a discriminating monopolist maximizes his profit by equating the MR in each of his markets to the MC for his output as a whole. A perfectly discriminating monopolist captures all the consumers' surplus for his output by equating his marginal price to his MC. A multiple-plant monopolist maximizes his profit by equating the MC in each of his plants to the MR for his output as a whole.

Neither a lump-sum nor a profit tax will affect the optimum price-quantity combination for a profit-maximizing monopolist. The imposition of either a specific or an ad valorem sales tax will result in a reduction of his output and an increase of his price. A revenue-maximizing monopolist maximizes his sales revenue subject to the condition that his profit does not fall below a minimum acceptable level. A profit tax may result in a reduction of his output and an increase of his price.

The profit of a duopolist or an oligopolist depends upon the actions and reactions of his rivals. Different theories are based upon different assumptions regarding market behavior. The Cournot solution is realized if each market participant maximizes his profit on the assumption that his rivals' output levels are unaffected by his actions. The collusion solution is realized if the market participants join together to maximize total industry profit. The Stackelberg solution is based upon the assumption that duopolists explicitly recognize the interdependence of their actions. Each desires to assume the role of either a leader or a follower, and market equilibrium is achieved if their desires are consistent. These three solutions are applicable for both homogeneous and differentiated products. The producers of differentiated products may find advertising profitable.

The market-shares solution is realized if a market participant follows the moves of his rivals in such a way as to maintain his historical share of total industry sales. The kinked-demand-curve solution is realized if a seller assumes that his rivals will follow his price reductions, but leave their prices unchanged in response to his price increases.

In monopolistic competition an individual seller possesses a negatively sloped demand curve for his distinct product, but his output constitutes such a small part of the total market that his actions do not have perceptible effects upon his rivals. However, simultaneous movements on the part of all sellers cause shifts of the individual demand curves. Short-run equilibrium is achieved when each seller has equated MR and MC. The number of firms within the industry increases or decreases sufficiently to drive the pure profit of the representative firm to zero in the long run.

A monopsonist faces a rising supply curve for an input. He may be the sole purchaser of a particular type of labor. The monopsonist's marginal cost of labor exceeds the wage rate, since he must increase the wage rate for all his employees in order to expand employment. The first-order condition for profit maximization requires that he employ labor up to the point at which the value of its marginal productivity equals its marginal cost. If the monopsonist is also a monopolist in his product market, the first-order condition requires that he equate the marginal-revenue product of labor to its marginal cost.

Duopsony and oligopsony are similar to duopoly and oligopoly in that there are no generally accepted behavior assumptions. Most theories of duopoly and oligopoly for undifferentiated products can be modified to cover duopsony and oligopsony. According to the Cournot behavior assumption each buyer selects his purchase level on the assumption that the other buyers are unaffected by his actions.

A single seller confronts a single buyer in bilateral monopoly. Price and quantity are determined either through the dominance of one participant, or through collusion and bargaining. The prices, quantities, and profits that would be achieved under conditions of monopoly, monopsony, and competition provide reference points for an analysis of bilateral monopoly. The competitive output level maximizes the joint profit of the buyer and seller, and bargaining may be restricted to a price for this quantity. Limits for price bargaining are constructed from assumptions about minimum acceptable profit levels.

EXERCISES

6-1. Determine the maximum profit and the corresponding price and quantity for a monopolist whose demand and cost functions are $p = 20 - 0.5q$ and $C = 0.04q^3 - 1.94q^2 + 32.96q$ respectively.

6-2. A monopolist uses one input, X, which he purchases at the fixed price $r = 5$ to produce his output, Q. His demand and production functions are $p = 85 - 3q$ and $q = 2\sqrt{x}$ respectively. Determine the values of p, q, and x at which the monopolist maximizes his profit.

6-3. Determine the maximum profit and the corresponding marginal price and quantity for a perfectly discriminating monopolist whose demand and cost functions are $p = 2,200 - 60q$ and $C = 0.5q^3 - 61.5q^2 + 2,740q$ respectively.

6-4. Let the demand and cost functions of a multiplant monopolist be $p = a - b(q_1 + q_2)$, $C_1 = \alpha_1 q_1 + \beta_1 q_1^2$, and $C_2 = \alpha_2 q_2 + \beta_2 q_2^2$ where all parameters are positive. Assume that an autonomous increase of demand increases the value of a, leaving the other parameters unchanged. Show that output will increase in both plants with a greater increase for the plant in which marginal cost is increasing less fast.

6-5. A revenue-maximizing monopolist requires a profit of at least 1,500. His demand and cost functions are $p = 304 - 2q$ and $C = 500 + 4q + 8q^2$. Determine his output level and price. Contrast these values with those that would be achieved under profit maximization.

6-6. Let the demand and cost functions of a monopolist be $p = 100 - 3q + 4\sqrt{A}$ and $C = 4q^2 + 10q + A$ where A is the level of his advertising expenditure. Find the values of A, q, and p that maximize profit.

6-7. Consider a duopoly with product differentiation in which the demand and cost functions are $q_1 = 88 - 4p_1 + 2p_2$, $C_1 = 10q_1$, and $q_2 = 56 + 2p_1 - 4p_2$, $C_2 = 8q_2$ for firms I and II, respectively. Derive a *price reaction function* for each firm on the assumption that each maximizes its profit with respect to its own price. Determine equilibrium values of price, quantity, and profit for each firm.

6-8. Consider a market characterized by monopolistic competition. There are 101 firms with identical demand and cost functions:

$$p_k = 150 - q_k - 0.02 \sum_{\substack{i=1 \\ i \neq k}}^{101} q_i \qquad C_k = 0.5q_k^3 - 20q_k^2 + 270q_k \qquad k = 1, \ldots, 101$$

Determine the maximum profit and the corresponding price and quantity for a representative firm. Assume that the number of firms in the industry does not change.

6-9. A monopsonist uses only labor, X, to produce his output, Q, which he sells in a competitive market at the fixed price $p = 2$. His production and labor supply functions are $q = 6x + 3x^2 - 0.02x^3$ and $r = 60 + 3x$ respectively. Determine the values of x, q, and r at which he maximizes his profit. Is the monopsonist's production function strictly concave in the neighborhood of his equilibrium production point?

6-10. Consider a bilateral monopoly for the produced good, Q_2, in which the buyer's and seller's production functions are $q_1 = 728q_2 - 3q_2^2$ and $q_2 = \sqrt{x}$ respectively. Assume that $p_1 = 6$ and $r = 3$. Determine the solutions that would prevail under conditions of monopoly, monopsony, and competition. Determine the limits for price bargaining under the assumption that the buyer can do no worse than the monopoly solution and the seller can do no worse than the monopsony solution.

*6-11. A monopolist will construct a single plant to serve two spatially separated markets in which he can charge different prices without fear of competition or resale between markets. The markets are 40 miles apart and are connected by a highway. The monopolist may locate his plant at either of the markets or at some point along the highway. Let z and $(40 - z)$ be the distances of his plant from markets 1 and 2 respectively. The monopolist's demand and production cost functions are not affected by his location:

$$p_1 = 100 - 2q_1 \qquad p_2 = 120 - 3q_2 \qquad C = 80(q_1 + q_2) - (q_1 + q_2)^2$$

Determine optimal values for q_1, q_2, p_1, p_2, and z if the monopolist's transport costs are $T = 0.4zq_1 + 0.5(40 - z)q_2$.

SELECTED REFERENCES

Andrews, P. W. S., *On Competition in Economic Theory* (New York: St. Martin's, 1964). A nonmathematical review and critique of imperfect-competition theories.

Baumol, William J., *Business Behavior, Value and Growth* (rev. ed.; New York: Harcourt, Brace & World, 1967). Part I covers oligopoly theory. Calculus and geometry are used.

Buchanan, Norman S., "Advertising Expenditures: A Suggested Treatment," *Journal of Political Economy*, vol. 50 (August, 1942), pp. 537–557. Also reprinted in R. V. Clemence (ed.), *Readings in Economic Analysis* (Cambridge, Mass.: Addison-Wesley, 1950), vol. 2, pp. 230–250. A geometric determination of the optimum advertising expenditure for a firm.

Chamberlin, E. H., *The Theory of Monopolistic Competition* (7th ed.; Cambridge, Mass: Harvard, 1956). The first statement of the problems of monopolistic competition and product differentiation. Geometry is used.

Cohen, Kalman J., and Richard M. Cyert, *Theory of the Firm* (Englewood Cliffs, N.J.: Prentice-Hall, 1965). Imperfect competition is covered in chaps. 10–13. Calculus and geometry are used.

Cournot, Augustin, *Researches into the Mathematical Principles of the Theory of Wealth*, trans. by Nathaniel T. Bacon (New York: Macmillan, 1897). The original statement of the Cournot solution. Also one of the first applications of mathematics to economics.

Efroymson, Clarence W., "A Note on Kinked Demand Curves," *American Economic Review*, vol. 33 (March, 1943), pp. 98–109. Also reprinted in Clemence, *Readings in Economic Analysis*, vol. 2, pp. 218–229. A nonmathematical discussion of kinked demand curves and full-cost pricing.

Fellner, William, *Competition Among the Few* (New York: Knopf, 1949). A nonmathematical discussion of oligopoly and bilateral monopoly. Contains an exposition of the Stackelberg solution.

Hicks, J. R., "Annual Survey of Economic Theory: The Theory of Monopoly," *Econometrica*, vol. 3 (January, 1935), pp. 1–20. Also reprinted in American

Economic Association, *Readings in Price Theory* (Homewood, Ill.: Irwin, 1952), pp. 361–383. A survey of the theories of imperfect competition developed during the late twenties and early thirties.

Kuenne, Robert E. (ed.), *Monopolistic Competition Theory* (New York: Wiley, 1967). These essays in honor of E. H. Chamberlin cover many aspects of his theory. Most of the essays use little mathematics beyond geometry.

Nicholls, William H., *A Theoretical Analysis of Imperfect Competition with Special Application to the Agricultural Industries* (Ames, Iowa: Iowa State, 1941). Contains largely nonmathematical descriptions of many different forms of imperfect competition. Particularly useful for the analysis of oligopsony.

Robinson, Joan, *The Economics of Imperfect Competition* (London: Macmillan, 1933). A pioneer study of monopoly, price discrimination, and monopsony in which many modern concepts were developed. The analysis is generally limited to geometry.

7
Welfare Economics

The objective of welfare economics is the evaluation of the social desirability of alternative economic states.   An economic state is a particular arrangement of economic activities and of the resources of the economy. Each state is characterized by a different allocation of resources and a different distribution of the rewards for economic activity.   Although the economist may not always be able to prescribe a method by which one state of the economy can be transformed into another, policy measures frequently will be available for changing an existing situation.   It is important to know in such cases whether the contemplated change is desirable.   Imagine, for example, that the economy can attain multi-market equilibrium at two different sets of commodity and factor prices. Since the desires of consumers and entrepreneurs are consistent at both equilibria, society can choose between them, if at all, only on welfare grounds.   The principles by which such problems can be solved fall within the domain of welfare economics.

The welfare of a society depends, in the broadest sense, upon the satisfaction levels of all its consumers.[1] But almost every alternative to be judged by welfare economists will have favorable effects on some people and unfavorable effects on others. Welfare comparisons would be simple if it were possible to aggregate the utilities of individuals into a single utility function. Unfortunately this operation cannot be performed. Interpersonal comparisons of utility are not possible. There is no obvious way to determine whether individual I or individual II derives more satisfaction from the consumption of a given bundle of goods.[2] Welfare comparisons on the basis of individual utilities are possible only in a very restricted sense. The economist can say whether a particular state of the economy involves an efficient allocation of resources, he can tell how to move from one state to another, and he can describe the consequences of such moves. The economist, however, has no more competence than anyone else to say that a particular move is desirable if it has unfavorable effects upon some members of society.

The Pareto conditions for maximum welfare and the possible fulfillment of these conditions under perfect competition are discussed in Sec. 7-1. The welfare implications of imperfect competition are outlined in Sec. 7-2. The failure of perfect competition to achieve the Pareto conditions when there are external effects in consumption and production is outlined in Sec. 7-3, and the attainment of the Pareto conditions through taxes, subsidies, and compensation is described in Sec. 7-4. Social welfare functions are considered in Sec. 7-5, and finally, the theory of second best is presented in Sec. 7-6.

7-1 PARETO OPTIMALITY AND THE EFFICIENCY OF PERFECT COMPETITION

An allocation is described by specific consumption levels for each consumer and specific input and output levels for each producer. Pareto optimality provides a definition of the economic efficiency of allocations that serves as the basis for much of welfare economics. An allocation is *Pareto-optimal* if production and distribution cannot be reorganized to increase the utility of one or more individuals without decreasing the utility of others. Conversely, an allocation is *Pareto-nonoptimal* if someone's utility can be increased without harming anyone else. Since indi-

---

[1] Statements of this kind are based on ethical beliefs or value judgments and cannot be proved. It is reasonable to postulate that the concept of social welfare transcends the more restricted notion of economic welfare. For obvious reasons the present analysis deals only with the latter.

[2] Ordinal utility functions are assumed throughout this chapter. The difficulty would not be eliminated by assuming cardinal functions, since measurability for individual consumers is neither necessary nor sufficient for interpersonal utility comparisons.

vidual utility levels cannot be compared, changes which improve the positions of some individuals but cause a deterioration in those of others cannot be evaluated in terms of efficiency; the net effects of the moves may or may not be beneficial. However, welfare can be said to increase (diminish) if at least one person's position improves (deteriorates) with no change in the positions of others. Clearly no situation can be optimal unless all possible improvements of this variety have been made.[1]

The conditions necessary for the attainment of Pareto optimality are derived in this section. These conditions are expressed in terms of physical input and output units without reference to a pricing system. Then it is demonstrated that the Pareto conditions will be achieved under perfect competition if (1) second-order conditions are satisfied for each consumer and producer, (2) no consumer is satiated, and (3) there are no external effects in either consumption or production. Pareto optimality for consumption and production are considered separately before conditions are formulated for an economy as a whole.

PARETO OPTIMALITY FOR CONSUMPTION

A distribution of consumer goods (including leisure and other withheld primary factors) is Pareto-optimal if every possible reallocation of goods that increases the utility of one or more consumers would result in a utility reduction for at least one other consumer. Pareto optimality will be achieved if each consumer's utility is a maximum given the utility levels of all other consumers. For illustration assume that there are only two consumers denoted by the first subscripts 1 and 2 and only two goods Q_1 and Q_2. The utility functions of the consumers are $U_1(q_{11},q_{12})$ and $U_2(q_{21},q_{22})$ where $q_{11} + q_{21} = q_1^0$ and $q_{12} + q_{22} = q_2^0$. Now assume that consumer II enjoys the level of satisfaction $U_2^0 =$ constant. In order to maximize the utility of consumer I subject to this constraint, form the function

$$U_1^* = U_1(q_{11},q_{12}) + \lambda[U_2(q_1^0 - q_{11}, q_2^0 - q_{12}) - U_2^0]$$

where λ is a Lagrange multiplier, and set its partial derivatives equal to zero:

$$\frac{\partial U_1^*}{\partial q_{11}} = \frac{\partial U_1}{\partial q_{11}} - \lambda \frac{\partial U_2}{\partial q_{21}} = 0$$

$$\frac{\partial U_1^*}{\partial q_{12}} = \frac{\partial U_1}{\partial q_{12}} - \lambda \frac{\partial U_2}{\partial q_{22}} = 0$$

$$\frac{\partial U_1^*}{\partial \lambda} = U_2(q_1^0 - q_{11}, q_2^0 - q_{12}) - U_2^0 = 0$$

[1] The present discussion is limited to static efficiency. No attention is paid to the welfare aspects of resource allocation over time, the time path of welfare, or the welfare aspects of alternative time paths for the economy.

and

$$\frac{\partial U_1/\partial q_{11}}{\partial U_1/\partial q_{12}} = \frac{\partial U_2/\partial q_{21}}{\partial U_2/\partial q_{22}} \tag{7-1}$$

The left-hand side of (7-1) is consumer I's RCS (rate of commodity substitution), and the right-hand side is II's. The RCSs of the consumers must be equal to achieve Pareto optimality in consumption.[1] If (7-1) were not satisfied, it would be possible to redistribute the goods in such a way as to increase I's utility without reducing II's. The argument is symmetric. Condition (7-1) also results from maximization of II's utility given a fixed level for I's. Thus, if (7-1) were not satisfied, it would also be possible to increase II's utility without reducing I's. The mathematical analysis for the two-consumer case is easily generalized for any number of consumers.

The argument can be presented in terms of an Edgeworth box diagram (see Sec. 5-1). The dimensions of the rectangle in Fig. 7-1 represent the total available quantities of Q_1 and Q_2 in a pure-exchange economy. Any point in the box represents a particular distribution of the commodities between the two consumers. For example, if the distribution of commodities is given by point A, the quantities of Q_1 and Q_2 consumed by I are measured by the coordinates of A, using the southwest corner O as the origin; the quantities consumed by II are measured by the coordinates of point A, using the northeast corner O' as the origin. The indifference map of I is drawn, using O as the origin, and the indifference map of II, using O' as the origin. The RCSs of the two consumers are equal where an indifference curve of I is tangent to an indifference curve of II. The locus of all such points is the *contract curve CC*. The mathematical form of the contract curve is given by (7-1), which is a function of q_{11} and q_{12}.

[1] Of course, the second-order conditions must also be fulfilled. It is postulated throughout the remainder of this section that the second-order conditions are fulfilled.

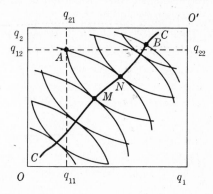

Fig. 7-1

The rates of commodity substitution are unequal at point A, and it is possible to increase the utility levels of both consumers by altering the existing distribution. If the final position (after a redistribution of Q_1 and Q_2) is between M and N, both consumers will have gained, since both will be on higher indifference curves than at A. If the final point is at M or N, one consumer will have gained without any deterioration in the other's position. If a point on the contract curve is reached, it is not possible to improve further the position of either consumer without a deterioration in the position of the other. According to the conditions of Pareto optimality any point from M to N is unambiguously superior to A. However, the evaluation of alternative points on the contract curve would involve an interpersonal comparison of utilities and is therefore not possible without an explicit ethical belief in one's ability to make such comparisons.

In Chap. 2 it was shown that each utility-maximizing consumer equates his RCS for Q_1 and Q_2 to their price ratio:

$$\frac{\partial U_i/\partial q_{i1}}{\partial U_i/\partial q_{i2}} = \frac{p_1}{p_2} \qquad i = 1, 2$$

Since prices are the same for all consumers, perfect competition implies that the RCSs are the same for all consumers. Thus, with the appropriate assumptions, perfect competition among consumers satisfies condition (7-1) and provides a state that is Pareto-optimal among consumers.

PARETO OPTIMALITY FOR PRODUCTION

Assuming that consumers are not satiated and that each individual's utility level is independent of the quantities consumed by others, an increment in the quantity of any consumer good without a decrement in the quantity of any other consumer good can lead to a utility increment for at least one consumer without utility decrements for others. Therefore, Pareto optimality among producers requires that the output level of each consumer good be at a maximum given the output levels of all other consumer goods.

Assume that there are two producers using two inputs to produce two goods with the production functions

$$q_1 = f_1(x_{11}, x_{12})$$

and

$$q_2 = f_2(x_{21}, x_{22})$$

where $x_{11} + x_{21} = x_1^0$ and $x_{12} + x_{22} = x_2^0$ are the available input quantities and q_1 and q_2 are the output levels. Maximize the output of good I subject to the constraint that the output of II is at the predetermined level q_2^0. Form the function

$$L = f_1(x_{11}, x_{12}) + \lambda[f_2(x_1^0 - x_{11}, x_2^0 - x_{12}) - q_2^0]$$

and set its partial derivatives equal to zero:

$$\frac{\partial L}{\partial x_{11}} = \frac{\partial f_1}{\partial x_{11}} - \lambda \frac{\partial f_2}{\partial x_{21}} = 0$$

$$\frac{\partial L}{\partial x_{12}} = \frac{\partial f_1}{\partial x_{12}} - \lambda \frac{\partial f_2}{\partial x_{22}} = 0$$

$$\frac{\partial L}{\partial \lambda} = f_2(x_1^0 - x_{11}, x_2^0 - x_{12}) - q_2^0 = 0$$

and

$$\frac{\partial f_1/\partial x_{11}}{\partial f_1/\partial x_{12}} = \frac{\partial f_2/\partial x_{21}}{\partial f_2/\partial x_{22}} \tag{7-2}$$

The left-hand side of (7-2) is I's RTS (rate of technical substitution) for X_1 and X_2, and the right-hand side is II's. The RTSs of producers must be equal to achieve Pareto optimality in production. If (7-2) were not satisfied, it would be possible to increase the output of one good without decreasing the output of the other. In fact, as the reader may verify, it would be possible to increase the outputs of both goods.

In Chap. 3 it was shown that each profit-maximizing producer equates his RTS for X_1 and X_2 to their price ratio:

$$\frac{\partial f_i/\partial x_{i1}}{\partial f_i/\partial x_{i2}} = \frac{r_1}{r_2} \qquad i = 1, 2$$

Since input prices are the same for all producers, perfect competition implies that their RTSs are the same. Thus, with the appropriate assumptions, perfect competition among producers satisfies condition (7-2) and provides an allocation that is Pareto-optimal among producers.

PARETO OPTIMALITY IN GENERAL

The Pareto conditions derived for consumers and producers are generalized and extended in a consideration of the economy as a whole. Consider an economy with m consumers, N producers, n primary factors, and s produced goods. For simplicity assume that each consumer consumes all produced goods, and each producer uses all primary factors and produces all goods. The consumers' utility functions are

$$U_i = U_i(q_{i1}^*, \ldots, q_{is}^*, x_{i1}^0 - x_{i1}^*, \ldots, x_{in}^0 - x_{in}^*)$$
$$i = 1, \ldots, m \tag{7-3}$$

where q_{ik}^* is the quantity of Q_k consumed by the ith consumer, x_{ij}^0 is his fixed endowment of the jth primary factor, x_{ij}^* is the amount that he supplies to producers, and $x_{ij}^0 - x_{ij}^*$ is the amount that he consumes. Production functions are given in implicit form:

$$F_h(q_{h1}, \ldots, q_{hs}, x_{h1}, \ldots, x_{hn}) = 0 \qquad h = 1, \ldots, N \tag{7-4}$$

where q_{hk} is the output of Q_k by the hth firm and x_{hj} is the amount of X_j which it uses. The aggregate amounts of primary factors supplied by consumers equal the aggregate amounts used by producers:

$$\sum_{i=1}^{m} x_{ij}^* = \sum_{h=1}^{N} x_{hj} \qquad j = 1, \ldots, n \tag{7-5}$$

and the aggregate consumption levels of produced goods equal their aggregate output levels:

$$\sum_{i=1}^{m} q_{ik}^* = \sum_{h=1}^{N} q_{hk} \qquad k = 1, \ldots, s \tag{7-6}$$

Pareto optimality will be achieved if the utility of each consumer is a maximum given the utility levels of all other consumers subject to the constraints (7-4), (7-5), and (7-6). Consider the maximization of consumer I's utility subject to these constraints. Form the Lagrange function

$$Z = U_1(q_{11}^*, \ldots, x_{1n}^0 - x_{1n}^*)$$

$$+ \sum_{i=2}^{m} \lambda_i[U_i(q_{i1}^*, \ldots, x_{in}^0 - x_{in}^*) - U_i^0] + \sum_{h=1}^{N} \theta_h F_h(q_{h1}, \ldots, x_{hn})$$

$$+ \sum_{j=1}^{n} \delta_j \left(\sum_{i=1}^{m} x_{ij}^* - \sum_{h=1}^{N} x_{hj} \right) + \sum_{k=1}^{s} \sigma_k \left(\sum_{h=1}^{N} q_{hk} - \sum_{i=1}^{m} q_{ik}^* \right)$$

where the λ_i, θ_h, δ_j, and σ_k are Lagrange multipliers. Setting the partial derivatives of Z equal to zero,

$$\frac{\partial Z}{\partial q_{1k}^*} = \frac{\partial U_1}{\partial q_{1k}^*} - \sigma_k = 0 \qquad\qquad \frac{\partial Z}{\partial x_{1j}^*} = -\frac{\partial U_1}{\partial (x_{1j}^0 - x_{1j}^*)} + \delta_j = 0$$

$$\frac{\partial Z}{\partial q_{ik}^*} = \lambda_i \frac{\partial U_i}{\partial q_{ik}^*} - \sigma_k = 0 \qquad \frac{\partial Z}{\partial x_{ij}^*} = -\lambda_i \frac{\partial U_i}{\partial (x_{ij}^0 - x_{ij}^*)} + \delta_j = 0 \quad (7\text{-}7)$$

$$\frac{\partial Z}{\partial q_{hk}} = \theta_h \frac{\partial F_h}{\partial q_{hk}} + \sigma_k = 0 \qquad\qquad \frac{\partial Z}{\partial x_{hj}} = \theta_h \frac{\partial F_h}{\partial x_{hj}} - \delta_j = 0$$

where $i = 2, \ldots, m; h = 1, \ldots, N; k = 1, \ldots, s;$ and $j = 1, \ldots, n$. The partials of the multipliers must also be set equal to zero; i.e., the constraints must be satisfied.

The conditions for Pareto optimality may be written in more familiar form. Solving (7-7) for σ_j/σ_k,

$$\frac{\sigma_j}{\sigma_k} = \frac{\partial U_1/\partial q_{1j}^*}{\partial U_1/\partial q_{1k}^*} = \cdots = \frac{\partial U_m/\partial q_{mj}^*}{\partial U_m/\partial q_{mk}^*} = \frac{\partial F_1/\partial q_{1j}}{\partial F_1/\partial q_{1k}} = \cdots$$

$$= \frac{\partial F_N/\partial q_{Nj}}{\partial F_N/\partial q_{Nk}} \qquad j, k = 1, \ldots, s \tag{7-8}$$

Conditions (7-8) state that the RCSs for all consumers and the RPTs (rates of product transformation) for all producers must be equal for every pair of produced goods. Imagine that (7-8) were violated for Q_j and Q_k so that RCS $= \frac{1}{3}$ for some consumer and RPT $= \frac{2}{3}$ for some producer. Three units of Q_j could be transformed into two units of Q_k by moving along the producer's transformation curve. If the consumer surrendered three units of Q_j (the position of all other consumers remaining unchanged), he would require only one unit of Q_k in exchange in order to remain on the same indifference curve and avoid a diminution of utility. The satisfaction level of this consumer could therefore actually be increased by performing the technological transformation of three units of Q_k into two of Q_j. Such an improvement is not possible if the RCSs and RPTs are equal.

Solving (7-7) for δ_j/δ_k,

$$\frac{\delta_j}{\delta_k} = \frac{\partial U_1/\partial(x_{1j}^0 - x_{1j}^*)}{\partial U_1/\partial(x_{1k}^0 - x_{1k}^*)} = \cdots = \frac{\partial U_m/\partial(x_{mj}^0 - x_{mj}^*)}{\partial U_m/\partial(x_{mk}^0 - x_{mk}^*)} = \frac{\partial F_1/\partial x_{1j}}{\partial F_1/\partial x_{1k}}$$
$$= \cdots = \frac{\partial F_N/\partial x_{Nj}}{\partial F_N/\partial x_{Nk}} \qquad j, k = 1, \ldots, n \qquad (7\text{-}9)$$

Conditions (7-9) state the RCSs for all consumers and the RTSs for all producers must be equal for every pair of primary goods. If this condition were violated for some consumer and some producer, it would be possible to increase the consumer's utility by an exchange between the consumer and producer.

Finally, solving (7-7) for δ_j/σ_k,

$$\frac{\delta_j}{\sigma_k} = \frac{\partial U_1/\partial(x_{1j}^0 - x_{1j}^*)}{\partial U_1/\partial q_{1k}^*} = \cdots = \frac{\partial U_m/\partial(x_{mj}^0 - x_{mj}^*)}{\partial U_m/\partial q_{mk}^*} = -\frac{\partial F_1/\partial x_{1j}}{\partial F_1/\partial q_{1k}}$$
$$= \cdots = -\frac{\partial F_N/\partial x_{Nj}}{\partial F_N/\partial q_{Nk}} \qquad \begin{array}{l} j = 1, \ldots, n \\ k = 1, \ldots, s \end{array} \qquad (7\text{-}10)$$

Conditions (7-10) state that the consumers' RCSs between factors and commodities must equal the corresponding producers' rates of transforming factors into commodities, i.e., their MPs (marginal products).[1] If (7-10) were violated for some consumer and producer, the consumer's utility could be increased by surrendering some of the factor for more of the commodity, or some of the commodity for more of the factor.

A Pareto-optimal state is described by the marginal conditions (7-8), (7-9), and (7-10) plus the additional condition that it is not possible to increase the utility of one or more consumers without diminishing the utility of others by discontinuing the production of one or more goods. It is assumed here that the latter condition is always fulfilled. Pareto

[1] The reader unfamiliar with the MP definition used in (7-10) should consult Sec. 3-8.

optimality is defined in terms of physical rates of substitution between factors and commodities without reference to market prices. The Lagrange multipliers δ_j $(j = 1, \ldots, n)$ and σ_k $(k = 1, \ldots, s)$ are efficiency prices; Pareto optimality would be achieved if all consumers and producers adjusted their rates of substitution to efficiency price ratios.[1] Any set of market prices for factors and commodities such that $r_j = \alpha\delta_j$ $(j = 1, \ldots, n)$ and $p_k = \alpha\sigma_k$ $(k = 1, \ldots, s)$, where $\alpha > 0$, will serve as efficiency prices and lead to a Pareto-optimal state. It is of interest for welfare economics to ask whether particular market prices are efficiency prices, or equivalently, to ask whether particular forms of market organization will lead to Pareto optimality.

PARETO OPTIMALITY UNDER PERFECT COMPETITION

It has been shown that under simple assumptions perfect competition among consumers will lead to Pareto optimality for consumers and that perfect competition among producers will lead to Pareto optimality for producers. These results can be generalized for the economy as a whole. The RCS between two commodities Q_k and Q_j equals their price ratio for every consumer if there is perfect competition among consumers:

$$\mathrm{RCS} = \frac{p_j}{p_k}$$

If there is perfect competition among entrepreneurs in commodity and factor markets,

$$p_j = \frac{r}{\mathrm{MP}_j} \qquad p_k = \frac{r}{\mathrm{MP}_k} \tag{7-11}$$

where for notational convenience it is assumed that there is only one primary factor, X. Its price is r, and MP_j and MP_k are its marginal products in producing Q_j and Q_k respectively. Since the same prices prevail for producers and consumers under perfect competition,

$$\mathrm{RCS} = \frac{p_j}{p_k} = \frac{r/\mathrm{MP}_j}{r/\mathrm{MP}_k} = \frac{1/\mathrm{MP}_j}{1/\mathrm{MP}_k}$$

$$= \frac{\text{marginal cost of } Q_j \text{ in terms of } X}{\text{marginal cost of } Q_k \text{ in terms of } X} = \mathrm{RPT} \tag{7-12}$$

which proves Pareto optimality.

Equation (7-12) would appear to hold even if (7-11) does not, provided that

$$\frac{p_j}{p_k} = \frac{r/\mathrm{MP}_j}{r/\mathrm{MP}_k} \tag{7-13}$$

---

[1] Efficiency prices are considered further within a linear-programming context in Sec. 9-2.

But (7-13) can hold without (7-11) only if

$$p_j = k \frac{r}{\text{MP}_j} \qquad j = 1, \ldots, s \qquad (7\text{-}14)$$

where $k \neq 1$ is a factor of proportionality, i.e., if prices are proportional to marginal cost $(= r/\text{MP})$. Equation (7-14) becomes

$$\frac{r}{p_j} = \frac{1}{k} \text{MP}_j \qquad (7\text{-}15)$$

The left-hand side of (7-15) equals the consumers' rate of substitution between Q_j and X; the right-hand side is $(1/k)$ times the producers' rate of transformation between Q_j and X. Conditions (7-10) are violated; the consumers' and producers' corresponding rates of substitution and transformation are not equal. Consumers do not provide the optimal amount of X (labor), and allocation cannot be Pareto-optimal.[1] Assume, for example, that price is three times MC, that is, $k = 3$. Let the RCS between labor and commodity Q_j equal 2 and the MP of labor, 6. A consumer would be willing to surrender an additional hour of leisure (work for an additional hour) if he received 2 more units of Q_j. But the application of an additional hour of labor would result in the production of 6 more units of Q_j. Thus the situation is not Pareto-optimal.

Perfect competition represents a welfare optimum in the sense of fulfilling the requirements of Pareto optimality unless one or more of the assumptions mentioned earlier in this section are violated. Second-order conditions must be fulfilled for all consumers and producers. If they were violated for one or more producers or consumers, the equality of the relevant rates of substitution or transformation would not ensure optimality. In fact, the point at which the rates of substitution and transformation are equal may be a "pessimum" rather than an optimum. The optimum is then represented by a corner solution (see Fig. 2-4a). Pareto optimality may not be achieved under perfect competition if one or more consumers are satiated. The marginal utility increments of a satiated consumer equal zero for each good, and his rates of substitution are not defined. Goods may be diverted from him to other consumers with no reduction of his utility and increases of their's. Illustrations of Pareto nonoptimality under perfect competition if external effects exist for consumption or production are given in Sec. 7-3.

[1] Since r/MP is the marginal cost of output (MC), (7-13) can be stated as

$$\frac{p_j}{p_k} = \frac{\text{MC}_j}{\text{MC}_k}$$

The above proof also implies that for an optimum, $p = \text{MC}$ for every commodity; the proportionality of prices and marginal costs is not sufficient.

There are cases in which perfect competition is Pareto-optimal, but some of the marginal equalities are not satisfied. Corner solutions may result even if all utility and production functions are of appropriate shape, provided that the consumers' RCSs are always greater (or smaller) than the corresponding producers' RPTs. One of the goods will not be produced, and Pareto optimality for the goods in question must be described in terms of marginal inequalities.

An additional difficulty is introduced by the fact that the analysis of Pareto optimality accepts the prevailing income distribution, i.e., the prevailing factor endowment. The problem of finding an optimal income distribution is not considered. It is conceivable that the norm of the perfectly competitive economy would lead to a situation in which a majority of individuals lived at a subsistence level or below. At point B in Fig. 7-1, consumer I is very well off, but consumer II is not. Since point B is on the contract curve, one could not improve one consumer's position without causing a deterioration in the position of the other. It is an efficient point and cannot be said to be inferior to any other point, such as A. The analysis of welfare in terms of Pareto optimality leaves a considerable amount of indeterminacy in the solution: there are an infinite number of points in Fig. 7-1 which are Pareto-optimal. The acceptance of the contract curve as representing welfare optima is already a value judgment. In order to judge the relative social desirability of alternative points on the contract curve, society must make additional value judgments which state its preferences among alternative ways of allocating satisfaction to individuals. Value judgments are ethical beliefs and are not the subject of economic analysis. They are taken for granted and can then be incorporated in economic analysis. The indeterminacy is the consequence of considering an increase in welfare to be unambiguously defined only if an improvement in one individual's position is not accompanied by a deterioration of the position of another. This indeterminacy can only be removed by further value judgments.

7-2 THE EFFICIENCY OF IMPERFECT COMPETITION

With few exceptions monopoly, oligopoly, monopsony, and other forms of imperfect competition will lead to Pareto-nonoptimal resource allocations. The marginal conditions realized under imperfect competition will normally violate the Pareto-optimal conditions given by (7-8), (7-9), and (7-10).

IMPERFECT COMPETITION IN CONSUMPTION

Imperfect competition will exist if one or more consumers are unable to buy as much of a commodity or sell as much of a factor as they desire without noticeably affecting its price. For illustration assume that there are two consumers, one factor, and two commodities. The utility functions are

$$U_1 = U_1(q_{11}, q_{12}, x_1^0 - x_1) \qquad U_2 = U_2(q_{21}, q_{22}, x_2^0 - x_2)$$

where x_i^0 is the factor endowment of the ith consumer, x_i is the quantity of factor that he supplies, and q_{ik} is his consumption of Q_k. Let the supply price of Q_1 depend upon the aggregate amount demanded: $p_1 = g(q_1)$ where $q_1 = q_{11} + q_{21}$ and $g'(q_1) > 0$. The budget constraints of the consumers are

$$rx_1 - g(q_1)q_{11} - p_2q_{12} = 0$$
$$rx_2 - g(q_1)q_{21} - p_2q_{22} = 0$$

Each maximizes his utility index subject to his budget constraint. Form the functions

$$L_1 = U_1(q_{11}, q_{12}, x_1^0 - x_1) + \lambda_1[rx_1 - g(q_1)q_{11} - p_2q_{12}]$$
$$L_2 = U_2(q_{21}, q_{22}, x_2^0 - x_2) + \lambda_2[rx_2 - g(q_1)q_{21} - p_2q_{22}]$$

and set the appropriate partial derivatives equal to zero:

$$\frac{\partial U_i}{\partial q_{i1}} - \lambda_i[p_1 + q_{i1}g'(q_1)] = 0$$

$$\frac{\partial U_i}{\partial q_{i2}} - \lambda_ip_2 = 0 \qquad -\frac{\partial U_i}{\partial(x_i^0 - x_i)} + \lambda_ir = 0 \qquad i = 1, 2$$

$$rx_i - g(q_1)q_{i1} - p_2q_{i2} = 0$$

and

$$\frac{\partial U_i/\partial q_{i1}}{\partial U_i/\partial q_{i2}} = \frac{p_1 + q_{i1}g'(q_1)}{p_2}$$

$$\frac{\partial U_i/\partial q_{i1}}{\partial U_i/\partial(x_i^0 - x_i)} = \frac{p_1 + q_{i1}g'(q_1)}{r} \qquad i = 1, 2 \qquad (7\text{-}16)$$

The consumers behave as duopsonists (see Sec. 6-5). Their equilibrium RCSs given by (7-16) reflect the marginal costs of acquiring additional quantities of Q_1 rather than p_1.†

If $q_{11} \neq q_{21}$, the marginal costs of Q_1 differ for the consumers, their RCSs differ, and the allocation of Q_1, Q_2, and X between them is Pareto-nonoptimal. If $q_{11} = q_{21}$, their RCSs are equal, but differ from the RPTs and MPs of producers which are equated to price ratios.

IMPERFECT COMPETITION IN COMMODITY MARKETS

For convenience limit attention to a single commodity, Q, and a single factor, X. Conditions (7-10) for Pareto optimality will be satisfied if

† Again it is assumed that the second-order conditions are fulfilled.

producers equate their MPs and consumers equate their RCSs to the factor-commodity price ratio:

$$MP = \frac{r}{p} = RCS \tag{7-17}$$

If it is assumed that consumers always satisfy (7-17), Pareto optimality will be achieved if producers equate price and MC (marginal cost):

$$p = \frac{r}{MP} = MC \tag{7-18}$$

If one or more producers fail to satisfy (7-18), the resultant allocation will be Pareto-nonoptimal. The equality of price and MC is a normal result under perfect competition, but it is an unusual result under imperfect competition.

The simple monopolist (see Sec. 6-1) equates MR (marginal revenue), which is less than price, to MC and thereby, creates a Pareto-nonoptimal allocation. The perfectly discriminating monopolist (see Sec. 6-2) is an exception to the rule that imperfect competition is Pareto-nonoptimal. He equates marginal price to MC. Conditions (7-17) and (7-18) are satisfied if p is appropriately interpreted as marginal price for both consumers and producer. In perfect competition both buyer and seller gain from trade; in perfectly discriminating monopoly all gains are absorbed by the seller. The income distributions which result from these two forms of market organization are quite different, but both are Pareto-optimal.

The revenue-maximizing monopolist (see Sec. 6-2) maximizes his sales revenue subject to the condition that his profit equal or exceed a minimum acceptable level. His minimum acceptable profit is generally less than his maximum monopoly profit, and his output level is generally higher than the level that would be achieved under simple monopoly. The revenue-maximizing monopolist would satisfy condition (7-18) if (1) his minimum acceptable profit equaled the profit that is earned at an output for which price equals MC and MC is increasing, and (2) his MR were nonnegative at this point. Since he has no particular motive to select such a point, the occurrence of both (1) and (2) would be a remarkable coincidence. In general, one cannot expect the revenue-maximizing monopolist to satisfy the conditions necessary for Pareto optimality.

Duopoly and oligopoly also will normally result in Pareto-nonoptimal allocations. Condition (7-18) is violated in all the cases considered in Sec. 6-3. In each case one or more of the market participants equate some form of MR to MC. The same comment applies for the analysis of monopolistic competition presented in Sec. 6-4.

IMPERFECT COMPETITION IN FACTOR MARKETS

Consider a factor market in which the sellers behave as perfect competitors. Conditions (7-10) for Pareto optimality will be fulfilled if each buyer of the input equates the value of his MP to the factor price:

$$pMP = r \qquad (7\text{-}19)$$

If one or more buyers fail to satisfy (7-19), the resultant allocation will be Pareto-nonoptimal. Condition (7-19) is normally satisfied under perfect competition, and normally violated under imperfect competition among buyers.

The monopsonist (see Sec. 6-5) equates the value of his MP to his marginal cost for the factor, which is greater than its price, and thereby, creates a Pareto-nonoptimal allocation. It is left as an exercise for the reader to formulate an analysis for a perfectly discriminating monopsonist parallel to the analysis for a perfectly discriminating monopolist, and to demonstrate that the resultant allocation is Pareto-optimal. Nearly all theories of duopsony and oligopsony involve equating the value of MP to some form of marginal input cost, and thereby, violate (7-19).

THE EFFICIENCY OF BILATERAL MONOPOLY

The markets thus far considered have imperfect competition on the seller's side and perfect competition on the buyers', or perfect competition on the sellers' side and imperfect competition on the buyers'. The term bilateral monopoly in its broadest sense covers markets in which there is imperfect competition on the part of both buyers and sellers.

The case of a monopsonistic buyer and a monopolistic seller is covered in Sec. 6-6. The specific outcome for such markets depends upon the relative bargaining strength of the participants. In Sec. 6-6 it was shown that input and output levels will be identical with those that would be achieved by perfect competition if the monopsonist and monopolist maximize their joint profit. The resultant allocation is Pareto-optimal. The distribution of their joint profit is immaterial from the viewpoint of Pareto optimality, although it may be rather important to them. This result is easily generalized to cover markets in which the aggregate number of buyers and sellers is greater than two provided that they maximize their joint profit.

7-3 EXTERNAL EFFECTS IN CONSUMPTION AND PRODUCTION

The conclusion that perfect competition leads to Pareto-optimal allocations is contingent upon the assumption that there are no external effects in consumption and production, i.e., that the utility level of a consumer does not depend upon the consumption levels of others and that the total cost of an entrepreneur does not depend upon the output levels of others. Pareto optimality may not be realized under conditions of perfect competition if there are external effects in consumption and production.

INTERDEPENDENT UTILITY FUNCTIONS

Assume that the utility level of one consumer depends upon the consumption of another. Extreme altruism may increase the satisfaction of the ith consumer if the consumption level of the jth consumer is raised. The desire to "keep up with the Joneses" may have the opposite effect.

Assume that there are two consumers with the utility functions

$$U_1 = U_1(q_{11}, q_{12}, q_{21}, q_{22})$$
$$U_2 = U_2(q_{11}, q_{12}, q_{21}, q_{22})$$

where $q_{11} + q_{21} = q_1^0$, $q_{12} + q_{22} = q_2^0$. In order to maximize the utility of I subject to the constraint that the utility of II is at the predetermined level $U_2^0 = $ constant, form the function

$$U_1^* = U_1(q_{11}, q_{12}, q_1^0 - q_{11}, q_2^0 - q_{12})$$
$$+ \lambda[U_2(q_{11}, q_{12}, q_1^0 - q_{11}, q_2^0 - q_{12}) - U_2^0]$$

and set the partial derivatives equal to zero:

$$\frac{\partial U_1^*}{\partial q_{11}} = \frac{\partial U_1}{\partial q_{11}} - \frac{\partial U_1}{\partial q_{21}} + \lambda \left[\frac{\partial U_2}{\partial q_{11}} - \frac{\partial U_2}{\partial q_{21}} \right] = 0$$

$$\frac{\partial U_1^*}{\partial q_{12}} = \frac{\partial U_1}{\partial q_{12}} - \frac{\partial U_1}{\partial q_{22}} + \lambda \left[\frac{\partial U_2}{\partial q_{12}} - \frac{\partial U_2}{\partial q_{22}} \right] = 0$$

$$\frac{\partial U_1^*}{\partial \lambda} = U_2(q_{11}, q_{12}, q_1^0 - q_{11}, q_2^0 - q_{12}) - U_2^0 = 0$$

and

$$\frac{\partial U_1/\partial q_{11} - \partial U_1/\partial q_{21}}{\partial U_1/\partial q_{12} - \partial U_1/\partial q_{22}} = \frac{\partial U_2/\partial q_{11} - \partial U_2/\partial q_{21}}{\partial U_2/\partial q_{12} - \partial U_2/\partial q_{22}} \qquad (7\text{-}20)$$

Equation (7-20) is the necessary condition for Pareto optimality. It generally differs from (7-8), which states that I's RCS must equal II's. Perfect competition results in the attainment of (7-8), but not of (7-20). Since the partial derivatives of the utility functions are functions of all variables, the optimum position of each consumer depends upon the consumption level of the other. For example, assume that the only external effect present in the two-consumer system is $\partial U_2/\partial q_{11} < 0$. Equation (7-20) becomes

$$\frac{\partial U_1/\partial q_{11}}{\partial U_1/\partial q_{12}} = \frac{\partial U_2/\partial q_{11} - \partial U_2/\partial q_{21}}{-\partial U_2/\partial q_{22}}$$

The RCS of consumer II must be greater for an optimal distribution than it would be in the absence of external effects.

It can be shown diagrammatically that condition (7-8) does not necessarily ensure Pareto optimality in the presence of external effects. Figure 7-2a and 7-2b give the indifference maps of consumers I and II respectively. Assume that in the initial situation I consumes the commodity batch represented by A and II consumes the batch represented by F. These points—at which their RCSs are equal—are reached by utility maximization carried out individually by the two consumers with no regard for possible external effects. Assume that I is not affected by II's consumption, and II's utility level is reduced by I's consumption of Q_1 (but not of Q_2). II's indifference map (solid curves) is drawn on the assumption that I's consumption is given by A. In their individual equilibrium situations I's utility index is 100, and II's, 80. Let the distribution of commodities be altered by some authority in such a way that the aggregate quantities consumed remain unchanged and that I moves to C and II to D. The utility level of consumer I has not been changed by this reallocation. However, the diminution of his consumption of Q_1 changes II's utility level for every commodity combination consumed by the latter: II's relevant indifference curves after the change in I's consumption are given by the dotted curves in Fig. 7-2b. Consumer II's utility level is increased to 90 since his new position is at D. One can conclude that II's utility level can be increased without diminishing I's utility level; hence the equality of the RCSs does not ensure Pareto optimality.

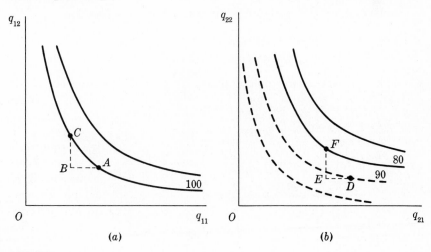

Fig. 7-2

PUBLIC GOODS

A quite different type of externality in consumption occurs when goods are consumed collectively. Each member of society gains satisfaction from the total output of a *public good*. No one's satisfaction is diminished by the satisfaction gained by others, and it is not possible for anyone to appropriate a public good for his own personal use, as is the case with ordinary goods.

The conditions for Pareto optimality given by (7-8) and (7-10) are not valid for public goods. New conditions must be formulated. No essentials are lost by the simplifying assumptions that there are two consumers, one producer, one ordinary good, one public good, and one primary factor. The consumers' utility functions are

$$U_i = U_i(q_{i1}, q_2, x_i^0 - x_i) \qquad i = 1, 2$$

where q_{i1} is the consumption of the ordinary good Q_1 by the ith consumer, q_2 is the total output of the public good Q_2, x_i^0 is the ith consumer's endowment of the primary factor X, and x_i is the amount that he supplies for production. The implicit production function is

$$F(q_1, q_2, x) = 0$$

where $q_1 = q_{11} + q_{21}$ is the output of Q_1 and $x = x_1 + x_2$ is the amount of X used in production.

Conditions for Pareto optimality are obtained by maximizing I's utility assuming that II's utility is at a predetermined level and that the production function is satisfied. Form the Lagrange function

$$Z = U_1(q_{11}, q_2, x_1^0 - x_1) + \lambda[U_2(q_{21}, q_2, x_2^0 - x_2) - U_2^0]$$
$$+ \theta F(q_1, q_2, x) + \delta(x_1 + x_2 - x) + \sigma(q_1 - q_{11} - q_{21})$$

where λ, θ δ, and σ are undetermined multipliers. Setting the partial derivatives of Z equal to zero,

$$\frac{\partial Z}{\partial q_{11}} = \frac{\partial U_1}{\partial q_{11}} - \sigma = 0 \qquad\qquad \frac{\partial Z}{\partial x_1} = -\frac{\partial U_1}{\partial(x_1^0 - x_1)} + \delta = 0$$

$$\frac{\partial Z}{\partial q_{21}} = \lambda \frac{\partial U_2}{\partial q_{21}} - \sigma = 0 \qquad\qquad \frac{\partial Z}{\partial x_2} = -\lambda \frac{\partial U_2}{\partial(x_2^0 - x_2)} + \delta = 0$$

$$\frac{\partial Z}{\partial q_2} = \frac{\partial U_1}{\partial q_2} + \lambda \frac{\partial U_2}{\partial q_2} + \theta \frac{\partial F}{\partial q_2} = 0 \qquad\qquad (7\text{-}21)$$

$$\frac{\partial Z}{\partial q_1} = \theta \frac{\partial F}{\partial q_1} + \sigma = 0 \qquad\qquad \frac{\partial Z}{\partial x} = \theta \frac{\partial F}{\partial x} - \delta = 0$$

It is assumed that the partial derivatives with respect to the Lagrange multipliers are also set equal to zero.

For ordinary goods (7-8) states that the RCS for every consumer must equal the corresponding RPT for every producer. Equations (7-21) imply that[1]

$$\frac{\partial U_1/\partial q_2}{\partial U_1/\partial q_{11}} + \frac{\partial U_2/\partial q_2}{\partial U_2/\partial q_{21}} = \frac{\partial F/\partial q_2}{\partial F/\partial q_1} \tag{7-22}$$

The sum of the RCSs of Q_1 for Q_2 for the consumers must equal the RPT of Q_1 for Q_2 in production. It is not necessary that the RCSs of the individual consumers be equal. Imagine that I and II have respective RCSs of 3 and 2 units of Q_1 per unit of Q_2, but that the producer's RPT is 4 units of Q_1 per unit of Q_2. Condition (7-22) is violated and the allocation of Q_2 and Q_1 is Pareto-nonoptimal. If I and II surrendered 3 and 2 units of Q_1 respectively, the producer could increase the output of Q_2 by more than 1 unit and thereby increase the utility levels of both consumers.

Equations (7-21) also imply that

$$\frac{\partial U_1/\partial q_2}{\partial U_1/\partial (x_1^0 - x_1)} + \frac{\partial U_2/\partial q_2}{\partial U_2/\partial (x_2^0 - x_2)} = -\frac{\partial F/\partial q_2}{\partial F/\partial x} \tag{7-23}$$

The sum of the RCSs of X for Q_2 must equal the reciprocal of the MP of X in the production of Q_2. Finally, solving (7-21) for δ/σ,

$$\frac{\delta}{\sigma} = \frac{\partial U_1/\partial (x_1^0 - x_1)}{\partial U_1/\partial q_{11}} = \frac{\partial U_2/\partial (x_2^0 - x_2)}{\partial U_2/\partial q_{21}} = -\frac{\partial F/\partial x}{\partial F/\partial q_1} \tag{7-24}$$

The RCS of X for Q_1 for each consumer must equal the MP of X in the production of Q_1. Condition (7-24) is the same as (7-10).

The analysis of public goods is easily generalized. If there is more than one primary factor, (7-9) is in force: the RCSs of all consumers and the RTSs of all producers must be equal for every pair of primary factors. If there is more than one ordinary good, (7-8) is in force: the RCSs of the consumers must equal the RPTs of the producers. If there are two public goods, their aggregate RCS, which may be expressed as the ratio of their aggregate RCSs for an arbitrarily selected ordinary good, must equal their RPT (see Exercise 7-11).

Public goods cannot be purchased and sold in the market in the same way as ordinary goods. No consumer can acquire a quantity of a public good that is exclusively his. There is little or no individual action that a consumer who desires more of a public good can take. Public

---

[1] Substitute $\lambda = \sigma/(\partial U_2/\partial q_{21})$ and $\theta = -\sigma/(\partial F/\partial q_1)$ in the equation for $\partial Z/\partial q_2$, divide through by $\sigma = \partial U_1/\partial q_{11}$, and rearrange terms.

goods normally are produced by public agencies on the basis of collective decisions and normally are financed by taxation.

EXTERNAL ECONOMIES AND DISECONOMIES

It was shown that the $p = \text{MC}$ criterion is necessary for Pareto optimality in the producing sector. The equality of price and marginal cost for all commodities and firms implies that the corresponding RPTs of different firms are the same. The RPT (the slope of the transformation curve) measures the opportunity cost or the real sacrifice, in terms of opportunities foregone, of producing an additional unit of a commodity. Until now this opportunity cost has been considered internal to the firm: in order to produce an additional unit of Q_j it has to sacrifice the production of a certain number of units of Q_k. The relevant measure of the sacrifice from society's point of view is the number of units of Q_k that society has to give up in order to produce an additional unit of Q_j. The opportunity cost is the same from the private and social points of view in the absence of external economies and diseconomies. If such external effects are present in the productive sphere, one must take into account the interdependence between the costs of the ith firm and the output of the hth (see Sec. 4-3).

Assume for simplicity's sake that there are only two firms with the cost functions

$$C_1 = C_1(q_1, q_2) \qquad C_2 = C_2(q_1, q_2) \tag{7-25}$$

where q_1 and q_2 are the output levels. The cost functions (7-25) express the existence of external effects. If each firm maximizes its profit individually, price will equal MC or

$$p = \frac{\partial C_1}{\partial q_1} \qquad p = \frac{\partial C_2}{\partial q_2}$$

The profit of each firm depends upon the output level of the other, but neither can affect the output of the other, and thus each firm maximizes its profit with respect to the variable under its control.

The welfare associated with production can be measured by the difference between the social benefit created and the social cost incurred. The social benefit derived from $q_1 + q_2$ units of the commodity can be measured by the total revenue $p(q_1 + q_2)$, i.e., by the amount that consumers are willing to pay for the output. The social costs are measured by the sum of the costs incurred by both entrepreneurs producing the commodity, $C_1(q_1, q_2) + C_2(q_1, q_2)$. In order to attain Pareto optimality, one must maximize the entrepreneurs' joint profits:

$$\pi = \pi_1 + \pi_2 = p(q_1 + q_2) - C_1(q_1, q_2) - C_2(q_1, q_2)$$

Setting the partial derivatives equal to zero,

$$\frac{\partial \pi}{\partial q_1} = p - \frac{\partial C_1}{\partial q_1} - \frac{\partial C_2}{\partial q_1} = 0$$
$$\frac{\partial \pi}{\partial q_2} = p - \frac{\partial C_1}{\partial q_2} - \frac{\partial C_2}{\partial q_2} = 0 \qquad (7\text{-}26)$$

The second-order conditions require that the principal minors of the relevant Hessian

$$\begin{vmatrix} -\dfrac{\partial^2 C_1}{\partial q_1^2} - \dfrac{\partial^2 C_2}{\partial q_1^2} & -\dfrac{\partial^2 C_1}{\partial q_1\,\partial q_2} - \dfrac{\partial^2 C_2}{\partial q_1\,\partial q_2} \\[2ex] -\dfrac{\partial^2 C_1}{\partial q_1\,\partial q_2} - \dfrac{\partial^2 C_2}{\partial q_1\,\partial q_2} & -\dfrac{\partial^2 C_1}{\partial q_2^2} - \dfrac{\partial^2 C_2}{\partial q_2^2} \end{vmatrix}$$

alternate in sign, or that

$$-\frac{\partial^2 C_1}{\partial q_1^2} - \frac{\partial^2 C_2}{\partial q_1^2} < 0 \qquad (7\text{-}27)$$

and

$$\left(-\frac{\partial^2 C_1}{\partial q_1^2} - \frac{\partial^2 C_2}{\partial q_1^2}\right)\left(-\frac{\partial^2 C_1}{\partial q_2^2} - \frac{\partial^2 C_2}{\partial q_2^2}\right)$$
$$-\left(\frac{\partial^2 C_1}{\partial q_1\,\partial q_2} + \frac{\partial^2 C_2}{\partial q_1\,\partial q_2}\right)^2 > 0 \qquad (7\text{-}28)$$

Inequalities (7-27) and (7-28) together imply

$$\frac{\partial^2 C_1}{\partial q_1^2} + \frac{\partial^2 C_2}{\partial q_1^2} > 0 \qquad \frac{\partial^2 C_1}{\partial q_2^2} + \frac{\partial^2 C_2}{\partial q_2^2} > 0$$

The partial derivatives $\partial C_1/\partial q_1$ and $\partial C_2/\partial q_2$ are the *private* marginal costs because they measure the rate of increase of an individual entrepreneur's total cost as his output level rises. Individual maximization requires that price equal private marginal cost and that private marginal cost be increasing. The sums $\partial C_1/\partial q_1 + \partial C_2/\partial q_1$ and $\partial C_1/\partial q_2 + \partial C_2/\partial q_2$ are *social* marginal costs because they measure the rate of increase of the industry's costs as the output level of a particular firm increases. Pareto optimality requires that price equal the *social marginal cost* of each entrepreneur and that *social marginal cost be increasing*. The equality of price and social marginal cost guarantees that the consumers' RCS will equal not the individual firms' RPTs but society's RPT, since the ratio of the social marginal costs measures, from society's point of view, the alternatives foregone by producing an additional unit of a commodity.

Assume that firm I experiences external economies and firm II experiences external diseconomies. Then $\partial C_1/\partial q_2 < 0$ and $\partial C_2/\partial q_1 > 0$. As a result, $\partial C_1/\partial q_1 + \partial C_2/\partial q_1$ in (7-26) can be made to equal price only if $\partial C_1/\partial q_1$ is smaller than under individual profit maximization. With

increasing MC this means that the firm which is the cause of external diseconomies should produce a lower level of output for welfare maximization than in the case of individual maximization.   By analogous reasoning the firm which is the cause of external economies should increase its
output.   These output changes can generally be accomplished by appropriate taxation and subsidization of the output levels of the firms
concerned.

Assume that the cost functions of the two firms are

$$C_1 = 0.1q_1^2 + 5q_1 - 0.1q_2^2 \qquad C_2 = 0.2q_2^2 + 7q_2 + 0.025q_1^2$$

Firm I experiences external economies and is the cause of external diseconomies; the converse holds for firm II.   Assuming that the price is
15 dollars and setting it equal to MC for both firms,

$$15 = 0.2q_1 + 5 \qquad q_1 = 50 \qquad \pi_1 = 290$$
$$15 = 0.4q_2 + 7 \qquad q_2 = 20 \qquad \pi_2 = 17.5$$

For Pareto optimality form the joint profit function

$$\pi = 15(q_1 + q_2) - 0.125q_1^2 - 5q_1 - 0.1q_2^2 - 7q_2$$

and set the partial derivatives equal to zero:

$$\frac{\partial \pi}{\partial q_1} = 15 - 0.25q_1 - 5 = 0$$

$$\frac{\partial \pi}{\partial q_2} = 15 - 0.20q_2 - 7 = 0$$

Here $q_1 = 40$, $q_2 = 40$, and $\pi = 360$.   The reader may verify that the
second-order conditions are satisfied.   Total profits are greater in this
case than under individual maximization

$$290 + 17.5 = 307.5 < 360$$

Individual maximization does not ensure Pareto optimality.   Pareto
optimality requires that the RCS equal the rate at which society can
transform one commodity into another.   In the absence of external
effects, the private and social rates of product transformation are identical.   In the presence of external economies or diseconomies individual
maximization results in the fulfillment of socially "wrong" or irrelevant marginal conditions.   Of course, aggregate profits *have* to be redis-
tributed among the individual firms.   Without such redistribution, some
firms would experience a diminution in their profits, and the resulting
position could not be said to be socially preferable.   In the present
example, 400 dollars accrue to firm I and -40 dollars to firm II as a result
of joint maximization.   A redistribution of any amount greater than

57.5, but less than 110, dollars from firm I to firm II will leave each better off than under individual maximization.

7-4 TAXES, SUBSIDIES, AND COMPENSATION

Sections 7-2 and 7-3 contain many examples in which market economies deviate from the marginal conditions necessary for Pareto optimality. Such economies usually can be led to Pareto optimality through the imposition of appropriate taxes and subsidies. Per unit taxes (subsidies) will decrease (increase) the levels of consumption and production activities by increasing (decreasing) their marginal costs if marginal costs are increasing. Accompanying lump-sum taxes and subsidies, which do not affect activity levels, may be used to distribute the gains from a movement to a Pareto-optimal allocation.

The achievement of Pareto optimality through taxation is illustrated for two specific cases: external effects in production, and monopoly. Unit taxes and subsidies are designed to lead market participants to observe the desired marginal conditions, and lump-sum taxes and subsidies are designed to leave consumers and producers at initial utility and profit levels. It is then demonstrated that positive net tax revenues provide social dividends that can be used to increase the utility of one or more members of society. Finally, compensation criteria are considered which go beyond the tax and subsidy criteria.

EXTERNAL EFFECTS IN PRODUCTION

If external effects are present, Pareto optimality normally can be achieved by imposing unit subsidies to increase the outputs of firms that generate external economies, and unit taxes to decrease the outputs of firms that generate external diseconomies. Return to the two-firm example presented in Sec. 7-3. Cost functions are

$$C_1 = 0.1q_1^2 + 5q_1 - 0.1q_2^2 \qquad C_2 = 0.2q_2^2 + 7q_2 + 0.025q_1^2$$

Firm I experiences external economies and is the cause of external diseconomies; the converse holds for firm II. Each firm equates its private MC to a competitive price of 15 dollars:

$$0.2q_1^0 + 5 = 15 \qquad q_1^0 = 50 \qquad \pi_1^0 = 290$$
$$0.4q_2^0 + 7 = 15 \qquad q_2^0 = 20 \qquad \pi_2^0 = 17.5$$

A Pareto-optimal allocation is determined by equating the social MC of each firm to the competitive price:

$$0.25q_1^* + 5 = 15 \qquad q_1^* = 40 \qquad \pi_1^* = 400$$
$$0.20q_2^* + 7 = 15 \qquad q_2^* = 40 \qquad \pi_2^* = -40$$

Let a tax of t dollars per unit be imposed on the output of firm I, and a subsidy of s dollars per unit be imposed on the output of firm II. Assume that each firm continues to equate its private MC to the competitive price:

$$0.2q_1 + 5 + t = 15 \qquad 0.4q_2 + 7 - s = 15 \tag{7-29}$$

The tax and subsidy are designed to achieve the Pareto-optimal outputs. Substituting $q_1 = 40$ and $q_2 = 40$ in (7-29), the appropriate values for the tax and subsidy are $t = 2$ and $s = 8$. Lump-sum taxes, L_1 and L_2, are imposed to leave the profits of the firms at their initial levels:

$$L_1 = \pi_1^* - \pi_1^0 - tq_1^* = 30$$
$$L_2 = \pi_2^* - \pi_2^0 + sq_2^* = 262.5$$

Since profits remain unchanged, the utility levels of those who receive the profits are unchanged by this move to Pareto optimality. A *social dividend*, S, is defined as the net tax proceeds:

$$S = tq_1^* - sq_2^* + L_1 + L_2 = 52.5$$

The social dividend may be used to increase the utility levels of one or more members of society.

MONOPOLY

Consider an economy in which a monopolist producing good Q is the only cause for deviation from Pareto optimality. The monopolist's demand and cost functions are $p = f(q)$ and $C = C(q)$. His profit-maximizing output and price, q^0 and p^0, are determined by equating MR and MC:

$$p^0 + q^0 f'(q^0) = C'(q^0) \tag{7-30}$$

His equilibrium is pictured as point E in Fig. 7-3. The monopolist's price is too high and his quantity too low for Pareto optimality. Pareto-optimal quantity and price, q^* and p^*, are determined by equating price and MC:

$$p^* = C'(q^*) \tag{7-31}$$

which occurs at point A in Fig. 7-3.

A unit subsidy will increase the monopolist's MR and may be used to induce him to expand his output to the Pareto-optimal level. The relevant equilibrium condition is

$$p^* + q^* f'(q^*) + s = C'(q^*) \tag{7-32}$$

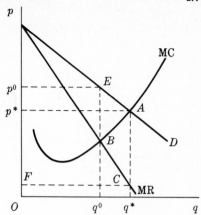

Fig. 7-3

Solve (7-32) for s utilizing (7-31) and the definition of MR:

$$s = -q^*f'(q^*) = p^* - \text{MR}^* \tag{7-33}$$

The desired unit subsidy equals the difference between price and MR at the Pareto-optimal output, the distance CA in Fig. 7-3. The monopolist's effective MR curve is shifted upward until it intersects the original demand curve at A.

The total subsidy is given by the area of the rectangle $FCAp^*$ in Fig. 7-3. The monopolist's cost increment for the move from q^0 to q^* is given by the area lying under his MC curve between these outputs, and his revenue increment from sales is given by the corresponding area lying under his MR curve. His profit reduction is the area CAB which lies between his MC and MR curves. In general,

$$\pi^0 - \pi^* = \int_{q^0}^{q^*} [f(q) + qf'(q) - C'(q)]\,dq \tag{7-34}$$

It is obvious from Fig. 7-3 that the subsidy exceeds the profit reduction. The imposition of a lump-sum tax equal to the area $FCBAp^*$ will leave the monopolist's profit at its initial level. In general, the lump-sum tax, L_M, is

$$L_M = \pi^* - \pi^0 + sq^* \tag{7-35}$$

The net cost of the movement to the Pareto-optimal output equals the monopolist's profit differential given by (7-34). A social dividend will remain if consumers may be taxed by a larger amount without utility reductions.

Assume that the income elasticity of demand for the commodity under consideration is zero for every consumer. In this case, the ordinary demand curve coincides with the compensated demand curve that passes through the monopoly equilibrium point (see Sec. 2-4). The area under the demand curve from q^0 to q^* gives the amount that consumers can pay while retaining the utility levels that they achieved under monopoly. The corresponding area under the MR curve gives the amount that they actually pay for a move from q^0 to q^*. The area that lies between the demand and MR curves is the total of lump-sum taxes, L_C, that can be collected from consumers leaving them at their initial utility levels:

$$L_C = \int_{q^0}^{q^*} [-qf'(q)]\, dq \qquad\qquad (7\text{-}36)$$

and the corresponding social dividend is the net tax collected from consumers and the producer:

$$S = L_C + L_M - sq^* \qquad\qquad (7\text{-}37)$$

Figure 7-3 shows that the social dividend is always positive under monopoly. The lump-sum taxes for consumers are given by the area $BCAE$, the net payment to the monopolist by the area BCA, and the social dividend by the area BAE.

The assumption of zero income elasticities is not necessary to secure a positive social dividend. Assume that each consumer has a positive income elasticity. The price reduction for Q will have positive income effects, consumers can pay the lump-sum taxes given by the area $BCAE$, the social dividend BAE can be achieved, and in addition each consumer can have a utility higher than his initial level.

Let the monopolist's demand and cost functions be

$$p = 240 - 8q \qquad C = 2q^2 \qquad\qquad (7\text{-}38)$$

Equating MR and MC,

$$\begin{aligned} 240 - 16q^0 = 4q^0 & \qquad q^0 = 12 \qquad p^0 = 144 \\ \mathrm{MR}^0 = \mathrm{MC}^0 = 48 & \qquad \pi^0 = 1{,}440 \end{aligned}$$

The Pareto-optimal quantity and price are obtained by letting price equal MC:

$$\begin{aligned} 240 - 8q^* = 4q^* & \qquad q^* = 20 \qquad p^* = \mathrm{MC} = 80 \\ \mathrm{MR}^* = -80 & \qquad \pi^* = 800 \end{aligned}$$

It is of interest to note that MR is negative for the Pareto-optimal solution in this case. The optimal unit subsidy and lump-sum tax are

$$s = p^* - \mathrm{MR}^* = 160 \qquad L_M = \pi^* - \pi^0 + sq^* = 2{,}560$$

Assume that all consumers have zero income elasticities for Q. The consumers' lump-sum taxes and the social dividend are

$$L_C = \int_{12}^{20} 8q\, dq = (4)(20)^2 - (4)(12)^2 = 1{,}024$$
$$S = L_C + L_M - sq^* = 384$$

COMPENSATION CRITERIA

Much of welfare economics concerns whether or not a movement from one allocation to another is socially desirable. Most economists agree that a movement is desirable if no one's utility is decreased and at least one person's utility is increased. Most changes would result in a reduction of someone's utility unless compensation is provided. Net subsidies were designed to provide compensation in cases considered earlier in this section. A number of economists have made potential rather than actual compensation the criterion for judging whether a change is socially desirable. Three prominent compensation criteria are:

The Kaldor criterion Allocation A is socially preferable to B if those who gain from A could compensate the losers (i.e., bribe them to accept A) and still be in a better position than at B.

The Hicks criterion Allocation A is socially preferable to B if those who would lose from A could not profitably bribe the gainers into not making the change from B to A.

The Scitovsky criterion Allocation A is socially preferable to B if the gainers could bribe the losers into accepting the change and simultaneously the losers could not bribe the gainers into not making the change.

Return to the example of external effects in production presented earlier in this section. A movement from an allocation in which each producer equates private MC and price to one in which each equates social MC and price would increase firm I's profit by 110 and reduce II's by 57.5. All three criteria are satisfied for this move. Firm I could pay 57.5 to II to bribe it into accepting the move, and II could not profitably pay I 110 to prevent the move.

The fundamental difficulty of compensation principles is that they refer to potential, rather than actual, welfare since they do not require that compensation actually be paid. In general, nothing can be said about the social preferability of A over B in the absence of actual compensation unless one is willing to make additional value judgments. Consider the case in which a change is contemplated from state A to state B. Some persons are affected unfavorably by the movement, and others benefit. Assume that there exists some redistribution of income which compensates the losers; assume moreover that the losers cannot bribe the gainers to oppose the change from A to B. There is no guarantee, however, that the redistribution that would compensate the losers will actually be carried out. The actual redistribution following the establishment of B may be such that the losers are not compensated. In addition, it is possible that the losers could have effectively blocked the move to B (by bribing the gainers) had they known the actual distribution that was going to be achieved. Under these circumstances it is not legitimate to say that the fulfillment of the Scitovsky criterion implies that state B is socially preferable to A. In general, the compensation criteria imply interpersonal comparisons that most economists strive to avoid.

7-5 SOCIAL WELFARE FUNCTIONS

The indeterminacy which remains if Pareto optimality is the only requirement for welfare optimization can be removed through the introduction of a social welfare function. A social welfare function is an ordinal index of society's welfare and is a function of the utility levels of all individuals. It is not unique, and its form depends upon the value judgments of the persons for whom it is a desirable welfare function. In certain cases it may be impossible to decide upon an acceptable form for the social welfare function by common consensus; it may then have to be imposed in dictatorial fashion. Whatever the case may be, its form depends upon the value judgments of its promulgators, since it expresses their views concerning the effect that the utility level of the ith individual has on the welfare of society. Moreover, the acceptance by an individual of the social welfare function for the purpose of solving the problem of distribution also involves a value judgment. The general form of the social welfare function is

$$W = W(U_1, U_2, \ldots, U_n) \tag{7-39}$$

where U_i is the level of the utility index of the ith individual.

DETERMINATION OF A WELFARE OPTIMUM

Assume that society consists of two individuals whose utility functions are

$$U_1 = U_1(q_{11}, q_{12}, x_1^0 - x_1) \qquad U_2 = U_2(q_{21}, q_{22}, x_2^0 - x_2)$$

where q_{ij} is the amount of the jth commodity consumed by the ith individual and x_i the amount of work performed by the ith individual. Assume that society's production function is

$$F(q_{11} + q_{21}, q_{12} + q_{22}, x_1 + x_2) = 0 \qquad (7\text{-}40)$$

Assume finally that the social welfare function is

$$W = W(U_1, U_2) \qquad (7\text{-}41)$$

The goal of society is to maximize (7-41) subject to the constraint given by (7-40). Form the function

$$W^* = W[U_1(q_{11}, q_{12}, x_1^0 - x_1), U_2(q_{21}, q_{22}, x_2^0 - x_2)]$$
$$+ \lambda F(q_{11} + q_{21}, q_{12} + q_{22}, x_1 + x_2)$$

and set its partial derivatives equal to zero:

$$\frac{\partial W^*}{\partial q_{11}} = W_1 \frac{\partial U_1}{\partial q_{11}} + \lambda F_1 = 0$$

$$\frac{\partial W^*}{\partial q_{12}} = W_1 \frac{\partial U_1}{\partial q_{12}} + \lambda F_2 = 0$$

$$\frac{\partial W^*}{\partial x_1} = -W_1 \frac{\partial U_1}{\partial (x_1^0 - x_1)} + \lambda F_3 = 0$$

$$\frac{\partial W^*}{\partial q_{21}} = W_2 \frac{\partial U_2}{\partial q_{21}} + \lambda F_1 = 0 \qquad (7\text{-}42)$$

$$\frac{\partial W^*}{\partial q_{22}} = W_2 \frac{\partial U_2}{\partial q_{22}} + \lambda F_2 = 0$$

$$\frac{\partial W^*}{\partial x_2} = -W_2 \frac{\partial U_2}{\partial (x_2^0 - x_2)} + \lambda F_3 = 0$$

$$\frac{\partial W^*}{\partial \lambda} = F(q_{11} + q_{21}, q_{12} + q_{22}, x_1 + x_2) = 0$$

It is assumed that the system of seven equations given by (7-42) can be solved for its seven variables. A welfare optimum is completely determined as a result of the introduction of distributional value judgments in the form of the social welfare function.[1] It can easily be verified that the resulting allocation is Pareto-optimal. Move the second terms of the first six equations in (7-42) to the right and then divide the first equation by the second and the third and the fourth equation by the fifth and sixth respectively:

$$\frac{\partial U_1/\partial q_{11}}{\partial U_1/\partial q_{12}} = \frac{F_1}{F_2} = \frac{\partial U_2/\partial q_{21}}{\partial U_2/\partial q_{22}} \qquad \frac{\partial U_1/\partial q_{11}}{\partial U_1/\partial (x_1^0 - x_1)} = \frac{F_1}{F_3} = \frac{\partial U_2/\partial q_{21}}{\partial U_2/\partial (x_2^0 - x_2)}$$

[1] In terms of the Edgeworth box diagram discussed in Sec. 7-1, the introduction of the social welfare function is equivalent to ranking all points on the contract curve from the point of view of social preferability.

The RCSs are the same for both consumers and equal the corresponding RPT. The rate at which consumers substitute leisure (the counterpart of work) for commodities equals the MP of labor. This proves Pareto optimality if the second-order conditions are also satisfied.[1]

SOCIAL PREFERENCE AND INDIFFERENCE

In an effort to create a social analog to individual indifference curves, economists have tried to derive contour lines in the commodity space which represent alternative combinations of aggregate quantities of commodities among which society as a whole is indifferent. *Scitovsky contours* are derived in the following fashion. Assume that all individuals enjoy specified levels of utility and that the outputs of all commodities but one are at specified levels. Then determine the smallest quantity of the remaining commodity necessary to meet the above specifications. The problem is expressed mathematically for a two-person, two-commodity economy as follows:

$$\text{Minimize } q_{11} + q_{21}$$

subject to

$$U_1(q_{11},q_{12}) - U_1^0 = 0$$
$$U_2(q_{21},q_{22}) - U_2^0 = 0$$
$$q_{12} + q_{22} = q_2^0$$

This problem can be solved by forming the function

$$V = q_{11} + q_{21} + \lambda_1[U_1(q_{11},q_{12}) - U_1^0] \\ + \lambda_2[U_2(q_{21}, q_2^0 - q_{12}) - U_2^0] \quad (7\text{-}43)$$

where λ_1 and λ_2 are Lagrange multipliers, and setting the partial derivatives with respect to q_{11}, q_{12}, q_{21}, λ_1, and λ_2 equal to zero. The minimum total quantity of Q_1 necessary to satisfy the conditions of the problem is generally determinate. For each possible value of q_2^0 a different optimal value of q_1^0 ($= q_{11} + q_{21}$) can be determined. The locus of all (q_1^0,q_2^0) points for given values of U_1 and U_2 forms a Scitovsky contour.[2]

---

[1] A social welfare function is analogous to the individual consumer's utility function. It provides a ranking—from society's or a dictator's point of view—of alternative positions in which different individuals enjoy different utility levels. It possesses the property that if a given social welfare function provides an acceptable ranking, so does any monotonic transformation of it. The reader may verify this proposition by proceeding analogously to the analysis in Sec. 2-3. Assume that the welfare function is $S = G(W)$ where $G' > 0$ and derive the first- and second-order conditions for a maximum.

[2] The reader may verify that points on a Scitovsky contour represent a Pareto-optimal distribution of commodities by finding the partial derivatives of (7-43).

If the individual indifference curves are convex, the Scitovsky contours will be convex. However, these contours are not "social" indifference curves, as it might appear from their shapes alone. A completely different Scitovsky contour is obtained if the specified values of U_1 and U_2 are changed. Take for example point A on the Scitovsky contour S_1 in Fig. 7-4. For any point on S_1 the total quantities of Q_1 and Q_2 must be distributed between the two consumers in such a manner that I enjoys the utility level U_1^0 and II the level U_2^0. But the quantities corresponding to A could also be distributed in a different manner, one that results in a utility level $U_1^{(1)}$ for I and $U_2^{(1)}$ for II. By carrying out the maximization process as indicated in (7-43) for these new values of U_1 and U_2, an entirely new set of points is determined, which describe a new Scitovsky contour corresponding to the different utility levels assigned to individuals. This new contour S_2 must have a common point with S_1 at A, but there is clearly no reason to expect that the two contours will coincide throughout their lengths. S_1 and S_2 may therefore either intersect at A (as in Fig. 7-4) or be tangent to each other. Neither case is consistent with the usual properties of indifference curves.

The explicit introduction of value judgments in the form of a social welfare function permits the derivation of contours with some desirable properties. Let the social welfare function be $W = W(U_1, U_2)$ in a two-person society. Find the Scitovsky contours corresponding to all distributions of utility (U_1, U_2) for which $W(U_1, U_2) = W^0$. These contours are shown in Fig. 7-5. The least ordinate corresponding to any value of q_1 represents the minimum amount of Q_2 necessary to ensure society the welfare level W^0. Therefore the envelope B of the Scitovsky contours in Fig. 7-5 is the locus of minimal combinations of Q_1 and Q_2

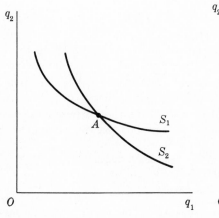

Fig. 7-4

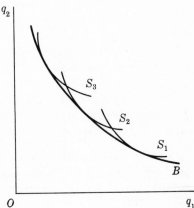

Fig. 7-5

necessary to ensure society the welfare level W^0 and is called a *Bergson contour*.[1]

The problem of finding the point of maximum welfare can thus be solved in two equivalent ways.

1. Each point on the aggregate transformation function defines a commodity combination that can be attained with the available resources. Even if only Pareto-optimal distributions of commodities are considered, a contract curve and thus an infinite number of ways in which utility can be distributed among consumers correspond to each point on the aggregate transformation function.[2] Find all possible ways of distributing utility among consumers corresponding to all points satisfying the transformation function. Of all these utility distributions choose the one for which $W(U_1, U_2, \ldots, U_n)$ is a maximum. The solution is obtained by examining points in the utility space.

2. Determine all Bergson contours. Each of these contours corresponds to a different welfare level. Choose that point on the aggregate transformation function which lies on the highest attainable Bergson contour. A solution is thus also obtained by examining points in the commodity space. The equivalence of the two procedures is obvious from the fact that both are equivalent to maximizing $W(U_1, \ldots, U_n)$ subject to the constraint given by the aggregate production function.

THE ARROW POSSIBILITY THEOREM

Arrow has investigated the formulation of social preferences. He describes individual and social preferences in terms of the rankings of alternative states formed by the relation "is at least as well liked as" (see Sec. 2-1). Individual utility and social welfare functions are special cases of this more general relation.

There are many ways in which social preferences may be formed from individual preferences. Social preferences might be determined by a dictator, or they might be determined by a majority vote of the individual members of society. Social preferences could be determined by vote, with the number of votes an individual casts depending upon the letter of the alphabet with which his surname begins. For example, people whose names begin with A cast one vote, those whose names begin with B cast two votes, and so on. It is obvious that not all conceivable

---

[1] See J. de V. Graaff, *Theoretical Welfare Economics* (London: Cambridge, 1957), chap. III. The felicitous terms *Scitovsky contour* and *Bergson contour* are due to Graaff. Bergson contours are nonintersecting in the absence of external effects but do not necessarily possess the "right" convexity.

[2] The geometric representation of the possible ways of distributing utility among two consumers corresponding to a given point on the aggregate transformation curve is called a *utility possibility curve*.

ways of translating individual preferences into social preferences are equally desirable, acceptable, or sensible. Arrow has stated five axioms which he believes that social preference structures must satisfy to be minimally acceptable. The axioms are approximately as follows:

Complete ordering As in the case of the individual, social preferences must be completely ordered by the relation "is at least as well liked socially as" and therefore must satisfy the conditions of completeness, reflexivity, and transitivity (see Sec. 2-1). The Pareto ranking, which states that allocation A is socially preferred to allocation B if at least one person's utility is higher in A and no one's utility is lower, is not complete and therefore does not satisfy this axiom.

Responsiveness to individual preferences Assume that A is socially preferred to B for a given set of individual preferences. If individual rankings change so that one or more individuals raise A to a higher rank and no one lowers A in rank, A must remain socially preferred to B. This axiom would be violated if there were some individuals against whom society discriminates in the sense that, when their desire for some alternative increases relative to other alternatives, the social desirability of that alternative is reduced.

Nonimposition Social preferences must not be imposed independently of individual preferences. If no individual prefers B to A and at least one individual prefers A to B, society must prefer A to B. This axiom ensures that social preferences satisfy the Pareto ranking. Let A be an allocation such that no member of society has a lower utility than at B and one or more members have higher levels. The nonimposition axiom requires that society prefer A to B.

Nondictatorship Social preferences must not totally reflect the preferences of any single individual; i.e., it must not be true that society prefers A to B if and only if the ith individual prefers A to B. If this axiom were violated, the ith individual would be a dictator.

Independence of irrelevant alternatives The most preferred state in a set of alternatives must be independent of the existence of other alternatives. Assume that when alternatives A, B, and C are available, society prefers A to B to C. If C were no longer available, it must not be true that society then prefers B to A.

Arrow's axioms reflect value judgments, but they appear reasonable and intuitively appealing to most economists. Unfortunately, his possibility theorem states that, in general, it is not possible to construct social preferences that satisfy all five axioms.[1]   Some sets of individual preferences will yield social preferences that satisfy the axioms, but there are sets of well-behaved individual preferences that will not.   If one of Arrow's axioms other than the complete-ordering axiom is discarded, social preferences that satisfy the remaining four axioms may be constructed from any well-behaved set of individual preferences.   If the nonimposition axiom is discarded, social preferences that always give the same ranking to each alternative may be imposed.   If the nondictatorship axiom is discarded, social preferences may be equated with the preferences of some individual.   If the independence-of-irrelevant-alternatives axiom is discarded, social preferences may be defined as some weighted average of individual preferences.

Another way around Arrow's dilemma is to limit individual preferences so that social preferences that satisfy all five axioms can always be constructed.   One possibility is to assume that all individuals always assign the same ranking to each alternative.   Other, more complicated, possibilities also exist.

7-6 THE THEORY OF SECOND BEST

A positive social dividend can always be achieved by a move from a Pareto-nonoptimal allocation to a Pareto-optimal allocation.   Therefore, the satisfaction of the Pareto conditions is often considered the welfare target toward which society should move.   It may well occur, however, that one or more of the Pareto conditions cannot be satisfied because of institutional restrictions.   A best welfare position is unattainable in this case, and it is relevant to inquire whether a second-best position can be attained by satisfying the remaining Pareto conditions.   The theory of second best says no: if one or more of the necessary conditions for Pareto optimality cannot be satisfied, in general it is neither necessary nor desirable to satisfy the remaining conditions.

The essential characteristics of the theory of second best can be illustrated for a simplified system with one consumer, one implicit production function, n commodities, and a fixed supply of one primary factor not desired by the consumer.   The results for this system are easily generalized to cover the more complete system presented in Sec. 7-1.   The necessary conditions for Pareto optimality are obtained by maximizing

---

[1] The proof of the possibility theorem is based upon advanced mathematics.   An intuitive proof is given by James Quirk and Rubin Saposnik, *Introduction to General Equilibrium Theory and Welfare Economics* (New York: McGraw-Hill, 1968), pp. 108–116.

the consumer's utility subject to the production function. Form the Lagrange function

$$L = U(q_1, \cdots ,q_n) - \lambda F(q_1, \cdots ,q_n,x^0)$$

and set its partial derivatives equal to zero:

$$\frac{\partial L}{\partial q_i} = U_i - \lambda F_i = 0 \qquad i = 1, \ldots , n \qquad\qquad (7\text{-}44)$$

where $U_i = \partial U/\partial q_i$ and $F_i = \partial F/\partial q_i$. It follows that

$$\frac{U_i}{U_j} = \frac{F_i}{F_j} \qquad i,j = 1, \ldots , n$$

If (7-44) is satisfied, the RCS for every pair of commodities will equal the corresponding RPT.

Assume that institutional conditions prevent the attainment of one of the conditions of (7-44), say the first. The failure to meet this condition can be expressed in various ways. One of the simplest is the assumption that

$$U_1 - kF_1 = 0 \qquad\qquad (7\text{-}45)$$

where k is a positive constant which differs from the optimal value of λ given by a solution of (7-44) and the production function.

The conditions for a second-best welfare optimum are obtained by maximizing utility subject to the aggregate production function *and* (7-45). Form the Lagrange function

$$L = U(q_1, \ldots ,q_n) - \lambda F(q_1, \ldots ,q_n,x^0) - \mu(U_1 - kF_1)$$

where λ and μ are both undetermined multipliers, and set its partial derivatives equal to zero

$$\frac{\partial L}{\partial q_i} = U_i - \lambda F_i - \mu(U_{1i} - kF_{1i}) = 0 \qquad i = 1, \ldots , n$$
$$\frac{\partial L}{\partial \lambda} = -F(q_1, \ldots ,q_n,x^0) = 0 \qquad \frac{\partial L}{\partial \mu} = -(U_1 - kF_1) = 0 \qquad (7\text{-}46)$$

A solution for this system cannot have $\mu = 0$.† Move the last two terms in each equation of (7-46) to the right-hand side and divide the ith equation by the jth:

$$\frac{U_i}{U_j} = \frac{\lambda F_i + \mu(U_{1i} - kF_{1i})}{\lambda F_j + \mu(U_{1j} - kF_{1j})} \qquad i,j = 1, \ldots , n \qquad (7\text{-}47)$$

† If $\mu = 0$, the first equation of (7-46) becomes $U_1 - \lambda F_1 = 0$ which contradicts the assumption contained in (7-45).

In general, nothing is known a priori about the signs of the cross partial derivatives U_{1i}, U_{1j}, F_{1i}, and F_{1j}. Therefore, in general, one may not expect any of the usual Pareto conditions to be required for the attainment of a second-best optimum.

The theory of second best has been used to question the desirability of policies which attempt to attain the Pareto conditions on a piecemeal basis for markets considered in isolation. The counterargument to this is that, though piecemeal policy is not valid in general, it is valid for many specific cases. Most of the Pareto conditions remain intact if utility and production functions are both separable so that $U_{ij} = F_{ij} = 0$ for $i \neq j$.† The parenthesized terms in (7-47) vanish if i or $j \neq 1$, and for the commodities other than Q_1

$$\frac{U_i}{U_j} = \frac{F_i}{F_j} \qquad i, j = 2, \ldots, n$$

Separability preserves the familiar Pareto conditions for all RCSs and RPTs that do not involve Q_1.

Proponents of piecemeal policy argue that the Pareto conditions provide reasonable guidelines for policy for Q_i, $i \neq 1$, unless Q_i is closely related to a good for which the Pareto conditions are violated. Consider the derivative for q_i in (7-46). The parenthesized term reflects the influence of the violated Pareto condition. If this term vanishes or is small relative to the other terms, it is argued that the violated condition may be ignored in the formulation of policy for Q_i. Chewing gum and railway locomotives, for example, are very distantly related in consumption and production. Therefore, policy for the locomotive industry should not be influenced by imperfect competition in the chewing-gum industry.

7-7 SUMMARY

The purpose of welfare economics is to evaluate the social desirability of alternative allocations of resources. In the absence of elaborate value judgments concerning the desirability of alternative income distributions, a simple value judgment is to consider a reallocation to represent an improvement in welfare if it makes at least one person better off without making anybody worse off. If it is not possible to reallocate resources without making at least one person worse off, the existing allocation is Pareto-optimal. The usual first-order conditions for Pareto optimality require that (1) the RCS of each consumer and the RPT of each producer be equal for each pair of commodities, (2) the RCS of each con-

---

† A function $f(x_1, \ldots, x_m)$ is separable if it may be written in the form $g_1(x_1) + \cdots + g_m(x_m)$ where in this notation g_i denotes a function of the single variable x_i.

sumer and the RTS of each producer be equal for each pair of primary factors, and (3) the RCS of each consumer and the MP of each producer be equal for each factor-commodity pair. Second-order conditions must also be fulfilled for Pareto optimality.

Perfect competition normally results in the fulfillment of the first-order conditions for Pareto optimality. It is in this sense that perfect competition represents a welfare optimum. It does not guarantee that the second-order conditions are fulfilled; nor does it ensure that the distribution of income (or of utility) is optimal in any sense. In addition, the definition of optimum welfare in terms of Pareto optimality leaves a certain amount of indeterminacy in the analysis, since every point on a contract curve is Pareto-optimal and one cannot choose between them without additional ethical judgments.

Imperfect competition among consumers or producers will normally lead to violations of the first-order conditions for Pareto optimality. Even if, by accident, consumers' RCSs were equal to producers' RPTs for all commodities, Pareto optimality would still not be attained as a result of divergences between consumers' RCSs for commodities and labor and the producers' corresponding rates of transforming labor into commodities. Perfectly discriminating monopoly and bilateral monopoly are exceptions. These forms of imperfect competition lead to Pareto-optimal allocations.

The first-order conditions for Pareto optimality must be modified in the presence of external effects in consumption or production. In general perfect competition will not lead to Pareto optimality if external effects are present. The equality of RCSs will not lead to Pareto optimality if utility functions are interdependent. Pareto optimality requires that the sum of the consumers' RCSs between a public good and an ordinary good equal the corresponding RPT for each producer. Price must equal social MC rather than private MC if there are external effects in production.

Systems of taxes and subsidies generally can be designed to lead a market economy from a Pareto-nonoptimal allocation to a Pareto-optimal one. Unit taxes and subsidies are used to make market participants observe appropriate marginal conditions, and lump-sum taxes and subsidies are used to secure a desired income distribution. Some economists have attempted to judge the social preferability of alternative allocations in terms of the ability of the gainers from a move to compensate the losers and the inability of the losers to bribe the gainers into not making the move.

The indeterminacy which remains in the analysis of Pareto optimality can be removed by explicitly introducing a social welfare function which states society's (or a dictator's) preferences among alternative distributions of utility among individuals. Rather than a single social welfare function there are many, each expressing the evaluations of different groups of people. A welfare optimum is determined by translating the social welfare function into the commodity space and finding a point on society's transformation function that lies on the highest Bergson contour. Such welfare optima are always Pareto-optimal. The Arrow possibility theorem states that, in general, it is not possible to construct social preferences from individual preferences without violating one or more of five axioms that most economists believe that social preferences should satisfy.

The theory of second best states that if one or more of the first-order conditions for Pareto optimality cannot be satisfied because of institutional constraints, in general it is neither necessary nor desirable to satisfy the remaining Pareto conditions. This theory has been used to question the desirability of policies to attain the Pareto conditions on a piecemeal basis.

EXERCISES

7-1. Consider a two-person, two-commodity, pure-exchange economy with $U_1 = q_{11}^{\alpha} q_{12}$, $U_2 = q_{21}^{\beta} q_{22}$, $q_{11} + q_{21} = q_1^0$, and $q_{12} + q_{22} = q_2^0$. Derive the contract curve as an implicit function of q_{11} and q_{12}. What condition on the coefficients α and β will ensure that the contract curve is a straight line?

7-2. An economy satisfies all the conditions for Pareto optimality except for one producer who is a monopolist in the market for his output and a monopsonist in the market for the single input that he uses to produce his output. His production function is $q = 0.5x$, the demand function for his output is $p = 100 - 4q$, and the supply function for his input is $r = 2 + 2x$. Find the values of q, x, p, and r that maximize the producer's profit. Find the values for these variables that would prevail if he satisfied the appropriate Pareto conditions.

7-3. Consider a two-person, two-commodity, pure-exchange economy with $U_1 = q_{11}^{\alpha} q_{12} q_{21}^{\gamma} q_{22}^{\delta}$, $U_2 = q_{21}^{\beta} q_{22}$, $q_{11} + q_{21} = q_1^0$, and $q_{12} + q_{22} = q_2^0$. Derive the contract curve of Pareto-optimal allocations as an implicit function of q_{11} and q_{12}. How does this differ from the contract curve for Exercise 7-1? Under what conditions will the two curves be identical?

7-4. Assume that the cost functions of two firms producing the same commodity are

$$C_1 = 2q_1^2 + 20q_1 - 2q_1q_2 \qquad C_2 = 3q_2^2 + 60q_2$$

Determine the output levels of the firms on the assumption that each equates its private MC to a fixed market price of 240. Determine their output levels on the assumption that each equates its social MC to the market price.

7-5. Determine taxes and subsidies that will lead the producer described in Exercise 7-2 to a Pareto-optimal allocation and leave his profit unchanged.

7-6. Determine taxes and subsidies that will lead the firms described in Exercise 7-4 to their Pareto-optimal output levels but leave their profits unchanged. What is the size of the social dividend secured by this change in allocation?

7-7. Consider an economy with two commodities and fixed factor supplies. Assume that the social welfare function defined in commodity space is $W = (q_1 + 2)q_2$ and that society's implicit production function is $q_1 + 2q_2 - 1 = 0$. Find values for q_1 and q_2 that maximize social welfare.

7-8. Assume that there are two consumers and two commodities. Let the utility functions be $U_1 = q_{11}q_{12}$ and $U_2 = q_{21}q_{22}$ with $q_{11} + q_{21} = q_1$ and $q_{12} + q_{22} = q_2$. Show that Scitovsky contours are given by $q_1q_2 = (\sqrt{U_1} + \sqrt{U_2})^2$.

7-9. Consider a society with seven individuals and three alternatives, A, B, and C. Society's preferences are determined by a system of voting in which each individual casts one vote for the alternative he favors. The alternative receiving the largest number of votes is declared to be society's choice. Construct an example in which this procedure violates Arrow's independence-of-irrelevant-alternatives axiom.

7-10. Consider a simplified economy with one consumer, one implicit production function, three commodities, and a fixed supply of one primary factor where

$$U = q_1q_2q_3 \qquad \alpha_1q_1 + \alpha_2q_2 + \alpha_3q_3 - x^0 = 0$$

Find values for q_1, q_2, and q_3 that maximize utility subject to the production function. Assume that institutional constraints result in a violation of one of the Pareto conditions so that

$$\frac{\partial U/\partial q_1}{\partial U/\partial q_3} = k\frac{\alpha_1}{\alpha_3}$$

where $k \neq 1$. Find second-best values for q_1, q_2, and q_3 as functions of k.

*7-11. Consider an economy with two consumers, two public goods, one ordinary good, one implicit production function, and a fixed supply of one primary factor that does not enter the consumers' utility functions. Determine the first-order conditions for a Pareto-optimal allocation. In particular, what combination of RCSs must equal the RPT for the two public goods?

SELECTED REFERENCES

Arrow, K. J., *Social Choice and Individual Values* (New York: Wiley, 1951). A treatise on the problems of constructing a social welfare function. Difficult for those unfamiliar with the mathematics of sets.

Bator, F. M., "The Simple Analytics of Welfare Maximization," *American Economic Review*, vol. 47 (March, 1957), pp. 22–59. A geometric exposition of some fundamental results of welfare economics.

Baumol, W. J., *Welfare Economics and the Theory of the State* (2d ed.; London: G. Bell, 1965). Contains a discussion of the welfare implications of perfect competition and monopoly and an analysis of some of the nineteenth-century literature on welfare. Mathematics is in appendixes.

Bergson, A., "A Reformulation of Certain Aspects of Welfare Economics," *Quarterly Journal of Economics*, vol. 52 (February, 1938), pp. 310–334. Also reprinted in R. V. Clemence (ed.), *Readings in Economic Analysis* (Cambridge, Mass.: Addison-Wesley, 1950), vol. 1, pp. 61–85. The first modern mathematical treatment of welfare economics.

Davis, Otto A., and Andrew B. Whinston, "Welfare Economics and the Theory of Second Best," *Review of Economic Studies*, vol. 32 (1965), pp. 1–14. Discusses situations in which the Pareto conditions are valid for second-best optima. Calculus is used.

Graaff, J. de V., *Theoretical Welfare Economics* (London: Cambridge, 1957). A treatise on welfare incorporating some modern theories. The mathematics is in appendixes.

Lipsey, R. G., and Kelvin Lancaster, "The General Theory of Second Best," *Review of Economic Studies*, vol. 24 (1956–1957), pp. 11–32. The first formal statement of the theory of second best. Calculus is used.

Quirk, James, and Rubin Saposnik, *Introduction to General Equilibrium Theory and Welfare Economics* (New York: McGraw-Hill, 1968). A modern treatment of welfare economics is presented in chap. 4. Advanced mathematical concepts are simplified and developed in the text.

Rothenberg, Jerome, *The Measurement of Social Welfare* (Englewood Cliffs, N.J.: Prentice-Hall, 1961). A detailed consideration of concepts of social welfare. Mathematics is mainly limited to calculus.

Samuelson, Paul A., *Foundations of Economic Analysis* (Cambridge, Mass.: Harvard, 1948). Chapter VIII contains a discussion of the social welfare function and the conditions for maximum welfare. The mathematics is mostly incidental.

———, *Collected Scientific Papers*, ed. by J. E. Stiglitz (Cambridge, Mass.: M.I.T., 1966), 2 vols. The utility feasibility function is developed in chap. 77, and public goods are covered in chaps. 92–94. Geometry and calculus are used.

Scitovsky, T., "A Reconsideration of the Theory of Tariffs," *Review of Economic Studies*, vol. 9 (1941–1942), pp. 89–110. Also reprinted in American Economic Association, *Readings in the Theory of International Trade* (New York: McGraw-Hill, 1949), pp. 358–389. The concept of Scitovsky contours was introduced and applied to international trade theory in this article.

8
Optimization over Time

The theories of consumption and production as presented in Chaps. 2 and 3 cover optimization for a single time period. In a short-run analysis entrepreneurs are assumed to possess plants of fixed size, but beyond this, the decisions of optimizing units for successive time periods are assumed to be independent. The consumer spends his entire income during the current period and maximizes the level of a utility index defined only for goods consumed during the current period. Similarly, the entrepreneur's production function relates inputs and outputs during the current period, and he maximizes his profit for the current period.

Time is introduced in both discrete and continuous terms in the present chapter. Multiperiod utility and production functions are defined, and the single-period theories of consumption and production are extended to cover optimization for T-period horizons. This introduction of time is accompanied by a number of simplifying assumptions. Time is divided into periods of equal length, and market transactions are assumed to be limited to the first day of each period. During the remaining days of each period the consumers supply the factors they have sold and consume the commodities they have purchased; entrepreneurs apply the inputs they have purchased and produce commodities for sale on the next marketing date.   The consumer's current expenditure is no longer bounded by a single-period budget constraint.   He may spend more or less than his current income and borrow or lend the difference.   Entrepreneurs also have the option of borrowing and lending.

The introduction of continuous time allows analysis of problems in which time itself is a relevant variable, such as the determination of an optimal life for a piece of durable equipment.   It is assumed that market transactions may take place at any point in time in the continuous analysis.

Multiperiod optimization is treated in the first six sections of this chapter.   The bond market and the concepts of compounding and discounting are described in Sec. 8-1.   Section 8-2 contains an extension of the theory of the consumer to the multiperiod, multicommodity case. Time preference and the effects of interest rates upon consumption expenditures over time are considered in Sec. 8-3.   Section 8-4 contains a brief discussion of how production theory can be extended to the multiperiod case, and an investment theory for the firm is developed in Sec. 8-5.   Bond-market equilibrium and interest-rate determination are covered in Sec. 8-6.   Time is treated as a continuous variable in the last two sections.   Continuous discounting is introduced and optimization criteria developed in Sec. 8-7.   The retirement and replacement of durable equipment is the subject of Sec. 8-8.

8-1 BASIC CONCEPTS

Multiperiod analysis requires the introduction of several new concepts to describe the methods and costs of borrowing and lending.

THE BOND MARKET

Borrowing and lending are introduced with the following simplifying assumptions: (1) consumers and entrepreneurs are free to enter into borrowing and lending contracts only on the first day of each period; (2) there is only one type of credit instrument: bonds with a one-period duration; (3) the bond market is perfectly competitive; (4) borrowers sell bonds to lenders in exchange for specified amounts of current purchasing power, expressed in terms of money of account; and (5) loans plus borrowing fees are repaid without default on the following marketing date.

These assumptions represent a considerable simplification of actual credit markets, but they allow the easy derivation of many basic results which can be extended to more complicated markets.   Each of the above assumptions can be modified to broaden the coverage of the analysis.

Assumption (1) follows from the discrete definition of time utilized in multiperiod analyses. This assumption is modified in Sec. 8-7. Assumption (2) could be altered by assuming the existence of different types of credit instruments, e.g., promissory notes and mortgages, with different maturities. Assumption (3) can be relaxed by drawing on the analysis of imperfect competition given in Chap. 6. Assumptions (4) and (5) can also be altered in a number of ways.

Let b_t be the bond position of some individual at the end of trading on the tth marketing date. The sign of b_t signifies whether he is a borrower or lender. If $b_t < 0$, he is a borrower with bonds outstanding and must repay b_t dollars plus the appropriate borrowing fee on the $(t + 1)$st marketing date. If $b_t > 0$, he is a lender who holds the bonds of others and will receive b_t dollars plus the appropriate borrowing fee on the $(t + 1)$st marketing date.

Since borrowing fees are also expressed in terms of money of account, they may be quoted as proportions of the amounts borrowed. On the $(t + 1)$st marketing date a borrower must repay $(1 + i_t)$ times the amount he borrowed on the tth. The proportion i_t is the market rate of interest connecting the tth and $(t + 1)$st marketing dates. Since the bond market is assumed to be perfectly competitive, the market rate of interest is not affected by the borrowing or lending of any single individual and is the same for all individuals. Interest rates are frequently expressed as percentages. If the interest rate is i_t, the borrowing fee is $100i_t$ percent of the amount borrowed. For example, the borrowing fee is 5 percent if $i_t = 0.05$.

MARKET RATES OF RETURN

Individuals desiring to borrow for a duration of more than one period can sell new bonds on successive marketing dates to pay off the principal and interest on their maturing issues. Similarly, lenders may reinvest their principal and interest income. Consider the case of an individual who invests b_t dollars on the tth marketing date and continues to reinvest both principal and interest until the τth marketing date. The value of his investment at the beginning of the $(t + 1)$st marketing date is $b_t(1 + i_t)$. If he invests the entire amount, the value of his investment at the beginning of the $(t + 2)$nd marketing date is $b_t(1 + i_t)(1 + i_{t+1})$. The value of his investment at the beginning of the τth marketing date is

$$b_t(1 + i_t)(1 + i_{t+1}) \cdots (1 + i_{\tau-1})$$

The total return on this investment is

$$J = b_t(1 + i_t)(1 + i_{t+1}) \cdots (1 + i_{\tau-1}) - b_t$$

Since the bond market is perfectly competitive, the average and marginal rates of return $(\xi_{t\tau})$ for this investment are equal and constant:

$$\xi_{t\tau} = \frac{J}{b_t} = \frac{dJ}{db_t} = (1 + i_t)(1 + i_{t+1}) \cdots (1 + i_{\tau-1}) - 1 \qquad (8\text{-}1a)$$

For example, if $\tau = t + 2$, $i_t = 0.10$, and $i_{t+1} = 0.06$,

$$\xi_{t,t+2} = (1.10)(1.06) - 1 = 0.166$$

Since the investor is earning interest on his previous interest income, the compound market rate of return exceeds the sum of the individual interest rates. It is interesting to note that only the levels of the interest rates, and not the order of their sequence, affect the market rate of return. The market rate of return remains 0.166 for $i_t = 0.06$ and $i_{t+1} = 0.10$.

It is convenient to define

$$\xi_{tt} = 0 \qquad (8\text{-}1b)$$

which states that an investor will earn a zero rate of return if he buys and sells bonds on the same marketing date. A positive return is earned only if bonds are held until the following marketing date. The market rates of return defined by (8-1) are applicable for borrowing as well as lending.

If the investor expects a constant rate of interest,

$$i_t = \cdots = i_{\tau-1} = i$$

Eqs. (8-1a) and (8-1b) become

$$\xi_{t\tau} = (1 + i)^{\tau-t} - 1$$

which can be evaluated from a compound-interest table for specific values of $(\tau - t)$ and i.

DISCOUNT RATES AND PRESENT VALUES

The existence of a bond market implies that a rational individual will not consider 1 dollar payable on the current $(t = 1)$ marketing date equivalent to 1 dollar payable on some future marketing date. If he invests 1 dollar in bonds on the current marketing date, he will receive $(1 + i_1)$ dollars on the second marketing date. One dollar payable on the second marketing date is the market equivalent of $(1 + i_1)^{-1} = 1/(1 + i_1)$ dollars payable on the first. It is possible to lend $(1 + i_1)^{-1}$ dollars on the first marketing date and receive 1 dollar on the second, or borrow $(1 + i_1)^{-1}$ dollars on the first and repay 1 dollar on the second. The ratio $(1 + i_1)^{-1}$ is the *discount rate* for amounts payable on the second marketing date. The *present value*, sometimes called the discounted value, of y_2 dollars payable on the second marketing date is $y_2(1 + i_1)^{-1}$ dollars.

Discount rates can be defined for amounts payable on any marketing date. In general, the discount rate for amounts payable on the tth marketing date is

$$[(1 + i_1)(1 + i_2) \cdots (1 + i_{t-1})]^{-1} = (1 + \xi_{1t})^{-1}$$

It follows from (8-1) that an investment of $(1 + \xi_{1t})^{-1}$ dollars on the first marketing date will have a value of 1 dollar on the tth.

An entire income or outlay stream can be expressed in terms of its present value, a single number. Consider the income stream y_1, y_2, . . . , y_τ where y_t is the income payable on the tth marketing date. The present value (y) of this stream is

$$y = y_1 + \frac{y_2}{(1 + \xi_{12})} + \cdots + \frac{y_\tau}{(1 + \xi_{1\tau})}$$

If all interest rates are positive, $(1 + \xi_{1t})$ increases and the present value of any fixed amount decreases as t increases. If all interest rates are 0.10, the present value of a dollar payable on the second marketing date is approximately 0.91 dollars, a dollar payable on the fifth is approximately 0.68, and a dollar payable on the tenth approximately 0.42.

The computation of present values allows an economically meaningful comparison of alternative income and outlay streams. Assume that the interest rate is 0.10 and consider two alternative two-period income streams: $y_1 = 100$, $y_2 = 330$, and $y_1 = 300$, $y_2 = 121$. The first income stream contains 9 dollars more than the second, but the second will be preferred at an interest rate of 0.10, since its present value (410 dollars) exceeds the present value of the first (400 dollars). The preferability of the second stream can be demonstrated by transforming it into a stream directly comparable to the first. The second income stream gives its holder 200 dollars more on the first marketing date than the first income stream. Let him invest these 200 dollars in bonds on the first marketing date. This leaves a spendable income of 100 dollars on the first marketing date and adds 220 dollars to his spendable income on the second. The transformed income stream is $y_1 = 100$, $y_2 = 341$, which is clearly preferable to the first income stream. This result can be generalized: regardless of how an income stream is transformed through borrowing and lending, an income stream with a greater present value can be transformed into a preferred stream.

8-2 MULTIPERIOD CONSUMPTION

A consumer generally receives income and purchases commodities on each marketing date. His present purchases are influenced by his expectations regarding future price and income levels, and he must tentatively plan purchases for future marketing dates. If his expectations prove correct and his tastes do not differ from the expected pattern, his tentative plans will be carried out on future marketing dates. If his expectations are not realized, he will revise his tentative plans. The present discussion is restricted to a consumer who formulates an integrated plan on the current marketing date for his consumption expenditures on n goods over a horizon containing T periods. His horizon is simply the period of time for which he plans on the current marketing date. It may be of any length, but for simplicity assume that it corresponds to the remainder of his expected lifetime. It is not essential that he actually know how long he will live; it is only necessary that he presently plan as if he did. If his life expectancy should change in the future, he would alter his horizon accordingly and revise his plans.

THE MULTIPERIOD UTILITY FUNCTION

In the most general case the consumer's ordinal utility index depends upon his planned consumption of each of the n goods in each of the T time periods:

$$U = U(q_{11}, \ldots , q_{n1}, q_{12}, \ldots , q_{n2}, \ldots , q_{1T}, \ldots , q_{nT}) \qquad (8\text{-}2)$$

where q_{jt} is the quantity of Q_j that he purchases on the tth marketing date and consumes during the tth period.

The construction of a single utility index does not imply that the consumer expects his tastes to remain unchanged over time. It only implies that he plans as if he knew the manner in which they will change. For example, he may know that a baby carriage will yield a great deal of satisfaction during the years in which he is raising his family and no satisfaction at all during the years of his retirement. The utility index (8-2) is not necessarily valid for the consumer's entire planning horizon. It merely expresses his present expectations. A change in his objective circumstances or subjective desires may cause him to revise his utility index on some future marketing date. A consumer who formulates his utility index on the expectation that he will become the father of a bouncing baby girl and in fact becomes the father of triplet boys will surely revise his utility index after the event. A consumer who discovers a desirable new commodity will revise his utility index to include this commodity.

THE BUDGET CONSTRAINT

The consumer expects to receive the earned-income stream $(y_1, y_2, \ldots , y_T)$ on the marketing dates within his planning horizon. Generally, his expected-income stream is not even over time. One possibility is a relatively low earned income during the early years of the consumer's working life, which increases as he gains training and seniority and reaches a peak during the middle years of his working life. His earned income may then begin to fall and become zero after retirement. Whatever his earned-income stream may be, it will seldom coincide with his desired consumption stream. Through borrowing and lending he is able to reconcile the two streams.

The consumer's total income receipts on the tth marketing date are the sum of his earned income and his interest income from bonds held during the preceding period: $y_t + i_{t-1}b_{t-1}$. His interest income will be positive if his bond holdings are positive and negative if his bond holdings are negative, i.e., if he is in debt. His expected savings on the tth marketing date, denoted by s_t, are defined as the difference between his expected total income and total consumption expenditures on that date:

$$s_t = y_t + i_{t-1}b_{t-1} - \sum_{j=1}^{n} p_{jt}q_{jt} \qquad t = 1, \ldots, T \qquad (8\text{-}3)$$

where p_{j1} is the price of Q_j on the initial marketing date and p_{jt} ($t = 2, \ldots, T$) is the price that he expects to prevail for Q_j on the tth marketing date. Similarly, i_1 is the rate of interest determined on the initial marketing date and i_t ($t = 2, \ldots, T - 1$) is the rate of interest that the consumer expects to prevail on the tth marketing date. The consumer's savings will be negative if his expenditures exceed his total income.

If the consumer is at the beginning of his earning life, his initial bond holdings (b_0) represent his inherited wealth. If he is revising his plans at a date subsequent to the beginning of his earning life, his bond holdings also reflect the results of his past savings decisions. To simplify the present analysis assume that he is at the beginning of his earning life and that $b_0 = 0$. On each marketing date the consumer will increase or decrease the value of his bond holdings by the amount of his savings on that date:

$$b_t = b_{t-1} + s_t \qquad t = 1, \ldots, T \qquad (8\text{-}4)$$

A "typical" consumer might dissave and go into debt during the early years of his earning life while he is earning a comparatively low income, buying a home, and raising a family; then save to retire his debts and establish a positive bond position during the remainder of his working life; and finally dissave and liquidate his bonds during retirement.

Taking (8-3) and (8-4) together, the consumer's planned bond holdings after trading on the τth marketing date can be expressed as a functions of his earned incomes, his consumption levels, prices, and interest rates:

$$b_1 = \left(y_1 - \sum_{j=1}^{n} p_{j1}q_{j1}\right)$$

$$b_2 = \left(y_1 - \sum_{j=1}^{n} p_{j1}q_{j1}\right)(1 + i_1) + \left(y_2 - \sum_{j=1}^{n} p_{j2}q_{j2}\right)$$

$$b_3 = \left(y_1 - \sum_{j=1}^{n} p_{j1}q_{j1}\right)(1 + i_1)(1 + i_2)$$

$$+ \left(y_2 - \sum_{j=1}^{n} p_{j2}q_{j2}\right)(1 + i_2) + \left(y_3 - \sum_{j=1}^{n} p_{j3}q_{j3}\right)$$

and in general, utilizing (8-1a),

$$b_\tau = \sum_{t=1}^{\tau} \left(y_t - \sum_{j=1}^{n} p_{jt}q_{jt}\right)(1 + \xi_{t\tau}) \qquad \tau = 1, \ldots, T \qquad (8\text{-}5)$$

The consumer's bond holdings after trade on the τth marketing date equal the algebraic sum of all his savings, net of interest expense or income, through that date with interest compounded on each.

In the single-period case the optimizing consumer would buy a sufficiently large quantity of each commodity to reach complete satiation if he did not possess a budget constraint. A similar situation would arise in the multiperiod case if there were no limitation upon the amount of debt that he could amass over his lifetime. The budget constraint for a multiperiod analysis can be expressed as a restriction upon the amount of the consumer's terminal bond holdings (b_T). He may plan to leave an estate (or debts) for his heirs, but for simplicity assume that he plans to leave his heirs neither assets nor debts. Evaluating b_T from (8-5), his budget constraint is:

$$b_T = \sum_{t=1}^{T} \left(y_t - \sum_{j=1}^{n} p_{jt}q_{jt}\right)(1 + \xi_{tT}) = 0$$

Dividing through by the constant $(1 + \xi_{1T})$ and moving the consumption-expenditure terms to the right, the consumer's budget constraint can also be written as

$$\sum_{t=1}^{T} y_t(1 + \xi_{1t})^{-1} = \sum_{t=1}^{T} \sum_{j=1}^{n} p_{jt}q_{jt}(1 + \xi_{1t})^{-1} \qquad (8\text{-}6)$$

since

$$\frac{1 + \xi_{tT}}{1 + \xi_{1T}} = \frac{(1 + i_t) \cdots (1 + i_{T-1})}{(1 + i_1) \cdots (1 + i_{T-1})}$$

$$= \frac{1}{(1 + i_1) \ldots (1 + i_{t-1})} = (1 + \xi_{1t})^{-1}$$

In the form (8-6) the budget constraint states that the consumer equates the present values of his earned-income and consumption streams.

UTILITY MAXIMIZATION

The consumer desires to maximize the level of his lifetime utility index (8-2) subject to his budget constraint (8-6).   Form the function

$$U^* = U(q_{11}, \ . \ . \ . \ ,q_{nT}) + \lambda \sum_{t=1}^{T} \left(y_t - \sum_{j=1}^{n} p_{jt}q_{jt}\right)(1 + \xi_{1t})^{-1}$$

and set its partial derivatives equal to zero:

$$\frac{\partial U^*}{\partial q_{jt}} = \frac{\partial U}{\partial q_{jt}} - \lambda(1 + \xi_{1t})^{-1}p_{jt} = 0 \qquad \begin{array}{l} j = 1, \ . \ . \ . \ , n \\ t = 1, \ . \ . \ . \ , T \end{array}$$

$$\frac{\partial U^*}{\partial \lambda} = \sum_{t=1}^{T} \left(y_t - \sum_{j=1}^{n} p_{jt}q_{jt}\right)(1 + \xi_{1t})^{-1} = 0$$

It follows that

$$-\frac{\partial q_{jt}}{\partial q_{k\tau}} = \frac{\partial U/\partial q_{k\tau}}{\partial U/\partial q_{jt}} = \frac{p_{k\tau}(1 + \xi_{1\tau})^{-1}}{p_{jt}(1 + \xi_{1t})^{-1}} \qquad \begin{array}{l} j, k = 1, \ . \ . \ . \ , n \\ t, \tau = 1, \ . \ . \ . \ , T \end{array} \qquad (8\text{-}7)$$

The consumer must equate the rates of substitution between each pair of commodities in every pair of periods to the ratio of their discounted prices.

The first-order conditions are similar to those for the single-period analysis.   Commodities are now distinguished by time period as well as kind, and discounted prices have replaced simple prices.   Once these modifications have been made, the second-order conditions are the same as those given in Sec. 2-7 for the general one-period analysis.   Income and substitution effects can be defined with respect to changes in the discounted prices of the various commodities on the various marketing dates if the interest rates remain unchanged.[1]

DEMAND FUNCTIONS

Solving the nT independent equations given by (8-7) and the budget constraint for the consumer's commodity demands,

$$q_{jt} = D_{jt}(p_{11}, \ . \ . \ . \ ,p_{nT}, i_1, \ . \ . \ . \ ,i_{T-1}) \qquad \begin{array}{l} j = 1, \ . \ . \ . \ , n \\ t = 1, \ . \ . \ . \ , T \end{array}$$

The consumer's demand for the jth commodity on the tth marketing date depends upon the price of each commodity on each marketing date and the interest rates connecting each pair of successive periods.   The

---

[1] More than one discounted price would change if one of the interest rates changed, since each interest rate enters the discount factors applicable for all prices on all the marketing dates following the date on which it is determined.

consumer's demand functions for bonds are obtained by substituting his commodity demand functions for the q_{jt}s in (8-5):

$$b_\tau = \sum_{t=1}^{\tau} \left\{ \left[y_t - \sum_{j=1}^{n} p_{jt} D_{jt}(p_{11}, \ldots ,i_{T-1}) \right] (1 + \xi_{tr}) \right\}$$
$$= b_\tau(p_{11}, \ldots ,i_{T-1}) \qquad \tau = 1, \ldots , T$$

If earned-income levels are treated as parameters, bond purchases are also functions of all prices and all interest rates.

The demand functions for commodities are again homogeneous of degree zero in prices and earned-income levels: if all actual and expected prices and earned-income levels change by the factor $k > 0$ *with all interest rates remaining unchanged*, the consumer's demand for each commodity on each marketing date will remain unchanged.[1]   The demand functions for bonds are homogeneous of degree one with respect to prices and earned-income levels.   From the zero-degree homogeneity of the commodity demand functions it follows that

$$b_\tau(kp_{11}, \ldots ,kp_{nT}, i_1, \ldots ,i_{T-1}) = \sum_{t=1}^{\tau} \left\{ \left[ky_t \right. \right.$$
$$- \sum_{j=1}^{n} kp_{jt} D_{jt}(kp_{11}, \ldots ,kp_{nT}, i_1, \ldots ,i_{T-1}) \right] (1 + \xi_{tr}) \right\} = kb_\tau$$

If every element in the consumer's earned-income stream and all prices should double, his planned commodity purchases would remain unchanged, and he would double his planned bond purchases.   However, since his bond holdings are measured in terms of the monetary unit of account, they will exchange for exactly the same physical quantities of commodities as before the doubling of the values of bond holdings and commodity prices.   The interest rates are independent of the monetary unit and must remain unchanged if commodity demands are to remain unchanged.

8-3 TIME PREFERENCE

Though much of the analysis of multiperiod consumption is formally identical with the analysis for a single period, the explicit introduction of time and interest rates presents a number of new problems.   Attention is centered upon the unique problems of multiperiod consumption by assuming that actual and expected commodity prices are fixed in value and remain unchanged.   The consumer's problem can then be stated as that of selecting an optimal time pattern for his consumption expenditures.

[1] The method of proof for this statement is the same as that utilized to prove the similar statement in Sec. 2-4.

THE CONSUMPTION–UTILITY FUNCTION

For pairs of commodities purchased on a particular marketing date, the first-order conditions given by (8-7) become

$$-\frac{\partial q_{jt}}{\partial q_{kt}} = \frac{p_{kt}}{p_{jt}} \qquad \begin{matrix} j, k = 1, \ldots, n \\ t = 1, \ldots, T \end{matrix} \qquad (8\text{-}8)$$

The consumer equates the rate of commodity substitution (RCS) between every pair of commodities purchased on a single marketing date to their simple price ratio. Thus, with regard to purchases on each marketing date, the consumer satisfies the first-order conditions for single-period utility maximization, with the exception of the single-period budget constraint. The consumer's optimization problem can be separated into two parts: (1) the selection of optimal values for his total consumption expenditures on the various marketing dates, and (2) the selection of optimal commodity combinations corresponding to the planned expenditures on each marketing date. Once the first problem has been solved, the consumer can solve the second by formulating T independent single-period problems with the optimal total consumption expenditures serving as single-period budget constraints.

Define c_t as the consumer's total expenditure for commodities on the tth marketing date:

$$c_t = \sum_{j=1}^{n} p_{jt} q_{jt} \qquad t = 1, \ldots, T \qquad (8\text{-}9)$$

The utility function (8-2), together with (8-9) and the $(n-1)T$ independent equations of (8-8), forms a system of $(nT + 1)$ equations in $(nT + T + 1)$ variables: U, q_{jt} $(j = 1, \ldots, n; t = 1, \ldots, T)$, and c_t $(t = 1, \ldots, T)$. Generally, nT of these equations can be utilized to eliminate the q_{jt}s, and the consumer's utility index can be expressed as a function of his consumption expenditures:

$$U = V(c_1, \ldots, c_T) \qquad (8\text{-}10)$$

Since (8-10) is constructed on the assumption that (8-8) is satisfied, it gives the maximum value of the utility index corresponding to each consumption-expenditure pattern.

The consumer's time-substitution rate:

$$-\frac{\partial c_\tau}{\partial c_t} = \frac{V_t}{V_\tau} \qquad t, \tau = 1, \ldots, T$$

is the rate at which consumption expenditure on the τth marketing date must be increased to compensate for a reduction of consumption expenditure on the tth in order to leave the consumer's satisfaction level unchanged. No generality is lost by limiting attention to the cases for which $\tau > t$. If the consumer's time-substitution rate is 1.06, his consumption expenditure on the τth marketing date must be increased at the rate of 1.06 dollars for each dollar of consumption expenditure sacrificed on the tth. In other words he must receive a premium of at least 0.06 dollars before he will postpone a dollars' worth of consumption expenditure from period t to period τ. This minimum premium is defined as the consumer's *rate of time preference* for consumption in period t rather than period τ and is denoted by $\eta_{t\tau}$:

$$\eta_{t\tau} = -\frac{\partial c_\tau}{\partial c_t} - 1 \qquad t, \tau = 1, \ldots, T \qquad \tau > t \tag{8-11}$$

The consumer's rates of time preference may be negative for some consumption time patterns; i.e., he may be willing to sacrifice a dollar's worth of consumption in period t in order to secure less than a dollar's worth in a later period. If expected consumption expenditures are 10,000 dollars on the tth marketing date and only 1 dollar on the τth, $\eta_{t\tau}$ would most likely be negative. The consumer's subjective rates of time preference are derived from his consumption-utility function and depend upon the levels of his consumption expenditures. They are independent of the market rates of interest and his borrowing and lending opportunities.

THE CONSUMPTION PLAN

The consumer's utility-maximization problem of Sec. 8-2 can now be reformulated using his consumption expenditures as variables. He wants to maximize the level of his consumption-utility index (8-10) subject to his lifetime budget constraint. Form the function

$$V^* = V(c_1, \ldots, c_T) + \mu \sum_{t=1}^{T} (y_t - c_t)(1 + \xi_{1t})^{-1}$$

and set its partial derivatives equal to zero:

$$\frac{\partial V^*}{\partial c_t} = V_t - \mu(1 + \xi_{1t})^{-1} = 0 \qquad t = 1, \ldots, T$$

$$\frac{\partial V^*}{\partial \mu} = \sum_{t=1}^{T} (y_t - c_t)(1 + \xi_{1t})^{-1} = 0 \tag{8-12}$$

Then

$$-\frac{\partial c_\tau}{\partial c_t} = \frac{(1 + \xi_{1t})^{-1}}{(1 + \xi_{1\tau})^{-1}} = 1 + \xi_{t\tau} \qquad t, \tau = 1, \ldots, T \qquad \tau > t \tag{8-13}$$

and substituting from (8-11),

$$\eta_{tr} = \xi_{tr} \qquad t, \tau = 1, \ldots, T \qquad \tau > t \tag{8-14}$$

The consumer in this case adjusts his subjective preferences to his market opportunities by equating his rate of time preference between every pair of periods to the corresponding market rate of return. If η_{tr} were less than ξ_{tr}, the consumer could buy bonds and receive a premium greater than necessary to maintain indifference. If η_{tr} were greater than ξ_{tr}, he could increase his satisfaction by selling bonds and increasing his consumption in period t at the expense of consumption in period τ. Though η_{tr} may be negative for some consumption-expenditure patterns, the observed (optimum) values of η_{tr} will always be positive if the interest rates are positive.

Second-order conditions require that the principal minors of the relevant bordered Hessian determinant alternate in sign:

$$\begin{vmatrix} V_{11} & V_{12} & -1 \\ V_{21} & V_{22} & -(1 + \xi_{12})^{-1} \\ -1 & -(1 + \xi_{12})^{-1} & 0 \end{vmatrix} > 0,$$

$$\begin{vmatrix} V_{11} & V_{12} & V_{13} & -1 \\ V_{21} & V_{22} & V_{23} & -(1 + \xi_{12})^{-1} \\ V_{31} & V_{32} & V_{33} & -(1 + \xi_{13})^{-1} \\ -1 & -(1 + \xi_{12})^{-1} & -(1 + \xi_{13})^{-1} & 0 \end{vmatrix} < 0, \cdots$$

$$\tag{8-15}$$

The reader may verify that the second-order conditions imply that the rates of time preference be decreasing.

For a numerical example consider a hypothetical consumer with a two-period horizon. Assume that his utility function is $U = c_1 c_2$ and that his actual and expected incomes are $y_1 = 10,000$, $y_2 = 5,250$. Form the function

$$V^* = c_1 c_2 + \mu[(10,000 - c_1) + (5,250 - c_2)(1 + i_1)^{-1}]$$

and set its partial derivatives equal to zero:

$$\frac{\partial V^*}{\partial c_1} = c_2 - \mu = 0$$

$$\frac{\partial V^*}{\partial c_2} = c_1 - \mu(1 + i_1)^{-1} = 0$$

$$\frac{\partial V^*}{\partial \mu} = (10,000 - c_1) + (5,250 - c_2)(1 + i_1)^{-1} = 0$$

If the interest rate is 0.05 (5 percent), the optimum consumption expenditures are $c_1 = 7,500$ and $c_2 = 7,875$. The consumer's rate of time preference for these expenditures equals the interest rate (market rate of return):

$$\eta_{12} = -\frac{dc_2}{dc_1} - 1 = \frac{c_2}{c_1} - 1 = \frac{7,875}{7,500} - 1 = 0.05$$

The second-order condition requires that

$$\begin{vmatrix} 0 & 1 & -1 \\ 1 & 0 & -(1 + i_1)^{-1} \\ -1 & -(1 + i_1)^{-1} & 0 \end{vmatrix} = 2(1 + i_1)^{-1} > 0$$

and is satisfied for $i_1 > -1$.

The two-period horizon case can be described graphically by giving a new interpretation to the conventional indifference-curve diagram. The consumer's earned-income stream is given by the coordinates of point A in Fig. 8-1. Let y^0 be the present value of this income stream. The consumer's budget constraint is

$$y^0 - c_1 - c_2(1 + i_1)^{-1} = 0$$

The locus of all consumption points with a present value of y^0 forms a straight line with negative slope equal to the market exchange rate, $(1 + i_1)$, between consumption expenditures on the first and second marketing dates. One dollar of income on the first marketing date can be transformed into $(1 + i_1)$ dollars of consumption expenditure on the second if the consumer lends at the market rate of interest. Likewise, $(1 + i_1)$ dollars of income on the second marketing date can be transformed into 1 dollar of consumption expenditure on the first if the consumer borrows at the market rate of interest. Assume that the consumer's budget constraint is given by the line labeled y^0 in Fig. 8-1. If he borrows on the first marketing date, he will move along his budget line going to the right of point A. If he lends, he will move along his budget line going to the left of point A.

The curves labeled $U^{(1)}$ and $U^{(2)}$ are members of the family of time indifference curves. Each is the locus of consumption expenditures yielding a given level of satisfaction. The slope of a time indifference curve is $-(1 + \eta_{12})$. These curves reflect the assumption that the rate of time preference is decreasing; i.e., the curves are convex as required by the second-order condition (8-15). The coordinates of the tangency point B give the optimal consumption expenditures. The consumer will buy AC

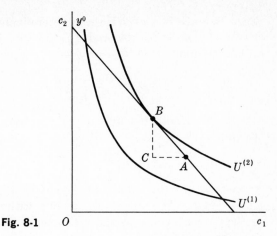

Fig. 8-1

dollars worth of bonds on the first marketing date and will spend the principal and interest, CB, for consumption goods on the second.

SUBSTITUTION AND INCOME EFFECTS

The effects of a change in the rate of interest upon the consumer's optimal consumption levels can be separated into income and substitution effects by methods similar to those employed in Sec. 2-6.

Assume that the consumer's horizon encompasses two marketing dates. In order to determine the effects of changes in the interest rate and earned-income levels, differentiate the first-order conditions (8-12) totally for $T = 2$:

$$
\begin{aligned}
V_{11}\, dc_1 + \quad & V_{12}\, dc_2 - \quad & d\mu = 0 \\
V_{21}\, dc_1 + \quad & V_{22}\, dc_2 - (1 + i_1)^{-1}\, d\mu &= -\mu(1 + i_1)^{-2}\, di_1 \\
-dc_1 - (1 + i_1)^{-1}\ & dc_2 \quad &= -dy_1 - (1 + i_1)^{-1}\, dy_2 \\
& & + (y_2 - c_2)(1 + i_1)^{-2}\, di_1
\end{aligned} \tag{8-16}
$$

The array of coefficients on the left-hand side of (8-16) is the same as the array for the last (and for $T = 2$, the only) bordered Hessian determinant of (8-15).

Using Cramer's rule to solve (8-16) for dc_1,

$$
dc_1 = -\mu(1 + i_1)^{-2} \frac{\mathbf{D}_{21}}{\mathbf{D}}\, di_1 + [-dy_1 - (1 + i_1)^{-1}\, dy_2
$$

$$
+ (y_2 - c_2)(1 + i_1)^{-2}\, di_1] \frac{\mathbf{D}_{31}}{\mathbf{D}} \tag{8-17}
$$

where $\mathbf{D}$ is the bordered Hessian determinant and $\mathbf{D}_{tr}$ is the cofactor of the element in its tth row and rth column. Dividing (8-17) through by di_1 and assuming that $dy_1 = dy_2 = 0$,

$$\frac{\partial c_1}{\partial i_1} = -\mu(1 + i_1)^{-2}\frac{\mathbf{D}_{21}}{\mathbf{D}} + (y_2 - c_2)(1 + i_1)^{-2}\frac{\mathbf{D}_{31}}{\mathbf{D}} \qquad (8\text{-}18)$$

Let y denote the present value of the consumer's earned-income stream:

$$y = y_1 + y_2(1 + i_1)^{-1}$$

An increase of y_1 by 1 dollar or of y_2 by $(1 + i_1)$ dollars will each increase y by 1 dollar. The rate of increase of c_1 with respect to a dollar's increase in the present value of the consumer's earned-income stream can be derived from (8-17):

$$\frac{\partial c_1}{\partial y} = \frac{\partial c_1}{\partial y_1} = (1 - i_1)\frac{\partial c_1}{\partial y_2} = -\frac{\mathbf{D}_{31}}{\mathbf{D}} \qquad (8\text{-}19)$$

A change of i_1 will alter the present values of the consumer's earned-income and consumption streams. Consider those changes of i_1 which are accompanied by changes in c_1 and c_2 such that the level of the consumer's utility index remains unchanged: $dU = V_1\,dc_1 + V_2\,dc_2 = 0$. Since (8-13) requires that $V_2/V_1 = (1 + i_1)^{-1}$, it follows that

$$-dc_1 - (1 + i_1)^{-1}\,dc_2 = 0$$

and from (8-16) it follows that

$$-dy_1 - (1 + i_1)^{-1}\,dy_2 + (y_2 - c_2)(1 + i_1)^{-2}\,di_1 = 0$$

Substituting into (8-17)

$$\left(\frac{\partial c_1}{\partial i_1}\right)_{U=\text{const}} = -\mu(1 + i_1)^{-2}\frac{\mathbf{D}_{21}}{\mathbf{D}} \qquad (8\text{-}20)$$

Substituting $-(y_1 - c_1)(1 + i_1)^{-1} = (y_2 - c_2)(1 + i_1)^{-2}$, which follows from the budget constraint, and utilizing (8-18) and (8-19), (8-17) may be written as

$$\frac{\partial c_1}{\partial i_1} = \left(\frac{\partial c_1}{\partial i_1}\right)_{U=\text{const}} + (y_1 - c_1)(1 + i_1)^{-1}\left(\frac{\partial c_1}{\partial y}\right)_{i_1=\text{const}} \qquad (8\text{-}21)$$

The total effect of a change in the rate of interest is the sum of a substitution and an income effect. The income effect equals the rate of change of consumption expenditure with respect to an increase in the present value of the consumer's earned-income stream weighted by his bond holdings multiplied by a discount factor.

The sign of the substitution effect is easily determined. From the first-order conditions $\mu > 0$, and from the second-order condition $\mathbf{D} > 0$. Evaluating $\mathbf{D}_{21}$,

$$\mathbf{D}_{21} = - \begin{vmatrix} V_{12} & -1 \\ -(1+i_1)^{-1} & 0 \end{vmatrix} = (1+i_1)^{-1} > 0$$

Therefore, the substitution effect with respect to c_1 in (8-18) is negative. The substitution effect with respect to c_2 is

$$\left(\frac{\partial c_2}{\partial i_1}\right)_{U=\text{const}} = -\mu(1+i_1)^{-2}\frac{\mathbf{D}_{22}}{\mathbf{D}}$$

Since $\mathbf{D}_{22} = -1 < 0$, the substitution effect with respect to c_2 is positive. An increase of the interest rate will induce the consumer to substitute consumption in period 2 for consumption in period 1 as he moves along a given time indifference curve. This follows from the fact that an increase of the interest rate is equivalent to an increase in the prices of commodities on the first marketing date relative to those on the second. If the consumer reduces consumption in period 1 and purchases bonds, his interest earnings will be greater, and he will be able to purchase a larger quantity of commodities on the second marketing date for each dollar's worth of purchases sacrificed on the first.

Although an increase of income may cause a reduction in the purchases of a particular commodity, it is difficult to imagine a situation in which an increase of income will cause a reduction in the aggregate consumption expenditure on any of the marketing dates. One can assume that $(\partial c_1/\partial y)_{i_1=\text{const}}$ is positive for all except the most extraordinary cases. If this is true, the direction of the income effect is determined by the sign of the consumer's bond position $(y_1 - c_1)$ at the end of trading on the first marketing date since the second term of (8-21) is of the same sign as $y_1 - c_1$. If the consumer's bond holdings are positive, an increase of the interest rate will increase his interest income and is equivalent to an increase of his earned income. If he is in debt, an increase of the interest rate will increase his interest expense and is equivalent to a reduction of his earned income. In this case both effects are negative, and the total effect, $\partial c_1/\partial i_1$, will therefore be negative. If his bond position is positive, the total effect will be positive or negative depending upon whether the value of the income effect is larger or smaller than the absolute value of the substitution effect.

8-4 MULTIPERIOD PRODUCTION

The theory of the firm can also be extended to the multiperiod case. The analysis of the entrepreneur is similar to that of the consumer, as in the single-period case.

THE MULTIPERIOD PRODUCTION FUNCTION

Production is seldom instantaneous. Generally, time must elapse between the application of inputs and the securing of outputs. Assume that (1) the entrepreneur buys inputs and sells outputs only on the marketing dates within his horizon, (2) he performs the technical operations of his production process in the time between marketing dates, (3) during the tth period he applies the inputs he purchased on the tth marketing date, and (4) on the $(t + 1)$st marketing date he sells the outputs secured during the tth period. These assumptions serve to define the time sequence of production. The following analysis could be based on many alternative sets of time-sequence assumptions without any major changes of its results.

Consider an entrepreneur who desires to formulate an optimal production plan for a horizon encompassing L complete periods and $(L + 1)$ marketing dates. Following the notation of Sec. 3-8, the entrepreneur's production function can be written in implicit form as

$$F(q_{12}, \ldots ,q_{s,L+1}, x_{11}, \ldots ,x_{nL}) = 0 \qquad (8\text{-}22)$$

where q_{jt} $(j = 1, \ldots ,s; t = 2, \ldots , L + 1)$ is the quantity of the jth output secured during the $(t - 1)$st period and sold on the tth marketing date and x_{it} $(i = 1, \ldots ,n; t = 1, \ldots ,L)$ is the quantity of the ith input purchased on the tth marketing date and applied to the production process during the tth period. Any outputs which the entrepreneur may sell on the initial marketing date are the result of past production decisions, and their levels enter (8-22) as constants rather than variables. On the $(L + 1)$st marketing date the entrepreneur plans to sell the outputs secured during the Lth period, but does not plan to purchase inputs, since he does not anticipate production in any period beyond the Lth. The multiperiod production function relates the input and output levels for all periods within the entrepreneur's planning horizon. The inputs applied during each period contribute to the production of outputs during all periods, and it is usually impossible to attribute a particular output to inputs applied during a specific period. However, it is possible to ascertain the effects of marginal variations and compute the marginal productivities of each input applied during each period with respect to each output secured during each period.

PROFIT MAXIMIZATION

The entrepreneur also faces a perfectly competitive bond market and is free to borrow and lend on the same terms as consumers. Given these opportunities, he will generally desire to maximize the present value of his profit from production subject to the technical constraints imposed by his production function. Form the function

$$\pi^* = \sum_{t=2}^{L+1} \sum_{j=1}^{s} p_{jt}q_{jt}(1 + \xi_{1t})^{-1} - \sum_{t=1}^{L} \sum_{i=1}^{n} r_{it}x_{it}(1 + \xi_{1t})^{-1}$$
$$+ \lambda F(q_{12}, \ldots ,x_{nL})$$

and set its partial derivatives equal to zero:

$$\frac{\partial \pi^*}{\partial q_{jt}} = p_{jt}(1 + \xi_{1t})^{-1} + \lambda \frac{\partial F}{\partial q_{jt}} = 0$$

for $t = 2, \ldots , L + 1; j = 1, \ldots , s;$

$$\frac{\partial \pi^*}{\partial x_{it}} = -r_{it}(1 + \xi_{1t})^{-1} + \lambda \frac{\partial F}{\partial x_{it}} = 0$$

for $t = 1, \ldots , L; i = 1, \ldots , n;$ and

$$\frac{\partial \pi^*}{\partial \lambda} = F(q_{12}, \ldots ,x_{nL}) = 0$$

It follows that

$$-\frac{\partial q_{jt}}{\partial q_{k\tau}} = \frac{\partial F/\partial q_{k\tau}}{\partial F/\partial q_{jt}} = \frac{p_{k\tau}(1 + \xi_{1\tau})^{-1}}{p_{jt}(1 + \xi_{1t})^{-1}} \qquad (8\text{-}23a)$$

for $t, \tau = 2, \ldots , L + 1; j, k = 1, \ldots , n;$

$$p_{jt}(1 + \xi_{1t})^{-1}\frac{\partial q_{jt}}{\partial x_{i\tau}} = -p_{jt}(1 + \xi_{1t})^{-1}\frac{\partial F/\partial x_{i\tau}}{\partial F/\partial q_{jt}} = r_{i\tau}(1 + \xi_{1\tau})^{-1}$$
$$(8\text{-}23b)$$

for $t = 2, \ldots , L + 1; j = 1, \ldots , s; \tau = 1, \ldots , L; i = 1, \ldots , n;$ and

$$-\frac{\partial x_{it}}{\partial x_{h\tau}} = \frac{\partial F/\partial x_{h\tau}}{\partial F/\partial x_{it}} = \frac{r_{h\tau}(1 + \xi_{1\tau})^{-1}}{r_{it}(1 + \xi_{1t})^{-1}} \qquad (8\text{-}23c)$$

for $t, \tau = 1, \ldots , L; h, i = 1, \ldots , n.$ Conditions (8-23a) require that the rates of product transformation (RPTs) equal the corresponding ratios of discounted output prices. By (8-23b) the discounted value of the marginal product of X_i applied during the τth period with respect to each output in each time period must be equated to the discounted price of X_i on the τth marketing date. Finally, (8-23c) requires that the rates of technical substitution (RTSs) equal the corresponding ratios of discounted input prices.

The second-order conditions are the same as those presented in Sec. 3-8 if each output and each input on each marketing date is defined as a distinct variable and simple prices are replaced by discounted prices.

Substitution effects may be derived for changes in each of the discounted prices, assuming that the interest rates remain unchanged.

An entrepreneur would not undertake single-period production if all inputs were variable and his maximum profit were negative. A similar limitation applies in the multiperiod case. If all inputs are variable, the entrepreneur will not undertake production at all if the discounted value of his profit from operations is negative. However, this restriction encompasses options not available in the one-period case. He may find it most profitable to undertake production, but to cease operations before the end of his planning horizon. The entrepreneur will not operate after the τth marketing date unless the present value of the added profit is nonnegative:

$$\sum_{t=\tau+1}^{L+1} \sum_{j=1}^{s} p_{jt}q_{jt}(1 + \xi_{1t})^{-1} - \sum_{t=\tau}^{L} \sum_{i=1}^{n} r_{it}x_{it}(1 + \xi_{1t})^{-1} \geqq 0$$

$$\tau = 1, \ldots, L \quad (8\text{-}24)$$

If (8-24) does not hold for some value of τ, the entrepreneur can earn more by investing all his funds in bonds on the τth marketing date than by continuing production. If (8-24) does not hold for $\tau = 1$, he will not undertake production at all.

Demand and supply functions can be derived in a manner similar to that used in Sec. 8-1 to derive consumer demand functions. The entrepreneur's demands for inputs, supplies of outputs, and demands for bonds on each marketing date can be expressed as functions of all prices and interest rates. The demand functions for inputs and supply functions for outputs are homogeneous of degree zero, and the demand functions for bonds are homogeneous of degree one with respect to all input and output prices.

8-5 INVESTMENT THEORY OF THE FIRM

The multiperiod production decisions of the firm are presented in a very general form in Sec. 8-4. The advantages and disadvantages of this formulation are similar to the advantages and disadvantages of the multiperiod consumption analysis contained in Sec. 8-2. The formal relationships between single-period and multiperiod production decisions are obvious, but many of the new problems arising from the introduction of time and interest rates are obscured by this formulation. Simplifying assumptions similar to those employed in Sec. 8-3 are utilized in the present section in order to bring the new problem to the forefront and derive some of the concepts and results of microeconomic investment theory. Specifically, it is assumed that entrepreneurs consider all current and expected input and output prices as known and constant and perform certain preliminary optimizations. It is then possible to treat the investment expenditures and revenues from sales on each of the marketing dates within the entrepreneur's horizon as the only variables and confine the analysis to an investigation of their interrelationships and the effects of the interest rates.

Special cases have played an important role in the development of microeconomic investment theory. Cases are frequently distinguished on the basis of input and output time structures. The simplest case is *point-input–point-output*, which covers investment in working capital: all inputs are purchased on one marketing date, and all outputs are sold on a subsequent marketing date. Tree growing and wine aging often serve as examples. The *multipoint-input–point-output* case covers the production of an output which requires the application of inputs during a number of successive periods.[1] Shipbuilding might fall into this category. The *point-input–multipoint-output* case covers an investment in a durable good which is purchased on one marketing date and is used for the production of outputs during a number of successive periods. Finally, there is the general *multipoint-input–multipoint-output* case. The first three cases are, of course, embraced by the fourth. In the present section attention is limited to the general and *point-input–point-output* cases.

THE INVESTMENT–OPPORTUNITIES FUNCTION

The entrepreneur's investment expenditure on the tth marketing date, denoted by I_t, equals the value of his input purchases on that date:

$$I_t = \sum_{i=1}^{n} r_{it} x_{it} \qquad t = 1, \ldots, L \tag{8-25}$$

His total revenue from sales on the tth marketing date, denoted by R_t, is

$$R_t = \sum_{j=1}^{s} p_{jt} q_{jt} \qquad t = 2, \ldots, L+1 \tag{8-26}$$

The definitions (8-25) and (8-26) require $2L$ equations.

Assume that an entrepreneur is given the levels for all his inputs and outputs except the inputs he purchases on the tth marketing date, and desires to minimize the present value of his investment expenditure on that date. To solve his constrained-minimization problem form the function

$$I_t^* = \sum_{i=1}^{n} r_{it} x_{it} (1 + \xi_{1t})^{-1}$$
$$+ \lambda^* F(q_{12}^0, \ldots, q_{s,L+1}^0, x_{11}^0, \ldots, x_{1t}^0, \ldots, x_{nt}^0, \ldots, x_{nL}^0)$$

[1] If time is treated as a continuous variable, the word *continuous* replaces *multipoint* in the titles of the special cases.

and set its partial derivatives equal to zero:

$$\frac{\partial I_t^*}{\partial x_{it}} = r_{it}(1 + \xi_{1t})^{-1} + \lambda^* \frac{\partial F}{\partial x_{it}} = 0 \qquad i = 1, \ldots, n$$

$$\frac{\partial I_t^*}{\partial \lambda^*} = F(q_{12}^0, \ldots, q_{s,L+1}^0, x_{11}^0, \ldots, x_{1t}, \ldots, x_{nt}, \ldots, x_{nL}^0) = 0$$

and

$$-\frac{\partial x_{it}}{\partial x_{ht}} = \frac{r_{ht}}{r_{it}} \qquad h, i = 1, \ldots, n \tag{8-27}$$

The first-order conditions are the familiar ones for single-period constrained cost minimization (see Sec. 3-2): RTSs are equated to fixed price ratios. The optimum intraperiod RTSs are independent of the interest rates. It is assumed that the entrepreneur always allocates his investment expenditure on the tth marketing date so that (8-27) is satisfied. Conditions (8-27) contain $(n - 1)$ independent equations for each marketing date, or a total of $L(n - 1)$ independent equations.

Now assume that the entrepreneur is given the levels for all his inputs and outputs except the outputs he sells on the tth marketing date, and desires to maximize the present value of his revenue from sales on this date. The first-order conditions for this constrained-maximization problem require that

$$-\frac{\partial q_{jt}}{\partial q_{kt}} = \frac{p_{kt}}{p_{jt}} \qquad j, k = 1, \ldots, s \tag{8-28}$$

The optimum RPTs for outputs sold on a given marketing date are also constants which are independent of the interest rates. It is assumed that the entrepreneur always adjusts his production so that (8-28) is satisfied. Conditions (8-28) contain a total of $L(s - 1)$ independent equations.

The entrepreneur's investment-opportunities function is constructed with the assumptions that (1) he satisfies his multiperiod production function, (2) he always equates his intraperiod RTSs to the fixed-input-price ratios, and (3) he always equates his intraperiod RPTs to the fixed-output-price ratios. His investment opportunities therefore are described by his production function (8-22) and Eqs. (8-25) to (8-28). The system as a whole contains $(Ls + Ln + 1)$ independent equations and $(Ls + Ln + 2L)$ variables. Assume that $L(s + n)$ of the equations can be used to eliminate the Ls q_{jt}s and the Ln x_{it}s. The revenues and investment expenditures are then related by a single implicit function:

$$H(I_1, \ldots, I_L, R_2, \ldots, R_{L+1}) = 0 \tag{8-29}$$

Given all the revenues and all but one of the investment expenditures, (8-29) gives the minimum value for the remaining investment expenditure. Similarly, given all but one of the revenues and all the investment expenditures, (8-29) gives the maximum value for the remaining revenue.

The entrepreneur possesses both external and internal investment opportunities: he can purchase bonds and he can invest in his own firm. His external rates of return are the same as those for consumers, as given by (8-1). In the general case, average internal rates of return cannot be defined in a manner parallel to average market rates of return, since it is not possible to attribute the entire revenue on the τth marketing date to the investment on any particular marketing date. Each revenue depends upon all the investment expenditures. However, marginal internal rates of return can be defined for any investment-revenue pair, assuming that all other investments and revenues remain unchanged. The *marginal internal rate of return*[1] from investment on the tth marketing date with respect to revenue on the τth, denoted by $\rho_{t\tau}$, is

$$\rho_{t\tau} = \frac{\partial R_\tau}{\partial I_t} - 1 = - \frac{\partial H/\partial I_t}{\partial H/\partial R_\tau} - 1 \qquad \begin{matrix} t = 1, \ldots, L \\ \tau = 2, \ldots, L+1 \end{matrix} \qquad (8\text{-}30)$$

Each of the marginal internal rates of return depends upon the levels of all the planned revenues and investment expenditures.

The marginal internal rate of return functions given above by (8-30) are independent of the market rates of interest and the entrepreneur's borrowing and lending opportunities. For given input and output price expectations, (8-30) provides a description in marginal terms of the objective technical framework within which the entrepreneur operates. For some investment and revenue combinations $\rho_{t\tau}$ may be negative.

THE INVESTMENT PLAN

The entrepreneur's maximization problem of Sec. 8-4 can now be expressed in terms of investment expenditures and revenues. From the set of investment and revenue streams that satisfy (8-29) he desires to select one that maximizes the present value of his profit stream. Form the function

$$\pi^* = \sum_{t=2}^{L+1} R_t (1 + \xi_{1t})^{-1} - \sum_{t=1}^{L} I_t (1 + \xi_{1t})^{-1} + \mu H(I_1, \ldots, R_{L+1})$$

---

[1] There is no generally accepted name for this concept. Friedrich Lutz and Vera Lutz, *The Theory of Investment of the Firm* (Princeton, N.J.: Princeton, 1951), use "marginal internal rate of return." Irving Fisher, *The Theory of Interest* (New York: Kelley and Millman, 1954), uses "marginal rate of return over cost." Other names for this or closely allied concepts include "marginal productivity of investment," "marginal efficiency of investment," and "marginal efficiency of capital."

and set its partial derivatives equal to zero:

$$\frac{\partial \pi^*}{\partial R_t} = (1 + \xi_{1t})^{-1} + \mu \frac{\partial H}{\partial R_t} = 0 \qquad t = 2, \ldots, L+1$$

$$\frac{\partial \pi^*}{\partial I_t} = -(1 + \xi_{1t})^{-1} + \mu \frac{\partial H}{\partial I_t} = 0 \qquad t = 1, \ldots, L$$

$$\frac{\partial \pi^*}{\partial \mu} = H(I_1, \ldots, R_{L+1}) = 0$$

where $\mu < 0$.† Substituting from (8-30), the first-order conditions require that

$$\rho_{tr} = \xi_{tr} \qquad \begin{matrix} t = 1, \ldots, L \\ \tau = 2, \ldots, L+1 \end{matrix} \qquad (8\text{-}31)$$

The entrepreneur must equate each of his marginal internal rates of return to the corresponding market rate of return.

The second-order conditions require that

$$\begin{vmatrix} H_{11} & H_{12} & H_1 \\ H_{21} & H_{22} & H_2 \\ H_1 & H_2 & 0 \end{vmatrix} < 0, \qquad \begin{vmatrix} H_{11} & H_{12} & H_{13} & H_1 \\ H_{21} & H_{22} & H_{23} & H_2 \\ H_{31} & H_{32} & H_{33} & H_3 \\ H_1 & H_2 & H_3 & 0 \end{vmatrix} < 0, \ldots \qquad (8\text{-}32)$$

where H_j is the first-order partial derivative of the implicit function (8-29) with respect to the jth variable and H_{jk} is the second-order partial derivative with respect to the jth and kth variables. All the above determinants must be negative.[1] These conditions must hold regardless of the order in which the $2L$ investments and revenues are listed.

Expanding the first determinant of (8-32),

$$2H_1 H_2 H_{12} - H_{22} H_1^2 - H_{11} H_2^2 < 0 \qquad (8\text{-}33)$$

The rate of change of the marginal internal rate of return for investment on the tth marketing date with respect to revenue on the τth is

$$\frac{\partial \rho_{tr}}{\partial I_t} = \frac{\partial^2 R_\tau}{\partial I_t^2} = -\frac{1}{H_2^3}(H_{11} H_2^2 - 2H_{12} H_1 H_2 + H_{22} H_1^2)$$

† The first-order conditions require that $\partial H/\partial R_t$ and $\partial H/\partial I_t$ be of opposite sign. The investment-opportunities function is assumed to be constructed so that $\partial H/\partial R_t > 0$ and $\partial H/\partial I_t < 0$ for the optimum production plan. If a solution were obtained with the signs reversed, it would only be necessary to redefine (8-29) as $-H$ to obtain the desired form.

[1] Second-order conditions require that the principal minors of the Hessian determinant of the second-order derivatives of π^* bordered by the first-order derivatives of $H(I_1, \ldots, R_{L+1})$ be alternately positive and negative. Conditions (8-32) are obtained by factoring out $\mu < 0$.

where $H_1 = \partial H/\partial I_t$ and $H_2 = \partial H/\partial R_\tau$. Since (8-33) must hold for the variables listed in this order and since $H_2 > 0$, (8-33) implies that

$$\frac{\partial \rho_{t\tau}}{\partial I_t} < 0 \qquad \begin{array}{l} t = 1, \ldots, L \\ \tau = 2, \ldots, L+1 \end{array} \tag{8-34}$$

Thus, the second-order conditions imply that all the marginal internal rates of return be decreasing.

If conditions (8-31) and (8-34) were not satisfied, the entrepreneur could increase the present value of his profit by either selling bonds and expanding internal investment or buying bonds and contracting internal investment.

POINT-INPUT–POINT-OUTPUT

In the simplest case the entrepreneur invests on one marketing date and receives the resultant revenue on the next.   He may repeat the production process over time, but his production on the first marketing date only affects his revenue on the second, and his effective planning horizon includes one full period and two marketing dates.

The entrepreneur's revenue can generally be stated as an explicit function of his investment expenditure:

$$R_2 = h(I_1) \tag{8-35}$$

In this special case all revenues on the second marketing date can be attributed to investment on the first, and it is possible to define an average internal rate of return:

$$\frac{R_2 - I_1}{I_1} = \frac{h(I_1)}{I_1} - 1$$

The average internal rate of return can be compared with the corresponding market rate of return i_1.

The entrepreneur desires to maximize the present value of his profit from operation:

$$\pi = R_2(1 + i_1)^{-1} - I_1$$

Substituting from (8-35), π can be stated as a function of I_1 alone:[1]

$$\pi = h(I_1)(1 + i_1)^{-1} - I_1$$

---

[1] Direct substitution and the use of a Lagrange multiplier are equivalent alternatives. The same result is obtained by maximizing

$$\pi^* = R_2(1 + i_1)^{-1} - I_1 + \mu[R_2 - h(I_1)]$$

(see Sec. A-3).

Differentiating,

$$\frac{d\pi}{dI_1} = h'(I_1)(1 + i_1)^{-1} - 1 = 0 \tag{8-36}$$

Rearranging terms and substituting from (8-1) and (8-30), the first-order condition becomes

$$\rho_{12} = i_1 = \xi_{12}$$

The entrepreneur equates his marginal internal rate of return to the corresponding market rate of return—in this case the market rate of interest.
    The second-order condition requires that

$$\frac{d^2\pi}{dI_1^2} = h''(I_1)(1 + i_1)^{-1} < 0$$

and if $i_1 > -1$,

$$h''(I_1) < 0 \tag{8-37}$$

The marginal internal rate of return must be decreasing.
    Imagine that (8-37) is satisfied, but $\rho_{12} > \xi_{12}$. The marginal return from borrowing funds for internal use exceeds their interest cost, and the entrepreneur can increase his profit by expanding investment. Conversely, if $\rho_{12} < \xi_{12}$, he is earning less on the marginal dollar of internal investment than he must pay for it, and he can increase his profit by contracting investment to buy bonds.
    By total differentiation of (8-36),

$$h''(I_1)\, dI_1 = di_1$$

and

$$\frac{dI_1}{di_1} = \frac{1}{h''(I_1)} < 0 \tag{8-38}$$

If the second-order condition is satisfied, (8-38) is negative: an increase in the rate of interest will cause the entrepreneur to reduce his investment expenditure.
    Possible shapes for the average and marginal internal return functions, labeled ARR and MRR respectively, are pictured in Fig. 8-2a. Both the average and marginal rates increase, reach a peak, and then decline as investment is increased. These curves possess the normal properties of average and marginal pairs (see Sec. A-2). If the interest rate is i_1^0, the entrepreneur will invest I_1^0 dollars. For this level of investment the marginal internal and market rates of return are equal (first-order condition), and the marginal internal rate is decreasing (second-order condition). The entrepreneur's total interest cost is given by the area $OI_1^0 A i_1^0$, his total return by $OI_1^0 BC$, and his net return by $i_1^0 ABC$.

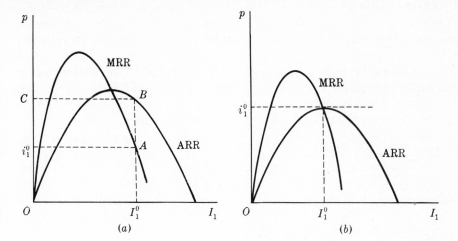

Fig. 8-2

In a perfectly competitive system the net return of the representative firm in each industry will be driven down (or increased) to zero by the entry (or exit) of firms. A long-run competitive equilibrium is pictured in Fig. 8-2b. The optimal investment of the representative firm is I_1^0. The average and marginal internal rates of return are equal, and the average internal rate of return now equals the rate of interest.

8-6 INTEREST-RATE DETERMINATION

The methods of Chaps. 4 and 5 can be utilized for an analysis of bond-market equilibrium, and interest-rate determination can be included within the general pricing process. A closer analogy with the earlier analyses of market equilibrium is obtained if the use of loanable funds rather than bonds is treated as the commodity for sale.[1] A demand for (supply of) bonds is equivalent to a supply of (demand for) loanable funds. An interest rate is the price of using loanable funds for a specified period of time. By convention, interest rates are expressed as proportions of the amounts borrowed, but they can be expressed in terms of money of account, as are all other prices. Let 100 dollars serve as a unit of purchasing power. An interest rate of i_t is then the equivalent of a price of $100i_t$ dollars per unit of purchasing power.

First, consider a partial-equilibrium analysis of the loanable-funds market. From the individual equilibrium conditions derived in Secs. 8-3 and 8-5 the current excess demand for loanable funds by each consumer and entrepreneur can be expressed as a function of the current and

---

[1] In the present analysis there is assumed to be no circulating money. Loanable funds represent general purchasing power expressed in terms of a money of account.

expected interest rates. It is convenient to use excess demand functions rather than demand and supply functions, since individual consumers and entrepreneurs may demand loanable funds at one interest rate and supply them at another.

A theory of interest-rate expectations must be formulated before market equilibrium can be determined. Many different expectation theories might be utilized. One possibility is to assume that individuals expect future interest rates to be at fixed levels regardless of the current interest rate; future interest rates then enter the current excess demand functions as constants rather than variables. Another possibility is the expectation that future interest rates will equal the current interest rate: $i_1 = i_2 = i_3 \cdots$. Still another possibility is the expectation that the current absolute change of the interest rate will be realized in the future: $i_1 - i_0 = i_2 - i_1 = i_3 - i_2 = \cdots$, or in general, $i_t = i_0 + t(i_1 - i_0)$. Each of these expectation assumptions allows the individual excess demands to be stated as functions of the current interest rate alone. An aggregate excess demand function is constructed by summing the individual functions. Since the individual excess demands are transformed into functions of the current interest rate before aggregation, it is not necessary that all individuals plan for horizons of the same length. An equilibrium current interest rate is one for which the excess demand for current loanable funds equals zero. It reflects time preference and the productivity of investment. In equilibrium the rate of time preference for each consumer and the marginal internal rate of return for each producer equal the interest rate.

The multimarket equilibrium theory of Chap. 5 can also be extended to include the interest rate and multiperiod expectations. Theories of price and interest-rate expectations must be introduced to allow the individual excess demands for each commodity and loanable funds to be expressed as functions of only current prices and the current interest rate.[1] Multimarket equilibrium is then determined by the requirement that the excess demand for every commodity and for loanable funds simultaneously equal zero.

The formulation of the mathematical requirements for specific cases of single-market and multimarket equilibrium is left as an exercise for the reader.

8-7 INVESTMENT THEORY AND THE ROLE OF TIME

Investment theory is characterized by the fact that time elapses between the application of inputs and the attainment of the resultant outputs.

[1] See J. R. Hicks, *Value and Capital* (2d ed.; Oxford: Clarendon Press, 1946), chap. XVI, for a specific theory of price expectations.

The multiperiod approach tends to obscure some of the time aspects of production. The variables are dated, but investment and revenue variations are limited to integral units of time. The discrete definition of time makes it difficult to deal with problems in which the elapsed time for which inputs are invested is of importance. The tools necessary for a continuous treatment of time are developed and applied in this section. The applications provide examples for the point-input–point-output, continuous-input–point-output, and point-input–continuous-output cases. The analysis of durable equipment in Sec. 8-8 provides examples for the continuous-input–continuous-output case.

CONTINUOUS COMPOUNDING AND DISCOUNTING

It is assumed that time is continuous and that transactions may take place at any point in time. A time period, such as a year, is necessary to provide a unit with which to measure time, but it has no other significance. Since elapsed time is now a variable, let $t = 0$ represent the present. The value $t = \tau$ now represents a point in time τ periods hence, where τ no longer need be an integer.

The concepts of Sec. 8-1 do not allow the determination of compound and present values for sums due on dates for which t is not an integer. Since time is assumed a continuous variable, interest is assumed to be compounded continuously. If interest were compounded once a year, an initial amount of w would increase to $w(1 + i)^t$ in t years. If interest were compounded twice a year, one-half of the annual interest rate would be applied every six months, and w would increase to $w(1 + i/2)^{2t}$ in t years. In general, if interest were compounded n times per year, w would increase to $w(1 + i/n)^{nt}$ in t years.

The effect of continuous compounding is obtained by letting $n \to \infty$. Let $z = (1 + i/n)^{nt}$. Instead of finding lim (z) as $n \to \infty$, it is convenient to take the natural logarithm and find lim $[\log (z)]$ as $n \to \infty$. The natural logarithm may be written as the quotient of two functions of n:

$$\log (z) = nt \log (1 + i/n) = \frac{\log (1 + i/n)}{1/nt} = \frac{h(n)}{g(n)} \qquad (8\text{-}39)$$

The numerator and denominator of (8-39) both approach zero as $n \to \infty$. L'Hôpital's rule[1] is employed to find the limit:

$$\lim_{n \to \infty} [\log (z)] = \lim_{n \to \infty} \frac{h'(n)}{g'(n)} = \lim_{n \to \infty} \frac{-(i/n^2)/(1 + i/n)}{-(1/n^2 t)}$$
$$= \lim_{n \to \infty} \frac{it}{1 + i/n} = it$$

[1] See the statement and application of L'Hôpital's rule given in Sec. 3-6.

and since the natural logarithm is a continuous function,

$$\lim_{n \to \infty} (1 + i/n)^{nt} = e^{it}$$

where the irrational number $e = 2.71828$ apx is the base of the system of natural logarithms.

If interest is compounded continuously, the value of principal and compound interest after t years of a present investment of w is we^{it} where i is the interest rate per year which is assumed to remain unchanged and where t may take any nonnegative value. The present value of the amount u payable at time t is ue^{-it} since a present investment of ue^{-it} in bonds will have a value of u at time t.

POINT AND FLOW VALUES

Production and consumption are assumed to take place continuously over time in the multiperiod framework. However, inputs are purchased, costs incurred, outputs sold, and revenues realized only on discrete marketing dates. These point values are easily generalized for the continuous framework. Transactions may take place at any point in time, and their values may be functions of the time at which they occur. For illustration, let R_T be a dollar revenue realized at time T, and let $R_T = R(T)$. The present value of the revenue is $R(T)e^{-iT}$ with the time derivative

$$\frac{d[R(T)e^{-iT}]}{dT} = [R'(T) - iR(T)]e^{-iT}$$

which is discounted marginal revenue with respect to time.

Inputs, outputs, costs, and revenues also may be realized as flows over time in a continuous analysis. Flows may occur at constant rates over time, or their rates may be functions of time. Consider a variable continuous revenue flow. Let $R = R(t)$ be the rate of the flow at instant t measured in dollars per year. No revenue is realized in an instant. However, a finite revenue is realized over a finite time interval. The present value of the revenue stream $R(t)$ from $t = 0$ through $t = T$, denoted by R_{0T}, is given by a definite integral:

$$R_{0T} = \int_0^T R(t)e^{-it}\, dt$$

The time derivative of the discounted revenue stream:

$$\frac{dR_{0T}}{dT} = R(T)e^{-iT}$$

is simply the present value of the rate of flow at $t = T$.

The notation used for a point value and the notation used for a rate of flow at a particular point in time are usually quite similar; $R(T)$ is used for both here. Their distinction, however, should be clear from the specific contexts in which they are used.

POINT-INPUT–POINT-OUTPUT

The simplest investment problem in which time is a variable occurs if all inputs are applied at one point in time and all outputs are sold at a later point in time. Imagine an entrepreneur engaged in the process of wine aging. He purchases a cask of grape juice for I_0 dollars and waits while it ferments and ages. Assume that fermentation and aging are costless processes so that his only other cost is foregone interest on his initial investment. Further assume that the sales value of the wine, a point value, is a function of the length of its aging period, $R(T)$.

The entrepreneur's optimization problem is to select an aging period, i.e., a value for T, that maximizes the present value of his profit:

$$\pi = R(T)e^{-iT} - I_0$$

Setting the derivative of π with respect to T equal to zero,

$$\frac{d\pi}{dT} = [R'(T) - iR(T)]e^{-iT} = 0$$

Dividing by $e^{-iT} \neq 0$ and rearranging terms,

$$\frac{R'(T)}{R(T)} = i \tag{8-40}$$

The entrepreneur must equate his proportionate marginal rate of return with respect to time $[R'(T)/R(T)]$ to his proportionate marginal rate of cost with respect to time (i).

The second-order condition requires that

$$\frac{d^2\pi}{dT^2} = [R''(T) - 2iR'(T) + i^2R(T)]e^{-iT} < 0$$

Substituting from (8-40) for i and multiplying through by $e^{iT}/R(T) > 0$,

$$\frac{R''(T)R(T) - [R'(T)]^2}{[R(T)]^2} < 0 \tag{8-41}$$

The proportionate marginal rate of return with respect to time must be decreasing; i.e., its derivative must be negative. If (8-40) and (8-41) are satisfied for $T = T^0$, the entrepreneur's marginal earnings from wine aging would exceed his earnings from investing $R(T)$ in the bond market if his investment period were slightly shorter than T^0, and would be less than bond earnings if it were slightly longer than T^0.

The effect of a change of the rate of interest upon the aging period can be determined by total differentiation of (8-40):

$$R''(T) \, dT - iR'(T) \, dT - R(T) \, di = 0$$

and

$$\frac{dT}{di} = \frac{R(T)}{R''(T) - iR'(T)} < 0 \tag{8-42}$$

The numerator of (8-42) is positive, and (8-41) together with (8-40) requires that its denominator be negative. An increase in the rate of interest will lead the entrepreneur to shorten his aging period, and a decrease will lead him to lengthen it.

CONTINUOUS-INPUT–POINT-OUTPUT

Consider an investment process in which an entrepreneur incurs a cost flow over time, but sells his entire output at a single point in time. An example is provided by an entrepreneur engaged in tree growing. He purchases a seedling for I_0 dollars at $t = 0$, incurs a cultivation cost flow of $G(t)$ dollars per year while the tree is growing, and sells the tree for $R(T)$ dollars at $t = T$. The present value of the entrepreneur's profit is

$$\pi = R(T)e^{-iT} - I_0 - \int_0^T G(t)e^{-it} \, dt$$

Setting the derivative of π with respect to T equal to zero,

$$\frac{d\pi}{dT} = [R'(T) - iR(T) - G(T)]e^{-iT} = 0$$

Multiplying by e^{iT} and rearranging terms,

$$\frac{R'(T) - G(T)}{R(T)} = i \tag{8-43}$$

The entrepreneur sells the tree when his proportionate marginal rate of return with respect to time net of cultivation cost equals the rate of interest.

The second-order condition requires that

$$\frac{d^2\pi}{dT^2} = [R''(T) - 2iR'(T) + i^2R(T) - G'(T) + iG(T)]e^{-iT} < 0$$

Multiplying by e^{iT} and rearranging terms,

$$[R''(T) - iR'(T) - G'(T)] - [iR'(T) - i^2R(T) - iG(T)] < 0$$

Substituting for $iR(T)$ from (8-43) shows that the second bracketed term equals zero, and the second-order condition may be written as

$$R''(T) - iR'(T) - G'(T) < 0 \qquad\qquad (8\text{-}44)$$

Substitute for i from (8-43) into (8-44) and multiply through by $1/R(T) > 0$:

$$\frac{[R''(T) - G'(T)]R(T) - R'(T)[R'(T) - G(T)]}{[R(T)]^2} < 0$$

which is the derivative of (8-43). The proportionate net marginal rate of return must be decreasing over time.

To determine the effect of an interest-rate change on the growing period differentiate (8-43) totally and solve for dT/di:

$$\frac{dT}{di} = \frac{R(T)}{R''(T) - iR'(T) - G'(T)} < 0 \qquad\qquad (8\text{-}45)$$

The numerator of (8-45) is positive, and (8-44) requires that the denominator be negative. As in the point-input–point-output case, an increase in the interest rate will cause the entrepreneur to shorten his growing period.

POINT-INPUT–CONTINUOUS-OUTPUT

Consider now a case in which a single investment, say in durable equipment, yields a revenue stream over time. For simplicity assume that the equipment earns revenue at a constant rate of R dollars per year during its life, and assume that the investment cost of the equipment is a continuous function of its life: $I_0 = I(T)$ where $I'(T) > 0$. The present value of the profit from operating the equipment is

$$\pi = \int_0^T Re^{-it}\, dt - I(T)$$

Setting the derivative of π with respect to T equal to zero,

$$\frac{d\pi}{dT} = Re^{-iT} - I'(T) = 0$$

and

$$Re^{-iT} = I'(T) \qquad\qquad (8\text{-}46)$$

The optimal life for the equipment occurs at a point at which the present value of the additional revenue from increased durability equals the marginal cost of durability.

The second-order condition for a maximum requires that

$$\frac{d^2\pi}{dT^2} = -iRe^{-iT} - I''(T) < 0 \qquad\qquad (8\text{-}47)$$

and is necessarily satisfied if the marginal cost of durability is increasing, i.e., if $I''(T) > 0$. The effect of the interest rate upon durability is obtained by differentiating (8-46) totally and solving for dT/di,

$$\frac{dT}{di} = \frac{TRe^{-iT}}{-iRe^{-iT} - I''(T)} < 0$$

since the denominator is negative by (8-47). Again, an increase in the interest rate will shorten the investment period, and a decrease will lengthen it.

8-8 RETIREMENT AND REPLACEMENT OF DURABLE EQUIPMENT

Further consideration of durable equipment based on another set of assumptions provides examples of continuous-input–continuous-output processes.

ASSUMPTIONS

Consider a machine used for the production of a single output, Q, which is sold for a competitive price, p, that is invariant over time. Let q_t denote the flow of output at instant t. The corresponding revenue flow is pq_t. The machine is purchased at $t = 0$ at the fixed cost I_0. The input cost flow, C_t, is a function of q_t, and the maintenance cost flow for the machine, M_t, is a function of both output flow and machine age:

$$C_t = C(q_t) \qquad M_t = M(q_t, t)$$

The machine can be sold for scrap when the entrepreneur no longer desires to use it for production. The scrap value of the machine at time T, S_T, is a decreasing function of the age of the machine: $S_T = S(T)$ where $S'(T) < 0$. The derivative $S'(T)$ gives the rate of loss of market value from continuing to use the machine, and is called *depreciation*.

The entrepreneur's optimization problem can be separated into two parts: (1) the determination of optimum input and output levels for each point in time while machines are in operation, and (2) the determination of optimal lives for one or more machines. Optimal input and output levels are considered first. Then criteria for an optimal lifetime are determined for a single machine and for an infinite chain of machines.

THE QUASI-RENT FUNCTION

Assume that the entrepreneur has decided to operate a machine from $t = 0$ through $t = T$. Given this decision the initial cost and scrap value of the machine may be ignored. The entrepreneur's problem is to maximize the present value of the *quasi-rent* flow from the operation of the machine, i.e., the difference between the present value of his sales revenue flow and the present value of his variable cost flow.   Since revenues and costs at different points in time are independent in the cases considered here, the entrepreneur can maximize the present value of his quasi-rent flow over the life of the machine by maximizing his rate of discounted quasi-rent flow at each point in time.   Furthermore, since the discount factor, e^{-it}, is a constant for any fixed value of t, the entrepreneur can achieve the desired result by maximizing his rate of quasi-rent flow at each point in time without discounting.

The entrepreneur's rate of quasi-rent flow at instant t, Z_t, is

$$Z_t = pq_t - C(q_t) - M(q_t,t) \qquad (8\text{-}48)$$

Setting the derivative of Z_t with respect to q_t equal to zero,

$$\frac{\partial Z_t}{\partial q_t} = p - \frac{dC_t}{dq_t} - \frac{\partial M_t}{\partial q_t} = 0$$

and

$$p = \frac{dC_t}{dq_t} + \frac{\partial M_t}{\partial q_t} \qquad (8\text{-}49)$$

The entrepreneur equates his rate of marginal cost flow, which in this case is a sum of input and maintenance costs, to his fixed rate of marginal revenue flow, p.   The reader may verify that the second-order condition requires that the sum of the marginal costs increase with output.

Assume that (8-49) may be solved for the optimum value of q_t as a function of t.   Substituting this function into (8-48), an optimal quasi-rent stream may be expressed as a function of t:

$$Z_t = Z(t)$$

The quasi-rent function gives the maximum quasi-rent obtainable at each point in time from the operation of the machine.   It is based upon the underlying optimal combinations of inputs and output.   The quasi-rent function holds for all values of t, and its form is unaffected by the selection of a particular value for machine life.   Thus, the quasi-rent function may be used for analyses of machine life without the explicit introduction of outputs, revenues, and costs.

RETIREMENT OF A SINGLE MACHINE

Consider an entrepreneur who desires to purchase one machine, invest his quasi-rent stream in the bond market at the going rate of interest, invest his scrap value in the bond market at the end of the machine's life, and then retire.   The present value of his profit from the operation of the machine is the present value of his quasi-rent stream, minus the cost of the machine, plus the present value of the scrap receipts:

$$\pi_1 = \int_0^T Z(t)e^{-it}\,dt - I_0 + S(T)e^{-iT} \tag{8-50}$$

Differentiating,

$$\frac{d\pi_1}{dT} = [Z(T) - iS(T) + S'(T)]e^{-iT} = 0$$

and

$$Z(T) + S'(T) = iS(T) \tag{8-51}$$

The entrepreneur will retire the machine when his marginal quasi-rent less depreciation flow equals the interest return from investing the scrap value in the bond market. The reader may verify that the second-order condition requires that the quasi-rent less depreciation flow decrease more rapidly than the alternative bond-market return and that an increase in the interest rate will hasten the machine's retirement.

REPLACEMENT FOR A CHAIN OF MACHINES

Consider an entrepreneur who plans for an infinite horizon and an infinite chain of machines succeeding each other. Assume that his quasi-rent function, initial cost, and scrap value function are the same for each machine except for dates, and assume that the planned lives of the machines are identical. The present value of the profit from the operation of the first machine is given by (8-50). The present values of the profits from the operation of the second and third machines are

$$\pi_2 = \int_T^{2T} Z(t - T)e^{-it}\,dt - I_0 e^{-iT} + S(T)e^{-i2T} = \pi_1 e^{-iT}$$

$$\pi_3 = \int_{2T}^{3T} Z(t - 2T)e^{-it}\,dt - I_0 e^{-i2T} + S(T)e^{-i3T} = \pi_1 e^{-i2T}$$

and in general,

$$\pi_k = \left[\int_0^T Z(t)e^{-it}\,dt - I_0 + S(T)e^{-iT} \right] e^{-i(k-1)T}$$

The present values of the profits from successive machines are identical except for discount factors that reflect the times over which their profits are earned.

The present value of the aggregate profit from an infinite chain of machines is

$$\pi = \sum_{k=1}^\infty \pi_k = \frac{\int_0^T Z(t)e^{-it}\,dt - I_0 + S(T)e^{-iT}}{1 - e^{-iT}}$$

where $1/(1 - e^{-iT})$ is the sum to infinity of the geometric progression $(1 + e^{-iT} + e^{-i2T} + e^{-i3T} + \cdots)$.† Setting the derivative of π with respect to T equal to zero,

$$\frac{d\pi}{dT} = \frac{\begin{gathered}[Z(T) - iS(T) + S'(T)]e^{-iT}(1 - e^{-iT}) \\ - ie^{-iT}\left[\int_0^T Z(t)e^{-it}\,dt - I_0 + S(T)e^{-iT}\right]\end{gathered}}{(1 - e^{-iT})^2} = 0$$

Multiplying by $e^{iT}(1 - e^{-iT})$ and rearranging terms,

$$Z(T) + S'(T) = \frac{1}{\delta}\left[\int_0^T Z(t)e^{-it}\,dt - I_0 + S(T)\right] \qquad (8\text{-}52)$$

where $\delta = (1 - e^{-iT})/i = \int_0^T e^{-it}\,dt$ is the present value of a one dollar income stream for T years. A machine is replaced when its marginal rate of quasi-rent flow per year net of depreciation equals the present value of the average return per year of a new machine net of its investment cost less the scrap value of the old machine. The bracketed term on the right-hand side of (8-52) gives a return for T years. Division by δ converts it to an annual basis. The second-order condition requires that the marginal return on the old machine be decreasing more rapidly than the average return on the new machine.

The first-order condition for the infinite-machine case (8-52) is quite different from the first-order condition for the one-machine case (8-51). Their difference reflects the difference in the options available to the entrepreneur. In the one-machine case he has a choice between continuing to operate the machine and investing its scrap value in the bond market. In the infinite-machine case he has a choice between operating an existing machine and operating a new machine.

8-9 SUMMARY

Consumers and entrepreneurs are assumed to have free access to a perfectly competitive bond market and may adjust their income and outlay streams over time through borrowing (selling bonds) and lending (buying bonds). An interest rate expresses the cost of borrowing, or income from lending, for a duration of one period, as a proportion of the amount borrowed or lent. Market rates of return for durations longer than one period are defined as compounds of the interest rates connecting pairs of successive periods. Discount rates are defined as the reciprocals of the corresponding market rates of return. An entire income or cost stream

† In general, consider the geometric progression a, ar, ar^2, ar^3, . . . in which the nth term is ar^{n-1}. If $r < 1$, the progression is convergent and its sum to infinity is $a/(1 - r)$. In the present case $a = 1$ and $r = e^{-iT} < 1$. See J. Blakey, *Intermediate Pure Mathematics* (London: Cleaver-Hume, 1953), pp. 66–68.

can be reduced to a single number, its present value, by multiplying each of its elements by the appropriate discount rate and summing.

The consumer's utility index is defined as a function of the quantities of n goods that he consumes during each of the T periods within his planning horizon. He desires to maximize the level of this index subject to a lifetime budget constraint, which requires the equality of the present values of his consumption and earned-income streams. First-order conditions require that he equate intraperiod and interperiod RCSs to discounted commodity price ratios. Second-order conditions follow from those for the n-commodity, single-period analysis. The consumer's present and planned commodity demands are functions of all current and expected prices and interest rates and are homogeneous of degree zero with respect to all prices and earned incomes. His demands for bonds are functions of the same variables, but are homogeneous of degree one with respect to all prices and earned incomes.

If prices are assumed to remain unchanged, the consumer's utility index can be expressed as a function of his consumption expenditures. The consumer's rate of time preference for consumption during period t rather than period τ ($>t$) is defined as the smallest premium which he will accept as compensation for postponing a marginal dollar's worth of consumption expenditure. The first-order conditions for constrained utility maximization require that the consumer equate his rates of time preference to the corresponding market rates of return. Substitution and income effects with respect to changes in the rate of interest can be defined analogously to the single-period case.

An entrepreneur is assumed to formulate a production plan for a planning horizon encompassing L periods and $(L + 1)$ marketing dates. On the tth marketing date he sells the outputs produced during the $(t - 1)$st period and purchases inputs for application to the production process during the tth period. He desires to maximize the present value of his net operating revenues subject to the technical rules specified in his multiperiod production function. First-order conditions require that he equate input and output substitution rates to discounted price ratios. Second-order conditions again follow from those for the general one-period analysis.

The analysis of the entrepreneur's investment problems can also be simplified by assuming that actual and expected prices remain unchanged and that he always combines inputs and produces outputs so that intraperiod RTSs and RPTs are equated to the appropriate price ratios. The entrepreneur's investment-opportunities function relates his investment expenditures and revenues on the assumption that he performs this preliminary optimization. Marginal internal rates of return are defined for each of the revenues with respect to each of the investments. First-order conditions require that each marginal internal rate of return be equated with the corresponding market rate of return. Second-order conditions imply that each of the marginal internal rates be decreasing. The general analysis is applied to the special case of point-input–point-output.

Single-market and multimarket equilibrium analyses can be extended to include the current interest rate and multiperiod expectations. In equilibrium the rate of time preference for each consumer and the marginal internal rate of return for each producer equal the interest rate.

A continuous framework is developed in which interest is compounded continuously, transactions may take place at any point in time, and time itself may be treated as a variable. This framework is used for three applications with the following results: (1) Point-input–point-output with input fixed and output variable; the marginal internal rate of return with respect to time equals the interest rate at the end of an optimal investment period. (2) Continuous-input–point-output with both input and output variable; the investment-period criterion is the same as (1) except that the marginal rate of return is calculated net of variable cost. (3) Point-input–continuous-output with input variable and output fixed; at the end of an optimal investment period the present value of the marginal revenue from lengthening the period equals the marginal cost of lengthening it.

The operation of durable equipment provides examples for the continuous-input–continuous-output case. A quasi-rent function gives the difference between revenue and variable cost flows at each instant of time. It is obtained by equating the sum of marginal input and maintenance cost flows to price. An entrepreneur will retire a single machine when his marginal quasi-rent less depreciation return equals the alternative interest return on scrap value. A machine within an infinite chain will be replaced when its marginal quasi-rent less depreciation return equals the average return net of investment cost for a new machine.

EXERCISES

8-1. Consider two alternative income streams: $y_1 = 300$, $y_2 = 321$, and $y_1 = 100$, $y_2 = 535$. For what rate of interest would the consumer be indifferent between the two streams?

8-2. A consumer purchases two goods over a two-period horizon. The consumer's multiperiod utility function is $U = q_{11}q_{21}q_{12}q_{22}$; his income stream is $y_1 = 800$, $y_2 = 220$; the interest rate is 0.10; and the fixed prices of the goods are $p_1 = 5$ and $p_2 = 25$. The consumer desires to leave no estate at the end of his horizon. Determine consumption levels for the two goods in the two periods that will maximize his utility.

8-3. A consumer's consumption-utility function for a two-period horizon is $U = c_1 c_2^{0.6}$; his income stream is $y_1 = 1,000$, $y_2 = 648$; and the market rate of interest is 0.08. Determine values for c_1 and c_2 that maximize his utility. Is he a borrower or lender?

8-4. A profit-maximizing entrepreneur uses one input, X, to produce one output, Q, over a two-period horizon. His multiperiod production function is $q_2 q_3^\gamma x_1^{-\alpha} x_2^{-\beta} - A = 0$ where all parameters are positive and $1 + \gamma > \alpha + \beta$. The subscripts refer to the dates on which inputs are purchased and outputs sold. The input and output have fixed prices of p and r respectively, and the market rate of interest is i. Express the entrepreneur's supply q_2 as a function of p, r, i, and the parameters. Show that $\partial q_2/\partial p > 0$, $\partial q_2/\partial r < 0$, and $\partial q_2/\partial i < 0$.

8-5. An entrepreneur invests on one marketing date and receives the resultant revenue on the next. The explicit form of his investment-opportunities function is $R_2 = 24 \sqrt{I_1}$, and the market rate of interest is 0.20. Find his optimum investment level.

8-6. Consider a bond market in which only consumers borrow and lend. Assume that all 150 consumers have the same two-period consumption-utility function: $U = c_1 c_2$. Let each of 100 consumers have the expected-income stream $y_1 = 10,000$, $y_2 = 8,400$, and let each of the remaining 50 consumers have the expected-income stream $y_1 = 8,000$, $y_2 = 14,000$. At what rate of interest will the bond market be in equilibrium?

8-7. Consider an entrepreneur engaged in a point-input–point-output wine-aging process. His initial cost is 20, the sales value of the wine is $R(T) = 100 \sqrt{T}$, and the rate of interest is 0.05. How long is his optimal investment period?

8-8. An entrepreneur is engaged in tree growing. He purchases a seedling for 4 dollars, incurs a cultivation cost flow at a rate of $G(t) = 0.4t$ dollars per year during the life of the tree, and sells the tree at $t = T$ for $R(T) = 4 + 8T - T^2$ dollars. The market rate of interest is 0.20. Determine an optimal length for his cultivation period, T. Apply the appropriate second-order condition to verify that your solution is a maximum.

8-9. An entrepreneur is considering the variable revenues and costs from the operation of a machine to produce the output Q which sells at the fixed price $p = 52$. His input cost flow would be at the rate $C_t = 5q_t^2$ dollars per year, and his maintenance cost flow would be at the rate $M_t = 2q_t + 3t$ dollars per year. Construct a quasi-rent function for the machine.

8-10. An entrepreneur plans for a one-machine horizon. He purchases the machine for 500 dollars. Its scrap value at time T is $S(T) = 500 - 40T$. The rate of interest is 0.05. The machine yields a quasi-rent flow at the rate $Z_t = 85 - 4t$ dollars per year. When should the entrepreneur retire this machine?

*8-11. An entrepreneur is engaged in a repeated point-input–point-output process. He invests I_0 dollars and receives a revenue of $R(T)$ dollars T years later. At T he will again invest I_0 dollars and receive another revenue of $R(T)$ dollars at $2T$. Assume that he repeats this cycle indefinitely. Interest is compounded continuously at the constant rate i. What is the present value of the entrepreneur's profit from such an infinite chain? Formulate his first-order condition for profit maximization. Compare this result with the first-order condition for the unrepeated case.

SELECTED REFERENCES

Allen, R. G. D., *Macro-economic Theory* (New York: St Martin's, 1967). Chapter 3 contains a discussion of investment theory using differential and integral calculus.

Carlson, Sune, *A Study on the Pure Theory of Production* (New York: Kelley and
    Millman, 1956).   Chapter VI contains a multiperiod production theory devel-
    oped with the aid of elementary calculus.
Fisher, Irving, *The Theory of Interest* (New York: Kelley and Millman, 1954).   A
    classic statement of many of the concepts of this chapter which contains verbal,
    geometric, and mathematical descriptions.
Friedman, Milton, *A Theory of the Consumption Function* (Princeton, N.J.: Princeton,
    1957).   Chapter II contains a theory of multiperiod consumption.   The
    remainder of the volume is devoted to its statistical verification.
Hicks, J. R., *Value and Capital* (2d ed.; Oxford: Clarendon Press, 1946).   Parts III and
    IV and the mathematical appendix contain multiperiod analyses.
Lutz, Friedrich, and Vera Lutz, *The Theory of Investment of the Firm* (Princeton, N.J.:
    Princeton, 1951).   A detailed study of many different investment problems in
    which time is treated as a continuous variable.   A knowledge of differential and
    integral calculus is helpful, but not absolutely necessary.
Modigliani, Franco, and Richard Brumberg, "Utility Analysis and the Consumption
    Function," in Kenneth K. Kurihara (ed.), *Post Keynesian Economics* (New
    Brunswick, N.J.: Rutgers, 1954), pp. 388–436.   A theoretical and empirical
    study of lifetime consumption patterns.   Some knowledge of calculus and
    mathematical statistics is required.
Smith, Vernon L., *Investment and Production* (Cambridge, Mass.: Harvard, 1961).   A
    detailed treatment of investment theory.   Geometry and calculus are used.

9
Linear Models

Chapters 2 through 8 cover a variety of situations in which individuals and economies optimize subject to constraints. The consumer maximizes utility subject to an income constraint. The producer maximizes profit subject to his production function. An economy maximizes social welfare subject to its transformation function. The calculus has been the major tool for the formulation and analysis of these constrained-optimization problems. There are constrained-optimization problems of interest to economists, however, for which the calculus does not provide an adequate tool. This chapter covers a broad class of such problems, namely, those in which the underlying functional relationships are linear.

The first partial derivatives of linear functions are nonzero constants and the second partial derivatives are zero. Thus, in general, neither the first- nor the second-order conditions for optimization within a calculus framework can be satisfied. A number of new tools have been developed within the last two or three decades that allow optimization within a linear framework. Linear programming and input-output analysis are the most important from the viewpoint of microeconomic theory.

Linear production functions are described in Sec. 9-1. The general concepts of linear programming are developed in Sec. 9-2 with examples drawn from linear production theory. A general method for the numerical solution of linear-programming systems is covered in Sec. 9-3. The two-person zero-sum game is described in Sec. 9-4. Applications of linear programming and the theory of games have little overlap. However, the formal structures of the two systems are quite similar. Input-output analysis, which serves as a basis for empirical multimarket systems, is the subject of Sec. 9-5.

9-1 LINEAR PRODUCTION FUNCTIONS

A linear production activity is a process by which one or more outputs are produced in fixed proportions by the application of one or more inputs in fixed proportions. It is homogeneous of degree one and thus yields constant returns to scale. If all inputs are increased (or decreased) proportionately, all outputs will be increased (or decreased) by the same proportion. A linear production function is formed from a collection of linear production activities that may be utilized simultaneously.

THE ONE-OUTPUT CASE

Consider a linear production activity by which a single output is produced from m inputs. The activity is completely described by a set of coefficients a_i $(i = 1, \ldots, m)$ which give the quantities of the inputs necessary to produce one unit of the output. Requisite input levels are uniquely determined for any specified output level:

$$x_i = a_i q \qquad i = 1, \ldots, m \tag{9-1}$$

The maximum output that can be secured from a specified set of input quantities is

$$q = \min_i \left(\frac{x_i}{a_i}\right) \qquad a_i > 0 \tag{9-2}$$

Each input can become the factor that limits output. It follows from (9-1) that the quantity x_i will support an output of x_i/a_i units, but all other inputs must be available in the appropriate amounts to achieve this output level. Therefore, the smallest x_i/a_i determines the maximum producible output level. Portions of the quantities of some inputs may remain unused because of a relative dearth of a limiting input.

Let the coefficients for a two-input activity be $a_1 = 2$ and $a_2 = 5$. An output of 1 unit requires $x_1 = 2$ and $x_2 = 5$, an output of two units requires $x_1 = 4$ and $x_2 = 10$, and so on. If an entrepreneur possessed 4

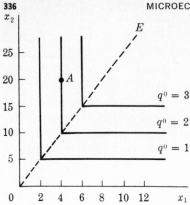

Fig. 9-1

units of the first input and 20 units of the second, he could produce 2 units of output:

$$q = \min (\tfrac{4}{2}, \tfrac{20}{5}) = 2$$

The first input is limiting, and the entrepreneur must leave 10 of his 20 units of the second unused. Figure 9-1 contains an isoquant diagram for this activity. The expansion path OE is the locus of points with x_1 and x_2 in the ratio $2:5$. Each isoquant makes a right angle at the expansion path. Starting from a point on the expansion path, an increment of one input without a proportionate increment of the other will not allow an increase of output. Point A with the coordinates $x_1 = 4$ and $x_2 = 20$ lies on the isoquant $q^0 = 2$.

Now assume that the entrepreneur has n distinct linear production activities that he can utilize individually or jointly for the production of his output. Let a_{ij} $(i = 1, \ldots, m; j = 1, \ldots, n)$ be the quantity of the ith input required to produce one unit of output using the jth activity. The outcomes of the activities are additive. Total output is

$$q = \sum_{j=1}^{n} q_j$$

where q_j is the quantity produced using the jth activity, and total input requirements are

$$x_i = \sum_{j=1}^{n} a_{ij}q_j \qquad i = 1, \ldots, m \qquad (9\text{-}3)$$

Composite input requirements per unit output, α_i $(i = 1, \ldots, m)$, are weighted averages of the coefficients for the individual activities:

$$\alpha_i = \sum_{j=1}^{n} \lambda_j a_{ij} \qquad i = 1, \ldots, m \qquad (9\text{-}4)$$

with $0 \leq \lambda_j \leq 1$ and $\Sigma_{j=1}^n \lambda_j = 1$ where $\lambda_j = q_j/q$ is the proportion of total output produced by the jth activity. Composite activities allow substitution among inputs that substantially changes the form of (9-2). The maximum output that can be secured from a specified set of input quantities is

$$q = \min_i \left(\frac{x_i}{\alpha_i} \right) \qquad \alpha_i > 0 \qquad\qquad (9\text{-}5)$$

The minimum ratio x_i/α_i is limiting, but the λ_j are selected to maximize the minimum ratio.

Assume that an entrepreneur can produce his output using two inputs and three activities with

$$a_{11} = 1 \qquad a_{12} = 2 \qquad a_{13} = 4$$
$$a_{21} = 8 \qquad a_{22} = 5 \qquad a_{23} = 3$$

Figure 9-2 is an isoquant diagram for this linear production function. The expansion paths for activities 1, 2, and 3 are OE_1, OE_2, and OE_3 respectively. Consider the isoquant for $q^0 = 3$. Points A, B, and C give input requirements if only one of the activities is used. The line segment AB gives the input requirements for all composite activities formed from activities 1 and 2 that can be used to produce 3 units. This is a special case of (9-4) with

$$x_1 = 3\alpha_1 = 3[\lambda + 2(1 - \lambda)]$$
$$x_2 = 3\alpha_2 = 3[8\lambda + 5(1 - \lambda)]$$

as λ varies from zero (point B) to one (point A). Similarly, the line segment BC gives input requirements for the composite activities formed from 2 and 3. Input substitution with composite activities is not possible to the left of OE_1, that is, for $x_2/x_1 > 8$. Only activity 1 will be employed, and some of X_2 will remain unused. To the right of OE_3, that is, for $x_2/x_1 < \frac{3}{4}$, only activity 3 will be employed, and some of X_1 will remain unused.

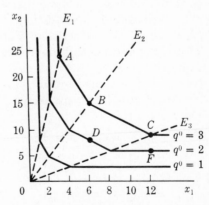

Fig. 9-2

The isoquants derived in Chap. 3 give x_2 as strictly convex functions of x_1, and have RTSs that are continuous and decreasing.   The isoquants in Fig. 9-2 give x_2 as convex (but not strictly convex) functions of x_1, and have RTSs that are discontinuous and nonincreasing.   Linear production functions will always generate isoquants of this general form.   The isoquants provide a graphic solution for (9-5); i.e., they give the maximum output levels that can be secured from each input combination.   Inefficient activities are eliminated.   A simple or composite activity is inefficient if some other simple or composite activity requires no more of any input and less of at least one input.   It is evident from Fig. 9-2 that combinations of activities 1 and 3 are inefficient.   Input requirements for $q^0 = 3$ are given by a line segment connecting A and C which lies above the line segments AB and BC.   Techniques developed in Sec. 9-3 allow the conclusion that combinations of all three activities will never be superior to pairwise combinations in the two-input case.

MULTIPLE-OUTPUT CASES

The concept of a linear production function is easily interpreted to accommodate more than one output.   Assume that each of s outputs is produced by a linear production activity using m inputs.   A particular output still may be produced by more than one activity.   Let a_{ij} be the quantity of the ith input required for the production of one unit of the jth output.   The input requirements for the production of a specified set of output levels is of the same form as (9-3):

$$x_i = \sum_{j=1}^{s} a_{ij}q_j \qquad i = 1, \ldots, m \tag{9-6}$$

where q_j is the specified quantity of the jth output.   Now substitution among outputs as well as inputs is possible.

Linear production activities may yield more than one output in the most general case.   Assume that each of n linear activities yields s outputs and uses m inputs.   Let z_j $(j = 1, \ldots ,n)$ denote the level of the jth activity.   The selection of a unit level for the activity is arbitrary as long as the outputs and inputs are in the appropriate proportions.   Let a_{ij} be the quantity of the ith output produced and b_{ij} be the quantity of the ith input required by one unit of the jth activity.   The outputs and inputs generated by a specified set of activity levels are

$$q_i = \sum_{j=1}^{n} a_{ij}z_j \qquad i = 1, \ldots, s$$
$$x_i = \sum_{j=1}^{n} b_{ij}z_j \qquad i = 1, \ldots, m \tag{9-7}$$

Composite activities again are defined as weighted averages of simple activities.

The tools thus far developed in this volume are of little use for the analysis of optimization with linear production functions. Linear programming, which is developed in the next two sections of this chapter, provides appropriate tools. Two sets of symbols are used in these sections. The symbols z, γ, and w are used in developing the general propositions of linear programming. These are replaced by the familiar symbols q, p, and r when the general propositions are applied to specific economic problems.

9-2 LINEAR PROGRAMMING: CONCEPTS

Linear programming covers problems in which a linear function is maximized or minimized subject to a system of linear inequalities including the requirement that the values of all variables be nonnegative. The general format is to find values for the variables z_j ($j = 1, \ldots, n$) that maximize

$$y = \gamma_1 z_1 + \gamma_2 z_2 + \cdots + \gamma_n z_n \tag{9-8}$$

subject to

$$a_{i1} z_1 + a_{i2} z_2 + \cdots + a_{in} z_n \leq k_i \qquad i = 1, \ldots, m \tag{9-9}$$

and

$$z_j \geq 0 \qquad j = 1, \ldots, n \tag{9-10}$$

where the parameters γ_j, a_{ij}, and k_i may be positive, negative, or zero.

The standard format given by (9-8) to (9-10) is quite general. If a linear function is to be minimized, the problem may be written in the standard format by maximizing its negative. If a constraint is of the form $\geq$, the inequality may be reversed to conform to (9-9) by multiplying through by -1. If the ith constraint is a strict equality, it may be represented by two weak inequalities, $\leq$ and $\geq$. The second inequality may then be reversed by multiplying through by -1.

THE FEASIBLE POINT SET

Any set of real numbers that satisfies (9-9) and (9-10) is a feasible solution for the linear-programming system. The collection of all feasible points in n-dimensional space (R^n) forms the *feasible point set* for the system.

It is useful to review some of the general properties of point sets in R^n before deriving the specific properties of feasible point sets.[1] A *con-*

---

[1] See also Sec. 5-4. The definitions of a closed set given here and in Sec. 5-4 are equivalent.

vex set has the property that every point on a straight-line segment connecting any two points in the set is also in the set. A *boundary point* has adjacent points that are in the set and adjacent points that are not in the set. All points adjacent to an *interior point* are in the set. A set is *closed* if it contains all its boundary points, and *open* if it contains none. The *null set* with no points and a set with a single point are both defined to be convex and closed. The set of all points in R^n is closed; it has no boundary points and includes them all. A set is *bounded from below* if there exists a set of n numbers, u_j, such that $u_j \leqq z_j$ $(j = 1, \ldots, n)$ for all points in the set. It is *bounded from above* if there exists a set of n numbers, v_j, such that $v_j \geqq z_j$ $(j = 1, \ldots, n)$ for all points in the set.

A linear equation such as the equality form of the ith constraint of (9-9) defines a *hyperplane* in R^n. A hyperplane is a line in R^2, a plane in R^3, and an $(n - 1)$-dimensional surface in R^n. If $a_{ij} = 0$, the hyperplane is parallel to the z_j axis. If $k_i = 0$, it includes the origin for R^n. The hyperplane defined by the ith constraint separates R^n into a *closed half-space*,

$$a_{i1}z_1 + a_{i2}z_2 + \cdots + a_{in}z_n \leqq k_i$$

the points of which satisfy the ith constraint and an *open-half space*,

$$a_{i1}z_1 + a_{i2}z_2 + \cdots + a_{in}z_n > k_i$$

the points of which violate the ith constraint. Half-spaces are convex sets, and closed half-spaces are closed convex sets. The point set which satisfies the jth nonnegativity constraint of (9-10) is also a closed half-space and therefore is closed and convex.

The points that satisfy each of the constraints of (9-9) and (9-10) considered individually form a closed convex set. A feasible solution for the programming system must satisfy all $(m + n)$ of the constraints. The feasible point set contains points that are in each of the $(m + n)$ sets formed by the constraints; i.e., it is the *intersection* of the $(m + n)$ sets. A theorem in point-set theory states that the intersection of a finite number of closed convex sets is itself a closed convex set. The nonnegativity constraints, (9-10), place lower bounds on the values of the variables. It follows that the feasible point set for a linear-programming system is always closed, convex, and bounded from below. This is important because the properties of such sets are well known.

For illustration, assume that an entrepreneur can use two linear activities to produce two outputs using three inputs. A unit of Q_1 requires 1, 1, and 2 units of X_1, X_2, and X_3 respectively. The respective input requirements for a unit of Q_2 are 3, 1, and 1. The entrepreneur possesses fixed quantities of the three inputs: $x_1^0 = 18$, $x_2^0 = 8$, and $x_3^0 = 14$. He may utilize smaller amounts, but he cannot secure additional quantities of the inputs. The entrepreneur's production opportunities are described by the following constraints:

$$\begin{aligned} q_1 + 3q_2 &\leqq 18 \\ q_1 + q_2 &\leqq 8 \\ 2q_1 + q_2 &\leqq 14 \\ q_1, q_2 &\geqq 0 \end{aligned} \qquad (9\text{-}11)$$

Each of the five constraints restricts solutions to a closed half-space. The nonnegativity constraints limit solutions to the nonnegative quadrant. It is convenient to limit consideration of the remaining constraints to this quadrant.

The relevant hyperplanes, lines in R^2, are plotted in Fig. 9-3. The first constraint of (9-11) limits solutions to points that lie on or below the line that contains points A and B, the second limits solutions to points that lie on or below the line that contains B and C, and the third limits solutions to points that lie on or below the line that contains C and D. The feasible point set is defined by the solid-line boundary $OABCD$. It is closed and convex, and in this example it is bounded from above as well as below. Every point in the set satisfies all five constraints given by (9-11), and every point not in the set violates one or more of the constraints. Point E ($q_1 = 5$, $q_2 = 4$) satisfies the first, third, and nonnegativity constraints of (9-11), but it is not feasible because it violates the second.

OPTIMAL SOLUTIONS

Once the feasible point set has been defined, the next task is to find a point in the set that maximizes the value of the objective function (9-8).

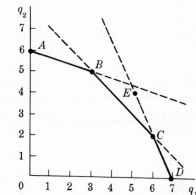

Fig. 9-3

Two additional concepts in point-set theory are useful for this purpose. An *extreme point* of a closed convex set is a boundary point that does not lie on a line connecting any pair of points in the set. Points O, A, B, C, and D in Fig. 9-3 are extreme points. A hyperplane that contains a boundary point of a closed convex set is a *supporting hyperplane* for the set if the entire set is in one of the closed half-spaces defined by it.

If the feasible point set is the null set, obviously there is no optimal solution for the programming system. If it contains a single point, that point is optimal regardless of the particular form of the objective function. If the feasible point set contains more than one point, it is necessary to find a point that maximizes the value of (9-8).

Assume that an optimal solution exists for the programming system given by (9-8) to (9-10). Let $(z_1^0, z_2^0, \ldots, z_n^0)$ be a point in the feasible set. Insert these values in (9-8) to obtain the corresponding value of the objective function, y^0:

$$y^0 = \gamma_1 z_1^0 + \gamma_2 z_2^0 + \cdots + \gamma_n z_n^0$$

Define a closed half-space which contains all points with objective function values no greater than y^0:

$$\gamma_1 z_1 + \gamma_2 z_2 + \cdots + \gamma_n z_n \leqq y^0 \tag{9-12}$$

and an open half-space which contains all points with values greater than y^0:

$$\gamma_1 z_1 + \gamma_2 z_2 + \cdots + \gamma_n z_n > y^0 \tag{9-13}$$

The selected point is optimal if (9-12) is a supporting hyperplane for the feasible point set. In this case there is no feasible point with a higher value for the objective function. If (9-12) is not a supporting hyperplane, the selected point is not optimal. In this case the set defined by (9-13) contains at least one feasible point with a value of y greater than y^0. Since a supporting hyperplane does not contain interior points of the feasible set, it follows that optimal points are always on the boundary of the feasible set. A theorem of particular importance for linear programming states that *a closed convex set which is bounded from below has one or more extreme points in every supporting hyperplane.*[1] This means that if a programming system has an optimal solution, there will be at least one extreme point that is optimal. The search for an optimal solution may be limited to a finite number of points since the number of extreme points is finite.

---

[1] A proof is given by G. Hadley, *Linear Programming* (Reading, Mass.: Addison-Wesley, 1962), pp. 62–63.

Assume that the entrepreneur whose production opportunities are described by (9-11) and pictured in Fig. 9-3 sells his output at the fixed prices p_1 and p_2, and desires to maximize his total revenue. The case in which $p_1 = 1$, $p_2 = 2$, and

$$y = q_1 + 2q_2$$

is pictured in Fig. 9-4a. The hyperplane defined by $y^0 = 7$ is the lowest broken line. It contains the extreme point D ($q_1 = 7$, $q_2 = 0$). The corresponding open half-space defined by (9-13) contains feasible points, A, B, and C, for example. Therefore, D is not optimal. Extreme point C ($q_1 = 6$, $q_2 = 2$) is in the hyperplane defined by $y^0 = 10$. The corresponding open half-space contains feasible points, and C is not optimal. Extreme point B ($q_1 = 3$, $q_2 = 5$) is optimal. It is contained in the supporting hyperplane defined by $y^0 = 13$. The corresponding open half-space contains no feasible points. The optimal solution occurs at an extreme point and is unique.

Figure 9-4b depicts the same feasible point set with different output prices and a different objective function: $p_1 = p_2 = 1$, and

$$y = q_1 + q_2$$

Extreme point A ($q_1 = 0$, $q_2 = 6$) is in the hyperplane defined by $y^0 = 6$. This point is clearly not optimal. Extreme points B and C, and all points on the intervening edge of the feasible set are contained in the optimal supporting hyperplane defined by $y^0 = 8$. There is not a unique optimal solution in this case. There are optimal boundary points that are not extreme points. Nonetheless, there are extreme points that are optimal.

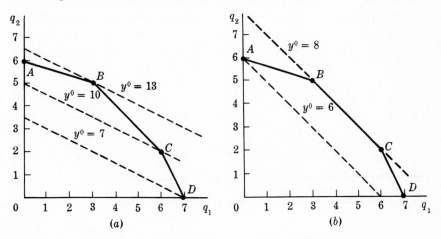

Fig. 9-4

The boundary of the feasible point set in Fig. 9-4 is the linear-programming counterpart of the product transformation curve defined for the continuous case in Sec. 3-5. In the continuous case a product transformation curve gives x_2 as a strictly concave function of x_1 with a rate of product transformation (RPT) that is continuous and increasing. For the linear-programming counterpart, x_2 is a concave (but not strictly concave) function of x_1 with an RPT that is discontinuous and non-decreasing. An optimum point for revenue maximization depends upon the ratio of the output prices in both cases.

Thus far, it has been assumed that optimal solutions exist. Consider the following programming system: maximize

$$y = 2z_1 + 3z_2$$

subject to

$$-3z_1 + 2z_2 \leqq 4$$
$$z_1 - 2z_2 \leqq 6$$
$$z_1, z_2 \geqq 0$$

This system is pictured in Fig. 9-5. All points that lie on or between the two constraint lines are feasible. The feasible point set is closed, convex, and bounded from below, but it is not bounded from above. There is no finite maximum for the objective function. It can be made ever larger by appropriately increasing the values of z_1 and z_2. Such a programming system is said to have an *unbounded solution*.

To prove existence of a finite optimal solution for a particular system or family of systems it is first necessary to prove that the feasible point set contains at least one point. If this is true, a sufficient condition for existence is that the feasible point set be bounded from above. If the values of the variables cannot be increased or decreased indefinitely, the value of the objective function cannot be increased or decreased indefi-

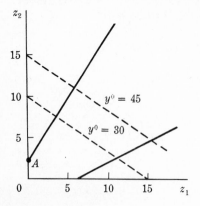

Fig. 9-5

nitely. Remember that all programming systems are bounded from
below. The existence of an upper bound is a sufficient, but not necessary,
condition for the existence of a finite optimal solution. Assume that the
objective function for the feasible point set pictured in Fig. 9-5 is
$y = -2z_1 + z_2$. The reader may verify that an optimal solution exists
at extreme point A ($z_1 = 0$, $z_2 = 2$) with $y = 2$.

For an illustrative proof consider the general system which underlies
the example in Fig. 9-4. An entrepreneur can use a linear activity for the
production of each of n outputs, he possesses fixed quantities of m inputs,
and he desires to maximize the revenue he obtains from selling his outputs
at fixed prices. The programming system is to maximize

$$y = p_1q_1 + p_2q_2 + \cdots + p_nq_n \tag{9-14}$$

subject to

$$a_{i1}q_1 + a_{i2}q_2 + \cdots + a_{in}q_n \leq x_i^0 \quad i = 1, \ldots, m$$
$$q_j \geq 0 \quad j = 1, \ldots, n \tag{9-15}$$

where a_{ij} is the quantity of the ith input required to produce a unit of the
jth output, and x_i^0 is the fixed available quantity of the ith input. The
a_{ij} are nonnegative, and each output requires a positive amount of at
least one input, that is, $a_{ij} > 0$ for at least one i ($j = 1, \ldots, n$). It is
assumed that all the p_j and x_i^0 are strictly positive.

Let v_j be the maximum amount of the jth output that can be produced if no other output is produced:

$$v_j = \min_i \left(\frac{x_i^0}{a_{ij}}\right) \quad a_{ij} > 0 \quad j = 1, \ldots, n$$

The assumptions that each output requires a positive amount of at least
one input, and that all $x_i^0 > 0$, and that all $a_{ij} \geq 0$ ensure that all $v_j > 0$.
The origin is feasible, but there are also nontrivial feasible points. For
example, $q_1 = v_1$ and $q_j = 0$ ($j = 2, \ldots, n$) is feasible. By construction, $v_j \geq q_j$ ($j = 1, \ldots, n$) for all points in the feasible set. The v_js
provide an upper bound for the set, and the existence proof is complete.
The family of programming systems given by (9-14) and (9-15) will
always have finite nontrivial optimal solutions.

DUALITY

The general linear-programming system is to find values for z_j ($j = 1$,
$\ldots, n$) that maximize

$$y = \gamma_1z_1 + \gamma_2z_2 + \cdots + \gamma_nz_n \tag{9-16}$$

subject to

$$a_{11}z_1 + a_{12}z_2 + \cdots + a_{1n}z_n \leqq k_1$$
$$a_{21}z_1 + a_{22}z_2 + \cdots + a_{2n}z_n \leqq k_2$$
$$\cdots\cdots\cdots\cdots\cdots\cdots\cdots\cdots\cdots\cdots \qquad (9\text{-}17)$$
$$a_{m1}z_1 + a_{m2}z_2 + \cdots + a_{mn}z_n \leqq k_m$$

and

$$z_j \geqq 0 \qquad j = 1, \ldots, n$$

An associated dual system is formed from the same coefficients: find values for w_i $(i = 1, \ldots, m)$ that minimize

$$y' = k_1w_1 + k_2w_2 + \cdots + k_mw_m \qquad (9\text{-}18)$$

subject to

$$a_{11}w_1 + a_{21}w_2 + \cdots + a_{m1}w_m \geqq \gamma_1$$
$$a_{12}w_1 + a_{22}w_2 + \cdots + a_{m2}w_m \geqq \gamma_2$$
$$\cdots\cdots\cdots\cdots\cdots\cdots\cdots\cdots\cdots\cdots \qquad (9\text{-}19)$$
$$a_{1n}w_1 + a_{2n}w_2 + \cdots + a_{mn}w_m \geqq \gamma_n$$

and

$$w_i \geqq 0 \qquad i = 1, \ldots, m$$

The initial system has m constraints and n variables; its dual system has n constraints and m variables. The initial objective function is maximized, and the dual objective function is minimized. The objective function coefficients and constraint constants are interchanged in the two systems, and the direction of the inequalities is reversed. The coefficient a_{ij} is in the ith row and jth column of the array for (9-17) and in the jth row and ith column of the array for (9-19). Duality is a symmetric relation. The reader may verify that the initial system is the dual of its dual.[1]

A system and its dual are related in a number of ways. Some of the more important duality theorems are stated here. *If a finite optimal solution exists for one of the systems, a finite optimal solution exists for the other. If feasible solutions exist for both systems, finite optimal solutions exist for both.* It is left as an exercise for the reader to demonstrate that no feasible solution exists for the dual of the system pictured in Fig. 9-5.

The variables of one system are associated with the constraints of the other. In Sec. 9-3 it is shown that the dual variable w_i gives the rate at which the initial objective function (9-16) will increase per unit

---

[1] Multiply (9-18) and (9-19) by -1 to put this system in the standard format, apply the rules given above to find its dual, and then multiply its dual objective function and constraints by -1. The resultant system is the same as that given by (9-16) and (9-17).

increase of k_i with k_h $(h \neq i)$ unchanged. It gives the marginal value of the ith constraint of the initial system measured in the same units as the objective function of the initial system.

Assume that optimal solutions exist and have been found for both systems. Let these be denoted by $z_1^*, \ldots, z_n^*$ and $w_1^*, \ldots, w_m^*$. A major duality theorem states that *the optimal value of a variable in one system is zero if the corresponding constraint in the other system is satisfied as a strict inequality, and nonnegative if the corresponding constraint is satisfied as an equality*:

$$
\begin{array}{lll}
a_{i1}z_1^* + \cdots + a_{in}z_n^* < k_i & \text{implies} & w_i^* = 0 \\
a_{i1}z_1^* + \cdots + a_{in}z_n^* = k_i & \text{implies} & w_i^* \geqq 0 \qquad (9\text{-}20) \\
& & i = 1, \ldots, m
\end{array}
$$

and

$$
\begin{array}{lll}
a_{1j}w_1^* + \cdots + a_{mj}w_m^* > \gamma_j & \text{implies} & z_j^* = 0 \\
a_{1j}w_1^* + \cdots + a_{mj}w_m^* = \gamma_j & \text{implies} & z_j^* \geqq 0 \qquad (9\text{-}21) \\
& & j = 1, \ldots, n
\end{array}
$$

An allied theorem states that *if the optimal value of a variable in one system is positive, the optimal values of the variables for the other system satisfy the corresponding constraint as an equality*:

$$
\begin{array}{lll}
w_i^* > 0 & \text{implies} & a_{i1}z_1^* + \cdots + a_{in}z_n^* = k_i \\
& & \qquad\qquad i = 1, \ldots, m \quad (9\text{-}22) \\
z_j^* > 0 & \text{implies} & a_{1j}w_1^* + \cdots + a_{mj}w_m^* = \gamma_j \\
& & \qquad\qquad j = 1, \ldots, n \quad (9\text{-}23)
\end{array}
$$

Insert the optimal z_j^* into (9-17), multiply the ith constraint by w_i^* $(i = 1, \ldots, m)$, and sum the resultant m constraints:

$$
\sum_{i=1}^{m} w_i^* \sum_{j=1}^{n} a_{ij}z_j^* = \sum_{i=1}^{m} w_i^* k_i \qquad (9\text{-}24)
$$

The equality follows from (9-22).† Insert the optimal w_i^* into (9-19), multiply the jth constraint by z_j^* $(j = 1, \ldots, n)$, and sum the resultant n constraints:

$$
\sum_{j=1}^{n} z_j^* \sum_{i=1}^{m} a_{ij}w_i^* = \sum_{j=1}^{n} z_j^* \gamma_j \qquad (9\text{-}25)
$$

---

[1] If $w_i^* > 0$, the corresponding constraint is an equality and remains an equality after multiplication. If $w_i^* = 0$, the corresponding constraint reduces to the trivial equality $0 = 0$ after multiplication. Thus, (9-24) is a sum of equalities.

The equality follows from (9-23). The left-hand sides of (9-24) and (9-25) are the same. Substituting from (9-18) into (9-24) and from (9-16) into (9-25),

$$y^* = \sum_{j=1}^{n} \gamma_j z_j^* = \sum_{i=1}^{m} k_i w_i^* = y'^* \qquad (9\text{-}26)$$

The optimal values of the objective functions for the two programming systems are equal.

Frequently in economics, the variables of an initial programming system are quantities, and the dual variables are imputed prices that would lead to an efficient allocation of resources. In some systems the imputed prices may be interpreted as competitive market prices. In other systems they are efficiency prices not realized in the market.

An illustration of duality in economics is provided by the system for the entrepreneur who produces n outputs from fixed quantities of m inputs. The initial system is given by (9-14) and (9-15). The dual variables are the rates by which the initial objective function, total revenue in dollars, would be increased per unit increase of each of the inputs considered individually, and are measured in dollars per input unit. The dual variables may be interpreted as imputed input prices, and are denoted by the familiar notation r_i ($i = 1, \ldots, m$).

The dual system is: minimize

$$y' = x_1^0 r_1 + \cdots + x_m^0 r_m \qquad (9\text{-}27)$$

subject to

$$\begin{aligned} a_{1j} r_1 + \cdots + a_{mj} r_m &\geq p_j \qquad j = 1, \ldots, n \\ r_i &\geq 0 \qquad i = 1, \ldots, m \end{aligned} \qquad (9\text{-}28)$$

The left-hand side of the jth constraint gives the unit production cost for the jth output in terms of the imputed input prices. The dual constraints state that unit cost equals or exceeds price (unit revenue) for each output. From (9-23) it follows that unit cost equals price for each output that is produced. The imputed input prices lead to efficiency in the sense that it is not possible for the entrepreneur to increase his profit by changing his output levels.

The dual objective function gives the value of the entrepreneur's input stocks in terms of the imputed input prices. By (9-26) the optimal value of his input stock equals his maximum revenue. If the owners of the input stocks were paid the imputed input prices, total revenue would be exhausted, and total profit would equal zero. If the optimal outputs satisfy the ith input constraint as a strict inequality, the entrepreneur will have an unused quantity of the ith input, and (9-20) states that its imputed price will be zero. Only scarce, i.e., fully utilized, inputs can have positive prices.

The dual system for the case shown in Fig. 9-4a is: minimize

$$y' = 18r_1 + 8r_2 + 14r_3$$

subject to

$$r_1 + r_2 + 2r_3 \geq 1$$
$$3r_1 + r_2 + r_3 \geq 2$$
$$r_1, r_2, r_3 \geq 0$$

The optimal solution for the initial system is $q_1^* = 3$, $q_2^* = 5$, $y^* = 13$. The equality holds for the first and second input constraints in the initial system, and the strict inequality holds for the third. An optimal solution for the dual system follows easily from (9-20) and (9-21). By (9-20), $r_3^* = 0$, and from (9-21)

$$r_1^* + r_2^* = 1$$
$$3r_1^* + r_2^* = 2$$

These equations have the solution $r_1^* = 0.5$, $r_2^* = 0.5$. An evaluation of the dual objective function confirms that $y'^* = 13$ as stated by (9-26).

9-3 LINEAR PROGRAMMING: SOLUTIONS

A number of general methods have been developed to obtain numerical solutions for linear-programming systems. The *revised simplex method*, which is presented here, is the most widely used and the most intuitively appealing for economists.

BASIC FEASIBLE SOLUTIONS

Few methods have been developed for the solution of systems of linear inequalities, but well-developed methods are available for the solution of systems of linear equations. Therefore, a first step is the conversion of (9-17) into a system of equations. Define m new variables z_j ($j = n + 1$, . . . , $n + m$) as the differences between the right- and left-hand sides of the constraints of (9-17). These variables allow the redefinition of the programming system (9-16) and (9-17): find values for z_j ($j = 1, \ldots, n + m$) that maximize

$$y = \gamma_1 z_1 + \cdots + \gamma_{n+m} z_{n+m} \tag{9-29}$$

subject to

$$
\begin{aligned}
a_{11}z_1 + a_{12}z_2 + \cdots + a_{1n}z_n + z_{n+1} &= k_1 \\
a_{21}z_1 + a_{22}z_2 + \cdots + a_{2n}z_n \qquad\quad + z_{n+2} &= k_2 \\
&\cdots \\
a_{m1}z_1 + a_{m2}z_2 + \cdots + a_{mn}z_n \qquad\qquad\qquad + z_{n+m} &= k_m \\
z_j \geq 0 \qquad j = 1, \ldots, n+m
\end{aligned}
$$

(9-30)

where $\gamma_j = 0$ $(j = n+1, \ldots, n+m)$. The new "slack" variables are also restricted to nonnegative values. When the equality holds for the ith relation of (9-17), $z_{n+i} = 0$. When the strict inequality holds, $z_{n+i} > 0$. The principal constraints are now given by a system of m linear equations in $(n+m)$ variables.

A set of nonnegative values for the $(n+m)$ z_j that satisfies (9-30) is a feasible solution for the programming system, i.e., is a point in the feasible set. Let (9-30) be reduced to m equations in m variables by setting the values of any n of the $(n+m)$ variables equal to zero. The reduced system forms a *basic feasible solution* (BFS) for the programming system if its determinant does not vanish and it can be solved for nonnegative values of the m included variables. A BFS for (9-30) is a feasible solution with not more than m variables at positive levels. Less than m will be positive if the solution values for one or more of the included variables equal zero; such BFSs are called *degenerate*.

A fundamental theorem of linear programming states that there is a one-to-one correspondence between BFSs and extreme points of the feasible point set.[1] If a finite optimal solution exists, there will always be one or more extreme points (BFSs) that are optimal. The search for an optimal solution can be limited to the finite number of BFSs for (9-30).

One solution method is to find all BFSs and to select the one (it may not be unique) that yields the highest value for the objective function. The equality form of the programming system pictured in Fig. 9-4a is: maximize

$$ y = q_1 + 2q_2 \tag{9-31} $$

subject to

$$
\begin{aligned}
q_1 + 3q_2 + q_3 \qquad\qquad &= 18 \\
q_1 + q_2 \qquad + q_4 \qquad &= 8 \\
2q_1 + q_2 \qquad\qquad + q_5 &= 14 \\
q_j \geq 0 \qquad j = 1, \ldots, 5
\end{aligned}
$$

(9-32)

where the q notation is retained for outputs. By omitting each pair of variables and solving for the remaining three, the reader can verify that

[1] A proof is given by Hadley, *op. cit.*, pp. 100–103.

this system has five BFSs:

$$
\begin{array}{lllllll}
(1) & q_3 = 18 & q_4 = 8 & q_5 = 14 & y = 0 & \text{(point } O) \\
(2) & q_2 = 6 & q_4 = 2 & q_5 = 8 & y = 12 & \text{(point } A) \\
(3) & q_1 = 3 & q_2 = 5 & q_5 = 3 & y = 13 & \text{(point } B) \\
(4) & q_1 = 6 & q_2 = 2 & q_3 = 6 & y = 10 & \text{(point } C) \\
(5) & q_1 = 7 & q_3 = 11 & q_4 = 1 & y = 7 & \text{(point } D)
\end{array}
$$

The corresponding extreme point in Fig. 9-4a is listed in parentheses following each BFS. The other five subsystems of three variables that can be derived from the equality constraints yield negative values for one or more of the variables and therefore are not feasible. For example, $q_1 = 18$, $q_4 = -10$, $q_5 = -22$ is a solution for the constraints, but it must be rejected because q_4 and q_5 are negative. As before, BFS (3) which corresponds to extreme point B is optimal.

GENERAL SOLUTIONS

Assume that a BFS has been found. Renumber the initial and slack variables so that those with the indices $1, \ldots, m$ are included in the BFS, and those with the indices $m + 1, \ldots, s$, where $s = n + m$, are excluded from it. If z_h is the slack variable for the kth constraint, the coefficients $a_{1h}, a_{2h}, \ldots, a_{mh}$ are zero except a_{kh} which is unity. Treat the excluded variables as constants, and move them to the right-hand side of (9-30). The equations are now in the form

$$
\begin{array}{l}
a_{11}z_1 + \cdots + a_{1m}z_m = k_1 - a_{1,m+1}z_{m+1} - \cdots - a_{1s}z_s \\
\cdots \cdots \cdots \cdots \cdots \cdots \cdots \cdots \cdots \cdots \cdots \cdots \cdots \cdots \cdots \cdots \cdots \cdots \cdots \cdots \quad (9\text{-}33) \\
a_{m1}z_1 + \cdots + a_{mm}z_m = k_m - a_{m,m+1}z_{m+1} - \cdots - a_{ms}z_s
\end{array}
$$

Using Cramer's rule to solve for the BFS variables in terms of the constants,

$$
z_j = \sum_{i=1}^{m} \beta_{ji} \left(k_i - a_{i,m+1}z_{m+1} - \cdots - a_{is}z_s \right)
$$
$$
j = 1, \ldots, m \quad (9\text{-}34)
$$

where $\beta_{ji} = \mathbf{D}_{ij}/\mathbf{D}$ is the cofactor $(\mathbf{D}_{ij})$ of the element in the ith row and jth column of the array of coefficients on the left of (9-33) divided by the determinant of the array $(\mathbf{D})$. From the definition of a BFS it follows that $\mathbf{D} \neq 0$. In the terminology of matrix algebra, the β_{ij} are the elements of the inverse of the matrix formed from the coefficient array for the BFS.

Equations (9-34) provide a general solution for the included variables in terms of the k_is and the excluded variables. They provide the

BFS values for the included variables on the assumption that the excluded variables are at zero levels:

$$z_j = \sum_{i=1}^{m} \beta_{ji} k_i \qquad j = 1, \ldots, m \qquad (9\text{-}35)$$

Another use for (9-34) is described later in this section.

THE REVISED SIMPLEX METHOD

Graphic solution methods fail when there are more than three dimensions, and complete enumeration of the BFSs is impractical if the numbers of equations and variables are large. The iterative revised simplex method described here has proved efficient for the numerical solution of linear-programming systems with large numbers of constraints and variables. This method is most easily described using the terminology for economic applications: the variables describe activities, the initial constraints describe resource limitations, the dual variables are resource prices, and the dual constraints compare unit costs and unit revenues. The general notation is used, and the methods are applicable for systems for which the terminology is inappropriate.

The revised simplex method begins with the selection of a BFS. Resource prices that would yield zero unit profits for the included activities are computed. Unit profit levels for the excluded activities are calculated from these prices. The BFS is optimal if potential profit levels are nonpositive for all excluded activities. It is not optimal if one or more of the excluded activities has a positive potential profit. In this case a new BFS is formed by including a profitable, formerly excluded activity and excluding one of the formerly included activities. The resource prices for the new BFS are computed, and the process continued until either an optimal BFS is found, or it is determined that no finite optimal solution exists.

The revised simplex method also may be described in terms of the feasible point set. Computations begin at an initial extreme point. Tests are made to determine whether the value of the objective function increases as a movement is made away from the initial extreme point along an edge of the feasible set. There is a one-to-one correspondence between the edges of the feasible set that join at the extreme point and the excluded activities. The extreme point is optimal if the value of the objective function cannot be increased by a movement along any edge. If one or more movements that increase the value of the objective function are possible, a movement is made along such an edge to an adjacent extreme point.[1] The process is repeated until an optimal extreme point

---

[1] It is possible for an edge to have zero length. In this case, an "adjacent" extreme point is coincident with the one under consideration.

is found, or it is determined that no finite optimal solution exists. The specifics of the revised simplex method are described by five steps.

Step 1   Select an initial BFS, and compute the β_{ij} for its general solution as given by (9-34). Again the included variables are numbered 1, . . . , m, and the excluded variables are numbered $m + 1$, . . . , s. If the feasible point set is null, no BFS exists, and the revised simplex method is not applicable. Otherwise, any BFS will provide a starting point. If $k_i \geqq 0$ $(i = 1, \ldots ,m)$, the origin in the space of productive activities is in the feasible set, and it provides a convenient initial BFS. This BFS includes the m slack activities with the values $z_i = k_i$ $(i = 1, \ldots ,m)$, and has $y = 0$. The general solution coefficients are $\beta_{ii} = 1$ and $\beta_{ij} = 0$ for $i \neq j$ $(i, j = 1, \ldots ,m)$. If another initial BFS is used, the values of the included variables may be computed from (9-35), and the objective function from (9-29).

Step 2   Compute the zero-profit resource prices implied by the initial BFS. Let w_i $(i = 1, \ldots ,m)$ denote the resource prices that will equate cost and revenue for each of the included activities:

$$a_{1j}w_1 + a_{2j}w_2 + \cdots + a_{mj}w_m = \gamma_j \qquad j = 1, \ldots , m \qquad (9\text{-}36)$$

The solution for this system of linear equations is

$$w_i = \beta_{1i}\gamma_1 + \beta_{2i}\gamma_2 + \cdots + \beta_{mi}\gamma_m \qquad i = 1, \ldots , m \qquad (9\text{-}37)$$

where the β_{ij} are the same coefficients computed for the general solution (9-34).† If the current BFS is optimal, the w_i provide an optimal solution for the dual system, and the duality theorems hold. If the current BFS is not optimal, the w_i will not provide an optimal solution for the dual system, and the duality theorems are inapplicable. In this case it is possible for some of the w_i's to be negative.

Step 3   Compute unit profit levels for the excluded activities. Unit profit, π_j, equals unit revenue less imputed unit cost:

$$\pi_j = \gamma_j - \sum_{i=1}^{m} a_{ij}w_i \qquad j = m + 1, \ldots , s \qquad (9\text{-}38)$$

† The coefficient array for (9-36) is the same as the array for (9-33) except that the rows and columns are transposed. The cofactor of the element in the ith row and jth column for the array of (9-33) is the same as the cofactor of the element in the jth row and ith column for the array of (9-36). The determinants of the two arrays have equal value.

If $\pi_j \leqq 0$ for all the excluded activities, the current BFS is optimal, and the computation is completed. In this case (9-38) implies that

$$a_{1j}w_1 + a_{2j}w_2 + \cdots + a_{mj}w_m \geqq \gamma_j \qquad j = m + 1, \ldots, s$$

(9-39)

which together with (9-36) provides a feasible and optimal solution for the dual system.[1] The optimal solution for the initial system is unique if $\pi_j < 0$ for all excluded activities, and not unique if $\pi_j = 0$ for one or more of the excluded activities. A means for finding other optimal BFSs in the latter case is described in Step 4 below.

The current BFS is not optimal if one or more of the excluded activities show a positive potential profit. The value of the objective function can be increased by letting a potentially profitable excluded activity assume a positive level. Select an excluded activity z_h with $\pi_h > 0$ for introduction into the BFS. If there are more than one, any will do. A commonly used procedure is to select one for which π_j is largest.

Step 4 Select a new BFS. Rewrite the general solution (9-34) with the excluded activity z_h explicit:

$$z_j = z_j^0 - \delta_j z_h \qquad j = 1, \ldots, m$$

(9-40)

where $z_j^0 = \Sigma_{i=1}^m \beta_{ji}k_i$ is the level of the jth included activity for the current BFS, and where $\delta_j = \Sigma_{i=1}^m \beta_{ji}a_{ih}$ is the change in the value of z_j per unit of z_h. As z_h assumes a positive value, the levels of the included activities will change in such a way as to maintain the equalities of (9-33). If $\delta_j > 0$, the introduction of z_h reduces the level of the included activity z_j. If $\delta_j = 0$, it leaves z_j unchanged, and if $\delta_j < 0$, it increases z_j. In geometric terms, (9-40) shows how the levels of the included activities are altered as a movement is made away from an extreme point along an edge of the feasible set.

If all $\delta_j \leqq 0$, no included-activity level is reduced by the introduction of z_h, there is no upper limit on the value of z_h, and the value of the objective function can be increased indefinitely. This condition will always arise at some point in the computations if the programming system has no finite optimal solution. It is a signal to stop the computational process.

If one or more $\delta_j > 0$, the corresponding z_j are reduced by increases of z_h. The value of z_h for which the level of such an activity becomes zero is determined by inserting $z_j = 0$ into (9-40): $z_h = z_j^0/\delta_j$. A larger value for z_h would make z_j negative which is not allowed by the constraints of

---

[1] If some $\pi_j > 0$, one or more of the constraints (9-39) will be violated. The w_i will not provide a feasible solution for the dual system. The w_i provide a feasible solution for the dual system if and only if the corresponding BFS is optimal.

the programming system. The maximum permissible value for z_h is the smallest value at which an included-activity level becomes zero:

$$z_h = \min_j \left(\frac{z_j^0}{\delta_j} \right) \qquad \delta_j > 0 \tag{9-41}$$

Let k be the value of j for which (9-41) is a minimum. If more than one activity level becomes zero so that there is not a unique k, a k corresponding to one of these may be selected arbitrarily. A new BFS is formed by including z_h and excluding z_k.†

The procedures used in this step will also allow the determination of all optimal BFSs for the case in which an optimal, but not unique, BFS is found in Step 3. A $\pi_h = 0$ indicates that an excluded activity can be introduced without changing the value of the objective function. Apply (9-41) for such an activity to determine which of the included activities would be excluded by its introduction. The resultant BFS is also optimal. If more than one excluded activity has a zero profit, the procedure may be repeated for each. The values of the variables for the alternative BFSs may be determined by the methods described in Step 5.

Step 5 Find values for the new BFS. It is possible to begin the computational process for the new BFS at Step 1 and calculate the β_{ij} and the values of the variables anew. However, certain theorems of linear algebra allow some computational shortcuts. Let a symbol with a zero superscript denote the value of a coefficient or variable for the current BFS, and a symbol without a zero superscript denote a value for the new BFS.

The coefficient π_h gives the increase in the value of the objective function per unit of z_h. Therefore, for the new BFS,

$$y = y^0 + \pi_h z_h \tag{9-42}$$

The value of z_h is given by (9-41). Values for the other BFS activities are determined by inserting the value of z_h into (9-40). By construction, $z_k = 0$. Interchange the newly included and newly excluded activities so that z_h takes the index k and z_k takes the index h.

The coefficient array as described by (9-33) for the new BFS is the same as the array for the old BFS except for the coefficients in the kth

---

† If $z_j^0 = 0$ and $\delta_j > 0$ for some $j = 1, \ldots, m$, (9-41) has the solution $z_h = 0$. The introduction of z_h will not increase the value of the objective function in this case. Nonetheless, the computational process should be continued in the same manner as if $z_h > 0$. Examples have been constructed in which the computational process cycles endlessly in this circumstance. However, cycling has not been reported for any practical application, and is ignored here.

column. A theorem of linear algebra makes computation of the new β_{ij} after such a change relatively easy. The coefficients for the kth row are

$$\beta_{kj} = \frac{\beta_{kj}^0}{\delta_k} \qquad j = 1, \ldots, m \tag{9-43}$$

By the method of selection for k, $\delta_k > 0$. The coefficients for the remaining rows are

$$\beta_{ij} = \beta_{ij}^0 - \delta_i \beta_{kj} \qquad i, j = 1, \ldots, m \qquad i \neq k \tag{9-44}$$

Finally, the resource prices implied by the new BFS are[1]

$$w_i = w_i^0 + \pi_h \beta_{ki} \qquad i = 1, \ldots, m \tag{9-45}$$

The computations now return to Step 3. Steps 3, 4, and 5 are repeated until either an optimal BFS is discovered in Step 3, or it is determined in Step 4 that no optimal BFS exists.

AN ILLUSTRATION

The revised simplex method is applied to obtain an optimal solution for the familiar example given by (9-31) and (9-32). A double notation scheme is used to keep track of the variables: the subscript $i.j$ identifies activity number i in the example which is numbered j for the computation process.

Step 1 The origin provides a convenient initial BFS. The solution (9-35) is

$$z_{3.1} = (1)(18) + (0)(8) + (0)(14) = 18$$
$$z_{4.2} = (0)(18) + (1)(8) + (0)(14) = 8$$
$$z_{5.3} = (0)(18) + (0)(8) + (1)(14) = 14$$

---

[1] By (9-37)

$$w_i = \sum_{j=1}^{m} \beta_{ji} \gamma_j$$

Substituting from (9-43) and (9-44), substituting γ_h from the old solution for γ_k in the new solution, and applying (9-37) for the old BFS,

$$w_i = \sum_{j=1}^{m} (\beta_{ji}^0 - \delta_j \beta_{ki}) \gamma_j + \beta_{ki} \gamma_h = w_i^0 + \beta_{ki} \left(\gamma_h - \sum_{j=1}^{m} \delta_j \gamma_j \right)$$

Substituting $\delta_j = \sum_{u=1}^{m} \beta_{ju} a_{uh}$ and utilizing (9-37) and (9-38),

$$w_i = w_i^0 + \beta_{ki} \left(\gamma_h - \sum_{j=1}^{m} \gamma_j \sum_{u=1}^{m} \beta_{ju} a_{uh} \right)$$

$$= w_i^0 + \beta_{ki} \left(\gamma_h - \sum_{u=1}^{m} a_{uh} w_u^0 \right) = w_i^0 + \beta_{ki} \pi_h$$

with

$$y = (0)(18) + (0)(8) + (0)(14) = 0$$

Step 2 From (9-37), the implied resource prices are

$$w_1 = (1)(0) + (0)(0) + (0)(0) = 0$$
$$w_2 = (0)(0) + (1)(0) + (0)(0) = 0$$
$$w_3 = (0)(0) + (0)(0) + (1)(0) = 0$$

A resource that is not fully utilized will always have a zero price.

Step 3 From (9-38), the unit profit levels for the excluded activities are

$$\pi_{1.4} = 1 - [(1)(0) + (1)(0) + (2)(0)] = 1 > 0$$
$$\pi_{2.5} = 2 - [(3)(0) + (1)(0) + (1)(0)] = 2 > 0$$

The value of the objective function can be increased by the introduction of either excluded activity. Since $\pi_{2.5} > \pi_{1.4}$, let $z_{2.5}$ be selected for introduction.

Step 4 The evaluation of (9-41) for $z_{2.5}$ is

$$\delta_{3.1} = (1)(3) + (0)(1) + (0)(1) = 3$$
$$\delta_{4.2} = (0)(3) + (1)(1) + (0)(1) = 1$$
$$\delta_{5.3} = (0)(3) + (0)(1) + (1)(1) = 1$$

and

$$z_{2.5} = \min\ (^{18}\!/_3, ^8\!/_1, ^{14}\!/_1) = 6$$

All three included activities are reduced by the introduction of $z_{2.5}$; $z_{3.1}$ becomes zero first and leaves the BFS.

Step 5 By (9-42),

$$y = 0 + (2)(6) = 12$$

and the values of the variables for the new BFS are

$$z_{2.1} = 6$$
$$z_{4.2} = 8 - (1)(6) = 2$$
$$z_{5.3} = 14 - (1)(6) = 8$$

By (9-43) and (9-44),

$$\beta_{11} = \frac{1}{3} \qquad\qquad \beta_{12} = \frac{0}{3} = 0 \qquad\qquad \beta_{13} = \frac{0}{3} = 0$$

$$\beta_{21} = 0 - (1)\left(\frac{1}{3}\right) = -\frac{1}{3} \quad \beta_{22} = 1 - (1)(0) = 1 \quad \beta_{23} = 0 - (1)(0) = 0$$

$$\beta_{31} = 0 - (1)\left(\frac{1}{3}\right) = -\frac{1}{3} \quad \beta_{32} = 0 - (1)(0) = 0 \quad \beta_{33} = 1 - (1)(0) = 1$$

and by (9-45) the imputed resource prices for the new BFS are

$$w_1 = 0 + (2)\left(\frac{1}{3}\right) = \frac{2}{3} \quad w_2 = 0 + (2)(0) = 0 \quad w_3 = 0 + (2)(0) = 0$$

The first resource is now fully utilized, and its price is positive. The computations now return to Step 3.

Step 3 From (9-38),

$$\pi_{1.4} = 1 - \left[(1)\left(\frac{2}{3}\right) + (1)(0) + (2)(0)\right] = \frac{1}{3} > 0$$

$$\pi_{3.5} = 0 - \left[(1)\left(\frac{2}{3}\right) + (0)(0) + (0)(0)\right] = -\frac{2}{3} < 0$$

This BFS is not optimal. The value of the objective function can be increased by the introduction of $z_{1.4}$.

Step 4 The evaluation of (9-41) for $z_{1.4}$ is

$$\delta_{2.1} = \left(\frac{1}{3}\right)(1) + (0)(1) + (0)(2) = \frac{1}{3}$$

$$\delta_{4.2} = \left(-\frac{1}{3}\right)(1) + (1)(1) + (0)(2) = \frac{2}{3}$$

$$\delta_{5.3} = \left(-\frac{1}{3}\right)(1) + (0)(1) + (1)(2) = \frac{5}{3}$$

and

$$z_{1.4} = \min\left(\frac{6}{\frac{1}{3}}, \frac{2}{\frac{2}{3}}, \frac{8}{\frac{5}{3}}\right) = 3$$

The second included activity, $z_{4.2}$, leaves the BFS.

Step 5 By (9-42),

$$y = 12 + \left(\frac{1}{3}\right)(3) = 13$$

and the values of the variables for the new BFS are

$$z_{2.1} = 6 - \left(\frac{1}{3}\right)(3) = 5$$

$$z_{1.2} = 3$$

$$z_{5.3} = 8 - \left(\frac{5}{3}\right)(3) = 3$$

By (9-43) and (9-44),

$$\beta_{21} = \left(\frac{-\frac{1}{3}}{\frac{2}{3}}\right) = -\frac{1}{2} \qquad \beta_{22} = \frac{1}{\frac{2}{3}} = \frac{3}{2}$$

$$\beta_{23} = \frac{0}{\frac{2}{3}} = 0$$

$$\beta_{11} = \frac{1}{3} - \left(\frac{1}{3}\right)\left(-\frac{1}{2}\right) = \frac{1}{2} \qquad \beta_{12} = 0 - \left(\frac{1}{3}\right)\left(\frac{3}{2}\right) = -\frac{1}{2}$$

$$\beta_{13} = 0 - \left(\frac{1}{3}\right)(0) = 0$$

$$\beta_{31} = -\frac{1}{3} - \left(\frac{5}{3}\right)\left(-\frac{1}{2}\right) = \frac{1}{2} \qquad \beta_{32} = 0 - \left(\frac{5}{3}\right)\left(\frac{3}{2}\right) = -\frac{5}{2}$$

$$\beta_{33} = 1 - \left(\frac{5}{3}\right)(0) = 1$$

and by (9-45) the imputed resource prices for the new BFS are

$$w_1 = \frac{2}{3} + \left(\frac{1}{3}\right)\left(-\frac{1}{2}\right) = \frac{1}{2} \qquad w_2 = 0 + \left(\frac{1}{3}\right)\left(\frac{3}{2}\right) = \frac{1}{2}$$

$$w_3 = 0 + \left(\frac{1}{3}\right)(0) = 0$$

The first two resources are now both fully utilized, and both have positive prices. Back to Step 3.

Step 3 From (9-38),

$$\pi_{3.4} = 0 - \left[(1)\left(\frac{1}{2}\right) + (0)\left(\frac{1}{2}\right) + (0)(0)\right] = -\frac{1}{2} < 0$$

$$\pi_{4.5} = 0 - \left[(0)\left(\frac{1}{2}\right) + (1)\left(\frac{1}{2}\right) + (0)(0)\right] = -\frac{1}{2} < 0$$

The current BFS is optimal and the solution process is completed. The current values of the w_i provide an optimal solution for the dual system. It is of interest to note that the potential profit levels for the excluded slack activities equal the negatives of the corresponding resource prices.

The initial BFS corresponds to extreme point O in Fig. 9-4a. It was determined that a movement along either edge (axis) away from O would increase the value of the objective function. A movement was made along the q_2 axis to extreme point A. It was determined that a movement from A along the edge toward B would increase the value of the objective function. A movement was made to extreme point B. Finally, it was determined that a movement away from B along either edge would decrease the value of the objective function.

9-4 THEORY OF TWO-PERSON, ZERO-SUM GAMES

The mathematical theory of games has been applied to market situations in which the outcome for each participant depends upon the actions of all. Games can be characterized by whether participants have an interest in behaving cooperatively or whether their interests are strictly competitive. Situations of duopoly, oligopoly, and bilateral monopoly often fit into the latter category.   Duopolists are in conflict if an action by one results in a diminution of the profit of the other.   The theory of games provides specific behavior assumptions which result in an equilibrium for such a market, though the equilibrium is quite different from the duopoly solutions given in Sec. 6-3.   It is convenient to discuss the theory of games at this point because linear-programming techniques can be used to obtain solutions for two-person, zero-sum games.

A DUOPOLY GAME

A game may consist of a sequence of moves as in chess, or it may consist of a single move on the part of each of its participants.   The present analysis is limited to single-move games.   In this context, a *strategy* is the specification of a particular move for one of the participants.   A duopolist's strategy consists of selecting a particular value for each of the variables under his control.   If price is his only variable, a strategy consists of selecting a particular price.   If price and advertising expenditure are both variables, a strategy consists of selecting particular values for both price and advertising expenditure.   Each participant is assumed to possess a finite number of strategies though the number may be very large.   This assumption rules out the possibility of continuous variation of the action variables.   The outcome of the duopolistic game, i.e., the profit earned by each of the participants, is determined from the relevant cost and demand relations once each of the duopolists has selected a strategy.

Games are classified on the basis of two criteria: (1) the number of participants and (2) the net outcome.   The first merely involves a counting of the number of participants with conflicting interests.   There are one-person, two-person, three-person, and in the general case, n-person games.   The second criterion allows a distinction between zero-sum and non-zero-sum games.   A zero-sum game is one in which the algebraic sum of the outcomes, e.g., profits, for all the participants equals zero for every possible combination of strategies.   If the net outcome of a game is different from zero for at least one strategy combination, it is classified as a non-zero-sum game.

A one-person, zero-sum game is uninteresting, since the player gains nothing, regardless of his strategy choice.   A monopolist or a monopsonist might be considered as the sole participant in a one-person, non-zero-sum game. The present analysis is restricted to two-person, zero-sum games and can be applied to a duopolistic market in which one participant's gain always equals the absolute value of the other's loss. In general, if I has m and II has n strategies, the possible outcomes of the game are given by the profit matrix

$$\begin{bmatrix} a_{11} & a_{12} & \cdots & a_{1n} \\ a_{21} & a_{22} & \cdots & a_{2n} \\ \cdots\cdots\cdots\cdots\cdots \\ a_{m1} & a_{m2} & \cdots & a_{mn} \end{bmatrix} \tag{9-46}$$

where a_{ij} is I's profit if I employs his ith strategy and II employs his jth. Since the game is zero-sum, the corresponding profit earned by II is $-a_{ij}$.

For a specific example consider the profit matrix

$$\begin{bmatrix} 8 & 40 & 20 & 5 \\ 10 & 30 & -10 & -8 \end{bmatrix} \tag{9-47}$$

If I employs his first strategy and II employs his second, I's profit is 40, and II's is -40. If I employs his second strategy and II employs his third, I's profit is -10, and II's is 10.

The duopolist's decision problem consists of choosing an optimal strategy. I desires the outcome (40) in the first row and second column of (9-47), and II desires the outcome (-10) in the second row and third column. The final outcome depends upon the strategies of both duopolists, and neither has the power to enforce his desires. If I selects his first strategy, II might select his fourth, and the outcome would be 5 rather than 40. If II selects his third strategy, I might select his first, and the outcome would be 20 rather than -10. The theory of games postulates behavior patterns which allow the determination of equilibrium in these situations. I fears that II might discover his choice of strategy and desires to "play it safe." If I selects his ith strategy, his minimum profit, and hence II's maximum, is given by the smallest element in the ith row of the profit matrix: $\min_j a_{ij}$. This is his expected profit from the employment of his ith strategy if his fears regarding II's knowledge and behavior are realized. I's profit will be greater than this amount if II fails to select his appropriate strategy. I desires to maximize his minimum expected profit. Therefore, he selects the strategy i for which $\min_j a_{ij}$ is the largest. His expected outcome is $\max_i \min_j a_{ij}$. He cannot earn a smaller profit and may earn a larger one.

II possesses the same fears regarding I's information and behavior. If II employs his jth strategy, he fears that I may employ the strategy corresponding to the largest element in the jth column of the profit matrix: $\max_{i} a_{ij}$. Therefore, II selects the strategy j for which $\max_{i} a_{ij}$ is the smallest, and his expected profit is $-\min_{j} \max_{i} a_{ij}$. The decisions of the duopolists are consistent and equilibrium is achieved if

$$\max_{i} \min_{j} a_{ij} = \min_{j} \max_{i} a_{ij}$$

Returning to the example given by (9-47), I will employ his first strategy. If II anticipates his choice, I's profit will be 5. If I employed his second strategy, and II anticipated his choice, his profit would be -10. II will employ his fourth strategy and limit his loss to 5. Every other column of (9-47) has a maximum greater than 5. In this case

$$\max_{i} \min_{j} a_{ij} = \min_{j} \max_{i} a_{ij} = a_{14} = 5$$

The duopolists' decisions are consistent, and an equilibrium is established. Neither duopolist can increase his profit by changing his strategy if his opponent's strategy remains unchanged.

Assume that the profit matrix is

$$\begin{bmatrix} -2 & 4 & -1 & 6 \\ 3 & -1 & 5 & 10 \end{bmatrix} \tag{9-48}$$

where I has two strategies and II has four. This profit maxtrix and its corresponding game problem can be simplified by introducing the concept of dominance. An inspection of (9-48) reveals that II will never employ his third strategy since he can always do better by employing his first, regardless of I's strategy choice. Each element in the third column is larger, and therefore represents a greater loss for II, than the corresponding element in the first. In general, the jth column dominates the kth if $a_{ij} \leq a_{ik}$ for all i and $a_{ij} < a_{ik}$ for at least one i. The fourth column of (9-48) is dominated by both the first and second columns. Dominance can also be defined with regard to I's strategies. In general, the ith row dominates the hth if $a_{ij} \geq a_{hj}$ for all j and $a_{ij} > a_{hj}$ for at least one j. Neither row of (9-48) dominates the other. A rational player will never employ a dominated strategy. Therefore, the profit matrix can be simplified by the removal of all dominated strategies.

Eliminating the third and fourth columns of (9-48), the profit matrix becomes

$$\begin{bmatrix} -2 & 4 \\ 3 & -1 \end{bmatrix} \tag{9-49}$$

Following the rules established above, I will desire to employ his second strategy, and II will desire to employ his first. These decisions are not consistent:

$$\max_i \min_j a_{ij} = a_{22} = -1 \neq 3 = a_{21} = \min_j \max_i a_{ij}$$

If the duopolists employ these strategies, the initial outcome would be $a_{21} = 3$. If II employs his first strategy, I cannot increase his profit by changing strategies. However, if I employs his second strategy, II can decrease his loss from 3 to -1 by switching to his second strategy. I can then increase his profit from -1 to 4 by switching to his first. II can then decrease his loss from 4 to -2 by switching to his first. The assumptions which lead to an equilibrium position for (9-47) result in endless fluctuations for (9-49).

MIXED STRATEGIES

A particular game may or may not have a solution if the duopolists select their strategies in the manner described above. The impasse presented by games such as (9-49) can be resolved by allowing the duopolists to select their strategies on a probabilistic basis. Let $r_1, r_2, \ldots, r_m$ be the probabilities with which I will employ each of his m strategies, where $0 \leq r_i \leq 1$ $(i = 1, \ldots, m)$ and $\Sigma_{i=1}^{m} r_i = 1$. Assume that he utilizes some random process to select a particular strategy. For example, if $m = 3$ with $r_1 = 0.3$, $r_2 = 0.1$, and $r_3 = 0.6$, he may assign the numbers 0 through 2 to the first strategy, 3 to the second, and 4 through 9 to the third; select a one-digit number by a random process; and employ the strategy that corresponds to the selected number. A random selection will not allow II to anticipate I's choice even if he knows I's probabilities.

II can randomize his strategy selection by assigning the probabilities $s_1, s_2, \ldots, s_n$ to his strategies, where $0 \leq s_j \leq 1$ $(j = 1, \ldots, n)$ and $\Sigma_{j=1}^{n} s_j = 1$. The duopolists are now concerned with expected, rather than actual, profits. A duopolist's expected profit equals the sum of the possible outcomes, each multiplied by the probability of its occurrence. For example, if II employs his jth strategy with a probability of one and I selects the probabilities $r_1, \ldots, r_m$, I's expected profit is $\Sigma_{i=1}^{m} a_{ij} r_i$.

The decision problem of each duopolist is to select an optimal set of probabilities. I fears that II will discover his strategy and that II will select a strategy of his own that will maximize his expected outcome, i.e., minimize the expected outcome for I. II has similar fears about I. The probabilities which the duopolists employ are defined as optimal if

$$\sum_{i=1}^{m} a_{ij} r_i \geqq V \qquad j = 1, \ldots, n \tag{9-50}$$

and

$$\sum_{j=1}^{n} a_{ij} s_j \leqq V \qquad i = 1, \ldots, m \tag{9-51}$$

where V is defined as the *value of the game*, The relations (9-50) state that I's expected profit is at least as great as V if II employs any of his pure strategies with a probability of one, and the relations (9-51) state that II's expected loss is at least as small as V if I employs any of his pure strategies with a probability of one. A fundamental theory-of-games theorem states that a solution [i.e., values for the rs and ss that satisfy (9-50) and (9-51)] always exists, and that V is unique.

If both duopolists select their strategies on a probabilistic basis, I's expected profit, E_1, can be determined from (9-50):

$$E_1 = \sum_{j=1}^{n} s_j \left(\sum_{i=1}^{m} a_{ij} r_i \right) \geq \sum_{j=1}^{n} s_j V$$

or

$$E_1 = \sum_{j=1}^{n} \sum_{i=1}^{m} a_{ij} r_i s_j \geq V \tag{9-52}$$

II's expected loss, E_2, can be determined from (9-51):

$$E_2 = \sum_{i=1}^{m} r_i \left(\sum_{j=1}^{n} a_{ij} s_j \right) \leq \sum_{i=1}^{m} r_i V$$

or

$$E_2 = \sum_{j=1}^{n} \sum_{i=1}^{m} a_{ij} r_i s_j \leq V \tag{9-53}$$

The middle terms in (9-52) and (9-53) are identical: I's expected profit equals II's expected loss. Combining (9-52) and (9-53):

$$V \leq E_1 = E_2 \leq V$$

which proves that

$$E_1 = E_2 = V$$

The expected outcome is the same for each of the duopolists and equals the value of the game if both employ their optimal probabilities. If I employs his optimal probabilities, his expected profit cannot be less than V, regardless of II's strategy choice. It will be greater than V if II employs a nonoptimal set of probabilities. Likewise, if II employs his optimal probabilities, his expected loss cannot be greater than V, regardless of I's strategy choice. It will be less if I employs a nonoptimal set of probabilities.

LINEAR-PROGRAMMING EQUIVALENCE

Optimal strategies for the duopolists and the value of the game can be determined by converting their game problems into a linear-programming format.   First,   consider   cases   in   which $V > 0$.   Define   the   variables

$$z_j = \frac{s_j}{V} \quad j = 1, \ldots, n \tag{9-54}$$

for duopolist II.   By this definition

$$\frac{1}{V} = z_1 + z_2 + \cdots + z_n \tag{9-55}$$

II desires to make his maximum expected loss as small as possible, or equivalently, he desires to make $1/V$ as large as possible.   His linear-programming equivalent is to find values for $z_j \geqq 0$ $(j = 1, \ldots, n)$ which   maximize   (9-55)   subject   to

$$a_{i1}z_1 + a_{i2}z_2 + \cdots + a_{in}z_n \leqq 1 \quad i = 1, \ldots, m \tag{9-56}$$

The relations of (9-56) are derived by dividing those of (9-51) by V and substituting from (9-54).

Define the variables

$$w_i = \frac{r_i}{V} \quad i = 1, \ldots, m \tag{9-57}$$

for duopolist I.   By this definition

$$\frac{1}{V} = w_1 + w_2 + \cdots + w_m \tag{9-58}$$

I desires to make his minimum expected profit as large as possible, or equivalently, he desires to make $1/V$ as small as possible.   His linear-programming equivalent is to find values for $w_i \geqq 0$ $(i = 1, \ldots, m)$ which   minimize   (9-58)   subject   to

$$a_{1j}w_1 + a_{2j}w_2 + \cdots + a_{mj}w_m \geqq 1 \quad j = 1, \ldots, n \tag{9-59}$$

The relations of (9-59) are derived by dividing those of (9-50) by V and substituting from (9-57).

The programming system for I given by (9-58) and (9-59) is the dual of the programming system for II given by (9-55) and (9-56).   The reciprocal of the value of the game is given by the maximum value for (9-55) which equals the minimum value of (9-58).   Using (9-54) and (9-57), the optimal probabilities for the duopolists are easily determined from the optimal values for the z_j and the w_i.

The linear-programming formulation facilitates a proof that solutions always exist for two-person, zero-sum games.   The proof proceeds by first establishing that finite optimal solutions always exist for the equivalent programming systems, and by then demonstrating that the optimal programming solutions provide a solution for the underlying game. Initially assume that all $a_{ij} > 0$. A feasible, but not optimal, solution for the programming system given by (9-55) and (9-56) is provided by $z_j = 0$ $(j = 1, \ldots, n)$. Let $a^0 = \min\limits_{i,j} a_{ij}$. A feasible solution for the programming system given by (9-58) and (9-59) is provided by $w_i = 1/a^0$ $(i = 1, \ldots, m)$. The existence of finite optimal solutions for the programming systems follows from a duality theorem stated in Sec. 9-2: If feasible solutions exist for a programming system and its dual, finite optimal solutions exist for both systems.

Let the optimum values of the programming variables be given by $z_1^*, \ldots, z_n^*$ and $w_1^*, \ldots, w_m^*$. At least one w_i^* must be positive since $w_i^* = 0$ $(i = 1, \ldots, m)$ is not feasible for (9-59). At least one z_j^* must be positive, for if all z_j^* were zero, all the constraints of (9-56) would be satisfied as strict inequalities. But then, as shown by the duality theorem expressed in (9-20), all w_i^* would equal zero, which has already been shown to be impossible. Since at least one w^* and at least one z^* must be positive, it is possible to equate the reciprocals of the optimal values of the objective functions (9-55) and (9-58):

$$V = \frac{1}{\sum\limits_{j=1}^{n} z_j^*} = \frac{1}{\sum\limits_{i=1}^{m} w_i^*}$$

and

$$V \sum_{j=1}^{n} z_j^* = V \sum_{i=1}^{m} w_i^* = 1$$

Substituting from (9-54) and (9-57),

$$\sum_{j=1}^{n} s_j = 1 \qquad s_j \geqq 0 \qquad \sum_{i=1}^{m} r_i = 1 \qquad r_i \geqq 0$$

which are the game probabilities. By substitution from (9-54) and (9-57) into (9-56) and (9-59), it is easily verified that these probabilities form a game solution as defined by (9-50) and (9-51).

Equations (9-52) and (9-53) define the value of the game as a weighted average of the elements of the profit matrix. It is necessary that V be positive in order to satisfy the nonnegativity requirements for the programming variables. However, in general, one cannot conclude that V is positive unless all the a_{ij} are positive. This difficulty is easily resolved by defining a modified game with a positive value. If one or more $a_{ij} \leqq 0$, select a number k with the property that $a_{ij} + k > 0$ for all

i and j, and add k to every element of the profit matrix. The value of the modified game exceeds the value of the initial game by k:

$$V' = \sum_{j=1}^{n} \sum_{i=1}^{m} (a_{ij} + k)r_i s_j = \sum_{j=1}^{n} \sum_{i=1}^{m} a_{ij}r_i s_j + k \sum_{j=1}^{n} \sum_{i=1}^{m} r_i s_j = V + k$$

(9-60)

and is positive by construction. The optimal probabilities for the initial and modified games are the same.[1] Therefore, a solution for the initial game can be obtained from a linear-programming solution for the modified game.

Return to the game given by (9-49). Let $k = 4$. The profit matrix for the modified game is

$$\begin{bmatrix} 2 & 8 \\ 7 & 3 \end{bmatrix}$$

II's linear-programming system is to find values for $z_1, z_2 \geq 0$ that maximize

$$\frac{1}{V'} = z_1 + z_2$$

subject to

$$2z_1 + 8z_2 \leq 1$$
$$7z_1 + 3z_2 \leq 1$$

An application of the methods of Sec. 9-3 gives the unique optimal solution $z_1 = 0.1$, $z_2 = 0.1$, $1/V' = 0.2$. Utilizing (9-54) and (9-60), II's optimal probabilities are $s_1 = 0.5$ and $s_2 = 0.5$ with $V = 1$. The reader may verify that the optimal solution for the dual programming system is $w_1 = 0.08$, $w_2 = 0.12$, which gives I's optimal probabilities as $r_1 = 0.4$ and $r_2 = 0.6$.

EXTENSIONS

An extension of the analysis to more complicated games is possible, but requires the use of mathematics beyond the scope of the present volume. An extension is a necessity for economic applications since the zero-sum requirement is seldom fulfilled in an actual market situation. The duopoly problem might be extended to a two-person, non-zero-sum game, or equivalently, to a three-person, zero-sum game in which the third person is an artificial entity—"Nature"—with outcomes equal to the

---

[1] See J. G. Kemeny, J. L. Snell, and G. L. Thompson, *Introduction to Finite Mathematics* (Englewood Cliffs, N.J.: Prentice-Hall, 1957), p. 291.

negative of the combined outcomes of the duopolists. The possibility of
coalitions arises in games containing three or more persons. For example,
the duopolists may act together in order to maximize industry profit.
In an oligopolistic market two or more of the participants may join
together to the detriment of their rivals. Unfortunately the convenient
linear-programming equivalence holds only for two-person, zero-sum
games.

9-5 THE INPUT–OUTPUT MODEL

The input-output model, sometimes called the Leontief model for its
originator W. W. Leontief, provides a linear multimarket analysis with
empirical orientation. Its assumptions represent a considerable simplification of the continuous multimarket equilibrium analysis given in Chap.
5. Utility functions are omitted, and consumer demands are usually
treated as exogenous without explicit regard to the equilibrium of individual consumers.[1] The industry, rather than the firm, is the unit of
production. Each industry uses a single linear production activity to
produce a single output. Both produced outputs and nonproduced
factors serve as inputs.

Output and price determination are first considered for general
input-output systems. The process of empirical implementation and the
special properties of empirical systems are then described. Finally,
alternative linear production activities are introduced, and the input-
output model is placed within a linear-programming format to allow
potential substitution among inputs.

OUTPUT DETERMINATION

Assume that an economy has m produced goods and n nonproduced factors. A linear production activity for the jth industry $(j = 1, \ldots ,m)$
gives the minimum quantities of the two types of inputs necessary to
secure one unit of the jth good: $a_{ij} \geqq 0$ $(i = 1, \ldots ,m)$ for the produced
inputs and $b_{ij} \geqq 0$ $(i = 1, \ldots ,n)$ for the factors. The output of the
ith industry, q_i, is absorbed by interindustry input uses and final consumption uses, y_i:

$$q_i = a_{i1}q_1 + a_{i2}q_2 + \cdots + a_{im}q_m + y_i \qquad i = 1, \ldots , m$$

---

[1] An "open" input-output system contains one or more exogenous sectors. All
sectors are endogenous in a "closed" system. Nearly all current analysis is for "open"
systems, and the description in the text is limited to these. The reader interested in
the properties of a closed system is referred to Wassily W. Leontief, *The Structure of
American Economy, 1919–1939* (2d ed.; New York: Oxford, 1951).

Moving the output variables to the left-hand side, the input-output balance equations may be written as

$$
\begin{aligned}
(1 - a_{11})q_1 - \quad a_{12}q_2 \quad - \cdots - \quad a_{1m}q_m \quad &= y_1 \\
-a_{21}q_1 + (1 - a_{22})q_2 - \cdots - \quad a_{2m}q_m \quad &= y_2 \\
\cdots\cdots\cdots\cdots\cdots\cdots\cdots\cdots\cdots\cdots\cdots\cdots\cdots\cdots \\
-a_{m1}q_1 - \quad a_{m2}q_2 \quad - \cdots + (1 - a_{mm})q_m &= y_m
\end{aligned}
\tag{9-61}
$$

The quantity of each good available for final consumption equals total output less interindustry input requirements.

Cramer's rule may be applied to express output levels as functions of final consumption levels if the determinant of the coefficient array of (9-61), $\mathbf{A}$, is not zero:

$$
\begin{aligned}
q_1 &= \beta_{11}y_1 + \beta_{12}y_2 + \cdots + \beta_{1m}y_m \\
q_2 &= \beta_{21}y_1 + \beta_{22}y_2 + \cdots + \beta_{2m}y_m \\
&\cdots\cdots\cdots\cdots\cdots\cdots\cdots\cdots\cdots \\
q_m &= \beta_{m1}y_1 + \beta_{m2}y_2 + \cdots + \beta_{mm}y_m
\end{aligned}
\tag{9-62}
$$

where $\beta_{ij} = \mathbf{A}_{ji}/\mathbf{A}$ is the cofactor of the element in the jth row and ith column of the array of (9-61), $\mathbf{A}_{ji}$, divided by the determinant of the array. Equations (9-62) provide a general solution for the input-output system (9-61) if $q_i \geqq 0$ $(i = 1, \ldots, m)$ whenever $y_i \geqq 0$ $(i = 1, \ldots, m)$. A necessary and sufficient condition for (9-62) to be a general solution is that $\beta_{ij} \geqq 0$ $(i,j = 1, \ldots, m)$. Existence conditions in terms of the a_{ij} are considered below. In the meantime limit attention to systems for which (9-62) is a general solution.

The coefficient β_{ij} for $i \neq j$ gives the direct and indirect input requirements for the ith good necessary to support one unit of final consumption of the jth. The direct requirement is a_{ij}. The indirect requirements are the inputs of i necessary to produce the inputs of the m goods necessary for j, the inputs necessary to produce those inputs, and so on. It follows that $\beta_{ij} \geqq a_{ij}$. The coefficient β_{jj} gives the direct and indirect input requirements of j for j and 1 to cover the unit of final consumption. It follows that $\beta_{jj} \geqq 1 + a_{jj}$.

Factor requirements are easily determined from output requirements:

$$
x_i = b_{i1}q_1 + b_{i2}q_2 + \cdots + b_{im}q_m \qquad i = 1, \ldots, n
$$

where x_i is the quantity of the ith nonproduced factor used as an input. Substituting for the q_j from (9-62),

$$
x_i = \gamma_{i1}y_1 + \gamma_{i2}y_2 + \cdots + \gamma_{im}y_m \qquad i = 1, \ldots, n
\tag{9-63}
$$

where

$$\gamma_{ij} = \sum_{h=1}^{m} b_{ih}\beta_{hj} = 0 \qquad \begin{array}{l} i = 1, \ldots, n \\ j = 1, \ldots, m \end{array} \tag{9-64}$$

The nonnegativity of the γ_{ij} follows from the nonnegativity of the b_{ih} and the β_{hj}. The coefficient γ_{ij} gives the quantity of the ith factor necessary to produce the quantities of the m goods which directly and indirectly support a final consumption unit of the jth good.

DECOMPOSABILITY

An input-output system is *decomposable* if it contains one or more self-sufficient groups of less than m industries each. Industries within a self-sufficient group do not require inputs from industries outside the group. The output levels of industries outside a self-sufficient group are independent of the output and final consumption levels of the industries within the group. The following five-industry system contains two self-sufficient groups:

$$\begin{bmatrix} a_{11} & a_{12} & a_{13} & a_{14} & 0 \\ a_{21} & a_{22} & a_{23} & a_{24} & a_{25} \\ 0 & 0 & a_{33} & a_{34} & a_{35} \\ 0 & 0 & a_{34} & a_{44} & a_{45} \\ 0 & 0 & 0 & 0 & a_{55} \end{bmatrix} \tag{9-65}$$

where the listed coefficients are positive. Industries 1 and 2 form a self-sufficient group. They secure inputs from each other, but not from the remaining three industries. The output levels of industries 3, 4, and 5 are unaffected by the output and final consumption levels of 1 and 2. Industries 1, 2, 3, and 4 form another self-sufficient group. They do not require inputs from 5, and 5's output level is independent of the output and final consumption levels of 3 and 4 as well as 1 and 2.

A decomposable input-output system can be solved by parts. If the coefficients of (9-65) are inserted in the balance equations (9-61), the fifth equation may be solved for q_5. Given q_5, the third and fourth equations may be solved for q_3 and q_4; and given q_3, q_4, and q_5, the first two equations may be solved for q_1 and q_2.

In general, the coefficient β_{ij} in (9-62) will equal zero if and only if the ith industry is outside a self-sufficient group which contains the jth. The direct and indirect requirements matrix that corresponds to (9-65) is

$$\begin{bmatrix} \beta_{11} & \beta_{12} & \beta_{13} & \beta_{14} & \beta_{15} \\ \beta_{21} & \beta_{22} & \beta_{23} & \beta_{24} & \beta_{25} \\ 0 & 0 & \beta_{33} & \beta_{34} & \beta_{35} \\ 0 & 0 & \beta_{43} & \beta_{44} & \beta_{45} \\ 0 & 0 & 0 & 0 & \beta_{55} \end{bmatrix}$$

where the listed coefficients are positive.   An *indecomposable* system contains no self-sufficient groups, and thereby, all the β_{ij} are positive.

An input-output system is *completely decomposable* if each industry is contained in a self-sufficient group of less than m industries.   For example,

$$
\begin{bmatrix}
a_{11} & a_{12} & 0 & 0 \\
a_{21} & a_{22} & 0 & 0 \\
0 & 0 & a_{33} & a_{34} \\
0 & 0 & a_{43} & a_{44}
\end{bmatrix}
$$

Industries 1 and 2 only secure inputs from each other, and industries 3 and 4 only secure inputs from each other.   Output levels for each group may be determined without regard to the output and final consumption levels of the other.   If a system is completely decomposable, $\beta_{ij} > 0$ for i and j in the same self-sufficient group, and $\beta_{ij} = 0$ for i and j in different groups.

EXISTENCE

The mere formulation of an input-output system does not guarantee that it has a general solution with $q_i \geqq 0$ $(i = 1, \ldots, m)$ for all $y_i \geqq 0$ $(i = 1, \ldots, m)$.   Two equivalent, but rather different, sets of necessary and sufficient conditions for the existence of a general solution are presented here.   The *Hawkins-Simon conditions*[1] require that all the principal minors of the coefficient array of (9-61) be positive:

$$
1 - a_{11} > 0, \quad \begin{vmatrix} 1 - a_{11} & -a_{12} \\ -a_{21} & 1 - a_{22} \end{vmatrix} > 0,
$$

$$
\ldots, \quad \begin{vmatrix} 1 - a_{11} & \cdots & -a_{1m} \\ \cdots\cdots\cdots\cdots\cdots\cdots \\ -a_{m1} & \cdots & 1 - a_{mm} \end{vmatrix} > 0 \quad (9\text{-}66)
$$

The first and subsequent inequalities of (9-66) require that $a_{ii} < 1$ $(i = 1, \ldots, m)$.   If $a_{ii} \geqq 1$ for some i, one or more units of i would be required to produce one unit of i.   No net output can be secured under such circumstances.   The last condition of (9-66) requires that the determinant of (9-61) be positive.   This implies that all the principal cofactors of (9-61) are nonnegative if a general solution exists.

An equivalent set of necessary and sufficient conditions for the existence of a general solution concerns the column sums of the input

---

[1] See David Hawkins and Herbert A. Simon, "Note: Some Conditions of Macroeconomic Stability," *Econometrica*, vol. 17 (July–October, 1949), pp. 245–248.

coefficients. These conditions require that there exist a set of numbers $d_j > 0$ $(j = 1, \ldots, m)$ such that

$$\sum_{i=1}^{m} d_i\, a_{ij} \leq d_j \qquad j = 1, \ldots, m \tag{9-67}$$

with the strict inequality holding for at least one j in each self-sufficient group of industries.[1] If a system is indecomposable, the strict inequality need hold for only one industry.

PRICE AND INCOME DETERMINATION

Applying the competitive condition that price equals unit cost for each industry,

$$p_j = a_{1j}p_1 + \cdots + a_{mj}p_m + b_{1j}r_1 + \cdots + b_{nj}r_n$$
$$j = 1, \ldots, m$$

where p_i $(i = 1, \ldots, m)$ and r_i $(i = 1, \ldots, n)$ are the prices of goods and factors respectively. By rearranging terms,

$$
\begin{aligned}
(1 - a_{11})p_1 - \quad a_{21}p_2 \quad - \cdots - \quad a_{m1}p_m &= v_1 \\
-a_{12}p_1 \quad + (1 - a_{22})p_2 - \cdots - \quad a_{m2}p_m &= v_2 \\
\cdots\cdots\cdots\cdots\cdots\cdots\cdots\cdots\cdots\cdots\cdots\cdots \\
-a_{1m}p_1 \quad - \quad a_{2m}p_2 \quad - \cdots + (1 - a_{mm})p_m &= v_m
\end{aligned}
\tag{9-68}
$$

where

$$v_j = b_{1j}r_1 + b_{2j}r_2 + \cdots + b_{nj}r_n \qquad j = 1, \ldots, m \tag{9-69}$$

is the *value added* per unit of the jth output.

The coefficient array on the left of (9-68) is the same as the array on the left of (9-61) except that the rows and columns are interchanged. The determinant values of the two arrays are equal, and the cofactor of the element in the ith row and jth column of one array equals the cofactor of the element in the jth row and ith column of the other. The solution of (9-68) for the p_js is

$$
\begin{aligned}
p_1 &= \beta_{11}v_1 + \beta_{21}v_2 + \cdots + \beta_{m1}v_m \\
p_2 &= \beta_{12}v_1 + \beta_{22}v_2 + \cdots + \beta_{m2}v_m \\
\cdots\cdots\cdots\cdots\cdots\cdots\cdots\cdots\cdots \\
p_m &= \beta_{1m}v_1 + \beta_{2m}v_2 + \cdots + \beta_{mm}v_m
\end{aligned}
\tag{9-70}
$$

where the β_{ij} are the same as the coefficients in (9-62) with rows and columns of the arrays interchanged. If (9-62) is a general solution for

[1] A proof is given by Lionel McKenzie, "Matrices with Dominant Diagonals and Economic Theory," in K. J. Arrow, S. Karlin, and P. Suppes (eds.), *Mathematical Methods in the Social Sciences, 1959* (Stanford, Calif.: Stanford, 1960), p. 50.

(9-61) with $\beta_{ij} \geqq 0$ $(i, j = 1, \ldots, m)$, it follows that (9-70) is a general solution for (9-68), that is, $p_j \geqq 0$ $(j = 1, \ldots, m)$ for all $r_i \geqq 0$ $(i = 1, \ldots, n)$.

Substituting from (9-69) and (9-64), (9-70) may be written as

$$p_j = \gamma_{1j}r_1 + \gamma_{2j}r_2 + \cdots + \gamma_{nj}r_n \qquad j = 1, \ldots, m \qquad (9\text{-}71)$$

The price of each good equals the value of the factors which are directly and indirectly required for its production. If (9-70) is a general solution, a necessary and sufficient condition that the prices of all goods be positive is that at least one factor with positive price be required for the production of at least one good in each self-sufficient group. An indecomposable system has the minimum requirement that one factor with positive price be required for the production of one good.

If an input-output system has only one nonproduced factor, its price may be set at unity, and (9-71) may be solved for the prices of produced goods in factor units. If a system has more than one factor, additional information is required for a determination of the r_i, and consequently, the p_j.

Income at market price equals the value of the final consumption levels. Substituting first from (9-71) and then from (9-63),

$$\sum_{j=1}^{m} p_j y_j = \sum_{i=1}^{n} \sum_{j=1}^{m} r_i \gamma_{ij} y_j = \sum_{i=1}^{n} r_i x_i$$

Income at market price equals income at factor cost, or put in another way, factor payments just exhaust the value of net output.

EMPIRICAL SYSTEMS

The input-output model serves as a social accounting framework as well as a tool for analysis. Systems with empirically derived coefficients have been established for many countries. The construction of an inter-industry transaction table for a base year is the major task of implementation. Transactions for the base year 1972 for a hypothetical economy with two industries and two factors are presented in Table 9-1. An industry's output distribution is described by its row, and its input purchases by its column. Reading across the first row, industry 1 used 2,000 million dollars of its output as an intra-industry input, delivered 6,400 million to industry 2 for use as an input, and delivered 1,600 million to the two final consumption sectors. Reading down the first column, the inputs of industry 1 consisted of 2,000 million dollars of its own output, 6,000 million of the output of industry 2, and 1,000 million of each factor, i.e., each value-added category. The *other* value-added category includes profits. Consequently, the value of the output of each industry equals the sum of its column entries as well as the sum of its row entries.

Table 9-1   Interindustry transactions, 1972
(In millions of dollars)

Industry	1	2	Final consumption Households	Other	Totals
1	2,000	6,400	1,000	600	10,000
2	6,000	4,800	4,000	1,200	16,000
Value added:					
Labor	1,000	3,200	.....	.....	4,200
Other	1,000	1,600	.....	.....	2,600
Totals	10,000	16,000	5,000	1,800	32,800

Two final consumption sectors are recognized in Table 9-1. The *other* sector includes all output deliveries other than those for current inputs and those to households. It includes deliveries to governments and foreign countries. Since the model is static, investment uses and inventory change are also included. The reader may verify that the sum of the final consumption totals, 6,800, equals the sum of the value-added (factor payment) totals.

A transactions table is stated in terms of monetary values for a base year. Its entries may be interpreted as physical units if it is assumed that each industry produces a single homogeneous output which is sold at a uniform price. The physical unit for each industry is the quantity of its output which could be purchased for one monetary unit during the base year. This definition sets the base-year price of each good and factor at unity.

Average input-output coefficients are computed by dividing the produced and factor inputs of each industry by its output level. The average coefficients are interpreted as the constant a_{ij} and b_{ij} of the general input-output model. Table 9-2 contains coefficients computed from Table 9-1. Since the sum of the column entries for an industry in Table 9-1 equals the industry's output level, the column sums of the coefficients in Table 9-2 equal one. Each industry in an empirical system requires

Table 9-2   Direct requirements per dollar of output, 1972

Industry	1	2
1	0.2	0.4
2	0.6	0.3
Labor	0.1	0.2
Other	0.1	0.1
Totals	1.0	1.0

Table 9-3   Direct and indirect requirements per dollar of final consumption, 1972

Industry	1	2
1	2.18750	1.25000
2	1.87500	2.50000
Labor	0.59375	0.62500
Other	0.40625	0.37500

factor inputs.   Therefore, the column sums of coefficients for produced inputs will be less than one:

$$\sum_{i=1}^{m} a_{ij} < 1 \qquad j = 1, \ldots, m$$

These column sums satisfy existence conditions (9-67) with $d_j = 1$ ($j = 1$, . . . ,m).   Thus, an empirical system always has a general solution with $\beta_{ij} \geqq 0$ ($i, j = 1, \ldots, m$) and $\gamma_{ij} \geqq 0$ ($i = 1, \ldots, n; j = 1, \ldots, m$).

The β_{ij} and γ_{ij} for the hypothetical economy are given in Table 9-3. Some 2.18750 units of good 1 and 1.87500 units of good 2 are required to support the delivery of one unit of good 1 to final consumption.   The corresponding direct and indirect factor requirements are 0.59375 units of labor and 0.40625 units of the other factor.   The sum of the direct and indirect factor requirements for each good equals unity as a result of the unit price definitions for empirical systems.

THE SUBSTITUTION THEOREM

If an input-output system has a general solution, produced and factor input levels are uniquely determined for any specified set of final consumption requirements.   There is no opportunity for substitution among inputs.   In Sec. 9-1 it is shown that a degree of input substitution is possible in the production of a good if more than one linear activity is available. The input-output model is easily extended to allow multiple production activities for each good.   No essentials are lost by assuming that each industry has the same number, u, of linear production activities.   Let a_{ij}^k denote the quantity of the ith good required to produce a unit of the jth using the kth activity for the jth, and let q_j^k denote the output level of the kth activity for the jth good.   The existence of multiple activities suggests that a prescribed set of final demands may be met by alternative sets of produced and factor input levels.

If an economy has only one scarce factor, it desires to minimize the quantity of that factor, x, necessary to meet its final consumption requirements. This optimization problem may be placed within the linear-programming format: select nonnegative output levels, $q_j^k \geqq 0$ ($k = 1$, . . . ,u; $j = 1$, . . . ,m), that minimize

$$x = \sum_{k=1}^{u} \sum_{j=1}^{m} b_j^k q_j^k \tag{9-72}$$

where b_j^k is the unit factor requirement of the kth activity for the jth good, subject to the conditions that the net output of each good be sufficient to meet its final consumption requirement:

$$\sum_{k=1}^{u} [(1 - a_{11}^k)q_1^k - a_{12}^k q_2^k - \cdots - a_{1m}^k q_m^k] \geqq y_1$$

$$\sum_{k=1}^{u} [-a_{21}^k q_1^k + (1 - a_{22}^k)q_2^k - \cdots - a_{2m}^k q_m^k] \geqq y_2 \tag{9-73}$$

$$\cdots \cdots \cdots \cdots \cdots \cdots \cdots \cdots \cdots \cdots \cdots \cdots \cdots$$

$$\sum_{k=1}^{u} [-a_{m1}^k q_1^k - a_{m2}^k q_2^k - \cdots + (1 - a_{mm}^k)q_m^k] \geqq y_m$$

Assume for the moment that $y_i > 0$ ($i = 1$, . . . ,m).

The feasible point set given by (9-73) and the nonnegativity constraints have several properties of interest. At least one activity for each good must be operated at a positive level in order to meet the positive consumption requirements. In general, a basic feasible solution (BFS) for a linear-programming system with m constraints has no more than m variables at positive levels (see Sec. 9-3). These properties taken together imply that every BFS for the programming system is an input-output system with one and only one production activity for each of the m goods. Each combination of m activities, one for each good, drawn from the um available activities constitutes an input-output system. There are u^m such systems. The systems which have general solutions provide the BFSs for the programming problem. The selection of an optimal BFS implies the selection of an optimal input-output system. To avoid trivial cases, limit attention to economies that have at least two feasible input-output systems.

The dual programming system[1] for (9-72) and (9-73) is to find values for $p_i \geqq 0$ ($i = 1$, . . . ,m) that maximize

$$I = \sum_{i=1}^{m} p_i y_i \tag{9-74}$$

---

[1] The initial system (9-72) and (9-73) is in the same format as the general dual system given by (9-18) and (9-19), and the dual system (9-74) and (9-75) is in the same format as the general initial system given by (9-16) and (9-17). The duality theorems of linear programming are symmetric and hold regardless of the classification of the two systems as initial and dual.

subject to

$$
\begin{aligned}
(1 - a_{11}^1)p_1 - \quad a_{21}^1 p_2 \quad - \cdots - \quad a_{m1}^1 p_m &\leqq b_1^1 \\
-a_{12}^1 p_1 \quad + (1 - a_{22}^1)p_2 - \cdots - \quad a_{m2}^1 p_m &\leqq b_2^1
\end{aligned}
$$

$$
\begin{aligned}
-a_{1m}^1 p_1 \quad - \quad a_{2m}^1 p_2 \quad - \cdots + (1 - a_{mm}^1)p_m &\leqq b_m^1 \\
(1 - a_{11}^2)p_1 - \quad a_{21}^2 p_2 \quad - \cdots - \quad a_{m1}^2 p_m &\leqq b_1^2
\end{aligned} \qquad (9\text{-}75)
$$

$$
-a_{1m}^u p_1 \quad - \quad a_{2m}^u p_2 \quad - \cdots + (1 - a_{mm}^u)p_m \leqq b_m^u
$$

The dual variables are the prices of the m goods measured in factor units. By rearranging terms, the constraints (9-75) may be written

$$
p_j \leqq \sum_{i=1}^m a_{ij}^k p_i + b_j^k \qquad k = 1, \ldots, u \qquad j = 1, \ldots, m
$$

This is the familiar condition that unit revenue (in factor units) is less than or equal to unit cost (in factor units) for each of the linear production activities. The duality theorem stated by (9-22) ensures the competitive condition that price equals cost for each activity operated at a positive level in the optimal input-output system, and (9-26) ensures the equality of the optimal values of income at factor cost (9-72) and income at market value (9-74).

The introduction of the possibility of substitution leads to questions about the constancy of empirical input-output coefficients. Will the coefficients remain at their observed base-year values as final consumption requirements change from their base-year values? The substitution theorem for input-output models answers: yes. Specifically, it states that an input-output system is optimal for all $y_i \geqq 0$ $(i = 1, \ldots, m)$ if it is optimal for any particular set of values for the y_is. This theorem follows easily from a parametric property of linear-programming systems: a change in the requirements for a system will leave the set of activities contained in its optimal BFS unchanged if they remain feasible.[1] Since the optimal input-output system has a general solution, its output levels will be nonnegative for all nonnegative final consumption requirements, and the substitution theorem is established. Output levels will be changed by changes in final consumption requirements, but the prices of goods are unaffected. The substitution theorem might be called the non-substitution theorem. Substitution is possible, but it is never observed

[1] This is evident for the general programming system given by (9-29) and (9-30). Its optimality criteria (9-39) do not contain the requirements (the k_i), and are unaffected by changes in their values. A proof of the substitution theorem is given by David Gale, *Theory of Linear Economic Models* (New York: McGraw-Hill, 1960), pp. 303–305.

in a one-factor economy. The substitution theorem is not valid for economies with more than one factor.

9-6 SUMMARY

A linear production activity is characterized by fixed proportions for input and output levels. A linear production function is formed from a number of linear activities that may be used simultaneously. Input substitution is possible if two or more linear activities are available for an output.

Linear programming covers the maximization of a linear function of n nonnegative variables subject to m linear inequality constraints. The nonnegative points in n-dimensional space that satisfy the constraints of a linear-programming system form its feasible point set. The set is closed, convex, and bounded from below. If a finite maximum value for the objective function exists, it will occur at one or more extreme points of the feasible point set. A finite maximum will exist if the feasible set is bounded from above and is not null.

A linear-programming system with n variables and m constraints has a dual system with m variables and n constraints. The variables of one system give the marginal values of the constraints of the other. The optimal values of the objective functions of the two systems are equal. In economics quantities are often the variables of one system, and prices the variables of the other.

Linear-programming constraints are converted to equations by adding "slack" variables. A basic feasible solution (BFS) is a nonnegative solution for the m constraint equations in m variables. There is a one-to-one correspondence between BFSs and extreme points of the feasible point set. The revised simplex method is an iterative procedure for the determination of an optimal BFS.

A duopolistic market is sometimes treated as a two-person, zero-sum game. Each duopolist selects probabilities for a finite number of strategies that maximize the expected value of his profit given the most unfavorable strategy choice on the part of his rival. The expected profit of one duopolist (which equals the expected loss of the other) equals the value of the game if both assign optimal probabilities to their strategies. Linear-programming methods can be used to obtain a numerical solution for a two-person, zero-sum game.

A single linear production activity is used for each of m goods in the input-output model. Produced outputs and nonproduced factors serve as inputs. A general solution for an input-output system gives outputs as linear functions of deliveries to final consumption. A system is decomposable if it contains one or more self-sufficient groups of less than m

industries.   Competitive (zero-profit) prices for the produced goods can be derived from factor prices.   Empirical input-output systems are based upon interindustry transaction tables.   The input-output model can be generalized to allow more than one activity per good.   The substitution theorem states that input substitution will not take place in an economy with multiple production activities if there is only one nonproduced factor.

EXERCISES

9-1. A linear production function contains four activities for the production of one output using two inputs.   The input requirements per unit output are

$$a_{11} = 1 \quad\quad a_{12} = 2 \quad\quad a_{13} = 3 \quad\quad a_{14} = 5$$
$$a_{21} = 6 \quad\quad a_{22} = 5 \quad\quad a_{23} = 3 \quad\quad a_{24} = 2$$

Plot isoquants for 1, 2, and 3 units of output.

9-2. Plot the feasible point set and use graphic methods to solve the following linear-programming system: maximize

$$y = 3z_1 - z_2$$

subject to

$$z_1 - 2z_2 \leqq 4$$
$$-z_1 - z_2 \leqq -6$$
$$z_1 + 2z_2 \leqq 12$$
$$z_1, z_2 \geqq 0$$

9-3. Form the dual system for the following linear-programming system: minimize

$$y = 6z_1 + 2z_2 + z_3$$

subject to

$$3z_1 + 2z_2 \quad\quad \geqq 10$$
$$z_1 + 5z_2 + z_3 \geqq 8$$
$$z_1, z_2, z_3 \geqq 0$$

9-4. The following programming system has an unbounded solution: maximize

$$y = 2z_1 + 3z_2$$

subject to

$$-3z_1 + 2z_2 \leqq 4$$
$$z_1 - 2z_2 \leqq 6$$
$$z_1, z_2 \geqq 0$$

Demonstrate that its dual system has no feasible solution.

9-5. Each of n linear activities yields s outputs and uses m inputs as described by (9-7).   An entrepreneur possesses fixed quantities of each of the inputs.   He desires to maximize his total revenue from the sale of the outputs at constant market prices.   Formulate his optimization problem as a linear-programming system, and derive its dual programming system.

9-6. Solve the following linear-programming system by complete enumeration of its BFSs: maximize

$$y = z_1 + 2z_2 + 3z_3$$

subject to

$$z_1 + 2z_2 + 4z_3 \leq 12$$
$$2z_1 \qquad + 2z_3 \leq 12$$
$$z_1, z_2, z_3 \geq 0$$

9-7. Use the revised simplex method to solve the following linear-programming system and its dual system: maximize

$$y = 3z_1 + 2z_2 + z_3$$

subject to

$$z_1 + 2z_2 + 4z_3 \leq 30$$
$$4z_1 + 2z_2 + z_3 \leq 60$$
$$z_1, z_2, z_3 \geq 0$$

9-8. How would the optimal solutions for Exercise 9-7 be altered if the constant for the second constraint were increased from 60 to 66 with the other parameters of the system unchanged?

9-9. Find optimal strategies for the participants in a two-person, zero-sum game with the following profit matrix:

$$\begin{bmatrix} 4 & -2 \\ -3 & 1 \end{bmatrix}$$

What is the value of the game?

9-10. The a_{ij} coefficients for a three-industry, input-output system are

$$\begin{bmatrix} 0.2 & 0.1 & 0.6 \\ 0.5 & 0.4 & 0.4 \\ 0.1 & 0.4 & 0.2 \end{bmatrix}$$

Use the Hawkins-Simon conditions to determine whether this system has a general solution.

9-11. Use the column-sum conditions given by (9-67) to determine whether the input-output system of Exercise 9-10 has a general solution.

9-12. The following interindustry transactions table was constructed for an economy for the year 1973:

Industry	1	2	Final consumption	Totals
1	500	1,600	400	2,500
2	1,750	1,600	4,650	8,000
Labor	250	4,800	.....	5,050
Totals	2,500	8,000	5,050	15,550

Construct tables similar to Tables 9-2 and 9-3 from this transactions table.

*9-13. A farm entrepreneur desires to maximize his profit from four linear production activities. Rye, barley, and corn are the respective outputs of the first three activities. Land, labor, and fertilizer are the inputs for each. Beef is the output of the fourth. Its inputs are labor, feeder cattle, and corn. The entrepreneur has fixed quantities of land and labor. He can purchase fertilizer and feeder cattle at fixed prices. He can sell rye, barley, and beef at fixed prices. He can neither buy nor sell corn. Formulate his optimization problem in the linear-programming format. Derive and interpret the dual system.

*9-14. Let the profit matrix of a two-person, zero-sum game have elements a_{ij} ($i = 1$, . . . ,m; $j = 1$, . . . ,n), and let r_i ($i = 1$, . . . ,m) and s_j ($j = 1$, . . . ,n) be the optimal probabilities for participants I and II respectively. Prove that these probabilities are also optimal for a game with profit elements $a_{ij} + k$ where k is a constant.

SELECTED REFERENCES

Baumol, W. J., *Economic Theory and Operations Analysis* (Englewood Cliffs, N.J.: Prentice-Hall, 1961). Linear programming and game theory are the subjects of chaps. 5 and 18 respectively.

Chiang, Alpha C., *Fundamental Methods of Mathematical Economics* (New York: McGraw-Hill, 1967). Linear models and the underlying mathematics are developed in chaps. 4, 5, and 18–20.

Dantzig, George P., *Linear Programming and Extensions* (Princeton, N.J.: Princeton, 1963). A comprehensive and advanced treatise on linear programming and related techniques.

Dorfman, R., P. A. Samuelson, and R. Solow, *Linear Programming and Economic Analysis* (New York: McGraw-Hill, 1958). An elementary presentation of linear programming and the input-output model.

Gale, David, *The Theory of Linear Economic Models* (New York: McGraw-Hill, 1960). An original approach to linear programming, games, and input-output. The necessary advanced mathematics are summarized in chap. 2.

Hadley, G., *Linear Programming* (Reading, Mass.: Addison-Wesley, 1962). A text with economic applications. Matrix algebra and point-set theory are used.

Leontief, Wassily W., *The Structure of American Economy, 1919–1939* (2d ed.; New York: Oxford, 1951). A description of the input-output model by its originator.

Miernyk, William H., *The Elements of Input-Output Analysis* (New York: Random House, 1965). An elementary nonmathematical description of empirical systems.

Neumann, J. von, and O. Morgenstern, *The Theory of Games and Economic Behavior* (2d. ed.; Princeton, N.J.: Princeton, 1947). The original application of the theory of games to economic behavior. Mathematical concepts are developed as needed.

Mathematical Review

This appendix contains a brief review of some of the mathematical concepts that are used in the text. Rigorous proofs are generally omitted; in fact, many statements are not proved at all.

The major tools of analysis are algebra and differential and integral calculus. The solution of simultaneous equations and the use of determinants are outlined in Sec. A-1. The fundamentals of differential calculus with respect to functions of a single variable are discussed in Sec. A-2. The analysis is extended to functions of many variables, and the applications of partial differentiation are discussed in Sec. A-3. The basic properties of integrals are reviewed in Sec. A-4, and the appendix ends with discussions of difference and differential equations in Secs. A-5 and A-6 respectively.

A-1   SIMULTANEOUS EQUATIONS AND DETERMINANTS

A system of n equations in n variables can be written as

$$
\begin{aligned}
a_{11}x_1 + a_{12}x_2 + \cdots + a_{1n}x_n &= b_1 \\
a_{21}x_1 + a_{22}x_2 + \cdots + a_{2n}x_n &= b_2 \\
\cdots \cdots \cdots \cdots \cdots \cdots \cdots \cdots \cdots & \\
a_{n1}x_1 + a_{n2}x_2 + \cdots + a_{nn}x_n &= b_n
\end{aligned}
\tag{A-1}
$$

where the as are coefficients and the bs constant terms. Any set of n numbers that preserves all n of the equalities in (A-1) when substituted for the xs is a solution for this system. A simple example of a system of simultaneous equations is

$$
\begin{aligned}
3x_1 - 5x_2 &= 11 \\
x_1 + 2x_2 &= 11
\end{aligned}
$$

Its only solution is $x_1 = 7$, $x_2 = 2$.

A determinant is a number derived from a square array of numbers according to rules to be specified. It is denoted either by vertical lines on both sides of the array from which it is calculated or by a boldface letter. If A denotes the array,[1] $\mathbf{A}$ denotes its determinant:

$$
\mathbf{A} =
\begin{vmatrix}
a_{11} & a_{12} & \cdots & a_{1n} \\
a_{21} & a_{22} & \cdots & a_{2n} \\
\cdots & \cdots & \cdots & \cdots \\
a_{n1} & a_{n2} & \cdots & a_{nn}
\end{vmatrix}
$$

The *elements* of the matrix A are the coefficients a_{ij} where the first subscript is the *row index* and the second subscript the *column index*. Thus a_{57} is the element in the fifth row and seventh column of the array.

The rule by which a determinant is calculated from an array is merely stated here.[2] Products of numbers (or elements) are formed from A such that each product contains one and only one element from each row and one and only one element from each column. Thus a determinant is defined only for square arrays. All such products can be written with the row indices in natural order $(1,2,3, \ldots ,n)$. Examples are the products $a_{11}a_{22} \cdots a_{nn}$ and $a_{12}a_{21}a_{33} \cdots a_{nn}$. If the number

---

[1] Any rectangular array of numbers is called a *matrix*. A matrix with m rows and n columns is of the order $(m \times n)$. An $(m \times 1)$ matrix is a column vector, and a $(1 \times m)$ matrix is a row vector. The terms "array" and "matrix" are used interchangeably.

[2] For more extensive discussion see A. C. Aitken, *Determinants and Matrices* (New York: Interscience, 1951), chap. II; S. Perlis, *Theory of Matrices* (Cambridge, Mass.: Addison-Wesley, 1952), chap. IV; or G. Birkhoff and S. MacLane, *A Survey of Modern Algebra* (rev. ed.; New York: Macmillan, 1953), chap. X.

of *inversions*[1] among the column indices is even, the sign of the product is left unchanged.   If the number of inversions among the column indices is odd, it is changed from minus to plus or from plus to minus.   The value of the determinant is the algebraic sum of all such products.   Consider the determinant

$$\mathbf{A} = \begin{vmatrix} a_{11} & a_{12} \\ a_{21} & a_{22} \end{vmatrix} = a_{11}a_{22} - a_{12}a_{21}$$

Only two products can be formed from the matrix A according to the rule stated above.   A negative sign precedes the second term, since it contains one inversion (an odd number) of the column subscripts when the row subscripts are written in natural order.[2]

If the matrix is[3]

$$\begin{bmatrix} 3 & 2 \\ -1 & 4 \end{bmatrix}$$

the determinant is $12 + 2 = 14$.

The above rule is very cumbersome if the matrix contains a large number of rows and columns.   Generally, a determinant is more easily evaluated by an expansion in terms of *cofactors*.   For any element a_{ij} of the matrix A form an array by striking out the ith row and the jth column of the original matrix.   The determinant of the remaining array, which contains $(n - 1)$ rows and $(n - 1)$ columns, is the *minor* of the element a_{ij}.†   The cofactor of this element is its minor multiplied by $+1$ if

[1] An inversion is an instance in which a lower index follows a higher one.   For example, the indices 1, 2 are in natural order; the sequence 2, 1 contains one inversion.   The sequence 1, 3, 2, 5, 4 contains two inversions, since it contains two instances in which a lower index follows a higher one: 3 comes before 2, and 5 before 4.   The sequence 4, 3, 2, 1, 5 contains six inversions.

[2] The same result is obtained by counting the number of inversions among row subscripts when the column subscripts are written in natural order.   The reader may check that if a matrix has n rows and n columns, the number of terms in the expression for its determinant is $n!$ (read "n factorial"), that is, $n \cdot (n - 1) \cdots 3 \cdot 2 \cdot 1$. See Aitken, *op. cit.*, pp. 26–36.

[3] The matrix or the array itself is written with square or round brackets.   The operation of forming the determinant, however, is indicated by vertical bars instead of brackets.

† The diagonal of the array running in northwest-southeast direction is the principal diagonal.   Minors of elements on the principal diagonal (i.e., of a_{11}, a_{22}, etc.) are called principal minors.   The principal minor of a_{11} in the original determinant $\mathbf{A}$ is a determinant of the order $(n - 1) \times (n - 1)$ and is denoted by $\mathbf{A}_{11}$.   The principal minor of a_{22} in the minor $\mathbf{A}_{11}$ is a determinant of order $(n - 2) \times (n - 2)$ and is denoted by $\mathbf{A}_{11,22}$.   This $(n - 2) \times (n - 2)$ determinant is itself a principal minor of the original determinant.

$(i + j)$ is even and by -1 if $(i + j)$ is odd. The determinant $\mathbf{A}$ can be written as

$$\mathbf{A} = a_{i1}\mathbf{C}_{i1} + a_{i2}\mathbf{C}_{i2} + \cdot\,\cdot\,\cdot + a_{in}\mathbf{C}_{in}$$

for any given row index i where $\mathbf{C}_{ij}$ is the cofactor of the element in the ith row and jth column. Similarly,

$$\mathbf{A} = a_{1j}\mathbf{C}_{1j} + a_{2j}\mathbf{C}_{2j} + \cdot\,\cdot\,\cdot + a_{nj}\mathbf{C}_{nj}$$

for any column index j. Since a determinant can be expanded in terms of any single row or column, the multiplication of any row or column of the array A by a number k changes the value of the determinant by the same multiple.

Imagine that the ith row of the matrix is multiplied by k. Then expanding the new determinant in terms of the ith row and denoting it by $\mathbf{A}^*$,

$$\mathbf{A}^* = ka_{i1}\mathbf{C}_{i1} + ka_{i2}\mathbf{C}_{i2} + \cdot\,\cdot\,\cdot + ka_{in}\mathbf{C}_{in} = k\mathbf{A}$$

The expansion

$$a_{i1}\mathbf{C}_{j1} + a_{i2}\mathbf{C}_{j2} + \cdot\,\cdot\,\cdot + a_{in}\mathbf{C}_{jn} \qquad \text{for } i \neq j$$

is an expansion by *alien cofactors* and equals zero.[1] Using this theorem it can be proved that adding a multiple of any row (or column) to any other row (or column) leaves the value of the determinant unchanged. For example, multiply the jth row by k, add it to the ith row, and denote the new determinant by $\mathbf{A}^{**}$. Expanding $\mathbf{A}^{**}$ in terms of its ith row:

$$
\begin{aligned}
\mathbf{A}^{**} &= (a_{i1} + ka_{j1})\mathbf{C}_{i1} + (a_{i2} + ka_{j2})\mathbf{C}_{i2} + \cdot\,\cdot\,\cdot + (a_{in} + ka_{jn})C_{in} \\
&= a_{i1}\mathbf{C}_{i1} + a_{i2}\mathbf{C}_{i2} + \cdot\,\cdot\,\cdot + a_{in}\mathbf{C}_{in} \\
&\qquad\qquad\qquad + k(a_{j1}\mathbf{C}_{i1} + a_{j2}\mathbf{C}_{i2} + \cdot\,\cdot\,\cdot + a_{jn}\mathbf{C}_{in}) \\
&= \mathbf{A}
\end{aligned}
$$

since the term in parentheses in the second equation is an expansion by alien cofactors and therefore equals zero.

The system of simultaneous equations in (A-1) can be solved by *Cramer's rule*, which states that the solution for x_j is given by the ratio of two determinants, the denominator being the determinant of the coefficients of the system of equations and the numerator being the determinant of the coefficients with the jth column replaced by the column of constant terms, provided that the determinant in the denominator does not vanish. First applying the rule that multiplying a column of the array multiplies the value of the determinant by the same number and then applying the rule that adding multiples of one column to some other

[1] See Birkhoff and MacLane, *op. cit.*, p. 286.

column does not alter the value of the determinant, the solution for x_1 is derived as follows:

$$x_1\mathbf{A} = \begin{vmatrix} a_{11}x_1 & a_{12} & \cdots & a_{1n} \\ a_{21}x_1 & a_{22} & \cdots & a_{2n} \\ \vdots & & & \vdots \\ a_{n1}x_1 & a_{n2} & \cdots & a_{nn} \end{vmatrix} = \begin{vmatrix} a_{11}x_1 + a_{12}x_2 & a_{12} & \cdots & a_{1n} \\ a_{21}x_1 + a_{22}x_2 & a_{22} & \cdots & a_{2n} \\ \vdots & & & \vdots \\ a_{n1}x_1 + a_{n2}x_2 & a_{n2} & \cdots & a_{nn} \end{vmatrix}$$

$$= \cdots = \begin{vmatrix} a_{11}x_1 + a_{12}x_2 + \cdots + a_{1n}x_n & a_{12} & \cdots & a_{1n} \\ a_{21}x_1 + a_{22}x_2 + \cdots + a_{2n}x_n & a_{22} & \cdots & a_{2n} \\ \vdots & & & \vdots \\ a_{n1}x_1 + a_{n2}x_2 + \cdots + a_{nn}x_n & a_{n2} & \cdots & a_{nn} \end{vmatrix}$$

$$= \begin{vmatrix} b_1 & a_{12} & \cdots & a_{1n} \\ b_2 & a_{22} & \cdots & a_{2n} \\ \vdots & & & \vdots \\ b_n & a_{n2} & \cdots & a_{nn} \end{vmatrix}$$

by substituting the column of constants from (A-1) for the sums in the first column. Denoting the determinant on the right-hand side by $\mathbf{A}_1$, the solution for x_1 is

$$x_1 = \frac{\mathbf{A}_1}{\mathbf{A}} \tag{A-2}$$

as stated. The expression (A-2) is meaningless if $\mathbf{A} = 0$. In this case no unique solution exists, and the rows of the array are *linearly dependent* or, equivalently, the matrix is *singular*.[1]

If the value of a determinant is zero, one of the equations can be expressed as a linear combination of the remaining ones. For example, the nth equation might then be obtained by multiplying the first equation by 6 and adding 3 times the second to the first. The nth equation contains no new information and can be omitted, because it depends linearly on the first $(n - 1)$ equations. For example, assume that the nth equation is a linear combination of the first $(n - 1)$ equations. The ith equation is

$$\sum_{j=1}^{n} a_{ij}x_j = b_i$$

[1] Denote by Σ (the Greek capital letter sigma) the operation of summing such that $\Sigma_{i=1}^{n}a_i$ is defined to mean $a_1 + a_2 + \cdots + a_n$. The rows of the matrix A are defined to be linearly dependent if it is possible to find a set of numbers $c_1, c_2, \ldots, c_n$ such that $\Sigma_{i=1}^{n}c_ia_{ij} = 0$ for all values of the index j, provided that the cs are not all equal to zero. It can be proved that the value of the determinant of the array is zero if and only if the rows (or the columns) of the array are linearly dependent. See Aitken, *op. cit.*, pp. 62 and 64.

and the nth is

$$\sum_{i=1}^{n-1} c_i \sum_{j=1}^{n} a_{ij}x_j = \sum_{i=1}^{n-1} c_i b_i$$

where the cs are constants not all equal to zero. Any set of xs which satisfies the first $(n-1)$ equations necessarily satisfies the nth. The last equation adds no new information. The system is reduced to $(n-1)$ equations in n variables. If no $(n-1)$-rowed minor vanishes, it is possible to solve for any $(n-1)$ variables in terms of the constant terms and the remaining variable.

If the original system of n equations is *homogeneous* (all constant terms equal zero), all the xs are zero if the determinant of the system is nonvanishing. According to Cramer's rule each x is expressed as a fraction. The denominator is nonzero by hypothesis. The numerator vanishes for every x, because all bs equal zero, and the determinant of any array with a column of zeros is itself zero. If the determinant vanishes, it is possible to solve only for the relative values of the variables, and the solution is unique except for a factor of proportionality. For example, if the system of simultaneous equations is

$$3x_1 - 4x_2 = 0$$
$$6x_1 - 8x_2 = 0$$

the determinant is $(3)(-8) - (6)(-4) = 0$. Hence the two equations are not independent, and the second equation can be omitted.[1] Then

$$3x_1 - 4x_2 = 0$$

or

$$\frac{x_1}{x_2} = \frac{4}{3}$$

Any set of values satisfies the system as long as the relation between x_1 and x_2 is as 4:3.† Numerical values for the variables can only be obtained by choosing an arbitrary value for one of them.

A-2 CALCULUS: FUNCTIONS OF A SINGLE VARIABLE

FUNCTIONS, LIMITS, CONTINUITY

The relation $y = f(x)$ (read "y is a function of x") means that a rule exists by which it is possible to associate values of the variable y with

---

[1] It does not matter which equation is omitted. Discarding the first leads to the same answer.

† The discussion in the previous paragraphs is intentionally not rigorous. Necessary and sufficient conditions for the solubility of a system of simultaneous equations are proved in any textbook on algebra. See Aitken, *op. cit.*, pp. 63–66, 69–71, or Perlis, *op. cit.*, pp. 45–48.

values of the variable x. Examples are $y = 1/x$, $y = 3x^2$, $y = \log \sin x$, and $y = 1$ when x is an odd integer and $y = 0$ for any other value of x. In each case values of y correspond to given values of x according to the rule of association specified in the form of the function.

A function may not be defined for all possible values of x: $y = 1/x$ cannot be evaluated for $x = 0$, and $y = \log \sin x$ cannot be evaluated for values of x for which $\sin x$ is negative. The subset of all real numbers for which a function is defined is a region called the *domain* of the function. Thus the function $y = x^2$ has all the real numbers as its domain. The function values corresponding to the x values in the domain may themselves constitute a subset of the real numbers. This region is called the *range* of the function. The above function has the nonnegative real numbers as its range.

The relation $y = f(x)$ is an *explicit* function, since y is expressed in terms of x. If the functional relation between y and x is denoted by $g(y,x) = 0$, y is an *implicit* function of x. Specifying a value of x implicitly defines a value of y such that the expression on the left-hand side reduces to zero when the appropriate values of x and y are substituted in it. The relations $y = x^2$, $y = ax + b$, and $y = \sqrt[3]{x}$ provide examples of explicit functions; the expressions $ax + b - y = 0$, $x^2 - y^2 = 0$, and $e^y + y - x + \log x = 0$ are examples of implicit functions. In order to rewrite an implicit function in explicit form it is necessary to solve the equation $g(y,x) = 0$ for y. This is not always possible. The implicit function $e^y + y - x + \log x = 0$ cannot be written in explicit form because the equation cannot be solved analytically for x or y. An explicit function can always be rewritten in implicit-function form. For example, the explicit function $y = 3x^4 + 2 \sin x - 1$ becomes $y - 3x^4 - 2 \sin x + 1 = 0$ in implicit form.

A function $f(x)$ is *convex* over the interval (a,b) if

$$f[\lambda x_1 + (1 - \lambda)x_2] \leqq \lambda f(x_1) + (1 - \lambda)f(x_2) \qquad \text{(A-3)}$$

for all $a \leqq x_1$, $x_2 \leqq b$, and all $0 \leqq \lambda \leqq 1$. It is *strictly convex* over the interval if the strict inequality holds in (A-3) for all $0 < \lambda < 1$. A function is *concave* over the interval (a,b) if

$$f[\lambda x_1 + (1 - \lambda)x_2] \geqq \lambda f(x_1) + (1 - \lambda)f(x_2) \qquad \text{(A-4)}$$

for all $0 \leqq \lambda \leqq 1$, and *strictly concave* if the strict inequality holds for all $0 < \lambda < 1$.

The left-hand sides of (A-3) and (A-4) give function values at points which are interpolations between the values x_1 and x_2. The right-hand sides give interpolations of the function values corresponding to x_1 and x_2. Strict convexity (strict concavity) over an interval means that for any

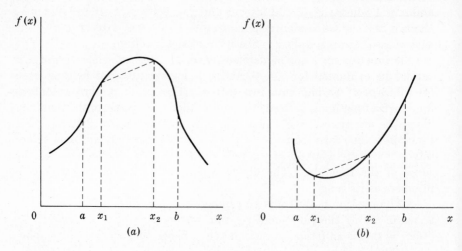

Fig. A-1

pair of x values in the interval, x_1 and x_2 with $x_1 < x_2$, the function values $f(x)$ for $x_1 < x < x_2$ lie below (above) the line segment connecting $f(x_1)$ and $f(x_2)$.   The function pictured in Fig. A-1a is concave over the interval (a,b).   The function in Fig. A-1b is convex over the interval (a,b).   In fact, it is convex over a wider interval.   A linear function satisfies the strict equalities in (A-3) and (A-4), and the two interpolations give identical values.   Thus, a linear function is both convex (but not strictly convex) and concave (but not strictly concave).

A sequence of numbers is a list or enumeration of numbers such as $1, 2, 3, 4, 5, \ldots$; or $1, \frac{1}{2}, \frac{1}{3}, \frac{1}{4}, \frac{1}{5}, \ldots$; or $2, 1, \frac{1}{2}, \frac{1}{4}, \frac{1}{8}, \ldots$; or $1, 0, -1, 0, 1, \ldots$.   Each number in a sequence can be assigned an index indicating how "far out" the number is in the sequence.   Thus in the third sequence above, $x_2 = 1$.   The sequence converges to a limit K if there exists a number K with the property that the numerical magnitude of the difference between K and an item in the sequence is arbitrarily small (can be made as small as one desires) if one takes an item in the sequence sufficiently "far out," i.e., an item with sufficiently high index, and if the difference remains at least as small for every item in the sequence with even higher index.   The first and fourth of the above sequences have no limit.   The second and third have the limit zero.

The explicit function $f(x)$ (or, what is the same thing, the variable y) approaches the limit L as x approaches the number a, if the value of the function can be made to be as near the number L as is desired by taking x values which are sufficiently close to a, and if the value of the function remains at least as near L for all x values even closer to a.   The process of finding the limit of $f(x)$ at $x = a$ may be visualized in the following manner.   Take successive values x_1, x_2, . . . , etc., of x that form a sequence converging to a.   Substitute these values of x in $f(x)$.   This results in a sequence of values $f(x_1)$, $f(x_2)$, . . . , etc.   If this sequence converges to a number L, $f(x)$ has the limit L at $x = a$.   A limit exists if L is finite.   The operation of taking the limit of $f(x)$ is denoted by $\lim_{x \to a} f(x) = L$.

The function $f(x) = 1 + 1/x$ approaches the limit 1 as $x \to \infty$ (x approaches infinity).   However, this result cannot be obtained by substituting ∞ for x in $1 + 1/x$ because $1/\infty$ does not equal zero. $A/B = C$ implies that $A = BC$.   If $1/\infty = 0$, then $1 = (\infty)(0)$.   Since this is untrue, the problem must be resolved by a different reasoning, namely by an application of the definition of the limit.   In fact, ∞ is not a number, but rather a direction.   Its appearance in a formula is equivalent to the command to list the positive integers in increasing order and go as far as possible, i.e., to take the limit.   The value of y can be made to differ from 1 by less than 0.1 by selecting a value for x greater than 10.   If $x = 20$, $1 + 1/x = 1.05$, which differs from 1 by only 0.05.   Likewise, y can be made to differ from 1 by less than 1/1,000,000 by selecting a value for x greater than 1,000,000.   The difference between the value of y and the number 1 can be made smaller than any prespecified number by taking an x that is sufficiently large.

The function $f(x)$ is continuous at the point $x = a$ if the following conditions are fulfilled: (1) $\lim_{x \to a} f(x)$ exists, (2) $f(a)$ exists, (3) $f(a) = \lim_{x \to a} f(x)$.†   The function is continuous in the interval $a < x < b$ if it is continuous at every point in the interval.   This definition of continuity implies that the function must be "continuous" in the everyday sense of the word: one must be able to draw the graph of the function without lifting the pencil from the paper.[1]

---

† At this point $x = a$ the value of the function must be finite, and this value must equal the limit of the function as x approaches a.   The function $y = 1$ when x is an odd integer and $y = 0$ for any other value of x is not continuous when x is an odd integer.   If $f(x)$ and $g(x)$ are two functions which are both continuous at $x = a$, then $f(x) + g(x)$, $f(x)g(x)$, and $f(x)/g(x)$ [provided that $g(x) \neq 0$] are also continuous.

[1] Note that a function that has "corners" or "kinks" but no gaps is continuous. The absolute value of a number x (denoted by $|x|$) is defined as follows:

$$|x| = x \qquad \text{if } x \geq 0$$
$$|x| = -x \qquad \text{if } x < 0$$

The function $y = |x|$ has a kink at $x = 0$, but is continuous.

THE DERIVATIVE

Assume that the function $y = f(x)$ is continuous in some interval. If the independent variable x changes by a small quantity Δx, the value of the function will change by the quantity Δy. Hence $y + \Delta y = f(x + \Delta x)$. The change in the value of the function can be expressed as

$$\Delta y = f(x + \Delta x) - f(x) \qquad \text{(A-5)}$$

Dividing both sides of (A-5) by Δx:

$$\frac{\Delta y}{\Delta x} = \frac{f(x + \Delta x) - f(x)}{\Delta x} \qquad \text{(A-6)}$$

The average rate of change of y per unit change of x for the interval x to $x + \Delta x$ is given by (A-6). For example, imagine that if one walks another half-hour, one covers an additional distance of 2 miles. The independent variable time is changed from x to $x + \frac{1}{2}$ hours; $\Delta y = 2$ miles, $\Delta x = \frac{1}{2}$ hour, and $\Delta y / \Delta x$ = average speed = 4 miles per hour. The derivative of $f(x)$, denoted by dy/dx, $f'(x)$, or $\dot{y}$, is defined as the rate of change of $f(x)$ as Δx approaches zero:

$$\frac{dy}{dx} = f'(x) = \lim_{\Delta x \to 0} \frac{f(x + \Delta x) - f(x)}{\Delta x}$$

The derivative is the rate of change or the speed in terms of the above example, or, to put it differently, the limit of the average rate of change (average speed) as Δx (the time interval) approaches zero. If the graph of $f(x)$ is plotted, the derivative calculated at the point $x = a$ is the slope of the curve representing $f(x)$ at the point $x = a$. The average rate of change is the slope of the secant between two points on the curve, and the derivative is the slope of the tangent to the curve at a given point. These concepts are illustrated by Fig. A-2.

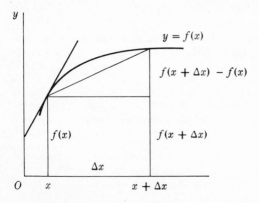

Fig. A-2

The derivative of a derivative is a second derivative, denoted by d^2y/dx^2, and is defined as

$$\frac{d^2y}{dx^2} = \lim_{\Delta x \to 0} \frac{f'(x + \Delta x) - f'(x)}{\Delta x}$$

The second derivative is the rate of change of the first derivative, i.e., the rate at which the slope of the function is changing. In terms of the previous example it is the acceleration or the rate of change of speed. Higher-order derivatives are defined similarly.

TECHNIQUES OF DIFFERENTIATION

To differentiate a function is to find its derivative. Some of the more important techniques of differentiation are stated below without proof:[1]

1. $f(x) = c$ (constant), $f'(x) = 0$
2. $f(x) = x^n$, $f'(x) = nx^{n-1}$
3. $f(x) = g(x)h(x)$, $f'(x) = g'(x)h(x) + g(x)h'(x)$
4. $f(x) = g(x)/h(x)$, $h(x) \neq 0$, $f'(x) = [g'(x)h(x) - g(x)h'(x)]/[h(x)]^2$
5. $f(x) = g[h(x)]$, $f'(x) = g'[h(x)]h'(x)$ (function of a function rule)
6. $f(x) = \log x$, $f'(x) = 1/x$ (log to base e)
7. $f(x) = \log [g(x)]$, $f'(x) = g'(x)/g(x)$ (log to base e)
8. $f(x) = e^{g(x)}$, $f'(x) = g'(x)e^{g(x)}$
9. $f(x) = a^x$, $f'(x) = a^x \log a$ (log to base e)
10. If $y = f(x)$ is single-valued and continuous, and can be written in inverse form as $x = g(y)$ such that $f'(x)$ is continuous and $\neq 0$, $f'(x) = 1/g'(y)$ or $dy/dx = 1/(dx/dy)$ (inverse-function rule).

MAXIMA AND MINIMA

A function of one variable $y = f(x)$ has a (relative) maximum at the point $x = a$ if $f(a) \geq f(x)$ for all values of x in a small neighborhood about the point a. The value $f(a)$ is not necessarily larger than values of $f(x)$ outside the small neighborhood about a. Similarly, $f(x)$ has a minimum at $x = b$ if $f(b) \leq f(x)$ for all x in a small neighborhood about b.

Sufficient conditions for maxima and minima can be indicated intuitively as follows. A function that has a maximum (or minimum) is, by definition, neither increasing nor decreasing at its extreme point. But the first derivative is the function's rate of increase. It must therefore equal zero at an extreme point. A function first increases, becomes stationary, and then decreases in the case of a maximum. Thus the

[1] Proofs can be found in any standard elementary text on calculus. See R. Courant, *Differential and Integral Calculus*, vol. I (2d ed.; New York: Interscience, 1936), pp. 136–140, 173, 175; or H. B. Fine, *Calculus* (New York: Macmillan, 1937), chaps. III and VII.

second derivative (the rate of change of the first derivative) is negative at a maximum. For similar reasons it is positive at a minimum. These conditions on the first and second derivatives are sufficient for maxima and minima.

A more rigorous proof of necessary and sufficient conditions runs as follows. Assume that $y = f(x)$ is a continuous function with continuous first- and second-order derivatives. The theorem of the mean states[1] that its average rate of change between two points (the slope of its secant) is equal to its derivative (slope of the tangent) evaluated at some point within the interval:

$$\frac{f(x + \Delta x) - f(x)}{\Delta x} = f'(x + \theta \Delta x) \qquad 0 < \theta < 1 \qquad (A\text{-}7)$$

If $f(x)$ is a maximum, $f(x + \Delta x) - f(x) \leq 0$. Then the fraction on the left-hand side of (A-7) is nonpositive for positive values of Δx and nonnegative for negative values of Δx. Let Δx approach zero from the right (i.e., through positive values). Then the limit of the fraction in (A-7) must itself be nonpositive. Letting Δx approach zero from the left (i.e., through negative values), the limit of the fraction must be nonnegative. But the limit of the fraction in (A-7) as Δx approaches zero is $f'(x)$; this must be neither positive nor negative and hence must equal zero. A necessary condition for a maximum or minimum is that the first derivative equal zero. This condition on the first derivative is the *first-order* condition for a maximum or minimum.

An additional condition must be fulfilled for a maximum or minimum. Expanding $f(x)$ in Taylor series[2] with remainder term about the point x,

$$f(x + \Delta x) = f(x) + \Delta x f'(x) + \frac{(\Delta x)^2}{2} f''(x + \theta \Delta x) \qquad 0 < \theta < 1 \tag{A-8}$$

Since $f'(x) = 0$ when $f(x)$ is a maximum, (A-8) becomes

$$f(x + \Delta x) - f(x) = \frac{(\Delta x)^2}{2} f''(x + \theta \Delta x) \tag{A-9}$$

This implies that $f''(x + \theta \Delta x)$ is nonpositive for all values of Δx within a small neighborhood of x. By the continuity of the second derivative $\lim_{\Delta x \to 0} f''(x + \theta \Delta x) = f''(x)$, and this must be nonpositive. Hence, the first derivative must equal zero, and the second derivative must be nonpositive for a maximum.[3] These conditions are necessary, but not suf-

[1] Proved in any standard text on calculus. See Courant, *op. cit.*, vol. I, pp. 102–104; or Fine, *op. cit.*, pp. 104–105.

[2] See Fine, *op. cit.*, pp. 208, 214–215, or any other standard text on calculus.

[3] Courant, *op. cit.*, vol. I, pp. 159–163.

ficient.   Their insufficiency is illustrated by the function $y = x^3$.   Its
first and second derivatives vanish at $x = 0$, yet the function has neither
a maximum nor a minimum at that point.   Sufficient conditions can be
stated as follows: a zero first derivative and a negative (positive) second
derivative implies that the function attains a maximum (minimum).
However, this statement does not provide necessary conditions, since
the second derivative may vanish although $f(x)$ attains a maximum or
minimum.   As an example consider the function $y = x^4$ which possesses
zero first and second derivatives at $x = 0$, yet has a minimum at that
point.

Necessary and sufficient conditions for a maximum (minimum) are
as follows: $f(x)$ attains a maximum (minimum) at $x = a$ if and only if
(1) $dy/dx = 0$ at $x = a$, (2) the first $(n - 1)$ (n even) derivatives are all
zero and the first nonzero derivative (the nth) is negative (positive) at
$x = a$.

In general, the maximum and minimum values of a function are
found by determining and solving the equation $f'(x) = 0$, then substituting the values of x for which the first derivative vanishes into $f''(x)$
and evaluating its sign.   If it is negative, the corresponding value of
$f(x)$ is a maximum; if it is positive, the corresponding value is a minimum.   If the second derivative is zero, there are three possibilities: (1)
$d^3y/dx^3 \neq 0$, (2) $d^3y/dx^3 = 0$ and $d^4y/dx^4 \neq 0$, or (3) $d^3y/dx^3 = 0$ and
$d^4y/dx^4 = 0$.   If (1) holds, the function has an inflection point (i.e., the
first derivative has an extreme value) rather than a maximum or minimum.   If (2) holds, the function has a maximum or minimum according
to whether the fourth derivative is negative or positive.   If (3) holds,
the signs of the fifth and sixth derivatives must be examined and (1)
and (2) applied with d^5y/dx^5 replacing d^3y/dx^3 and d^6y/dx^6 replacing
d^4y/dx^4.

The examples in Chaps. 2 through 8 are limited to functions which
fall into a class with the property that the second derivative is nonzero
for extreme values.   Necessary and sufficient conditions for functions in
this class involve only the first and second derivatives.   The above refine-
ment involving higher-order derivatives is not mentioned in the text,
but should be kept in mind.   The conditions on the second derivative
are the *second-order* conditions.

The satisfaction of the first-order condition at a point in an interval
in which a twice-differentiable function is strictly concave (strictly convex) is necessary and sufficient for the existence of a maximum (minimum)
at that point.   If the case of the vanishing second derivative mentioned
in the last paragraph is ignored, the proof is easy.   The second derivative
of a strictly concave (strictly convex) function is strictly negative (strictly
positive) over the interval, which satisfies the second-order condition for

a maximum (minimum).[1]   Consider the case of a strictly concave function. Select two distinct x values, x_1 and x_2, in the interval. Rewrite (A-4) as a function of λ,

$$g(\lambda) = f[\lambda x_1 + (1 - \lambda)x_2] - \lambda f(x_1) - (1 - \lambda)f(x_2) > 0$$

for $0 < \lambda < 1$, with the limiting values $g(0) = 0$ and $g(1) = 0$. It follows from the continuity of $f(x)$, and hence the continuity of $g(\lambda)$, that $g(\lambda)$ has a maximum in the closed interval $0 \leqq \lambda \leqq 1$. The first-order condition for this maximum is

$$g'(\lambda) = f'(x)(x_1 - x_2) - f(x_1) + f(x_2) = 0$$

where x represents $\lambda x_1 + (1 - \lambda)x_2$. The second-order condition is[2]

$$\frac{d^2 g(\lambda)}{d\lambda^2} = f''(x)(x_1 - x_2)^2 < 0$$

which implies that $f''(x) < 0$. The proof that $f''(x) > 0$ in an interval in which $f(x)$ is strictly convex is similar.

Allied theorems state that if $f''(x) > 0$ over an interval, $f(x)$ is strictly convex over the interval, and if $f''(x) < 0$ over an interval, $f(x)$ is strictly concave over the interval. These theorems provide an easy means of testing the convexity or concavity of particular functions. For example, consider the function $f(x) = x^3 - 3x^2 + 3x$. Its second derivative is $f''(x) = 6x - 6$ which is negative for $x < 1$ and positive for $x > 1$. Hence, $f(x)$ is strictly concave for $x < 1$, and strictly convex for $x > 1$.

If $f(x)$ is strictly convex or strictly concave over an interval, there cannot be more than one point within the interval at which the first-order condition is satisfied. This is easily proved by contradiction. Assume that $f(x)$ is strictly concave and that $f'(x_1) = f'(x_2) = 0$ with $f(x_1) \geqq f(x_2)$. It follows from concavity that

$$f[\lambda x_1 + (1 - \lambda)x_2] > \lambda f(x_1) + (1 - \lambda)f(x_2)$$
$$\geqq \lambda f(x_2) + (1 - \lambda)f(x_2) = f(x_2)$$

For a value of λ sufficiently close to 0 this states that $f(x) > f(x_2)$ where x is within a small neighborhood of x_2, which contradicts the assumption that $f(x_2)$ is a maximum within such a neighborhood. Satisfaction of the

---

[1] An example of the troublesome exception is provided by the function $f(x) = -x^4$. It is strictly concave as the reader may verify by plotting it. Its derivative, $f''(x) = -12x^2$, is strictly negative for all real values of x except at the point $x = 0$ where it vanishes.

[2] The function of a function rule for second derivatives is used. In general, if $\phi(x) = \psi[h(x)]$, $\phi''(x) = \psi''[h(x)]h'(x)^2 + \psi'[h(x)]h''(x)$.

first-order condition is necessary and sufficient for the attainment of a unique global maximum within a concave interval of $f(x)$. Similarly, satisfaction of the first-order condition is necessary and sufficient for the attainment of a unique global minimum within a convex interval of $f(x)$.

AVERAGE AND MARGINAL CURVES

Assume that $R = pq$ and

$$p = \frac{R}{q} = f(q)$$

The functional relationship $p = f(q)$ is frequently referred to as an average curve.[1] The curve the ordinate of which measures the rate of change of R (the change at the margin) is the marginal curve or the curve marginal to $p = f(q)$. Substituting the value $f(q)$ for p in $R = pq$ and differentiating with respect to q

$$\frac{dR}{dq} = f(q) + qf'(q) \tag{A-10}$$

Let q be restricted to nonnegative values. The relationship (A-10) implies that the marginal curve will lie below the average curve if the average curve is decreasing and above it if the average curve is increasing, since $f'(q) < 0$ and $q > 0$ imply $f(q) > dR/dq$ for all positive values of q and conversely for $f'(q) > 0$. Hence the average curve is rising when the marginal curve is above the average, and the average is falling when the marginal is below the average. It also follows that if the average curve has an extreme point [i.e., a point at which $f'(q) = 0$], the marginal curve intersects the average curve at this point.

If $q = 0$ is in the domain of $f(q)$, (A-10) becomes

$$\frac{dR}{dq} = f(0) \tag{A-11}$$

The value of p from the average curve is $p = f(0)$. Hence the average curve and the curve marginal to it intersect at the point where they both meet the p axis. The slope of the average curve is $dp/dq = f'(q)$, and the slope of the marginal curve is

$$\frac{d^2R}{dq^2} = f'(q) + f'(q) + qf''(q) = 2f'(q) + qf''(q)$$

If the average curve is a straight line, $f''(q) = 0$, and the slope of the marginal curve is twice the slope of the average curve. On the basis of

[1] The relation $p = f(q)$ is an average curve because it relates values of q to the average values (with respect to q) of the variable R. An economic example is provided by the demand curve where q is quantity sold, p is price, and R is total revenue.

this information the marginal curve can be constructed diagrammatically with ease if the average curve is given.

A-3 CALCULUS: FUNCTIONS OF MANY VARIABLES

PARTIAL DERIVATIVES

The definitions of a limit and continuity are easily generalized to a function of n independent variables

$$y = f(x_1, x_2, \ldots, x_n)$$

The partial derivative of y with respect to x_i is

$$f_i = \frac{\partial y}{\partial x_i} = \lim_{\Delta x_i \to 0} \frac{f(x_1, x_2, \ldots, x_i + \Delta x_i, \ldots, x_n) - f(x_1, x_2, \ldots, x_n)}{\Delta x_i}$$

which is the rate of change of the function with respect to x_i, all other variables remaining constant. The techniques of differentiation are the same as those for a function of a single variable; all variables other than x_i are treated as constants. For example, if

$$y = 3x_1 x_2^2 + x_2 \log x_1$$

then

$$\frac{\partial y}{\partial x_1} = 3x_2^2 + \frac{x_2}{x_1} \quad \text{and} \quad \frac{\partial y}{\partial x_2} = 6x_1 x_2 + \log x_1$$

Higher-order derivatives are determined by successive partial differentiation; $\partial^2 y/\partial x_i^2$ is the partial derivative of f_i with respect to x_i, also denoted by f_{ii}; $\partial^2 y/\partial x_i \, \partial x_j$ is the partial derivative of f_i with respect to x_j (one of the second cross partial derivatives) and is denoted by f_{ij}. For the previous example

$$\frac{\partial^2 y}{\partial x_2 \, \partial x_1} = 6x_2 + \frac{1}{x_1}$$

If the first and second cross partial derivatives are continuous, $f_{ij} = f_{ji}$. The partial derivatives of the implicit function $f(x_1, x_2, \ldots, x_n) = 0$ are obtained by assuming that $y = f(x_1, x_2, \ldots, x_n)$ and calculating $\partial y/\partial x_1$, $\partial y/\partial x_2$, etc.

THE TOTAL DIFFERENTIAL

For a function of a single variable

$$\frac{dy}{dx} = f'(x)$$

The symbol dy/dx denotes the derivative and was not interpreted as a fraction composed of the quantities dy and dx. Defining dx as an increment or change in the independent variable, dy can be defined as

$$dy = f'(x)\, dx \qquad \text{(A-12)}$$

This is the *differential* of $f(x)$. At a given point x^0 the value of the function is $y^0 = f(x^0)$, and (A-12) can be rewritten in terms of deviations from this point as

$$y - y^0 = f'(x^0)(x - x^0) \qquad \text{(A-13)}$$

which is the equation of the tangent to $y = f(x)$ at the point (x^0, y^0). Hence, (A-12) is the general form of the equation of the tangent to the function. For small changes of x (A-13) gives the approximate value of the corresponding change of $f(x)$.

The *total differential* of a function of n variables is defined as

$$dy = f_1\, dx_1 + f_2\, dx_2 + \cdots + f_n\, dx_n \qquad \text{(A-14)}$$

which is the general form of the equation of the tangent plane (or hyperplane) to the surface (or hypersurface) defined by $y = f(x_1, x_2, \ldots, x_n)$. It also provides an approximate value of the change in the function when all variables are permitted to vary, provided that the variation in the independent variables is small. The *total derivative* of the function with respect to x_i is

$$\frac{dy}{dx_i} = f_1 \frac{dx_1}{dx_i} + \cdots + f_i + \cdots + f_n \frac{dx_n}{dx_i}$$

or the rate of change of y with respect to x_i when all other variables are permitted to vary and where all x_j are specified functions of x_i.

The second differential of $y = f(x_1, x_2, \ldots, x_n)$ is obtained by taking the total differential of (A-14):

$$d^2 y = \sum_{i=1}^{n} \sum_{j=1}^{n} f_{ij}\, dx_i\, dx_j \qquad \text{(A-15)}$$

which provides an approximate value of the change in the change in the value of the function when all variables are permitted to vary within a small neighborhood.

Assume that $y = f(x_1, x_2)$, $x_1 = g(w_1, w_2)$, and $x_2 = h(w_1, w_2)$. The partial derivatives of y with respect to w_1 and w_2 are determined by the *composite-function rule* derived below. Taking total differentials

$$dy = \frac{\partial y}{\partial x_1}\, dx_1 + \frac{\partial y}{\partial x_2}\, dx_2 \qquad \text{(A-16)}$$

$$dx_1 = \frac{\partial x_1}{\partial w_1}\, dw_1 + \frac{\partial x_1}{\partial w_2}\, dw_2 \qquad \text{(A-17)}$$

$$dx_2 = \frac{\partial x_2}{\partial w_1}\, dw_1 + \frac{\partial x_2}{\partial w_2}\, dw_2 \qquad \text{(A-18)}$$

and substituting (A-17) and (A-18) into (A-16) and collecting terms on dw_1 and dw_2,

$$dy = \left(\frac{\partial y}{\partial x_1}\frac{\partial x_1}{\partial w_1} + \frac{\partial y}{\partial x_2}\frac{\partial x_2}{\partial w_1}\right) dw_1 + \left(\frac{\partial y}{\partial x_1}\frac{\partial x_1}{\partial w_2} + \frac{\partial y}{\partial x_2}\frac{\partial x_2}{\partial w_2}\right) dw_2 \quad \text{(A-19)}$$

The expression (A-19) is itself a total differential in which the first term in parentheses equals $\partial y/\partial w_1$ and the second one equals $\partial y/\partial w_2$. Hence

$$\begin{aligned}
\frac{\partial y}{\partial w_1} &= \frac{\partial y}{\partial x_1}\frac{\partial x_1}{\partial w_1} + \frac{\partial y}{\partial x_2}\frac{\partial x_2}{\partial w_1} = f_1 g_1 + f_2 h_1 \\
\frac{\partial y}{\partial w_2} &= \frac{\partial y}{\partial x_1}\frac{\partial x_1}{\partial w_2} + \frac{\partial y}{\partial x_2}\frac{\partial x_2}{\partial w_2} = f_1 g_2 + f_2 h_2
\end{aligned} \quad \text{(A-20)}$$

If the independent variables of a function $f(x_1,x_2)$ are themselves functions of some other variables w_1 and w_2, $f(x_1,x_2)$ is differentiated partially with respect to w_1 and w_2 according to (A-20). This is the *composite-function rule*. By further differentiation of the first equation of (A-20),

$$\frac{\partial^2 y}{\partial w_1\, \partial w_2} = f_{11}g_1g_2 + f_{12}(g_1h_2 + g_2h_1) + f_{22}h_1h_2 + f_1g_{12} + f_2h_{12}$$

Given the implicit function $f(x_1,x_2, \ldots ,x_n) = 0$, the partial derivative $\partial x_j/\partial x_i$ is obtained by first finding the total differential

$$f_1\, dx_1 + f_2\, dx_2 + \cdots + f_n\, dx_n = 0$$

dividing by dx_i

$$f_1\frac{dx_1}{dx_i} + f_2\frac{dx_2}{dx_i} + \cdots + f_j\frac{dx_j}{dx_i} + \cdots + f_i + \cdots + f_n\frac{dx_n}{dx_i} = 0$$

and setting all differentials other than dx_j and dx_i equal to zero. Then

$$f_j\frac{\partial x_j}{\partial x_i} + f_i = 0$$

and

$$\frac{\partial x_j}{\partial x_i} = -\frac{f_i}{f_j} \quad \text{(A-21)}$$

Equation (A-21) is the *implicit-function rule*. By further differentiation of (A-21),

$$\begin{aligned}
\frac{\partial^2 x_j}{\partial x_i^2} &= -\frac{f_j[f_{ii} + f_{ji}(\partial x_j/\partial x_i)] - f_i[f_{ij} + f_{jj}(\partial x_j/\partial x_i)]}{f_j^2} \\
&= -\frac{f_{ii}f_j^2 - 2f_{ij}f_i f_j + f_{jj}f_i^2}{f_j^3}
\end{aligned}$$

ENVELOPES

Let $f(x,y,k) = 0$ be an implicit function of the variables x and y. The form of this function is assumed to depend on the magnitude of the parameter k. In general, $f(x,y,k) = 0$ describes a curve in the xy plane. A different curve corresponds to each possible value of k. The envelope of this family of curves is itself a curve with the property that it is tangent to each member of the family. The equation of the envelope is obtained by taking the partial derivative of $f(x,y,k)$ with respect to k and eliminating k from the two equations

$$f(x,y,k) = 0$$
$$f_k(x,y,k) = 0$$

This method of obtaining the envelope is generally applicable, provided that $f_{kk} \neq 0$ and $f_x f_{yk} - f_y f_{xk} \neq 0$.†

MAXIMA AND MINIMA WITHOUT CONSTRAINTS

The definitions of maxima and minima are similar to those for a function of a single variable. Necessary and sufficient conditions are difficult to derive. Only sufficient conditions are stated here.[1] It is sufficient for a maximum or minimum that all first-order increments in the function be zero and all second-order increments be negative for a maximum and positive for a minimum. First-order increments are given by (A-14); dy must be zero for all values of the dx_i's ($i = 1, \ldots, n$). This implies that $f_1 = f_2 \cdots f_n = 0$. Second-order increments are given by (A-15). The quadratic form (A-15) must be *negative definite* for a maximum and *positive definite* for a minimum; that is, d^2y must be negative for a maximum and positive for a minimum for all values of the dx_i's except $dx_i = 0$ for all i.

The Hessian determinant of the second partial derivatives is

$$\begin{vmatrix} f_{11} & f_{12} & \cdots & f_{1n} \\ f_{21} & f_{22} & \cdots & f_{2n} \\ \cdot & \cdot & \cdots & \cdot \\ f_{n1} & f_{n2} & \cdots & f_{nn} \end{vmatrix}$$

The quadratic form (A-15) is negative definite if and only if the principal minors obtained by deleting the last $(n - i)$ rows and $(n - i)$ columns

---

† For proof see W. F. Osgood, *Advanced Calculus* (New York: Macmillan, 1925), pp. 186–193; Fine, *op. cit.*, pp. 272–274.

[1] See W. F. Osgood, *op cit.*, pp. 173–179; R. G. D. Allen, *Mathematical Analysis for Economists* (London: Macmillan, 1938), chap. XIX; P. A. Samuelson, *Foundations of Economic Analysis* (Cambridge, Mass.: Harvard, 1948), appendix A.

$(i = n - 1, n - 2, \ldots, 0)$ of the Hessian alternate in sign:

$$f_{11} < 0, \quad \begin{vmatrix} f_{11} & f_{12} \\ f_{21} & f_{22} \end{vmatrix} > 0, \quad \begin{vmatrix} f_{11} & f_{12} & f_{13} \\ f_{21} & f_{22} & f_{23} \\ f_{31} & f_{32} & f_{33} \end{vmatrix} < 0,$$

$$\ldots, \quad (-1)^n \begin{vmatrix} f_{11} & f_{12} & \cdots & f_{1n} \\ f_{21} & f_{22} & \cdots & f_{2n} \\ \cdots & \cdots & \cdots & \cdots \\ f_{n1} & f_{n2} & \cdots & f_{nn} \end{vmatrix} > 0 \quad \text{(A-22)}$$

The quadratic form is positive definite if and only if the principal minors are all positive.[1] In this volume the second-order conditions are usually expressed in terms of the principal minors of the Hessian determinant.

Extreme values are determined in a manner analogous to that employed in the single-variable case. The n equations $f_1 = 0$, $f_2 = 0$, $\ldots$, $f_n = 0$ are solved for the n variables x_1, x_2, $\ldots$, x_n. The signs of the principal minors of the Hessian are calculated for each solution. If their signs are as required for a maximum (minimum), the function $f(x_1, x_2, \ldots, x_n)$ attains a maximum (minimum) for that solution.

CONVEX AND CONCAVE FUNCTIONS

The function $f(x_1, x_2, \ldots, x_n)$ is convex over an interval if

$$f[\lambda x_1^{(1)} + (1 - \lambda)x_1^{(2)}, \lambda x_2^{(1)} + (1 - \lambda)x_2^{(2)}, \ldots, \lambda x_n^{(1)} + (1 - \lambda)x_n^{(2)}]$$
$$\leqq \lambda f(x_1^{(1)}, x_2^{(1)}, \ldots, x_n^{(1)}) + (1 - \lambda)f(x_1^{(2)}, x_2^{(2)}, \ldots, x_n^{(2)})$$

for all pairs of points $(x_1^{(1)}, x_2^{(1)}, \ldots, x_n^{(1)})$ and $(x_1^{(2)}, x_2^{(2)}, \ldots, x_n^{(2)})$ in the interval and all $0 \leqq \lambda \leqq 1$. The function is strictly convex if the strict inequality holds for all $0 < \lambda < 1$. The function is concave over the interval if

$$f[\lambda x_1^{(1)} + (1 - \lambda)x_1^{(2)}, \lambda x_2^{(1)} + (1 - \lambda)x_2^{(2)}, \ldots, \lambda x_n^{(1)} + (1 - \lambda)x_n^{(2)}]$$
$$\geqq \lambda f(x_1^{(1)}, x_2^{(1)}, \ldots, x_n^{(1)}) + (1 - \lambda)f(x_1^{(2)}, x_2^{(2)}, \ldots, x_n^{(2)})$$

and strictly concave if the strict inequality holds for $0 < \lambda < 1$.

By advanced methods it can be proved that if a twice-differentiable function is strictly concave (strictly convex) over an interval, the second-order conditions for a maximum (minimum) will be satisfied at every point in the interval. In addition there cannot be more than one maxi-

---

[1] The numbering of the variables is arbitrary. The sign conditions on the principal minors imply that all minors of given order are of the same sign. For example, in the two-variable maximum case the conditions $f_{11} < 0$ and $f_{11}f_{22} - (f_{12})^2 > 0$ imply that f_{22} is negative.

mum (minimum) within the interval. Thus, the satisfaction of the first-order conditions at a point within the interval is sufficient for the existence of a unique global maximum (minimum) at that point.

The determinants given by (A-22) provide a means for testing for the convexity or concavity of particular functions. If the determinants alternate in sign as shown for (A-22) over an interval, the corresponding function is strictly concave over the interval. If the determinants of (A-22) are all positive over an interval, the function is strictly convex over the interval. For example, consider $f(x_1,x_2) = 2x_1^{0.5}x_2^{0.4}$. Evaluating the first two determinants of (A-22),

$$f_{11} = -0.5x_1^{-1.5}x_2^{0.4}$$
$$f_{11}f_{22} - (f_{12})^2 = 0.08x_1^{-1}x_2^{-1.2}$$

It follows that $f(x_1,x_2)$ is strictly concave for $x_1 > 0$, $x_2 > 0$, in this case.

CONSTRAINED MAXIMA AND MINIMA

Many maximum and minimum problems in economics are such that the independent variables are not permitted to take on all possible values; the variables are "constrained" to satisfy some side relation. The constrained-maximum problem is to maximize the function $f(x_1,x_2, \ldots ,x_n)$ subject to the constraint that only those values of $x_1,x_2, \ldots ,x_n$ that satisfy the equation

$$g(x_1,x_2, \ldots ,x_n) = 0$$

are admissible. For example, the function

$$f(x_1,x_2) = (x_1 - 1)^2 + (x_2 - 2)^2$$

has an unconstrained minimum at the point $x_1 = 1$, $x_2 = 2$. However, if this function is subject to the requirement that $x_1 - x_2 - 2 = 0$, its minimum value is achieved at the point $x_1 = \frac{5}{2}$, $x_2 = \frac{1}{2}$. The function $f(x_1,x_2)$ defines a surface in three-dimensional space. The equation $x_1 - x_2 - 2 = 0$ defines a straight line in the horizontal x_1x_2 plane. The constrained-minimum problem is one of finding the lowest point of the surface defined by $f(x_1,x_2)$ such that this point is above the straight line defined by the constraint. These concepts are illustrated with reference to a maximum problem in Fig. A-3. The unconstrained maximum occurs at the point M. The constraint is given by the line AB. All points on the surface other than those lying above the line AB, namely the points along the curved line PNQ, are irrelevant. The constrained maximum occurs at the point N. The result will generally differ from the unconstrained case, and the constrained maximum will

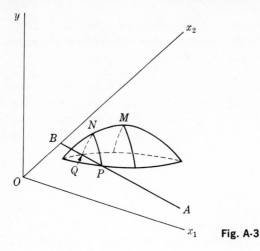

Fig. A-3

generally be lower than the unconstrained maximum. It, of course, cannot be higher.

Method 1 If it is possible to solve the equation

$$g(x_1, x_2, \ldots , x_n) = 0$$

for one of the variables, say $x_1 = h(x_2, \ldots , x_n)$, the solution for x_1 can be substituted in $f(x_1, x_2, \ldots , x_n)$ to give $f[h(x_2, \ldots , x_n), x_2, \ldots , x_n]$ which is a function of $n - 1$ variables. Denote this function by $H(x_2, \ldots , x_n)$. The maximization of $f(x_1, x_2, \ldots , x_n)$ subject to the constraint is equivalent to the unconstrained maximization of $H(x_2, \ldots , x_n)$ with respect to $x_2, \ldots , x_n$. The constrained-maximum problem is thus reduced to an unconstrained one that is handled in customary fashion.

Method 2 The procedure outlined above involves a loss of symmetry depending upon which variable is expressed in terms of the others from the constraint. A more general procedure involves the use of *Lagrange multipliers*. Form the function

$$V = f(x_1, x_2, \ldots , x_n) + \lambda g(x_1, x_2, \ldots , x_n)$$

This function contains the $(n + 1)$ variables $x_1, x_2, \ldots , x_n$ and λ, which is an undetermined Lagrange multiplier (different from zero). Maximizing V is equivalent to maximizing $f(x_1, x_2, \ldots , x_n)$, subject to $g(x_1, x_2, \ldots , x_n) = 0$. In addition, $f(x_1, x_2, \ldots , x_n)$ is identically equal to V only for those values of the variables that satisfy the constraint.

The first-order conditions require that the first partial derivatives of V must vanish for both maxima and minima. This condition gives $(n + 1)$ equations in $(n + 1)$ variables

$$\frac{\partial V}{\partial x_1} = f_1 + \lambda g_1 = 0$$

$$\cdots \cdots \cdots \cdots \cdots$$

$$\frac{\partial V}{\partial x_n} = f_n + \lambda g_n = 0 \qquad\qquad \text{(A-23)}$$

$$\frac{\partial V}{\partial \lambda} = g(x_1, x_2, \ldots, x_n) = 0$$

The last equation ensures that the constraint is satisfied. The solution of this system of simultaneous equations gives the point or points at which $f(x_1, x_2, \ldots, x_n)$ achieves a maximum (or minimum) subject to $g(x_1, x_2, \ldots, x_n) = 0$.†

Second-order conditions require that the quadratic form

$$\sum_{i=1}^{n} \sum_{j=1}^{n} f_{ij} \, dx_i \, dx_j$$

be negative for a maximum (positive for a minimum) for all values of the dxs that satisfy

$$g_1 \, dx_1 + g_2 \, dx_2 + \cdots + g_n \, dx_n = 0$$

other than $dx_i = 0$ for all i. Form the determinants

$$\begin{vmatrix} V_{11} & V_{12} & g_1 \\ V_{21} & V_{22} & g_2 \\ g_1 & g_2 & 0 \end{vmatrix}, \begin{vmatrix} V_{11} & V_{12} & V_{13} & g_1 \\ V_{21} & V_{22} & V_{23} & g_2 \\ V_{31} & V_{32} & V_{33} & g_3 \\ g_1 & g_2 & g_3 & 0 \end{vmatrix}, \ldots,$$

$$\begin{vmatrix} V_{11} & V_{12} & \cdots & V_{1n} & g_1 \\ V_{21} & V_{22} & \cdots & V_{2n} & g_2 \\ \cdots & \cdots & \cdots & \cdots & \cdots \\ V_{n1} & V_{n2} & \cdots & V_{nn} & g_n \\ g_1 & g_2 & \cdots & g_n & 0 \end{vmatrix}$$

which are obtained by bordering the principal minors of the Hessian determinant of second partial derivatives of V by a row and a column containing the first partial derivatives of the constraint. The element in the southeast corner of each of these arrays is zero.

† If the function V were formed by writing $f - \lambda g$ rather than $f + \lambda g$, the only difference would be a change in the sign of λ.

The second-order conditions for a constrained maximum will be satisfied if these bordered determinants alternate in sign, starting with plus; i.e., the signs of the determinants from left to right must be $+$, $-$, $+$, etc. The second-order conditions for a constrained minimum will be satisfied if they are all negative. These conditions together with (A-23) are sufficient for constrained maxima and minima.[1]

By advanced methods it has been proved that $f(x_1, x_2, \ldots, x_n)$ cannot have more than one constrained maximum (minimum) in an interval if the determinantal conditions for a constrained maximum (minimum) hold over the interval. In this case the satisfaction of conditions (A-23) is sufficient for the existence of a unique global maximum (minimum) within the interval.

The Lagrange-multiplier technique may be generalized to cover cases in which a function is maximized or minimized subject to more than one constraint provided that the constraints are consistent and the number of constraints is smaller than the number of variables. Consider the maximization or minimization of $f(x_1, x_2, \ldots, x_n)$ subject to $g(x_1, x_2, \ldots, x_n) = 0$ and $h(x_1, x_2, \ldots, x_n) = 0$. Form the function

$$Z = f(x_1, x_2, \ldots, x_n) + \lambda g(x_1, x_2, \ldots, x_n) + \mu h(x_1, x_2, \ldots, x_n)$$

where λ and μ are both undetermined Lagrange multipliers. First-order conditions for both maxima and minima require that

$$\frac{\partial Z}{\partial x_1} = f_1 + \lambda g_1 + \mu h_1 = 0$$
$$\cdot \cdot \cdot \cdot \cdot \cdot \cdot \cdot \cdot \cdot \cdot \cdot \cdot \cdot \cdot \cdot$$
$$\frac{\partial Z}{\partial x_n} = f_n + \lambda g_n + \mu h_n = 0$$
$$\frac{\partial Z}{\partial \lambda} = g(x_1, x_2, \ldots, x_n) = 0$$
$$\frac{\partial Z}{\partial \mu} = h(x_1, x_2, \ldots, x_n) = 0$$

Second-order conditions require that the quadratic form of second-order partials be negative for a maximum (positive for a minimum) for all nontrivial sets of values of the dxs that satisfy

$$g_1 \, dx_1 + g_2 \, dx_2 + \cdots + g_n \, dx_n = 0$$

and

$$h_1 \, dx_1 + h_2 \, dx_2 + \cdots + h_n \, dx_n = 0$$

---

[1] See Samuelson, *op. cit.*, appendix A; Allen, *op. cit.*, chap. XIX; and for a rigorous treatment of some aspects of this problem, G. Debreu, "Definite and Semi-definite Quadratic Forms," *Econometrica*, vol. 20 (April, 1952), pp. 295–300.

Border the following principal minors of the Hessian of Z with the first partials of the two constraints

$$\begin{vmatrix} Z_{11} & Z_{12} & Z_{13} & g_1 & h_1 \\ Z_{21} & Z_{22} & Z_{23} & g_2 & h_2 \\ Z_{31} & Z_{32} & Z_{33} & g_3 & h_3 \\ g_1 & g_2 & g_3 & 0 & 0 \\ h_1 & h_2 & h_3 & 0 & 0 \end{vmatrix}, \ldots, \begin{vmatrix} Z_{11} & \cdots & Z_{1n} & g_1 & h_1 \\ \cdots & \cdots & \cdots & \cdots & \cdots \\ Z_{n1} & \cdots & Z_{nn} & g_n & h_n \\ g_1 & \cdots & g_n & 0 & 0 \\ h_1 & \cdots & h_n & 0 & 0 \end{vmatrix}$$

In the two-constraint case, the second-order conditions for a maximum will be satisfied if the above determinants alternate in sign, starting with minus, and those for a minimum will be satisfied if they are all positive. If there are $m < n$ constraints, border the principal minors of order $(m + 1)$ through n with the partial derivatives of the m constraints. The second-order conditions for a maximum will be satisfied if the determinants alternate in sign, starting with the sign of $(-1)^{m+1}$, and those for a minimum will be satisfied if all the specified determinants have the sign of $(-1)^m$.

IMPLICIT-FUNCTION THEOREM AND JACOBIANS

Assume that the implicit function $f(x,y) = 0$ is continuous and has continuous first partial derivatives. Consider a point (x^0, y^0) for which $f(x^0, y^0) = 0$ and assume that $f_y(x^0, y^0) \neq 0$. The *implicit-function theorem* states that there exists a neighborhood of points about (x^0, y^0) such that for any x value in the neighborhood there corresponds a *unique* y value in the neighborhood with the property that $f(x,y) = 0$. The implicit-function theorem thus asserts the existence, under the stated conditions, of a unique solution, $y = \phi(x)$.† It gives a sufficient condition for the *local univalence* of solutions. Solutions may exist if $f_y(x^0, y^0) = 0$, but if f_y vanishes throughout an entire neighborhood, then no unique solution exists in that neighborhood. This is true *a fortiori* if f_y vanishes identically.

An example where $f_y(x^0, y^0) = 0$, but where a unique solution exists nevertheless, is given by $f(x,y) = (x - y)^2$. The equation $(x - y)^2 = 0$ possesses the unique solution $y = x$; yet $f_y = -2(x - y) = 0$ at any point satisfying the original equation. An example where $f_y(x,y) = 0$ throughout a neighborhood is given by $f(x,y) = x - 1$. It is clear that $f(x,y) = 0$ is satisfied by $x = 1$ and any value of y; hence no unique solution exists.[1]

The question of the existence of a locally unique solution for n simultaneous equations in n unknowns requires a generalization of the

---

† Moreover, the solution is differentiable under the stated conditions.

[1] For rigorous proofs and geometric arguments see Courant, *op. cit.*, vol. II, pp. 111–122.

implicit-function theorem and the concept of the *Jacobian*. Consider the system of simultaneous equations

$$
\begin{aligned}
f^1(x_1,x_2, \ . \ . \ . \ ,x_n) &= y_1 \\
f^2(x_1,x_2, \ . \ . \ . \ ,x_n) &= y_2 \\
& \cdots \cdots \cdots \\
f^n(x_1,x_2, \ . \ . \ . \ ,x_n) &= y_n
\end{aligned}
\tag{A-24}
$$

The Jacobian of (A-24) is the determinant of the first partial derivatives of the functions f^i and is denoted by

$$
\mathbf{J} = \frac{\partial(y_1,y_2, \ . \ . \ . \ ,y_n)}{\partial(x_1,x_2, \ . \ . \ . \ ,x_n)} =
\begin{vmatrix}
\dfrac{\partial y_1}{\partial x_1} & \dfrac{\partial y_1}{\partial x_2} & \cdots & \dfrac{\partial y_1}{\partial x_n} \\
& \cdots \cdots \cdots \cdots & & \\
\dfrac{\partial y_n}{\partial x_1} & \dfrac{\partial y_n}{\partial x_2} & \cdots & \dfrac{\partial y_n}{\partial x_n}
\end{vmatrix}
\tag{A-25}
$$

The appropriate generalization of the implicit-function theorem is the following: If the functions $f^i(x_1,x_2, \ . \ . \ . \ ,x_n)$ $(i = 1,2, \ . \ . \ . \ ,n)$ are continuous and possess continuous first partial derivatives and if the Jacobian (A-25) is nonvanishing at the point $(x_1^0,x_2^0, \ . \ . \ . \ ,x_n^0)$ satisfying (A-24), then, in some neighborhood about the point $(y_1,y_2, \ . \ . \ . \ ,y_n)$ there exist unique inverse functions $x_i = \phi^i(y_1,y_2, \ . \ . \ . \ ,y_n)$, $(i = 1,2, \ . \ . \ . \ ,n)$. As in the case of the simple implicit-function theorem, no general assertion may be made if the Jacobian vanishes at $(x_1^0,x_2^0, \ . \ . \ . \ ,x_n^0)$. However, if $\mathbf{J} = 0$ in an entire neighborhood about $(x_1^0,x_2^0, \ . \ . \ . \ ,x_n^0)$, local univalence does not hold. The proof of this theorem is suggested by the following argument for the two-variable case. Consider the equations

$$
f(x_1,x_2) = y_1 \tag{A-26}
$$
$$
g(x_1,x_2) = y_2 \tag{A-27}
$$

If the Jacobian does not vanish, not all partial derivatives may equal zero. Assume that $f_1 \neq 0$. Then by the implicit-function theorem

$$
x_1 = \phi(x_2,y_1) \tag{A-28}
$$

Substituting in (A-27),

$$
F = g[\phi(x_2,y_1),x_2] - y_2 = 0 \tag{A-29}
$$

Then

$$
\frac{\partial F}{\partial x_2} = g_1\phi_1 + g_2 \tag{A-30}
$$

Substituting (A-28) in (A-26),

$$G = f[\phi(x_2,y_1),x_2] - y_1 = 0$$

Since G is identically equal to zero, its partial derivative with respect to x_2 also equals zero:

$$\frac{\partial G}{\partial x_2} = f_1\phi_1 + f_2 = 0 \tag{A-31}$$

Solving (A-31) for ϕ_1 and substituting its value in (A-30),

$$\frac{\partial F}{\partial x_2} = g_1\left(-\frac{f_2}{f_1}\right) + g_2 = \frac{f_1g_2 - f_2g_1}{f_1} \tag{A-32}$$

Since by hypothesis the Jacobian (the numerator) and f_1 do not vanish, $\partial F/\partial x_2 \neq 0$ and (A-29) can be solved for x_2. Therefore

$$x_2 = h(y_1,y_2) \tag{A-33}$$

Substituting (A-33) into (A-28) gives the solution for x_1.

A second relevant theorem states that the existence of a function $H(y_1,y_2, \ldots ,y_n) = 0$, that is, functional dependence among the equations of (A-24), is necessary and sufficient for the Jacobian of (A-24) to vanish throughout a neighborhood of the point $(x_1^0,x_2^0, \ldots ,x_n^0)$. The proof of sufficiency can be suggested as follows. Assume that there exists a functional dependence $H(y_1,y_2) = 0$. Taking the total differential,

$$H_1\,dy_1 + H_2\,dy_2 = 0$$

Substituting for dy_1 and dy_2 their values obtained by differentiating (A-26) and (A-27) and collecting terms,

$$(H_1f_1 + H_2g_1)\,dx_1 + (H_1f_2 + H_2g_2)\,dx_2 = 0$$

Since this must hold for all values of dx_1 and dx_2, the bracketed terms must each equal zero:

$$H_1f_1 + H_2g_1 = 0 \qquad H_1f_2 + H_2g_2 = 0$$

Moving the second terms to the right-hand side and dividing the first equation by the second,

$$\frac{H_1f_1}{H_1f_2} = \frac{-H_2g_1}{-H_2g_2}$$

or

$$f_1g_2 - f_2g_1 = 0 \tag{A-34}$$

The left-hand side of (A-34) is the Jacobian which equals zero.

As an example, consider the functions

$$x_1^2 - 2x_2 - 2 = y_1$$
$$x_1^4 - 4x_1^2x_2 + 4x_2^2 = y_2$$

The functional dependence between them is given by $(y_1 + 2)^2 - y_2 = 0$. The Jacobian

$$\frac{\partial(y_1,y_2)}{\partial(x_1,x_2)} = \begin{vmatrix} 2x_1 & -2 \\ 4x_1^3 - 8x_1x_2 & -4x_1^2 + 8x_2 \end{vmatrix}$$
$$= (-8x_1^3 + 16x_1x_2) - (-8x_1^3 + 16x_1x_2) = 0$$

vanishes identically.

If the functions (A-26) and (A-27) are linear, the first theorem reduces to the familiar proposition that the determinant of the array of coefficients must be nonvanishing. This condition is fulfilled if the number of equations equals the number of variables and if the equations are not functionally dependent. If the Jacobian of a system of linear equations vanishes, the equations are linearly dependent (see Sec. A-1).

A-4 INTEGRALS

The integral of a function $f(x)$ is another function $F(x)$ which has the property that its derivative equals $f(x)$; $F'(x) = f(x)$. An integral is unique except for an arbitrary additive constant c, since a constant vanishes on differentiation. Thus if $F(x)$ is an integral of $f(x)$, so is $F(x) + c$. Integration is the process of finding the integral and is in a sense differentiation in reverse. The integral $F(x) + c$ is known as the indefinite integral and is denoted by

$$\int f(x)\, dx = F(x) + c$$

The techniques for finding the indefinite integrals of various kinds of functions can be difficult. Some of the simple rules of integration are stated below without proof:[1]

1. $f(x) = g'(x)$, $\int f(x)\, dx = g(x)$
2. $f(x) = g(x) + h(x)$, $\int f(x)\, dx = \int g(x)\, dx + \int h(x)\, dx$
3. $f(x) = cg(x)$ (c a constant), $\int f(x)\, dx = c\int g(x)\, dx$
4. $f(x) = x^k$ ($k \neq -1$), $\int f(x)\, dx = x^{k+1}/(k + 1)$
5. $f(x) = 1/x$, $\int f(x)\, dx = \log x$
6. $f(x) = e^{ax}$, $\int f(x)\, dx = \dfrac{1}{a} e^{ax}$
7. If $x = g(u)$, then $\int f(x)\, dx = \int [g(u)]g'(u)\, du$

[1] See Courant, *op. cit.*, vol. I, pp. 141–143, 207–210.

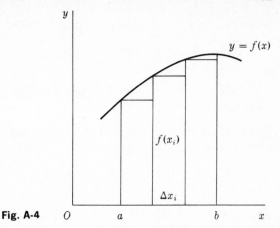

Fig. A-4

Integration can be used to calculate the area under a curve. The function $f(x)$ is plotted in Fig. A-4. To calculate the area between the x axis and the curve between points a and b, subdivide the distance $(b - a)$ into segments of width Δx_i, and then erect rectangles of height $f(x_i)$ over each segment. The height of each rectangle is the value of the function evaluated at the left-hand boundary of each segment. The required area A is approximately $\Sigma f(x_i)\,\Delta x_i$.† As the width of the rectangles becomes smaller, the expression $\Sigma f(x_i)\,\Delta x_i$ comes closer to the true area A. In fact,

$$A = \lim_{\Delta x_i \to 0} \Sigma f(x_i)\,\Delta x_i$$

provided that this limit exists.[1] Now change the right-hand-side boundary b of the area under consideration to a variable boundary x. The area from a to a variable right-hand-side boundary x is a function of x and will be denoted by $A(a,x)$. A somewhat larger area would result if the right-hand-side boundary were somewhat farther to the right, i.e., if this boundary were $x + \Delta x$. The resulting area will be denoted by $A(a,x + \Delta x)$. The difference between these two areas is

$$A(a, x + \Delta x) - A(a,x) = A(x, x + \Delta x)$$

The area between the points x and $x + \Delta x$ is also given by the width of the interval Δx multiplied by the value of the function $f(x)$ at some point

† The sum of these rectangles underestimates the area under the curve. If the height of the rectangles were given by the value of the function corresponding to the right-hand boundary of each segment, the approximation would overestimate the correct area. Either method is permissible for the analysis.
[1] The limit exists if the function $f(x)$ is continuous.

between x and $x + \Delta x$.   Denote this value of x by x_0:

$$A(a, x + \Delta x) - A(a,x) = f(x_0)\, \Delta x$$

or

$$\frac{A(a, x + \Delta x) - A(a,x)}{\Delta x} = f(x_0)$$

When Δx approaches zero, $x + \Delta x$ approaches x, and hence x_0 approaches x, since x_0 is between x and $x + \Delta x$.   Taking limits

$$\frac{dA}{dx} = \lim_{\Delta x \to 0} \frac{A(a, x + \Delta x) - A(a,x)}{\Delta x} = f(x)$$

This proves that the derivative of the area under a function is the function itself or that the integral of a function is the area under it.   The area $A(a,b)$ is the *definite* integral of $f(x)$ between the points a and b.   If $F(x)$ is an indefinite integral of $f(x)$, the definite integral between a and b is

$$\int_a^b f(x)\, dx = F(b) - F(a)$$

An example of definite integration is provided by

$$\int_0^b \alpha e^{-rx}\, dx = -\frac{\alpha e^{-rb}}{r} + \frac{\alpha}{r} = \frac{\alpha(1 - e^{-rb})}{r}$$

The limits of integration may be functions of a variable x as in $g(x) = \int_{\psi_1(x)}^{\psi_2(x)} f(x,y)\, dy$.   In this case the integral's derivative is

$$g'(x) = \int_{\psi_1(x)}^{\psi_2(x)} \frac{\partial f(x,y)}{\partial x}\, dy - \psi_1'(x)f[x,\psi_1(x)] + \psi_2'(x)f[x,\psi_2(x)]\dagger$$

A-5 DIFFERENCE EQUATIONS

Consider the sequence of numbers 1, 4, 9, 16, 25, etc., and denote them by $y_1, y_2, \ldots, y_t, \ldots$.   The first differences of this sequence are $\Delta y_1 = y_2 - y_1 = 3$, $\Delta y_2 = y_3 - y_2 = 5$, $\Delta y_3 = y_4 - y_3 = 7$, etc.   The second differences are the differences between the first differences or $\Delta^2 y_1 = \Delta y_2 - \Delta y_1 = 2$, $\Delta^2 y_2 = \Delta y_3 - \Delta y_2 = 2$, etc.   In this particular sequence of numbers the second differences are constant and equal 2. This can be written as

$$\Delta^2 y_t = 2 \tag{A-35}$$

---

† Courant, *op. cit.*, vol. II, pp. 219–220.

Equation (A-35) can also be written as the difference between two first differences, or

$$\Delta y_{t+1} - \Delta y_t = 2 \tag{A-36}$$

Each of the first differences in (A-36) can be written as the difference between two members of the sequence, or

$$(y_{t+2} - y_{t+1}) - (y_{t+1} - y_t) = y_{t+2} - 2y_{t+1} + y_t = 2 \tag{A-37}$$

Equation (A-37) is a *difference equation;* it is expressed in terms of the differences of a sequence of numbers. It relates the $(t + 2)$nd member of the sequence to the $(t + 1)$st and the tth members. In general, difference equations relate the tth member of a sequence to some previous members. The general linear difference equation of nth order with constant coefficients is

$$a_0 y_t + a_1 y_{t-1} + a_2 y_{t-2} + \cdots + a_n y_{t-n} + b = 0 \tag{A-38}$$

Equation (A-38) is linear because no y is raised to any power but the first and because it contains no products or other functions of the ys. It is an nth-order equation because the most distant value of y upon which y_t depends is y_{t-n}. Thus (A-37) is a linear difference equation of second order with constant coefficients. A difference equation is homogeneous if $b = 0$. Equation (A-37) is nonhomogeneous.

THE NATURE OF THE SOLUTION

The homogeneous first-order equation is

$$y_t = a y_{t-1} \tag{A-39}$$

Given the information that $y_0 = 2$, $y_1 = 2a$ can be determined from (A-39) by substituting the value of y_0 on the right-hand side. Then $y_2 = a(2a) = 2a^2$. In this fashion it is possible to calculate the value of y for any value of t. This procedure is cumbersome and can be avoided by finding a general solution for the difference equation. A general solution is an expression, usually a function of t, which gives the value of y_t immediately upon substitution of the desired value of t. A function of t must be found such that $y_t = f(t)$. Any such function is a solution if it satisfies the difference equation. In the first-order case the solution $f(t)$ must satisfy[1]

$$f(t) = af(t - 1) \tag{A-40}$$

[1] A difference equation can also be regarded as defining y as a function of t. To every value of t there corresponds a value of y with the proviso that the independent variable t can take on only integral values, i.e., 0, 1, 2, 3, etc.

In addition the solution must also be consistent with the *initial conditions*. The initial conditions are a statement about the value of y at one or more specified points in the sequence. The number of initial conditions must be the same as the order of the equation in order to obtain a complete solution. Only one initial condition is necessary in the first-order case. This was given by $y_0 = 2$ in the previous example. The problem is to find the solution or solutions that satisfy the difference equation and then to select the solution that also satisfies the initial conditions.[1] Subsequent discussion is confined to linear difference equations of first and second order with constant coefficients.

HOMOGENEOUS FIRST-ORDER EQUATIONS

Equation (A-39) can be written as

$$\frac{y_t}{y_{t-1}} = a \qquad \text{for all } t$$

Therefore,

$$y_t = \frac{y_t}{y_{t-1}} \frac{y_{t-1}}{y_{t-2}} \cdots \frac{y_2}{y_1} \frac{y_1}{y_0} y_0 = a^t y_0$$

The term a^t is itself a solution since it satisfies (A-39):

$$a^t = a(a^{t-1})$$

If $f(t)$ is a solution, so is $cf(t)$ where c is a constant. Thus assume that the general solution is $y_t = ca^t$. This satisfies the difference equation because

$$ca^t = a(ca^{t-1})$$

The parameter a is given by the difference equation and c is determined on the basis of the initial condition such that the general solution ca^t is consistent with it. In the previous example the initial condition was given by $y_0 = 2$. $y_0 = ca^0 = c = 2$, and the general solution is $y_t = 2a^t$.

HOMOGENEOUS SECOND-ORDER EQUATIONS

The homogeneous linear second-order equation is

$$ay_t + by_{t-1} + cy_{t-2} = 0 \tag{A-41}$$

---

[1] In the subsequent discussion, most proofs are omitted, and the ones given are sketchy at best. The reader is referred to W. J. Baumol, *Economic Dynamics* (2d ed.; New York: Macmillan, 1959), chaps. 9–13; and S. Goldberg, *Introduction to Difference Equations* (New York: Wiley, 1958), chaps. II–III.

Any function of t is a solution if it satisfies the difference equation. A solution is provided by x^t where x is a number as yet undetermined, as can be verified by substituting x^t into (A-41):

$$ax^t + bx^{t-1} + cx^{t-2} = 0 \qquad\qquad\qquad (A\text{-}42)$$

and dividing through by x^{t-2}

$$ax^2 + bx + c = 0 \qquad\qquad\qquad (A\text{-}43)$$

Equation (A-43), called the *characteristic equation*, is a quadratic and is solved by the customary formula

$$x = \frac{-b \pm \sqrt{b^2 - 4ac}}{2a} \qquad\qquad\qquad (A\text{-}44)$$

This generally gives two values of x: x_1 and x_2. Then x_1^t and x_2^t are both solutions of (A-42).† The general solution of the homogeneous second-order difference equation is $k_1 x_1^t + k_2 x_2^t$ where k_1 and k_2 are constants determined in accordance with the initial conditions. Two initial conditions are needed in the second-order case. Assume that these are $y_0 = 3$ and $y_1 = 4$. Then

$$k_1 x_1^0 + k_2 x_2^0 = k_1 + k_2 = 3$$
$$k_1 x_1^1 + k_2 x_2^1 = k_1 x_1 + k_2 x_2 = 4$$

This system of equations can be solved for k_1 and k_2, since x_1 and x_2 are already known.

In some cases $b^2 - 4ac$ is negative. This introduces a complication because, according to (A-44), one would have to take the square root of a negative number.[1] In such a case the solution is obtained by a different method and involves the trigonometric functions sine and cosine. The solution is merely stated here. Introduce the following notation:

$$v_1 = -\frac{b}{2a}$$
$$v_2 = -\frac{b^2 - 4ac}{2a}$$
$$R = \sqrt{v_1^2 + v_2^2}$$

---

† If $b^2 - 4ac = 0$, the two roots of the quadratic equation are not distinct, i.e., $x_1 = x_2 = -b/2a$. Then set $x_1^t = (-b/2a)^t$ and $x_2^t = t(-b/2a)^t$. See Baumol, *op. cit.*, pp. 186–190.

[1] The square root of a negative number is an imaginary number, denoted by the letter i, for example, $\sqrt{-16} = 4i$. The quantity x (sum of a real and an imaginary number) is a complex number. See for example, *ibid.*, pp. 191–205.

Find the angle z the sine of which is $v_2/\sqrt{v_1^2 + v_2^2}$ and the cosine of which is $v_1/\sqrt{v_1^2 + v_2^2}$.† The solution is

$$y_t = R^t[w_1 \sin (tz) + w_2 \cos (tz)] \tag{A-45}$$

where w_1 and w_2 are constants determined in the usual fashion in accordance with the initial conditions.

NONHOMOGENEOUS EQUATIONS

Two steps are required to find the solution of a nonhomogeneous difference equation. The first one is to find the solution $f(t)$ of the corresponding homogeneous equation. The second one is to find the *particular solution* denoted by $g(t)$. The final general solution is $f(t) + g(t)$. Finding the particular solution is illustrated with reference to a second-order equation. The nonhomogeneous equation is

$$ay_t + by_{t-1} + cy_{t-2} + d = 0 \tag{A-46}$$

The solution of the homogeneous part of (A-46) is $k_1 x_1^t + k_2 x_2^t$. To find a particular solution substitute in (A-46) $y_t = K$ (constant) and solve for K:

$$aK + bK + cK + d = 0$$

and

$$K = \frac{-d}{a + b + c} \tag{A-47}$$

provided that $a + b + c \neq 0$. Then the general solution is

$$y = k_1 x_1^t + k_2 x_2^t + \frac{-d}{a + b + c} \tag{A-48}$$

where k_1 and k_2 are now determined in accordance with the initial conditions. If $a + b + c = 0$, assume that the particular solution is $y_t = Kt$, substitute this in (A-46), and solve for K. Then the general solution is $y_t = k_1 x_1^t + k_2 x_2^t + Kt$, provided that $-b - 2c \neq 0$. If $-b - 2c = 0$, substitute Kt^2 and proceed analogously. In the first-order case either $y_t = K$ or $y_t = Kt$, and in the second-order case either $y_t = K$, or $y_t = Kt$, or $y_t = Kt^2$ leads to the correct particular solution.

A-6 DIFFERENTIAL EQUATIONS

An equation in which the variables are derivatives is called a *differential equation*. Examples are given by (1) $dy/dt = 17$, (2) $d^2y/dt^2 + b \, dy/dt + cy = 0$ and (3) $dy/dt + by^2 = c$. Equations (1) and (2) are linear differential equations because they are linear in y and its derivatives.

---

† The angle z can be determined by using tables of trigonometric functions.

Equations such as (3) are nonlinear and are not considered here.[1] The general nth-order linear differential equation with constant coefficients is

$$a_0 \frac{d^n y}{dt^n} + a_1 \frac{d^{n-1}y}{dt^{n-1}} + \cdots + a_n y + b = 0 \qquad \text{(A-49)}$$

This equation is homogeneous if $b = 0$. The homogeneous first-order equation is

$$\frac{dy}{dt} = by \qquad \text{(A-50)}$$

A general solution is a function $y = f(t)$ that satisfies the equation and yields the value of y upon substitution of a value of the independent variable t. As in the case of difference equations, solutions must also satisfy initial conditions.

The solution of (A-50) can be obtained by integration. Treating dy and dt as differentials, (A-50) may be written as

$$\frac{dy}{y} = b \, dt$$

Integrating both sides,

$$\int \frac{1}{y} \, dy = \int b \, dt$$

It follows that

$$\log y = bt + c \qquad \text{(A-51)}$$

where c stands for the constant of integration which is determined from initial conditions. From (A-51) the solution for (A-50) is

$$y = e^{bt+c} = ke^{bt}$$

where $k = e^c$. Given the initial condition $y = y_0$ when $t = 0$, it follows that $k = y_0$, and the solution is

$$y = y_0 e^{bt}$$

The derivation of solutions to higher-order equations has many similarities to the corresponding derivations for difference equations. For any differential equation of the form of (A-49) a solution is provided

[1] These equations are also called ordinary differential equations since the derivatives occurring in them are total derivatives. Equations containing partial derivatives are called partial differential equations. These latter are rarely encountered in economic applications.

by $e^{\lambda t}$ where λ is an as yet undetermined number. In the second-order case, $a d^2 y/dt^2 + b\, dy/dt + cy = 0$, the substitution of $e^{\lambda t}$ yields

$$a\lambda^2 e^{\lambda t} + b\lambda e^{\lambda t} + ce^{\lambda t} = 0$$

Dividing by $e^{\lambda t}$,

$$a\lambda^2 + b\lambda + c = 0$$

which is the same quadratic characteristic equation as (A-43), encountered in the solution of second-order difference equations. Since the quadratic yields, in general, two roots λ_1 and λ_2, the general solution will be of the form $y = k_1 e^{\lambda_1 t} + k_2 e^{\lambda_2 t}$. Given the initial conditions $y = y_0$ and $dy/dt = y_0'$ when $t = 0$,

$$y_0 = k_1 + k_2 \qquad y_0' = k_1\lambda_1 + k_2\lambda_2$$

and the constants are

$$k_1 = \frac{y_0' - \lambda_1 y_0}{\lambda_1 - \lambda_2} \qquad k_2 = -\frac{y_0' - \lambda_2 y_0}{\lambda_1 - \lambda_2}$$

if $\lambda_1 \neq \lambda_2$. If the solution to the characteristic equation is a pair of complex numbers $\lambda = \theta_1 \pm \theta_2 i$, the solution of the second-order differential equation becomes

$$y = e^{\theta_1 t}(k_1 \cos \theta_2 t + k_2 \sin \theta_2 t)$$

where k_1 and k_2 are determined, as before, from the initial conditions.

The particular solution for a nonhomogeneous differential equation is found in the same way as for difference equations: assume that $y = K$ (constant) provides a solution. Substitute this trial solution in

$$a\frac{d^2 y}{dt^2} + b\frac{dy}{dt} + cy + d = 0$$

and solve for K, provided that $c \neq 0$.† The general solution is, as before, the sum of the particular solution and the solution to the homogeneous equation.

EXERCISES

A-1. Use Cramer's rule to solve the following system of simultaneous equations:

$$
\begin{aligned}
2x_1 + 3x_2 \qquad &= 13 \\
x_1 + x_2 + x_3 &= 0 \\
5x_1 - 6x_2 + x_3 &= -13
\end{aligned}
$$

---

† If $c = 0$, one assumes $y = Kt$; if b is also equal to zero, the trial particular solution becomes Kt^2. See also Sec. A-5.

A-2. Differentiate the following functions:

(a) $f(x) = 6x^3 + 2x^2 - x + 12$.
(b) $f(x) = 4\sqrt{x}$.
(c) $f(x) = e^{-x}(x - 2)$.
(d) $f(x) = 4x^3/(2x^2 - x)$.
(e) $f(x) = \log(x^{-3})$, (log base e).

A-3. Determine the values of x at which the following functions possess maximum and minimum values:

(a) $f(x) = x^2 - 2x + 5$.
(b) $f(x) = x^3 - 27x^2 + 195x + 3$.
(c) $f(x) = \log(x^2 - x + 1)$.

A-4. Determine whether the following functions are strictly convex, strictly concave, or neither over the specified intervals:

(a) $f(x) = x^2 - 3x + 4$, for $x =$ any real number.
(b) $f(x) = \log x$, for $x > 0$ (log base e).
(c) $f(x) = e^{ax}$, for $x \leq 0$.
(d) $f(x) = x^3 - 2x^2 + x$, for $x \geq 0$.

A-5. Determine f_{11} and f_{12} for the following functions of two variables:

(a) $f(x_1,x_2) = x_1^2 x_2^2 - x_1 x_2 + 3x_1 - 2x_2$.
(b) $f(x_1,x_2) = \log(2x_1 + 3x_2)$.
(c) $f(x_1,x_2) = x_2^{x_1}$.

A-6. Take the total differential of $y = 2x_1 x_2^2 + x_2 e^{x_3} + \log x_1$.

A-7. Construct the envelope of the family of curves in the xy plane given by $y - 2x^2 - xk + k^2 = 0$.

A-8. Find values for x_1 and x_2 which maximize

$$f(x_1,x_2) = 5x_1 + 10x_2 + x_1 x_2 - 0.5x_1^2 - 3x_2^2$$

A-9. Let $f(x_1,x_2) = Ax_1^\alpha x_2^\beta$, where A, α, $\beta > 0$, be defined for the domain x_1, $x_2 > 0$. Demonstrate that the function is strictly concave within its domain if and only if $\alpha + \beta < 1$.

A-10. Find values for x_1 and x_2 that maximize $f(x_1,x_2) = x_1^2 x_2$ subject to the requirement that $5x_1 + 2x_2 = 300$. Demonstrate that the appropriate second-order condition is satisfied.

A-11. Demonstrate that the simultaneous equations

$$x_1^2 + 4x_1 x_2 + 4x_2^2 = y_1$$
$$x_1 + 2x_2 = y_2$$

do not possess solutions of the form $x_i = \phi^i(y_1,y_2)$, $i = 1, 2$.

A-12. Find $\int f(x)\, dx$ if

(a) $f(x) = x^2 - 2x$.
(b) $f(x) = (2x + 1)/(x^2 + x)$.
(c) $f(x) = ae^{-bx}$.

A-13. Evaluate the definite integral $\int_6^{10} (2x + 3)\, dx$.

A-14. Solve the following nonhomogeneous difference equations:

    (a) $2y_t - y_{t-1} - 6 = 0$ and $y_0 = 10$.

    (b) $y_t + 3y_{t-1} - 4y_{t-2} - 20 = 0$ and $y_0 = 10,\, y_1 = 19$.

A-15. Solve the homogeneous second-order differential equation:

$$\frac{d^2y}{dt^2} + 5\frac{dy}{dt} + 6y = 0$$

where $y_0 = 6$ and $y_0' = 3$.

SELECTED REFERENCES

Aitken, A. C., *Determinants and Matrices* (New York: Interscience, 1951). A concise reference work that is too difficult for the beginner.

Allen, R. G. D., *Basic Mathematics* (New York: St. Martin's, 1964). A modern text of particular interest to economists.

———, *Mathematical Analysis for Economists* (London: Macmillan, 1938). A survey of the calculus with many economic illustrations.

Baumol, W. J., *Economic Dynamics* (2d ed.; New York: Macmillan, 1959). Chapters 9–13 contain an introduction to linear difference equations and chap. 14 contains an introduction to differential equations.

Courant, R., *Differential and Integral Calculus* (2d ed.; New York: Interscience, 1936), 2 vols. A classic treatise. Highly recommended as a reference for advanced students.

Goldberg, S., *Introduction to Difference Equations* (New York: Wiley, 1958). A beginning text with many examples drawn from economics.

Goursat, E., *A Course in Mathematical Analysis*, vol. I, trans. by E. R. Hedrick (Boston: Ginn, 1904). A classic treatise. Recommended for intermediate and advanced students.

Hadley, G., *Linear Algebra* (Reading, Mass.: Addison-Wesley, 1961). Determinants are covered in chap. 3.

Milne-Thompson, L. M., *The Calculus of Finite Differences* (London: Macmillan, 1933). Chapters XI–XVII contain a comprehensive treatment of difference equations.

Osgood, W. F., *Advanced Calculus* (3d ed,; New York: Macmillan, 1935). A text more advanced than Allen.

Perlis, S., *Theory of Matrices* (Cambridge, Mass.: Addison-Wesley, 1952). A specialized treatment of determinants and matrices.

Samuelson, Paul A., *Foundations of Economic Analysis* (Cambridge, Mass.: Harvard, 1948). A mathematical approach to economic theory. An appendix contains a survey of some of the mathematical tools employed in the text. The treatment will prove difficult for all but advanced students.

Woods, F. S., *Advanced Calculus* (new ed.; Boston: Ginn, 1934). A text recommended for advanced students.

Index

Index